Language of the Underworld

DAVID W. MAURER

Language of the Underworld

Collected and Edited by

Allan W. Futrell & Charles B. Wordell

Foreword by

STUART BERG FLEXNER

THE UNIVERSITY PRESS OF KENTUCKY

1981

"Schoonerisms: Some Speech-Peculiarities of the North-Atlantic Fisherman," June 1930; "Carnival Cant: A Glossary of Circus and Carnival Slang," June 1931; "The Argot of the Underworld," December 1931; " 'Junker Lingo,' By-Product of Underworld Argot," April 1933; "The Lingo of the Good-People," February 1935; "The Argot of the Underworld Narcotic Addict," Parts 1 and 2, April 1936, October 1938; "Underworld Place-Names," Parts 1 and 2, October 1940, February 1942; "The Argot of Forgery," December 1941; "The Argot of the Faro Bank," February 1943; " 'Australian' Rhyming Argot in the American Underworld," October 1944; "The Argot of the Three-Shell Game," October 1947; all reprinted from *American Speech* © by The University of Alabama Press.

"The Lingo of the Jug-Heavy," *Writer's Digest*, October 1931. "Prostitutes and Criminal Argots," *American Journal of Sociology*, January 1939. "Marijuana Addicts and Their Lingo," *American Mercury*, November 1946. Copyright 1946 by The American Mercury, Inc. "The Argot of the Dice Gambler," *Annals of The American Academy of Political and Social Science*, May 1950. Copyright, 1950, by The American Academy of Political and Social Science. "The Argot of the Racetrack," *American Dialect Society*, November 1951; "The Argot of the Craft," from *Kentucky Moonshine*. Copyright © 1974 by The University Press of Kentucky.

"The Argot of Narcotic Addicts," from David W. Maurer and Victor H. Vogel, *Narcotics and Narcotic Addiction*, 4th edition, 1973. "The Con Man and His Lingo," from David W. Maurer, *The American Confidence Man*, 1973. Courtesy of Charles C Thomas, Publisher, Springfield, Illinois.

Library of Congress Cataloging in Publication Data

Maurer, David W
    Language of the Underworld

    Includes bibliographical references and index.
    1. Crime and criminals — Language (New words, slang, etc.) 2. Subculture — Slang. 3. Cant. I. Futrell, Allan W. II. Wordell, Charles B. III. Title.
HV6085.M38   364.3'0141   79-57574
ISBN 0-8131-1405-5

CONTENTS

146879

ACKNOWLEDGMENTS

We wish to thank the following for their assistance in the preparation of this book:

American Speech, Writer's Digest, The Annals of the American Academy of Political and Social Science, American Journal of Sociology, and Charles C Thomas Publishing Company for their permissions to reprint materials; Cary and Marie Robertson, Angela Settle, Helen Ellison, and Priscilla Robertson for volunteer assistance as readers and Michael Misbach for his clerical assistance.

FOREWORD

In 1930-1931 four articles appeared which served notice that a brilliant and prolific young scholar was on the scene, a scholar with a new subject and a new approach. His name was David W. Maurer. The new subject was the argot of subcultural groups; the approach was fieldwork in the living language of subcultures.

In the fifty years since these first pieces appeared David Maurer has explored his subject in more than two hundred books, papers, and articles which have influenced the course of American language scholarship and had a strong influence on modern sociology and anthropology. This collection contains the most important of Professor Maurer's shorter pieces dealing with criminal subcultures (including those first four), many of which are in otherwise hard-to-obtain or in out-of-print publications. These fascinating scholarly articles and glossaries are a harvest of years of brilliant and painstaking lexicographic research. More important, with Maurer's other works they have broken new ground, sowed the seeds of sociolinguistics, and contributed to modern social and cultural anthropology. They are part of a seminal body of work that has changed forever our concept of our language and culture.

Maurer began his first linguistic investigation in the late 1920s while doing research at sea for Clarence Birdseye (which explains why "Speech Peculiarities of the North Atlantic Fishermen" was one of his first articles). When he began his linguistic work, the completed *Oxford English Dictionary*, *American Speech*, and the Linguistic Society of America were all less than five years old, Hans Kurath was just projecting fieldwork for *The Linguistic Atlas of the United States and Canada*, and Mencken's *The American Language* (which Maurer was to help Raven McDavid update and revise into a one-volume edition some forty years later) was still a comparatively slim volume with no fourth edition or supplements. Such basic works as Bloomfield's *Language*, the *Dictionary of American English*, and even Merriam-Webster's Second Unabridged edition were not to appear until the next decade, and Mathews's *Dictionary of Americanisms* was almost three decades away.

In fact, when Maurer began his pioneering work, observation of our non-standard language was limited almost solely to members of the American Dialect Society, regional dialects were still often discussed as "quaint," and social dialects were practically untouched. Many language societies, scholarly groups, and teachers' associations were still imitating eighteenth-century British usage inherited through handbooks, or recommending Greek and Latin models. Descriptive lexicography (defining words in terms of behavior patterns) was a theory rather than a practice, even though the techniques of descriptive linguistics had been developed by such anthropologists as Sapir and Bloomfield, with both of whom Maurer studied. A reliable dictionary of American slang had not yet been written. Most slang, not to mention all four-letter words, was banned from most newspapers, magazines, and books. Though some anthropologists and linguists had studied the language and culture of primitive tribes far removed in time or place from twentieth-century America, no respected scholar wanted to devote his life to studying the "illiterate" occupational, social, or other speechways of modern culture.

Maurer, of course, did not know in the late 1920s that such major works, scholars, and interests were in the future, that he would be a leader and a major influence rather than merely a maverick. What he probably missed most was not scholarly equals or good scholarly source material but a tape recorder to record the speech he heard, for tape recorders were also some twenty years in the future, and he had to rely on memorizing, copious notes, and minimal shorthand transcriptions during the first half of his research career. I well recall my own experience as Maurer's student assistant during his early experiments with getting professional criminals to speak into a rather primitive wire recorder which I operated in a separate room since the thieves he was working with refused to be seen and possibly identified by a third person. Even after he began using a recorder he had to develop special techniques to cure his informants of "mike-fright," then far more prevalent than today.

Breaking new scholarly ground with his fieldwork and publications on the living language of criminal subcultures, Maurer had to feel his own way, to develop his own methods, set up and prove or disprove his own theories. The pieces collected here are in chronological order and show his growth, his ever-improving methods, and his expanding ideas. With the encouragement of such people as H. L. Mencken and Louise Pound his work slowly gained acceptance. At the same time it grew from an all-consuming interest in the words he heard and defined to a description of the behavior within the groups that used them, and finally to a unified understanding of subcultures, their place in society and their influence on it.

Along the way he learned to supplement his fieldwork interviews with contemporaries by delving into older literature such as that of the Spanish picaresque writers and the Elizabethan playwrights; in fact, he got his doctorate from Ohio State University in comparative literature of the seventeenth century. In addition, he sought out very old criminals in order to develop a historical perspective on modern argot and criminal behavior. He has developed ever more adroit interviewing techniques (which he has generously shared with other social scientists) and improved methods of checking and cross-checking his material with an ever-widening group of informants.

He realized very early that, since he was basing his work on interviews in the field, his research must be so well documented and verified that there could be no question of its authenticity or of the meaning and use of the words he traced. Thus he never depended on single informants but has conducted in-depth interviews with as many of each subculture as feasible, up to several hundred on some projects. The quantity, scope, and accuracy of his work is awesome when one remembers that he takes nothing from other sources, that all research is original research done in the field.

Seldom have a man and his work been so well suited. Collecting material while living on North Atlantic fishing boats, running down moonshiners, studying safecrackers, confidence men, and counterfeiters, meeting with drug addicts, prostitutes, pickpockets, and dice and card manipulators on their own grounds and on their own time takes a great deal of physical stamina and a strong personality, as well as mental ability. Maurer is big, with large shoulders and strong arms and hands, a man who can help pull in a heavy fishing net in freezing weather or push a car out of a muddy backroad on the way to an illegal still.

With a gleam in his eye (to Maurer fieldwork is a challenge) and an anti-stuffshirt sense of humor, he does not expect everyone else to be a scholar. He can talk about more than books with his informants: besides being a professor of linguistics (now retired) and widely published, he is a part-time farmer, a onctime breeder and trainer of guard dogs, and an avid trout fisherman. He admires sharp wits and skills wherever he finds them. Like an anthropologist, he comes not to judge but to learn; he attempts to be objective, yet becomes so involved in the language of each subculture he studies that he becomes immersed in its life. Thus, addicts, counterfeiters, prostitutes, pickpockets know they are talking to a scholar who not only records their speech but who knows, understands, and tries to interpret their personal and group behavior patterns. To many criminals he has become a unique contact from the straight life, bringing them some understanding of its attitudes and values — just as to the generations of students he has taught and trained, and to criminologists, linguists, and sociologists, he has brought some insight into the attitudes and behavior of professional criminals. A man with less stamina, less strength of personality, a lesser understanding of people could not have accomplished the work Maurer has, no matter how well trained or how intelligent.

Thus, early in his linguistic career, he became the leading expert in criminal argot, "the argot man." He seems at times to be the first scholar actually to *listen* to criminals and other subcultural groups. He is certainly the first to have gathered, analyzed, and presented large blocks of their speech in a useful, systematic way. Thus, as this collection so amply demonstrates, Maurer was the first to report, define, and trace many items of criminal argot, while at the same time contributing many etymologies for that part of our general language, especially slang, that comes from the underworld. Since many terms he discovered as criminal argot years ago have since become common terms, his work has wide lexicographical validity. His argot work also produced the first serious record of marijuana users ("Marijuana Addicts and Their Lingo," 1946) and a major examination of the narcotic addict's language and subculture, long before "the drug culture" was a popular subject. He also corrected the widely held misconception that rhyming slang came from Australia (it was still incorrectly called "Australian rhyming slang" when his "Australian Element in American Criminal Argots" was first published, in 1944, before Julian Franklyn's excellent 1960 *Dictionary of Rhyming Slang* explaining Cockney rhyming terms).

More important than such lexicographical "firsts," however, is that Maurer's glossaries have been a source almost all modern dictionaries of the English language have drawn upon, there being few if any that do not now include words he first reported and defined. In addition, his body of work has become a major source for many books on the American language, be they on slang or other specialized dictionaries or histories and discussions of the language itself.

Since the mid-1930s, Maurer's work has also contributed much to the work of law enforcement officials, criminologists, psychologists, social workers, to all who must know the language of the subcultural groups with which they work in order to be effective. This aspect of Maurer's contribution began in 1935 when Dr. Victor H. Vogel, then medical officer in charge of the newly established drug-treatment center of Lexington, Kentucky, invited him to teach his staff about addicts' argot, this probably being the first time a language expert was used in law-enforcement rehabilitation work. Since then, Maurer has worked closely, often as a team member, with several criminologists, sociologists, psychologists, and professionals in other fields on a wide variety of projects, contributing linguistic research and insights.

On the lighter side, since the publication of his "Lingo of the Jug-Heavy" in *Writer's Digest* in 1931, Maurer's glossaries, articles, and books have been a major source for fiction writers, playwrights, and filmmakers. Thus those of us who work directly or indirectly in the American language owe him the greatest of debts.

He has also had a constructive influence outside the field of criminal argot and lexicography. As this collection again shows, fairly early in his work he found it necessary to relate argot words to the subculture that uses them, to define the words in terms of the group's behavioral pattern. He increasingly includes behavioral, cultural, and psychological details in his writing so the reader will understand the context and ambience of the vocabularies. Thus by the late 1940s he was simultaneously defining and examining the words and the behavior patterns of criminal subcultures.

As he continued to listen to and analyze a growing number of argots he began to see the full spectrum and depth of language in relation to behavior. He noted both the basic unifying elements and the wide differences between specific argots and between specific subcultures. He found that argots were not primarily secret communications used to deceive outsiders but rather one aspect of group identity. He saw that argot was not an isolated lexical phenomenon but a major facet, force, and expression of all subcultures. He explored the genesis of argots and the reasons for and methods of their social distribution. Thus his work had expanded beyond that of a lexicographer. He had narrowed the gulf between linguistics, sociology, and anthropology, and his work was beginning to influence these fields. It had slowly grown from the words themselves to a description and understanding of various subcultures and to an overall concept of subculture itself. (The wide sociolinguistic importance of his work is shown by the fact that some articles in this collection were first published not in linguistic journals but in such publications as the *American Journal of Sociology* and the *Annals of the American Academy of Political and Social Sciences.*)

Using language as the key to subculture, Maurer has shown that professional crime is much more than individual lawbreaking, that it is actually a way of life within certain subcultures. He has also shown that crime is not a mere facet of the life of some groups but is the entire way of life. He has shown that professional criminals are not necessarily social or psychological abnormalities but that they are often fully integrated and well-adjusted members of their own societies. He has shown that subcultures are not monolithic but that each has its own social stratification — hierarchies within subcultures.

Mainly, however, Maurer's work has thrown considerable light on cultural pluralism in America. He has made effective use of cultural indices and has demonstrated that the American language, like American culture, is not homogeneous, and his pioneer work in sociodialects continues to contribute to many fields. He who started out with the North Atlantic fishermen has indeed caught some fascinating fish and showed us that the waters of linguistics are deeper than we had imagined.

STUART BERG FLEXNER

INTRODUCTION

This book is a selection of David W. Maurer's writings drawn from the more than two hundred books, monographs, articles, and professional papers he has contributed to the study of the American language. These studies represent a unique area of scholarship in which he has concentrated—studying subcultures by investigating the speech patterns of their members. During the past fifty years he has undertaken synchronic language studies of specific subgroups, his observations often culminating in the recording of a basic lexicon and the objective defining of terms used by the various groups. He has studied the speechways of police officers, religious orders, occupational groups, sportsmen, Gypsies, businessmen, criminals, and many others, the list including over a hundred subcultures.

The term subculture itself demands some explanation since it has enjoyed expanded usage over the past several years, carrying with it some ambiguity which accompanies many frequently used terms. Maurer thinks of a subculture as a group of individuals—such as social, occupational, ethnic, or racial groups—who share certain common attitudes, associations, behavior patterns, and speech patterns. A subculture is largely a social phenomenon in that rigid geographical bounds do not necessarily restrict it, though clusters of its members may confine themselves to certain locales. A subculture, contrary to some sociological theory, is not necessarily a deviant group; it is, rather, any cohesive social microsystem that has certain cultural indices in contrast to those of the macrosystem constituting the dominant culture. For example, we would probably not consider a group of boys hanging around a hamburger joint a subculture; we might, however, consider a fraternal order a subculture, not because it is formalized or appears to be more respectable, but because it has definite consistent indices of ethics, morals, and ideals. Cultural indices, therefore, are quite useful in distinguishing subcultures, and Maurer has often employed them to such an end.

The dominant culture consists of a multiplicity of subcultures characterized by minimal differences in these indices from one subculture to the next. Criminal subcultures, by contrast, overlap the dominant culture in varying degrees but can likewise be distinguished from it, as Maurer points out in *Whiz Mob: A Correlation of the Technical Argot of Pickpockets with Their Behavior Pattern* (1955, 1964): "Even though these subcultures intermingle at many points with the dominant culture, and in some instances—like that of the moonshiner in the agricultural south—are almost indistinguishable from it, they all have in common one factor which differentiates them from the dominant culture. They are all parasitic" (p. 11). These criminal subcultures with this "parasitic" characteristic stand apart from other subcultures and are often referred to in the aggregate as the "underworld."

The term underworld is of dubious validity since it imposes a misleading structure on criminal subcultures. Maurer has explained the nature of professional criminal groups and delineated their relationship to noncriminal groups by using the term subculture:

> It would appear that much can be gained from going a little beyond current psychiatric and sociological concepts of professional crime to the point where we recognize it as a cluster of subcultures, some of them, like the culture of pickpockets which we are about to comment upon, very ancient. It is helpful if we visualize the dominant culture as bounded by a large circle with these subcultures, projected as very small circles, clustering about the rim of the large one. Thus some of these small circles will be largely within the dominant culture, some encysted wholly within it, some only slightly within it, and others barely touching the periphery so that for all practical purposes they are outside it. We might then think of the position of these circles as indicative of the degree to which the criminal cultures are absorbed and accepted by the dominant culture, if we bear in mind that this degree will vary substantially with geography as well as with social structure. (*Whiz Mob,* p. 10)

Maurer, however, cautions the reader that "while this sort of image is mechanical and oversimplified, it may . . . enable us to handle abstract concepts, the referents for which are not yet isolated" (*Whiz Mob,* p. 11). Sociologist David O. Arnold distorts Maurer's use of this imagery in his article entitled "Subculture Marginality,"[1] in which he claims Maurer is guilty of "turning a convenient abstraction into a supposed picture of reality, of taking vague boundary lines and going over them with a heavy crayon." He also ignores the context in which Maurer is writing when he paraphrases him as saying "that all subcultures are differentiated from the dominant culture by being parasitic," when Maurer actually says that all *criminal* subcultures are parasitic.

In effect, Arnold has assigned to Maurer a model of subculture that is not Maurer's. On the one hand, he has taken Maurer's imagery too literally, failing at once to heed his caution and to realize his sensitivity to shading, or overlapping, among subcultures; and, on the other hand, Arnold misconstrues observations pertaining to a certain group of subcultures as applying to all subcultures. After building and razing a model for Maurer, Arnold delineates his own model of subcultures that, on comparison, appears to be largely a loose paraphrase of Maurer's: "Thus we can have, at one extreme, subcultures sharing almost no elements of the national culture — Gypsies might be an example of such a subculture — and at the other extreme subcultures hav-

---

1. David O. Arnold, "Subculture Marginality," in *The Sociology of Subcultures,* ed. David O. Arnold (Berkeley, Calif., Glendessary Press, 1970), pp. 82-84.

ing few or no truly unique elements but only variant patterns—here we might look to regional or class subcultures for examples. And of course all possible combinations could occur between these extremes" (p. 84).

Maurer had already expanded his concept of subculture in *Whiz Mob* thus:

For example, the subculture of the professional stick-up men would be partly within but mostly without the dominant culture; the subculture of the professional gambler is largely within the bounds of the dominant culture, and in some places—like Nevada—could be entirely within it. The big-time confidence men are flexible and are equally at home in their own subculture or in the dominant culture—in fact, they are able to simulate behavior within the dominant culture to a high degree of perfection. On the other hand, a criminal subculture like that of the Gypsies touches the dominant culture so slightly that for all practical purposes it is completely outside. (p. 11)

The two models do not conflict; Maurer has simply limited his, in this context, to those subcultures that pilfer the resources of the dominant culture for their existence. By doing this, Maurer has set up a workable analogy of the "underworld" to the "dominant culture." Consequently, Arnold's misconceptions are not presented here by way of criticism so much as they are for the sake of disclaiming any legitimation his interpretation of Maurer's use of the term might have introduced.

It is essential that the reader understand that by "criminal" we mean a professional criminal, and not simply a "deviant" member of the dominant culture. A professional criminal is one who practices an established criminal craft as a primary means of his support, is recognized by other criminals of the same vocation as being knowledgeable in the field, lives by the code of behavior of his specific group, and uses the specialized secret or semisecret language—the argot—indigenous to his group. His attitudes and behavior patterns are only partly those of the dominant culture but in significant respects are those of the parasitic subculture. Maurer sees professional criminals as normally belonging to one of the following four major divisions of the underworld: 1) the grifters, those who live by their wits and manual skills; 2) the heavy rackets people, those who practice crimes of violence or use the threat of violence; 3) the lone wolves, those who work most effectively by themselves without organization; and 4) the quasi-criminals, such as prostitutes and criminal drug traffickers, those who become criminals as a result of implementation of laws by the dominant culture. All these divisions are labeled "deviant" by members of the dominant culture's power structure which has the political authority to do so. That power structure generally does not distinguish members of the dominant culture "gone wrong" from professional criminals. These occasional or nonprofessional criminals, however, are not the subject of any of the language studies included here.

Subcultures comprised of professional criminals go far back into human history. Many commentators have observed that there is a high rate of professional crime in the United States, Canada, and Mexico as compared to modern Europe. They generally fail to realize, however, that since the sixteenth century the criminal subcultures of Europe have been systematically imported to the New World. This came about through the use of legal deportation, the sentencing of criminals to exile ("remittance men"), the voluntary exodus of professional criminals to escape apprehension by the law, and the development of a system of indentured servitude, many of the servants being recruited from prisons, jails, and almshouses. Professional criminals moving into the New World found that the techniques perfected in Europe in an economy of scarcity could be adapted to an economy of great abundance resulting in high profits to the criminals. Along with their way of life they brought their argots, some of which were likewise adapted to the language of the New World. As the news of this criminal bonanza spread, it attracted increasing numbers of professional criminals from Europe, Africa, and Asia, and still does as we see in the current growth of the Mafia. This migration of criminals extending over a period of some four hundred years combined with the dynamics of frontier life helps to explain the high incidence of professional crime in America as contrasted to its relatively low incidence in Europe.

Studies of criminal argots, therefore, have significance for scholars. First, all criminals do not speak the same argot; an awareness of this fact is essential to an understanding of the multicultural nature of the underworld and, by analogy, the pluralism existing throughout American culture. Maurer, who has never been *on the rackets* himself, has studied sociolects within the criminal phase of American culture and has observed that the American language, like the behavior patterns of the various individuals and groups that use it, is not homogeneous. His findings can be of special value in establishing this awareness since he defines the argot terms from the point of view of the culture in which they are used.

Second, slang often originates in the underworld, sometimes getting extensive usage there before diffusing. This phenomenon is apparent when one reads some of Maurer's earlier works in which many words presently enjoying wide usage in the dominant culture are described as criminal terms. A more mature examination of this phenomenon can be seen in his major article "Slang," in the current *Encyclopaedia Britannica*. Francis Grose's *A Classical Dictionary of the Vulgar Tongue* (1785), the first comprehensive dictionary of English slang, contains many criminal canting terms, and Stuart Flexner and Harold Wentworth's *Dictionary of American Slang* (1960), a classic itself, is derived, in many respects, from studies of criminal speech.

Criminals' language has been a topic of interest for many years, studies of it perhaps merited on the basis of this attention alone. A study of the *Rotwelsch* of rogues appeared in the early part of the sixteenth century, one edition of which was edited by Martin Luther. Such well-known writers as Thomas Dekker, Ben Jonson, Henry Fielding, Charles Dickens, and Damon Runyon either studied the language of criminals or used it extensively in their writings. Eric Partridge has produced entire dictionaries of criminal terms from historical and literary sources, and Goldin, O'Leary, and Lipsius's *Dictionary of American Underworld Lingo* (1950) is primarily a collection of general criminal speech gathered in prison.

Maurer, however, contributes a new dimension to the study of criminal language. For many years his articles and glossaries have served as scholarly sources for anthropologists, linguists, sociologists, lexicographers, etymologists, psychologists, criminologists, creative writers, specialists in police work, and others. The material is presented with a broad understanding of human nature, often with an element of humor; but, more important, it is presented with objectivity and authenticity. He bases his work on a close study of the living language and the people who use that language naturally. This is in contradistinction to the criminals sometimes serving as subject matter for romantic film and fiction, or those purportedly supplying the basis for bold sociological conjecture. The most useful contribution he has made to the field, therefore, may be the sources and materials he uses and his methods of securing information from them. A brief examination of these should give the reader a better understanding of the significance of this collection.

Previous researchers have depended largely upon police information, printed and literary sources, or upon a single language informant to obtain materials for their studies. Maurer, on the other hand, gathers his materials from the criminals themselves, approaching a subculture much as an anthropologist does. The basic materials consist of narratives delivered in the vernacular by operating professionals, other knowledgeable members of the subculture, or persons with long and intimate contact with a particular subculture. These narratives, often extending over a total of many hours, consist mainly of accounts of life in the subculture, focusing on the principal criminal activity. They constitute a linguistic corpus for subsequent analysis and description.

These materials are usually collected in the native habitat of the criminal, though in some cases good informants are interviewed while in prison. The criminal free in society, however, usually makes a better informant for reasons Maurer explains in several of his works, especially in *The American Confidence Man* (1974) and *Whiz Mob*. A major reason worthy of mention here is that the vast majority of convicts are not professional criminals. A tape recorder is used whenever possible, but before the days of portable electronic devices, the corpus was recorded in shorthand or memorized for later transcription.

In addition to verbal narration, written materials are often contributed by informants who are interested and are known to be reliable. These consist of letters, documents, autobiographical narratives, and collections of stories or anecdotes. Some highly intelligent and well-read informants often engage in extensive discussion of both linguistic and behavioral issues.

Maurer selects his informants carefully with a view toward acquiring competent operators, preferably those who have grown up in the subculture and can speak from long experience. Often they are from families including other professionals, and they have always been *turned out* by someone older. These people supply the raw data from which the study is ultimately prepared and may range in number from a very few as in "The Lingo of the Good People" to several hundred as in "The Argot of the Criminal Narcotic Addict."

Since Maurer's methods differ widely in time frame as well as with each subculture he studies, any description of methodology we give here can be nothing more than an overview, synthesized and somewhat oversimplified. For instance, questionnaires such as those used in conventional sociological and linguistic surveys are not very effective in this area of study and are rarely used; however, facsimiles of them have been used when the situation called for it. Though no rigid methodology can be described, certain guidelines employed with varying degrees of consistency can be noted, even if these procedures may not always follow the order in which they are presented here.

The techniques he uses for contacting desirable informants would constitute material for a separate study. Many of these people come to Maurer by way of referrals from judges, physicians and surgeons, attorneys, detectives, *fixers,* and others; however, most are referred by professional criminals who have already become interested in the work and have previously served as subjects themselves. But in all cases informants are checked out in advance through confidential sources who can supply useful information about the subject before he is approached. This enables Maurer not only to select the best qualified but also to profit from the effect his investigative interest has upon the ego of the potential informant. Thus, when the informant is finally approached he may respond favorably to the attention that he has received. Those who are *hot,* or currently wanted by the police, are usually excluded. His main interest, however, is in the subject's intelligence, his professional standing, and his competence as an informant; few ordinary convicts meet these qualifications. Accounts of specific criminal acts not covered by the statutes of limitation are avoided and always discouraged. Certain hazards are naturally inherent in this phase of the investigation so only those researchers with special training and experience should conduct these interviews. Moreover, at this stage the investigator may experience some culture shock, so care must be taken to avoid value judgments.

The standard procedures of interviewing used in linguistics and anthropology are adapted to the situation at hand. Maurer always identifies himself fully and never uses subterfuge of any kind. He often gives as a reference another individual whom the informant may know, but this is not essential. As the interviewer, his first responsibility is to arouse an interest on the part of the informant and to cultivate cooperation based on this interest. Intelligent criminals usually respond readily to this approach in the course of a series of interviews and sometimes become quite enthusiastic about the project.

For several reasons, Maurer never pays informants. First, most professional criminals have a good income and would not be impressed by a small fee. Second, payment would put a commercial value on production and might encourage the introduction of spurious material. Third, if the subject does not have a high level of interest in the work, Maurer places little stock in the value of his assistance. The exception to this policy is that he generally deposits tobacco money in the account of a prisoner-informant as a matter of courtesy. Books, magazines, and other reading material play an even more important role in enhancing the convict's interest. If it can be arranged, Maurer will sometimes provide the convict with a typewriter and has often received excellent material as a result.

The time and place of an interview are usually set by the informant and care is taken to maintain his privacy and to keep his involvement confidential. When women are interviewed, steps are taken to avoid subjecting them to suspicion by male intimates. For example, if a pickpocket is living with a female shoplifter, the courteous approach to interviewing the shoplifter would be through her man, the pickpocket, who might even arrange for interviews. However, it would not be wise to approach a big-time mobster on the heavy rackets for an interview with his woman. Women on the grift often have not only a separate craft but also a good deal of autonomy in making decisions on their own; on the heavy rackets, women may be kept separate from the affairs of the man or at least be under strong compulsion from the code of *omertá* and usually do not have a racket of their own. There may be a wide variation according to circumstances which the investigator must assess carefully in advance. In all interviews Maurer avoids acquiring information that might get the informant into trouble, and he strives to maintain the dignity and protect the self-image of the subject.

Interviews in prison have the advantage of assuring that the informant will be available; however, as a rule only convicts selected because of their specialized knowledge are chosen. Professional criminals doing time may be under great tension and reluctant to talk about their work for personal or legal reasons, which must be respected. Some men who decline to be interviewed in prison can be approached successfully after release, and a friendly interest in the man coupled with casual correspondence often prepares the way for subsequent cooperation. Techniques in this area vary with the personality and circumstances of the informant. It cannot be overemphasized that being in prison does not necessarily qualify a person as a professional criminal, and nonprofessionals are, as much as possible, sifted out of Maurer's list of informants.

Most interviews, especially the initial ones, do not involve direct questioning. In later phases of the study, however, the informant may work over a manuscript with Maurer, and direct questioning is freely accepted. A tape recorder is a great convenience, but permission is secured before using one. Moreover, it is never concealed nor surreptitiously used, although sometimes only the microphone is exposed since the presence of the tape recorder may tend to inhibit some subjects. Also, some people alter their speech patterns if they become self-conscious about being recorded; most informants, however, ignore the microphone and speak naturally. It may take a short period for the informant to lapse into the argot, but Maurer often precipitates this by taking the initiative in using argot himself. Interviews range anywhere from two to six hours in length, and the same informant may be interviewed repeatedly. Some informants may eventually be asked to comment on material from other informants, who always remain anonymous, especially in the later stages of a study where verification is important. Oftentimes, an informant who is interested will enlist the help of one or more of his acquaintances. In most cases, it is important to interview individuals in various parts of the country, and it is often best to conduct the interview in the city where the individual lives or visits as a base of operations. In the case of *road men* it is often most convenient to interview them by appointment in a large urban center at times when they are not actively working.

In an analysis of the corpus, two areas receive the most attention. First, behavior pattern is noted with special reference to variations, including the modus operandi among other culturally important indices. At this point, conferences with specialized detectives such as con-squad men, pickpocket squad men, loft-squad men, or homicide and robbery specialists may be helpful.

Second, the linguistic patterns are studied with special attention given to phonology, syntax, and lexicon. Phonology is usually noted only when it is characteristic of or exclusively significant in the argot. For example, among old-time opium users the standard term *fun* /fUn/ is a measure of opium, employed by dealers, amounting to about 5.79 grains; opium weights are calibrated in *fun*. In the West and the Midwest this is recoded as /fUn/, but on the East coast it is either /fUŋ/ or /fɔŋ/. This means that a certain pronunciation is recorded in a given area, but it does not necessarily indicate that all argot speakers in the area employ this phonology. The total phonology of the speaker is usually not important in argot studies, since each speaker normally uses the regional dialect with which he grew up. Most individuals maintain this phonology during their lifetime, though some *road workers* vary it unconsciously as a result of contact with speakers from other areas. Some big-time con men are skilled at imitating regional dialects and foreign brogues, but these are the rare exception. Some minor argots such as *ceazarney* /kiazarni/ and *alfalfa* are based entirely on phonemic distortion, but these are more artificially than socially generated.

Syntax is usually indicated with the entry or is obvious from the idioms listed, fragmentary or incomplete paradigms being so labeled. For example, among professional gamblers, especially horse players, the verb *to win* for first, second, and third person singular and plural, past, present, and future consists of one form: *win*. It is interesting to note that this usage of *win* is consistent among touts in bookie joints and at racetracks all over the country.

The proper placement and use of prepositions often serve as a sort of union card that unconsciously reveals a person's involvement in the subculture. A big con operator might *cut into* a mark in order to get him to participate in the con game, but he is not likely to *cut him in* on the score. An uninitiated racetrack enthusiast might exclaim that a certain horse is *in the lead* whereas a horse trainer or jockey would be inclined to say that he is *on the lead,* meaning either that the horse is winning the race or that he is running on his "lead" leg. Likewise, a pickpocket *on the whiz* might sometimes declare himself *out* of a certain *touch* but *in* on another, and his mob must have an *in* with the local police or political organization in order to work in the first place. This latter example illustrates the compulsion for some rackets to create neosemanticisms by converting one part of speech to another; in this case using a preposition as a noun. More frequently, however, a verb is converted to a noun—"He is on the take"—or vice versa—"He greased the fuzz and stayed out of stir." Though it is common for people to use malapropisms without chance of diminishing their intended meaning, in a criminal subculture such a practice signals the hearer that something is not right. Some years ago, for instance, Maurer played a tape of himself talking to a superb pickpocket squad detective proficient in the argot of the *whiz* only to have the pickpockets for whom he was playing the tape declare immediately that they knew Maurer was talking to the fuzz.

Many other syntactic phenomena of these argots are reflected in the quoted corpus of illustrations, and since the overall structure of argots is commonly close to the basic pattern of spoken colloquial American English, only contrasting elements are noted. In some argots variations in intonation, stress, and juncture are significant, but often these are too subtle to permit generalizations, especially since all argots are primarily spoken and seldom written. In some of the included studies—the pickpocket glossary, for example—Maurer has indicated shifts in stress where this may be helpful in clarifying the syntactic pattern.

Since lexicon is basic to any argot, it receives the most attention. Each sense under every entry is defined mainly in terms of the behavior pattern. These definitions are carefully constructed on an inclusive-exclusive formula to clarify the relation of the term and its semantics to the subculture. At this stage the assistance of intelligent informants is essential.

Meanwhile, some attention must be given to spelling, since terms not listed in conventional dictionaries are frequently encountered. In spite of all circumspection, mistakes often creep in and when they are discovered they may be corrected in later publications. For example, some years ago Maurer recorded the pickpocket phrase *super-and-slang* meaning watch and chain, and he assumed the spelling would be *super.* After talking to an old-time pickpocket, however, he recorded the term *kettle* for watch, the reference being to the size of the old-fashioned case which was often stripped of the works and sold for the gold therein. He then realized that super should be *souper* which reflected a kind of whimsical humor. Other old-time pickpockets later verified this form, although most pickpockets are not proficient at spelling. Again, the original spelling of the term *greefo* for marijuana was changed to *griefo*. While working in Mexico Maurer recorded the term *pótacion de guaya* (drink of grief), a concoction made by soaking the ripe seed pods of the *cannabis indica* in a bottle of wine or brandy. It then became clear that *greefo* should be spelled *griefo*. He also recorded such variations as *griffa, griffo, reefo,* and *riffa,* which may suggest a relationship to the term *reefer* (marijuana cigarette). The later telescoped form, *pota guaya,* is probably the source for the currently popular term *pot*.

Other variants in the spelling of certain words will appear from time to time in these chapters, but no attempt has been made to standardize them in this publication. Maurer indicates that there are probably other such spellings that have not come to his attention. In transcribing the lexicon, there is always the danger of assuming that the spelling of the argot term would follow the conventional spelling for standard English terms with similar phonology; therefore, arbitrary decisions must sometimes be made. This may be due to a lack of understanding of the cultural metaphors of the terms or a lack of awareness of the history of the metaphor involved. In the spelling of some argot words from foreign languages, Maurer tries to ascertain the appropriate foreign spelling, but this is not always successful. For example, *gee* /gi/ (gum opium) is probably spelled *ghee* since it seems to be derived from the Hindustani *ghee* (dark-colored butter). The term *gee* as in *heavy-gee* (a safecracker) is a homophone but comes from the French proper name Guy. Maurer suggests that his recording of Chinese argot terms, notably common among old-time opium users, which he has collected both from Chinese and from Americans who have associated with Chinese, into English graphics is largely arbitrary and leaves a good deal to be desired.

The last stage in argot collection is the verification of materials gathered, analyzed, and classified. This is done with the help of competent informants who have a comprehensive understanding of their own profession and subculture. This verification is usually done in writing and preferably in conference with each individual, though it can also be done by mail if the person doing the verification is not available for a personal conference. The lexicon, complete with definitions and behavioral details, is set up with about four entries to the page and includes pertinent questions about each entry which can be answered by checking a number or by writing a brief comment in the blank space provided. This work is time-consuming but is carried out with considerable care. Where there are disagreements on information Maurer must resolve them; in many cases this necessitates further fieldwork. While no single informant will know all the argot or be familiar with all the cultural material discussed, there must be substantial agreement on essential points before the material can be considered authentic.

Because he is dealing with loosely defined, dynamic, and sometimes unstable subcultures, Maurer must make generalizations in which there is some calculated risk. It should be noted that the use of a word by a professional criminal does not necessarily establish it as an argot term, for it must be known or used by a number of operators within a subculture to be classified as such. It follows then that no argot is ever completely recorded nor can any description of a subculture be considered definitive. Maurer would be the first to say that his argot studies are not to be thought of as exhaustive. They are, rather, suggestive with the thought that they may be useful to others, since the language is the key to the subculture.

Studies of criminals are popular in sociological circles, since professional criminals constitute, in many ways, clearly defined segments of society and are therefore often considered ideal subjects for study. In this sense they provide a desirable arena for the study of group behavior, a paramount concern of sociologists. This arena has often been bounded by prison walls, and, even though prison would seem to be a logical place to study general criminal speech, sociologists have consistently presupposed the existence of language as an omnipresent entity pervading all parts of society, and they have, consequently, largely ignored it as one of the keys to group behavior.[2] The need persists, however, for in-depth study of prison as a subculture and as a separate speech community. One excellent step in this direction is the book by Joanne and Nathan Kantrowitz, *Stateville Names* (in preparation). Another large project is now under way in a West Coast prison by Inez Cardozo-Freeman of Ohio State University.

So it has not been until recently that sociologists and linguists have teamed up to discover that people have a tendency to code-switch — automatically alter their speech patterns — when going from one social role or situation to another, much as bilinguals exercise diglossic skills as they move from one linguistic setting to another. Maurer has reported this phenomenon operating in criminal subcultures. He has put to rest the myth that criminals' argots are secret languages used principally to deceive. Argots, while secret or semisecret, are mainly used as a means of identification by members of the in-group who have knowledge of the sociolect of the subculture. However, when a professional criminal converses with a member of the dominant culture he avoids argot and, insofar as he is able, speaks in the social dialect dictated by the social frame in which he finds himself. Just as behavior patterns of criminals differ from those of the dominant culture, so does argot differ from legitimate English; however, the nature of these differences often does not conform to what is generally believed or expected. Therefore, the analysis of criminal argots from a combined sociological and linguistic perspective can shed considerable light upon the behavior patterns of the criminals who use them. The same technique may be useful in studying other language groups.

2. Pier Paolo Giglioli, "Introduction," in *Language and Social Context,* ed. Pier Paolo Giglioli (New York: Penguin, 1977), p. 7.

With two or three exceptions, these selections of Maurer's work concentrate on studies of criminal subcultures. The relevance of these individual exceptions is explained in the headnotes to the articles. Most of the articles included here have two introductions. The first has been written by Maurer especially for this book and is intended to place the argot or the material presented in its proper historical perspective or to describe the circumstances surrounding the writing of the article or the study of the argot. The second introduction is the one that appeared when the article was first published, included here so that the reader can get an idea of Maurer's perspective at the time. The arrangement of the selections is chronological according to the date first published. The book can then be viewed as a series of synchronic studies of entire semantic sets which have functioned in various time frames reflecting at once the development of Maurer's insights on the nature of argot and, by extension, the changing behavior patterns of professional criminals.

ALLAN W. FUTRELL

1

Speech Peculiarities of the North Atlantic Fishermen

This study—actually a rather crude word list—is included for several reasons despite its shortcomings by current standards. First, it reflects the general state of language study in academia in 1930, when Bloomfield's *Language* had yet to appear, and Mencken's *The American Language,* then a slim volume, was regarded as a rather spicy and off-color publication. The study of regional dialects was almost respectable, and Hans Kurath was just organizing fieldwork for the *Linguistic Atlas of the United States and Canada,* now, some fifty years later, being completed under the able direction of Raven McDavid. Observations on variant language found in subcultures were presented somewhat discreetly to the exclusive membership of the American Dialect Society. These notes on the living language seldom reached the classroom, for English professors taught the language as it "should be," and not as it actually was.

Geographical dialects were regarded as "quaint"; the social dialects were scarcely recognized at all; the terms *sociolinguistics* and the *sociology of language* had yet to be coined. Anthropologists and linguists tended to limit their observations to safe areas such as the speech of so-called primitive tribes. It was hardly in the genteel tradition of the Modern Language Association to recognize an occupational language like that of the deep-sea fishermen as worthy of serious attention. Furthermore, this occupation included a heavy quota of Newfoundlanders and Nova Scotians, together with immigrants from Ireland, Northern England, and Scotland, as well as Scandinavians, some Holland Dutch, Portuguese, Italians, and a few Spaniards. Although the basic language on most vessels was English, there was little interest in the study of the speech of these seamen, most of whom could have been classified as illiterate immigrants.[1]

I suspect that a study of this polyglot occupation would have tried even the

1. A recent study (in *National Science Magazine,* March 1979) indicates a survival of this ancient and clannish subculture transplanted to the West Coast where the specialized language is still used and where Italian and Portuguese are the dominant code languages employed over a sophisticated network of electronic communication.

skills of a modern researcher well trained in the subtleties of descriptive linguistics. I not only lacked training but had little insight into the depth and significance of the linguistic elements involved, for I was a sort of jackleg fisheries engineer working for Clarence Birdseye on production problems at sea. This was well before Birdseye's name had become a household word, and just after he had invented the quick freeze process now universally used. He was interested in modernizing production methods which, at that time, had changed little since the seventeenth century. In those days, fishing was done largely from fore-and-aft rigged schooners, graceful but antiquated, that were frequently powered by auxiliary diesel engines, and some steam trawlers that were often refitted from World War I minesweepers. This crude equipment was a far cry from the sophisticated fishing vessels used today, especially along the Pacific and Alaskan Coast. The language reflects some of the crude methods and equipment used in that day, though some of it has been adapted to changing times. Many of today's West Coast fishermen were transplanted from New England fishing centers. Observations on language were a minor luxury somewhat incompatible with rigorous and demanding work on deck.

A second reason for the inclusion of this work is that its publication brought me into immediate and personal contact with people like the pioneer dialectologist Louise Pound and that perennial disturber of the peace, H. L. Mencken, both of whom firmly believed that there were treasures to be discovered in what was then regarded as linguistic slumming.

Finally, while working with the fishing fleet, I made my first contact with criminal argots. The fishing ground and eastern seaports were infiltrated with professional rum runners and skilled European smugglers who were in the process — though we did not realize it at the time — of forging the prohibition rackets which brought together the skills and aptitudes of many criminal subcultures to produce what is romantically called "syndicated crime" today. Friendly contacts with the rum fleet at sea, off the islands of St. Pierre and Miquelon, and in various ports allowed me to hear, for the first time, spoken criminal argots. Also, some of these contacts were later very useful to me in initiating a study of the speech patterns used within various criminal subcultures. The fishing fleet, of course, was in no way criminal, but some individual fishermen and ex-fishermen were involved directly or indirectly in smuggling.

Nearly fifty years later I hardly know what motivated my publishing this article. I suspect that I smelled something rather yeasty in the linguistic ferment which was bubbling beneath the tight lid of literary purism.

• • •

THE life of the deep-sea fisherman of the North Atlantic is by no means a rosy one, despite the recent alleviating innovations of radio and powered vessels. Some six of his seven days are spent at sea, jogging when the weather is rough and fishing in the lulls between gales and storms. On the seventh the catch is unloaded at Gloucester, Boston, or Halifax and the evening of that day is given over to the dismal recreation of women and rum; the next day he is back again to the sobering influence of physical danger and gruelling toil. From his viewpoint his life is a dreary one, entirely devoid of the romance which is popularly supposed to associate itself with a sea-going life. His home is a ninety-foot vessel and his world a brief circle of treacherous grey. He laughs at "the lure of the sea"—he fishes because he can do nothing else. His speech is as hard and as bleak as his life. He is not troubled with too vivid an imagination, but he does have a sense of humor—coarse and dry though it may be—which makes existence tolerable.

The number of nationalities and races represented in this regional industry is almost unlimited. Aboard the *Princeton*, a steam trawler out of Boston, I found twenty-two men representing fourteen different nationalities; none were native-born citizens of the United States, and the skipper alone was a naturalized citizen. This cosmopolitan crew is not an exception, but fairly representative. The foreign element in crews always runs high with the nordic element predominating, and the majority of this of English or Irish stock. New Foundland and Nova Scotia contribute the bulk of seamen, though Englishmen and Irishmen from the other side are numerous, and the firemen (aboard the steam trawlers) are almost inevitably Spanish. The Latin element is heavily represented. French—both Continental and Canadian—Spanish, Italian, and Portugese fishermen ply out of the ports whose most blatant boast is of pure and undefiled Americanism. In Boston, Maverick Square, the lower end of Sumner Street, and Havre and Liverpool Streets form the centre of this foreign sea-going community. In Gloucester, at the upper end of Commercial Street, a straggling but sizable Italian and Portuguese quarter has established itself. Most of these men engage in forms of close-in fishing, returning home each night, but there is one large sea-going dragger out of Gloucester, the *Amelia Pereirra*, which is manned from skipper to cook by Portuguese. The skipper alone, one Abilone Pereirra, speaks English.

In the face of this tremendous foreign influence in the fishing industry, it is strange that foreign words and idioms have not made a place for themselves in the lingo of the craft; however, it will be noticed in the list to follow[1] that most of the words are of dialectal English extraction. While I do not attempt to completely explain this fact, I offer the following suggestions which may, in part, account for it. First, these foreigners came to America with their craft already well-established—the Portuguese were famous fishermen before Cape Cod was known to exist—and have, in their own languages, an adequate technical vocabulary. Second, what word-borrowing does go on takes place *from* rather than *into* English. The foreigners sell their fish over an American Exchange (where, by the way, the English language only is permitted), their vessels are rigged and repaired in American sail-lofts, they frequently speak American fishermen on the grounds, and the matrix of the population with whom they mingle ashore is well sprinkled with native Americans. At present the radio is also an important factor in introducing English for, in addition to the regular radio programs which are received aboard almost all fishing vessels, Station WHDH, the monotonous "voice from home" broadcasts daily market reports, hails, and bits of gossip or news from vessel to vessel and from shore to the grounds. At any rate, whatever the cause may be, the language aboard those boats where dialects of English are spoken remains almost wholly of English extraction, and the adoption of foreign words and phrases is rare. Now for the list.

All hands, n.   Everyone; not necessarily confined to the crew.
allow, v.   To think, to suspect, to take for granted.
bachelor man, n.   Bachelor.
back, n.   The 'top' portion of the trawl.   (See *otter trawl*.)
bank, or *banks*, n.   Any 'shoal' water (usually 10–110 fathoms deep) or the bottom under that shoal water. *Fishing banks* include any shoal water where fish feed or breed.
basket, n.   A container, made of canvas stretched over a steel frame, about twice as deep as it is wide, and usually square at the top, which holds some 150 pounds of fish. It is used for hoisting fish out of the hold when unloading and may be used to lower such small fish as herring, blinks, or butterfish into the hold.

---

[1] In this list I have purposely neglected the great body of sea-language which has already been pretty thoroughly cataloged, and have concerned myself mainly with those terms directly connected with the workaday language of the fisherman.

be civil, v.   To behave.

belly, n.   That part of the cod-end of the trawl which drags on the sea bottom while the net is being towed.

bend, v.   To attach by tying or splicing a rope; also, specifically to wind the foot-rope cable with rope.

beam trawler, n.   A powered vessel (erroneously so called) which is equipped with otter trawls and machinery for setting and towing them.   Probably correctly called *steam trawlers* although *beam trawler* is favored by general usage.

betimes, adv.   Right away, early, now and then.

blinks, n.   Undersized or culled mackerel.

blare, v. or n.   The crying of birds or a baby, or may be used to indicate the sound of a steam or compressed-air whistle.

blocks, n.   Round cross-sections of timber with holes in the centre through which a cable is run.   They are spaced at convenient intervals all the way across the foot-rope and serve to keep the net from being torn while towing over rough bottom.   Sometimes called *rollers.*

bosom, n.   Considered by some fishermen to be the portion of single-mesh netting between the belly and the footrope.

break, v.   To cut, as rope or hair.   " 'Ey, you, 'oo broke yer 'air orf?"

break water, v.   To awaken or get out of bed.

breeze up, v.   To blow a gale.   "We allowed she'd breeze up, so we was after puttin' her 'ead inter th' norwest an' shortenin' sail."

bull-hides, n.   One or more green cowhides which are lashed to the belly of the net to ease the chafing on the bottom.

busy to work, adv. phr.   Busily at work.

catch a trip, v. phr.   To take a satisfactory quantity of fish; sometimes *catching a good trip* implies also that the fish brought a good price, that the trip was prosperous.

checkers, n.   Temporary adjacent enclosures or pens on deck to keep the fish from sliding about when the vessel rolls; there are usually four in the form of a divided square.   The heavy planks of which they are made are called *checkerboards.*

chicken halibut, n.   A young halibut weighing up to 25 pounds, and much esteemed as a delicacy.

civil morning, n. phr.   A fine morning.

clever morning, n. phr.   A nice morning.

cod-end, n.   The bag at the apex of an otter trawl which collects the fish.

cod-end knot, n.   An ingenious knot for keeping the cod-end closed until it is filled with fish and then releasing it after the bag has been hoisted aboard.

cold, v.   To chill a lobster after it has been boiled.

cold-cock, v.   To kill when used of vermin; when applied to a man it usually means to stop, to knock unconscious, to disable.

coloring, n.   Tattooing on the person.

complaint of the flesh, n. phr.   Sickness.

cruise, v. or n.   1. To make a journey either on shore or at sea; 2. the journey itself.

dab, n.   A species of flatfish resembling the sole.

dismal, adj.   Used of a person to mean crabbed or crusty.

dirty, adj.   Of the weather, stormy, blowy, or even foggy; of a vessel, meaning that she takes seas aboard to a troublesome extent in heavy weather.

dong, n.   The male organ.

doors, n.   Otter boards (see *otter boards*).

doughboys, n.   Heavy dumplings cooked in broth or with vegetables.

down, adv.   North, or North along the coast.

dragger, n.   A small powered sailing vessel equipped with a small variety of otter trawl.   As distinguished from a beam trawler, this vessel is smaller, carries only one net, and fishes from the starboard side only.

dragging guts to the bear, v. phr.   Applied to dragging the heavy wet bull-hides aft to be put in pickle after a trip has been caught.   Sometimes it is jocularly known as *the blessed Savior dragging guts to the bear*.   (The origin of this phrase has puzzled the writer considerably and he would appreciate any light which readers might be able to throw on it.)

family duties, n. phr.   Intercourse by a married couple.

fat, adj.   Used to describe certain fish, especially the herring, shad, or menhaden when they reach a state of perfect health between spawning seasons.

fetch up, v.   To ram, to collide, to run aground; used of the trawl when it catches on an obstruction on the bottom.

fit-out, n.   A handline or line-trawl; any tackle for taking fish by hook and line.

footrope, n.   The rope (usually a cable bound with rope) which stretches across the mouth of the otter trawl and holds the wings together.   It is in a plane parallel to that of the horizontal plane of the headrope, but trails some distance behind it.

found, n.   Food and bedding furnished aboard a vessel, in addition to pay, or a share in the catch.   "He's after gittin' fifty dollars a month, stock, and found."

friend-girl, n.   Girl friend, sweetheart.

gallows, n.   Heavy steel bars, curved until they resemble horse-collars, which support the blocks through which the wires run from the winch to the net.   There are four on a *beam trawler*, one on each quarter, while the *draggers* have only two, fore and aft, on the starboard side.

get good weather, v. phr.   To have good weather.

grum, adj.   Having a sorrowful facial expression.

gurry, n.   The entrails and other waste parts of fish.

hake, n.   (Sometimes called *white hake*.)   The whiting.

hail, n.   The total number of pounds of fish which a vessel may *have* in her hold at the time a declaration is made; daily *hails* are sent in by most company-owned boats each day by radio.

hard bottom, n.   Rough or jagged bottom.   Geographically, that area known as "the Northern Edge."

haul-back, v. or n.   1. To retrieve the trawl by starting the winches and winding the cables on the drums.   2. The act of taking in the trawl and hoisting it aboard.

headrope, n.   The cable or rope running between the wings across the mouth of the net.   It is above and somewhat forward of the footrope.

heave, v.   1. To toss or throw an object. 2. To haul, as on a rope.

herring-snapper, n.   A New Foundlander or Nova Scotian; sometimes an inhabitant of Maine.

hold prayer, v.   To conduct any kind of religious services.

industrious girl, n. phr.   A corruption of 'girl industrial worker.'

ice-pan, n.   Sea ice in cakes; sometimes indicates "pancake-ice' in the process of formation.

inside clothes, n.   Underwear. Also the heavy work clothing worn under oilskins.

iron, n.   A swordfish harpoon.

jig, v.   To gig or spear a fish by artificial light.

jimbo, n.   (Sometimes *jumbo*).   The stem-staysail.

jog, v.   To keep a vessel into the wind, and under steerage way if she is powered, when the weather is too rough to fish.

keep school, v. phr.   To conduct a school or class; also used in *keep meeting* or *keep church.*

kitchen-barroom, n.   In the old days (before Prohibition) it was the custom for fishermen to live ashore in a boarding and rooming house where there was always a barrel of liquor on tap (and on sale) in the kitchen. Although the kitchen-barroom has now taken on something of the flavor of a speakeasy, it is still an indispensable institution in Gloucester.

lay, n.   The relationship or agreement between vessel-owners and fishermen with regard to the proportionate share of each in the catch.   The *lays* of every type of vessel are different.

lavendar Jesus, n. phr.   A choice bit of profanity, probably a variation of 'blue Jesus.'

lean, adj.   The opposite of *fat,* used to describe fish which are poor after the spawning season.

macaroni, n.   Clay bottom which collects in the nets in peculiar tube-like formations.

mackerel-boat, n.   A small boat some twenty feet or more in length which is towed astern of the *mackerel seiner*; it carries the small gasoline engine for *pursing* the seine.

mackerel-seine, n.   A large, fine-meshed, bag-shaped, circular seine with which a school of mackerel is surrounded and captured.

mackerel-seiner, n.   A vessel equipped for taking mackerel.

Maid, n.   An intimate form of direct address.

make a set, v. phr.   To set, tow, and haul-back the trawl.

make fish, v. phr.   To preserve fish, usually by splitting and pickling or drying them.   Also used of preparing fish for the table.

maul, v.   To make tangible love to either sex.

Miss, n.   A polite form of direct address.

muff-diver, n.   A pervert of either sex who is addicted to cunnilinctus.

mug-up, v. or n.   1. To get a snack with tea or coffee between meals. 2. The snack itself, which is taken in the galley after each set if there is time.

My maid, n. phr.   A polite form of direct address.

nippers, n.   Any small voracious vermin, especially body lice.

(to be) on lobsters, v. phr.   To be taking or dressing lobsters.

(to be) on heavy fish, v. phr.   To be making large catches in rapid succession.

(the) other side, n.   Europe.   "Larry seed a God's plenty o' beam-trawlin afore he left th' other side."

otter trawl, n.   A drag-net in the shape of a large flat bag, approximately 114 feet wide at the mouth and some 90 feet from the mouth to the apex, or cod-end, where the fish collect.   As it is towed over the bottom astern of the vessel the mouth, or "wings" are held open by water-pressure against two otter-boards, or doors, one on either side.

overhaul, v.   To successfully assail a woman's virtue.

pansy, n.   A man with inherent homosexual characteristics.

paralyzed, adj.   Dead drunk.

parson, n.   1. A minister or priest.   2. Anyone who appears particularly dignified.

penboards, n.   Boards which are used in constructing pens (see *pens*) which are built up as needed at sea and torn down as the catch is unloaded.

pennywrinkle, n.   The periwinkle; also the hermit-crab which often inhabits the periwinkle shell.

pens, n.   Bins in the fish-hold built of boards and used for keeping the various grades of fish separate; they also serve to keep the cargo from shifting.

pickle, n.   Brine for preserving fish.

piece, n.   1. A firearm of any kind, including a pistol.   2. A young girl, often implying that she is a prostitute.   3. Copulation. (See *skin*).   4. The male organ.

pinny, n.   Pinafore.

poor, adj.   Used of persons who have died.   "Poor Charley were a wonderful fine handliner, he were."

Portagee, n.   Portuguese.

pox, n.   Any kind of veneral disease.

proud, adj.   Pleased.

purse, v.   To draw up a seine by means of *a pursing rope* which works like the string in a purse.

put a face on, v. phr.   To spoil one's good looks.   "Tighten up them foresheet blocks, er by th' Lord Jesus I'll put a face on ye."

redjacks, n.   Light but waterproof leather boots; before the advent of rubber boots they were worn universally by the fishermen, and are still quite popular.

ripper, n.   A short sharp knife for dressing fish.

rummy, n.   Anyone who is habitually drunk.

sail-loft, n.   A wharf for rigging and outfitting fishing vessels.

salt-fishing, part.   To catch, dress, split, and pickle fish in tubs aboard the vessels; now almost a thing of the past because of the market for fresh fish.

salt-water-pigeon, n.   A painful infection which sets in about the hairs on the wrists as a result of salt water coming in contact with skin which has been chafed by oilskins.

sanders, n.   Sandpipers, especially young ones.

say a few, v. phr.   To talk a little; to say a little something.

scent, n. or v.   Perfume; the act of perfuming.

schrod, n.   Haddock which are too small to be filleted.

seed-lobster, n.   A female lobster carrying eggs under her tail.

set, v.   1. To get the net in position for towing.   2. To plant the garden.

sewer, n.   A sink of slime and ooze in the ocean bottom.

shack, n.   The quarters of the radio operator.

shag, or *shag-fish*, n.   Cod which have been split, salted, and cured in the sun.

shine, n.   A mixture of alky splits and water which is used as an intoxicating drink.

sing out, v.   To speak or to call.

site, n.   A place as fisherman aboard a fishing vessel.

skin, n.   A delectable bit of feminine flesh.   " 'Twere a wonderful fine piece o'skin I 'ad me in 'Alifax."

skins, n.   Oilskins, waterproof clothing.

skinyard, n.   An exchange of spicy or vulgar stories.

shift, n.   A change of clothes.

shocking, adj.   Surprising.

slapjacks, n.   Heavy rough shoes with wooden soles, used when fishermen are working on deck in fine weather.

sling, n.   A rope or cable looped at each end which is used to hoist the cod-end aboard.

slipshods, n.   Slapjacks.

slit, v.   To cut the fish open from the gills to the anus with one quick flip of the knife; may also be applied to the entire dressing process.

snapper, n.   Any undersized marketable fish.

sparks, n.   The radio operator.

Spk or *Spick*, n.   A Spaniard.

split, v.   1. To cut a fish in two equal halves from head to tail, usually removing the backbone in the process.   2. The divide a single haul of fish into several sections to facilitate hoisting aboard; this is known as *splitting the bag*.

string of gear, n. phr.   Sexual equipment.

sweetness, n.   Sugar.

terrible, adj.   Used of a person to indicate strength or size.

trash, n.   The non-food-fish taken in the net.

tree, n.   A bush, as *raspberry tree, blueberry tree*.

tronch the garden, v. phr.   To prepare and plant a garden.

twanging or *twang*, v, or n.   The crying of a baby.

twine, n.   Netting, especially that of which the otter trawl is made.

twine-loft, n.   A place for making and mending trawls, seins, etc.

vessel, n.   As distinguished from the *beam-trawler* or *steam-trawler* proper, any wooden schooner-rigged fishing boat, either with or without power.

warp, n.   The line by which the iron of a swordfish harpoon is fastened to the shaft.

whore's egg, n.   A small spiny crustacean esteemed by the Italians as a delicacy.

widow lady, n.   A widow.

widow man, n.   A widower.

wire, n.   1. The cables, some 150 fathoms in length, which are used to tow the trawl.   2. Used to designate that portion of the cable which is 'out,' that is, off the drum; this length is always kept to approximately three times the depth of the water, that is, in 40 fathoms of water the actual amount of *wire* is 120 fathoms.

wonderful, adj. Very.

you, pro. Used excessively as a term of direct address, even among persons who know each other.

In addition to the above list there are certain other peculiarities in the speech of the fishermen which can hardly be classed as idioms or dialect —though they are, probably, an integral factor in the dialect—but must, as a sop to pedantry, rather be treated as the marks of ignorance and illiteracy. They consist mainly in distortions of (1) verbs, and (2) pronouns.

In most verbs there is a tendency to reverse the customary order of person and number, especially in the present tense. The past and compound tenses are formed heaven only knows how, with the premium seemingly on bizarre variety. Rather than attempt to give a list of isolated mutilated verb forms, I present sample conjugations of a common verb or two in present and past tenses, which will serve to illustrate (though hardly to explain) the plan of mutilation.

To see (past participle, seed)
Indicative

Present	Imperfect	Present Perfect	Past Perfect	Future
I sees	I seed	I has seed	I had seed	(regular)
you sees	you seed	you has seed	you had seed	
he see	he seed	he have seed	he had seed	
we sees	we seed	we has seed	we had seed	
you sees	you seed	you has seed	you had seed	
they sees	they seed	they has seed	they had seed	

To do (past participle, doed—pronounced *dōōd*)
Indicative

Present	Imperfect	Present Perfect	Past Perfect	Future
I does (doos)	I doed or done	I has doed	I had doed	(regular)
you does	you doed or done	you has doed	you had doed	
he do	he doed or done	he have doed	he had doed	
we does	we doed or done	we has doed	we had doed	
you does	you doed or done	you has doed	you had doed	
they does	they doed or done	they has doed	they had doed	

While this tendency does produce some weird effects, the confusion is hardly so great as might be imagined, for after all the verb-needs of the fishermen are simple enough to be amply supplied by the tenses here included; ideas in the subjunctive are beyond both his needs and his capacities, but I have no doubt that if he did suddenly wish to express himself in that mode, he could concoct tenses in the pluperfect or future perfect which would make up in originality what they lacked in grace.

The distortion of pronouns is more regular, perhaps, than that of verbs. In general, the tendency is to interchange subject pronouns for object pronouns, and *vice versa;* any sundry deviations from this generalization may be accepted, I suppose, as linguistic sports, for want of a better explanation. The following examples will illustrate: "They was after givin' it to *we*"; "*us* do be havin' a wonderful fine time"; "Carey was after tellin' I th' trut', I do allow." There is also the substitution of *he* or *she* for the impersonal pronoun *it* as "*He* do be breezin' up outer th' norwest" and "That last comber, *she* were after bein' a awful sea."

I purposefully omit any notes on pronunciation, despite the fact that this is probably the most fascinating element in the language of the fishermen, for it has in it the roll and boom of the sea. But it is too vast and complicated a subject to attack in a short article; in fact, I am not sure that it can be successfully analyzed even by a very thorough study, because of the heterogeneous nature of the crews. Every bay and cove and inlet on the coasts of Labrador, New Foundland, and Nova Scotia has its own particular brogue, and often an individual dialect. These brogues are so distinctive that an up-and-coming native who has cruised about extensively can place a stranger's locale quite accurately by hearing him speak. But once the fisherman drifts away from home, he associates with men from other locales and the edge is taken from his native brogue. Even after a liberal and intimate acquaintance with the seamen, I found myself unable to put my finger on the subtle phonetic differences in the speech of natives from different parts, although I could detect that the differences were there; hence I leave the study of pronunciation and enunciation among the fishermen to an abler and more painstaking scholar than myself.

2

Circus and Carnival Argot

The American circus constituted a peripatetic subculture, a kind of world of make-believe, which visited every town of any size in the country during the warmer months. It differed from the much smaller European circus which was often family owned and operated. Its extravagance, its collection of esoteric performers, its large menagerie, its inclusion of grifters to trim the public, its rapid and efficient mobility, and most of all its size, set it apart. At the time this article was written the heyday of the circus was declining, and the general public was beginning to lose interest. Motion pictures were supplying powerful year-round competition. The better shows were consolidating and operating under contract from a fixed base, as did the Ringling Brothers and Barnum and Bailey Circus in Florida. As of 1930, most adults who attended circuses claimed they did so only for the enjoyment of the children they brought with them. It did not take a Freudian psychiatrist, however, to observe that the circus appealed to the childlike element in all adults even more strongly perhaps than it did to the children.

Though the circus was to some extent an occupational subculture, it was also a total way of life for the members and their families, who had little contact with the world outside the tanbark. There were four social divisions within this small world. First, there was the management. Its members not only exploited all the employees but, at the same time, exercised a certain paternal authority over them which often included compassion; generosity, however, was rare. Families of the management frequently traveled in a special railroad car or motorized van. In fact, Zack Terrell, later the owner of the Cole Brothers Circus, acquired the private railroad car belonging to the steel tycoon Charles M. Schwab and traveled with his equestrian wife amidst the splendor of Italian marble bathrooms, hand-carved mahogany furniture, and luxurious bedrooms, to the undying envy of every other circus owner.

Second, there were the performers, who likewise traveled with their families, their complicated equipment, and their trained animals. Many of these were genuine artists and superb entertainers. Their children were legion in a child's paradise.

Third, there were the laborers, generally known as razorbacks, who did the rough and heavy work connected with setting up and tearing down the circus. Many of these were expert teamsters since circuses which traveled by train used scores of four- and six-horse *snatch teams* to move the heavy wagons to and from the railroad yards and in the inevitable parade through the streets of small and medium-sized towns. Also, many laborers were experienced riggers, experts at moving and installing heavy equipment, often possessing prior experience as seamen on sailing ships. There were carpenters, masons, plumbers, electricians, blacksmiths, wheelwrights, cooks, stable hands, and even musicians, who doubled in brass. Often there was a contingent of American Indians, usually stoically disapproving of circus life but sparking the Wild West show. In contrast to management and the performers, who usually showed a high degree of successful adaptation to their environment, the laborers often manifested symptoms of acute social and psychological maladjustment. The circus was their escape from adult reality, which meant the responsibilities of family life. They clung to it for emotional security. They lived in a hard male world where the safety valves were whiskey, gambling, and an occasional whore.

Finally, most circuses carried grifters. These were flat-jointers, short-change artists, pickpockets, and short-con men who preyed upon the local citizenry and paid the management a percentage of the take. Their conflicts with local law were amicably disposed of by the official circus *mender* or *patch*. The grifters were strictly professional and very effective at their individual rackets. They represented a subculture within a subculture and in general held themselves superior to the other circus personnel, who, in turn, looked down upon them as undesirables. While the grifters had only a minimal status outside the *privilege car* (the rolling headquarters of the management where the grifters congregated to drink and socialize), it was this group—particularly the short-con operators—that especially interested me and that opened the way for a later intensive study of their subculture in and out of circuses.

The circus constituted the first full-fledged subculture which I encountered, and there I made many contacts that facilitated later studies. Incidentally, George Milburn's excellent study of circus argot ("Circus Words," *American Mercury,* November 1931) appeared just after the publication of this piece, though I was unaware that he was working on the subject until after my article was published.

• • •

ROMANCE is fading from the road show.   Seventy-five years ago a circus was manned, propelled, defended by flesh and blood. The performers lashed straining horses over thirty miles or more of treacherous roads between stands; the same performers and the same horses, aided perhaps by a few extra laborers, unloaded the wagons, set up the show, gave two or three performances, licked the inevitable native rowdies, and proceeded to the next stand without balking at the personal hardship involved.   In that day the life produced a sturdy and valiant personnel; those who could not use their fists as well as their heads soon dropped by the wayside, along with those who could not drive six horses or swing a sledge.   As the weaklings dropped, so were the daring attracted; daring and strength in physical achievement begot daring and strength in verbal expression, and by the time the American circus was ready to pass from the horse-and-wagon stage to the railroad-era, it was manned by a type half roughneck, half gentleman, and spoke a jargon as swaggering and as picturesque as itself.   During a period of forty years or so this type flourished, always sapped and enervated, however, by ever-increasing mechanical aids.   Steam engines did the hauling, elephants and horses loaded and unloaded, canvas was hauled up with steam winches or powerful teams of horses, the work was specialized, living quarters for the crew and personnel improved, the customer was treated with some degree of consideration—and now it is all changed.   The modern circus or carnival is a motorized caravan, groomed by skilled mechanics, and carrying performers each of whom is an expert in his or her profession.   These performers live in good hotels along the way, or, as in the case of those large circuses operated by the Ringling interests, are cared for in comfortable quarters aboard the trains, while even the razor-backs or canvas-men eat tasty food served in a clean mess-tent. Profanity is, to a large extent, eliminated from the business; courtesy is shown between employer and employee, and, to an even more marked degree, from employee to customer.   For the circus, like other big business firms, has adopted the idea of "service," and the customer's comfort is second only to his capacity to pay.[1]   This commercialization

---

[1] It should be noted that carnivals as a class have not progressed so rapidly as circuses in the process of becoming modernized.   The carnival also has the reputation of evading the law whenever possible.

—so some of the old-timers feel—has emasculated modern showman-ship, and along with it modern circus and carnival slang. However that may be, there yet remains plenty of glamour and of grief in the road-show business and its jargon still retains a redeeming modicum of romance. Indeed, few occupations have so colorful a technical vocabulary; few take such flagrant liberties with the mother-tongue; few are so baffling and yet so fascinating in the obscurities of distorted speech.

The reasons for this are legion. To mention only the most obvious, we have, in the first place, a group of people from all parts of the world, civilized and uncivilized. Riders from Potato Gulch rub elbows with French acrobats, Polish strong men, South American equestrians, Italian musicians, Negro laborers, American Indians, Japanese tumblers, Australian or African savages, and foreign freaks without end. Some sort of universal language is necessary, and, indeed, inevitable. Then, strong as are the bonds cementing members of the troupe together, there are always cliques and counter cliques which wish to preserve what privacy they may regarding their respective affairs. This leads to jargons within a jargon; but the private lingo soon loses its protective quality and is absorbed into the general hodge-podge of speech. And this same principle may be applied to the whole show as opposed to the general public; for so many fake games of chance, tricks to catch customers, and shady deals of all sorts depend upon the customer's ignorance of what is going on, that some form of secret communication is indispensable. This type of language changes rapidly, for obvious reasons; but it is continually fed by the profound contempt which all show-people feel for the "rubes." Then, too, shows travel all over the world, and pick up useful words in all the far corners; the business attracts numerous flashy individuals with a flair for the unusual, the bizarre, in dress and manner and speech; what is more, the professional showman loves his work and delights in coining lively words and phrases to describe its various technicalities—and so on without end.

As might be expected, the high birth-rate in show-lingo is equalled by a death-rate sufficient to insure the survival of none but the fittest. Words appear today and sink into oblivion tomorrow. When a word is singularly apt, it may stick for a year or five years or twenty years, accordingly as it fulfills the demands of varying conditions and circum-stances. Some words approach immortality in their ability to make adjustments. A few of them had ancestors in the Roman circus; others were bandied about over medieval Europe with the mystery and miracle players; still others were contributed by troupes of Renaissance strolling players; various others have worked their way in through modern foreign languages—French, Spanish, Mexican; but the great bulk of them are sharp-edged and lack the polish of time; they had their birth in garish, teeming, earthy America.   These which follow represent the residue of the sifting process—the fit which have survived —the essence of modern circus lingo.

May I here express my appreciation for the interest taken in this article by Mr. Tim Limerick, whose long experience with road shows has been the source of most valuable criticism and suggestion.

ace, 1. n.   A one-dollar bill.   2. adj.   One who performs any particular act exceptionally well.

(to) advertise, v.   To attract undesirable attention by raising a rumpus in a public place.   "Mac gets plastered, and tries to advertise in a grab-joint when the cops git him."

advance agent, or *agent,* n.   The man who travels ahead of a show for the purpose of locating lots, procuring licenses, arranging for advertising, and "fixing" city or village officials.

Annie-Oakley, n.   A meal ticket, named for Annie Oakley, Buffalo Bill's famous woman rifle-shot, who could throw a playing card into the air and make it look like a punched meal-ticket.

b. r., n.   The common term for "bankroll."   "According to reports from Charlie Chatman, he has been adding considerable to the b. r."

bally-show, n.   One which "opens" (see *opening*) regularly—about once an hour, with repeat performances.

battery-whip, n.   A whip with an electrified lash, used in handling animals.   "In some states a trainer ain't allowed to carry a gun in the parade, so he has to keep the cats off with a battery-whip.

beddy, n.   A winter hangout for an individual connected with the circus or carnival. "This spring weather makes me itch to leave the winter beddy and get with it again."

benny, n.   An overcoat.

big-tom, n.   The cat (usually in the center) on a cat-rack which is heavily loaded and bigger than the rest to make a deceptive target.   His size makes him easy to hit, while the weight prevents him from going down.   See *cat-rack.*

biz., n.   The common term for "business."

bloomer, n.   A town which fails to respond to the show business, or one in which small profits are made.   "Marion, Indiana, is always a bloomer for me."

(to) blow, v.   1. intr.   To give a big prize, by mistake or through failure of a mechanical device, to a customer playing a "set-joint" or other game of chance.   See *set-joint* and "go wrong."

2. tr.   To beat a hotel by leaving without paying the bill.   "We was fixin' to blow that one, but the guy was so nice we hadn't the heart."

blow-off, n.   The first sale or sales, on which no profit is made, but which serve to stimulate business for a *pitchman.*   See *pitchman.*

bluebirds, n.   Regarded as a sign of coming spring, hence a symbol of optimism. "Business is fair, but I ain't seen any bluebirds around yet."

blues, n. General admission seats in a circus. "Guess you'll have t' set in the blues, lady."

boss, n. One who evaluates stolen articles for thieves; usually not a professional pawn-broker.

caravan, n. A carnival troupe with all the baggage and equipment.

carnifolks, n. Persons who engage in the carnival business.

carnival-louse, n. A hanger-on who follows a carnival, but who has nò official connection with it.

cat-den, n. A cage of lions.

cat-rack, n. A game of skill which consists of throwing base-balls at a row of grotesque cats mounted on a frame. "George is taking in the dough on his cat-rack." See *big-tom*.

century, n. A one-hundred-dollar bill, or one hundred dollars in smaller denominations.

cheaters, n. Eye-glasses. "We got his leather and a pair of cheaters."

cleaner, n. One who "cleans sticks" in a set-joint, i. e. the man who takes paid players aside and recovers the money or prizes which they have won to make an impression on the crowd. See *stick* and *set-joint*.

cold, adj. Used to characterize a town which doesn't respond readily; one in which small profits are made. Profitable towns are indicated as "red." See *red* and *bloomer*.

(to) cool him off, v. phr. To take a "monkey" aside and console him when he has lost so that he will not complain to the police or cause a disturbance in front of the joint. "If you don't take that monkey for a walk and cool him off, he's going to squawk." The "cooling" process sometimes consists of blackjacking.

concessionaires, or *concessioners*, n. Those who have bought various concessions from a circus or carnival.

connection, n. The narrow enclosed passageway from the menagerie into the main tent. "Bill's stalling the push in the connection."

cooch-show, or *coochie-show*, n. A show, often run by a "Doc" or patent-medicine man, which exhibited the so-called "hoochie-coochie dance" as an attraction. Now almost obsolete.

(to) crack, v. To speak. "He tried to crack to the copper, but the cop cut him short."

(to) cut him in, v. phr. To take another man into business temporarily. "Business was good, so we cut him in for a couple of days."

den, n. 1. A consignment of rattle-snakes for snake-eaters or snake-shows; dens come in two sizes: a ten-dollar den which contains fifty snakes, and a five-dollar den which contains twenty-five.

2. A cage for animals.

deuce, n. A two-dollar bill.

dip, n. A pickpocket.

Doc., n. A quack who runs a medicine show, or "pitches" patent medicines. Used to avoid prosecution for assuming the title "Dr."

dolly, n. A small, portable derrick, usually mounted on a motor truck.

donnicker, n. A toilet or water-closet.

double-saw, or *double-saw-buck*, n. A twenty-dollar bill. See *saw-buck*.

drag, n. 1. The train or cars used to transport a circus or carnival.

2. A street.

(to) duck him in, v. phr.   To draw on an unsuspecting victim in a game of chance. "You get him over here, and we'll duck him in."

fin, n.   A five-dollar bill.

fixer, n.   1. Legal representative of the circus or carnival who acts as mediator between the show and local officials.   2. An "illegal" representative whose business it is to buy protection from local police.

(to) flash, v., tr.   To show a stolen article to one capable of evaluating it.   "I'm going to flash it to the boss and see what it's worth."   See *boss.*

(to) flash for the crowd, v. phr.   To give a valuable prize at a set-joint for the purpose of interesting the crowd.   See *throw a cop.*

(to) flop, v.   To sleep or stay over night.

flop-house, n.   A cheap rooming house or hotel.

(to) frame, v.   To prepare, set up, or build anything.   "We got up early so's we could frame the joint, i. e., unload and set up the place of business."   See *set-joint.*

(on the) front, prep. phr.   Before or in front of a joint.   The man who "works on the front" usually does nothing else but "make openings"—that is, repeat the ballyhoo for his particular joint.   See *openings.*   Sometimes a man "grinds on the front" which means that he does not "make openings" regularly, but keeps up a continual and repetitious barking for the joint.   See *grinder.*

geek, n.   A freak, usually a fake, who is one of the attractions in a pit-show. The word is reputed to have originated with a man named Wagner of Charleston, W. Va., whose hideous snake-eating act made him famous.   Old-timers still remember his ballyhoo, part of which ran:

> "Come and see Esau
> Sittin' on a see-saw
> Eatin' 'em raw!"

See *pit-show.*

get in (or *out*), v. phr.   Orders given to "sticks" indicating that they shall "get in" or "get out" of the play according to the way business is going.   "Sticks" are set-ups who win in order to attract "live ones," and as the number of "live ones" increases, the "sticks" are removed.   As the number of "live ones" dwindles, "sticks" are introduced to stimulate play.   See *sticks, cleaner, live one.*

(to) get the wrinkles out of your belly, v. phr.   To get acquainted with a new show and become accustomed to the life.

(to) get with it, v. phr.   To return to one's business with the show.   "These warm spring days make me want to get with it again."

(to) gilly, v.   To charter a few cars and move a small show by rail.

gilly show, n.   A small show which owns no trucks, but must be "gillied" from stand to stand.

gimmick, n.   1. Any dishonest device for regulating a game of chance so that the customer may be made to win or lose at the will of the operator.   "We had a slick gimmick on our set-joint."

2. Any small, un-named device of any sort such as a gimcrack or a gadget "Where's the gimmick that turns on this fan?"

(to) go in the back way, v. phr.   To practise pederasty.

(to) go in the bushes, v. phr.   To have sexual intercourse.

(to) go up the dirt road, v. phr.   To practise pederasty.

(to) go wrong, v. phr.   For a joint to "break" or "blow"; that is, to allow the customer to win a prize which the operator did not intend him to win.   "The joint went wrong that night and I lost a lot of slum."

governor, n.   The owner, or "main guy" of a show.

grab-joint, n.   A restaurant or eating stand.

grift, n.   Concessions of crooked gambling joints, short-change, etc., which used to be sold by circuses and carnivals to men known as "grifters" who were well-organized and successful.

grifter, n.   One who buys concessions of "grift."

grinder, n.   A barker who talks continually in front of one show or joint.   Contrasted to one who "makes openings" at regular intervals.

grind-show, n.   One which shows continually, but has no regularly repeated performances; example, a *pit-show,* or freak-show.

gummy, n.   1. Glue sold by pitchmen.   2. A pitchman who sells glue.   See *pitchman.*

gypsy camp, n. phr.   The tent or booth of a fortune-teller.   "There's a new mitt-reader in the gypsy camp today."

(to) handle, v,   To direct the "sticks" during the time that they are gambling; this must be done so that the customers do not suspect anything.   "Mac is too careless in handling them sticks."

(to) heel a hotel, v. phr.   To slip into the room of a friend who is staying at a hotel in a single room.   The "heeler" sleeps there all night with his friend and goes out in the morning without paying.

herbalist, n.   A quack doctor whose specialty is medicines made from herbs and plants.   "Chief Running Elk is one of the best herbalists in the country."

home-guard, n.   The native of a town who puts up a stand near the circus lot, thereby giving the outsiders competition.

hoofer, n.   A negro.

hostile, adj.   Angry, surly, disinclined.

(to) hustle, v.   1. To peddle or sell any article temporarily.   "Johnny's hustling gummy now."   2. To prostitute one's self.   "I guess she has to hustle a little now to get along."

hustler, n.   1. A peddler or *pitchman* who has no special line, but "hustles" anything that another pitchman will pay him for.   2. A prostitute.

info, n. or v.   1. Information.   2. To inform or notify.   "Bill infoes from Kansas City that everything is rosy."

jack-pot, n.   A gambling device working on the same principle as a *three-marble tiv,* except that it uses a coin.   See *tiv.*

jam-man, n.   A pitchman who has no professional ethics; i.e., one who will box up axle-grease and sell it for salve, or sell colored and perfumed water for hair tonic.   Restricted to *pitchmen.*

jig, n.   A Negro.

jig-show, or *jig-opry,* n.   A negro minstrel.

Johnny-come-lately, n. phr.   A greenhorn in the pitch business.   "I may be only a Johnny-come-lately, but I know that much."

jump, n.   The trip that a road-show makes from one stand to another.

keister, n.   A pitchman's case in which he carries his stock.   His outfit is usually referred to as his "tripes and keister."   See *tripes.*

law, n.   Any local officers such as policemen, sheriff, or constable.

leaf, n.   The "paper business."   "I hear that Hutchinson has quit the leaf and gone to working fountain pens."   See *paper-business.*   Restricted to *pitchmen.*

leather, n.   Pocketbook.   "I made that monkey for his leather."

live-one, n.   A native who is playing at a set-joint.   The natives watch the "sticks" win prizes or money until, stimulated by their seeming success, they become "live-ones" and join in the play.   As soon as there are sufficient "live-ones" to make the game profitable for the operators, the "sticks" are told to "get out"—cease playing.

lookout, n.   An outside man who takes disgruntled losers in charge and consoles them to prevent their laying in a complaint.   "That's Johnny over there. He watches for squawks and cools them off."

lot-reader, n.   The man who "reads the lot" after the show has packed, thus making sure that nothing is left behind and that everything is cleaned up satisfactorily.

lucky-boy, n.   A virile but lazy young man who travels with a show, supported by a girl who is working; a kind of male gold-digger.

lugger, n.   One who is paid to "lug in" customers to a certain show or joint. He may be a native or one of the show people.

main drag, n. phr.   The main street in a town.   Sometimes called the "main stem."

main guy, n. phr.   The "governor" or owner of a show.

(to) make, v.   1. To rob.   "We just made that dude for his roll."   2. To accomplish anything.

(to) make a joint, v. phr.   1. To set up or "frame" a joint.   2. To call at a hotel or place of business.

(to) make a stall, v. phr.   To stop anyone and engage him in conversation; used especially of prostitutes.

med. show, n. phr.   A medicine show consisting of a quack or "Doc" and several entertainers.

mender, n.   A claim-adjuster who travels with a show to take care of any claims or complaints which customers may raise against the show.   "Who's doing your mending now?"   See *patch.*

midway, n.   The main street in a circus or carnival.

mitt, n.   A palmist.   (Short for mitt-reader.)

(to) mix in the tip, v. phr.   For one pitchman to remain in the crowd during the "tip" or spiel which another is making.   Often the one in the crowd will question the other so as to bring out the merits of his wares, or start the crowd by making a purchase.

mob, n.   The group of men employed by one joint.   "Only two of Bert's mob are out tonight."

moll, n.   A girl; does not necessarily have any unsavory connotation.

monkey, n.   A rube (native) that has been taken in or fleeced.   "That monkey looks like a squawk."

mugman, or *mugsnapper,* n.   An itinerant photographer.

nuts, n.   Drop, in the sense of having someone covered with a gun.   "He had the nuts on me, so I gave in."

(to) office, or *give the office,* v. phr.   To tip someone off.   "We gave him the office and he kept mum."

open spot, n. phr.   A town which is not closed against *pitchmen.*   See *pitchmen.*

openings, n.   The ballyhoo which goes with all shows repeating their performances regularly, such as wild west shows, or wrestling and boxing shows.   The openings are usually divided into the "first opening" and "second opening"; the first consists of the material calculated to draw a crowd about the "front"; after a crowd has collected and has heard the advertisement of the show, the natural tendency is for many of them to drift away.   The "second opening" is then made for the purpose of calling them back and herding them in.   This method is in contrast with the "grind shows" which have no regular performances, but exhibit freaks in a *pit-show* or *platform-show.*

p.c., n.   The usual term for *percentage-wheel,* a gambling device which paid off on a one-to-six or a one-to-twelve percentage; thus a dime on No. 6 paid sixty cents—thirty cents to the customer and thirty cents to the house.   The *p.c.* is now obsolete, but its principle is still used in a game which substitutes small and large compartments for numbers; the large compartments (into which a ball is thrown) pay small prizes and the small compartments pay large ones.   Red, green, and black balls are used to further complicate the system.

pad, n.   The subscription blank upon which a "sheet-writer" takes orders.   Restricted to *pitchmen.*   See *paper-boys.*

paper-boys, n.   1. Pitchmen who sell magazines.   2. Pitchmen who sell books of tickets, each redeemable for certain kinds of merchandise, comparable to the "thrift-book" system.

peep-show, n.   A bawdy-house performance which differs from the European peep-show in that the prostitute picks a likely-looking rube who, unaware that anyone is watching, furnishes the entertainment for the prostitute's friends or even a paying audience.

peg-joint, n.   A gambling device operated with numbered pegs, the numbers being concealed until after the customer plays, on the same principle as a punch-board.

pipe, n. or v.   A word of very loose usage, signifying (1) a letter or spoken message, (2) a leisurely conversation over business matters, or an exchange of personalities, or (3) to send a message, to engage in conversation.   Restricted to *pitchmen.*   "I saw Charlie Morgan in Memphis and we had a few pipes." "Andy Miller shoots a pipe from Louisville that he is doing well there." "Bill Johnson pipes from Frisco that times are hard."   The column of letters for *pitchmen* in *The Billboard* is known as "Pipes for Pitchmen."

pipefest, n.   A leisurely conversation held by several pitchmen when they congregate in a hotel or rooming house.

pit-show, n.   An exhibition of freaks displayed in a "pit" built of boards or canvas, around the top of which is a walk for the customers.   "Go over and throw your lamps on that new tattoo-man in Jenk's pit-show."

(to) pitch, v.   To sell or vend articles, either on the show lot or on the streets of towns.   Pitchmen are frequently seen occupying the doorways of vacant store rooms in cities.

pitchman, n.   A vendor who "pitches" his wares, as described above. *High pitchmen* sell from an automobile or wagon, while *low pitchmen* set up their "tripes and keister" to do business on the ground.

plant-show, n.   Short for plantation-show, a negro minstrel show.

plaster, n.   Any cheap novelties, such as small statutes, etc., made from plaster-paris, and given as prizes at the various joints.

poke, n.   Pocketbook.   "See if you can make that sap for his poke."

possom-belly, n.   A compartment built underneath an animal-cage, slung between the front and rear axles, which is entered by a trap-door in the floor of the cage.

privilege-car, n.   A restaurant-car equipped to serve show people on long jumps; often it served as a lounge where gambling was promoted and the show people fleeced by a house-man representing the circus or carnival owner.   The *privilege-car* is now a thing of the past.

(to) pull the sticks, v. phr.   To take the set-ups out of a game of chance so that the "live-ones" may be fleeced.

punk, n.   A youngster in the show business.   "I was just a punk then, and hadn't got the wrinkles out of my belly."

(to) put out, v. phr.   1. To give a prize to a customer at a gambling joint.   2. For a woman to prostitute herself.

razor-backs, n.   Laborers to do the heavy work connected with a road show.

(to) read the lot, v. phr.   To inspect the show-lot after the show has packed for lost articles, money, or equipment left behind.

reader, n.   A license or permit for the operation of a show or any of its co ncessions.   State-, county-, and city-readers are required before a show can oper ate.   See also *soldier-reader.*

red, adj.   Describes a town where excellent business is done; just opposite of *cold.*

route-card, n.   A table or schedule issued to show people giving the "stands" for about ten days in advance.

rum-dum, adj.   No-account, shiftless.

sap, n.   A *monkey,* or rube that has been taken in.

saw-buck, or *saw,* n.   A ten-dollar bill.   "I just saw two saws and a fin in that sap's roll."

secretary, n.   Any accountant or bookkeeper with a show.

set-joint, n.   A gambling device operated with a numbered wheel and arrow-spindle.   These are always fitted with a *gimmick* which prevents the customer from winning too often, or which may be used by the operator to lead the customer on until he will place a large bet, when the operator applies the *gimmick* and the customer loses.

shack, n.   A brakeman on a freight-train.

shake-down, n.   A bribe or payment from a show or its concession-men to local authorities.

(to) shake down, v. phr.   To collect a shake-down.   "See those two dudes? They're going to try to shake us down."

shakes, n.   An earthquake.   "I hear they had a little shakes over in Los Angeles yesterday."

sheetie, n.   Short for *sheet-writer.*   A *paper-boy,* or *paper-writer.*   See *paper-boy.*

shoot, v.   To say or write something pertaining to *pitchmen.*   See *pipe.*

show-letter, n.   The weekly report of a show, often published in *The Billboard.*

(*to*) *slice*, v. To reduce the width of a parade. Restricted to circuses. "When we came to the bridge, the parade-master saw we'd have to slice it."

(*to*) *slough the joint*, v. phr. 1. To close up business for the day or at the end of a stand. 2. For the law to close down a show or gambling joint.

slum, n. Cheap goods to be given as prizes in joints; slum usually wholesales at thirty to sixty cents per gross.

snatch-team, n. A strong, active team of horses used to supplement other teams on bad ground. Restricted to circuses. "They took a snatch-team down and hauled the cage out."

soldier-reader, n. A free pitchman's license granted to an ex-service man.

(*to*) *spin*, v. To be able to speak a language or dialect fluently. "I used to could spin the grifter's lingo, but I've forgot it now."

(*to*) *spot*, v. To put the wagons in their proper places before a show begins.

squawk, n. A *monkey* who registers a complaint over losses he has suffered while gambling.

(*to*) *stall the push*, v. phr. To gather the crowd about one show and attempt to herd them in.

stand, n. A town or city where a show stops to give performances.

(*to*) *stand him on his ear*, v. phr. To procure credit at a store or from an individual. "Bill stood him on his ear for a double-saw, and never paid it."

stick, n. An individual—sometimes a local rube—hired by the operator of a *set-joint* to win flashy prizes so that the crowd will be induced to gamble. When the "live ones" have been started, the *sticks* are removed and deliver their winnings to a man outside who has no apparent connection with the joint. This process is known as "cleaning the sticks," and the man is a "cleaner." *Sticks* are also known as *cappers* or *boosters*.

straight-man, n. A medicine-show performer who works "straight," i.e., without make-up.

subscriptionists, n. *Paper-boys.*

suit-case outfit, n. A *gilly-show* which is figuratively so small that it can be packed in a suit-case.

super, n. A stolen watch.

t.b., n. Total blank. Said of a town which is "cold" or a "bloomer."

(*to*) *take him for a walk*, v. phr. To get a disgruntled gambler away from the joint and "cool him off."

thin, adj. Short of money. "We were pretty thin by the time we got to Indianapolis."

(*to*) *throw a cop*, v. phr. To allow a "stick" or even a customer to win a valuable prize. Sometimes called *throwing a prize*, or *throwing out a prize*. See *flash*.

tips, n. "Starters" who buy the first tickets to a show or sideshow in order to start the crowd in.

tiv, n. Usually known as a *three-marble tiv*. A gambling device using red and black marbles.

towner, n. A native of the town in which the show is playing. Also anyone not connected with the show.

trick, n. The show, or outfit. "The last trick I was on the grub was awful."

tripe, n. Short for tripod. Used by *low pitchmen* to hold the "keister."

(*to*) *turn the push*, v. phr. To conduct the crowd through a show so that there are no stragglers.

walk-around, n.   The path or wooden walk from which patrons of a *pit-show* view the attractions.

walk-through show, n. phr.   A *pit-show.*

(to) watch the tips, v. phr.   To stand by watching a *pitchman* do business; by derivation, to idle about.

wedged, part.   Stuck or stranded in a hotel without money to pay the bill.

white-stone worker, n. phr.   A *pitchman* who "works" synthetic diamonds or rhinestones.

(to) work, v.   To sell or deal in any commodity.   Restricted to *pitchmen.*

ADDENDA

mend, v. To resolve complaints against the show; to buy off local police, usually in advance.

paper business, n. Work by pitchmen who sell block subscriptions to magazines, valuable books, coupons, and so on.

patch, n. A *mender* or fixer for a road show.

sheet-writer, n. A *paper boy* or one who works the *leaf.*

three marble tiv, n.phr. A flatjoint involving the rolling of balls into holes or receptacles on a board.

tip, 1. v. Act of stimulating a group to gather and enter a show or game. 2. n. The speech or spiel made by the *starter.* 3. n. The crowd itself.

3

The Argot
of the Underworld

This study presents a kind of general survey of specialized language used by professional criminals in the United States and Canada as of 1930-1931. Only about half of the collected material could be published in that particular issue of *American Speech*. I naively imagined that I would publish the second half the following year and would then leave the underworld argots and move on to something else. I had no inkling that nearly fifty years later I would still be working on the second half, for the volume of uncollected material was tremendous.

Today many of the terms in this glossary are familiar in the dominant culture. This is due to the gradual diffusion of the criminal subcultures and their exploitation in fiction and motion pictures, which, incidentally, were very slow to use authentic language. Today, this situation seems to be changing, with some motion picture script writers either following the careful work done by fiction writers in depicting authentic social dialects or doing independent research on their own when producing an original script — usually the former. In many cases, argot words well known in the dominant culture are replaced by others in the subculture. In 1931 most of the terms in this study were confined to criminal subcultures and were not known in the dominant culture.

It is interesting to note that the first quoted statement by a criminal in the article (discussing a con game called the *pay-off*) represents one of the earliest descriptions of this racket and was my first acquaintance with the big-con rackets. In a sense I was well prepared for this since I was already in touch with old-time circus grifters who were instructing me in short-con techniques. Subsequent contact with both short-con workers and some of the best big-con operators enabled me to write *The Big Con: The Story of the Confidence Man and the Confidence Game,* which was published in 1940. This book has been through several editions and currently appears as *The American Confidence Man* (Springfield, Ill.: Charles C. Thomas, 1974).

At this time I had no idea of the full spectrum of criminal argots. Based upon my rather limited view, I concluded that few if any of the canting terms contained in the seventeenth-century writings of Dekker, Greene, and others had survived into the twentieth century. Subsequent research, however, has turned up a number of survivals in either form or meaning, or both. These occur largely among the various types of thieves, as contrasted to con men, stickup men, safecrackers, and the like.

Fieldwork for this study was quite difficult. Questionnaires were not effective in this fieldwork largely because of the complex sociopsychological tendencies to protect secrecy and to exclude outsiders. Confronted with the sizable word list necessary in a questionnaire, a criminal is likely to be disturbed by the amount of information already revealed, for one of the basic axioms of professional criminals is, "Never wise up a sucker." Furthermore, any criminal observed working on such a questionnaire might be subject to social pressures of an unpleasant nature. Although nowadays professionals tend to be perhaps a little less secretive, the questionnaire is still impractical, partly because of a deep-seated association of this kind of thing with investigative reporting. There were no portable sound-recording devices, and the use of pencil and paper in the presence of a criminal tended to terminate the interview abruptly. All data had to be temporarily memorized and reproduced after each interview. Fortunately, I enjoyed a limited sponsorship and cooperation from some members of an influential midwestern syndicate, although I was hardly qualified by training or experience to fully exploit these resources.

• • •

Acknowledgment: To Warden Thomas and Deputy Warden Woodard for their courtesy in giving me access to the Ohio State Penitentiary over a period of some nine months while I was collecting material, and to the prisoners (whose names I have, at their own request, agreed not to mention) who were kind enough to allow me to draw upon their professional knowledge and experience.

PART I

OUR modern American underworld differs little in spirit from that of Greene and Dekker, of Cervantes and Aleman. It is true that the technique of rogue and officer have changed; Dekker's glossary of "canting language"—complete though it was, for Dekker spent enough of his life in jail to be thoroughly conversant with his material—has given way to a succession of argots in the latest of which, so far as I can determine, not a single one of his words has survived; the social status of the criminal (and of the accused criminal) has been remarkably altered; politics, prohibition, and the general decay of so-called morality are tending to efface any sharp line which may have existed between criminality and respectability. But despite these superficial changes, the forces which mold the language of the underworld remain much the same from one age to another.

Though the argot treated in this study seldom reaches the layman except as it is filtered through celluloid or woodpulp, it is spoken fluently—and not without some professional pride—by the initiate of the underworld, and constitutes an American dialect of considerable though undetermined proportions; it is peculiar in that there are few colloquial variations; it appears to be pretty well standardized from coast to coast and from the Gulf well into Canada. However, it should not be assumed that all those who know the argot speak nothing else; many of the big-time crooks and racketeers are well educated—I have it from one who should know that "often their tastes are comparable to those of a cultured and prosperous business man who enjoys literature, travel, art, and music"—and speak standard English except when they are in the company of lower-class hoodlums who use the vernacular exclusively.

The good Thomas Dekker, who made the first serious effort to record English thieves' cant, was troubled somewhat by what appeared to him to be a total absence of grammar. Says he in his *Lanthorne and Candle Light* (1608):

Now as touching the Dialect or phrase itselfe, I see not that it is grounded upon any certaine rules; and no mervaile if it have none, for sithence both the Father of this new kinde of learning, and the Children that study to speake it after him, have bene from the beginning and stil are, the Breeders and Nourishers of a base disorder, in their living and in their manners: how is it possible they should observe any Method in their speech, and especially in such a Language as serves but onely to utter discourses of villainies?

But his reasoning that villainous subject matter justifies anarchy in language was but a bit of seventeenth-century sophistry. As a matter of fact, the underworld cant of Dekker's day, like the argot of our own, followed the same general rules of grammar to which the contemporary literary English was subject. There are a few notable deviations, but the structure of the language is, on the whole, patterned after our more respectable dialects. The significant point is, I think, the tendency to form idioms which, because of their vagueness and multiplicity of sense, often defy exact translation. But all underworld argot is largely a matter of vocabulary; once one has an equivalent for a slang or cant word, it is easy enough to unravel the sense.

Let us examine several examples of the argot *in situ* to gather some idea of its general characteristics, principally its machine-gun staccato, its hard timbre, its rather grim humor, its remarkable compactness. The first example will illustrate especially well the last-named quality. The particular swindle discussed here is known as *the pay-off;* I am told that it is so called because "it proves that no matter how worldly-wise a man may be, he can always be made to 'pay off' when he tries to obtain something for nothing." An expert contributes the further note to the effect that "it is always easier to inveigle an intelligent man than a country habitant." It is less frequently known as *the sure-thing* or *wire-tapping.*

I have just found a customer for the pay-off, well heeled. Let's go to the big store and line up the props and frame the layout for the score. We should be good for five or six x-rays and the nut will be only a few yards. We can line up four or five set-ups at a G apiece and use the big store's phone for relay on the doggies. We can use the delayed-wire stall and let him cash in on a few small bets and then line him up for the final pay-off. We can frame a pinch for the mope. That will be forty as there will be no beef. We can then go to the big store to meet the nut and figure our end.

A sentence-by-sentence translation would read something like this:
(1) I have just found a person with plenty of money whom we can
swindle.   (2) Let's go to the swindlers' headquarters and arrange to
get the scenery used to set up an imitation broker's office and lay our
plans for swindling him.   (3) We should be able to make fifty or
sixty thousand dollars while our expenses will be only a few thousand
dollars.   (4) We can hire four or five men to pose as broker's clerks for
a thousand dollars apiece, and use the headquarters phone to get true
results on the horse races.   (5) We will pretend to him that we
can delay the telegraphic reports of the races, and make bets of the
winning horses after each race has been run.   After the bets are made
reports of the winners will be wired.   Allow him to place a few bets on
winning horses and win a small amount each time.   An accomplice
who poses as a bookmaker on the races pays the small bets so that the
victim is convinced that the scheme is on the square and will be willing
to plunge a large amount on one race for what he thinks will be a
large winning.   (6) We will have stalls (accomplices) to pose as
detectives and raid the establishment just as the victim puts down the
large bet.   In the excitement of the pretended raid, the bookmaker
walks out with the money while the raiders take the victim out of the
establishment as if he is under arrest.   Outside they frighten the
victim with threats of exposure and imprisonment for operating a
gambling establishment, and if possible persuade him to leave town.
(7) That will be fine, for if the victim leaves town there will be no
complaint made to the police.   (8) Then we will go back to headquarters where we will pay the expense of hiring the stalls, the scenery,
the offices, etc. and divide the remainder.

In this case three men are planning what is called a *stone tail
elevation* (following persons wearing valuable diamonds and holding
them up in some deserted spot).   A complete glossary[1] of the terms
necessary to translate these items will be found farther on in this
article.

Let's get a line on some stones and elevate them.   Tomorrow night the opera
season starts, opening at the Auditorium with Maria Jeritza in "La Tosca."
Plant near the in and case all the boilers for parties loaded with ice.   Now
when you make a party that is stoned heavy, I.C. the boiler and tab the plates.
Go to a pay station so there will be no tail on the call and get the boiler club and

---

[1] Because of the necessity for dividing this article into two sections, some words
must be omitted from the glossary to Parts I and II.   They will be included in the
glossary accompanying Parts III and IV to be published in a later issue.

info on the boiler and plates.   Come here as soon as you score the info and I will be jake with a hot boiler and a brace of roscoes.   We will ramble back to the Auditorium to pick them up, and when they mope we will tail them till we hit a spot to hoist, where we will elevate.   I will keep them covered while you clean. Fan the boiler pockets for oscars.   When blowing kill the spark and take the screw.   If we do not hit the spot to elevate before they hit the kip, we will elevate as they step in the kip.   I have a scratch market for the ice on the spot.

Here are some instructions for *making a stone box mark:*

In this building I am giving you the dope on, there is a stone wholesaler. The mark is on the fourth.   There are two ins but both are bugged.   Shell door peter with duster and keister.   Shell door bugged.   Make your in from overhead in mouthpiece's office as floor is clean.   Use the can-opener on the back of the box to clean it.   Nail the stones but blow the slum.   The building is cold after ten and you have eight hours to score before a rumble.   Split out on the mope and connect at my plant.   If you want to drop your end, I will have a scratch bidder.

The foregoing job is, of course, to be pulled without the owner's knowledge.   The following one, however, which is known as an *inside stone hoist* is accomplished with the connivance of the owner who will not receive a percentage of the loot, but will collect heavily from the insurance company.

I have just been given an ice mark.   The prop is in on the frame for the hoist at chow time.   Wants no end.   He guarantees fifty yards of unset stones.   He will beef for a hundred grand insurance.   He will be single O at chow time. Tomorrow give it the O.O. and line the lam while I go and make arrangements for a hot boiler.   Give me a ring at my plant after the O.O. and we will make a meet for the frame.

The following item outlines plans for *making a set-up jug mark* which is similar to the preceding job in that "inside assistance" is given the yeggs.   This time the cashier cooperates so far as to give the safe-blowers a key and the lay-out of the bank, vaults, burglar alarms, location of money and bonds, etc.   However, the *heavymen* are doing the *scratch-pusher* a favor, for when they leave they will, in return for his assistance, carry off his books and thereby conceal his shortage incurred while playing the races with the bank's money.

I was chinning a scratch-pusher for a straw jay, who has dropped a lot of the jay's scratch on the doggies.   He wants the jay taken over on the heavy and his books nailed with the scratch.   He says the jay carries thirty to forty yards working scratch besides the stiffs. The jug has a three-plate V. and a duster. Inside a fireproof hall with a top keister and a flunk. The books are in the bottom of the peter. Nail them when you blow. He will mit you a screw for a double and that's the in. The V. has a comb bug so you can use a jumper for a short. Use the keister torch on the V. and when in punch the hall. I have a stiff-point lined up for 85; you'll get the office when it's forty.

Perhaps we might add that in this case the information is being relayed to the yeggs by a *ten-per*—an individual who finds prospects and acts as a go-between if necessary for ten percent of the haul.

This last item is interesting because it gives a behind-the-scenes version of a victim being "taken for a ride"—an event which is given space in almost every city newspaper every day.

Johnny Oakes, whose mob monicker was "Timber" was in Dutch. The finger was put on him for speaking out of turn to his twist. The mob decided that, for safety's sake, Timber must go riding. Skivers and Skats drew the job of sneezing Timber and chopping him down. Skivers and Skats were rambling down the drag when they I.Cd. Timber pushing pills in a pill-joint. They curbed the boiler and rambled into the pill-joint with their roscoes in their coat kicks and fronted Timber. They officed him out to the boiler and as soon as he hit the boiler they cleaned him of his protection. Skivers took the wheel and Skats acted as cover on Timber. Then they high-balled to the timbers and stopped and made Timber get out. Skats said, "This is curtains for you, Timber." Timber asked why he was riding. He was then infoed that his chatter to his twist of his capers was 30 for him, and the rest of the mob said 40. Skivers said, "We'll give you a break for your agate and let you play rabbit. If you make it, why 40; if not, it's 30. When I give you the office, scram and we will let you make 100 before chopping. That is your only out." Timber was given the office and scrammed for his agate, but the wipers got into action and chopped him down. 30 for Timber.

Now that we have had a brief sample of the actual argot in use, let us proceed to the glossary where it can be examined more closely in full detail. Only about half the total collected glossary can be presented in this issue.

PART II

GLOSSARY

ace, n. A one-dollar bill.
after the beef, adv. phr. After the report goes in to the police. "It's your funeral after the beef."
ahead of the beef, adv. phr. Before the report of a crime goes in to the police.
alki, n. Alcohol.

alki cooker, n. phr.   One who has charge of distilling alcohol.

anchor on prop, n. phr.   A stock pin with a safety catch attached.   See *prop.*

angle, n.   An idea or method of procedure.   "That angle's got me queered."

artillery, n.   1. A dope addict's hypodermic outfit; a needle and accessories.
2. Firearms of any description.   See *rosco, oscar, heater, rod, gat, heat, belly-gun, Tommy.*

backs, n.   Counterfeit money printed on one side only of onion skin paper.   Back-print silk thread is placed between the fronts and backs and the two pieces are pasted together.   The counterfeit is then ready for the "shover" to pass. "Here's a couple of backs you can shove."

batty, adj.   Insane; "to have a screw loose."   See *stir-bugs.*

(to) beef, v.   (to) protest; another carry-over from the war.

(to) bible, v.   To swear; to take oath.

a big day, n. phr.   Visiting day at the penitentiary.

big house, n. phr.   The penitentiary.   East Coast, *up the river, stir* or *bighouse;* mid-west, *stir* or *big-joint;* West Coast, *bighouse.*

big store, n. phr.   Confidence men's headquarters.

bindle-stiff, n.   A bum who carries a bundle of belongings, usually tied in a hand-kerchief, or wrapped in paper.   "Hard times bring back the bindle-stiffs."

big top, n. phr.   A bank.   See *jay, jug.*

biscuit shooter, n. phr.   A waitress.

bit-borrower, n.   One who does not repay loans.   "No. 66710 is a bit-borrower right."

black V., n. phr.   Fire-proof iron vault, always painted black.

(to) blot out, v. phr.   To kill.   " 'Dutch' was blotted out by the town clown."

(to) blow, v.   1. To *lam*, to make a getaway.   "When the smoke cleared, the Frisco Kid had blown."   2. For the moon to go down.   "Flatten out till the Oliver blows."

blow-off, n.   The end or finish.   "We'll drop in for the blow-off."

(to) blow a box, v. phr.   To blow a safe.

body snatcher, n. phr.   A kidnapper.

boiler, n.   An automobile.   "That boiler is hot; ditch it."

box, n.   A safe of any kind.   "Pete taught me to blow a box."   East Coast, *peter;* Midwest, *peter;* West Coast, *crib* or *box.*

booster, n.   A shoplifter.

breast kick, n. phr.   The inside pocket of a vest or coat.

breech kick, n.   The side pocket in pants.   "I never carry soup in my breech kick."

(to) breeze, v.   To beat it, to blow, to get away.   "Breeze, breeze, damn it, somebody's wrong here."

briars, n.   Hack-saw blades.   "We'll get you the briars in cigars."

broad, n.   *Moll.*   See *Moll.*

buck, n.   1. A Catholic priest.   "He's no buck, you rum; he's an Episcopalian."
2. A dollar piece.

bug, n.   A burglar alarm.   "Douse that bug if you can find the connection."

bugged, part.   Wired to a burglar alarm.   "The joint was bugged and we got a tumble."

(to) bump, v.   To die.

(to) bump off, v. phr.   To kill.   "We don't want to bump no one off."

buried, part.   Confined without hope of release.   "They'll bury him for that."
Mid-west, *settled;* Pacific Coast, *lagged.*

burns, n.   A Burns detective.

c note or *century,* n.   A hundred-dollar bill.

can, n.   The police station, or jail.   Also called *the box,* or *piss-house.*

can opener, n. phr.   An instrument, made of chilled steel and shaped like a large
can opener.   After a small hole has been drilled in a safe, the blade is inserted
and a piece is cut from the safe just as one cuts out the top of a can.   This
instrument can be used only on thin-walled safes.   It is especially valuable in
private residences where the use of explosives would lead to immediate
discovery.

cannon, n.   1. A pickpocket.   2. A gun.   1. East coast, *cannon;* Mid-west,
whiz or *cannon;* West Coast, *guns.*

cannon-ball peter, n.   A round or cylindrical steel burglar-proof safe with laminated
steel doors that can be opened only by the acetylene torch.

cap, n.   A fulminate cap that is attached to a fuse, which, when exploded, sets
off the nitro-glycerin; a so-called dynamite cap.

(to) case, v.   To watch; a pawnshop expression, probably a pun on watch-case.
"Let him case the joint."

charging out, part. phr.   A mob or gang ready to go to work.   "We was just
charging out when in steps 'Frisco.' "

check-cop, n. phr.   A gluey substance placed in the palm of the hand to enable one
to steal chips of any kind in a gambling game.

chisler, n.   A small-time thief who declares himself in on someone's else racket.

chive, n.   (pronounced shiv.)   A knife.   "A file makes a A-1 chive, if you grind
it right."

chopper, n.   A machine-gunner for a mob; a *torpedo.*

(to) clean the poke, v. phr.   To take the money out of a pocketbook and throw the
pocketbook away.

clown, n.   1. A *town clown,* or constable.   2. A rotter, a cheapskate.

cokie, n.   A cocaine addict or snow-bird.

cold-slough, n.   An apartment or house when no one is at home.   To make a cold
slough is to successfully enter and pull a job in an uninhabited dwelling, during
the daytime; at night is known as burglary.

(to) collar, v.   To arrest.   "That shamus tried to collar him."

collared, part.   Arrested; taken into custody by an officer.

college, n.   A penitentiary.   "He was just released from college."

combo, n.   The combination of safe or vault.

con man, n. phr.   One who works a confidence game.

cook, n.   An expert at rolling and cooking opium pills.

(to) cop a lam, v. phr.   To make one's getaway.   See *lam, on the lam.*

(to) cop a sneak, v. phr.   To take advantage of an opportunity to run away.   See
(to) cop a lam.

copper-hearted, adj.   Deceitful; yellow; a natural stoolpigeon; a squealer.   "That
copper-hearted fink slugged him."

(to) crash, v.   To enter a home or business place forcibly.   "We were just waitin'
to crash a hock shop."

crown, n.   A tiara or coronet; an ornamental head-dress set with jewels.

(to) cuff it, v. phr.   To charge it or credit it.   "Cuff it, and I'll square with you later."

cush, n.   1. Bribe money.   2. Profit from a deal.   3. Money or pay in general, usually easily made.   "Got the cush?"

cut, n.   A share.   "He was given a cut of ten per cent."

cutor, n.   A twenty-five-cent piece.   See *quetor*.

cutter, n.   A prosecuting attorney.

D. A., n. phr.   The district attorney.

dance hall, n.   The death-house of a penitentiary; so called because of the continual pacing of the condemned man.

damper, n.   A cash-register.   "Let's have what's in the damper too."

daub, n.   A color compound to mark cards while playing.

declared in., v. phr.   Given a share.   When a person who did not participate in a job but who possesses dangerous knowledge regarding it, he may be "declared in" as a precaution.

demier, n.   A ten-cent piece.

deuce, n.   A two-dollar bill.

dinah, n.   Dynamite.   "Nix on the dinah; I'll take stew every time."

dinger, n.   The bell-alarm outside banks; a *bug*.

a dip, n. phr.   A portion of snuff, used freely in penal institutions.   See *snoose*.

(to) do the book, v. phr.   To serve a life sentence.

door-matter, n.   A petit larceny thief; one who would steal a door-mat.   "Oh, he's only a door-matter."

double saw, or *double saw-buck*, n. phr.   Twenty-dollar bill.

drag, n.   A street.

(to) draw, v.   To be sentenced for a certain term.   "Bill drew life on the installment plan."

(to) drill, v.   1. To shoot.   "Red drilled him right there."   2. To walk (see *playing soldier*).   "Bill and me was drilling on the drag."

driving alki, part. phr.   Driving an *alki car* from one city to another; liquor running.   "Jake was driving alki when they knocked him off."

dummy, n.   Bread in penal institution.   See *punk*.

duster, n.   A sheet-iron door between the outer door of a safe and the inner compartments.   "That shot cracked the duster."

elbow, n.   A policeman.   East Coast, *shamus*, *fuzz*, or *goms;* Mid-west, *law* or *works;* West Coast, *elbow*.

end, n.   A share or cut in a theft or division of money, loot, etc.   "My end of that is four grand."

eye, n.   A pinkerton detective; sometimes called a "pink."   "He's an eye."

(to) fall out of Cleveland, v. phr.   To be arrested and convicted in Cleveland.   "Johnny fell out of Cleveland."

(to) fall for the elevation, v. phr.   To be convicted of highway robbery.

(to) fall for the general principle, v. phr.   Framed and kangarood to the penitentiary; convicted on general principles, though innocent of the specific offence for which one is tried.   "The old general principle gets all ex-cons."

(to) fall for the heavy, v. phr.   To be convicted of safe blowing or entering a bank or vault.   "I fell for the heavy and drew a fin in Joliet."

(to) fall for a hot car, v. phr.   To be convicted of auto stealing.

(to) fall for a jug, v. phr.   To be convicted of robbing a bank.

(to) fall for the owl, v. phr.   To be convicted of burglary of a residence.   "Jake hadn't been off the heavy a week when he fell for the owl."

(to) fall for paper hanging, v. phr.   To be convicted of forgery.

(to) fall for receiving, v. phr.   To be convicted of having stolen property in one's possession.   "That fuzey bibled he caught me with the rocks, so I fell for receiving."

(to) fall for a seven-up, v. phr.   To be convicted of burglarizing a general store.

(to) fall for the slough, v. phr.   To be convicted of house breaking in the day time.

(to) fall for the tools, v. phr.   To be convicted of having burglar tools.

(to) fan, v.   To search; so-called from running one's hand over a victim's person to find out where his pocketbook or weapon is kept.   "When Joe turns on the heat, you fan him."

Fed. rap., n. phr.   To do time in a U. S. Government prison.   "He took a fed. rap. for peddling snow."

felt out, v. phr.   Sounded; pumped.   "He was felt out about the pay roll."

feeler, n.   A question asked with idea of gaining information.

(to) fill (him) in, v. phr.   To add an extra man to a gang for a special job.   "We didn't like him, but we filled him in anyway."

fin, n.   1. A five-dollar bill.   2. A five-year sentence.

(to) finger.   1. v.   To point out; to identify a criminal.   "The finger was put on him and he was collared."   "They fingered me; that's how I come to be here."   2. n.   A stoolpigeon or informer.   "He's a finger for the eye."

fink, n.   A strike guard employed by mines or factories.   "Finks are tougher than regular clowns, usually."

fire-proof peter, n. phr.   An iron safe for protection against fire.   Not burglar proof.

five C note, n. phr.   A five-hundred-dollar bill.

five C note or five yards, n. phr.   A five-thousand-dollar bill.

(to) flatten out, v. phr.   To lie low; to hide.

flunk, n.   A steel compartment with a thin iron door in a safe.

(to) fly a kite, v. phr.   To smuggle a letter out of a prison.   "Sure, that screw'll fly your kite for a buck."

fourth of July, n. phr.   A gun battle.   "I was ready to put on a fourth of July if the law showed up right then."

freight, n.   Bribe money.   "He had to put out ten G's for freight."

frill, n.   A girl or woman.   Also *skirt, muff, twist, moll, jane.*

front, n.   The clothes one is wearing.   "That's a punk front you're putting up, Hank."

fronts, n.   Counterfeit money printed on one side only of onion-skin paper.   A front print.   See *backs.*

full of larceny, adj. phr.   Open for bribe.   "He is full of larceny and you can do business with him."

fuzey, n. A policeman who is especially diligent in enforcing the law. "That fuzey would arrest his own mother."

gaper, n. A small circular mirror held in the palm of the hand while playing cards or dealing. "Why couldn't he win? He had a check cop and a gaper."

gelt, n. Money in general.

ginger-bread door, n. A safe door with ornate trimmings which have nothing to do with strengthening the door. "Ginger-bread don't bother me none."

girl, n. A male degenerate with feminine ways; a fairy; a fruit.

(to) give the O. O., v. phr. To give the "once over"; to scrutinize sharply. "Hey, give that bird the O. O. and what do you say?"

(to) give a tumble, v. phr. To suspect. "I never gave a tumble Rose would fall for Dago Sam."

glim, n. A light or a match. "Douse the glim, there!"

(to) glom, v. To steal; to gather in. "We glommed them rocks up on Park Avenue."

go-between, n. One who carries money from racketeers to officials for protection from arrest.

(to) go gandering, v. phr. To be out looking for someone or something. "We went gandering for a peterman." Sometimes known as "playing the bird with the long neck."

(to) go to the kip, v. phr. To go to bed. See *(to) hit the kip*.

gonger, n. An opium pipe.

gopher, n. An iron safe. "He punched the gopher open."

gopher mob, n. phr. Vault tunnelers; a gang which makes a business of digging into vaults from underneath.

gorilla, n. A hoodlum or thug.

grand or *G.*, n. A thousand-dollar bill; see *yard*.

grease, n. 1. Money paid for protection; bribe money. 2. Nitro-glycerine.

(to) grease, v. To bribe. "You'll have to grease the clown for that job."

greased, adj. Bribed or fixed. "He was well greased."

(to) grift, v. To work at some underworld profession.

grifter, n. A cheap crook.

hack, n. 1. A watchman; usually restricted to merchant-policemen and differentiated from the municipal constables or police. "Sorry we had to blot that hack." 2. A pen guard.

half-a-buck, n. A fifty-cent piece.

half a C or *half-century*, n. phr. A fifty-dollar bill. "That job's worth half a C or nothing."

(to) hang paper, v. phr. To forge and pass checks.

hangout, n. An undercover rendezvous for a mob.

hard money, n. Metal money; "iron money."

hard stuff, n. phr. Metal money.

(to) have a fall, v. phr. To be arrested. "Haven't seen Joe lately; suppose he's had a fall?"

heat, n. 1. Excitement; trouble. "He left a lot of heat behind him." "He was always in the heat." 2. The vicinity of trouble. "Let's blow out of the heat." 3. The "drop" or "nuts" with a gun.

heater, n. A fireman. East Coast, *rod, heat;* Mid-west, *oscar, roscoe,* or *rod;* West Coast, *heat, rod.*

heist (or *hoist*), n. A holdup or robbery. Largely restricted to the liquor running business. "He was buried for the heist." East Coast, *heist,* Mid-west, *elevation* or *hoist;* West Coast, *highjack.*

(*to*) *heist* (or *hoist*), v. To hold up a person, or to rob at the point of a gun. "We heisted them for three hundred cases."

heel, n. Sneak thief; a term of contempt. East Coast, *gyp;* Mid-west, *heel;* West Coast, *heeler.*

heister, n. A high-jacker or a highway-robber. Variation of *hoister.* East coast, *heister* or *gorilla;* Mid-west, *heister* or *elevator;* West Coast, *highjacker.*

high-jacker (*hijacker, hyjacker*), n. One who robs liquor-runners of their cargo.

(*to*) *hit the gonger,* v. phr. To smoke opium.

(*to*) *hit the hay,* v. phr. To go to sleep.

(*to*) *hit the kip,* v. phr. To go to bed.

hoister, n. A high-jacker or highway-robber. Variation of heister.

hop-head, n. phr. An opium addict.

(*to*) *horn in,* v. phr. To muscle in.

hot, adj. 1. Any stolen object is said to be hot. 2. To be pursued by the law. "He was hot and had to lam."

hot boiler, n. phr. A stolen automobile. "I fell for a hot boiler in Minneapolis, back in '24."

hot car farm, n. phr. A garage, or place outside a city where motor numbers and external appearances of stolen cars are changed. "Pete ran that hot car farm but he never took the rap for it."

hot car hustler, n. phr. An automobile thief.

hot shot, n. phr. A fast freight train.

hot slough, n. phr. An inhabited apartment or dwelling which is the object of a robbery.

hot-spot, n. The electric chair.

hot-squat, n. phr. 1. The electric chair. 2. Death by electrocution. "He took his hot-squat like a man."

hooker, n. A prostitute.

hoop, n. A ring.

hoosegow, n. A jail; also known as the *can* or *box.*

hustler, n. A loose term meaning: 1. A prostitute. 2. A specialist in some unlawful enterprise.

ice, n. Diamonds.

in, n. 1. The entrance to a building. "Where's the in to this joint?" 2. An introduction. "Give us an in to the chief, will you?"

(*to be*) *in the benny,* v. phr. To have one's coat on.

(*to be*) *in the kick,* v. phr. To be in the pocket. "Lamp the bulge in the kick."

(*to be*) *in the lid,* v. phr. To have one's hat on.

(*to be*) *in the strides,* v. phr. To have one's pants on.

inside man, n. phr. The man who does the inside work; sometimes known as the mechanic. Usually restricted to safe-blowing.

Italian football, n. phr. A bomb, often also called a pineapple.

jake, adj. All right. "Everything's jake now."

jakey, or *jake,* n.   Jamaica Ginger.

james, n.   A jimmy or a bar for forcing entrance.   "Come here, James."   East Coast, *stick* or *james;* Mid-west, *james* or *bar;* West Coast, *james.*

jay, n.   A bank.   "I want to run over to Youngstown to put in a night on that jay we spotted."   East Coast, *tomb* or *jug;* Mid-west, *jug* or *jay;* Pacific Coast, *jug* or *big-top.*

John Fate, n. phr.   Fate or circumstances.   "It's about time John Fate grinned at me."

jug, n.   A bank.   See *jay.*

jug hoister or *heister,* n. phr.   One who holds up banks.   See *hoist.*

a jug heavy, n. phr.   A man who specializes in blowing bank safes.   "George is a good mechanic but he'll never make a jug heavy.   He'd better stay on the small stuff."   East Coast, *box-worker* or *iron-worker;* Mid-West, *heavyman* or *peterman;* West Coast, *cribman* or *boxman.*

junker, n.   A dope fiend or addict.

kangarood, v.   Framed; convicted and imprisoned on a trumped-up charge.

keister, n.   A steel inner compartment of a safe for valuables, with a steel door made of several laminated plates.   There are generally three to seven steel plates in thickness for safety.   "Can we use can-opener on this keister?"

(to) kick back, v.   To return stolen money or valuables.   "Kick back that scratch."

kindergarten, n.   A college or university.

king, n.   The warden of a penitentiary or prison.

kite, n.   A letter or note, usually smuggled out of an institution and delivered surreptitiously.

(to) knock off, v. phr.   To arrest a suspect or raid an unlawful establishment.   "His joint was knocked off."

knowledge-box, n.   A school house.

kosher, adj.   All right, reliable, to be trusted; from the Yiddish word for "clean," as applied to food.   "He is kosher."

label maker, n. phr.   One who counterfeits labels of different makes of whiskies and liquors; usually an engraver of some skill.

lag, n.   A term in the penitentiary.   "I'm not doing a long lag this time."

lammister or *lamster,* n.   One who is wanted by the police; one who is "on the lam."   Mid-West, *red-hot;* West Coast, *corner-turner.*

(to) lay off, v. phr.   To let go; to quit.   "Lay off that rod, you dirty dog!"

law, n.   A policeman, deputy sheriff, constable, etc.   Sometimes referred specifically as John Law.

life on the installment plan, n. phr.   An indeterminate sentence.   "He must have some weight; he got life on the installment plan."

loft worker, n. phr.   A cloth thief, who robs cloth factories on a large scale.

lower deck, adv. phr.   Riding on the blind baggage coach.   "Guess we'll have to go lower deck to Chi this time."

(to) make the queer, v. phr.   To be engaged in counterfeiting.   See *shoving the queer, (to be) on the queer, queer.*

mark, n.   A place designed to be robbed.   "The mark was at the corner of Mill and Lamont."

market for stiffs, n. phr.   The office of a questionable broker or "fence" where stolen bonds, stocks and securities can be sold.

McCoy, adj. 1. Pure, reliable, O. K. "This is McCoy." "He is McCoy."
2. Nitroglycerin used to blow safes; probably named for a well-known nitro man in the oil fields of Pennsylvania. "This bird has used McCoy on this job."

moll-buzzer, n. A pickpocket who robs women, i.e., who buzzes the molls.

moll, n. 1. A gangster's sweetheart or mistress. 2. Any girl whether associated with the underworld or not.

(to) mope, v. To stroll, to walk. "Joe moped into the plant like nothing was up."

M. P., n. A mounted policeman.

mouthpiece, n. A lawyer.

moocher, n. A beggar on the street.

muff, n. A girl or woman.

mumbly-pegs, n. phr. A girl's legs. "Long time since I seen any classy mumbly-pegs."

(to) muscle in, v. phr. To attempt to infringe upon the territory or profits of a rival gang.

mutt, n. A yellow gangster; a hoodlum unworthy of the steel of a really tough individual. A term of contempt.

(to) nail, v. To arrest. "They nailed me right on the border."

needle-beer, n. Beer that has had alki or ether injected into it.

noise, n. Dynamite or nitro-glycerin used for blowing safes.

nut, n. Cost, debt, expense. "He was on the nut (in debt for) his boiler." "I got two grand and the nut (expenses) for that job."

nut college, n. phr. An insane asylum.

o. b. or *obie*, n. The Post Office. "Up there in the sticks there wasn't even an o. b."

(to) office, v. To warn or tip off someone; to give him inside information.

oliver, n. The moon.

on the Erie, prep. phr. To be listening; to have one's ears open. A humorous play on the name of a railroad. See *I. C.*

(to be) on the heavy, prep. phr. To be engaged in blowing safes.

(to be) on the hipe, prep. phr. To be practising the short change racket.

(to be) on the I. C., v. phr. 1. To be on the lookout; a whimsical usage of the abbreviation for "Illinois Central." He was on the I. C. for the law."

(to be) on the lam, v. phr., also *to lam* or *(to) take a lam*. To be wanted by the police, to be on the run from the authorities; to be running away from anything. "You ought to have seen him lamming out of that stiff-joint." "Bell's on the lam in Detroit now."

(to be) on the peter, v. phr. To be a peterman or safe blower; so-called either because "pete" or nitro-glycerin is used in this business or because certain types of safes are known as "peters." See *cannon-ball peter.*

(to be) on the queer, v. phr. To be engaged in counterfeiting money. See *shoving.*

(to be) on the racket, v. phr. To be a racketeer of some kind.

(to be) on the rats, v. phr. To be engaged in robbing box-cars or rattlers.

on the shake, prep. phr. Attempting to extort money. "He was on the shake and that was why he was put on the spot by the gamblers."

(to be) on the skin, v. phr. To be a professional fur-thief.

on the square, prep. phr. Honest.

(to be) on the whiz, v. phr.   To be operating as a pick-pocket.

oscar, n.   A pistol.

out, n.   A way to freedom or a means of getaway.   "No outs this way, buddy."

O'Shaugnessy pardon, n. phr.   Death; so-called because the O'Shaugnessy Undertaking Co. takes charge of most of the Catholic bodies. This expression is restricted to the Ohio State Penitentiary. "Well, Slim just wised me that old John got an O'Shaugnessy pardon last night."

outside man, n. phr.   One who stands outside on guard while a job is being pulled inside a building.

pan-handler, n.   A beggar or bum who asks for small sums of money on the street.

paper, n.   Marked cards. "I smell paper in this little party."

paper-hanger, n.   A forger. East Coast, *bill-poster;* Mid-west, *paper-hanger;* Pacific coast, *scratcher.*

pay master on a convoy, n. phr.   The man who makes contact with officials and police and pays them to allow liquor-laden cars to pass through without police interference.

pay-off, n.   1. The time to divide the loot or profit on a deal. "Thursday's the pay-off, or we'll know the why-for."   2. A confidence man. "Watch him, he's a pay-off."

pedigree, n.   A police record.

penny-weighter, n. phr.   1. One who substitutes paste gems for valuable jewels; a term which originated in hock-shops and jewelry stores of questionable reputation.   2. A diamond thief.

persuader, n.   A black-jack.

(to) pike, v.   To look at. "Pike the eye, there."

pilot man, n. phr.   One who drives the lead car in a booze convoy.

pineapple, n.   A bomb.

piss-house, n.   The police station.

plant, n.   1. A hide-out. "He went to the plant until the heat blew over."   2. An establishment where opium is cooked or liquor made. "They knocked off our plant yesterday."   3. A place where swag is hidden until it is safe to pass it to the *fence.*

(to) play with the squirrels, v. phr.   To be an inmate of an insane asylum.

(to) play the bird with the long neck, v. phr.   See *to go gandering.*

(to) play the match, v. phr.   To engage in a confidence game. "Tony's slick at playing the match."

plinger, n.   A bum or street beggar who "plings" or "mooches" passers-by.

pogey, n.   The hospital of a penal institution. " I got it soft here in the pogey."

poke, n.   A pocketbook.

poly, n.   A politician.

Pontius Pilate, n. phr.   A judge.

prat kick, n. phr.   The hip pocket.

prohi, n.   A prohibition agent.

(to) promote, v.   To plan or line up a touch. "No use to promote anything around here. Sam always queers it."

prop, n.   A stick pin of some value. When a safety catch is attached the pin is called *anchor on prop.* "I like that ice but there's an anchor on prop."

(to) punch, v.   To open a safe or door by force. "Red punched that box pronto."

punk, n.   Bread in a penal institution.

(to) put the finger on, v. phr.   To identify or point out a person.   "The dicks put the finger on him."

(to) put (him) on the grease, v. phr.   To scold, admonish, berate, bawl out.   "He was put on the grease by his brother."

quetor, n.   A twenty-five cent piece.   See *cutor.*

racket, n.   A word of numerous and loose usages, some of which are: 1. The extortion of money from victims by threatening force.   2. The conversion of otherwise legitimate organizations—such as labor unions—into vehicles for extortion.   3. Any unlawful occupation or profession.   4. Any honest means by which a person makes a living.   "You've got a soft racket, Professor."   5. In general, the activities of the underworld against society.

ranked, part.   Exposed or found out.

rap, n.   1. A prison term.   2. A trial in criminal court.

rapper, n.   A witness in criminal court.   See *sucker.*

rattler, n.   1. A train, especially a freight train.   2. A boxcar.   "He always meets the midnight rattler."

reader, n.   A warrant for arrest.   "That fuzey bribed a reader and they fingered me at the piss-house."

reader with a tail, n. phr.   A warrant for arrest with a reward attached.   "I hear they've put a tail on that reader for our torpedo."

red, n.   A penny.

ref, n.   A reformatory.

rib, n.   1. A girl.   "Who's yer rib, Bill?"   2. A term for the small of the back or the midriff where an enemy is likely to stick a gun.   "All around is dicks and I feels a gun stuck in my rib."

(to) ride, v.   To cause someone to be unfairly convicted and imprisoned; to frame; to kangaroo.   "He did that so's to ride me to the big house and he could lam with the rocks."

ridge, n.   A gold coin of any denomination.

rod, n.   A gun, usually a pistol.   "Give him the rod, Bill."

rodman on a convoy, n. phr.   A gunman who protects a booze-laden car from being held up or high-jacked.   "He used to be a rodman on the convoy, but he didn't have the guts for that job."

rope, n.   A necklace.   "Get this rope to the fence before we fall for receiving."

(the) rope, n. phr.   1. Execution by hanging.   2. The death penalty, regardless of the means of execution.

rosco, n.   A pistol.   "No one moved for a rosco."

(to) root with the oliver, n. phr.   To work while the moon is down, or concealed beneath a cloud.   "Come on, while we can root with the oliver."

(to) root against the oliver, v. phr.   To work while the moon is shining.   "There'll be plenty of heat if we have to root against the oliver."

(to) rumble, v. or *(to) give a rumble,* v. phr.   To notive, to suspect, to look at.   "Johnny said the hack rumbled him (or gave him a rumble) so he blew."

(to) run the roads down, v. phr.   To go over the highways with a machine and figure out the best roads for the getaway.   This is always a preliminary precaution taken before a big job.

rung up, adj. phr.   To have the appearance altered.

sand, n. Sugar in a penal institution.

saw buck, n. A ten-dollar bill.

scatter, n. A saloon, resort, or blind pig. "His scatter was given a play by all the heavy mobs."

schoolmate, n. A fellow convict. An ex-schoolmate is a convict from one's "alma mater."

(to) score, v. To succeed in accomplishing any object. "Bull's scored that time."

scratch, n. Paper money. "Don't mess with that iron money; get the scratch."

scratcher, n. A forger or *paper hanger*.

screw, n. 1. A guard in a penitentiary. 2. A key.

second story man, n. phr. A house prowler; one who climbs into second story windows.

second story work, n. phr. Porch climbing at the dinner hour to avoid detection by the inhabitants of the house.

(to be) set in, v. phr. To have protection, and be safe from interference by the law. "Bull is sure set in with coppers in Buffalo."

settled, part. Sent to prison. "He fell for the tools in St. Louis and they settled him."

settled wrong, part. phr. Convicted, though innocent; framed; kangarood.

seven up hustler, n. phr. One who robs general stores.

seven-up, n. A general store.

shack, n. A mine guard; also a freight-brakeman. "The shacks have Tommies."

(to) shake, or *to shake down*, v. phr. 1. To extort money from someone. "We shook him plenty." 2. To search a victim. "Shake him, Bill."

shake-down, n. Money extorted by agents of the law on threats of arrest or exposure. "That John Law can't pull a shake-down in here."

shamus, n. A policeman.

Shaw-Davis pardon, n. phr. Death; so called because the Shaw-Davis Undertaking Co. handles most of the Protestant bodies at the Ohio State Penitentiary. The term is restricted to this institution.

shell V., n. phr. A steel vault with a thin-one-plate door, always painted white. "I'd rather work on a shell V. than a cannon-ball any day."

shill, n. A come-on man or persuader in some game. "Let him go with it; he's only a shill to get the big boys in."

short, n. 1. A trolley-car. "Split up and get on a short if you can." 2. A short-circuit used to avoid setting off a burglar alarm.

shoving the queer, part. phr. Passing counterfiet money. See *on the queer*.

shyster, n. Any attorney.

simple simon, n. A diamond in a man's tie.

six-hat and fifty-shirt, adj. phr. An expression analogous to the more common "strong back and a weak mind," meaning that the person to whom the adjective is applied has shoulders out of all proportion to the capacity of his cranium.

skin-joint, n. phr. A fur store.

sky pilot, n. A Protestant minister.

skin worker, n. phr. A fur thief.

skins, n. Furs. See *skin worker* and *on the skin*.

skinny, n. A ten cent piece. "Shootin' a skinny this time; it's all I've got left."

skipper, n.   1. The police captain of a precinct.   "That skipper'll need plenty of grease."   2. The deputy warden of a penal institution.   Also known as the dep.

slang, n.   A watch chain.

slough worker, n. phr.   One who robs apartments, flats, etc. in day time.

slugs, n.   Bullets or buck-shot.   "Joe got a bellyful of slugs that time."

slum, n.   Jewelry.   See *slum joint*.

slum-joint, n.   A jewelry store, ironically so-called with the inference that the merchandise of the jeweler is "slum," i.e., the very cheap trinkets which one sees given away by set-joints at carnivals and circuses.   East-coast and Midwest, *slum-joint;* West Coast, *ice-house*.

slum worker, n. phr.   One who approaches passers-by and sells them cheap watches and jewelry as valuable jewelry.

small fry, n. phr.   A bootlegger who sells by the drink or bottle.   Restricted to liquor men.   "There's only small fry down on Havre St."

(to) smoke, v.   To shoot; to shoot at.   "I smoked them guys a plenty."

sneak-gate, n.   A steel-barred gate in vaults, inside the vault door, that is used in day time when the vault door is open.   It is to safeguard the vault in day time, without the bother of keeping the vault door closed.

(to) sneeze, v.   To kidnap.   "He was sneezed and shook down for 5 X-rays."

sneezed, part.   Arrested, collared, knocked off.

snoose, n.   Snuff.   "Bill chews snoose like an old-timer now."

snow-bird, n.   A cocaine addict.

soldier, 1. n.   An "outside man" on a heavy job.   2. v.   *To soldier*.   To stand watch as an "outside man."   "I started soldiering for Max; he was the heavy then."

soup, n.   Nitro-glycerin or "pete."

souper or *super*, n.   A watch.

spindle, n.   The steel bar to which the combination of a safe is attached.

(to) splurge it, v. phr.   To live fast and loose on the proceeds of a job.

(to) spot someone, v. phr.   To place someone on the spot to be killed.   "You spot him and the chopper'll do the rest."

spreader, n.   An instrument for spreading bars on prison windows.   "Someone's making a spreader in here."

(to) spring, v.   To obtain a release or discharge from jail or the penitentiary; also used to mean bail.   "It took ten G's to get sprung."

square cop, n. phr.   A cop that gives one a square deal.

(to) square a rap, v. phr.   To "*fix*" or bribe authorities so that charges may be dropped.   "The boss squared my rap so I didn't have to take a fall that time."

stall, n.   One who shades the wire from being seen while the theft is being made.

stool, n.   An informer or stoolpigeon; a rat; a squealer; a cat.

(to) stem in, v. phr.   To drill a hole in the door of a safe to give easy access to explosives, or to force the dog of a combination.   Restricted to safe-blowers.   "I was just stemming in when in stepped the clown."

stew, n.   Nitro-glycerin.

steer-joint, n.   A gambling joint that has *steerers, shills*, etc., therefore one where the patron always loses.

steerer, n.   A *shill*, or *come-on* man in a gambling joint.

stick-man, n.   A croupier in a gambling joint.

stiff joint, n. phr.   A bond office or brokerage.

stiffs, n.   Bonds or negotiable securities.

(to) sting, v.   To make a theft.   "That's the second time Bull stung that guy."

stir-bugs, adj. phr.   Crazy from confinement and punishment, temporarily.   "He went stir-bugs on that last bit."

stir, n.   The penitentiary.   "Sugar'll be in the stir again before long.   He's a habitual."

stir-agent, n.   A shyster lawyer who hangs about a penal institution to pick up any business he can.

stones, n.   Diamonds or gems.

string, n.   The fuse for setting off a fulminate cap.   "Give us about a yard of that string."

sucker, n.   1. The victim of a hold-up or robbery.   2. A witness in criminal court.

sure-thing worker, n. phr.   One of a gang of several men, who are supposed to have inside information on horse races, fights, etc.   "The sure-thing worker," sells supposedly authentic tips.   East Coast, *big conner* or *short conner;* Mid-west, *sure-thing man;* West Coast, *wire-worker* or *con man*.

swamped, part.   Surrounded and surprised.   Arrested by a large force.   "They swamped us that time."

(to) tab a kite, v. phr.   To write a letter, usually one which is to be smuggled out of prison or "flown."

tail, 1. n.   A reward for the arrest of a criminal.   "The D. A. issued a reader with a tail for Jack."   2. v.   To follow.   "He was tailed to his plant and collared."

ten per-center, n. phr.   One who finds promising prospects for a gang and receives ten per cent of the loot.   Sometimes called a "ten-per."

thimble, n.   A stolen watch.

(to) throw slugs, v. phr.   To engage in a gun battle.   "There was Red and Thommy out in the street a-throwing slugs."

timer, n.   A safe or vault with a time lock, which allows the combination to be worked only after a certain time of day.   "That one's a timer; lay off it."

tip, n.   Inside information; a warning; an "office."   See *office*.

Tommie Gee, or *Tommie G.*, n. phr.   A machine gun operator.   "He was a Tommie Gee for Red's mob."

Tommy, n.   A machine gun; a term carried over from the war.   "They had Thompson Tommies."

(a) ton of law, n. phr.   A hefty policeman.

(to) top off, v. phr.   To execute; to assassinate.   See *(to) top*.

(to be) topped, v. phr.   To be electrocuted or hanged.   "That bird in the dance house is to be topped in September."

torch man, n. phr.   One who enters safes or vaults by burning with the acetylene torch.

(to) torch a squib, v. phr.   To light the fuse to a charge of nitro-glycerin.   "I had just lit a match to torch the squib when I heard steps behind me."

torpedo, n.   A machine gunner for a mob or gang.   Also known as a *chopper.* "Guess the chief wants Bill for the new torpedo."

touch, n.   A job or a prospective job.   "Sam kites me some dope on a touch in Cleveland."

town clown, n. phr.   Marshal or constable in a small town or village.   Differentiated from the "coppers" or "bulls" of the city police forces.

trigger-man, n.   A gunman or body guard for a racketeer; always selected for his coolness of nerve and his speed and accuracy with a gun.

(to) tumble, v.   To be seen or found out.   "We tumbled once on that job, so we passed it up."

(to) turn on the heat, v. phr.   To cover someone with a gun.   "You turn on the heat and I'll fan him."

twist or *twist and twirl,* n. phr.   A girl.   Said to be of Australian origin.

two-time loser, n. phr.   A prisoner who has been convicted twice.   "He's a two-time loser; got the book the second time."

underneath, adv. phr.   Riding the rods underneath the coaches of a passenger train; differentiated from "riding the rods" under freight cars.   "The dicks collared us while we were still underneath."

upper deck, adv. phr.   On top of a passenger train.   "It's damned cold traveling upper deck."

V., n.   A safe.   See *black V.*

violin case, n. phr.   The case for carrying a machine gun.   Actual violin cases are often used, but sometimes a specially-constructed case resembling a violin case is employed.

ways, n.   Shares or cuts.   "We split that five ways, don't forget."

weight, n.   Pull or political influence.   "He'll never do his bit; he's got too much weight."

(to) weed out, v. phr.   To take more than a rightful share in loot or profit.

whiskers, n.   The U. S. Government or a federal officer.

whiskey cutter, n. phr.   One who dilutes and adulterates good whiskey, making four bottles of whiskey out of what was originally two bottles of whiskey or other liquor.

whiz, n.   A pick-pocket.

wholesaler, n.   One who sells nothing less than a case at a time.   He deals principally in case lots.   Restricted to liquor-runners.

why-for, n.   The reason why.   "Now I'm gonna give you the why-for."

whiz-mob, n.   A pickpocket mob or gang.   "That whiz-mob from———will be over again tonight."

wipe, n.   A handkerchief.   "Give him your wipe, Joe, he looks like a slaughter house."

wire, n.   The one who purloins the purse or valuables while the *shade* distracts the victim's attention.   Restricted to pickpockets.

(to) wise, v.   To inform someone.   "Go wise the mob the why-for."

(the) works, n. phr.   The death penalty.   See *hot squat, the rope.*

works, n.   A policeman of any kind.   "He's works."

worm, n.   Silk.   "Two cars of worm due here tomorrow."   "He's on the worm lately."

worm worker, n. phr.   A silk thief.

wrong, adj.   Deceitful, unreliable, untrustworthy.   A stoolpigeon is said to be "wrong."   It is always a term of contempt.   "He was put on the spot for being wrong."   "He's wrong, I tell you."

X-ray or *ten yards*, n.   A ten-thousand-dollar bill.

yard, n.   A thousand-dollar bill.   See *grand*.   "We want five yards for that job."

yegg, n.   A safe-blower or peterman.

yentzer, n.   A cheater.   From the Yiddish.   "No mob will fill him in as he is a yentzer."

4

The Lingo
of the Jug-Heavy

The *jug-heavy* (or safecracker) is a relatively small but highly specialized sub-culture within the *heavy rackets* of the underworld. Here is a small portion of the argot used by safecrackers in the late 1920s and early 1930s, first published in *Writer's Digest* for use in film and fiction. While today some of these terms have filtered out into the dominant culture, in 1931 this argot was entirely restricted to the small in-group of specialized professional bank-blowers.

In those days, bank-blowing was a lucrative activity, and the *heavy gees* were highly skilled in their craft. Banks were selected carefully to assure maximum proceeds. The jobs were rehearsed to a fine level of perfection and executed with great precision. The top man seldom went to prison. Today such bank burglaries are rare since, with the exception of a few doing long prison sentences, the old-time safecracker has disappeared. The decline in this profitable craft was due largely to the institution of federal insurance applied to all banks, the result of which was almost certain conviction in federal court of any safecracker who could be definitely connected with a bank job.

Nevertheless, there are occasional reports of *heists* (if we may use the term rather loosely) which bear all the elements of the craft used by the old-time *box-men*. The largest robbery of this kind ever in the United States was a 4.3 million dollar job pulled off at the Purolator Security Incorporated Armored Express Company in Chicago in 1974. The biggest *gopher job* to come to my attention, however, was performed by French professionals at the main branch bank of the Société Générale in Nice. Over 10 million dollars in currency and valuables was taken in this job, and by police reports it is obvious that these French professionals were not only expert but also used all the organizational talents commonly attributed to old-time American *jug-heavies*.

Modern safecrackers have altered the modus operandi drastically and work mostly on safes in business or industry. Some use highly sophisticated electronic techniques, as contrasted to the old-timers who supplied information for this study. At that time both nitroglycerin and dynamite were the chief agents of entry. Present-day safecrackers also do some very crude work, often bludgeoning an office safe with sledgehammers and punches or burning it with an acetylene torch; it is not uncommon for them to abandon a safe after failing to crack it.

The subculture of the old-time safecracker was an extremely tight one which excluded the bunglers and included only the masters. These men were skilled machinists and electricians who often manufactured their own tools. They were also meticulous organizers who knew how to bring several aspects of their plans together with consummate timing to produce a perfect job. Although they used explosive force in their work, it was a source of pride that they seldom killed or injured anyone.

Most of them were trained before 1900 and learned their craft on small-time banks and post offices before they graduated to the big time. Each safe-cracker was *turned out* by an older safecracker who taught the craft with rigorous discipline. Their general custom was to stash the loot after a big job and spend several weeks or months in the hobo jungles, riding the freights and appearing to be harmless derelicts. This was probably a holdover from earlier days when they depended on the railroads for transportation and the careful timing of passing freights to cover the noise of the blast. I have heard that some of them actually worked as trainmen or depended on trainmen for information about the shipment of cash. When they felt safe in the hobo jungles, they would reunite, or they would pick up the loot and spend a season in some northern fishing camp or recreation center where they could live high and plan their next job.

•   •   •

THE jug-heavy is the aristocrat of thieves. His specialty is blowing banks, but his professional pride does not prevent him from engineering a *stone tail elevation* or an *inside stone heist* by way of tiding himself over the depression.

Like all other professionals he has built up a technical vocabulary for his own private use—an argot that ambitious writers of underworld fiction seem to have overlooked. This is because the *peterman*'s occupation is "closed" to the outsider, and being by necessity a man of few words, his lingo seldom if ever gets into print.

When magazine writers do put occasional phrases of the jug-heavy into print they sound strange because the writer inserts them in their full literal spelling while the jug-heavy himself says these phrases with poor pronunciation and sliding over of syllables, such as relegating "the" to "t' " and "with" to "wid," "wi'," or "wit'."

AFTER THE BEEF. adv. phr. After the report goes into the police. "It's your funeral after the beef." "Try to see him ahead of the beef."

ARTILLERY. n. 1. A dope addict's hypodermic outfit; a needle and accessories. 2. Firearms of any description. Also *rosco, oscar, heater, rod, gat, heat, belly-gun, Tommy*.

To BIBLE. v. To swear; to take oath.

BIG TOP. n. A bank. See *jay, jug*.

BLACK V. n. Fireproof iron vault, always painted black.

To BLOW. v.i. 1. To lam, to make a getaway. "When the smoke cleared, the Frisco Kid had blown." 2. For the moon to go down. "Flatten out till the Oliver blows."

To BLOW A BOX. v. phr. To blow a safe.

BOX. n. 1. A safe, especially a large safe or vault. 2. Police station or jail.

BOX-MAN. n. A professional safe cracker or a bank burglar.

BUG. n. A burglar alarm. "Ding that bug if you can find the connection."

BUGGED. part. Wired to a burglar alarm. "The joint was bugged and we got a tumble."

BURNS. n. A Burns detective.

CAN OPENER. n. An instrument made of chilled steel and shaped like a large can opener. After a small hole has been drilled in a safe, the blade is inserted and a piece is cut from the safe just as one cuts out the top of a can. This instrument can be used only on thin-walled safes. It is especially valuable in private residences where the use of explosives would lead to immediate discovery.

CANNON-BALL PETER. n. phr. A round or cylindrical steel burglar-proof safe with laminated steel doors that can be opened only by the acetylene torch.

CAP. n. A fulminate cap that is attached to a fuse, which, when exploded, sets off the nitroglycerin; also dynamite cap.

To CASE. v.t. To watch; of pawnshop origin, probably a pun on watchcase. "Let him case the joint."

CHARGING OUT. v. phr. Said of a mob or gang ready to go to work. "We was just charging out when in steps 'Frisco.' "

To COLLAR. v.t. To arrest. "That shamus tried to collar him."

COLLEGE. n. A penitentiary. "He was just released from college."

COMBO, or COMB. n. The combination of a safe or vault.

COPPER-HEARTED. adj. Deceitful; yellow; a natural stoolpigeon; a squealer. "That copper-hearted fink slugged him."

To CRASH. v.t. To enter a home or business place forcibly. "We were just waitin' to crash a hock shop."

CROWN. n. A tiara or coronet; an ornamental headdress set with jewels.

CUSH. n. 1. Bribe money. 2. Profit from a job. 3. Money or pay in general, usually easily made. "Got the cush?"

D.A. n. The district attorney.

DECLARED IN. part. phr. Given a share. When a person who did not participate in a job but who possesses dangerous knowledge regarding it may be "declared in" as a precaution.

DINAH. n. Dynamite. "Nix on the dinah; I'll take stew every time."

DINGER. n. The bell-alarm outside banks; a bug.

DOUBLE. n. Key made from the original for illicit purposes.

To DRAW. v.t. To be sentenced for a certain term. "Bill drew life on the installment plan."

DRILL. v. (usually passive). To receive a specified prison sentence, as to get "drilled" for five years.

DUSTER. n. A sheet-iron door between the outer door of a safe and the inner compartment. "The shot cracked the duster."

ELBOW. n. A policeman (Pacific Coast). Midwest: *law, works*; East Coast: *shamus, fuzz, goms*.

EYE. n. A Pinkerton detective; sometimes called a "pink." "He's an eye."

To FALL FOR THE HEAVY. v. phr. To be convicted of safe blowing or entering a bank or vault. "I fell for the heavy and drew a fin in Joliet."

To FALL FOR A JUG. v. phr. To be convicted of robbing a bank.

To FALL FOR RECEIVING. v. phr. To be convicted of having stolen property in one's possession. "That fuzzy bibled he caught me with the rocks, so I fell for receiving."

To FALL FOR THE TOOLS. v. phr. To be convicted of having burglar tools.

To FAN. v.t. To search; so-called from running one's hand over a victim's person to find out where his pocketbook or weapon is kept. "When Joe turns on the heat, you fan him."

To FILL (HIM) IN. v. phr. To add an extra man to a gang for a special job. "We didn't like him, but we filled him in anyway."

FIRE-PROOF PETER. n. phr. An iron safe for protection against fire. Not burglar proof.

FLUNK. n. A steel compartment with a thin door in a safe.

FORTY. adv. An expression meaning "Everything is OK."

FOURTH OF JULY. n. phr. A gun battle. "I was ready to put on a fourth of July if the law showed up right then."

FULL OF LARCENY. adj. phr. Open for bribe. "He is full of larceny and you can do business with him."

FUZZY. n. A policeman who is especially diligent in enforcing the law. "That fuzzy would arrest his own mother."

GINGERBREAD DOOR. n. A safe door with ornate trimmings which have nothing to do with strengthening the door. "Gingerbread don't bother me none."

To GLOM. v.t. To steal; to gather in. "We glommed them rocks up on Park Avenue."

To GO GANDERING. v. phr. To be out looking for someone or something. "We went gandering for a peterman." Sometimes known as "playing the bird with the long neck."

GOPHER. n. An iron safe. "He punched the gopher open."

GOPHER MOB. n. phr. Vault tunnelers; a gang that makes a business of digging into vaults from underneath.

To GREASE. v.t. To bribe. "You'll have to grease the clown for that job."

HACK. n. 1. A watchman; usually restricted to merchant-policemen and differentiated from the municipal constables or police. "Sorry we had to blot that hack." 2. A pen guard.

HARD STUFF. n. phr. Metal money.

To HAVE A FALL. v. phr. To be arrested. "Haven't seen Joe lately; suppose he's had a fall?"

HEAT. n. 1. Excitement; trouble. "He left a lot of heat behind him." "He was always in the heat." 2. The vicinity of trouble. "Let's blow out of the heat." 3. The "drop" with a gun. "Turn on the heat, Joe."

HEAVY RACKETS. n. Those enterprises involving violence or the threat of violence to take money, as contrasted with the *grift*.

HOT. adj. 1. Any stolen object is said to be "hot." A *hot boiler* is almost always used for the getaway after a job. 2. To be pursued by the law. "He was hot and had to lam."

IN. n. 1. The entrance to a building. "Where's the in to this joint?" 2. An introduction. "Give us an in to the chief, will you?"

INSIDE MAN. n. phr. The man who does the inside work; sometimes known as the mechanic. Usually restricted to safe blowing.

JAY. n. A bank. "I want to run over to Youngstown to put in a night on that jay we spotted." Far West: *jug*; Midwest: *jug* or *jay*; East Coast: *tomb* or *jug*. A *straw jay* is a county or small-town bank.

JUG-HEAVY. n. A man who specializes in blowing bank safes. "George is a good mechanic but he'll never make a jug-heavy. He'd better stay on the small stuff."

JUMPER. n. A wire used to divert the alarm circuit while working in a bank.

KEISTER. n. A steel inner compartment of a safe for valuables, with a steel door made of several laminated plates. There are generally three to seven steel plates in thickness for safety. "Can we use a can opener on this keister?" 2. A suitcase: A *keister torch* is an acetylene torch which can be carried in a suitcase.

MARK. n. A place designated to be robbed. "The mark was at the corner of Mill and Lamont."

MARKET FOR STIFFS. n. phr. The office of a questionable broker or "fence" where stolen bonds, stocks, and securities can be sold. A stiff-joint.

McCOY. adj. 1. Pure, reliable, OK. "This is McCoy." "He is McCoy." 2. n. Nitroglycerin used to blow safes; probably named for a well-known nitroman in the oil fields of Pennsylvania. "This bird has used McCoy on this job."

MECHANIC. n. A professional safe blower; often literally a master mechanic with the skills of a machinist, electrician, metallurgist, etc.

To MOPE. v.i. To stroll, to walk. "Joe moped into the plant like nothing was up."

NOISE. n. Dynamite or nitroglycerin used for blowing safes.

NUT. n. Cost, debt, expense. "He was on the nut (in debt) for his boiler." "I got two grand and the nut (expense) for that job."

To be ON THE HEAVY. v. phr. To be engaged in blowing safes.

To be ON THE LAM. v. phr. Also *to lam* or (to) *take a lam,* (to) *cop a lam*; to be wanted by the police, to be on the run from the authorities, to be running away from anything. "You ought to have seen him lamming out of that stiff-joint." "Bill's on the lam in Detroit now." Pacific Coast: *corner-turner, lammister*; Midwest: *red-hot, on the lam*; East Coast: *lambster* or *lamster.*

To be ON THE PETER. v. phr. To be a peterman or safe blower, so-called either because "pete" or nitroglycerin is used in this business or because certain types of safes are known as "peters." See *cannon-ball peter.* Pacific Coast: *cribman* or *boxman*; Midwest: *heavyman* or *peterman*; East Coast: *boxworker, ironworker.*

OUT. n. A way to freedom or a means of getaway. "No outs this way, buddy."

OUTSIDE MAN. n. phr. One who stands outside on guard while a job is being pulled inside a building. A *soldier.*

PEDIGREE. n. A police record.

PETER. n. A safe. Pacific Coast: *crib* or *box.*

To PUNCH. v.t. To open a safe or door by force. "Red punched that box pronto."

READER WITH A TAIL. n. phr. A warrant for arrest with a reward attached. "I hear they've put a tail on that reader for our torpedo." A *tail* is also used to designate someone following behind. "Let's put a tail on him."

RIDGE. n. A gold coin—of any denomination.

To ROOT WITH THE OLIVER. v. phr. To work while the moon is down or concealed behind a cloud. "Come on, while we can root with the oliver."

To ROOT AGAINST THE OLIVER. v. phr. To work while the moon is shining. "There'll be plenty of heat if we have to root against the oliver."

To RUMBLE, or to GIVE A RUMBLE. v. phr. To notice, to suspect, to look at. "Johnny said the hack rumbled him (or gave him a rumble) so he blew."

To RUN THE ROADS DOWN. v. phr. To go over the highways with a machine and figure out the best roads for the getaway. This is always a preliminary precaution taken before a big job.

SCRATCH. n. Paper money. "Don't mess with that iron money; get the scratch." A *scratch-pusher* is a cashier, *working scratch* is the day's receipts in a bank or business house.

SCREW. n. A key.

SHELL V. n. A steel vault with a thin one-plate door, always painted white. "I'd rather work on a shell V than a cannon-ball any day."

SIX-HAT AND FIFTY-SHIRT. adj. phr. An expression analogous to the more common "strong back and a weak mind," meaning that the person to whom the adjective is applied has shoulders out of all proportion to the capacity of his cranium.

SLUM JOINT. n. phr. A jewelry store, ironically so-called with the inference that the merchandise of the jeweler is "slum," i.e., the very cheap trinkets that one sees given away by set-joints at carnivals and circuses. West Coast: *ice house.*

SNEAK-GATE. n. A steel-barred gate in vaults, the inside vault door that is used in daytime when the vault door is open. It is to safeguard the vault in daytime, without the bother of keeping the vault door closed.

SOLDIER. 1. n. An "outside man" on a heavy job. 2. v.i. *To soldier.* To stand watch as an "outside man." "I started soldiering for Max; he was the heavy then."

SOUP. n. Nitroglycerin or "pete."

SPINDLE. n. The steel bar to which the combination of a safe is attached.

To SPLURGE IT. v. phr. To live fast and loose on the proceeds of a job.

To STEM IN. v. phr. To drill a hole in the door of a safe to give easy access to explosives, or to force the dog of a combination. Restricted to safe blowers. "I was just stemming in when in stepped the clown."

STEW. n. Nitroglycerin made by softening dynamite in warm water and squeezing it until the "soup" is freed from the sawdust and clay base and can be skimmed off the top.

STIFFS. n. Bonds or negotiable securities.

STIR. n. The penitenitiary. "Sugar'll be in the stir again before long. He's a habitual."

STONES. n. Diamonds or gems. Also *ice.* A *stone tail* or *elevation* is a job that is pulled by "tailing" "heavily stoned" persons from an opera or theatre to a convenient spot where they are robbed at the point of a gun.

STRING. n. The fuse for setting off a fulminate cap. "Give us about a yard of that string."

SWAMPED. v.t. Surrounded and surprised. Arrested by a large force. "They swamped us that time."

TEN PERCENTER. n. phr. One who finds promising prospects for a gang and receives 10 percent of the loot. Sometimes called a "ten-per."

THIRTY. n. The end; a termination of anything, usually unfavorable. Probably borrowed from newspapermen.

TIMER. n. A safe or vault with a time lock, which allows the combination to be worked only after a certain time of day. "That one's a timer; lay off it."

TORCH MAN. n. phr. One who enters safes or vaults by burning with the acetylene torch.

To TORCH A SQUIB. v. phr. To light the fuse to a charge of nitroglycerin. "I had just lit a match to torch the squib when I heard steps behind me."

TOWN CLOWN. n. phr. Marshal or constable in a small town or village. Differentiated from the "coppers" or "bulls" of the city police forces.

V. n. A safe. See *black V*.

To WEED OUT. v. phr. To take more than a rightful share in loot or profit.

X-RAY or TEN YARDS. n. A ten-thousand-dollar bill. Other denominations, *demier* or *skinny*, ten cents; *cutor* or *quetor*, twenty-five cents; *fin*, five dollars; *sawbuck* or *saw*, ten dollars; *double saw*, twenty dollars; *C* or *C note*, one hundred dollars; *yards*, *G*, or *grand*, one thousand dollars.

5

Junker Lingo: By-Product of Underworld Argot

This is probably one of the first published records of the argot of the underworld narcotic addict who at that time inhabited a subculture that was tightly closed to outsiders. This was because the Harrison Narcotic Act (1914) carried exorbitantly severe prison sentences which put all the people involved in drug trafficking in constant fear of arrest and conviction. I culled this material while working on other aspects of criminal argots during the 1930s when I occasionally encountered an addict or dealer. I felt apologetic about the amount of material collected but decided to publish it anyway since I could find no other studies. In fact, in 1935 the chief comprehensive reference work on drugs was *The Opium Problem* by Terry and Pellens (1928), a conservative medical book that made no reference either to a subculture or to argot usage within it.

In the next issue of *American Speech* I was surprised to find a response to this article from Victor Folke Nelson, a professional writer doing a term in Sing Sing. In his "Addenda to 'Junker Lingo,' " Nelson made the following comment:

While it is true, as Mr. Maurer states, that the narcotic addict and the peddler of drugs are extremely reticent creatures who build up a wall of secrecy which is very difficult to penetrate, it is likewise true that the average addict or peddler is a vastly illiterate person whose linguistic needs are quite adequately supplied by a few hundred words. Perhaps two hundred of these are terms which pertain largely or wholly to drugs and their use; and Mr. Maurer has done well indeed to discover so many of them. After twenty years of association, off and on, with drug-addicts, I can assure him that his vocabulary is fairly accurate and comprehensive.

Obviously, there was a good deal more to be learned about the language and behavior patterns of addicts who supported their habits by crime than either Nelson or I realized at the time.

In 1935 I discussed the nature of criminal subcultures and argots over a national radio hookup, and following the lecture I received a long distance call at the station from Victor H. Vogel, medical officer in charge of the newly established drug treatment center at Lexington, Kentucky. He told me his staff had no knowledge of this argot but would like to learn more about it, so he invited me to come to Lexington and use the institution as a base for further research. This I did with more complete results than I had been able to produce up to that time, as will be seen in subsequent chapters.

• • •

A drug addict of necessity lives in a more or less restricted world of his own. He has cultivated certain peculiarities of speech which are variations of the conventional underworld argot. The origins of most of these terms are either quite obvious, or so obscure as to make speculation uncertain.

Among the addicts dope in general is known as *gow, junk,* or *peter* (any kind of *knockout drops*). Addicts who belong to no specific class — often those who do not use exclusively any type of drug — are said to be *junkers* or *from Mt. Shasta.* When one has contracted the habit or is under the immediate influence of the drug, he is *all lit up, on the gow,* or *hitting the gow.* Drugs are sold by *peddlers* and *ice-tong doctors* (illegal practitioners who also sell dope) and the *rations* — usually sold at a standard price of $1.00 — are designated, according to the type of drug involved, as *checks, bindles,* or *O.Z.'s.*

Specific types of dope most frequently used in America are morphine, cocaine, opium and its derivative laudanum, heroin, and marijuana. Cocaine is known as *C., snow, coke, happy dust, heaven dust. Bernice* or *burnese* is crystallized cocaine prepared for inhaling into the lungs. To *go on a sleigh-ride* is to inhale the *bernice* and experience the consequent exhilaration. A cocaine addict is called a *snowbird,* a *cokie,* or a *snifter.* Opium is referred to specifically as *O., mud,* or *hop,* and the addict is known as a *hophead, pipe-smoker,* or *cookie.* The pipe through which most addicts get the effect of opium is a *gong,* a *gonger,* or a *stem; Yenshee* (perhaps the only word connected with opium traffic which is of Chinese origin) is the residue left in the pipe after it has been smoked. When the opium addict is smoking he is said to be *hitting the gong, kicking the gonger, kicking the gong around,* or *lying on his hip.* The preparation of opium for smoking is known as *cooking a pill* or *rolling a pill* and the opium den is called a *hopjoint.* Morphine is referred to as *M.* or a *slumber party* and heroin, represented by *H.,* is known as *courage pills* when it is prepared in tablet form.

Cocaine, opium, and heroin, it should be noted, are taken either through the stomach or by inhalation through the lungs, while morphine is more frequently taken by direct injection into the blood. The hypodermic needle and its accessories used for the injection of narcotics are called the *gun* or *artillery.* If the addict cannot obtain the regulation needle he may construct an *emergency gun* from a medicine dropper and safety pin; the flesh is punctured with the pin, which is then used to enlarge the opening enough to allow the insertion of the nozzle of the dropper. The injection of dope is referred to as a *bang in the arm* or a *shot in the arm*. The *main line* is the blood vessel into which the injection is made; and the injection itself, immediately after being introduced, is called a *speedball*. The feeling of exhilaration or lassitude that ensues is known as the *jab-off*.

An addict who is endeavoring to break himself of the drug habit voluntarily is *kicking the habit*. A *torture chamber* is a jail or other institution where he may be confined without access to narcotics. When an addict who for some reason cannot obtain dope through the usual channels becomes desperate, he may *throw a wingding* (feign a highly realistic fit in public) in the hope that the doctor who is summoned will administer narcotics to quiet him; professional *wingdingers* are addicts who make a practice of obtaining their narcotics in this manner.

Federal narcotic agents are the bane of addicts, for they cut off the source of supply by arresting the *peddlers*. These agents, hated alike by *peddler* and addict, are called *whiskers, gazers,* or *uncles*.

If the reader is impressed by the meagerness of the vocabulary presented here, let me remind him that the narcotic addict is a reticent creature at best and that the addict's fear that his supply will be cut off and the peddler's fear of arrest combine to build up a wall of secrecy which is most difficult to penetrate. The material presented here, meager though it is, represents the cullings of more than a year's research among underworld characters. There exists, I feel sure, a much more extensive means of communication among those addicted to this vice and the men who supply the drugs, but it remains for someone with more fortitude than I to uncover it in its entirety.

6

The Lingo
of the Good People

Good people were, in the 1930s, old-timers or professionals who had *packed the racket in.* The word was applied in the singular as well as the plural; for example, "Joe is good people." Some of the material for this study was collected from several life-termers in large penitentiaries in the days when a life term often meant exactly that. Others who contributed were retired thieves, circus grifters, and sure-thing operators. Most of the informants were over seventy years of age. The article's main interest lies in the fact that it distinguishes the various individual criminal craftsmen who flourished around 1880-1900 from the organized underworld which developed during prohibition. The informants were mostly from the eastern part of the United States and had primarily been involved in unorganized crime, including murder, as opposed to the big-time racketeers who contributed to the "Argot of the Underworld" and "Lingo of the Jug-Heavy." Many of the older terms are accompanied by their modern equivalents, so that the change in the argot as well as the social structure of crime becomes clear.

• • •

TO the modern gangster an old-timer is *good people.* It has occurred to me that it might be interesting to revert lingusitically thirty years or so to an age when highly organized gangdom had no voice in the government; when the automobile and the machine gun were unthought of as tools of crime; when crooks talked in terms of dollars instead of thousands; when crime, in short, was in the horse-and-buggy stage and had not yet become one of the major industries of this great republic. Even as the countless generations of criminals who preceded them, the *good people* had their argot. Around 1900 when the present-day elderly *good people* were criminal Dapper Dans, their lingo was the last word in linguistic nobbiness. Now it is faded and quaint; it lacks the businesslike rat-a-tat-tat of the modern argot; sometimes it has a definite charm and again it is just stale.

In this article I have attempted to bring together many notes on the older argot which have come to my attention during several years of rather close contact with the American underworld, as it is represented in the artificial culture of prisons and as it occurs in situ in some of our larger cities. In addition, in order that this may not sink to the level of collection of verbal fossils, I have tried, wherever possible, to link the dead with the living, to present the lingo of the *good people* as a stage in the development of the racy argot now spoken wherever those outside the law congregate.[1] I am aware that the relationships which I have pointed out may not always be true; but when dealing with argot that seldom if ever reaches print while it is fresh, one is handling very treacherous material; besides, in most instances, I have been compelled to depend upon my own ingenuity, amplified by considerable assistance from underworld figures whose linguistic training often leaves much to be desired. Hence, I shall welcome any suggestions or corrections which the reader may be kind enough to make.

Four trends are visible in the older argot, as can be readily seen by consulting the accompanying glossary. One cannot say much more, for, in the light of what little reliable information is available regarding the language spoken on the fringes of society, it is rather dangerous to make generalizations.

The first trend brings about the death of certain words, especially those reflecting technique and equipment which have been outmoded. For instance, *drag* (in the sense of a horse-drawn cab) no longer plays any part in the life of gangsters who run the roads down in *hot boilers; cluck* (counterfeit metal money) finds no place in a modern *scratch-spot* where boys who are *on the queer* are handsomely equipped to print anything from twenty dollar bills to fake government bonds and really can't bother making silver dollars; a *gooseberry* (a line full of clothes), once a source of clean linen to criminals who rode the *side-door pullmans,* is no longer meaningful to crooks who ride in drawing rooms and wear handmade shirts over monogrammed nether garments. There are other words which are slowly but surely becoming obsolete[2] in the argot because they originally were of dialectal or colloquial origin and had connotations to the old-timers which are not obvious to the moderns; for instance, *hole in the wall, sixer,* and *gully-miner* — all of Western origin.

The second trend preserves words with little or no change in meaning. The words in the glossary which are accompanied by no statement to the con-

---

1. In relating this material to the modern argot, I have drawn heavily upon Mr. George Milburn's "Convicts Jargon," *American Speech* 6 (1931): 436-42; and my own studies, "The Argot of the Underworld," *American Speech* 7 (1931): 99-118; "Carnival Cant: A Glossary of Circus and Carnival Slang," *American Speech* 6 (1931): 327-37; "The Lingo of the Jug Heavy," *Writers' Digest* (Oct. 1931); "Junker Lingo, By-Product of the Underworld Argot," *American Speech* 9 (April 1933): 27-28; and upon unpublished material now in my files.

2. In the glossary I have used the word *obsolete* to mark those words which, to the best of my knowledge, have disappeared or are disappearing from modern argot, though they may remain in legitimate speech. However, I wish to emphasize that one is on treacherous ground here, and many words which appear to be obsolete are merely dormant; they crop out sometimes with a disconcerting lack of regard for the scholar who has just solemnly pronounced them dead.

trary are still in use, though often they have acquired modern synonyms which may be more popular than the older form. The development of such synonyms is often the first step in the death of the original term, which becomes just one of a number of convenient phrases and may eventually lose its usefulness. For instance, such words as *moll* and *auntie* or *aunt* have been prevalent in crook lingo for centuries; on the other hand, such expressions as *gull, woody* (in the Elizabethan sense), and *trimmer* were all well-known terms to the *good people* but have not passed on to the moderns; the present generation has junked them, for all their centuries of service, and adopted such phrases as *scissors-bill, stir-bugs,* and *lemon* or *stoolo.*

The third trend gives new meanings to old words. As illustrations we have words like *stiff* (now meaning a negotiable security except in the compound *working stiff*), *kite* (now restricted to a letter smuggled out of prison), *heeler* (which has ceased to mean a bouncer and has taken on various meanings), and *angel* (which has, so to speak, become its own antonym). The form of the word has remained identical, but the meaning, sometimes following obvious metaphorical patterns, sometimes without obvious links, has changed or reversed itself.

The fourth trend we find in words which have pulled themselves up by the their bootstraps and now occupy a place in colloquial if not in elegant English. In a sense they have been elevated to respectability, even though most of them suffer from the anemia that inevitably attacks slang words of an older vintage. Samples from this numerous group are *dink,* which once meant a *lady-killer, dinky,* once meaning nobby or natty, and *candy-kid,* once a *dink* whose *lady friend* generously supported him. It is surprising to note the number of faded argot expressions which have been, at one time or another, popular phrases and have eventually achieved respectability. We need only to look about us to see this process going on. Such words as *on the spot, go for a ride, rub-out, moll, big shot, scram, chiseler,* etc., have slipped from the underworld to the front page and are rapidly making their way from wood pulp to glazed paper. This transfer is the basis of the only generalization which I feel safe in making about underworld argots. As soon as argot words become popular with respectable people, they gradually cease to function in the underworld; and by the time an underworld phrase has established itself firmly in print, it is practically dead in the argot, and a new word has taken its place.

AGUE. Loss of nerve under stress; *cold feet.* (Obs.)

ALL TO THE GOOD. Successful, applied to any kind of criminal work. (Obs.) 'That Wells-Fargo trick must be *all to the good* by now.' Analogous to the modern *score.*

ALL WOOL AND A YARD WIDE. Genuine or reliable. (Obs.) Modern *McCoy, square.*

To ALLOT. To divide spoils according to a prearranged agreement. (Obs.) Modern *cut, lay.*

ANCHOR. n. A reprieve or stay of execution. v. (passive only) For a prisoner to be temporarily saved from execution by a stay. See LIFESAVER, LIFEBOAT. In modern pickpocket argot specialized to indicate a safety catch on a stickpin.

ANGEL. The victim or prospective victim of criminals. (Obs.) Modern *sucker, scissors-bill.* (In modern theatrical slang, an *angel* is someone who can be persuaded to finance a show.)

To ANGLE. 1. To meander about. (Obs.) 2. To be searching for a *job* that will yield some loot. (Obs.) The word persists in modern argot meaning to suppose, to estimate, to calculate.

To ANTE UP. To even up a score against an enemy. (Obs.) Modern *to pay off.*

APPLE BUTTER. A crook's *line* which he uses to lure the victim and conceal his real intentions. (Obs.)

AUNTIE. The *madame* or *housemother* in a brothel.

BADGER GAME. A swindling or blackmail racket similar to the modern racket known by the same name.

BAG. An informer or stool pigeon. (Obs.) Modern *fink, rat, ratter, stool, wrong, bogus.*

BALL. A dollar, especially silver. (Obs.) Modern *wheel, ace, buck,* etc.

To BANG. To fornicate.

BANG-TO-RIGHTS. Red-handed. Modern *to get a dead-bang rap.*

BARKER. A noisy, boisterous person. (Obs.) Now survives only in its specialized circus and carnival usage.

BARON. 1. The cop assigned to a hotel beat. (Obs.) 2. The beat proper. (Obs.)

BATS. 1. Temporary insanity resulting from solitary confinement. (Obs.) Modern *stir-bugs* or *stir-simple.* 2. Delirium tremens.

To BATTER. To *panhandle* passers-by. (Obs.) Modern *to mooch* or *panhandle, to put the sleeve on (someone).*

BEACH COMBER. A cheap crook who lives from hand to mouth; one without much initiative. (Obs.) Modern *petty larceny.*

BEAK. A judge. Modern *Pontius Pilate, monk* (judge of the supreme court).

BEEF. Meaningless chatter; gossip. Modern criminals have specialized it to mean a report turned in to the police as in *after the beef, ahead of the beef,* etc.

To BELCH. To confess, or carry information to the police. Modern *to squawk, to turn stool, to fink.*

BIG CORNER. The lion's share of loot from a job. Modern *big end, big cut.*

BIT. A prison sentence. Now apparently supplanted by *stretch* and *jolt,* and by specialized words for sentences of varying lengths.

BLACK-GOLD or BLACK-GOLD SOUPER. A watch of inferior quality.

BLANKET STIFF. A hobo or migratory worker who carries a blanket roll (*crum*) and is distinguished from his more lowly cousin, the *bindle stiff,* who carries all his belongings in a handkerchief or paper bag. Persists only in hobo lingo.

BLOOMER. A safe which, after it has been blown, is found to be empty, or which does not yield enough to pay for the trouble. 'We pulled a *bloomer* in Boston that night.' (Almost obsolete, except with old-timers.) Modern *blank* or *blank peter. Bloomer* is current in circus slang signifying a town which does not pay expenses.

To BLOW. 1. (transitive only) To welcome a friend; to entertain friends. (Obs.) *To blow* now means to leave in a hurry; perhaps there is a different metaphor involved. 2. (passive only) To be caught red-handed. (Obs.) See BANG-TO-RIGHTS.

BLOWN-IN-THE-GLASS STIFF. 1. A reliable associate. (Obs.) 2. A skilled crook. (Obs.) Modern *McCoy, the real McCoy, jake, right.*

BOARD STIFF. A man who carries an advertisement for a living. (Obs.) Modern *sandwich man.*

BOILED DINNER. A tough Irishman. (Obs.) Modern *harp.*

BOILER-MAKER. A criminal dandy; one who has a way with the women; a *candy-kid.*

BOOKED. To have one's record in the possession of the police; now specialized to mean arraigned. Modern *tabbed, pedigreed.*

BOOSTER. A shoplifter. Since this racket has of recent years been largely appropriated by women, the modern argot favors the form *twist booster.*

BOOTLEG. Prison coffee. (Obs.) Modern *moke* or *jamoke.*

To BRACE. To beg; *to panhandle; to batter.* (Obs.)

To BRASS UP. To portion out the loot according to the *lay.* Modern *cut.*

To BREAK A LEG. To be arrested or convicted of a crime. (Obs.) Analogous to the modern *fall* in such idioms as *to fall for the heavy, to fall for a hot boiler,* etc.

BUCK. 1. A dollar. Modern *wheel, ace, casenote, check.* 2. A priest.

BUG. A prostitute. (Obs.) Modern *hustler, hooker.*

BUGHOUSE. An asylum for insane or feebleminded. Modern *nut college.*

BULL. 1. A serving of meat in a prison. 2. A police officer (uniformed).

BULL-BUSTER. A crook who habitually resists arrest. Modern *a Dillinger.*

BULL-CON. A convincing but unreliable *line. Salve, apple butter.*

BUM. Anything which is not genuine. Modern *phoney, prop, scratched.*

BUM or ON THE BUM. To be wounded.

BUNDLE. 1. A woman. (Obs.) 2. A package sent from home to a prisoner. 3. The loot from a burglary. 4. Any stolen property.

To BUNG. To strike with the fist. *Bunged* or *bunged up,* beaten.

BUNGER. A bruise or a black eye.

BURIED. To be convicted of a crime. Modern *fall, settled, to get the book. Buried* now means sentenced to life, or given a long term without hope of parole.

BUST. Any burglary. (Obs.) Modern *hotslough job, cold-slough job, owl job, crash,* etc., with specialized meanings.

BUSTER. A jimmy-bar used by burglars for forcing entrance. (Obs.) Modern *james, stick, bar.*

BUTCH KICK. The hip pocket. Perhaps a variation of the modern *breech kick,* meaning side pocket.

BUZZARD. A small-town constable or local peace officer. Modern *town clown.*

BUZZER. A sneak thief or pickpocket. Survives only in the phrase *moll-buzzer.*

CADET. 1. A pimp. 2. One who supplies girls for the white slave traffic.

To CALL THE TURN. To identify a criminal at headquarters during the showup. Modern *finger, put the finger on, spot.*

CANDY or CANDY-KID. One who has a way with women. A *dink,* a *boiler-maker.*

CARB. Money. (Obs.) See DUST.

CARD. A cutup or prankster.

CELL 99. A mythical cell where unidentified dead are said to be kept; hence, any unidentified corpse.

CENTRAL OFFICE. The old Mulberry St. Police Station in New York City.

CHALKED. Confined in a cell with one's record, or parts of it, chalked on the outside. Modern filing systems have made this practice obsolete except in areas which are backward.

CHAMOIS-PUSHER. A boxer. (Obs.) Modern *leather-pusher.*

CHARLIE ADAMS. The jail at East Cambridge, Mass.

CHEESY. Of an inferior quality. Modern *rum, rummy.*

CHICK. Prison fare. Modern *gooby.*

CHINK. Metal money; loose change. (Obs.) Modern *ridge, coin.*

CHIPPY. A girl, equivalent to the slang term *chicken. Chippy* has now acquired an unsavory connotation and is practically the equivalent of prostitute.

CHRISTMAS. A railroad detective. (Obs.)

CHURCH HYPOCRITE. A crook who is skilled in pious posing, a VESTRY THIEF, *q.v.* (Obs.)

CLAM. A *sucker;* a prospective victim; a *come-on.*

To CLIMB A PORCH. To burglarize a dwelling. The modern *climb* designates a burglary which must be accomplished as an *outside job.*

To CLOUT. To steal from markets and stores as a sneak thief. Cf. modern *heel, heeler, gyp, booster.*

CLUBHOUSE. The municipal police station. Modern *piss house, crummy, can.*

CLUCK. Counterfeit money (metal). Modern *phoney ridge, queer.* Modern counterfeiters make very little bad metal money.

CODGER. One of *the boys;* a *cove;* a companion in crime. (Obs.)

COFFIN VARNISH. *Rotgut* whisky.

COLD MEAT PARTY. A wake where refreshments are served. (Obs.)

COMEBACK. 1. Resistance on the part of the victim. 2. An unforeseen reversal of a situation reacting to the crook's disadvantage.

To COME HOME. To be released from prison. Modern *get a ducat, hit the bricks, get sprung.*

COME-ON. A prospective victim.

CON. (variant of *bull-con*) A lie. Perhaps there is some connection between this term and the modern *conner* and *short-conner* applied to big-time swindlers.

CONNY. One who leads *suckers* to a gambling joint. Modern *shill, steerer, come-on man.*

COOLER. A cell in solitary confinement. Now, though not used in the argot, a common slang term for jail. Modern *sol* or *the hole.*

COPPED OUT. Arrested. See modern *cop* in its various senses.

COPPER JOHN. The prison at Auburn, N. Y. Modern *copper* means *good time* or time taken off a sentence for good behavior; it may also mean a stool pigeon. There may be some connection.

To COSS. To sleep. (Obs.) Modern *plow the deep, pound the bell.*

To CRACK. 1. To break into a building. 2. To shoot with a pistol. 3. To speak.

CRAPPER. A depreciative name for a penitentiary. (Obs.) Modern *stir, big house,* etc.

CRAVEN HUNTER. An underworld busybody; a *Crowley's anvil.* (Obs.) Both terms said to be of British origin.

CREEPER. A prostitute who robs inebriated patrons. Modern *roller.*

CREEPERS. Gumshoes worn by burglars. Modern *sneakers.*

CRIB. A saloon where crooks gather. (Obs.) Modern *plant, kip, gun joint. Crib* is now restricted to safeblowing, where it is a term for a special type of vault.

CRIMP. A solicitor or runner for cheap lodging houses. (Obs.)

CROAKER. A doctor. Now restricted to a prison physician.

CROWLEY'S ANVIL. 1. A malicious gossip; one who talks too much. (Obs.) 2. A stool pigeon. (Obs.)

CRUM or CRUMMY. 1. A hobo's *bindle* or the roll carried by a *blanket stiff.* 2. Any of numerous species of body vermin, especially a louse.

To CRUSH. To break out of jail, to escape. Modern *lam, take a powder, take an A.D., pull a Dillinger, take it on the heel and toe, blow stir.*

CURRYNACKER. A woman street vendor. (Obs.)

CUSH. Cash. Now also specialized to mean bribe money or profits from a criminal enterprise.

CUTTINGS. Shares of stolen property. Modern *cut, end.*

DAMP POWDER. A fourflusher; one whose elaborate plans never materialize.

DAMPER or DAMPER-GETTER. A sneak thief, especially one who specializes on cash registers *(dampers).*

DECKHAND. Any household servant, especially a kitchen maid. (Obs.)

To DIE. 1. To cease criminal work because of pressure from the law; to drop out of a gang temporarily. 2. To leave the underworld and go straight.

DINGE. A smoke-colored negro or mulatto.

DINGLE. The back room in a saloon, often used as a hangout for crooks.

DINK. A *dude;* a *boiler-maker;* one who dresses in the latest manner; one especially successful with women. Obsolete in the argot. In slang it is wholly deprecatory.

DINKY. Chic, natty, high-toned. Obsolete in the argot, but the term has degenerated in slang and acquired a wholly opposite meaning. See HINKY-DINK.

DIP. A pickpocket, especially that member of the gang now designated as the *wire.* Modern *guns, cannons,* or *whiz.*

To DISCHARGE. When a gang member withdraws (voluntarily or involuntarily) from a job and foregoes his usual *cut,* he is said to have been *discharged.* The same term applies when any gang member withdraws before a fellow member is arrested so he will not have to contribute to the *defense fund.* Modern *to cut (someone) out.*

DIVORCED. A euphemistic expression indicating that two persons are not living together because one (or both) of them is doing time. The modern *to kiss off a moll* carries the same meaning, with the implication the man has *ditched* his imprisoned mistress.

DOE. A child, especially the prospective victim of a *snatch* or *sneeze* gang. The term is still popular, I am told, with kidnapers. Both *snatch* and *sneeze,* however, are modern words.

DOSS HOUSE. A cheap boarding or rooming house.

To DOUBLE UP. To share one's cell with another prisoner.

DRAG. 1. A jimmy-bar or tool for forcing entrance. (Obs.) 2. A horse-drawn vehicle. (Obs.) 3. A street. Modern *field of wheat.*

To DROP. To apprehend or arrest. Cf. modern *knocked off, sneezed, dropped.*

DRUM. A saloon or speakeasy. (Obs.) Now used only to designate a prison cell.

DUMP. A penitentiary. Giving way to *big house, stir.*

DUST. n. Valuables or money; loot. (Obs.) v. To clear out in a hurry. Modern *to lam,* or *take it on the lam.*

DUSTER. A *lamster;* sometimes applied to a criminal who jumps bail to escape trial. Modern *corner-turner.*

FALLBACK. 1. A crook without much self-reliance; one who frequently *falls back* on his friends for assistance. 2. A friend in trouble.

FALL GUY. One who bungles his work and usually gets caught; a clumsy thief. This word now means one who is made the goat, one who involuntarily *takes the rap* for the rest of the gang.

FALL MONEY. A fund raised by criminals to meet bail, pay lawyers, etc. Modern *defense fund.* While formerly criminals *chipped in* to raise this fund, it is now the practice in many localities to force the victims of various rackets to raise defense funds for any gang member who falls afoul of the law. Modern *fall money* often indicates the reserve fund

a criminal carries to effect his release if he is caught.

FEATHERS. A bed. Modern *kip, roses red, soogan.*

A FEW. A short sentence, usually fifteen days or less; *to be on the rock pile.*

To FILL IN or FILL OUT. To plan an *inside job* with the aid of an accomplice who *lines up* the *marks* (good prospects for burglars). See modern expressions *to front, to feel, front, feeler,* etc.

FINGER. An officer of the law; especially a uniformed policeman. See modern use as a verb meaning to identify; now being supplanted by *made* or *pegged.*

To FLAG. (tr. only) To *lay off* a prospective victim; to refuse to harm any passer-by. The modern word means to halt, as *to flag* a taxi, or to assume *a flag,* or alias.

FLAT or FLATFOOT. A detective or plainclothes man. Modern *dick, clubs-and-sticks.*

FLAT JOINT. A professional gambler's setup or establishment. Modern *steer joint.*

FLAT-WORKER. A burglar who enters apartment houses. Modern *hot-slough-worker* or *cold-slough-worker,* and many other specialized terms.

FLAWNY MAN. One who sells paste jewelry for genuine. Modern *slum-worker,* largely restricted to circus and carnival slang.

To FLICKER. 1. To die. 2. To *pass out* or faint away; to be knocked out.

FLIMFLAM. n. A clever trick to outwit a sucker. v. To extract money from a victim by trickery.

FLIMFLAM-WORKER. One who swindles his victims by trickery; a pickpocket or short-change-worker. Now largely restricted to circus slang. Modern *to be on the hipe.*

FLIP. Insolent or impudent.

FLOGGER. An overcoat. (Obs.) Modern *benny.*

FLOGGER STIFF. One who steals overcoats from vestibules or other public places. (Obs.)

To FLOP. To be arrested. Modern *fall* in its various combinations probably is related to this expression. *To flop* now means to fail to receive consideration by the parole board or by the governor.

FLOP GAME. A confidence game in which the victim is induced to put his money in a box or package and then is deceived with a similar package containing worthless paper.

FLYING JIB. A drunk man; *three sheets in the wind.*

FRITZER. Something which is not genuine or will not pay. Modern *phoney, bogus, n.g.*

FRONT or FRONT OFFICE. 1. The warden's office in a prison. 2. The place where prisoners are questioned in a municipal police station. 3. When a prisoner has been interviewed by the warden or other officer, he is said to have been *up front* or to have *come front.*

FRONT. A watch and chain. Modern *souper and slang. Front* now applies only to a suit of clothes.

GAME. Wounded or disabled. See BUM.

GASH. 1. The mouth. Modern *north-and-south, kisser.* 2. An unsavory name for a woman; a prostitute; a *chippy.*

GAYCAT. A young apprentice who does odd jobs and makes himself generally useful to criminals, especially by getting tips and by *feeling out* jobs for professionals. In modern gangs, restricted to *lookouts, soldiers, outside men.*

GERVER or GARVER. A safe-cracker. (Obs.) Modern *jugheavy, yegg, heavy, peterman, boxworker, ironworker, cribman, boxman, heavyman.*

GHOST. A respectable attorney who surreptitiously advises gangsters' lawyers for a substantial fee. Any lawyer is a *mouthpiece* to modern crooks.

GLAD-HANDER. A backslapper; a *yes man.* Modern *mitt-glommer.*

GOB. The mouth. See GASH.

GOOSE. A Jew. Probably alluding to the Jewish custom of using goose grease for cooking. See SHEANY.

GOOSEBERRY. A clothesline on which a washing is drying. Obsolete, except among bums and hoboes, and in circus slang.

To GO OUT or GO HOME. To be discharged from prison upon completion of a sentence. Modern *draw a ducat, hit the bricks.* When a prisoner is about to be released, he is said to be *short-timing it.*

GOPHER MAN. A burglar who tunnels into a building or warehouse. In modern argot he is a member of a *gopher mob* which tunnels under banks for the purpose of blowing the vault.

GORILLA. A *bad* criminal; one who will kill if he is caught in a tight place. In the modern argot the term signifies one who does the *dirty work* (killing) for an organized gang. A *rubber, Tommy Gee, wiper.*

GRAFT. Any job entailing little risk and yielding a good profit. Modern *racket* (in a special sense) or *easy racket.*

GRAFTER. A pickpocket; a *dip.* Modern *guns* or *cannons.*

GRAVEL TRAIN. A political fixer or agent who mediates between the law and the underworld. Modern *polly* or *right polly.*

GREEN GOODS. Any worthless stocks, bonds, or securities. Modern *stiffs.*

GREEN-GOODS-WORKER. A *short-conner* or swindler who sells fake securities.

GRIFTER. A circus swindler. The term now includes any unlawful activity and carries a contemptuous implication.

GUAGER. One who deals in stolen property. Modern *fence* (no longer popular), *uncle, unk, stop.*

GULL. A prospective victim; a *sucker.* This word appears to have been popular with criminals since the late sixteenth century; *sucker* and its numerous synonyms, however, seem to have supplanted it and it does not appear in modern argot.

GULLY-MINER. 1. A smalltime confidence man. (Obs.) 2. One who works a *gully mine,* i.e., who works hard without much profit and changes localities often.

GUM, GUMSHOE, or GUMSHOE WORKER. 1. A burglar or sneak thief. 2. A stool pigeon; one who spies on crooks and then informs the police. (Obs.) Modern *rat, squealer, cat, stool.*

GUMS. Sneakers worn by burglars.

GUN. A pickpocket; a *dip.* Modern *guns* or *cannons.*

GUN MOLL. A female pickpocket.

GUNSMITH or GUN-MAKER. One who trains young criminals, especially pickpockets.

GUY. A smart aleck; a fourflusher. Survives principally in such combinations as *wise guy* and *fall guy.*

HANDOUT. 1. A meal given a tramp. Modern *lump.* 2. A job which is especially easy. (Obs.) Modern *pipe.*

HARNESS. 1. Steel re-enforcements on the outside of a safe, vault, or strongbox. 2. A policeman's *(harness bull)* uniform.

HEELED. 1. Intoxicated. 2. *Flush;* carrying a large amount of money; usually appears as *well heeled.* Modern *to be in the stepping dough, sitting pretty, to splurge it* or *splurge it on the line.* 3. Armed.

HEELER. 1. A ward politician who uses strong-arm methods. 2. The bouncer for a gambling joint or brothel. (Obs.) The word now refers (1) to one who avoids paying his hotel bills and (2) to a sneak thief who steals from rooms or apartments.

HINKY-DINK. n. The Clark Street district in Chicago. adj. Excellent; having *class* or quality. Modern *forty.*

HIPPED. 1. Caught napping; whipped. 2. To be covered with a gun.

To HIT THE POT. To get drunk.

HOLE IN THE WALL. A disreputable establishment where crooks gather. (Obs.) Modern *joint, plant, spot.*

HONEY. A negro wench. Now extended to any attractive girl, or to anything excellent or impressive, as modern *sweetheart.*

HOOKS. Hands. Modern *ivory bands, mitts, dukes.*

HOOLIGAN. A tough character; a hoodlum. The term persists in standard English, but is seldom used in modern argot.

HOP. Opium. Modern *mud, O., pen-yen, tar.*

HOPPER or HOPPY. Anyone who is deformed or crippled.

HOPS. Prison tea.

HOP TALK. Hot air; *bull-con;* talking through one's hat, or retailing fictitious adventures. One who indulges in *hop talk* is now called a *ring-tailed cat* or a *fuzzy-tail.*

HOSPITAL. A euphemism for prison or jail. Such expressions as *to break a leg* are analogous. (Obs.) The metaphor survives in the modern *to get well* for being released.

To GET HOURS. To be ordered by the law to leave town on short notice. Modern *to get an s.p. with a floater.*

HOUSEMAN. A burglar. See FLAT-WORKER.

HOUSE-PROWLER. One who locates prospects for burglars. Modern *feeler, front, ten-per, ten-percenter.*

HUNK. Vengeance.

HUSTLER. A prostitute.

ICE or ICY MITT. A cold or hostile reception.

INKPOT. A hangout for criminals. (Obs.) Modern *gun joint, plant, meet, kip.*

To JABBER. To wander about looking for someone or something. Modern *to gander, to play the bird with the long neck, to gun.*

JAIL ARITHMETIC. Figures which have been juggled to cover a shortage in one's accounts.

JAP. A negro. (Obs.) See DINGE, HONEY.

To JERRY or GIVE (HIM) THE JERRY. To strike someone; to knock someone out. Modern *to sap cold, to lay among the sweet peas.*

To JOB. (tr. only) To convict an innocent man; *to railroad* a man to prison to get him out of the way or to protect someone else. Cf. modern *settled wrong, framed, kangarooed, to take a bum beef* or *bum rap.*

JOCKEY. One who steals valuable horses, especially race horses. (Obs.)

JOHN or JOHN BATES. A rube; a greenhorn; a *sucker;* a *joskin.*

JOHNNY. One who associates with theatrical folk, especially women.

JOHN YEGG. A personification of YEGG, *q. v.*

JUG or STONE JUG. A jail or prison. Modern argot applies this word, by metaphor, to banks and bank vaults. Its most recent form is *jay.* See modern *tomb, big top, jugheavy, heavyman.*

JUNGLE. 1. A hobo camp along the railroad. 2. Prison. (Obs.)

To KEEP TAB ON. To follow a prospective victim. Modern *to tail* or *to put a tail on.*

KETTLE. A stolen watch. Modern *souper* or *hot souper.*

KIP. A rooming house of questionable character; one where underworld characters hang out. This word, while still retaining its older meaning in some cases, has acquired a variety of meanings: a residence, one's home address, bed, bedroom, etc. Modern crooks frequently use it to distinguish their living quarters from their *plant,* where they hide out until trouble blows over.

KITE. 1. A prostitute. Modern *hooker, hustler, quiff, muff.* 2. A letter smuggled out of prison This is the usual present meaning.

To KITE A CHECK. To write a check when there is no money in the bank, on the assumption that money can be raised by the time the check comes through.

To LAY OUT. To subdue a victim by force, especially with the fists or a blackjack. Modern *to sap cold, to persuade.*

To LAY PAPER or to LAY BAD PAPER.

To pass forged checks or securities. See modern *paper-hanging* and *plastering.*

LEATHER. A pocketbook or billfold.

LEERY. Suspicious or afraid. Modern *wise.*

LEMON POOL or LEMON GAME. A dishonest pool game by which unsuspecting players are victimized.

LIFESAVER or LIFEBOAT. A reprieve, pardon, or stay of execution. See ANCHOR.

LIGHTNING. *Rotgut* whiskey.

LIMBER. Ready and able to fight.

LIMBO. Prison.

To LOSE A MAN or DROP A MAN. To have one of the gang arrested or sentenced to prison.

LOUSE. 1. A smalltime crook or petty thief. 2. A contemptible person; a cheater or *beefer.*

LOVER. A *boiler-maker;* a *candy-kid;* one who is kept by his girl friend, usually a prostitute.

LUSHER. A prostitute who preys on drunken patrons. Modern *roller* or *rolling hustler.* A *lush-worker* is now a professional thief who robs drunks.

MACK. A man supported by a prostitute; a pimp. See BOILER-MAKER, LOVER, etc.

MAIN SQUEEZE or MAIN STEM. 1. The chief or leader of a gang. 2. The head of any organization. Modern *big shot, wheels, chief, brains.*

To MAKE THE BOOST. To be released before one's sentence is up; to get time off for good behavior. See modern *copper, good time,* etc. Modern usage favors *spring,* ignoring its earlier restriction to bail.

MARKS AND CREDITS. The grading system by which *good time* or *copper* (time off the original sentence) is computed in penitentiaries.

To MASH. 1. To successfully storm a lady's virtue. 2. To beat up someone severely.

To MEASURE. To subdue by force. See to LAY OUT, to MASH.

MEET. A rendezvous where criminals gather before or after a job. In modern argot, the *meet* is usually quite distinct from the *plant* and the *kip.*

To MESS. To fight.

MESSER. A strong-arm man; a professional bully; a bouncer.

METER. A suitcase or *kiester.* (Obs.) Modern *saratoga.*

MISSION STIFF. 1. A bum or smalltime crook who hangs around missions and subsists on what they give him. 2. A term of contempt applied to reformed criminals.

MOLLY. A prostitute.

MONICKER. A genuine name, as distinguished from an alias. Modern *handle, flag.*

MOONLIGHTER. A burglar. See modern *rooting with the oliver, rooting against the oliver,* etc.

To MUCK. To make love in a forceful fashion; to maul a woman.

MUG. n. 1. The face or mouth. 2. A tough or hoodlum. v. To subdue with violence. Modern *mug* means to photograph at police headquarters.

MUSH. A stolen umbrella (restricted to petty thieves and pawnbrokers).

To NAB. To arrest. Modern *glommed, knocked off, sneezed.*

NANCY. A homosexual or male degenerate. Modern *girl, sill.*

NERVE-UP or NERVER-UP. A *gate-crasher;* one who enters prizefights, etc., without a ticket.

NICK. n. A successful job. Modern *score.* v. To complete a job successfully.

NIFTY. adj. or adv. Insolent; cocky; without proper respect for those in authority.

To NIP. To arrest. See NAB.

NIPPERS. Handcuffs.

NOTCH or NOTCH GIRL. A prostitute.

NOTCH HOUSE. A brothel.

OLD MAN. 1. The chief or head of a gang. Modern *wheels, big shot.* 2. The warden of a prison. Modern *king.*

To BE ON THE GOG. To lack stability; to be unreliable. Modern *wrong.*

To BE ON THE GUN. To practice thievery. In modern parlance this phrase is restricted to pickpockets.

To BE ON THE ROCK PILE. To be serving a short sentence, usually in a workhouse.

To BE ON THE SPUD. A variation of the *green goods* game; to swindle with fake securities.

To BE ON THE TURF. To be down and out. Restricted to prostitutes.

PACKET or PACKAGE. When a man is drunk he is said to be carrying *a good heavy packet* or *a swell package.* (Obs.)

PAD. 1. Sleeping quarters or a bed. (Obs.) See

modern *kip* and its variants. 2. A lock or pad-lock.

PAD MONEY. 1. Room rent or a hotel bill. (Obs.) 2. Any living expenses. See modern *nut, meet the nut,* etc.

PANEL-WORKER. An advance accomplice (usually a girl posing as a servant) to locate and acquire loot. Modern *a twirl fronting for an owl mob.*

PANHANDLER. A street beggar with a hard-luck story.

PAPER. A cigarette paper. Modern *blanket* or *sheet.*

To PEACH. For a crook *to squeal* to authori-ties. (Obs.) Modern *turn copper, fink, to do a solo.*

PEELER. A uniformed policeman. (Obs.) Modern *shamus, fuzzy, elbow, works,* etc.

PENNYWEIGHTER. One who steals gold or silver plate. Still survives in mining camps to designate one who steals very small quantities of gold, as opposed to a high-grader who ap-propriates any big nuggets which he sees in the sluice boxes. Present usage restricts it to a jewel thief, or a jeweler who substitutes paste gems for genuine ones.

PETERMAN. A thief who uses drugs or liquor to subdue his victim. (Obs.) See modern *roll.* Specifically (restricted to waterfronts) one who shanghaies men for vessels. Modern *peterman* is restricted entirely to the safe-blowing racket.

PHONEYMONICKER or PHONEYMONICA. An alias.

To PICK UP. To arrest. See modern *to have a fall,* or *to fall for.*

PIE WAGON. The police patrol. Modern *paddy.*

PIG. n. A yellow crook; a stool pigeon. (Obs.) Modern *rat, mutt, grifter, lemon, wrong, stoolo.* v. To be released from responsibility for a crime committed by the gang by giving advance notice and foregoing any share in the loot. (Obs.) See modern *to cut (someone) out.*

PIPE. n. A victim who is easy to rob because he is drunk; the victim of a *peterman.* v. To observe. Now used in carnival lingo with numerous shades of meaning.

POKE-A-MOKE. A swindling racket similar to the modern *pay-off* or *sure thing,* practiced widely by *short-conners.* (Obs.)

PORK DUMP. The Clinton Prison, N. Y.

PRAT-DIGGER. A pickpocket, one who ex-ploits the *prat kick.* Modern *whiz, cannons.*

PRAT LEATHER, LEATHER, or POKE. A wallet.

PROP MAN. A pickpocket or *snatcher* who lifts stickpins containing valuable stones. (Obs.) Survives in such phrases as *anchor on prop.*

PRUSSIAN. One who habitually employs a *punk kid,* or apprentice. (Obs.) Modern *jocker.*

PUFF. Dynamite or nitroglycerine used for safeblowing. (Obs.) See modern *stew, pete, dinah, soup,* etc.

PUNK. 1. Prison bread. Modern *dummy.* 2. A male homosexual.

PUNK KID. An apprentice who works with any crook, or who travels with a beggar. The word survives as *punk,* especially on the circus lot, where it means a novice. An old-time cir-cus man once defined the word for me as 'a kid who hasn't got the wrinkles out of his belly yet.'

PUSH or BIG PUSH. A crowd. Now largely restricted to circus and carnival lingo. The modern underworld seems to favor *crush.*

QUAD. Prison.

QUALITY. Anyone who makes a good appear-ance or who has certain admirable attributes. Modern *classy, ritzy, McCoy, a swell front.*

QUEER. 1. A job which does not yield a profit. (Obs.) Modern *bloomer.* 2. Counter-feit money. See modern *on the queer, shoving the queer,* etc. 3. A male homosexual.

RAG. A paper dollar. Modern *ace* or *buck.*

RAGS. Paper money. (Obs.) Modern *scratch, geetis.*

RAP. Charges preferred against a crook. Now extended to mean a prison term or a trial.

RAT. A stool pigeon, a *pig.*

RED-NECK. 1. A variant of *roughneck;* any honest working man. (Obs.) 2. One who be-longs to a labor union or sympathizes with union men in a strike.

To REEF A POKE or REEF A LEATHER. To steal a wallet by squeezing up (i.e., *taking a reef in*) the lining of the victim's pocket until the wallet can be reached or falls out.

RIGHT. Reliable; free from any connections with the police. Still used in this sense, and in variants like *a right scratch drop for ice,* etc. Its antonym *wrong* appears to be an addition of the modern underworld.

To BE IN RIGHT or SIT IN RIGHT. To have political protection or political pull. Cf. modern *fixed, greased*.

RINGER. 1. An alarm bell. (Obs.) Modern *bug*. 2. A person who closely resembles another, as in the modern slang phrase, *a dead ringer*.

RIPPER. 1. A degenerate who molests, rapes, or mutilates women in parks or other secluded spots; probably from Jack the Ripper. 2. A shrewd or lucky fellow who 'gets away with murder'; *a smart fellow*.

ROCK. A dollar, especially a silver dollar. Now restricted to mean a diamond or other valuable stone.

ROUGHNECK. Any honest citizen; a hardworking fellow. Modern *sucker, scissors-bill, honest stiff, honest John, working stiff*.

ROUNDER. A stool pigeon, i.e., one who always looks around. The word survives in the modern phrase *to round on a tail*, meaning to turn on someone following or to turn when spoken to.

To ROUST. To crowd a victim preparatory to picking his pocket. Modern *to stall*.

RUNNER. 1. A pimp. 2. A *punk* used to carry information, or as a lookout. Modern *soldier, outside man, gaycat*.

SAILS. The ears. Modern *bells*.

To SAIL or BE SAILING. To be on the lookout. Modern *to be on the I.C. and Erie* or *on the Erie Canal*.

SALT CREEK. Execution. (Obs.) A euphemized form of the prospector's well-known but inelegant saying. Modern *stretching rope, topping, wiping, going riding, hot squat, hot spot, frying*, or *burning* (the last four restricted to electrocution), etc. The phrase is now generalized to mean any uncomfortable situation.

SALVE. A line of talk calculated to gain the sympathy of officials or used in establishing an alibi. See SOFT SOAP, APPLE BUTTER.

SAWDUST. 1. Explosives, especially dynamite. (Obs.) 2. Prison bread.

SCOFFER. A glutton; one who has no control over his appetite. (Obs.) Although the noun is not now in use, the verb *to scoff* is a common term for eating, especially in a prison.

SHACK or SHAG. A railway brakeman or mine guard used in strikes. Modern argot has transferred this word to prison guards, and in looser sense to special deputies or pay-roll guards.

SHAFTS. The legs. (Obs.) Modern *mumbly pegs* (restricted to women's legs).

SHARK. One who waylays and robs drunks. A *peterman* (in the obsolete sense).

SHEANY or SHEENY. 1. A Jew. 2. Anyone from whom it is difficult to extract money.

SHEBANG. Dive where criminals meet. Modern *joint, spot, meet*.

SHOESTRING. A bluff.

SHUFFLE. Counterfeit money. Modern *queer, backs, paper*.

SIDE-KICK. One's pal. In modern argot a side pocket in the coat; it is doubtful if there is any connection.

SINGER. A stool pigeon or trusty who carries tales to the administration. (Obs.)

SIXER. 1. A jail sentence of six months. 2. A revolver or six gun. (Obs.) Modern *roscoe, oscar, rod, heat, heater, iron*.

SKY. The pocket. Now supplanted by the circus term *kick* as in *breech kick, prat kick*, etc.

SKY-BLUE or SKY. Prison soup, so called because of its thin, clear quality.

SLAB. The counter in a store or bank. (Obs.)

SLANG. A watch chain.

SLAVEY. A *punk* or apprentice. (Obs.)

SLEEPY HOLLOW. The prison at Trenton, N. J.

To SLOPE. 1. To make a getaway. 2. To move on to another town. Modern *lam, mope, blow,* etc.

To SLUSH or SLUSH UP. To drink. Modern *tiddletywink*.

IN SOAK. 1. In prison. 2. In pawn.

To SOAK. 1. To serve a long term in prison. See modern *lag, buried, to get the book*. 2. To hock or pawn something. 3. To blackjack. Modern *to sap*.

SOFT SOAP. Same as SALVE, *q.v.* Also used as a verb.

To SOUND. To run the hands over a victim to locate valuables or weapons. (Obs.) Modern *fan*.

SOUPER-TWISTER. One who snatches watches; a pickpocket who specializes in watches. Although the term survives in the modern argot, *thimble-worker* appears to be favored.

SPARK. A diamond. Modern *ice, rocks, simple-simon.*

To SPILL. (tr. only) To confess or to turn state's evidence. It occurs in numerous combinations such as *spill the beans, spill the works,* etc. Now common as slang. Modern *to kick through, to cough up, to squawk, to fink.*

SPINORTY. A distortion of *sporty;* natty; up-to-date; liberal with money.

SPLIT. The agreement by which the loot is divided. Modern *lay.*

SPOT or ONE-SPOT. 1. A dollar, as in *five-spot, ten-spot,* etc. 2. A one-year prison term. Modern *boffo. Five-spot, ten-spot,* etc., have a corresponding significance, the analogy being to various monetary denominations. See the same process in modern *fin*—$5 bill—(five-year sentence), *saw* or *sawbuck* (ten years), *double saw* (twenty years).

To SPRING. To provide bail for an arrested person. Modern argot, while it retains this meaning, extends the term to any act releasing or liberating a prisoner by any means, including a jail delivery.

SQUARE. Honest or incorruptible.

To SQUARE A SUCKER. To reimburse a victim to avoid prosecution. Modern *to have a blowback.*

To STAKE. To loan or give money to someone.

STAKE GRUB. Jail or prison rations. Modern *chow* or *gooby.*

To STALL. To throw a victim off guard before picking his pocket; see ROUST. The *stall* in a pickpocket gang is now often called a *front* or a *front gee.*

To STAND OUT. To cite a convict for breaking regulations. Modern *to banner* or *to get a banner.*

STAND-UP. The lineup at police headquarters where suspects are identified. (Obs.) Modern *lineup, showup.*

STATE or STATE TOBACCO. Tobacco sold to convicts.

To STEER. To lead a victim into a trap, especially in gambling. See modern *steerer, shill, come-on man,* etc.

STEERER. An *inside man* or tipster who locates prospects for robbers or safeblowers. Now restricted to gambling, in the sense of a

lure for *suckers.* The modern tipster is known as a *ten-per* man, or a *ten-percenter.*

STICK. A match. Modern *torch,* taken up from safeblowers' argot in such phrases as *torch a squib, torch a string,* etc. (i.e., to light with an acetylene torch).

To STICK AND SLUG. A battle cry exhorting gangsters to greater efforts when engaged in a gang fight.

STICKER. A reliable and genuine friend. Modern *McCoy, like-that.*

STIFF. 1. A confederate or accomplice in any criminal activity; a *cove;* a *codger.* Modern *one of the boys.* 2. A prospective victim; one who is not initiated into the underworld; a legitimate person.

STONE-GETTER. One who specializes in burglaries involving diamonds. (Obs.) Modern *stone man* or *stone-heister.* A specialized group are known as *stone-tail-and-elevation men.*

STOWAWAY. A smalltime politician or ward heeler who is placed on numerous municipal pay rolls under an assumed name. (Obs.)

STRAP. A blackjack. Modern *sap, jack, persuader, leather.*

STRING. A group of people; *three-string, four-string,* etc., according to the number. (Obs.)

STRONG-ARM MAN. A crook who commits violent crimes. (Obs.) Modern *gorilla, hoodlum, mug, Tommy Gee, wiper, rubber.*

STUDENT. Same as a *stowaway.* (Obs.) Modern argot seems to have no equivalents for these terms.

STUFF. Loot.

SUPER. A tramp who makes his way by soliciting churches or religious organizations; a *mission stiff.*

SURE-THING GAMBLER. A cheap hanger-on at race tracks who bets only with gullible persons. In the modern argot the original meaning has been lost and the phrase refers only to certain complex swindling games worked by *short-conners.* See modern *wire tapping, sure-thing game, wire working,* etc.

SWAG. 1. A hobo's *bindle* or travelling kit. (Obs.) Modern *bindle* or *balloon.* 2. Loot such as silverware and jewelry, so called because it was often done up in a cloth like a hobo's *bindle.* Modern *jam.*

To SWAP. To kiss.

SWELL. A general term of approbation, applied especially to anything costly. Applied to individuals, it conveys the idea of success and wealth.

To SWITCH. 1. To change or reverse one's position. 2. To turn informer to the police. Modern *to fink*.

TALL. Anything proper or fastidious. (Obs.) See SWELL and QUALITY for analogous expressions.

TANK. One with a large capacity for drink.

TEDDY. An Irishman. Modern *harp, chaw*.

THIMBLE-RIGGER. A shell-game-worker. Now largely confined to circus and carnival usage. Not to be confused with modern *thimble-worker*.

THIRD-RAIL. A pickpocket or luggage thief who works passenger trains.

To THROW (SOMEONE) DOWN. To desert a friend when he is in trouble. Modern *to kiss (someone) off* (usually restricted in use to a person of the opposite sex).

TICKET. 1. A warrant for arrest. Modern *reader, reader-with-a-tail*, or *general*. 2. A pardon or certificate of release given a prisoner when he is discharged. Modern *ducat*.

TINKER. A smalltime housebreaker or sneak thief. (Obs.)

TITLE-TAPPER. A swindler who borrows money with forged deeds as security.

TOADSKINS. Paper money. Now largely restricted to circus and carnival usage. Modern argot favors *scratch*.

To TOAST. To live well without any visible means of support. Modern *sitting pretty, to splurge it on the line*.

TOMMY-BUSTER. A man who makes short shrift with women; one who takes them by storm.

TOMRIG or TOMMY. An unsavory name for a young girl.

TONY. Excellent; stylish; having *class* or *quality*. Same as *hinky-dink*.

TOUT. n. A tipster or *steerer*. (Obs.) Now restricted to sport tipsters, especially at a race track. v. To furnish tips or *inside* information to crooks. (Obs.)

TRACK THIRTEEN WITH A WASHOUT. A life sentence. Modern *to get the book, to be buried*.

TRICK. A successfully executed job. Now largely restricted to prostitutes. Modern *score*.

TRIMMER. A yellow gangster; one who carries water on both shoulders; a stool pigeon. (Obs.)

TROLLEY. 1. The grapevine telegraph by which information is spread in prisons. 2. An actual cord used for purposes of communication between cells.

To TWIST. 1. To steal a watch by breaking the chain. See SOUPER-TWISTER. 2. To roll a cigarette.

UNCLE. A pawnbroker, especially one who will dispose of stolen goods. Modern *fence* or *right drop*.

To BE UNDER COVER. To be in hiding until trouble blows over. Modern *to be hot, to be on the lam*.

UNFORTUNATE. Said of one of the gang who has been sent to prison. See modern *to take a fall, to have a fall, to fall for the owl*, and other variants.

To UNSLOUGH. To unbutton, especially the trousers.

To GO UP THE RIVER. To serve time in Sing Sing. Modern argot has generalized the phrase to apply to any prison sentence.

To VAG. To sentence a known criminal for vagrancy when no definite charges can be brought against him.

VALENTINE. A short sentence, imposed when the judge could have given a longer one.

VESTRY THIEF. 1. A sneak thief who robs churches. 2. A swindler who poses as a religious person in order to contact pious, unsuspecting folk who have money.

WASHOUT. A life sentence. (Obs.) Modern *buried, settled, lagged, to get the book*. See TRACK THIRTEEN.

To WEED. To fleece a victim. (Obs.)

To WHIPSAW. To baffle a victim or an enemy. (Obs.)

WHITE-LINER. One who is addicted to grain alcohol. Modern *gas-hound*.

WILLY. A homosexual man; a pervert. Modern *girl, nola, wolf, sill, guncell*.

WINDOWS. Eyeglasses. (Obs.) Modern *cheaters*.

WIRES. The political connections which may be used to quash an indictment or prevent a criminal's being brought to trial.

WISE. Clever; shrewd; intelligent.

WISE GUY. One who impersonates an officer

and *shakes down* other crooks. (Obs.) In modern argot any bluffer or fourflusher. Although officers are often impersonated by modern crooks there seems to be no word for that type of criminal.

WOOD. A mace (wooden) as differentiated from the *strap,* or leather blackjack.

WOODY. Foolish; crazy; especially with reference to dementia brought on by drugs or by confinement. See modern *stir-bugs, stir-simple.*

To WORK. To ply any unlawful trade. The verb seems to be fading out of modern argot, but the euphemistic idea survives in many compounds like *skin-worker, hot-slough-worker, hot-heap-worker,* etc.

YAP. A *sucker;* one easily victimized. Modern *sucker, scissors-bill.* Survives in modern argot only in *Yap-town* (Cleveland).

YEGG or YEGGMAN. One who burglarizes stores and breaks open safes. *Yeggman* is now practically obsolete, but *yegg* is still occasionally used to designate a safeblower. I am told that the word originally had no connection with safeblowing but referred to the desperate nature of this type of criminal *(yek-man* or *yegg-man* is reported to have been the name for professional killers employed by Chinese tongs). Compare the etymology given in the 2nd edition of *Webster's.* Modern *peterman, jugheavy, boxman, heavyman, ironworker, cribman, jayheavy.*

7

The Argot of the
Underworld Narcotic Addict

This chapter includes both part one (1936) and part two (1938) of a work I published on the argot of underworld drug addicts. (In 1935 or 1936 Dr. Alfred Lindesmith gave me a brief list of argot terms collected largely in Chicago.) It was, I believe, one of the earliest systematic examinations of the language of this subculture which differed from other criminal subcultures in its rather recent origin. It was created synthetically by the passage of the Harrison Narcotic Act in 1914. There was, however, an earlier group of opium smokers, largely Chinese, which served as a kind of nucleus about which the new subculture centered. The reason for this was that in each community the local Chinese were the source to which addicts turned when the law went into effect. Many terms relating to the consumption of opium were still in active use, and many passed over into the argot of the needle addict.

At that time, there were two distinct classes of addicts. First, there was the noncriminal addict who secured drugs from legitimate or semilegitimate medical sources and concealed this habit from the rest of the community in which he lived. These addicts, while they may have been technically law violators, were in no other sense criminal, did not associate freely, and did not have an argot. Some of them, nevertheless, had been longtime opium smokers. We have no way of knowing the size of this class of addicts, although it must have been legion.

The second class of addicts included those who supplied their habits by crime. It is this group that is represented in this chapter since they formed a subculture and developed a substantial and well-defined argot. A majority of these appear to have been criminals before they took up drugs and used their criminal expertise to insure a regular supply of drugs, usually morphine, heroin, cocaine, or opium. Others supported their habits by resorting to crime after becoming addicted, but these were usually inept nonprofessionals who used crude criminal tactics to acquire as much money as they could. They practiced largely petty larceny, mugging, embezzling on a small scale, and became parasitic on their families and friends.

It is interesting to note that in those days crimes committed by both groups were almost entirely nonviolent since the drugs were full strength and were taken in rather large quantities. My own estimate at that time was that most morphine addicts took from two to eight grains of morphine every twenty-four hours. If we consider that five grains of morphine would readily kill a nonuser, we get some indication of the size of the habits involved. When addicts were on drugs in those days they felt too good to bother anyone; in fact, they wanted to *coast* or relax completely. When they did not have drugs they were in a state of collapse and incapable of committing violent crimes. Today, of course, the situation is much different. Heroin, the main hard drug used, is usually cut to about 3 percent, which is very weak indeed, and its use or deprivation does not deter most users from violent acts. Furthermore, new drugs of the stimulant and hallucinogenic type produce very different effects on users. Drugs such as the amphetamines, DMT, and PCP, as well as cocaine when used to the point of producing severe hallucinations, are increasingly associated with violent crimes, often of a bizarre nature.

In 1937 the Marijuana Tax Act was passed and marijuana was classed with the narcotic drugs, though it was not a true narcotic. By that time, it was in rather wide use in a burgeoning secondary subculture of its own. It should be noted that in those days the users of hard drugs shunned marijuana smokers whom they regarded as noncriminal, unstable, and unreliable. Many of the marijuana terms recorded here are distinctly derogatory.

At this time the drug subculture was tight, and noticeable diffusion had not yet developed. When the subculture began to diffuse about 1949, however, the drugs, behavior patterns, and the argot went with it and penetrated the dominant culture on a large scale. The changes in this subculture will be treated in greater detail in a later chapter.

• • •

PART I

Acknowledgment: To certain underworld figures connected with the narcotic traffic, the federal men in the Public Health Service, to stool pigeons and informers employed by the Department of Justice, all of whose names must obviously be withheld, for the assistance they rendered in preparing this study. I am especially indebted to Dr. Victor H. Vogel, United States Public Health Service, for his assistance in getting informants and to Dr. Edward H. Carleton, of the Dorsey Clinic, Louisville, Kentucky, for his careful attention to medical and anatomical details.

For several years during which I have been collecting and publishing information relative to languages outside the law, I have suspected the existence of a professional argot among underworld narcotic addicts, but investigation into that field seemed impossible because of the fear psychosis which every underworld addict develops, and because the gangs which control the narcotic traffic have shown a decided disapproval of academic snooping.

All the symptoms of a well-developed argot were obvious. If safe-blowers, pickpockets, short-conners, and various other underworld professions had developed well-defined argots motivated by professional pride, protection from outsiders, and the technicalities of their work,[1] it seemed logical that addicts and peddlers with their constant fear of betrayal, with their elaborate and effective underground facilities for transmitting both information and narcotics, and with the almost frenzied clannishness which goes with addiction, should have developed an argot of their own.

Furthermore, I had observed occasional expressions in the vocabularies of other underworld figures which seemed to be discarded argot words of a secret or semisecret nature which might be the outcroppings of a specialized language common to narcotic addicts. Over a period of some three years I noted these words and made an attempt, certainly not very fruitful, to obtain others. Since there is, as I shall point out a little later on, almost no connection between addiction and big-time criminals, and since I was getting most of my information from underworld figures who stood rather high in their professions, there were no channels through which to penetrate the wall of hostile silence which confronted me. But I collected such

---

1. These are, of course, only a few of the motives involved in the formation of an argot. A subsequent study now in preparation will attempt some explanation of the social, psychological, and linguistic factors which enter into argot formation.

information as I could get and published a few notes[2] which, I felt, treated the subject in a most inadequate manner. I still suspected the existence of a larger body of argot which remained tantalizingly beyond reach. Shortly after this, Victor Folke Nelson contributed a list of fifteen additional expressions which appeared to indicate a well-defined argot,[3] along with a complaint very similar to mine—that he could not get addicts to talk.

Subsequently, however, it has been possible for me to establish several connections with the world of the addict. These connections varied sufficiently in viewpoint and geographical distribution to supply, I think, a rather significant cross section of the addict's argot. Once the notes were collected, they were subjected to a rigorous checking by underworld addicts and by persons intimately connected with the narcotic racket. Hence the resulting study, though not complete—for it is folly to suppose that any argot can be recorded fully—represents a fairly accurate sample of a body of argot hitherto inaccessible to the linguist, and sheds some light on the psychology of the addict as reflected in his lingo.

It is suggested that the reader, as he peruses the glossary following, keep in mind several points relative to the addict's position in American underworld life. First, big-time gangsters, racketeers, and the criminal aristocrats do not use narcotics. When a gangster becomes addicted (as he rarely does) he is eliminated immediately because he menaces the safety of the organization. Second, narcotics have little connection with violent crime. Addicts often have a record of minor crimes, but few of them habitually go armed and only the cocaine addict, when cornered, is reputed to be dangerous, which I am inclined to believe is the exception rather than the rule. Third, the narcotic racket is controlled by gangsters of a vicious type, not addicted themselves, who prey upon the addict and racketeer the peddler. They spread the habit mercilessly, for it enlarges their market; since the collapse of prohibition, they have expanded the narcotic traffic until it is our largest illicit industry. Fourth, there is nothing romantic about the life of pitiful illusion and misery which the addict leads, popular conceptions to the contrary notwithstanding. The addict is usually psychopathic and certainly socially inadequate. Last, the argot spoken by this group appears to differ considerably from other underworld argots. Addicts are almost fanatically clannish and tend to keep the argot well within their own fraternity; this argot does not seep out as rapidly as the argot coined by other underworld cliques and consequently has had very little influence upon the great body of lingo common to the American underworld.

2. 'Junker Jargon,' *American Speech*, VIII (1933), No. 2, 27–28.
3. 'Addenda to Junker Lingo,' *American Speech*, VIII, No. 3, 33–34.

ALL LIT UP. To be under the influence of narcotics. Also *coasting, floating, hitting the gow, in high, on the gow, on the stuff, picked up,* some with specialized meanings. Usually restricted to addicts who use the needle. Cf. GOWED, JABOFF.

ARTILLERY. The hypodermic needle used to inject narcotics. Also *Bay State, emergency gun, gun, hype, joint, Luer, nail, needle* (1). Cf. EMERGENCY GUN, NEEDLE (2), DROPPER.

BAMBOO. An opium pipe. See GONG.

BANG. A shot of narcotic injected hypodermically. Usually restricted to morphine, cocaine, or heroin. Also *bang in the arm, fix-up, geezer, jolt, pop, shot, skin shot, vein shot.* All these terms indicate a *ration* of dope prepared for injection, in contrast to *bindle, check, deck,* etc., which indicate dope as it is sold or transferred before putting it into solution. Cf. BANG IN THE ARM, TO FIRE, SKIN SHOT, SPEED BALL, TO BLOW A SHOT.

BANG IN THE ARM. A shot of narcotic, most commonly morphine or cocaine, injected directly into the vein, as contrasted to *skin shot.* However, the term also appears to be generalized and may, according to the context, indicate any injection of narcotic (see BANG). A string is wrapped around the arm and held tight with the teeth until the blood congests in a large vein; dope injected into this vein goes immediately, upon release of the string, to the heart where the effect is instantaneous; it excites, then depresses, the central nervous system, circulation, and respiration. When morphine is used, the addict is usually conscious of an unusual and very satisfying clearness of the mind. Cocaine and heroin produce tingling sensations of varying degrees, usually of great intensity and extending over the entire body. This type of shot is not used as a rule by the amateur; the hardened addict uses it almost exclusively. Also *jolt.* For further information, see BLOW A SHOT, GUTTER, JABOFF, MAIN-LINER, SPEED BALL, VEIN SHOT, VERIFICATION SHOT.

BAY STATE. A hypodermic needle. See ARTILLERY.

BEAT THE GONG. To smoke opium. See GONG, HIT THE GONG.

BERNICE OR BURNESE. Crystallized cocaine prepared for direct inhalation. The crystals stick on the inner respiratory surfaces, especially of the nose and throat, where they mix with the mucous secretions and are partly absorbed, partly swallowed. Bindles are usually put up in cigarette papers all ready for *sniffing* or *blowing.* Conditioned addicts refer to this method of taking dope as 'wasting it' because much more dope is used than would be necessary to get the same effect through the hypodermic needle with a *vein shot.* Also *C., happy dust, heaven dust, snow.* Cf. BLOWING, CHARLIE COKE, COASTING, SNIFTER.

BIG MAN. The brains behind a dope ring; the one who seldom takes the rap. Most narcotic rings are controlled by gangsters of a vicious type, often with sound local political connections. The *big man* wholesales dope to peddlers and may racketeer peddlers for protection and the privilege of selling. Cf. IN FRONT OF THE GUN.

BINDLE. A quantity of dope prepared for sale, as contrasted to a *ration,* or shot of dope to be injected. Both bindles and rations vary widely; the bindle according to the source of purchase, the ration according to the taste of the addict and the degree of adulteration to which the narcotic has been subjected. Restricted to morphine, heroin, and cocaine users. Also *cap, card, check, cigarette paper, cube, deck, O., Oz., piece.* Cf. BANG, RATION, SHORT PIECE, TURKEY.

BIRD'S EYE. A half-size *ration* of dope to be injected hypodermically. Usually restricted to morphine, cocaine, or heroin. Probably so called from the constriction of the pupils and glassy appearance of the addict's eyes immediately after injection. See RATION.

BLACK STUFF. Opium, as contrasted to *white stuff* (morphine). Not used to refer to opium after it has been prepared or *cooked* for smoking, when it becomes a *pill* or *yen-pok.* Also *gee-yen, gum, hop, li-yuen, mud, O.* (2), *pen-yen, rooster brand, san-lo, tar, yen-shee,* with specialized meanings. Cf. CHEF, COOK A PILL, GREEN ASHES.

To BLOW A SHOT. To waste dope by missing a vein with the hypodermic. Not to be confused with *blowing,* q.v. Restricted to *vein-shooters.* Cf. BANG IN THE ARM.

BLOWING. Inhaling narcotics, especially *bernice.* Also *sniffing.* Cf. BERNICE, SNIFTER.

BO-BO-BUSH. Marajuana. See GREEFO.

BOOTS-AND-SHOES. A down-and-out addict who has literally sold or pawned all his clothes to buy dope. All underworld addicts eventually 'go boots-and-shoes.' Also *dugout, geed up.* Cf. BUNK YEN, CIRCUS, COTTON-SHOOTER.

BRODY. A feigned spasm to elicit sympathy and perhaps dope from a physician. See CIRCUS.

To BUG. To inject a shot of coal oil, tobacco juice, or strong disinfectant into the flesh. This produces a vicious swelling which is used to secure sympathy and a shot from doctors or druggists. Frequently it results in abscesses or amputation. Cf. CIRCUS, TO MAKE (5), TO MAKE A CROAKER FOR A READER, WHITE ANGEL.

BUM STEER. A specialized form of the common underworld idiom. Addicts use it to refer to various tricks for smuggling dope into a jail or penitentiary. For instance, dope is planted on a confederate, who is stationed before the institution in a car. The guards are notified that there is a man outside in a car with a machine gun. The confederate is arrested and taken inside for investigation while the search for the machine gun proceeds. Once the confederate is inside with the dope, he relays it to the *trolley* or *grape-vine* which exists in most institutions for the dissemination of narcotics. Cf. GRAPEVINE, PLANT (2), TRAINED NURSE, TROLLEY.

BUNK YEN. The tendency shown by a down-and-out addict to hang around a den even though he has no money for a *lay.* Restricted to opium addicts. Cf. BOOTS-AND-SHOES, LAY (1).

BURNESE. Variant of *bernice,* q.v.

C. Cocaine. Also *bernice, coke, happy-dust, heaven-dust, snow,* Cf. H., M., O.; OLD STEVE, SPEED BALL.

CAP. A bindle of heroin or morphine sold in capsules which are, incidentally, often concealed by the peddler in his rolled-up shirt cuffs, heroin in one sleeve, morphine in the other. See BINDLE.

CARD. A bindle of opium peddled by sticking small pills of the gum on the under side of a card. Specialized to the opium traffic. See BINDLE.

CARTWHEEL. A feigned spasm. See CIRCUS.

CEMENT. A general term covering any kind of illicit narcotics. This term seems to be restricted to dope as it passes into commerce, and is not used as a synonym for *gow, mojo,* etc., which terms refer rather to the dope as used by the addict. Apparently restricted to New York and vicinity. Cf. GOW.

CHARLIE COKE. A cocaine addict. Also *cokie, snifter, snowbird.* Cf. BERNICE, COASTING.

CHEATER. An attendant in a den who is skillful at mulcting the addict of his shot as it is administered. He does this by pinching up a flap of flesh on the addict's arm, then running the needle completely through this flap and into his own thumb. The addict feels the needle enter, but the attendant gets the effect. Cf. CHEF, TO MAKE (3).

CHECK. A bindle of narcotics. See BINDLE.

CHEF. The attendant in an opium den. He *cooks the pill* for the addict. Also *cook.* Chefs often have a bad reputation among addicts, for they *make* the addict for any narcotics he may have as soon as the drug takes effect. Cf. COOK A PILL, GEE-YEN, GREEN ASHES, LAYOUT, TO MAKE (3).

To CHILL. To submit to arrest without struggling or resisting. Cf. GUZZLED, PLANT (2).

CHINO. A Chinese. Incidentally, while much of the opium traffic in America is still in the control of Chinese, they seldom deal in other forms of drugs, and those of the older generation refuse to take narcotics through the needle. Most Chinese who deal in opium are also addicts.

CHUCK HABIT or CHUCK HORRORS. The enormous appetite which the addict develops under the *cold turkey* system. He eats ravenously for several days or even weeks. Cf. COLD TURKEY, MEDICINE, PANIC MAN.

CIGARETTE PAPER. A bindle of heroin. See BINDLE.

CIRCUS. A feigned spasm enacted in public in the hope that a physician will administer narcotics. Also *Brody, cartwheel, figure eight, twister, wing-ding.* Cf. BOOTS-AND-SHOES, TO BUG, TO MAKE (5), TO MAKE A CROAKER FOR A READER.

COASTING. The exhilarating sensation produced by cocaine. Also *floating, to go on a sleigh ride.* Cf. ALL LIT UP, BERNICE.

COKE. Cocaine. Practically obsolete among underworld addicts. See C.

COKIE. A cocaine addict. Not widely used by underworld addicts. See CHARLIE COKE.

COLD TURKEY. Treatment of addicts in institutions where they are taken off drugs suddenly without the 'tapering off' which the addict always desires. Cf. CHUCK HABIT, KICK THE HABIT, MEDICINE, MR. FISH, PANIC MAN, TORTURE CHAMBER.

CONNECTION. A peddler who knows an addict and from whom the latter can make a purchase. Cf. CONNECTOR, TO CUT (SOMEONE) IN, GO-BY, HIT, MARK A CONNECTION, SCORE A CONNECTION.

CONNECTOR. A go-between who establishes relations between addicts and peddlers, often for a share of the dope purchased. Cf. CONNECTION, TO CUT (SOMEONE) IN.

COOK. The attendant in an opium den. See CHEF.

To COOK A PILL. To prepare a *pill* of opium for smoking. This is done by holding the *pill*, impaled on a long steel needle (*yen-hok*), over an alcohol flame. Usually this is done by the *chef* or attendant so that the addict may be free to get the entire effect of the one large puff he inhales. Also *tchi.* Cf. CHEF, GEE-YEN, GREEN ASHES, LAYOUT, TO ROLL A PILL, YEN-HOK, YEN-POK.

COOKER. The receptacle, usually a spoon, which is used to boil the solution before it is taken into the needle. Restricted to morphine, cocaine, or heroin users. Cf. COTTON.

COOKIE. 1. An opium addict. See HOP HEAD. 2. The *chef* or attendant in a den

who *cooks the pill* for the smoker. See CHEF.

COTTON. The wad of cotton placed in the cooking spoon and used as a filter for dissolved bootleg morphine as it is drawn up into the needle. Cf. COOKER, COTTON-SHOOTER.

COTTON-SHOOTERS. Down-and-out addicts who hang around other addicts in order to pick up the *cottons* which they discard. If they collect enough cottons they can soak out the residue of narcotic which remains and eventually get enough for a shot. Cf. BOOTS-AND-SHOES, COTTON.

COURAGE PILLS. Heroin in tablet form. See H. Cf. CIGARETTE PAPER.

CROAKER. An addict's term, common also among other underworld folk, for a physician. In underworld argot, specialized to mean a prison doctor. Cf. ICE-TONG DOCTOR, MAKE A CROAKER FOR A READER, READER.

CUBE. 1. Crude bootleg morphine. See M. 2. A bindle of morphine cut in cubic form. Theoretically, a cube should contain an ounce but purchases of this size must be relatively rare. Most ounce cubes are cut into smaller portions, and are still sold as *cubes.* Cf. BINDLE, OZ., SHORT PIECE.

To CUT (SOMEONE) IN. When an addict cannot identify himself sufficiently to buy from a peddler, he may *cut* another addict *in,* that is, give him a ration or a share of the ration for making the purchase. Cf. CONNECTION, CONNECTOR.

DEADWOOD. The thing an addict fears most: to be trapped by an agent posing as a *panic man.* Many addicts find it very difficult to resist a plea for dope from another addict who is desperate. Cf. CHILL, GUZZLED, TO MAKE (1), PAID OFF IN GOLD, PANIC MAN.

DEALER. A peddler. Often restricted to a druggist who is amenable to persuasion. Cf. PEDDLER.

DECK. A bindle of morphine, cocaine, or heroin. See BINDLE.

DO-RIGHT-PEOPLE. 1. Nonaddicts. Also, *square John.* 2. Legitimate people or those with no criminal connections. 3. The taxpayers (prison argot).

DREAM-STICK. An opium pipe. See GONG.

DROPPER. The inevitable medicine dropper used by the poorer class of addicts to construct a makeshift hypodermic. Cf. EMERGENCY GUN.

DUGOUT. An addict who has reached the bottom; one who is, as the saying goes among addicts, 'lame, lazy, and crazy.' See BOOTS-AND-SHOES.

EMERGENCY GUN. An improvised hypodermic constructed from a medicine-dropper and a safety-pin or other sharp instrument (*spike*). The flesh is punctured by the pin and the fluid injected under the skin from the dropper. Cf. ARTILLERY, GEE, NEEDLE, SPIKE (2).

FIGURE EIGHT. A feigned spasm, or *wing-ding*. See CIRCUS.

To FIRE. To inject dope from a hypodermic. See BANG.

FIX-UP. A ration of dope, especially one which has just been taken. See BANG, RATION. Cf. BINDLE.

FLIPPED. Knocked out by some kind of knock-out shot administered by an attendant or by another addict who then *makes* his victim for any narcotics he may have. Also *taken*. Cf. HOT SHOT, TO MAKE (3), PETER.

FLOATING. Under the influence of narcotics, especially cocaine. See COASTING.

To be FROM MOUNT SHASTA. To be addicted to narcotics. Also *hooked, to hit the gow, on drugs, on the gow, on the mojo, on the stuff*.

FUN. (Usually pronounced *foon*.) A *ration* or *pill* of opium. Restricted to opium users. Cf. RATION.

GAZER. A Federal narcotic agent. Also *whiskers, uncle*. Cf. DEADWOOD, PAID OFF IN GOLD.

GEE or GEE RAG. The packing (usually carefully made of cigarette-paper and thread) between the needle and the medicine-dropper of an *emergency gun*. This joint must be quite tight to prevent the entrance of air and leakage of liquid. Cf. EMERGENCY GUN.

GEED UP. Down and out. Applied to a *dugout* or an addict who has gone *boots-and-shoes*, q.v.

GEE-YEN. Opium which precipitates in very small quantities in the stem of the pipe. This is retrieved sometimes by the *chef* who may refine it and sell it again. See BLACK STUFF. Cf. CHEF, GREEN ASHES, YEN-SHEE-GOW.

GEEZER. A shot of narcotic injected hypodermically. See BANG.

GET THE HABIT OFF. To indulge in narcotics; to satisfy a desire intensified by abstinence. See HABIT.

GO-BY. When an addict wants to make a purchase but cannot identify himself, he is said to *get the go-by*, that is, the peddler refuses to talk business to him. For related terms cf. CUT (SOMEONE) IN, MARK A CONNECTION, SCORE A CONNECTION.

GOD'S MEDICINE. Morphine. See M.

GONG. An opium pipe. Also *bamboo, dream-stick, gonger, hop stick, joy stick, saxophone, stem, stick*. Cf. BLACK STUFF, HIT THE GONG, HOP HEAD.

GONGER. Variant of *gong*, q.v.

To GO ON A SLEIGHRIDE. To experience the exhilaration from inhaling crystallized cocaine. See COASTING.

GOW. Dope in general, especially dope used hypodermically; probably of Chinese origin, but no longer restricted to opium. Also *junk, mojo, stuff*. Cf. BINDLE, BLACK STUFF, C., CEMENT, GREEFO, H., M., O., RATION.

GOWED. Having too much dope, in which case the effect is spoiled and the addict goes into a sort of stupor. Also *jammed, overcharged, purring*.

GOWSTER. A narcotic addict, especially one who uses heroin, morphine, or cocaine. Also *hop head, junker*. Cf. ALL LIT UP, CHARLIE COKE, FROM MOUNT SHASTA, GUTTER, REEFING MAN.

GRAPEVINE. The underground system by which messages circulate in prisons and, of necessity, the channel through which the addict makes contact with the peddler either inside or outside the walls. Cf. BUM STEER, TROLLEY.

GREEFO. Marajuana dried and prepared for smoking in cigarettes. Also *bo-bo-bush, muggles*. Cf. POTIGUAYA, REEFER.

GREEN ASHES or GREEN MUD. Ashes left from incompletely burning opium. *Chefs* often intentionally leave some of the opium unburned, then retrieve it by combing the ashes with a *yen-hok* when the customer is not looking. Cf. BLACK STUFF, CHEF, COOK A PILL, GEE-YEN, ROOSTER BRAND, YEN-SHEE-GOW.

GUM. Old-fashioned gum-opium which is dissolved and taken internally like laudanum. Not commonly used by underworld addicts. See BLACK STUFF.

GUN. A hypodermic needle. See ARTILLERY, EMERGENCY GUN.

GUTTER. A conditioned addict who shoots narcotics into a vein where the blood, which has been congested, carries it immediately to the heart. The hardened addict always prefers this to a *skin shot*, q.v. Also *main-liner, vein-shooter*. Cf. BANG IN THE ARM.

GUZZLED. Arrested. Apparently refers rather to the addict than to the peddler, who is *knocked off*. Cf. TO CHILL, DEAD-WOOD, GAZER, KNOCKED OFF, PAID OFF IN GOLD.

H. Heroin. Also indicated by any word in which the letter *h* is initial or conspicuous. These words are inserted into the argot extemporaneously and as a rule do not become permanent. The same linguistic device is used to refer to other drugs, especially morphine. An addict once approached a medical friend of mine and inquired if there wasn't a beer tavern nearby where they had 'music.' He thought the name of the place was 'Maxwell' and it wouldn't cost a fellow a lot of 'money' to have some fun. The addict was feeling out the doctor for a shot of morphine, or for directions as to where he could get one. Also *courage pills, witch hazel*. Cf. C., CUBE, M., O., OLD STEVE, SPEED BALL.

HABIT. A word used widely and loosely by addicts in a confusing variety of idioms, each capable of expressing a shade of meaning not always clear to this investigator. Perhaps the most common usage indicates a period of abstinence or deprivation; thus a *thirty-six-hour habit* indicates that the addict has had no dope for thirty-six hours, by which time he is probably *in a panic*, with all the bodily secretions flowing freely. See GET THE HABIT OFF, KICK THE HABIT, SMOKE THE HABIT OFF for spe-

cialized meanings. Cf. COLD TURKEY, KICK-BACK, MEDICINE, PANIC MAN.

HAPPY DUST. Cocaine, especially *bernice*. See C.

HAWKS. Guards in Federal prisons.

HEAVEN DUST. Cocaine, especially *bernice*. See C.

HIPPED. An opium addict who has smoked on one side so long that one hip is slightly atrophied. Also *thin hips*. Cf. LAY, TO LIE ON THE HIP.

HIT. A word from the very cryptic and compact peddler-addict argot, used when delivering dope to the addict. While a direct translation is difficult, it signifies in general that the sale is consummated. Cf. CONNECTION, TO MAKE (4), MEZONNY, MIZAKE THE MIZAN, RIZOLIN, SIZENDIZUP.

To HIT THE GONG. To take opium through a pipe. Also *beat the gong, kick the gong, lay, lie on the hip*. Cf. GONG.

To HIT THE GOW. 1. To be addicted to narcotics. See FROM MOUNT SHASTA. 2. The act of taking dope. Cf. ALL LIT UP, TO HIT THE GONG, GOW, GOWSTER.

To HIT THE STUFF. 1. To be addicted to narcotics. See FROM MOUNT SHASTA. 2. The act of taking dope.

HOOKED. Addicted to narcotics. See ALL LIT UP, FROM MOUNT SHASTA.

HOP. Opium. Not to be confused with *hops*, a common underworld term for tea. See BLACK STUFF, GOW.

HOP HEAD. An opium addict. Now almost obsolete among underworld addicts. Modern terms are *cookie, pipe-smoker, yen-shee-kwoi*. The term shows a tendency to become generalized to include all narcotic addicts. See GOWSTER. Cf. BLACK STUFF, HOP.

HOP JOINT. An opium den. Cf. LAY (1).

HOP STICK. An opium pipe. See GONG.

HOT SHOT. Cyanide or other fast-working poison concealed in dope to do away with a dangerous or troublesome addict. The *hot shot* kills the addict, in contrast to *flipping him* or *taking him*. Cf. FLIPPED, MICKEY FLYNN, PETER.

HYPE. The hypodermic needle used to inject narcotics. See ARTILLERY.

ICE-TONG DOCTOR. An illegal practitioner who also sells dope. Cf. CROAKER,

DEALER, TO MAKE (5), MAKE A CROAKER FOR A READER, READER, WHITE ANGEL.

IN FRONT OF THE GUN. To peddle narcotics with the understanding that the peddler 'takes the rap' if he is arrested, thus protecting the *big man* for whom he works. Cf. BIG MAN, KNOCK-OFF, PEDDLER.

IN HIGH. The peak of exhilaration. Restricted to morphine, heroin, and cocaine, usually to heroin or cocaine if hyperactivity is maintained for very long. See ALL LIT UP.

IRON HOUSE. A city jail. Most other underworld terms are also used by addicts. Cf. TORTURE CHAMBER.

JABOFF. The feeling of extreme exhilaration following immediately after a *vein shot* or a *verification shot*. The dope moves in a compact body directly along a large vein to the heart, where the effect is very sudden and powerful. The addict first experiences extreme euphoria, followed very shortly by depression of the heart and respiration, then usually unconsciousness. Also *pickup*. Cf. ALL LIT UP, BANG IN THE ARM, GUTTER, SPEED BALL.

JAM. An overdose of dope. See GOWED.

JOINT. A hypodermic needle complete. See ARTILLERY.

JOLT. A shot of narcotic taken directly into the vein. See BANG IN THE ARM.

JOY-POPPER. A person, not a confirmed addict, who indulges in an occasional shot of dope. However, *joy-popping* is usually the beginning of a permanent addiction. If the *joy-popper* has trouble establishing the desire and pleasure from indulging it, he is called a *student*. Cf. PLEASURE JOLT.

JOY STICK. An opium pipe. See GONG.

JUNK. 1. Narcotics in general. See GOW. 2. Often used to refer specifically to morphine. See M.

JUNKER. A narcotic addict. See GOWSTER.

KICK-BACK. The addict's almost inevitable return to narcotics after *kicking the 'habit*. Expert medical opinion now is that confirmed addicts are practically incurable; that amateurs, beginners, accidental addicts taken in the early stages, have some chance to be reclaimed. Cf. COLD TURKEY, KICK THE HABIT, MEDICINE, TO SMOKE THE HABIT OFF.

To KICK THE GONG or KICK THE

GONGER. To smoke an opium pipe. See HIT THE GONG.

To KICK THE HABIT. To stop using drugs.

KNOCK-OFF. The arrest of a peddler by a Federal agent. Apparently distinguished in usage from *guzzled*, and *paid in gold*. Cf. TO CHILL, DEADWOOD, IN FRONT OF THE GUN.

LAY. 1. A place to lie down and smoke opium. Cf. HOP JOINT. 2. The act of smoking. See HIT THE GONG. 3. The privilege of indulging one's self in a den, as 'How's chances for a lay?' Restricted to opium. Cf. BUNK YEN, LAY-DOWN, to LIE ON THE HIP.

LAY-DOWN. The price an addict pays for a *lay* in a den. Restricted to opium traffic.

LAYOUT. The outfit an opium smoker or *chef* uses, including pipes, *suey-pow, yen-hok, toy, yen-pok, yen-shee-gow*, and an alcohol lamp. Cf. CHEF, COOK A PILL, GONG.

LENT. Japanese fibrous morphine just being introduced on the West Coast; practically unknown to most American addicts as yet. Cf. M.

To LIE ON THE HIP. To be smoking opium. Opium is usually taken in a reclining position with the addict lying on his side. See HIT THE GONG. For supplementary notes see CHEF, HIPPED, LAY.

LI-YUEN. A high-quality smoking opium. See BLACK STUFF.

LUER. A hypodermic needle. See ARTILLERY.

M. Morphine. Also *cube, junk, God's medicine, lent, white stuff*. Cf. C., H., O.; BLACK STUFF, CUBE, OLD STEVE, SPEED BALL.

MAIN LINE. The vein, usually in the forearm near the elbow, or in the instep, into which the *gutter* fires the dope. Cf. BANG IN THE ARM.

MAIN-LINER. An addict who shoots narcotics into his veins. For further details see BANG IN THE ARM, GUTTER.

To MAKE. A term varying widely in meaning according to the context. As a verb it is always transitive. 1. For an agent to trap a peddler. Cf. DEADWOOD. 2. For authorities in an institution to detect a prisoner's addiction. Cf. TRAINED NURSE, WEASEL. 3. For someone to rob an addict of his supply of dope. Cf. CHEATER, FLIPPED. 4. For an addict to purchase dope from a peddler. Cf. HIT, TO MARK A CONNECTION. 5. To obtain drugs from a physician. Cf. TO BUG, CIRCUS, TO MAKE A CROAKER FOR A READER. There are other senses which are very difficult to isolate and define.

To MAKE A CROAKER FOR A READER. To persuade a physician, by one means or another, to write a prescription for narcotics. Cf. TO BUG, CIRCUS, CROAKER, ICE-TONG DOCTOR, TO MAKE (5), READER.

To MARK A CONNECTION or MARK FOR A CONNECTION. To locate or make contact with a peddler. An addict who has *marked a connection* knows where he can get dope when he wants it. Cf. CONNECTION, HIT, TO MAKE (4).

MEDICINE. Drugs necessarily administered to 'taper off' an addict who is or has been *kicking the habit* in an institution. Cf. COLD TURKEY, KICK THE HABIT.

MEET. An appointment arranged between an addict and a peddler. Cf. CONNECTION, HIT, TO MARK A CONNECTION.

MEZONNY. A cryptic peddler-addict idiom which is difficult to translate; it conveys the idea that one 'has his money working,' i.e. is about to *score a connection* or receive dope from a peddler. See HIT.

MICKEY FLYNN or MICKEY FINN. A knockout dose (often cigar ashes in a carbonated drink) administered to an addict or a sucker. See PETER.

MIZAKE THE MIZAN. To *score a connection* and buy dope from a peddler. Perhaps a corruption of the phrase 'make the man.' See HIT, MAKE (4).

MOJO. Dope of any kind, but especially morphine, heroin, or cocaine. See GOW.

MR. FISH. An addict who gives himself up to Federal officials voluntarily and goes to prison in an effort to break himself of the habit. Also *self-starter*. Cf. HABIT.

MUD. Opium before it is rolled into pills for smoking. See BLACK STUFF.

MUGGLES. Marajuana leaves before they are made into cigarettes, or *reefers*. See GREEFO.

NAIL. A hypodermic needle. See ARTILLERY.

NEEDLE. 1. The entire hypodermic, or *joint*. 2. The hollow needle alone, often carried by addicts because it is easier to conceal. See ARTILLERY, EMERGENCY GUN.

O. 1. Among addicts who use the needle it refers to an 'ounce' or *piece* of dope, especially of morphine. See CUBE, OZ., SHORT PIECE. 2. I have heard an opium addict use it with reference to opium, but have not been able to verify it as a widely used term. See BLACK STUFF. Cf. C., H., M.

OLD STEVE. One of several terms which may refer to morphine, heroin, or cocaine. Also *Racehorse Charlie, sugar, sweet stuff, trained nurse, white nurse*. Cf. C., H., M., SPEED BALL.

ON DRUGS. Addicted. See FROM MOUNT SHASTA.

ON THE GOW. 1. Addicted to narcotics. See FROM MOUNT SHASTA. 2. Used of an addict who is under the immediate influence. See ALL LIT UP.

ON THE MOJO. Addicted to narcotics. See FROM MOUNT SHASTA.

ON THE STUFF. 1. Addicted to narcotics. See FROM MOUNT SHASTA. 2. Under the immediate influence. See ALL LIT UP.

OVERCHARGED. Having taken too much dope. See GOWED.

OZ. An ounce of narcotics, especially a bindle of morphine. See BINDLE, O., PIECE, SHORT PIECE. While bindles of morphine are frequently indicated as 'ounces,' it seems unlikely that this much actually changes hands at one purchase, especially among the poorer class of addicts. Sometimes these Oz.'s have been shaved and become *short pieces*. More frequently, however, bootleg morphine is so heavily adulterated that an ounce does not give the full narcotic effect. Cf. RATION.

P. G. Paregoric, which contains about 1.88 grains of opium per fluid ounce. Skilled addicts can 'cook' the opium out of it with two fires, one underneath to vaporize the camphor, alcohol, etc., and one on top to consume these ingredients as they bubble up from the compound.

PAID OFF IN GOLD. Arrested by a Federal agent who has persuaded an addict or peddler to sell him some dope. Once the dope has changed hands and the agent has flashed his badge, he is said to have *paid him off in gold*. Cf. DEADWOOD, GAZER, GUZZLED, KNOCK-OFF.

PANIC MAN. An addict who is desperate

for narcotics. Since the bodily secretions are dried up by opiates, their absence in the system of a confirmed addict causes an intense and unnatural flow which can be stopped only by further application of narcotics. Furthermore, taking an addict off narcotics suddenly often has a severe aphrodisiac effect on him. Hence he is literally 'in a panic' for dope. Cf. CIRCUS, DEADWOOD, SNEEZED DOWN.

PAPER. A smuggled bindle wrapped in thin tinfoil and placed inside a postcard which has been slit with a razor blade and then smoothed under a hot iron. The postcard may then be mailed to a prisoner. See TRAINED NURSE.

PEDDLER. An illicit dealer in narcotics. Cf. BIG MAN, DEALER, IN FRONT OF THE GUN, KNOCK-OFF, PAID OFF IN GOLD.

PEN-YEN. A generic term for opium. See BLACK STUFF.

PETER. Knockout drops given an addict when he is *flipped* or *taken*. Also *Mickey Flynn*. Probably taken over metaphorically from the safe-blower's argot for nitroglycerine, although the term has had a long and respectable use meaning gunpowder. Cf. FLIPPED, HOT SHOT.

PICKUP. The exhilaration following an injection of narcotics, especially a *vein shot*. See JABOFF. Also the same as *coasting, floating*.

PICKED UP. Under the immediate influence of narcotics. See ALL LIT UP.

PIECE. An 'ounce' of narcotics, especially of morphine. Subject to the qualifications listed under *Oz*. See BINDLE.

PILL. A *ration* of opium prepared for smoking. See YEN-POK.

PIPE SMOKER. An opium addict. See HOP HEAD.

PLANT. 1. Narcotics hidden away, either on the person or secreted in a *plant* or hiding place. 2. To smuggle narcotics into jail by using a plant, or confederate who, with dope concealed on him, allows himself to be arrested. See BUM STEER, TO CHILL.

PLEASURE JOLT. An occasional indulgence by one who is not a confirmed addict. See JOY-POPPER.

POISON ACT. The Federal Narcotic Act.

POP. An injection of narcotics. See BANG.

POTIGUAYA. Marajuana leaves after the pods have been removed; crude marajuana. Cf. GREEFO.

PURRING or PURRING LIKE A CAT. Having taken too much dope. See GOWED.

RACEHORSE CHARLIE. Morphine, heroin, or cocaine. See OLD STEVE.

RATION. A *shot* of dope, usually contrasted to a *bindle*, q.v. The size of the ration varies with the type of dope, the length of time the addict has been using it, and the tolerance he has built up. It is probable that few addicts take more than one grain at a shot, and from three to five rations a day, although most of them believe that they take much more than they really do. Bootleg narcotics are so heavily adulterated that the addict must use a great deal to get the desired effect. Cf. BANG, BINDLE, BIRD'S EYE, FIX-UP, FUN.

READER. A physician's prescription for narcotics. Not to be confused with the common underworld usage of the same term with a variety of other meanings. Also *script, writing*. Cf. ICE-TONG DOCTOR, TO MAKE A CROAKER FOR A READER.

REEFER. A marajuana cigarette. Also *twist*. Cf. GREEFO, REEFING-MAN.

REEFING MAN. A marajuana addict, or a *twister*. Cf. GREEFO, REEFER.

RIZOLIN. Peddler-addict argot meaning, perhaps, 'the stuff is rolling,' i.e., 'your order is filled.' See HIT.

To ROLL A PILL. To prepare opium for smoking by rolling up a small wad of it between the palms. Cf. COOK A PILL.

ROOSTER BRAND. An euphemism for cheap bootleg opium refined from *yen-shee* or *green ashes*, a little higher in quality than *san-lo*. Cf. BLACK STUFF, CHEF, GEE-YEN, GREEN ASHES.

SACH. A method of concealing dope. The addict who anticipates arrest may soak some part of his garments, usually his shirttail, in a saturated solution of morphine, heroin, or cocaine. This is his *trained nurse* who 'takes care of him' while he is in jail. See TRAINED NURSE.

SAN-LO. The lowest grade of bootleg opium, refined and worked over from *yenshee*. See ROOSTER BRAND.

SAXOPHONE. An opium pipe. See GONG.

SCORE or SCORE A CONNECTION or SCORE FOR A CONNECTION. To purchase narcotics from a peddler. See MARK A CONNECTION, CONNECTION.

SCRIPT. A prescription for narcotics. See READER.

SELF-STARTER. An addict who voluntarily places himself in an institution where he hopes to *kick the habit*. See MR. FISH.

SHORT PIECE. An 'ounce' or *bindle* of narcotics, especially morphine and cocaine, which has been shaved with a razor blade or otherwise reduced before it reaches the addict. Cf. BINDLE, CUBE, OZ.

SHOT. A ration of narcotics, injected hypodermically. For further notes, see BANG, RATION.

SHOT IN THE ARM. 1. A *vein shot* or injection of narcotics into the blood stream directly. See BANG IN THE ARM. 2. A *skin shot,* q.v.

SIZENDIZUP. Peddler-addict argot, impossible to translate literally; the general import is that the coast is clear and the sale may proceed. See HIT.

SKIN SHOT. An injection of narcotics beneath the skin. Also *shot in the arm*. Addicts agree that this type of shot produces a milder but more lasting effect than the *vein shot,* q.v. *Skin shots* are as a rule preferred by beginners; see BANG IN THE ARM.

SKIN YEN. The desire for a *skin shot,* q.v.

To SMOKE THE HABIT OFF. For an addict to recuperate by indulgence after a period of abstinence. Cf. HABIT, KICK-BACK.

SNEEZED DOWN. For an addict to be abducted and held without dope in order to elicit information from him. Probably a modified application of the current underworld term *sneeze* for kidnapping. Cf. GUZZLED, PANIC MAN.

SNIFFING. Inhaling narcotics, especially *bernice*. See BLOWING.

SNIFTER. A cocaine addict who inhales *bernice*. See BERNICE, CHARLIE COKE.

SNOW. Cocaine. Practically obsolete among underworld addicts. See C.

SNOWBIRD. A cocaine addict, especially a *snifter*. See CHARLIE COKE.

SPEED BALL. A very powerful shot composed of morphine or heroin mixed in equal parts with cocaine. Cf. BANG, C., H., M.

SPIKE. 1. The needle from a hypodermic outfit. See NEEDLE (2). 2. The nail, pin, hook, or other substitute for the needle in an *emergency gun*, q.v.

To SPOT FOR SOMEONE. To act as lookout for an addict while he takes a shot in a public place or in a prison where a guard may see him.

SQUARE JOHN. Any nonaddict. Not to be confused with current underworld usage. See DO-RIGHT-PEOPLE.

STEM. An opium pipe. See GONG.

STICK. 1. A home-made opium pipe constructed from a wide-mouthed bottle and rubber tubing. 2. Variant of *dream-stick, hop stick, joy stick*. See GONG.

STOOL. An addict-informer who is used by the government for persuading addicts to sell part of their rations, then turning them over to a Federal agent. Cf. PAID OFF IN GOLD.

STUDENT. An amateur addict who has difficulty in establishing the habit satisfactorily. Cf. JOY-POPPER.

STUFF. A generalized term for narcotics. Now becoming obsolete. See GOW.

SUEY-POW. A sponge for cooling and cleaning an opium pipe. See LAYOUT.

SUGAR. Heroin, cocaine, or morphine. Both this term and *sweet stuff* are much used at present in jails and prisons to disguise conversations about dope. However, their very popularity will guarantee rapid extinction, for they must very soon become known. See OLD STEVE.

SWEET STUFF. Morphine, cocaine, or heroin. See OLD STEVE, SUGAR.

TAKEN. Knocked out with drugs; addicts are often *taken* when they are known to be carrying a supply of narcotics on their persons. See FLIPPED.

TAR. Opium. See BLACK STUFF.

TCHI. To roll a *pill* of opium and prepare it for smoking. See COOK A PILL.

THIN HIPS. An old-time opium addict, one who has smoked lying on one side for so long that his hips are of unequal size. See HIPPED.

TORTURE CHAMBER. A jail or other institution where an addict cannot obtain dope. Cf. BUM STEER, COLD TURKEY, IRON HOUSE, SNEEZED DOWN.

TOY. A small lockbox in which opium is kept. See LAYOUT.

TRAINED NURSE. Narcotics smuggled into jail with an addict to 'take care of him' while he is there. Also *paper, sach, writing.* Cf. BUM STEER, TO MAKE (2) , PLANT (2) .

TROLLEY. The secret channels through which dope and other articles are distributed within prisons; sometimes an actual string or wire stretched between cells. Cf. GRAPEVINE.

TURKEY. A bindle of bad dope, or a fake capsule found to contain only sugar or chalk. Not to be confused with *cold turkey.* Cf. BINDLE.

TWIST. A marajuana cigarette. See REEFER, TWISTER (2) .

TWISTER. 1. A feigned spasm. See CIRCUS. 2. One who rolls his own *twists,* or marajuana cigarettes or, by extension, a marajuana addict. See REEFING MAN.

UNCLE. A Federal narcotic agent. See GAZER. Not to be confused with current underworld meanings, a politician who sponsors criminals or a receiver for stolen property.

VEIN SHOT. An injection of narcotics directly into the blood stream. See BANG IN THE ARM.

VEIN-SHOOTER. One who pumps narcotics directly into the blood-stream; hence a hardened addict. See GUTTER.

VERIFICATION SHOT. A type of vein shot in which the blood is drawn up into the needle where the addict can watch it mix with the dope. The most rapid and satisfying type of shot for the experienced addict. See BANG IN THE ARM.

The WEASEL. A Federal agent in Atlanta who is widely known among addicts for his ability to *make* a man: to sense that a prisoner uses narcotics and catch him when he does. Cf. MAKE (2) .

WHISKERS. A Federal narcotic agent. See GAZER.

WHITE ANGEL. A nurse or other attendant in an institution, especially one who can be persuaded to slip an addict a shot when he is *in a panic.* Not to be confused with *trained nurse* or *white nurse.* Cf. MEDICINE.

WHITE NURSE. A term loosely used, like several others, to mean cocaine, heroin, or more frequently, morphine. See OLD STEVE.

WHITE STUFF. 1. Morphine. See M. Cf. BLACK STUFF. 2. A cotton field, or, by extension, chain-gang labor. There is a punning maxim among underworld addicts to the effect that 'you mustn't fall in Dixie, for white stuff will flip a junker'; that is, an addict mustn't get arrested in the South, for he can't stand penal labor.

WING-DING. A feigned fit or spasm. See CIRCUS.

WITCH HAZEL. Heroin. See H.

WRITING. 1. A letter written on porous woodpulp paper which has first been soaked in a saturated solution of drug. The letter is mailed to a prisoner and statements in it like 'Helen asked about you,' 'Carrie is in town,' or 'Mildred still loves you,' inform the recipient that heroin, cocaine, or morphine respectively has been *put in writing.* He may then soak out the drug, cook down the resulting solution, and fill his hypodermic. See TRAINED NURSE. 2. A prescription for narcotics. See READER.

YEN. Same as *habit,* q.v., except that it is often restricted to opium users. However, the term also enjoys a wide usage with reference to all types of drugs, as in the idiom *skin yen.*

YEN-HOK. The long steel needle upon which a pill of opium is cooked. See COOK A PILL, LAYOUT.

YEN-POK. The *pill* of opium after it is prepared for smoking. See COOK A PILL, LAYOUT.

YEN-SHEE. The residue left in the pipe after the opium has been smoked. It usually contains some unconsumed opium which may be retrieved by the *chef* and reworked. See BLACK STUFF. Cf. GREEN ASHES.

YEN-SHEE-GOW. A cup-shaped scraper for removing opium residue or *yen-shee,* from the bowl of the pipe and retrieving the unburned opium for further use. See CHEF, GREEN ASHES, LAYOUT.

YEN-SHEE-KWOI. An opium addict. See HOP HEAD.

PART II†

T HIS study is an extension of *The Argot of the Underworld Narcotic Addict*[1] and, while it is complete in itself, it has seemed advisable to cross-reference many of the terms to the previous study; those terms marked with an asterisk[2] refer to entries in Part I where additional or related information is available. The introductory material dealing with the position of the addict in underworld life may be taken as applying to this study also.

It should not be assumed that all the terms listed here have been coined since the publication of the 1936 article; while many of them are apparently of very recent coinage, it is probable that most of them were simply not recorded in the previous study; a careful check shows no evidence that any of the previously printed terms have become obsolete.[3] Only by checking these lists at intervals over the next ten or fifteen years will it be possible to determine how rapidly the argot changes and what factors most strongly influence change. However, the argot of so-called criminal narcotic addicts is the least stable of any of the criminal argots I have examined. The addicts are constantly 'steaming the lingo up'; this tendency (perhaps concomitant to addiction) complicates collection and makes the formation of definitions based on usage most difficult.[4] It produces an

† Acknowledgement: To Dr. Alfred R. Lindesmith of Indiana University, for extensive assistance in the initial fieldwork; to Dr. Lawrence Kolb and Dr. Pescor of the United States Public Health Service for assistance; to Dr. Victor H. Vogel of the Medical Staff of the University of Colorado, Dr. A. Guiglia of the Medical Staff of the University of Louisville, and Dr. Clyde Vanneter of the Medical Staff of the Ohio State University, for attention to medical and anatomical details; to Professor Franklin Edgerton of Yale and Professor Thomas Pollock of the Ohio State University for etymological advice; and to the underworld figures whose intelligent co-operation has made this study possible.

1. *American Speech*, April, 1936.
2. A few terms marked ** refer to brief addenda published in *American Speech*, October, 1936, p. 222.
3. Because of the very rapid decline of opium smoking, the opium argot is known only to a dwindling fraternity; very few youngsters now begin on the pipe. This means that the argot of that group is on the way to obsolescence. Already, much of the terminology has been loosely transferred to needle-addiction, frequently without a full knowledge of the original meanings of the words transferred.
4. After close association with addicts' argot for several years, I am still unable to isolate and define the numerous shades of distinction which addicts make in the use of some very common words—for instance, *habit, high*, and their related idioms. Dr. Lindesmith, who is intimately acquainted with addiction from a sociological viewpoint, has experienced the same difficulty.

infinite number of words and idioms which enjoy only a brief life among certain individuals or cliques, or which are used only a few times by one addict, then dropped. This study includes only words which enjoy a wide and thoroughly established usage within the fraternity. On the other hand, addicts' speech reveals some of the forces which operate in the formation of argots much more clearly than do the more stable criminal lingoes.

In this study quite a few semantic suggestions are offered, most of them explained in terms of metaphor. While none of these can be guaranteed, they have been published only after a very careful investigation; many more have been suppressed because the evidence supporting them is hardly conclusive. Since the meanings of argot words and idioms must often be explained in terms of the life-relationships which the words express, it has seemed advisable to include some descriptions (often more sociological than linguistic) of these life-relationships.[5] A mere word-list from a culture so obscure as that of the underworld addict would have little real meaning to the uninitiated without these descriptive notes.

GLOSSARY

AB. or ABB. An abscess which forms in the arms or legs of conditioned needle-addicts as a result of infections induced by impure drugs or unsterile needles. These abscesses are difficult to heal as long as the addict is *on drugs,** but clear up when he goes *off,* leaving characteristic deposits of scar-tissue about the veins. See *up and down the lines.* Cf. *To bug.**

AD. or ADD. A narcotic addict, especially a needle-addict. Apparently restricted to Chicago and vicinity. Also *bird-cage hype, chippy, cokomo, dope-hop, gow-head, Hoosier-fiend, hype, hypo-smecker, jabber, junk-hog, knocker, main-line shooter, needle-fiend, pipe-fiend, pipie, pleasure-smoker, pleasure-user, smecker, viper, yenshee-boy,* some with specialized meanings. See *gowster,** *hop-head.** Cf. *do-right John.*

To Be AROUND THE TURN. For an addict who is *kicking the habit** to have passed through the most distressing of the withdrawal symptoms (see *panic-man**) which reach their height in from thirty-six to seventy-two hours after the last *ration.** Also *over the hump* 1. Cf. *to break the habit, to carry, to cat-nap* 1, *to fold up, to hold, sick, yenshee-baby.*

To ASK FOR THE COTTON. To borrow another addict's *cotton** in order to squeeze out the residue of narcotics for a very small shot. An indication that the borrower is short of money. See *cotton-shooter,** *Charley Cotton, Cotton Brothers, rinsings, cotton-habit.*

To Be AWAY FROM THE HABIT. To be *off drugs,** or to be *off.*[6] Also *to break the habit* 1, *to catch up, to fold up, on*

5. For more extensive notes on the close interdependence between the life-situation of the addict and his argot, see Lindesmith, A. R., *The Nature of Opiate Addiction,* The University of Chicago Press, 1937, Chapter V.

6. This freedom from the habit is of course only temporary. There is to date no known cure for addiction once it is firmly established; while occasionally accidental addicts stop permanently, underworld addicts almost inevitably *kick-back.** Although research is going on constantly on this problem, medical authorities do not yet agree on the exact nature of drug addiction. The attitude of the addict is reflected in the following excerpt from a ballad:

the up and up, washed up. Cf. *to play around* 2.

To BACK UP. 1. (tr.) To distend the vein into which the addict intends to inject narcotics by holding up the circulation with a string or rope and massaging the skin over the vein. Restricted to *vein-shooters.** Also *to bring up.* See *bang in the arm.** 2. (intr.) To refuse to make a *connection* or to take drugs because of suspicion that the peddler or the addict is a *stool-pigeon.* See *to blow the meet, chill* 2.**

To BANG. See *to shoot.*

BELT. 1. The exhilaration experienced when narcotics are taken; euphoria. Also *bing* 2, *boot, drive, jab-off,** kick.* 2. More specifically, the terrific 'jolt' which follows a *vein-shot** when the mass of injected narcotics reaches the heart. Also *bing, boot, drive, kick.* See *bang in the arm.**

BENDING AND BOWING. See *high.*

BERNIES. (Probably var. of BERNICE*) 1. Cocaine crystallized for inhalation. 2. Cocaine allegedly obtained from Dr. Bernie, probably a mythical character. Restricted to Chicago and vicinity. See *bernice.**

BIG-SHOT CONNECTION. A peddler who distributes large amounts of narcotics; one who prospers because he has protection from the law. See *connection,** big-man.**

BING. 1. A *ration* of narcotics injected hypodermically. Also *bingo, bird's-eye* 4, *fix, gee* 3, *go, jab-pop, load, penitentiary-shot, pick-up, pin-shot, point-shot, prod, prop,* some with specialized meanings. See *bang in the arm.** 2. See *belt.*

BINGO. See *bing* 1.

BIRD-CAGE HYPE. A very poor underworld addict who has trouble supporting his habit. Probably so-called because this type of addict often lives in a *bird-cage* or *bird-cage joint,* a very cheap lodging house with chicken-wire netting separating the small sleeping compartments. Transients who live in these establishments are called *bird-cage stiffs.* There is also a saying that when an underworld addict is down and out, 'he has a bird-cage on one foot and a boxing glove on the other'—a humorous variant of 'a boot on one foot and a shoe on the other.' See *boots and shoes,** ad.*

BIRD'S-EYE. 3. A very small quantity of drugs. 'When Whitey brought the cap I took just a tiny little bit—a bird's-eye—and gave the rest to him.' 4. A small quantity of solution held in the hypodermic needle for another addict who is *playing around* and does not trust himself to take a larger shot. Equivalent to the word 'butts' on a cigarette. 'Save me two or three points of that for a bird's-eye.'

The BIZ, BIZZ, or BUSINESS. 1. An outfit for taking drugs hypodermically; it consists of a hypodermic needle or some homemade substitute, a medicine-dropper, a cooking-spoon, and a piece of cotton for filtering purposes. Also *factory* 1, *joint* 3, *lay-out* 2, *machinery, the works.* Cf. *engine, lay-out* 1.** 2. The hypodermic needle. Also *harpoon, point, tom-cat,* with specialized meanings. 3. Narcotics. 4. The 'third degree' administered by the police.

BLOCK. 1. A *cube* of morphine; any portion of an ounce as sold in a *bindle,** usually 2 to 5 grains. 2. Crude bootleg morphine.

BLOOD-SUCKER. A physician. See *to write scrip.*

To BLOW A SHOT. 2. To waste a shot by spilling the solution.

To BLOW THE MEET. To fail to keep

'I wish I had never seen morphine,
I wish I had never seen coke;
I wish that the hop in that last lonely pop
Was a dream that would go up in smoke.
Do you think I would ever take one more?
Do you think that I really would?
If you do you are right, I'm afraid that you are,
For you bet your life that I would. . . .'

an appointment, usually because of suspicion either on the part of the addict or the peddler. Cf. *paid off in gold,* stool-pigeon, to back up* 2.

BOO-GEE. 1. The tissue-paper packing or *gee-rag** used to make an air-tight connection between the medicine-dropper and the *joint** or needle. Also *shoulder.* See *gee* 3.

BOOT. See *belt.*

BOW-SOW. Narcotics. Restricted to West Coast. See *cotics.*

To BREAK or BREAK THE HABIT. 1. To *kick the habit.** See *away from the habit.* 2. To suffer severe localized withdrawal symptoms. 'I always break the habit in my stomach,' says the opium addict. See *panic-man.**

BRICK or BRICK-GUM. Crude *gum** or gum opium before it is *rolled* for smoking. Also *black-stuff,* gee* 2, *grease, leaf, leaf-gum, skamas.* Cf. *canned-stuff, to roll a pill.**

To BRING UP. See *to back up* 1.

To BUILD UP THE HABIT. To gradually increase one's tolerance to narcotics by increasing the dosage. Cf. *junk-hog.*

BULL-HORRORS. A kind of delirium suffered by conditioned addicts, especially cocaine addicts, in the later stages of addiction.[7]

BUNK-HABIT. 1. The desire to hang about an opium den even though one is without the price of a *lay.** 2. An opium habit.

BURNED OUT. A sclerotic condition of the veins present in most conditioned addicts. See *ab., up and down the lines.*

The BUSINESS. See *the biz.*

To BUST THE MAIN-LINE. To inject narcotics intravenously. Also *to shoot, to take it in the line, to take it main.* See *vein-shot,* bang in the arm,* channel.* '. . . From my dropper I'll shake the dust, From my spike I'll scrape the rust, And my old main-line I'll bust . . .'

CANNED-STUFF. Commercial smoking opium put in tins. Specific brands are *Lem Kee, San Lo,** etc. Cf. *brick.*

To CARRY. For a ration of narcotics to support an addict for a specified length of time without any discomfort from diminishing euphoria. See *to fix, to hold, junk-hog.*

To CAT-NAP. 1. To get small (and very welcome) snatches of sleep during the withdrawal period. Cf. *to be around the turn.* 2. To nod or doze as a result of too large a ration of narcotics. See *high.*

To CATCH UP or To Be CAUGHT UP. See *to be away from the habit.*

CECIL. Cocaine. See *cotics.*

CHANNEL. A vein or *main-line** into which a *vein-shooter** injects the narcotic solution. See *to go into the sewer, to bust the main-line.* Cf. *to go in the skin.*

CHARGED. Var. of OVERCHARGED.* Stupefied or drowsy as a result of having taken more narcotics than necessary to produce euphoria. This condition is accidentally produced through failure to judge the quantity or strength of narcotics properly. Also *coasting* 2, *to play the nod.* See *junk-hog, high.*

CHARLEY COTTON. One of the mythical Cotton Brothers, C., H., and M. Cotton. See *Cotton Brothers, rinsings.*

CHINESE NEEDLE WORK. An euphemistic expression for using or dealing in narcotics. Also *embroidery, Dr. White.*

CHIPPY. See *pleasure-user.*

CHIPPY-HABIT. A type of indulgence in which the user takes only a small amount of narcotic at irregular intervals; although this type of user is not technically an addict, his *habit* usually develops without his knowledge and he finds himself *hooked** before he is aware of it. Also *coffee-and habit, cotton-habit, hit-and-miss habit,* some with specialized meanings.

To CLOUT or To ROOT ON THE DERRICK. To steal, especially as a sneak-

---

7. Probably induced by the addicts' constant fear of *deadwood,** or betrayal and arrest, followed by consequent withdrawal distress and deprivation of narcotics. Addicts of the underworld live in a perpetual state of emotional excitement, with fear and anticipation predominating. These fears imbed themselves in the subconscious and are released in grotesque forms when the addict is in a state of delirium. See *the leaps.*

thief. Most underworld addicts live by thievery of one sort or another; some are big-time professional thieves; most of them remain small-timers and barely succeed in supporting their habits. Other types of thievery in which addicts are prominent are: *boosting* or *rooting on the boost* (shoplifting); *rooting on the cannon* or *on the gun,* etc. (picking pockets); and, more rarely, *short-conning* (working small-time confidence games). Addicts very rarely are connected with violent crime or with the *heavy rackets.*

COASTING. 2. To be in a state of stupor or semi-stupor induced by too large a dose of narcotics, especially cocaine. See *charged, high.*

COFFEE-AND HABIT. A form of *chippy-habit.* The jocular inference is that it is really no habit at all.

COKOMO or KOKOMO. A cocaine addict. See *ad.*

CONNECTION DOUGH. The price of a *bindle* of narcotics. Also *mezonny* 2,** *score dough.* See *connection.**

COOKING-SPOON. Var. of COOKER.* See *spoon.*

COTICS. Any kind of narcotics. Also *Dr. White, dynamite, fu, gee* 2, *gee-fat, G.O.M., gonger* 2, *goods, goof-ball, goznik, grease, hemp, hocus, Indian-hay, leaf, leaf-gum, Lem-Kee, Mary Warner, McCoy, medicine* 2, *merchandise, mezz, Miss Emma, skamas, Old Steve*, *tea, Texas-tea, viper's-weed, weed,* with specialized meanings.

COTTON BROTHERS. The *cotton** used by addicts; occurs in such phrases as 'Where are the Cotton Brothers?' which is one way of *asking for the cotton, q.v. Charley Cotton* is cotton saturated with cocaine solution; *M. Cotton* is that containing morphine solution; *H. Cotton* is that containing heroin.

COTTON-HABIT. A small, irregular habit which a very poor addict (*cotton-shooter**) may support by begging the *cottons** from more prosperous addicts. See *to ask for the cotton, chippy-habit.*

CROCK. 1. An opium pipe. 2. The bowl of an opium pipe. Restricted to Midwest. See *log.*

To CUT. To adulterate drugs, usually

with sugar of milk. This is done by the peddlers and dealers, or by the bootleg manufacturers, sometimes by all three. Cf. *to shave, junk-hog.*

CUTERED PILL. A strong, unpalatable smoke obtained when the bowl of the opium pipe is too hot or too full of *yenshee,** or when the *pill** contains too much badly refined *yenshee.* Cf. *suey-pow.**

To DABBLE. To indulge irregularly in narcotics. See *chippy-habit, to play around.*

DINGHIZEN. The inevitable medicine dropper which is in the *lay-out* of the needle-addict. Also *dripper, dingus, fake, fake-a-loo.* Cf. *emergency-gun,** *the biz, to lip the dripper.*

DINGUS. See *dinghizen.*

DO-RIGHT JOHN. A non-addict. A combination of *do-right people** and *square-John.** Also *square-apple.*

DOPE-HOP. A prison-term for a drug addict. Addicts seldom use the term *dope* with reference to narcotics; it appears to be almost taboo. See *ad.*

DR. WHITE. A euphemism referring to drugs or drug-addiction. 'Only Dr. White can help me.' Alludes to cocaine, morphine, or heroin. See *white-stuff,** *cotics.*

DRIPPER. See *dinghizen.*

DRIVE. See *belt.*

TO DRIVE IN. To deliver narcotics to an addict who is in jail or prison via the *trolley.** See *finger, finger of stuff, keyster-plant, bum-steer,** *to shoot the curve* 2.

DYNAMITE. 1. Bootleg dope with an unusually high narcotic content. See *cotics.* Cf. *McCoy.* 2. A knock-out dose given to an addict under the guise of narcotics. See *peter.**

EIGHTH-PIECE. See *piece.*

EMBROIDERY. See *Chinese needle-work.*

ENGINE. An outfit for preparing and smoking opium. Also *hop lay-out, joint* 4, *saddle-and-bridle.* See *lay-out** for details. Cf. *the biz.*

EYE-OPENER. The first injection of the day, often taken in bed. The addict usually wakes up *sick* because the euphoria from his last injection has worn off. Cf. *to laugh and scratch.*

FACTORY. 1. A needle-addict's *lay-out.* See *the biz.* 2. A wholesale distributing depot for peddlers where *caps** are filled.

FAKE or FAKE-A-LOO. The medicine dropper, probably so-called because so often it is used as a substitute for the regulation glass tube in constructing a home-made hypodermic. Many addicts prefer the home-made needle because the rubber bulb makes it easier to control the injection. See *dinghizen.*

To FEEL THE HABIT COMING ON. See *to be sick.*

FINGER or FINGER OF STUFF. A rubber finger-stall or condom filled with narcotics and swallowed or concealed in the rectum. Also *keyster-plant.* See *to drive in.*

FINK. See *stool-pigeon.*

FIRE-PLUG. A large *pill** or *ration** of smoking opium, as distinguished from the common *yen-pok.** The *pill* is usually about the size of a very large pea; some addicts roll it in a cone-shape so that it fits snugly into the eye of the pipe. It is cooked on the *yen-hok.** Cf. *brick, cotics.*

FIX. Var. of FIX-UP.* A ration of narcotics, especially one to be injected. See *bing.*

To FIX. To take narcotics; usually infers that the addict takes enough to *fix him up,* or restore him to the state which he has come to regard as normal. 'Let's go in the can and fix.' See *to carry, to smoke the habit off.** Cf. *junk-hog.*

To FOLD UP. To stop taking narcotics. See *to be away from the habit.*

To FRAME A TWISTER or A TOSS-OUT. To feign a spasm in order to obtain narcotics from a doctor. Also *to put the croaker on the send for a jolt, to throw a meter.* See *circus.**

FU. 1. Marijuana, or cannabis indica. 2. The drug contained in the ripe seed-pods of the female flowering hemp plant.[8] Also *goof-ball, greefo,** *hemp, Indian-hay, Mary Warner, mezz, muggles,** *mutah, tea, Texas-tea, viper's-weed, weed.* See *to vipe, cotics.*

To GAP. To begin to manifest withdrawal symptoms. The addict yawns frequently and may drool. See *to be sick.*

GAPPER. An addict in need of narcotics. See *to gap.*

GEE. 2. Pronounced both [gi] and [dʒi], with opium smokers favoring [gi]. Smoking opium, especially refined or reworked opium. Probably from the Hindustani *ghee,* refined butter.[9] Most smokers believe it to be a Chinese word, but apparently it is not,[10] although it seems to have entered America through the Chinese. Many addicts, probably influenced by the oriental pronunciation, pronounce all *gee*-words [gi]; others, perhaps influenced by g. (abbreviation for *gow,** *grease,** *gonger,** *gum,** etc. and paralleled by

---

8. Although medical authorities are somewhat dubious about classifying marijuana as a true narcotic, a new Federal law now considers it such.

Because of the close relationship between 'swing' music and marijuana, the drug has had much sensational publicity and is used widely in small doses to release the sexual rhythms essential to a complete response to 'swing.' Such recent song-hits as 'Texas Tea Party,' 'The Chant of the Weed,' 'Smokin' Reefers,' 'Reefer Man,' 'Viper's Drag,' 'Viper's Moan,' etc., reflect, in a very thinly disguised manner, the close relationship between drug-aroused sexual desire and popular dance music; through the dance-hall and the brothel much of the argot associated with this drug has passed into the popular vocabulary. Most addicts of opium, heroin, morphine or cocaine remain aloof from marijuana addicts and do not use their argot.

9. The word was probably applied to opium by Hindu addicts, brought to China with the traffic, and entered America with many other Chinese terms associated with opium addiction. Dr. Franklin Edgerton of Yale states: 'The derivation . . . seems to me very plausible.'—Letter, January 25, 1938. Such derivation is made more plausible by the numerous metaphorical names for opium made in English on the basis of consistency—*gum, tar, grease, black-stuff, brick-gum,* etc.

10. Dr. Edgerton states: 'I have been unable to learn of its (gee) existence in Chinese. Neither of my colleagues, Dr. George Kennedy and Professor Li Fang-Kuei, know of the existence of any such word.'—Letter, January 25, 1938.

H,* M,* and C*), or by the older *gee 4*, favor [dʒi]. Cf. *boo-gee, gee 2, gee 3, geezer,* *gee-fat, geed-up,* *gee-rag 2, gee-stick, gee-yen.* *3. A ration of narcotics exclusive of opium. Perhaps an extension of *gee 2*, but more probably an abbreviation (g.) of 'guy' or 'geezer.' Occurs in other argots in combinations like *right-gee, wrong-gee, torch-gee, Tommy-gee*, etc. Pronunciation apparently now confused with *gee 2* [gi]. See *gee** and *gee-rag 2* where it is now impossible to be certain whether the derivation is from *g.* (abbreviation for *granny*) or from *gee 2*.

GEED UP. 2. Same as *coasting 2*. See *high*.

GEE-FAT. Probably var. of *gee-yen.** The *yenshee** which forms in an opium pipe, often reclaimed, refined, and re-sold. See *cotics, brick*. Cf. *cutered pill*.

GEE-RAG. 2. The packing (often a handkerchief) used to make the connection airtight between the stem and the bowl of an opium pipe. Cf. *boo-gee*.

GEE-STICK. An opium pipe. See *log*.

To GET ONE'S YEN OFF. To allay withdrawal distress with narcotics. It should be noted that *yen** applies strictly to withdrawal distress and would hardly be used to indicate the desire (largely psychological) which an addict might feel for narcotics after he had been *away from the habit* for some time.

GO. A *ration* of narcotics. Restricted to needle-addicts. Also *gee 3*. See *hing 1*. Cf. *short-go*.

To GO IN THE SKIN. To indulge in *skin-shooting** as contrasted to *vein-shooting.** Also *S.S.* Cf. *to back up*.

To GO INTO THE SEWER. To take narcotics intravenously. See *to back up*.

GOODS. Narcotics as they pass into commerce. Restricted to *big-men,** and not used by addicts. Also *merchandise*. See *cotics*.

GOOF-BALL. Marijuana. See *fu, to vipe*.

G.O.M. Morphine. Literally, 'God's own medicine,' a phrase borrowed from legitimate medicine. See *cotics*.

GONGER. 2. Any opium derivatives. Restricted to the West Coast. See *cotics*.

GONGOLA. An opium pipe. See *log*.

To GOW. To remove the *yen-shee** from an opium pipe. See *yen-shee-gow.**

GOW-HEAD. Originally an opium addict, but now generalized to include all forms of addiction except marijuana.

GOZNIK. Narcotics. Restricted to the West Coast. See *cotics*.

GREASE. Smoking opium before it is rolled into *pills.** See *brick, cotics*.

GREEN PILL. See *cutered pill*.

GROCERY-BOY. 1. An addict who has drugs but is hungry and wants food. 2. An addict who has developed a large appetite as an aftermath of his withdrawal symptoms. See *chuck-habit,** *dug-out.***

HALF-PIECE. See *piece*.

HARPOON. The hypodermic needle. See *the biz 2*.

To HAVE A CHINAMAN (or A MONKEY) ON ONE'S BACK. See *to be sick*.

To HAVE A HABIT. See *to be sick*.

To HAVE A YEN. See *to be sick*.

HIGH. Var. of IN HIGH.* To be well fortified with drugs; usually implies that the addict is noticeably under the influence of drugs. May also mean stupefied or *charged* from an overdose or a badly timed shot. Usage is so loose that the sense must be determined from the situation. The same is true of the following equivalents: *bending and bowing, coasting 2, full of poison, geed-up 2, leaping, leaping and stinking, lit, polluted, shot-up, stepping high, to cat-nap 2*. See *all lit up.**

HIGH-HAT. 2. A large *pill** of smoking opium. See *fire plug*. 3. A large opium-lamp.

To Be HIT. To begin to feel the effects of a narcotic injection; euphoria in the early stages.

HIT-AND-MISS HABIT. See *chippy-habit*. Apparently restricted to the East Coast and Mid-west.

To HITCH UP THE REINDEER. To prepare the *lay-out* for an injection of cocaine. Also *to make a spread, to spread the joint*. Cf. *to go on a sleighride,** and the compounds of *snow.**

HOCUS. A *ration* of cocaine, morphine, or heroin in solution, ready for injection. See *cotics*.

To HOLD. 1. (tr.) See *to carry*. 2. (intr.) To have drugs for sale, especially on one's person. 'Are you holding?' Applies only to peddlers.

HOOSIER FIEND. An inexperienced addict; a yokel who has become addicted, perhaps accidentally, and doesn't know he is *hooked** until he is deprived of drugs and develops withdrawal distress.

HOP LAY-OUT. An opium smoker's *lay-out*. See *engine*. Cf. *lay-out* 2.

HOP-TOY. Var. of TOY.* A container for smoking opium.

HUMMING-GEE BOWL. The bowl of an opium pipe; whimsical legend has it that it is made of bone from the human skull. See *log*.

HYPE. 1. A narcotic addict, especially a needle-addict. 2. or HYPO. An injection of distilled water or some non-narcotic solution given addicts while they are *kicking the habit**; some addicts believe that this relieves withdrawal distress. See *needle-fiend*.

HYPO-SMECKER. A needle-addict. See *ad*.

ICE-CREAM HABIT. See *chippy-habit*.

INDIAN-HAY. Marijuana. See *fu, to vipe*.

IRON-CURE. The *cold-turkey** treatment usually administered in jails and prisons; the addict is taken off drugs suddenly and allowed to *kick his habit out* on the floor of his cell. Also the *steel-and-concrete cure*. See *quarry-cure*.

To JAB. To take drugs hypodermically. 'I've smoked and I've jabbed.'*

JABBER. A needle-addict. See *ad*.

JAB-POP or JAB-POPPO. A *ration* of drugs injected with the needle. See *bing* 1.

JOINT. 2. The hollow needle, or a substitute. See *tom-cat*. 3. The hypodermic outfit including all accessories. See *lay-out* 2, *the biz*. 4. The opium smoker's outfit complete. See *engine*.

JUNK-HOG. An addict who indulges to great excess—excess being a relative matter, for it is difficult to determine an 'average' consumption of narcotics. In order to sustain a habit an addict must take a carefully measured *ration** at regular intervals spaced so as to ward off withdrawal distress. From 2 to 10 grains of morphine every 24 hours seems to be sufficient to support most conditioned addicts. Most of them claim, or sincerely believe, that they take much more than they really do, either because of the heavy adulteration to which bootleg drugs are subjected, or in order to acquire status as the supporter of an *oil-burning habit*. The highest dosage I have recorded is 64 grains every 24 hours, an amount which must be viewed with some suspicion. See *to cut, to shave, high*.

To KEEP THE MEET. To keep an appointment with an addict or peddler as scheduled. Addicts are fanatically punctual about *keeping the meet*. If the other party does not appear on the minute, they leave quickly on the assumption that an arrest may have taken place. See *meet, to blow the meet*.

KEYSTER-PLANT. A device for smuggling drugs into prisons, or for concealing them once they have been smuggled in. Also *finger of stuff*. See *to drive in*.

KICK. 1. See *belt*. 2. Var. of KICK THE HABIT.* To go *off drugs.** 'They threw me into a cell in the band-house and I kicked her cold-turkey.'

KNOCKER. A person, usually an addict who is temporarily *off drugs,** who criticises those who are addicted.

LAMP-HABIT. 1. An excessive or continuous desire for opium. An addict with such a desire is said to have a *lamp-habit* because he likes to see the alcohol lamp used in opium-smoking lit continuously. 2. By extension, an excessive desire for any drug. Also *oil-burning habit*. See *junk-hog*. 3. A slight *habit** acquired by breathing the smoke and vapor from the lamps in an opium den. May also have the same inference as *coffee-and habit*.

To LAUGH AND SCRATCH. To take narcotics hypodermically; injections, especially intravenous injections, produce a prickly or itchy sensation over the addict's entire body; this reaction is particularly noticeable when he has been *off drugs* temporarily, or when he does not get his *ration* on time. Cf. *eye-opener*.

LAY. 4. A *ration* of narcotics, not restricted to opium.

> '. . . And there's that lay of M,
> My good old pipe and stem,
> Good God how I love them. . . .'

LAY-DOWN JOINT. A *hop-joint** or opium den, especially one which supplies the drug and all necessary equipment. See *lay-down.**

LAY-OUT. 2. By extension from *lay-out,** the hypodermic and all accessories. See *the biz.* Note that the following quotation qualifies the term in order to specify the original meaning:

'. . . Ten thousand hop lay-outs, all inlaid in pearl,
Every hop-head fiend will bring along his girl.
Every junkie with a habit
Will be jumping like a rabbit,
Down at the cocaine jubilee. . . .'

LEAF or LEAF-GUM. See *brick, cotics.*

LEAPING AND STINKING. See *high.*

LEAPS. A state approximating delirium tremens resulting from excessive and continued use of cocaine; these hallucinations range from the unspeakably horrible to the whimsical and harmless. Some addicts contentedly dig gold out of the floors; others herd bizarre menageries about with them; one informant always has the same kind of *leaps*—an endless procession of white rats which come popping backward through the keyhole. See *bull-horrors.*

LEM-KEE. A commercially prepared smoking opium. See *canned-stuff, brick, cotics.*

LEMON-BOWL. 1. A hollowed-out lemon rind fitted to the bowl of an opium pipe to make the opium more mild. Some addicts prefer an orange rind, or *orange-bowl.* 2. An opium pipe so equipped. See *log.*

LINE. The *main-line** or vein into which the addict injects narcotics. See *channel.*

To LIP THE DRIPPER. To suck all the air out of the *dinghizen* before taking a shot; addicts commonly test for air by getting the dropper to stick to their lip or tongue-tip; when a regulation hypodermic is used, this procedure is of course superfluous. Beginning addicts are usually careful to remove all air because they fear the consequences of an air-bubble in the bloodstream. As addicts become conditioned they grow more and more careless about such trifles and take

not only air, but quantities of foreign matter in suspension into the bloodstream. Dr. Lindesmith reports one addict who broke off the tip of his needle in the vein-wall and 'lost' it while trying to extract it; he appeared to suffer no immediate effects from this piece of steel in his bloodstream. While most addicts filter bootleg narcotics before injecting them, they do it largely because they do not want to stop up their needles with grit or splinters. Cf. *needle-trouble, boogee.*

LIT. Var. of ALL LIT UP.* See *high.*

'. . . After I do this bit,
In my old Morris chair I'll sit,
Oh, Gee! How I'll get lit. . . ."

LOAD. A *ration* of narcotics. Restricted to needle-addicts. See *bing* 1.

LOADED. See *high.*

LOBBY-GOW or LOB. A hanger-on, usually an addict, at a den or place where addicts habitually gather; he runs errands and frequently acts as a *connector.** See *to be on the send.*

LOG. An opium pipe. Also *crock, gongola, gee-stick, humming-gee bowl, lemon-bowl* 2. See *gong.**

LONG-TAILED RAT. See *stool-pigeon.*

LOUSE. See *stool-pigeon.*

MACHINERY. See *the biz.*

To MAIN-LINE. To inject narcotics into the vein. 'If you can main-line a cube of that stuff, it is on the house.' See *main-liner.**

MAIN-LINE SHOOTER. A *vein-shooter.**

To MAKE A SPREAD. To spread out the equipment for taking narcotics; hence, to prepare for a period of indulgence. May refer to a gathering of addicts who indulge together.

MARGIN-MEN. Dope runners who transport narcotics in wholesale quantities between the *big-men** and the *dealers.** Probably so-called because they operate on a narrow margin, paying off the *big-men** as soon as they collect from the *dealers.** It is profitable but risky work, for it is understood that the *margin-man* 'takes the rap' for the *big-man* if he is caught. See *to roll stuff.* Cf. *to pitch.*

MARY WARNER. Marijuana. See *fu, to vipe.*

McCOY. Medicinal drugs; hence chemically pure drugs as contrasted to bootleg drugs. See *cotics.* Cf. *dynamite* 1.

MEDICINE. 2. Morphine. See *cotics.*

MEET. An appointment, usually with a dealer or peddler. See *to keep the meet, to blow the meet.*

MERCHANDISE. See *goods.*

MEZZ. Marijuana. Probably derived from the name of a well-known 'swing' conductor and composer. See *fu, to vipe.*

MISS EMMA. Morphine. See *cotics.*

MOUTH-HABIT. 1. A narcotic habit which is satisfied by taking narcotics orally. Found chiefly among beginners and accidental addicts; held in contempt by experienced addicts. Sometimes *gowsters** are made by first establishing a mouth-habit unconsciously, then being induced to transfer the desire to the needle. Also *scoffing.* Cf. *needle-habit.* 2. Specifically, an opium habit which is sustained by swallowing the *yen-pok** with black coffee.

MOUSE. See *stool-pigeon.*

MUTAH. Marijuana. See *fu, to vipe.*

NARCOTIC-BULLS. Federal narcotic officers. See *gazer.**

NARCOTIC-COPPERS. See *narcotic-bulls.*

NEEDLE-FIEND. 1. An addict who takes narcotics through the hypodermic. See *ad, needle-yen.* 2. An addict who makes a kind of fetish out of the needle and enjoys dallying with the needle when using it, often pricking himself several times preliminary to actually taking the drug. Such an addict gets pleasure from inserting an empty needle or taking injections of water, aspirin, or amytal when he cannot get drugs. Cf. *needle-shy.*

NEEDLE-HABIT. A narcotic habit which is satisfied with the hypodermic needle. Cf. *mouth-habit.*

NEEDLE-SHY. A phobia, either permanent or temporary, which manifests itself in a revulsion against using the hypodermic needle or seeing it used.

NEEDLE-TROUBLE. Mechanical difficulties in making an injection; usually caused by clogging of foreign matter, breakage, or leakage of air. Cf. *boo-gee, to lip the dripper.*

NEEDLE-YEN. 1. A desire for narcotics taken hypodermically. 2. A desire for dallying with the needle as described under *needle-fiend.*

To Be OFF. Var. of To Be OFF DRUGS.* To be temporarily freed from the habit. Cf. *to be on.*

OIL-BURNING HABIT. A ravenous appetite for drugs; probably a metaphorical variant of *lamp-habit,* perhaps related to *oil-burner* from race-track argot.

To Be ON. Var. of To Be ON DRUGS.* To be addicted and actively indulging the habit; refers to a regular consumption and not to *joy-popping** or a *chippy-habit.*

To Be ON THE SEND or TO HAVE SOMEONE ON THE SEND. To obtain drugs through a runner or intermediary who makes the connection for a fee or for a share of the purchase. See *connector,** *connection-dough, lobby-gow.*

To Be ON THE UP AND UP. See *to be away from the habit.*

ORANGE-BOWL. 1. See *lemon-bowl* 1. 2. See *lemon-bowl* 2. 3. A large half-orange shell scraped thin and used as a shade for an opium lamp; this shade reflects the heat and enables the addict to *tchi** the *pill** evenly all over.

To Be OVER THE HUMP. 1. See *to be around the turn.* 2. To build up a state of euphoria until the maximum of pleasure is reached. Once a cocaine addict is *over the hump,* he says he is *coasting** or *in high.*

PANIC. A scarcity of drugs in a certain city or locality as a result of a raid at the source of supply. Cf. *big-shot connection, to shoot yenshee.*

PAPER. Var. CIGARETTE PAPER.* A bindle of drugs, especially *burnese** or heroin.

PENITENTIARY-SHOT or PEN SHOT. See *pin-shot, point-shot* 2.

To PICK (SOMEONE) UP. To provide narcotics for an addict, or to administer a shot.

PICK-UP. 1. A *ration* of narcotics, usually injected. See *bing* 1. 2. See *bing* 2.

PIDDLE. Var. of PITAL.* A hospital or sanatorium where a drug addict may be treated. Also *pogie.*

PIECE. 2. Theoretically an ounce of drugs, especially morphine. Among dealers or wholesalers a *piece* seems to indicate a full ounce; among addicts it seems to have a wide and loose usage meaning a large *bindle** of varying size; few underworld addicts ever purchase a full ounce at one time. Such terms as *half-piece, quarter-piece, eighth-piece* seem to retain the meaning half-ounce, quarter-ounce, etc.

PIN-SHOT. An injection of narcotics made with a safety-pin or other sharp instrument and a medicine dropper; an opening is made in the skin with the pin and the dropper forced under the skin. Distinguished from *point-shot* 1, *q.v.* This usually results in a *skin-shot.** Also *penitentiary shot.*

PIPE-FIEND. An opium smoker. The word *fiend* appears to be an archaic argot word now replaced by more modern synonyms; it survives in such combinations as *pipe-fiend, needle-fiend,* etc. The term *dope-fiend,* while it has become almost standard English, is practically taboo among underworld addicts.[11] Also *pipie, gowster,** hop-head,** yenshee-boy.*

PIPIE. See *pipe-fiend.*

To PITCH. To retail narcotics in small quantities. Also *to push, to shove, to shove shorts, to push shorts,* with somewhat specialized meanings. Cf. *to roll stuff, margin-man.*

PLANT. 3. Equipment for taking narcotics, or materials from which such equipment can be made, concealed about the person or in one's cell in prison. See *bundle.***

To PLAY AROUND. 1. To begin to take small *pleasure-shots* now and then and to cultivate a *chippy-habit.* Also *to dabble.* 2. For an addict who is *off* drugs to return to them little by little with every intention of being very careful not to *kick-back;** however, he usually wakes up *sick* some morning and finds himself with a *habit.*

To PLAY THE NOD. Var. of To GET THE SCRATCH AND THE NOD. See *charged.*

PLEASURE-SMOKER. One who smokes opium irregularly but does not become addicted; a genuine *pleasure-smoker* is not merely *dabbling* or playing around; he smokes irregularly for a period of years without becoming addicted, or never becomes addicted. Cf. *joy-popper,** chippy-habit.*

PLEASURE-USER. The same as *pleasure-smoker* except that it is generalized to include all types of drugs. See *chippy-habit.*

POGIE. A hospital. See *piddle.*

POINT. 1. The hollow needle through which the injection is made. See *lay-out* 2, *point-shot* 1. 2. Any substitute for a hypodermic needle, especially a sewing-machine needle. See *tom-cat.*

POINT-SHOT. 1. A type of injection taken when a hypodermic needle has been broken and cannot be replaced. The point of the needle is inserted into the vein or under the skin and the glass shank of a medicine-dropper slipped down over it so that the solution can pass into the blood when the bulb is pressed. Distinguished from *pin-shot.* 2. An injection taken with a substitute for the hollow needle, especially a sewing-machine needle from power sewing machines used in prisons. See *tom-cat, pin-shot.*

POISON. A physician who will not sell narcotics to an addict. Cf. *right-croaker.*

POLLUTED. See *high.*

POTIGUAYA. The seed-pods of marijuana after the leaves have been stripped; crude marijuana. Erroneously defined in Part I.

PROD or PROP. See *bing* 1.

To PUFF. See *to roll the log.*

---

11. I have never heard an addict refer to himself or another addict (unless he meant to be insulting or jocular) as a *dope-fiend.*

'I'm gonna take my gal along,
We'll kick around the gong.
She'll sing that pipe-fiend song. . . .'

To PUSH. To peddle narcotics, especially as a sub-agent or small-time dealer. See *to pitch.*

To PUSH SHORTS. The same as *to push,* with the inference that the peddler handles *shorts* or *short-pieces;** hence that he deals in small quantities.

To PUT THE CROAKER ON THE SEND FOR A JOLT. See *to frame a twister.*

QUARRY-CURE. One form of *cold-turkey** treatment in which the addicts are worked in the stone-quarry while they are *kicking the habit.** Restricted to the Chicago Bridewell and to addicts who have done time there. See *iron cure, steel-and-concrete cure.*

QUARTER-PIECE. See *piece.*

RAT. See *stool-pigeon.*

READER WITH A TAIL. Var. of READER.* A prescription for narcotics, probably illegally issued, which is being traced by narcotic agents. See *to write scrip.*

To REGISTER. (tr. or intr.) To apply a very slight suction to the hypodermic needle before injecting the narcotic; by this method the addict assures himself by the showing of blood in the glass that the needle has struck the vein and avoids *blowing his shot.** One aspect of *verification-shooting.**

RIGHT-CROAKER. A physician or dentist who will sell drugs to an addict; one who will *sail,* or *turn,* or *write scrip.* While most underworld addicts buy bootleg dope from peddlers, quite a number seem to be able to persuade a certain type of doctor (often addicted himself) to supply them. Cf. *to bug.*

RINSINGS. The residue of solution remaining in the *cotton** after an addict fills his hypodermic. See *to ask for the cotton.*

R.F.D. DOPE-HEAD. An itinerant addict who depends for his narcotics upon small-town or country doctors.

To ROLL THE LOG. To smoke opium. Also *to puff, pleasure-smoker.* See *log, to hit the gong.**

To ROLL STUFF. To transport narcotics in wholesale quantities. See *margin-man.*

To ROOT ON THE DERRICK. See *to clout.*

SADDLE-AND-BRIDLE. An opium smoker's *lay-out.** See *engine.*

To SAIL. See *to turn.*

SATURDAY-NIGHT HABIT. See *chippy-habit.*

To SCOFF. To take narcotics through the mouth; an archaic underworld term meaning to eat. See *mouth-habit.*

SCORE-DOUGH. The price of a *bindle* of narcotics. Also *connection-dough.* Cf. *to be on the send.*

SCRIP. Var. SCRIPT.* A prescription for narcotics. See *to write scrip.*

To SEND. To smoke marijuana. See *fu, to vipe.*

To SHAVE. To reduce a *piece* or *cube* of narcotics as it passes from dealer to dealer or from addict to addict. This term applies to morphine only; the shaving is done with a razor blade along the flat sides of the cube. Other types of narcotics are *cut.*

To SHOOT. To take narcotics hypodermically, either intravenously or under the skin. Also *to bang.** Cf. *channel.*

'. . . Oh shoot no more the main lines, Oh shoot no more today. . . .'

To SHOOT THE CURVE. 1. To purchase drugs from a peddler. 2. To connive in prison to secure certain privileges, often drugs. See *to drive in.*

To SHOOT YENSHEE. To inject a solution of any form of opium, but especially that made from *yenshee,** *gee-yen,** or the residue accumulated in a *gee-rag* 2. Injected intravenously, it satisfies an opium or morphine habit temporarily; injected under the skin, it usually causes an abscess. Most addicts resort to it only when there is a *panic.*

SHORT. Var. of SHORT-PIECE.* A small quantity of drugs sold by a small retailer or peddler. See *to push shorts.*

SHORT-GO. A small or undersized injection; the implication is that the dealer has short-weighted the addict. See *bird's-eye, go.*

SHOT UP. Under the influence of narcotics. See *high.*

SHOULDER. See *boo-gee.* Restricted to Mid-West.

To SHOVE. See *to pitch.*

To SHOVE SHORTS. See *to push shorts, to pitch.*

To Be SICK. To manifest withdrawal distress, for a description of which see *panic-man.** Many addicts are *sick* even when they are not actually deprived of drugs or *kicking the habit;** as each injection wears off, they have a mild attack of withdrawal symptoms, which disappear as soon as they take narcotics. The term *sick* is often specialized to the early-morning craving which conditioned addicts like to satisfy before they arise. Also *to feel the habit coming on, to have a habit, to have a yen, to have a monkey (or a Chinaman) on one's back, to gap.*

SKAMAS. Smoking opium. See *brick, cotics.*

SMECK or SMACK. A *bindle** of drugs, especially a *card** of opium.

SMECKER. A narcotic addict. See *ad.*

To SNEEZE IT OUT. To *kick the habit;** cold-turkey.** So-called because the addict's withdrawal distress may take the form of violent sneezing. A guard in prison may say 'You shot it in, now sneeze it out,' when an addict begs for narcotics.

To SNORT. To inhale *burnese** and experience the consequent exhilaration. See *snifter.**

SPOON, or COOKING-SPOON. The spoon (or substitute *cooker,** such as the lid of a tobacco tin) in which the narcotic solution is 'cooked,' usually with a match.[12]

To SPREAD THE JOINT. See *to make a spread.*

SQUARE-APPLE. See *do-right John.* Restricted to the West Coast.

S.S. A *skin-shot.** See *to go into the skin.*

STASCH. Var. of SACH.** Probably a hybrid word resulting from a combination of *sach* or *satch* (from saturate) with *cache.* A concealed *plant** of narcotics, usually one which an addict keeps as a last resort in case of arrest. The variety of these plants is limited only by the ingenuity of the addict. The most popular is paper or a piece of cloth—often one of the garments—soaked in a saturated solution and dried.

STEEL-AND-CONCRETE CURE. See *iron-cure.*

'We must slap them in the hole,
On the concrete let them roll,
That will fix them, Dr. H———
You've said it, Dr. K———.'

STEPPING HIGH. See *high.*

To STOOL. To act as a *stool-pigeon.*

STOOL-PIGEON. A government informer.[13] Also *long-tailed rat, fink, rat, mouse,* and several other terms which are unprintable. Cf. *paid off in gold.**

To TAKE A SWEEP or TAKE A SWEEP WITH BOTH BARRELS. To inhale *bernice** or crystallized cocaine.

To TAKE IT IN THE LINE. To take narcotics intravenously. See *to back up* 1, *channel.*

To TAKE IT MAIN. To take narcotics intravenously. See *to back up* 1, *channel.* 'Do you take it main, or are you a skin-shooter?'

---

12. 'Cooking' is done to insure complete solution and to raise the temperature of the solution to the degree at which the addict gets full pleasure from the injection. Some addicts bring it to a boil, then let it cool.

'. . . To me she'll sweetly croon,
"Daddy, here's your joint and spoon,
Now chase away your gloom.
They are your consolation."
We'll live so happily,
I'll bang her and she'll bang me,
Among my souvenirs. . . .'

13. Almost always an addict, held in equal contempt by the underworld and the federal agents; he works sometimes for money, but usually for immunity from arrest, a shorter sentence than his offense would warrant, certain privileges (sometimes drugs) which he desires, or protection from the death sentence which addicts or dealers may pass upon him. Because of the close fraternal spirit among addicts, an especial hatred is reserved for those who turn traitor. It should be noted that a *bona fide* agent or officer, even though he uses trickery in making an arrest, is not a *stool-pigeon.*

TEA or TEXAS-TEA. Marijuana. See *fu, to vipe*.

TEA-MAN. A *reefer-man** or marijuana addict. See *fu, to vipe*.

THREE-DAY HABIT. 1. See *chippy-habit*. 2. A *habit** which has not been appeased with narcotics for a period of three days, by which time the addict is in a *panic*. Cf. *to be sick*.

To THROW A METER. See *to frame a twister*.

TOM-CAT. The needle from a power sewing-machine (used in prisons) substituted for the regulation needle in making an *emergency-gun.** See *point-shot* 2, *boo-gee, pin-shot*.

TOSS-OUT. See *to frame a twister*.

To TURN. To consent to sell narcotics to an addict. Also *to sail, to write scrip* (when applied to physicians). See *right-croaker*. Cf. *to push*.

To TURN IN or TURN UP. Same as *to stool*, with the implication that the arrest takes place.

TWISTER. 3. A *speed-ball** or *whiz-bang*. 4. A fit of violent retching or vomiting of blood or mucus during withdrawal distress. 5. A *ration* of narcotics. See *bing* 1.

UP AND DOWN THE LINES. A phrase indicating that the addict has ruined his veins by accumulating deposits of scar-tissue. Also *burned out*. 'Boy, I've been up and down the lines; I'd give plenty for your arms.' See *ab*.

To VIPE. To smoke marijuana cigarettes. A special technique of inhalation is used and beginners are often 'taught' to smoke by girl employees or 'hostesses' who see to it that the customer's inhibitions are broken down and that he is convinced of the aphrodisiac effect of the drug. Marijuana is usually consumed in com-

pany with the opposite sex except among perverts. Also *to send*. See *fu*.

VIPER. A marijuana smoker. See *fu, to vipe*.

VIPER'S WEED. Marijuana. See *fu, to vipe*.

V.S. Var. VEIN-SHOT.** 1. Narcotics injected intravenously. 2. A *vein-shooter.** See *channel*.

WASHED UP. To be temporarily *off drugs.** See *to be away from the habit*.

WEED. Marijuana. See *fu, to vipe*.

WEEK-END HABIT. An irregular type of habit which is satisfied by taking narcotics in small doses for two or three days consecutively, then quitting for several days. Most practised by beginners, by former addicts who are *playing around*, or by addicts who are regularly employed and can indulge the habit only over the week-end. One type of *chippy-habit*.

WHIZ-BANG. 1. A powerful *vein-shot** composed of morphine or heroin mixed in equal parts with cocaine. 2. Any *vein-shot* in which there is a mixture of drugs.

To WRITE SCRIP. 1. For a physician to supply an addict regularly with narcotics by prescription. 'A croaker out in Peoria is writing scrip for me.' 2. See *to turn*.

YEN-SHEE BABY. The difficult bowel movement following a period of indulgence in opiates. Opium or opium derivatives dry up all bodily secretions, constipate the addict, and cause the sex-urge to abate or entirely disappear; withdrawal releases all bodily secretions in abnormal quantities and converts the addict into a *panic-man.** Cf. *to be sick*.

YEN-SHEE-BOY. Probably var. of YEN-SHEE-KWOI.** An opium addict.

YEN-SHEE-QUAY or QUOY. See *yen-shee-boy*.

8

Prostitutes and Criminal Argots

Vast changes have taken place in the subculture of prostitutes in the forty years since this study was made. During this time we have seen the passing of the parlor house, the ascendancy of the pimp, often black, over the traditional madam, and the emergence of a class of "call girls" far superior to the old-time "house girls" in intellect, appearance, and social mobility. Some of these changes have come about in response to the emergence of large-scale amateur competition, but the more important variations are perhaps best reflected in society's changed attitude toward prostitution. For instance, in the 1930s the word *prostitute* itself was taboo and was expunged from the description of the *dramatis personae* of a hit Broadway play. Prostitution was not discussed socially in mixed company and, incredible as it may seem, there were many middle-class women who hardly believed in its existence. Today all this is changed and the prostitute is freely and sometimes quite accurately portrayed in novels, motion pictures, and television. More often, however, she is romanticized or sensationalized, but the taboo on her appearance has been lifted.

The old-time prostitute was, with a few notable exceptions, a bovine type of low intelligence, no education, negative personality, and emotional immaturity. She was not expected to talk to customers and could not function on the social levels expected of prostitutes and call girls today. Contrary to popular opinion, her language was not predominantly pornographic, although she did have access to some of the taboo words which were then used almost exclusively by males. In those days these words were socially and legally taboo; today they are likely to occur not only in the latest best seller but in the feature sections of good newspapers. The terms included in this glossary had questionable status in the United States mails, even in a technical article, for in 1939 a severe censorship was still being enforced by the postmaster general, whose severity was usually surpassed only by his lack of linguistic and literary expertise. Today they seem almost quaint against the background of permissiveness which is part of the so-called sex revolution. The relation of language to behavior as part of this phenomenon is discussed in some detail in *American Speech* 51 (1976):5–24.

• • •

ABSTRACT: Current linguistic field work among prostitutes indicates that they have developed relatively little of the professional argot so characteristic of other criminal professions. This situation is explained in terms of the underworld setup in which prostitutes work and in the light of certain social, economic, and psychological factors which normally enter into argot-formation.

M OST of us do not need to peruse the reports of prosecutor Thomas Dewey's recent investigation to realize that prostitution is a flourishing institution in modern America. It is recognized as one of the oldest professions and has for centuries been associated with crime and the underworld. Today it constitutes one of our most widespread criminal activities. Yet it differs from other criminal and semicriminal occupations in that it lacks a well-developed argot. In fact, the results of several years' casual investigation in many American cities followed by two years' intensive work in one of the most extensive districts in the country are largely negative. There is always the possibility that a great body of secret argot remains untapped, but I do not believe so. At present I am prepared to go so far as to say that, with the exception of a few words indigenous to the profession, prostitutes are quite without the technical vocabulary which characterizes all other criminal groups.

The speech of prostitutes varies with their geographical derivation, their backgrounds, their education, and the social stratum in which they happen to work. While it is difficult to generalize, for it is dangerous to assume anything like a speech-norm, one might classify their speech as low-grade colloquial American. It is cheap and tawdry, well sprinkled with trite slang culled from popular songs and cheap magazines. Of the thousands of specimens I have examined, few rise above an illiterate or semiliterate level. Discarded argot words from other criminal professions are prominent; in fact, because of their natural contacts with both the underworld and the respectable upperworld, prostitutes are unconscious entrepreneurs of secondhand argot; through them much of it enters the language on more respectable levels. But they lack the sophistication to make and acquire an artificial language for themselves. The argot vocabulary that applies strictly to the profession appears to consist of less than fifty words, as compared to the hundreds and even thousands used by other groups such as grifters, thieves, heavy-men, underworld narcotic addicts, and homosexuals. Excepting occasional individual forays into picturesque profanity or obscenity, their speech is colorless. One looks in vain for the sinister vivacity of language found in so many of the groups operating outside the law.

At first thought this is surprising. But it can be explained, I think, in terms of the underworld setup in which prostitutes work and in the light of certain social, economic, and psychological factors which normally enter into argot-formation.

If we review the position of the prostitute in the crime world, eliminating those ladies of easy virtue who frequent night clubs or decorate bachelor apartments and confining ourselves to those honest professionals who sell a standard article at a set figure, we see that she has three choices. She may work *on the line* in a house supervised by a *madam*; she splits her earnings with the house and pays an exorbitant price for food, lodging, medical service, and police protection. Where white slavery or its equivalent exists, all the houses are tightly organized under gang control; if she does not work for the organization, she cannot work at all. Between the gangs and municipal henchmen, she is exploited into a life of abuse and poverty. Or, if she is more fortunate, she may work in a *call-house,* living to herself, but being constantly and exclusively available to one proprietor by telephone. She makes fair money but the market is limited, the overhead is high, and her earning days are numbered. Or, in a city where the racket is unorganized, she may *work the streets,* or share a room or *crib* with a companion, making her own peace with the local authorities.

Whatever system a prostitute may work under, she never develops a sense of trade, of group solidarity, of gang morale. She must always work as an individual, even when the machinery is highly organized. Consequently, she is perpetually on the defensive. Her rivals steal her customers, her employers exploit her, her patrons abuse her. She is never permitted to develop professional independence, which appears to be the first essential in the formation of criminal argots.

Argots originate in tightly closed cliques, in groups where there is a strong sense of camaraderie and highly developed group solidarity based primarily on community of occupation. Since prostitution, by its very low position in the hierarchy of the crime world and by virtue of its internal organization, denies the prostitute all claim to true professional status, it is obvious that professional pride is largely lacking as a motive for argot.

This stunting of professional growth by external forces has wider implications. Under our present social setup the prostitute is never able to overcome the social stigma which dogs her. She develops serious feelings of inferiority, which other criminal groups either never know or rationalize so successfully that they become sources of personal power. Hence while other groups, hardly aware that they are anything but legitimate, express their criminal smugness through mutually intelligible argot, she struggles for status and security in a world which is not her own.

Furthermore, other more highly trained criminals rise to their positions through successive stages of apprenticeship. They admire their superiors, imitate them, and work hard to master technique. Their training is rigorous, the demands upon them tremendous. They either go up or out. For the prostitute there is none of this. Once in her profession, she is taught submission by her pimp, who beats her thoroughly and regularly thereafter lest she forget her place; eventually both violence and submission become part of her badly warped sex psychology. There is no incentive, no advancement. Her speech never takes on the color manifest in the lingoes of underworld folk who are working up in the criminal world.

Prosperity is a powerful factor in the birth of criminal argot. When a given profession is making money, it tightens the protective walls about itself; it attempts to stand aloof and isolated. Increased specialized technical activity gives birth to a host of new words and phrases. Growing contempt for the law, other gangsters, and the *scissors-bill,* or decent citizen, breeds a vicious attitude of superiority; as a result, much the same sort of importance is attached to language as is attached to the secret rites of a fraternal order. The fact that the gang prospers makes it a target for underworld reprisals and *shakedowns* from the police. This external pressure tightens the organization, builds morale, and makes for a vicious circle of success. Prosperous criminals usually spend lavishly; they grow bitterly cynical and, at the same time, both sentimental and extravagant. They take what they want and shape it to their own ends. Language is no exception. They mold their sinisterly jocose professional argots into grotesque and bizarre forms partly as a result of the braggadocio born of financial and political power.

The speech of the prostitute is subject to no such pressure. She has no organization; her needs for secrecy are few, if any; she seldom if ever participates in the spoils of big-time crime. Her earnings are never more than enough to maintain her on a very modest level; more often she skirts the edge of poverty. Consequently, the tendency to "splurge" linguistically is either atrophied or missing altogether.

There is a further economic aspect of prostitution which differentiates it from other branches of crime. Most criminals, by one method or another, take what they want from their victims; the prostitute sells a standard service and depends heavily on simple commercial good-will. The sale is a simple matter, the approach stock. Since the customer must want to buy before he can be sold, the burden on the girl's ingenuity is a very light one. If one man doesn't buy, another may. There is neither incentive toward a classification of her patrons nor a psychological approach based on such a classification. Other skilled professionals depend heavily on a shrewd analytical and psychological approach, and the technical elements involved become the essence of their argots.

Nor is the work of the prostitute technical in the sense that it is for other criminals. Her function is purely biologic, and, while she has some training in performing that function, it is usually of the simple trial-and-error type. Her pimp teaches her what he has learned from other women; once she succeeds in pleasing him, she assumes that her patron will be equally delighted. But her vocabulary for discussing technique is no more adequate than that of the average semiliterate farm wife. It is limited, unscientific, vague, popular rather than professional. Perhaps it is out of deference to the self-conscious prudery of many of her patrons that she often avoids the more common crudities; perhaps it is her thwarted maternal sentiment which leads her to discuss the sex act with her patrons—when she refers directly to it at all—in patent, diminutive euphemisms. However, when she does step over the line into the salty language which Allan Walker Read[1] records in his "folk epigraphy," she does it with a vengeance and a high art. But that is not argot.

Aside from those professional elements already mentioned, there are several personal elements which interfere with the formation and growth of argot. First, prostitutes differ from other underworld folk in that they are readily reducible to a norm. Most of them are of low middle-class origin with rural or small-town backgrounds. The odor of respectability still clings faintly about them; hence the jealousy with which they guard their true identities, and the fact that they have no last names. They bring with them speech-habits firmly fixed in childhood; the only noticeable change is an effort to conform a little more closely to the obvious characteristics of city-talk.

Second, most of them are socially inadequate; great numbers of them find compensation in liquor and drugs. Their egos have shrunk, in contrast to the megalomaniac tendencies so apparent in other underworld folk. They indulge in a thousand pitiful compensatory artifices. They wear cheap, sensational evening dress even though they live in a brothel. They make themselves up lavishly. They assume high-toned names. Blonde types bleach out their hair and pose as English; brunettes, mulattoes, and Jewesses like to pass as Spanish. They claim kinship or friendship with distinguished-looking strangers whose framed photographs adorn their dressing-tables. They dramatize themselves in synthetic autobiographies which eventually they come to believe; some even couch these autobiographies in doggerel and cherish fond hopes of fame through publication. They all aspire to marriage; many of them achieve this solution to their life-problem. All these manifestations indicate a yearning for respectability which is not so evident among other professional criminals. It does not occur to the successful racketeer that he is not respectable; he is simply not legitimate. His language reflects pride in his station, a delight in competent technique, a sinister sense of humor, a sort of linguistic cynicism. Not so with the prostitute. Her underlying desire to conform contributes heavily to inability, or perhaps, disinclination, to form an argot.

Third, by comparison with other professional criminals, prostitutes are not generally of very high intelligence. They represent the residue of girls who are either unable or unwilling to find a place in any other occupation. They are not regularly employed in the legitimate sense because they are incapable of any but the simplest tasks. Those who survive the profession long enough to

1. *Lexical Evidence from Folk Epigraphy in Western North America: A Glossarial Study of the Low Element in the English Vocabulary* (Paris, 1935).

grow old in it spend their declining years over a scrub bucket. This is hardly the type of mind which produces the subtle, flickering, humorous metaphors which characterize the lingoes of other criminal professions. It requires a sprightliness of mind, a kind of creative imagination, if you will, to toy so adeptly with language, to take so obvious a pleasure in the nuances of euphuism in a minor key.

I have tried to outline briefly some of the reasons why the results of research in this field are largely negative, why our largest criminal class does not manifest linguistic tendencies which appear to be natural and indigenous to other criminal groups. If I have seemed to attach undue importance to these results, it is only because at present we know so little about the factors which motivate and produce criminal argots that even negative notes should receive rather careful scrutiny. It is only through a painstaking analysis of all the meager evidence available that we may eventually better understand the intricate jigsaw that is language.

BAG. A douche bag, standard field equipment for all prostitutes.

BED-READY. Sexually aroused.

B.F. A pimp. Also *jelly bean, p.i.*

BLACK BOTTLE. Poison, often used as a means of suicide.

To BLOW (YOU) OFF. To hold intercourse through the mouth.

BURNT. Having contracted any venereal disease.

CALL HOUSE. An assignation house to which girls are called to serve a selected clientele.

To CARRY THE TORCH. To have one's love unrequited, as a prostitute for a pimp.

CIRCUS. A sexual exhibition for customers. Also *dig, gazupie, show.*

COLD BISCUIT or COLD POTATO. An unappealing customer, or one who is difficult to arouse.

CREEPER. An accomplice (usually under the bed) who steals from the customer's clothes.

DATE. A customer.

DIG. See *circus.*

To DO IT. To hold sexual intercourse. See *trick.*

To EAT PUSSY. Cunnilingus. Also *hair-pie, sixty-nine.*

FAMILY TRADE. An arrangement whereby a very limited clientele supports several girls in an apartment.

FRENCH. Intercourse through the mouth; *French-date* and *French-girl* are analogous to parallel compounds under *straight.*

To GO IN THE BROWN. See *go up the dirt road.*

GOBBLEGOO. A prostitute who prefers intercourse through the mouth.

To GO UP THE DIRT ROAD. To practice pederasty. Also *go in the brown.*

HOOKER. A prostitute. Also *hustler.*

HUSTLER. See *hooker.*

JACK-ROLLER or LUSH-ROLLER. A prostitute who robs drunken customers.

JELLY BEAN. See *B.F.*

To LAY THE NOTE. To pay a prostitute.

LUSH-ROLLER. See *jack-roller.*

MUFF-DIVER or HIGH-DIVER. A customer (or pimp) who derives his pleasure from cunnilingus.

ONE-WAY GIRL. A prostitute who does not practice perversion with men.

ON THE LINE. Working in the red-light district or in a common house.

ORPHAN. A prostitute without a pimp.

OUTLAW. A prostitute who does not give her earnings to her pimp.

PARLOR-HOUSE. One in which a customer dances with the girls in a "parlor" and selects one there.

P.I. See *B.F.*

To POUND THE PAVEMENT or To POUND THE BLOCKS. To solicit as a streetwalker.

PUBLIC ENEMY. A customer's wife.

SIL. A prostitute's female lover (jail).

SIXTY-NINE or SIX-TO-NINE. Mutual cunnilingus.

To SPIT (YOU) OUT THE WINDOW. For a prostitute to refuse to swallow semen after ejaculation in the mouth.

STRAIGHT. Normal sexual intercourse; a *straight date*, a customer who wants normal intercourse; a *straight girl*, one who does not practice perversions. Compare *French*.

THREE-WAY GIRL. A prostitute who will take normal intercourse, intercourse through the mouth, or practice passive pederasty.

TRICK. The act of holding intercourse for money.

(A) TRIP AROUND THE WORLD. A tongue-bath.

TWO-WAY GIRL. A prostitute who takes intercourse normally or through the mouth.

To UNBETTY. To unbutton a customer. Also *unslough*.

To UNSLOUGH. See *unbetty*.

PART II

The following words relate to prostitution but are not generally used by prostitutes. They are current in general underworld speech and especially in borderline professions which in one way or another come into close contact with prostitutes — tramp musicians, narcotic addicts, white slavers. Words from the more highly specialized argots are omitted. Note the depreciatory implications of many of the terms.

BEAN-JAMMERS. Toughs who brawl in a house so that the police will close it.

BEE-DRINKER. A girl who receives a percentage of the large bills she runs up on customers in a restaurant.

BENNY HOUSE. A house that caters to perverts. See *slide*.

BLADDER. An unattractive prostitute. Also *beetle, blister, boat-and-oar, body-snatcher, broken car, bum curtain, cat, curb-sailor, dog, doll, hay-bag, nanny, nautch girl, oak door, pisga rib steak, round-heels, sloop-of-war, swinging door, tabby, tart, tomato*, each expressing varying degrees of unattractiveness.

BLOWER. A *french-girl*. Also indicated by the phrase *she stoops to conquer*.

BOTTLE HOUSE. A house where drinks are sold. Also *shock house*.

BOTTLER. A girl who works in a bottle house.

BOX-COAT. A pimp. Also *barber, bludger, boilermaker, bung, bung-kite, buzzard, calf, custom-made man, fish and shrimp, he-madam, Latin lover, Louis, lover, mack, McGimp, salmon-man, star boarder, sweetback*.

BULL PEN. A cheap house. Also *cathouse, hook-shop, nanny-shop, nautch house*.

CLIP JOINT. An establishment that uses girls to lure prospects for robbery or swindling rackets.

DOG-AND-BELL. An expensive house.

KING-BUNG. Proprietor of a house; sometimes a white slaver.

LANDLADY. Proprietress of a house. Also *aunt, madam, mother*.

To LAY THE LOG. To hold intercourse.

LEATHER. 1. The anus. 2. To practice pederasty.

MAGGOT. A white slaver.

ON THE TURF. Down and out (applied to prostitutes).

OOM PAUL. A man who derives pleasure from cunnilingus.

THE OLD THING. Syphilis.

PANEL-HOUSE. A house where customers are systematically robbed.

RAN-TAN. Profits from prostitution (restricted to white slavers).

RIDING ACADEMY. A cheap hotel where one may take a prostitute.

ROULETTE WHEEL. A woman's rectum.

STREETWALKER. A girl who works on her own and solicits on the street.

SHE STOOPS TO CONQUER. See *blower*.

The SLIDE. An establishment where male homosexuals dress as women and solicit men. Not to be confused with a *benny house,* which employs women. Some *benny houses* will provide a boy or man for special orders.

TISH. 1. Money in a prostitute's stocking. 2. A trick played on prostitutes by grifters, who appear to slip a large bill into the girl's stocking; when she takes it out later, it is only a piece of tissue paper.

TRICK-A-TRACK. An exhibition in which prostitutes figure. Also *trip to the Red Sea.*

TURQUOISE. A woman who will practice pederasty.

WAY DOWN SOUTH IN DIXIE. The act of "Frenching" a man. Also *cop a bird, lay the lip.*

9

Place Names
of the Underworld

This material is largely self-explanatory. Some of these place names were well established before the criminals took them over; others were originated by the criminals and have remained within the subculture. Although most of the cities are on railway lines marking the well-traveled East-West, West-East migratory routes followed by professional criminals, the names survive among present-day criminals who travel by car or plane. A few persist in the lingo of citizens' band enthusiasts (Bean Town, K.C., Nap-Town), but these names were generally prevalent before the CB operators picked them up so that we might conclude that, on the whole, there seems to be little if any connection between the place names used by criminals and those used in citizens' band communications.

• • •

THE tendency to coin suitable or humorous names for particular places is almost universal. Underworld folk, like persons in legitimate society, delight in applying names that appropriately express the "personality" of a city or voice the reaction of professional criminals to it. All professionals have the tendency to coin or corrupt place names, but pickpockets and *heavy-gees* (criminals who employ violence, specifically, safe blowers) seem most inclined to this activity.

Since the professional criminal is, generally speaking, a city child, most of his place names apply to cities rather than to smaller towns, unless those small towns enter into the experience of the profession as a whole. In addition to specific place names, the organized criminal recognizes four general classifications of the types of city in which he works, namely: *right, wrong, airtight,* and *rip-and-tear.* In the *right* city, the professional can operate freely by paying regular tribute to the city administration through the *fixer.* In a *wrong* one, the professional receives no protection for his rackets—a rather rare phenomenon in the United States. An *airtight* city protects organized gangs resident in the city—as long as they do not operate locally, which gives the illusion of a crime-free city. In *rip-and-tear* locales, certain mobs are given temporary carte blanche for a price, for which they may operate freely, knowing that members of other gangs in the city at the time will be rounded up to "take the rap" for the protected mob.

Behind many underworld place names there is a little anecdote or wisecrack which accounts for the name. Thus Cincinnati is known as *Death Valley* because pickpocket mobs have observed that "it is hotter than hell in the summertime and if you're not careful, you'll starve to death there." St. Paul has long borne the name of *Home* to thieves, pickpockets, con men, and professionals in the heavy rackets because they were once all welcome to make it their headquarters as long as they did not operate locally; Toledo, Ohio, on the other hand, offering similar courtesies from the days of Brand Whitlock into the era of the modern Purple Mob, has never been honored with so affectionate a monicker. Cedar Rapids, Iowa, is known far and wide as *The Hurdy Gurdy* because of a quaint custom once practiced by the police there. Pickpockets commonly carry their *fall-dough* (cash reserve to be used only in case of arrest) sewed up in the seams of their clothes. The detective force, knowing this, instituted a solemn ceremony which the pickpockets called the *hurdy gurdy* (why, I have never been able to discover); the detectives stripped all pickpockets naked, cut their clothes to ribbons in search of caches of money, returned the bundle of rags to the unfortunate thieves, then forced them to swim the Cedar River on their way out of town. And so on.

THE KIRK. Albuquerque, N.M.

THE STORMY END OF THE Q. Billings, Mont.

CITY OF THE DEAD. Brooklyn, N.Y.

GRANTSVILLE. Richmond, Va.

DOLLAR BILLS AND BRICK HOUSES. Baltimore, Md.

HOME OF THE CHIRPERS or HOME OF THE CHIRPS. Toronto, Canada.

THE VILLAGE. Chicago, Ill.

BEAN TOWN, Boston, Mass.

THE SLEEPY TOWN or THE SLEEPY CITY. Philadelphia, Pa.

LOUSE-TOWN. Columbus, Ohio.

BRASS. Butte, Mont.

MILL CITY or FLOUR TOWN. Minneapolis, Minn.

THE PEG. Winnipeg, Canada.

CRAW TOWN or THE CRESCENT CITY. New Orleans, La.

MOREAL. Montreal, Canada.

THE ROCK. Little Rock, Ark.

THE VAPOR CITY. Hot Springs, Ark.

C.B. Council Bluffs, Iowa.

KAW TOWN or K.C. Kansas City, Kan.

DODGE. Ft. Dodge, Iowa.

THE HUT. Terra Haute, Ind.

THE CITY. New York, N.Y.

YAP TOWN. Cleveland, Ohio.

THE SAINTY BURG. St. Paul, Minn.

THE SPOKES. Spokane, Wash.

CINDERS or SMOKEY TOWN or PIG IRON. Pittsburgh, Pa.

BUBBLES. Hot Springs, Ark. (rare)

THE BURG. Pittsburgh, Pa.

THE CAP. Washington, D.C

CARSON. Carson City, Nev. (The State Penitentiary is located there.)

CRAW-FISH TOWN. New Orleans, La.

CROWN CITY. Pasadena, Calif.

D.B.Q. Dubuque, Iowa.

E-TOWN. Evansville, Ind.

HIGHBROW. Boston, Mass.

THE HUB. Boston, Mass.

JACKTOWN. Jacksonville, Fla.

JOE-TOWN. St. Joseph, Mo.

JOLLY. Joliet, Ill.

KEY or THE KEY. Milwaukee, Wis.

L. Elmira, N.Y.

THE LAKE. Salt Lake City, Utah.

LUNGER [lʌŋɡer] or [lʌŋer]. Denver, Colo.

MIMMIE. Miami, Fla.

MINNIE. Minneapolis, Minn.

MOLLIE. Mobile, Ala.

THE MORGUE. Philadelphia, Pa. Criminals do not regard Philadelphia as a very lively city, which probably accounts for this bit of hyperbole.

MOSSBACK. Portland, Ore. The etymology of this name is obscure. Notes from readers would be welcome.

MURPHY. Murfreesboro, Tenn. (Important to criminal addicts because there is a *junk connection* there.)

NAP-TOWN. Indianapolis, Ind.

ON THE HILL. Natchez, Miss. This is an old-time gambler's term and probably distinguishes modern Natchez, situated on a high bluff, from old-time Natchez (and particularly the notorious tenderloin district at the foot of the bluff) which was commonly known as Natchez-under-the-hill.

PADUKE. Paducah, Ky.

THE PORT. 1. La Porte, Ind. (Reputedly a hideaway for Chicago criminals.) 2. Newport, Ky. (Formerly a hideout for Cincinnati gangsters.)

ROME. Richmond, Va. Probably so-called because it is built on several hills.

SACK or THE SACK. Hackensack, N.J.

THE SIZZLING-POT. Yuma, Ariz.

STIRVILLE. Ossining, N.Y. (Sing Sing State Prison). Also humorously known as Stirville-on-the-Hudson.

SUGARTOWN. Salt Lake City, Utah. (So-called because the State Penitentiary there is traditionally known as The Sugar House.)

T.O. Toledo, Ohio.

THE WALLOWS. Walla Walla, Wash.

WIGGINS. Erie, Pa. This name apparently derives from an obscure pun. If someone is *on the Erie* (itself a pun on *ear*) he is listening, or trying to overhear a conversation. When someone has an ear cocked for another's conversation, he is said to be *wiggins*, and such a person is called an *ear-wigger.*

THE ZOO. Kalamazoo, Mich.

Mr. Blackwell has kindly supplied me with two variants for New York City, *The Big Smear* and *The Big Onion*, from his own list of criminal place-names.

10

The Argot of Forgery

The basic structure of the traffic in forged documents as of 1941 is recorded here. In 1958 E. H. Lemert, the only American sociologist to investigate forgery, interviewed seventy-eight amateur and semiprofessional forgers of very low quality in prison and erroneously concluded that forgery as a racket was dead. I do not agree with his findings since the production and passing of forged paper has increased tremendously in volume up to the present time. It has followed the fundamental pattern described in this chapter with some improvements and refinements. The annual take, while impossible to compute, has increased spectacularly.

In the past ten years, however, a new class of forger has emerged who uses sophisticated electronic equipment to produce company checks or government checks of large denomination with the great advantage that they are as genuine as any other check processed by that computer. These forgers often lack any underworld connection and are often middle or lower-middle class employees who have been trained to operate computers. An interesting case in point is that of a government functionary from Hyattsville, Maryland, who wrote himself government checks on a computer totaling approximately $850,000 which he cashed and spent. He received a six-year prison sentence which he has reportedly dismissed as a small price to pay for his experience.

Likewise, in the area of government assistance and welfare many people without criminal backgrounds have learned to forge the necessary papers and identifications to tap the United States Treasury for considerable amounts of money. The *New York Times* (May 16, 1978) reported that fraud involving forgeries of this type amounts to twelve billion dollars a year. The *New York Times* (May 7, 1978) also reported forgery by middle-class businessmen such as the bank employee who withdrew $30,000 to gamble, the stock brokerage official who played the stock market with the company's money, and the government employee who programmed a $50,000 payroll check to himself. The *Louisville Courier-Journal* (June 14, 1978) reported the arrest in Los Angeles of a woman charged with fraudulently collecting $240,000 in welfare payments during the past seven years; added to this sum is an undetermined number of other items such as food stamps and medical services. This fraud was accomplished by using eight sets of forged IDs buttressed by forged driver's licenses and social security cards.

While the computer did not invent crime it has, nevertheless, made forgery temptingly available to an ever-escalating class of amateur forgers who have no prior criminal experience. The great convenience of this corruption is that no signs remain, only code numbers on electronic tape which can be erased at will. At the same time, it makes available to professional forgers a sophisticated technology with which to complement years of experience and highly developed grift sense. This connection is almost, if not quite, fool-proof.

•   •   •

THE BUSINESS of making and passing spurious checks is subject to sharp division of labor. On the one hand are the skilled craftsmen (*makers, designers,* or *connections*) who produce forged checks in wholesale quantities; these men are really a species of counterfeiter with an argot closely resembling that of counterfeiters. On the other hand are the *passers* who have specialized in distributing bad checks; their techniques suggest some of those used by confidence men and their argot is related to that of *the grift*. The *connection* seldom tries to pass his own product, while the *passer,* unless he is unusually skilled or pressed by circumstances, does not manufacture the checks to be passed. In this study about one hundred of the technical terms of the *passer's* argot will be considered.[2]

The racket itself is a most lucrative one. Bad checks in excess of $100,000,000 per year (according to my informants) are made by *connections* and distributed to *passers,* although by no means all of these checks are actually put into circulation. The racket is very dangerous for two reasons: First, it preys not so much upon the unprotected individual as upon organized business, which has taken steps to protect itself; second, it does not employ the *fix* so universally as do other branches of *the grift,* which of course means that it is open to severe and well organized prosecution.

The *passer* is distinguished from most other *grifters* in that he usually operates as a 'lone-wolf.' In most cases, he starts as an amateur and

---

1. Acknowledgments are hereby accorded the professional forgers (whose names cannot be given here) who cooperated so generously in the production of this study. Illustrative quotations have been supplied by professionals and do not necessarily reflect the opinion of the writer. I must also recognize the assistance of my wife, Barbara S. Maurer, both in field-work and in the tedious work of verification.

2. In this study only the senses which apply specifically to forgery are given. Many of these terms have numerous applications in general underworld argot, in prison argot, and in the specialized argots of various criminal professions, but no attempt is made to register the variant meanings here.

makes his first contact with the organized racket when he goes to prison. It is here that he perfects his technique and learns the professional argot—a rather unusual linguistic situation within *the grift*. As a rule he has little occasion to use it outside prison walls.

His work is done in the intervals (averaging perhaps one to two years) between prison sentences. Because of his frequent *falls* he suffers from chronic *bull horrors;* there is deeply imbedded in his mind a fear of stoolpigeons.[3] This causes him to keep to himself, avoiding the hangouts frequented by other *grifters*. Often he is a drug addict. Perhaps his solitary habits explain the relative paucity of argot emanating from his profession.

There are, of course, many types of *passer,* each with his own specialty and each constantly working out new aspects of the racket in order to keep ahead of the law. Following are two samples of the argot *en bloc,* taken from men of long experience:

I

—— was one of those gees who always stayed in a burg over a Sunday after he'd made a Saturday spread. He's wandering around in the skid-road when he's pulled into a gyp joint. He lets this guy sell him a Simple Simon hoop with a lumb of carbon in it as big as a chunk of coal. He gets by with it and gets a dub or more in change. Meanwhile he meets some wrong twist and figures he'll use her in working the broad joints. Then what does he do but get lushed up with this twist and tell her about the hoop. She wants the hoop and when he don't come across, she sneaks out of the joint and fingers him. . . .

II

I had a good connection and a machine and plenty I.D. But the heat was on the pay-chees I had been laying, so I chased Whiskers all day and wound up with a bunch of assorted stiffs. I figured the alarm sheets were out ahead of me so I ditched all the paper but the Whiskers stiffs. I had a good front, so I had no trouble papering the burg with these stiffs. They were all for forty bucks and some odd scatter. I also had a jug stiff for five C's, but I donickerized it because I knew the Pinky had my mug scattered around the jugs. I blew the burg that same night with about six yards and teamed up with —— for a Saturday night spread.

GLOSSARY

ALARM SHEET. 1. A warning issued by any protective organization which is trying to apprehend a *passer* or forger. See *scrip* 1. 'I walked up to the window with a check in my hand and noticed a teletyped alarm sheet there with my own description on it.'

2. Periodical publications of merchants' associations bearing descriptions of forgers and their activities. See *scrip* 1.

BLOW-BACK. Money refunded to a victim in order to forestall prosecution. *Paperhangers* use this method less frequently than do other types of *grifter*.

3. The stoolpigeon constitutes a much more potent danger to the forger than to any other criminal because of the *alarm sheets* which are broadcast as he works. Thus the stoolpigeon needs only report the presence of a certain forger in a certain city, and detectives can arrest him immediately on the strength of charges, photographs, and fingerprints already on file.

The large protective agencies discourage it, but small hotels and stores can usually be *fixed* in this manner. The *blow-back* is most frequently used to *square a beef on a stir stinger*, that is, to accept parole from a certain prison with the knowledge that the criminal will be moved immediately to another city to face an old charge which can be *fixed* with a *blow-back*. 'Send a kite to the twist and have her raise dough for a blow-back and mail it with a sob story. He might fall for it if he hasn't been burnt lately." Cf. *sticker* 2.

The BOOK. A telephone directory, especially the yellow 'classified' section from which the *passer* compiles his sucker list. 'Paperhangers often compare notes on the book in order to exchange pushovers.' Cf. *pushover*.

BOUNCER (sucker word). A bad check. Used by *paperhangers* only when quoting an outsider who does not know the argot. 'The guy said he had enough bouncers to paper his house.'

BRIAR. Among forgers, a jeweler's saw which can be rolled compactly and hidden in a fountain pen, or concealed between the upper teeth and the gums. Carried by many *paperhangers* in the hope that they can escape from the police holdover before they are transferred to the county jail, from which escape is more difficult.

BROAD JOINT. A store which sells women's apparel. 'Prospects are always pretty good in a broad joint as women managers fall for a pretty check and a good line of chatter.'

BUILD-UP. 1. The purchase made, the presentation of the identification papers, etc. which precede the passing of forged *paper*.
2. The confidence talk which convinces the merchant about to be victimized.
3. The character assumed by the *paperhanger*. See *front*. Also *the business* 2.

BULL HORRORS. A jittery condition which *passers* (along with some other types of criminal) develop as a result of the constant fear of being identified and arrested. *Bull horrors* probably account for the many superstitions in which *paperhangers* believe, i.e., going past a police station will bring on arrest before nightfall; meeting a cross-eyed person brings bad luck; throwing one's hat on a bed will bring on disaster; meeting an ex-convict with whom one has served time presages arrest, etc. Cf. *jitney worker*.

BURNT UP. (Business institutions) so well protected that they are difficult or impossible to victimize with forged checks. 'Hotels are so burnt up that it hardly pays to try to lay a stiff there.'

The BUSINESS. 1. A *paperhanger's* outfit comprising checks, identification papers, fountain pen, and sometimes ink-pads, check protector, stamping outfit, etc. Also *lay-out*.
2. The confidence talk which goes with passing the check. 'I gave him the business when I came back to pick up the suit.' Also *build-up* 2.
3. Questioning or examination at the hands of the merchant or his credit manager. 'The credie gave me the business and then fell for the stiff.'

CERT. A forged certified check, considered the very best thing in bad *paper* by the professional. They are difficult to make and difficult to pass because certified checks are not often used in ordinary commercial channels; hence they require a special *build-up* and are usually used for down payments on automobiles, in the purchase of real estate, etc. See *stiff* 1.

To CHASE WHISKERS. 1. To follow the mailman, rifling mailboxes for bills which can be used to cash checks as described under *store worker*.
2. To rifle mailboxes for government checks, now largely W P A checks. See *Whiskers stiff*.

To COLLY. To understand. 'There's fuzz in the back. Don't you colly?'

CONNECTION.[4] 1. A professional forger, often also a counterfeiter, who supplies the *paperhanger* with forged checks in lots of 100 or more at $1.00 to $2.00

---

4. One informant notes: 'I have always thought that someone in the game should invent terms which would differentiate the various meanings of this word. *Connection* is too broad, too general, and is in use for all sorts of rackets and schemes.'

apiece, made out in the names and amounts specified by the *passer,* and mailed, expressed, or supplied personally to the operator. If the *paperhanger* is well known, he can get all the checks he needs on credit; otherwise he pays cash. This type of *connection* is well equipped to supply anything from a government bond to a $100 bill or a forged will. 'Connections for hot paper are usually closely related to connections for queer and junk and any good connection can start one on the right path to a fence.' See *designer.*

2. An ordinary printer who can be induced to supply an operator with blank checks printed in the name of a non-existent business; the operator then does his own forging with a fountain pen, a check-protector, and a stamping outfit.

CONSENT JOB (rare). An inside job in which the sales-person in a store will accept a bad check in return for a percentage. Cf. *finger's end.*

To COP A PLEA. To plead guilty (general). *Paperhangers* usually plead guilty at the earliest opportunity so that they will be safely in prison before their record catches up with them. Some prefer to work in states like Wisconsin or Washington which do not have grand-juries and where consequently there is no delay for an indictment. Cf. *sticker.*

CREDIE [krɛdɪ]. A credit manager. See *Joe Goss.*

CREDS. Credentials. See *I.D.*

CROAK SHEET. An insurance policy such as may be obtained by mail and used as identification. Seldom used by professionals, favored by amateurs and smalltimers. Cf. *I.D.*

DAMPER. A cash-register (general) but specialized by *paperhangers* to mean a bank. Also *jug.*

DAMPER PAD. 1. A check-book.

2. A bank-book. 'That was a sweet set-up. I had the guy's own I.D. and his damper pad too.'

DESIGNER (rare). One who makes plates

for money, checks, or bonds; a counterfeiter. *Maker* is the commonly used term. 'A man on the racket who used *designer* would be accused of being highbrow.' See *connection* 1. Cf. *scratcher, sheet-and-scratch man.*

DIG. A hiding place for contraband. See *plant* 2.

THE EYE. The Pinkerton Detective Agency, or a representative of that agency. 'The Eye is easier fixed than a W.J. Why? Because his racetrack activities make him a natural for the fix.' Also *Pinky.* Cf. *W.J.*

FAKE. Loosely used for a forged check or other spurious document. (See *stiff* 1.) This does not refer to its spurious nature, but is a general term used when one cannot remember or does not wish to refer to any particular object, or rarely, when he wishes to conceal the topic under discussion. Synonymous with 'thingamajig' in legitimate usage.

FALL DOUGH. Money concealed on the person to be used in case of arrest. The *paperhanger* differs from other *grifters* in that he seldom *fixes* directly or through a *fixer* since, once arrested and identified, there are so many complaints against him from other stores or communities that it would be impossible to *fix* them all. He uses his *fall dough* to make it easier for him when he goes to jail or to the penitentiary. 'I know what a C-note in fall dough will do for me when I check into the big-house.' Cf. *the fix.*

FIDDLE. Clipped form of FIDDLE AND FLUTE. A suit of clothes, one of the favored purchases of the *paperhanger* who wishes to cash a forged check. Also *frock.* Not to be confused with *front,* q.v.

FINGER'S END[5] (rare). The 10 per cent share given the accomplice for a *consent-job,* q.v.

The FIX. An arrangement whereby, for a percentage paid to the officers of the law, *paperhangers* are permitted to work (rare). 'Milwaukee was at one time on

---

5. One operator comments: 'There should be another word used for this idea. *Finger,* properly speaking, is one who squeals, snitches, puts the finger on a guy, etc. There is another term denoting this *cut* for an accomplice but I cannot recall it, try though I have for several days.' I have been unable to locate it, if it exists.

the fix list. A lawyer there who was related to Arnold Rothstein guaranteed that if there was a sneeze during the spread, he would spring.' Cf. *blow-back, fall dough.*

FLASH. See *front.*

FLOP or FLOP JOINT. 1. When the racket calls for a transient address, the *paperhanger's flop* is a leading hotel where he registers under the name he is using on his checks. He does not live here, but in a small obscure hotel. Cf. *plant* 1.

2. When the racket calls for local status, the *flop* is an apartment in a rather exclusive residence district. If the racket calls for a *build-up* of weeks or even months, the criminal may occupy this apartment and become well established in the community; otherwise, he never fraternizes or develops local contacts.

FLOP PLANT. A place of concealment for extra *paper* made out in one identification, used by a *passer* while he is working with *paper* made out in another name. As contrasted to the *keister* plant, it is a place of concealment in the hotel room, under the rug, beneath the mattress, or in the hollow bed posts. Cf. *plant* 2.

To FLY A FLAG or CARRY A FLAG. To go under an alias.

FRIDAY FACE. A gloomy face; a 'sourpuss.' Probably so called because the *paperhanger* does most of his work on Saturday and is often broke by Friday.

FROCK (obsolescent). See *fiddle.*

FRONT. Any clothing, conversation, etc., which a *paperhanger* uses to make his identification seem authentic. Also *flash.* See *scissorbill front, white-collar front, working-stiff front.*

FRONT OFFICE. Primarily a prison phrase, but specialized by forgers to mean detective headquarters. "The fuzz picked me up on S.P. and took me into the front office for a round."

GAGERS. [gedʒɚz]. The eyes. 'When Camera-Eye McCarthy levels his gagers on you, you might as well cop out.'

To GET A RANK. See *to rank a play.*

To GO FOR A STIFF. For a merchant to accept a forged check. 'He had so much larceny in him that he went for that stiff a-flying.'

GRAB JOINT. A cheap store usually located on the *skid-road* and characterized by an employee standing out in front to pull customers in. Because of the very high profits made by these stores, they are willing to take a chance on cashing a check in order to make a sale. Also *gyp joint, jerk joint.*

GYP JOINT. See *grab joint.*

To HANG ONE'S SELF. 1. See *to rank a play.* 'The poor sap had the mark sold on the stiff, then hung himself by gabbing too much.'

2. To make a bad impression. 'The rapper got all balled up on the stand, but the beak had made up his mind on account of my record and practically told the jury to settle me. So you see I hung myself without opening my trap.'

To HAVE A TAIL. For a *paperhanger* to be followed by someone (usually a detective) while he is working or between operations. 'And if a merchant refuses a stiff, the paperhanger often gets so thoroughly convinced that he has a tail that he will blow the burg even though he has spent a week arranging for the Saturday spread.'

HEKTOGRAPH SIG. A signature lifted from a genuine check or a letter with a gelatine substance; a genuine ink signature will yield two or three very convincing signatures in the hands of a skilled operator; however, this method is used only by one who happens to know that an individual has a large checking account, and who signs a personal check with the hektograph, opens a commercial account in a local bank, and waits for the forged check to clear.

HOLD. See *sticker* 2.

HOOSIER STIFF. See *sucker stiff.*

I.D. The identification used by *paperhangers* to make their checks convincing. For big jobs, these papers may be prepared and supplied by the *connection;* usually the operator supplies his own in the form of letters mailed to his local address, a driver's license, etc. 'A passer never offers to show his I.D. until the credie asks for it.' Cf. *croak sheet.*

INSIDER. The inside coat pocket where a *paperhanger* usually carries his paper and his identification. See *prat kick.*

JERK JOINT. See *grab joint*.

JITNEY WORKER. A small-time worker who specializes in very small checks—often $5.00 or less—because he is not likely to be returned and prosecuted for so small an amount. 'The professional looks with some scorn on a jitney worker, although he is often an operator who was at one time up in the dough but has lost his nerve due to frequent falls and jolts. He has an aggravated case of bull and stir horrors.' Cf. *bull horrors*.

JOE GOSS. The credit manager or any individual authorized to O.K. a check. From the Australian rhyming argot *Joe Goss, the boss*. '. . . she says to him right in front of the female Joe Goss, "Why, dear, can't you write the lady a check to make up the difference?" ' Also *credie*.

JUG. See *damper*. 'Most paperhangers stay clear of the jugs because they can make you too easy.'

JUG STIFF. A cashier's check forged on an out-of-town bank. See *stiff* 1.

KEISTER PLANT. A false bottom or secret compartment in a suitcase or bag, used to conceal the *paper* which a *passer* does not wish to carry on his person. 'I always stash my paper in a keister plant, but I don't know why. It is very obvious but it eases my conscience.' See *plant* 2.

KID-GLOVE WORKER. 1. See *paperhanger*. 2. Any white-collar criminal.

LAY. The act of passing a forged check. '. . . any store displaying the Burns protective sign is always good for a lay. . . .' To LAY. To cash a forged check.

LAY-OUT. See *the business* 1. 'He tried to cuff him for a new lay-out, but the gee wouldn't stand for it.'

LUSH STIFF. A worthless check passed by a legitimate citizen or non-professional on a non-existent account, using his real name and passing it at a place where he is known. Usually he is intoxicated. 'An Honest John will sometimes lay a lush stiff when he is all lushed up.' See *stiff* 1.

MACHINE. A check protectograph.

MAKER. See *designer*.

MISS PANTYWAIST. *See store dick* 2.

MR. FAKUS. See *store dick* 1.

NUT STIFFS. Small checks passed at the end of a Saturday *spread* or on a Sunday for the purpose of paying traveling expenses. 'Nut stiffs are mostly for, say, $30, and are given for $22.50 or $25.00 purchases. They are passed to joints which can't be made for a large score, but are reasonably safe for this amount.' See *stiff* 1.

OSCAR. 1. See *store dick* 2.
2. A hotel clerk.

PAPER. See *stiff* 1.

PAPERHANGER. A professional who passes forged checks. Also *kid-glove worker*, *passer*, *paper-pusher*, *pusher*, *shover*, the last three terms being reserved for men who pass counterfeit money.

To PAPER THE BURG. To pass a quantity of forged checks. See *to plaster the burg*.

PASSER. See *paperhanger*.

PAY-CHEE. A pay-check, usualy forged on paper exactly like that used by some local industry, with simulated watermarks, often with serial numbers fitting into the company's account, and sometimes forged in the names of employees taken from the pay-roll. Some *passers* manufacture their own *pay-chees* in an emergency. See *stiff* 1.

PINKY. See *The Eye*.

P.L. A forged personal check. See *stiff* 1.

PLANT. 1. An address, usually a hotel room, where the *passer* is registered under a name which he is not using on checks. Here the operator hides the *paper* which he is not using on his immediate racket; contrary to popular belief, he usually carries on his person the checks being used immediately. Cf. *flop*. 1.
2. Generalized to any hiding place for *paper*, such as a false bottom in a suitcase, a secret pocket, a locker in a bus or railroad station (used only by amateurs and smalltimers), or, on occasion, the U.S. mail. It should be emphasized that while these *plants* are used by most professionals, their actual value is largely psychological because a *paperhanger* does not often have trouble while he is actually laying the check, but is arrested as the aftermath of work he has done weeks or even months in the past. Also *dig*, *flop plant*, *keister plant*.

3. A safe place, such as a rented apartment, office, or locker where a *passer* takes his purchases until he is ready to leave town; he may or may not take some of this merchandise with him.

To PLASTER THE BURG. Essentially the same as *to paper the burg* with the distinction that *plastering* implies rather carefully planned, large-scale operations.

POCKET OUTFIT. A small portable stamping outfit for simulating a 'certified' stamp or a company name stamp.

PRAT KICK. The hip pocket. This term and *insider* are borrowed from pickpockets and are usually the only terms generally used by *paperhangers* for pockets, since these two pockets are the ones where the check-book and *paper* are carried.

PUSHER or PAPER-PUSHER. See *paperhanger*.

PUSHOVER. A merchant who can always be counted upon to cash forged checks; a perpetual sucker whose name is handed about from one professional to another. 'Every burg has its pushovers. They are often located on the skid-road.' Cf. *the book*.

To RANK A PLAY. To excite suspicion and have a check refused. 'One time I forgot the name I was using and had to look at the stiff. That little slip ranked the play.' Also *to get a rank, to hang one's self* 1.

RAPPER. 1. The victim of a forged check who files a complaint in police court. 'If the stiff is laid on a flop-joint it's a cinch to fix the rapper and square the beef.'

2. A representative or agent (*finger-man*) for the victim; he identifies the criminal in court or in a police line up.

SATURDAY SPREAD. The grand finale to each week of preparation. Most forged checks are passed on Saturday afternoon or evening, after the *passer* has taken pains to be sure that the banks are closed and that there are no employees remaining in the bank. He has made all his purchases, arranged to have his merchandise delivered to a temporary address, or agreed to call for purchases already made on Saturday afternoon, at which time he floods the town with *paper* and moves rapidly on to the next city which he has selected. Cf. *Sunday take*.

SCATTER. The odd change on a check. 'Most stiffs are for so much and some odd scatter as they look better that way.'

SCISSORBILL FRONT. Clothing, etc., enabling the operator to pose as a workingman. This outfit may call for blue or white overalls and a battered lunch box. See *front*.

SCRATCH. A pen, especially a fountain pen.

SCRATCHER. 1. The man who actually makes the forged checks (usually with a pen).

2. Any penman who makes forged documents. Also *pen-pusher, writer of sad short stories* (prison argot). Cf. *designer, sheet-and-scratch man*.

SCRIP. 1. The description of a check worker as it is given to the law or as it appears on the *alarm sheets* sent out to merchants. Credit managers are trained to observe carefully the characteristics of all persons cashing large checks and professionals often *beat* these *scrips* by dressing to appear heavier or lighter than they really are, by using such simple disguises as mustaches and eyeglasses or by varying their mannerisms. See *alarm sheet*.

2. See *stiff* 1.

SHAMUS [ʃɑməs]. A private detective hired to protect a department store. 'The big stores with a shamus are always a pushover for the false-arrest racket.' Cf. *store dick* 1.

SHEET-AND-SCRATCH MAN A *paperhanger* who makes his own *paper*. 'In less than a year he went from P.L.'s to a sheet-and-scratch man.' Cf. *designer, scratcher*.

SIG. The signature on a forged check. See *hektograph sig*.

SIG CARD. Any card, such as a Western Union collect-card, bearing the *paperhanger's* signature for comparison when he endorses the forged check. See *I.D.*

SKID-ROAD or SKID-ROW. The cheap business district in any city; largely current on the West coast. (Probably by extension from the San Francisco water-front.) 'The district around Mission and Howard Streets would be a good example of the skid-road. It is an old-time word.'

SOUR PAPER. Forged checks, especially after one has been caught passing them. 'This is his third jolt for sour paper.' See *stiff* 1.

SPREAD. The act of passing a number of forged checks in a very short time, then leaving town. See *Saturday spread*.

To STAND A CHECK. For a racket to be well enough organized to withstand a check-up by phone. 'This pay-chee racket will stand a check, for we'll have the voice on the other end for an O.K.' Also used in referring to a long-distance check-up on forged certified checks; the *passer* can stand one such *check*, then must cease operations with those particular checks.

STICKER. 1. A warrant for arrest. 'The paperhanger probably has more stickers on him when he checks in stir than any other type of criminal.'

2. A detainer sent to a prison when a known forger or *paperhanger* is to be released; thus he may be re-arrested and held on a previous charge. Also *hold*. See *blow-back*. Cf. *to cop a plea*.

STIFF. 1. A forged check. Also *paper, scrip* 2. Cf. *cert, fake, jug stiff, lush stiff, nut stiff, pay-chee, P.L., sour paper, sucker stiff*, each with specialized meanings.

2. A negotiable bond, usually forged or stolen.

3. A letter (prison argot also).

STIFF-MARKET. 1. A *connection*.

2. A broker who will handle stolen or forged bonds.

STORE DICK or HOUSE DICK. 1. The store detective employed by large department stores. Also *Mr. Fakus*. Cf. *shamus*.

2. The floorwalker in a department store. Also *Mr. Fakus, Miss Pantywaist, Oscar*.

STORE WORKER. A woman *paperhanger* who takes monthly bills (rifled from mail boxes by a male accomplice) to the department stores from which they emanate and claims that she has been sent by her 'friend' (the recipient of the bill) to settle the account. She offers a forged check on an out-of-town bank for an amount considerably larger than the bill and pockets the change. See *to chase Whiskers* 1.

SUCKER STIFF. A forged check used by an amateur. Also *Hoosier stiff* (rare). See *stiff* 1.

SUNDAY TAKE. The profit from checks cashed on Sunday. Most professionals work exclusively on Saturday, but some (especially those who drive) arrange their rackets so that they can make expenses from checks cashed in filling stations, drug stores, and used car lots on Sunday. 'Your real professional doesn't go much for the Sunday take.' Cf. *Saturday spread*.

THE VOICE. A *paperhanger's* partner who answers the phone in a rented office in order to give verification to the identification used in the build-up. Most professionals do not use a partner.

WHISKERS STIFF. 1. A legitimate government check taken from the mails. See *to chase Whiskers* 1.

2. A forged government pay-check. See *to chase Whiskers* 2.

WHITE-COLLAR FRONT. Clothing, talk, and identification which convinces a merchant that the *paperhanger* is a salesman, accountant, or other prosperous white-collar worker. See *front*.

W.J. A Burns Detective Agency operative. 'The paperhanger does not have a great fear or respect for the W.J. and I have often heard it said that any store displaying the Burns protective sign is always good for a lay . . . probably because the merchant has more faith in the W.J. than the forger has.' Cf. *The Eye*.

WORKING-STIFF FRONT. Clothing, etc. used to convince the merchant that the *paperhanger* is a farmer or rural person. See *front*.

11

The Argot
of the Faro Bank

Well into the twentieth century faro was a very popular game in the United States, and the portrait of the huge Bengal tiger, which signified that a game was available, appeared everywhere—on the premises of casinos, bars, private clubs, fraternal orders. Although poker was probably played with greater frequency, more money passed through the faro banks because of its popularity among the high rollers. It was a rather complicated and exciting game at which a compulsive gambler could lose large amounts rapidly. It also had a reputation for being susceptible to manipulation by crooked dealers, crooked owners, crooked players, or all three simultaneously.

Today it is not played widely, though a few large casinos still maintain a bank for those who wish it, and I note that various suppliers who furnish professional gamblers with a great variety of cards and dice, both legitimate and marked or loaded, still market several varieties of expensive dealers' boxes and even more expensive faro shears for trimming *humps* and *wedges.* This indicates the faro bank is still alive and well in certain obscure localities.

I became interested in faro in the late 1930s when I was collecting material on confidence men for *The Big Con.* My interest in this subculture was twofold. First, there was then still a lucrative confidence game based on faro called *the last turn. Touches* of up to $50,000 were not uncommon in this game. Second, many of the big-time confidence men were fascinated by faro, often gambling heavily upon it. When they were *flush,* they could become spectacular suckers for it. This aspect of the game was interesting since most of these confidence men were expert cheaters at faro and liked to match wits with the dealer, who was a past master at chicanery. It would not be unusual for ten players—six of whom were con men—to be busily cheating the house as well as each other, while the dealer trimmed everybody if he could. All old-time faro players had numerous systems which they used from time to time, but none of these were really effective without the aid of the sharp wit and the skilled hand.

With the recent revival of legitimate gambling on the East Coast as well as in the Southwest, it is not unlikely that faro may be revived, for it is a fast and exciting game where large amounts of money change hands in short order. Today, with planeloads of suckers being ferried on gambling junkets to casinos, with larceny in the general public at a high level, and with loose cash flying around in unprecedented quantities, it may be only a question of time until some smart casino operator brings all three together in a happy nostalgic combination. The old Bengal tiger may stalk again behind the iron bars of his picture frame.

•   •   •

THERE IS no such thing as an honest professional gambler; he must be able to improve perceptibly upon the law of averages if he wishes to live. And most professionals live very well. They constitute a large block within the *grift*[2] and are accepted by the fraternity along with thieves, pickpockets, confidence men, etc. The status of the big-timers is rather high; some are straight gamblers, some are part-time confidence men, and some are full-time confidence men who gamble a little on the side.[3] Beneath the big-timers are hordes of small fry who grind away at their little games and hope to rise in the world some day. All of them, big and little, are cannibalistic in that they prey upon all other underworld types; a big-time criminal flush with his *end* of a *touch* is their special dish. But the wealthy legitimate gambler or would-be gambler is the prime and never-failing source of revenue. The gambler, like the confidence man, looks for the solid citizen with enough larceny in him to make him a good *mark*.

Professional gamblers work together in mobs, with partners, or alone, usually under the protection of expert *fixers* who iron out any legal difficulties. Their argot is closely tied into that of the *grift* in general, although each type of gambler has something of a specialized argot and

1. Acknowledgments: To my wife, Barbara S. Maurer, for valuable assistance in the field-work as well as in subsequent editorial work; to the old-time gamblers who have given generously of their knowledge of faro; to the confidence men for notes on *the last turn;* to Mr. Clayton Rawson of New York, who is now preparing a significant work on modern gamblers and gambling; and to both Mr. Joseph Blackwell, Jr., and Mr. Clinton Sanders of Richmond, Virginia, who brought to bear their wide knowledge of the argot of the underworld gambler in verifying, criticising, and supplementing my notes. I should also indicate my indebtedness to that distinguished old gentleman, The Duke of Bedford, for persuading me to record this colorful aspect of the American vernacular before it passes entirely from the scene.

2. For a brief definition of the *grift* and a delineation of its ramifications, see the present writer's introduction to 'The Argot of Confidence Men,' *American Speech*, 15: 113 ff. (1940).

3. The confidence-element as well as some sleight-of-hand is indigenous to most dishonest gambling; these factors will be treated in some detail in subsequent studies.

even individual mobs sometimes show a tendency toward usage which is not generally used throughout the fraternity;[4] this last is especially true of mobs who work together as a unit over a considerable period of time. Much of the gambler's argot seeps out into general underworld speech and some of it into the language of legitimate folk; in fact almost everyone who gambles at all, even to the extent of a friendly game of poker or craps, knows a little of it. The great body of it, however, remains the property of the professional and is preserved within the circle of the initiate.

So much for gamblers in general. Since faro may be regarded as the grand-daddy of all professional gambling in this country, perhaps it is the proper point of departure for a series of studies on gamblers' argot. The game, which is very ancient, seems to have been brought to the French possessions in the New World around 1700 after a stormy history in Europe.[5] It spread up the Mississippi and its tributaries and was the backbone of the tremendous gambling industry of the Middle West and South. Then it moved to the East and the Far West and, during the 19th century, became probably the most lucrative as well as the most crooked of all gambling games.[6] Most people today, even those conversant with

4. Most of the argot included in this study (which presents only a sampling of about one hundred technical terms) is strictly that of the faro players; a few words which enjoy extended or more generalized usage will be so indicated in the Glossary. Most of the better-known standard terminology, such as 'faro,' 'faro-box,' 'faro-banker,' 'faro-dealer,' 'dealer's box,' etc., which is defined in standard reference works has been omitted in favor of more esoteric material.

5. For a summary of what is known of the history of faro, together with details of the game and a brief glossary, see Herbert Asbury's *Sucker's Progress: An Informal History of Gambling in America*, Dodd, Mead & Company, New York, 1938, Chapter I.

6. Many readers will recall seeing the large framed color-print of a Bengal tiger (often realistically ensconced behind iron bars set in the frame) in the windows of saloons, lodge-halls, etc. This indicated—and usually still does—a faro game on the premises. In this connection, one informant adds: 'Your mention of the picture of the Bengal tiger brings to mind something old Eddie Duchin (Double-Dealing Eddie) pointed out to me in Seattle one night over twenty years ago. He was at that time past seventy and five cold winters and had been dealing for over fifty years, having pulled his first turn in a place owned by his uncle on St. Charles St. in the Crescent City. He was to faro what Nick the Greek is to dice and Tony Sanguinetti is to poker. He told me how the Bengal tiger was first introduced into America (it had been in use in southern Italy for many years) and how it served as an office (secret signal) between professionals. This signal was arranged by about twenty dealers and keepers who were run out of New Orleans during a reform drive, and it was agreed that certain markings on the picture of the tiger would be known to them alone, and not known to the owners of the game. One could walk up to a window in a strange town and glance at the picture and find his office. The right eye marked with red in the center meant that the house was rank and hard to beat because of spotters; the left eye meant that the house was easy to beat, etc. Eddie stated that after most of that first mob had died, been hung, or killed, that the office was passed on to close friends. That night I saw him take several yards out of the play as the man back of the can making the spread and covering the come-ons was well known to Eddie, however, not a gesture or a nod or any kind of office did I see pass across the spread. . . .'

gaming, believe the game to be extinct; however, it is not. It has become a gambler's game and some professionals who would not think of playing poker or bridge for fun are so fascinated by the game that they are virtually 'suckers' for it.

Also, it has fallen into the hands of confidence men who have built about it a successful swindle called *the last turn*.[7] Many a wealthy man who likes to gamble has learned about it to his sorrow; the nationally known ex-bootlegger who was moved from Cincinnati to Chicago and fleeced of $50,000 is typical of the *marks* for whom these men play. Within an hour's drive of the place where I now write, a *last-turn store* staffed by expert *shills* and using big-time confidence men as *ropers,* is going full blast in the midst of genteel resort surroundings. So, although faro is not dead, it has withdrawn from popular patronage to such an extent that many persons who consider themselves gamblers have never seen it played.

Honest faro is probably the fairest of banking games, since there is a very small percentage in favor of the bank; however, honest faro has not been played in this country for many, many years. We are concerned here with faro as the gamblers know it—a cut-throat game in which dishonesty knows no bounds either on the part of the house or the players. It has become a kind of high-powered sport where experts at cheating[8] try to beat a game run by men who must be even more expert if they wish to stay in business. And of course when it is run as a con-game, there is no game at all—just props, actors, and a well-heeled *mark.*

The argot of the faro bank should be of some philological interest, since it is the source for many idioms in standard American, as well as the fountain-head from which much of the argot of other more modern rackets appears to stem. As American criminal argots go, it is very old.

---

7. For details of this swindle see D. W. Maurer's *The Big Con: The Story of the Confidence Man and the Confidence Game,* Bobbs-Merrill, Indianapolis and New York, 1940, Chapter 8.

8. The inveterate faro player is not only adept at cheating but almost a mystic about cards and—although few admit it—very superstitious, a fact which is amply reflected in the numerous 'systems' for beating the bank which are indicated in the following Glossary. Many more of these systems undoubtedly exist, but players do not like to divulge them, especially if they happen to believe in their efficacy. On reading this statement, an informant adds the following interesting instance of superstition on the part of a dealer: 'I once knew a (faro) dealer at the Bank Club in Reno, who also dealt at the Owl Club in Mexicali, and of all things he was a Turk whom we called "The Rug Rider" and "Alcazabby." He was as fine a dealer as ever pulled a case card from a can. Down near the Overland Hotel was an old woman named "Ma" McGinty, who sold sheets to the divorcées and hustlers that came to Reno to trim and be trimmed in turn. Well, every night "The Rug Rider" would visit "Ma" at her stand, buy a *New York Times,* and give "Ma" a silver dollar. He did this regularly every night just before going on shift at the Bank Club. It was a known fact that "The Rug Rider" could not read English, he could not even read in his own language. . . .'

Following are two samples of it *en bloc*, taken from men who have bucked the tiger for over fifty years.

I

Some losers never beef when playing the bank, and blow about every bet, but they bleed inwardly. Some beef when playing and pound the checks on the lay-out, and cuss the old gut-puller, and say to him, 'The old thing would be in your way' or anything that would make a dealer sore, but a good dealer likes to hear an egg beef, and never says a word back but just keeps on winning about every bet the mark bets, and believe me it makes your Irish blood boil when you keep on getting whipsawed about every other turn.

In Hot Springs, one Saturday night about two o'clock in the morning we took stock, and when we turned ourselves over we found twelve fish—two pale-faces, and one saw. Honey O'Neil says, 'We'll play the saw and hold the two for Sunday jack. I'll do the playing,' he says, 'as I feel very lucky and besides the bank owes me plenty.'

Honey changed the saw in and blowed it. Then he said, 'Weed me the deuce, it's better to be behind the six than have two bucks.' So I gave him the rest of the jack, and what he did do to that old gut-puller Andy Grainger from Louisville, whose brother was Mayor there for so long! Well, when Honey cashed in we had 2800 smackers off of that two bucks. The bank did not open on Sunday, so we played around Johanna Bryant's roadhouse all day Sunday and until Monday noon. Then we came to town to finish the old tiger, and Andy was there, smiling as usual, and he took both of us for the works. 'Honey,' I said, 'Now I feel normal again, and that will be my last play at the old bank, so help me God. . . .'

II

You know the bank is about through as a money-getter around gambling houses, as it is only played in certain spots in the country. The new element coming up now don't know how to play it. Craps is fast action and that is what counts now-a-days. Faro is hard to learn how to play. You have to get your jack down fast, and when there are about ten playing and all the checks are out and all the colors, and some players are playing the same colors, you have to be smart to the bank to keep track of your checks. There might be a smarty who would nail you for a bet now and then. And if you find a bet on a dead card, you can take it if the dealer leaves it there for a minute or two. Then he sets it in the rack—but very seldom does he get the chance. A bet left on a dead card is called a sleeper. Old-timers tell big yarns about big winnings off a small sleeper. Here is one about a big winning.

Out in Tonopah, which was a boom town, they slung up houses overnight. Well, it was like this: When they put the roof on the joint where the tiger was, they left a little knot-hole in the roof. When the sun would shine through this hole in the afternoon, it would shine on the lay-out and make a spot about the size of a check. The dealer there was very nearsighted, and a certain rounder there knew it, so when the spot got on a winning card, he told the dealer to pay the white check. The dealer did, and the rounder won a grand on the light that came through the knot-hole, and the nearsighted dealer never knew that he wasn't paying a white check bet. So goes the tiger. . . .

GLOSSARY

BEHIND THE SIX. 1. The money drawer, often located behind the six-card on the faro *lay-out*. 2. Broke or short of funds, since one's money has gone into the drawer.

BOTH ENDS AGAINST THE MIDDLE

or TO PLAY BOTH ENDS AGAINST THE MIDDLE. A nonsense phrase used by faro players.[9] 'It is just a saying. When some egg is watching you play the bank and asks you what you are playing, you would say, "Both ends against the middle. So what?" '

BRACED. Said of a gambling house or gambling game which maintains very high odds in favor of the house by means of crooked games, dealers, etc. Also *brace game*. Not restricted to faro, but almost inevitably implied with relation to faro because of the nature of the game.

To BREAK EVEN. To bet against the bank according to the system whereby one card is backed to win twice and lose twice, or to win four times and lose four times.

To BREAK OFF. For a card to fail to win after winning two or more times; thus if the ace has been bet to win three times and wins, then loses on the next play, the players say that the ace *broke off*.

To BUCK THE TIGER. To play faro.

To CALL THE TURN BOTH WAYS FROM THE CASE CARD. To name correctly the cards in the *last turn*. Thus if a player had bet his money on an ace-tray or a tray-ace combination, and the last three cards were ace, deuce, tray, he would be paid two for one on the bet.

CAN. A faro dealer's metal dealing box; a faro-box. See *tell-box*.

CASE or CASE-RACK. A small abacus or counting rack used to keep a record of the cards in the order they are pulled out of the box during one deal at faro. Also *case-keeper* 2. Cf. *tab*.

CASE CARD. The fourth and last card of any one denomination drawn from the dealer's box; thus if three jacks have been played, the remaining one is the *case card*.

CASE-KEEPER. 1. The man who operates the *case* at faro. 2. The *case*, q.v.

CAT-HOP.[10] The *last turn* at faro if it happens to contain a pair and a *case card*, q.v. Cf. *the last turn*.

CHECK-RACKED. Refused one's winnings in a gambling house; sometimes because the player has broken the bank; sometimes because the house suspects the player of cheating. Not restricted to faro.

CHOPS. A system of progressive betting in faro in which the player adds a check when he wins and removes one when he loses. Barred in many gambling houses.

To COLD DECK. To introduce a stacked deck into the play. Not restricted to faro; in fact, much more commonly heard nowadays in connection with other types of card game. Used with reference to faro when it is played with the pack held in the dealer's hand (rarely) in which case the dealer would also use all the other tricks of the card manipulator. In the old days, faro dealers depended entirely upon their skill in stacking and dealing from the hand. Also *to put the ice in, put the chill in* or *put the cooler in*.[11]

COLD GAME. A game which is so thoroughly *snaked* that the player has no chance of winning. Not restricted to faro.

COLORS. A system of betting in faro by which the player bets all black cards to win and all red cards to lose, or *vice versa*, the player following one color-combination throughout the entire deal or reversing it once or more if he chooses.

COPPER. A small disc resembling a checker which is placed on a stack of

---

9. Asbury (p. 13) mentions *both ends against the middle* as a method of trimming faro cards for dishonest dealing. While I have been unable to verify this as contemporary usage, Asbury's work is quite sound historically and it is probable that his sense is the primary one, the present one being derivative.

10. *Cat* and *cat-harpen* are given by Asbury (p. 15) but I have been unable to find these variants among contemporaries. They are both probably obsolete.

11. Since the use of stacked decks, as well as the various methods of stacking and introducing them into play are, nowadays, much more widely known in other games than faro, a mere mention of the practice is made here. In subsequent studies, it will receive detailed treatment.

faro checks, thus betting them to lose.[12] Cf. *to cop, copper on and copper off.*

To COPPER A BET. To bet a card in faro to lose by placing a *copper* on the checks.

COPPER ON AND COPPER OFF. A dishonest system of beating the *faro bank* from the outside, probably invented by Kid Stevens and Jerry Daley, and worked by a mob of four, one of whom *keeps cases* while the others play. The *look-out* always shifts his eyes off the *lay-out* just as the card is being pulled by the dealer and at this instant one of the players, watching the dealer also, sees if that card is going to win; if so, he pulls the *copper* off a stack of checks previously bet to lose, and takes the bet; if the card is going to lose, he leaves the *copper* there and collects. The player moves the *copper* with a looped hair which he controls with his right hand. Stevens, Daley, and two other con-men still operating traveled over the country taking touches averaging $7,000 to $10,000 from each house they visited.

To COPPER THE ODDS. To bet all odd *case cards* to lose. A player may also *copper* the entire deal, thus betting every odd card to lose, which is known as *coppering the odds and playing the evens,* or *odd-even,* q.v.

COURT-SKIN. See *paint-skin.*

CROSS COLORS. A variation of the *colors* system in faro. The player reverses his color system at will throughout the deal.

DEAD CARD. Any card on the faro *lay-out* which no longer *has action* because the dealer has already drawn the four cards corresponding to it in the various suits, or because it happens to be the first or last card drawn.

The DOUBLE-ODD. A method of cheating for the house in faro by surreptitiously introducing two extra cards which the dealer can control. See *the odd.*

The DOUBLE-OUT. A betting system in which the *case card* is played to fall the

same way that the third card falls; it may also be applied to cards other than the *case card.*

To DRIVE THE HEARSE. To keep a record of the cards played at faro, using a *case.* Also *to keep cases.*

FARO BANK. 1. A gambling house where a faro game is set up. 2. The 'bank' for the game of faro; that is, the capital with which the proprietor backs the game. 3. The game of faro (obsolescent).

FISH-HOOK CARD. The seven on a faro *lay-out.* Not restricted to faro, but has varying meanings in some other games.

GUN-TURN. Two fives drawn from the box in a single *turn.* So-called from an old pickpocket saw:
'Two fives together
What the mark had in his leather. . . .'
Also *pickpocket-turn.*

GUT-PULLER. A faro-dealer. Probably so-called because pulling cards from the dealer's box suggests the act of gutting crayfish and other crustaceans by selecting the middle fin of the tail and pulling out the large intestine with it.

HANGMAN'S TURN. A combination consisting of a jack and a king drawn in a single *turn.* Reputedly so called from an old-time faro dealer named Jack King who was hanged for murder.

To HAVE ACTION. For any card to win or lose at faro. All cards in the dealer's box except the *soda* and the *hock* have the power to win or lose, according to the order in which they are drawn from the box.

HEARSE-DRIVER. The *case-keeper* in a faro game.

HEEL or **HEELER.** A player who consistently makes *heel-bets,* q.v.

HEEL-BET or **HEELED BET.** A type of *string bet* in faro whereby the player bets one card to win and one to lose, or two to win and two to lose.

To HEEL A STRING. To place a *copper* on the bottom of the checks when a *string bet* is made, thus *coppering* the first card and automatically playing it

---

12. Asbury (p. 15) indicates that this disc is made of copper. While this may have been true long in the past, it no longer holds; however, Asbury's note may give a clue to the origin of the term.

to lose while the last card included in the *string bet* is played to win.

HIGH LAY-OUT. A dishonest faro *lay-out* which is approximately one inch higher than the square *lay-out*. It is used with a *tell-box* which is held flush with the *high lay-out;* by manipulating his box, the dealer can make the cards move out of the box and into the *lay-out* or back, thus controlling the *turn*. Largely used for youngsters or 'suckers' who are not familiar with the standard *lay-out*.

HOCK CARD. Also HOCK, HOC. The last card in a faro dealer's box; like the *soda* card, it does not *have action*.

HUMPS. Cards in a faro deck which have been trimmed so that the dealer may locate and manipulate them at will. The trimming is done with special *shears* and may follow any of a number of patterns— all the cards stripped except the aces or other desired cards, certain cards with rounded edges, etc.[13] No longer restricted to faro. Also *strippers, wedges.* Cf. *shears.*

ICE. A stacked deck. See *to cold deck.*

The INSIDE. Participation in a game as a member of the staff of a gambling house, as contrasted to participation as an independent player. 'There is no game that can't be beaten either from the inside or the outside.' Not restricted to faro.

INSIDE CORNER. A type of faro bet taking in three cards; so called because the check is placed on the 'inside corner' of any card, thus indicating the other two cards in the *lay-out* to be included.

KANGAROO CARD or To BET THE KANGAROO CARD. A system for betting the first card at faro. The player bets his money on the card which, added to the *soda* card, will total eleven. Thus if the *soda* card was four, the *kangaroo* card would be seven.

To KEEP CASES. See *to drive the hearse.*

The LAST TURN. 1. The last three cards in a faro dealer's box, the two *having action,* and the hock card which is 'dead'. 2. A confidence game based upon faro.

LAY-OUT. A suit of thirteen spades, pasted or painted upon a board, cloth, or table-top, and used for faro. Other suits are rarely used.

LOOK-OUT. The dealer's assistant who watches for cheating and sees that the dealer does not overlook any bets, a task which, when several players are playing various systems simultaneously, may become quite complicated.

To LOSE OUT. For a given card to lose on the fourth play after having already lost three times in one deal.

To MAKE A BRUSH. To build up a small initial bet into a considerable sum. Also *to play a shoestring.* Not restricted to faro.

MARKER. A square token, usually of ivory or some synthetic, provided by the house and used by the faro player as a substitute for money provided his credit is good. He announces the value of each *marker* as he bets and is required to settle in cash after each deal, returning the *markers* to the bank.

MEDICINE TURN. The combination of the queen and nine, falling together in that order in a single *turn*. Probably so called from a play on the word 'quinine'.

The ODD. A method of cheating for the house; the dealer introduces an extra card which he can control to win 'sure' bets. See *the double-odd.*

ODD-EVEN. See *to copper the odds.*

The OLD THING. A *faro bank,* or the game of faro. The implication is that the game is *braced.* In argot sample I there is a pun on the secondary meaning of this term ('The old thing would be in your way') which is *syphilis.* This is not specialized argot.

ONE ON THE LAY-OUT AND THREE IN THE HAND. The *three-one* system

---

13. In his discussion of trimmed cards (p. 13) Asbury says that some of the 'most popular' forms included *hollows, rounds, rakes, concave,* and *convex,* but he does not describe these forms. While they were undoubtedly used at one time, I can find no survival of them in modern practice. One old-time dealer, now past eighty, says they are not now used. '*Strippers* just about covers everything today,' he said.

at faro, as used by a cheap gambler. See *three-one.*

ONE SIDE AGAINST THE OTHER. A faro system whereby the player bets the ace, two, three, four, five, and six to lose and the king, queen, jack, ten, nine, eight to win, or *vice versa.* The seven is usually barred.

OPEN BET. A faro wager playing a given card to win, so called because there is no *copper* placed upon it.

The OUTSIDE. As contrasted to *the inside,* participation in a gambling game as a patron. If a professional is 'beating the game from the outside' he is posing as a 'sucker' in order to fleece the house. See *the inside.*

PAINT-SKIN. Any court-card, as contrasted to spot-cards. Also *red-skin, court-skin.* Not restricted to faro but much used by faro players.

PICKPOCKET-TURN. See *gun-turn.*

To PLAY A SHOESTRING. See *to make a brush.*

To PLAY THE EVENS. A faro system by which the gambler plays the even *case cards* to win.

To PLAY ON VELVET. To gamble with money won from the bank. Not restricted to faro.

To PLAY THE BANK. To play faro.

POT. A faro bet taking in four cards.

RED-SKIN. See *paint-skin.*

ROUNDER. A gambler who plays largely with *stake-money,* q.v. Not restricted to faro, but faro etiquette requires that a *rounder* who wins give the other *rounders* $10 to $25 to *play the bank* for him.

SAND TELL-BOX. A faro dealer's box constructed to manipulate cards which have been slightly sanded on the backs. See *tell-box.*

SAND-TELL LIQUID. A liquid dressing used by faro dealers to prepare ordinary poker cards for use in a *sand tell-box;* it simulates sanding on the backs of the cards, thus permitting manipulation in the box.

SECOND BUTTON. A system whereby the faro player bets the *case card* to fall as the second card fell; the *case-keeper* records and gives out this information.

To SHADE. To conceal any desired movement, especially the manipulation of cards or any gambling devices. Not restricted to faro.

SHEARS. A precision cutting instrument used for trimming cards for dishonest dealing. Also used by dealers for squaring up cards after they have been used; faro cards cost $1.50 per pack and dealers like to conserve them. Evans lists one in the *Secret Blue Book* 'equipped with micrometer attachment' at $50.00.

SHORT-FARO. A simplified form of faro, much faster than straight faro and operrating with a higher percentage in favor of the bank.

SINGLE-OUT. A faro system whereby the gambler plays a card to fall in exactly the reverse of the order in which it previously appeared.

SLEEPER. A bet placed on a 'dead' card on the faro *lay-out.* In some houses it belongs to any player who notices it and picks it up.

To SNAKE A GAME. 1. To surreptitiously obtain the faro dealer's deck and mark it; this is usually done only when a box is not used; old-timers sometimes beat the bank by this method in bygone days. 2. To set up a dishonest game for fleecing 'suckers.' Not restricted to faro.

SNAKE TELL-BOX. A type of dishonest dealer's box. See *tell-box.*

SNAP. A temporary faro game set up in a gambling room or elsewhere, usually with a small amount of capital.

To SNOWBALL THE LAY-OUT. To distribute white checks all over the faro *lay-out;* the mark of a cheap gambler.

SODA CARD or SODA. The first card that shows face up in a faro dealer's box; like the *hock* card, it has no action, but is shown before any bets are made.

SPLITS. A pair of cards falling together in a single *turn;* in honest faro, this is the only advantage which the dealer maintains over the players, for the bank takes half of all the money bet on that *turn,* hence the term, indicating that the bank 'splits' the money with the players.

SQUARE-DECKER. A faro dealer who wins for the house by stacking the deck according to the systems which he has observed various players using. He is of course a skilled manipulator of cards, and nowadays may be found dealing other games than faro.

SQUARE GAME. An honest faro game (rare). The implication is that the dealer is using a 'squared deck' which has been so trimmed with the shears that cheating is minimized and players are likely to receive a 'square deal.' Cf. *humps*.

STAKE MONEY. Money borrowed by a gambler so that he can continue his play, or money given him by by-standers who believe that his luck is due to change; if he wins, he repays the loan and divides the profits. See *rounder*.

To STAND PAT TO STAND OFF AND SWITCH EVERY TIME YOU HAVE ACTION. A faro system by which the player lets all his bets ride until he has action, then reverses all remaining bets. Also known as the *stand pat* system.

STRING BET. A type of bet in which the checks are 'strung' along from one card to several others, usually consecutively, as from the deuce to the king. See *to heel a string*.

STRIPPERS. Cards trimmed for dishonest dealing. Not restricted to faro. See *humps*.

STRONGER THAN (THE) NUTS. A very crooked gambling game, literally one which shows a higher percentage for the operator than the shell-game (*the nuts*); automatically true of all faro games today.

To BE STUCK. To go broke trying to beat the *faro bank*.

SURE THING BET. A type of bet which the 'sucker' believes he cannot lose; much used in connection with the *last turn*, q.v. Regarded by some faro players as a 'sucker word' but used freely as argot by other types of gambler.

TAB. A printed score-sheet on which faro players can record the behavior of various cards as they win or lose throughout the game; the *case-keeper* records only one deal at a time. Marking this score sheet is called 'keeping tabs.'

TELL-BOX. One type of dealer's box for faro. An intricate and effective internal mechanism enables the dealer not only to 'tell' the location of the cards, but to manipulate the cards in order to deal seconds, etc. The H. C. Evans Co. of Chicago offers one in their *Secret Blue Book* at $35.00, with other 'Special Boxes' priced from there on up.[14]

THREE-ONE. A faro system by which the player bets a given card to win after it has lost three times during the deal.

The TIGER. A *faro bank*.

TRAYDEUCER. A combination of a three and a deuce drawn in a single faro *turn*.

TURN. In faro, the drawing of two cards from the dealer's box, one of which wins while the other loses. Since neither the *soda* nor *hock* cards have any action, there are twenty-five *turns* in a deal.

To TWIST THE TIGER'S TAIL. To play faro.

VELVET. Money which a gambler wins from the house. Not restricted to faro.

WEDGES. Cards trimmed with faro *shears* for use by dishonest dealers. See *humps*.

WHIPSAWED. Having lost at two different bets in the same *turn* at faro. Clever dealers know how to lead a player into this situation.

WHITE-SKIN. A spot-card as contrasted to a court-card. Not restricted to faro. Cf. *paint-skin*.

To WIN OUT. For a given card in faro to win the fourth time after having already won three times during the deal. Cf. *to lose out*.

---

14. Asbury (pp. 13-14) gives some history of the development of the dealer's box and notes that *tongue-tell* boxes sold in the 1840's for $125.00 to $175.00. He lists other types (now obsolete among faro dealers) as the *top-sight tell*, the *end-squeeze*, the *screw-box*, the *needle-squeeze*, the *lever-movement*, the *coffee-mill*, and the *horse-box*. Mr. Rawson indicates that some professional magicians use a *needle-box*, which may be a variant of the *needle-squeeze* referred to by Asbury.

12

The Australian Element
in American Criminal Argots

There is a widespread myth among professional criminals in America that rhyming slang came into this country from Australia, and indeed a number of successful Australian criminals have migrated to the United States since about 1900. Of the 349 terms collected from American criminals, only 3 percent are found to be of Australian origin, while 48 percent appear to be of British origin, and 49 percent of American origin. Most American criminals, however, firmly believed that all rhyming slang was Australian, and they characterized it as *Aussi lingo*. With the help of Sidney Baker, the well-known Australian lexicographer, and a number of American criminal informants, the situation was, I think, considerably clarified in 1944.

The rhyming slang in spoken British English seems to have been popular around 1820, though some examples occur in print well before that date. It was not then, nor has it ever been, the usage of a predominantly criminal subculture in England but simply a language fad common in the Cockney area of London. It is interesting, however, to note that in modern British detective fiction many criminals speak Cockney and often employ rhyming slang. In fact, it seems to be an accepted literary convention that criminals in Britain use this language. Note that in Shaw's *Pygmalion* Eliza Doolittle's father not only speaks Cockney like Eliza but has definite criminal tendencies even though they are crude and unspecialized. Subsequently, numerous novels and films have followed this trend.

Incidentally, much of the fieldwork for this study was done via the *grapevine*, a very effective method of communication among criminals for transmitting information accurately and rapidly. It involved the collaboration of numerous informants, both inside prison and out, who worked on the project with considerable interest. While I had used the *grapevine* in other connections, this is the first attempt I made to use it systematically for the collection and verification of data.

I have commented on rhyming slang in other places (*American Notes and Queries,* 1942; *American Mercury,* October 1946). There is a wide interest in this subject in England, and perhaps the leading authority on British rhyming slang is Julian Franklyn, who wrote the excellent *Dictionary of Rhyming Slang* (1960). In 1978 Inez Cardozo-Freeman made a survey of the incidence of rhyming argot at the maximum security state prison at Walla Walla, Washington. She produced a considerable number of new terms as well as variants on old ones, which indicates that the processes described here are still viable and operative. The Seattle area was one of those intensively surveyed in 1944. (Inez Cardozo-Freeman, "Rhyming Slang in a Western Prison," *Western Folklore* 37 [1978]:296–305.)

The reader will note evidence of censorship which seems quaint today. For instance, words like *bottle and glass, rattle and hiss, Colonial puck,* and others do not include the actual rhyming term in the definition, since such words could not appear in print. It should be easy for any reader to restore such puritanical lapses to their pristine earthiness.

• • •

O NE CANNOT work long in American criminal argots without encountering stray bits of rhyming argot (*turtle-doves*, gloves), a type of cant used by British (and especially Cockney) thieves for more than a century.[2] American criminals refer to this type of argot as 'Australian,' and most of them believe that it stems from Australia. This belief is not illogical, since many expert criminals hail from Australia and since the rhyming argot is most widely used on the West Coast. Over a period of years I have been collecting this argot and noting its geographical distribution; recently I forwarded several hundred selected items to Mr. Sidney J. Baker, the Australian lexicographer, for checking against Australian usage. The results are given in the following pages.

First, a word about this argot and its use in the United States. Briefly, its notable features are the following: Each meaning is expressed by a pair of words the second of which rhymes (or rhymes imperfectly) with the meaning. The predominant rhythm of these pairs is either iambic or trochaic and usually carries over into the meaning, *dinky-dirt*, a shirt. The key word (a shirt) is not expressed but is left for the hearer to supply. There is frequently—too frequently to be coincidental—a connection between the sound and the sense, or between the imagery and the sense, or both. There is a tendency (notably less pronounced than in Australia) to clip one term and allow the other to carry the meaning even though it no longer rhymes, as *twist*, a girl, from *twist and twirl*. There is a marked lack of technical meanings, indicating that rhyming argot has never been specialized to any criminal craft; the more highly specialized crim-

---

1. Acknowledgments: To Mr. Clinton Sanders, of Norfolk, Va., and Mr. Joseph Blackwell, Jr., of Richmond, Va. for their assistance in contributing numerous additions to my word-list from their unpublished files. Mr. Sanders deserves credit for ingeniously devising the system for estimating the concentration of the so-called Australian argot by percentage. He has enlisted the assistance of others with intimate knowledge of the argots used within the prisons mentioned in this study. Once these percentages were estimated, it is notable that few of the informants who subsequently checked them disagreed materially with them. Acknowledgments are also due the men, who, over a period of ten years, have supplied and checked the basic materials of this word-list and supplied me with notes on the incidence of the rhyming argot in various localities.

2. Eric Partridge has included some modern Cockney rhyming slang in his useful *Dictionary of Slang and Unconventional English*, London, 1938.

inals do not use much of it. It is seldom used 'straight' but appears a phrase at a time intermixed with established American argots, to which it seems inferior in strength and color. It is predominantly an 'institutional argot' (an argot of prisons), although on the West Coast and especially in San Francisco it is current among many non-criminal groups. It differs from other argots in that it has a remarkably clear-cut geographical distribution.

With regard to the geographical distribution of 'Australian' argot, four points are significant: 1. It is most prevalent on the West Coast, especially in the vicinity of larger cities. 2. In spreading out over the country (assuming a West-East movement) it follows the well-worn travel-routes of criminals. 3. It appears in isolated prisons, but is notably absent from surrounding colloquial usage, except in areas like Chicago where criminal recidivists and convicts with West-Coast experience are common. 4. There is a relatively weak concentration of the argot in the larger East-Coast cities.

The rhyming argot enjoys most of its popularity within prison walls. The following table will perhaps give some idea of its concentration within the institutions and localities where it occurs in measurable quantities. For purposes of estimation, the rhyming argot was allotted a basic vocabulary of 500 words, although it is considerably larger if all the rarer coinages are included; this figure was kept in mind when estimating the concentration of rhyming argot in the speech of criminals in any given area. Although the figures in the table are given as percentages, they have actually only a sort of index value; they give a crude but, I think, fairly accurate idea of the relative degrees of concentration of this type of criminal speech.[3]

TABLE SHOWING RELATIVE CONCENTRATIONS OF SO-CALLED AUSTRALIAN ARGOT IN VARIOUS AREAS OF THE UNITED STATES

City	Percent
1. San Francisco and vicinity	10
Concentrations within the San Francisco area	
Alcatraz Federal Prison[4]	20

---

3. Very accurate figures arrived at as a result of a statistical break-down of argot elements in any given locality are highly desirable, but under present working conditions would seem virtually impossible to secure. A complete analysis of the argot used in any one prison system would be most helpful as a point of departure for further investigation of linguistic problems connected with the criminal.

4. Alcatraz is theoretically a 'silent house.' However, as one informant who has served time there comments, 'There is no way to keep hooks from talking, and even if there was, they still have their knowledge of the lingo.'

Folsom Prison (Recidivists' Prison)[5]	25
San Quentin Prison	20
2. Los Angeles and vicinity	05
3. Seattle and vicinity	05
4. Chicago and vicinity	05
5. New York and vicinity	05
6. Kansas City and vicinity	04
Concentrations within the Kansas City area	
Leavenworth Federal Prison[6]	04
Addicts' Prison at Leavenworth	04
Kansas State Prison (Lansing)	02
7. Atlanta Federal Prison	02
8. Georgia State Prison[7]	01
9. Boston and vicinity	05
10. Reno and vicinity[8]	03
11. New Orleans and vicinity	01
12. Salt Lake City and vicinity[9]	05
13. San Diego and Mexicali area[10]	03
14. Texas Prison System[11]	07

The areas listed, including both cities and prisons, hold relatively heavy percentages of criminals. British criminals generally work out of East-Coast port cities, while Australian criminals seem to concentrate on the West Coast, although many, especially confidence-men and thieves

---

5. Several men who know Folsom Prison believe that an estimate of 25% is too high, but all agree that more rhyming argot is used there than anywhere else. Since these estimates are only relative, the figure has been allowed to stand.

6. It will be noted that the percentage of rhyming argot is higher here than in other Federal Prisons in the Mid-West and the East; presumably this is because many of the Leavenworth men have had contact with the Chicago underworld.

7. While rhyming argot is not indigenous to Georgia, some is brought to the State prison by recidivists from Atlanta who have remained in Georgia and have run afoul of the State laws; relatively few professional criminals with Federal records remain in Georgia.

8. Criminals moving East from the San Francisco area like to stop over at Reno to rest up after prison sentences, and to try their luck at the gaming tables.

9. This area apparently owes its high percentage to the fact that many West-Coast criminals who 'pack the racket in' go there to settle down. 'For many years the Lake was known as a right city and it still has the reputation of being a good place to cool off in,' comments one professional. 'Many retired prostitutes and wealthy madams go there to live when they go off the racket.'

10. Here the situation parallels that at Reno; the criminal moving East from the Los Angeles area pauses in this area to gamble and get his breath. Some are picked up and sent to the Nevada State Prison, carrying the rhyming argot there.

11. The Texas prisons contain a rather high percentage of men who have done time on the West Coast. Between Mexicali and New Orleans there are very numerous *cooling-off spots* or hide-outs for West-Coast criminals. In addition, many thieves from the West Coast work the territory comprising Texas, Oklahoma, Arkansas, and Louisiana.

working England, South America, and the Continent, appear in Boston and New York; both occur in very small numbers compared to native American criminals. By the same token, these seaports, both East and West, are points of departure for American criminals who work the steamships and tourist cities of Europe and the Mediterranean on the one hand and China, Australia, and the Far East on the other. Thus it is obvious that American criminals are not at all dependent upon immigrant criminals from either England or Australia for their knowledge or rhyming argot.[12]

Now for a few remarks on the use of rhyming argot in Australia, condensed from extensive notes supplied me by Mr. Sidney Baker, who is perhaps better equipped than anyone else to deal with that subject. First, we must remember that Australia, even as our own early colonies,[13] was heavily settled by transported British criminals; in fact, transportation did not cease there until 1868. The result was that much criminal and semi-criminal slang was absorbed by the general population. Until about 1880 Australia was mainly a man's country; thereafter a relative balance between the sexes was established. There has been a terrific carry-over from the early days, which can be noted, for instance, in the strong masculinization of hypochoristic forms and the marked decolorization of numerous vulgarisms, but principally in the few categories into which Australian slang may be divided; it is rather a *lingua franca* of the public than the possession of special groups.[14] There appears to be developing

---

12. In this regard, it is interesting to note that few specialized criminals use much of this argot. Those who do know it appear to have learned it in prisons or from British or Australian criminals whom they have met in their travels. One informant suggests: 'The roving British and Australian thief have played their part in bringing the lingo to the racketlands of America, but the ones who have really brought the Australian lingo into our stream of speech have been the roving American thief and the good-time bims (chorus girls and fortune hunters) who have played between Frisco, Shanghai, and Sydney for the past fifty years. While we are on the subject let me tell you that the majority of the first-class hookers and the big-shot hooks and first-class con men and hustlers of Frisco, Seattle, Los Angeles, and other Western cities know the ports of the Orient as you know the Campus at Louisville.' The rhyming argot carries words for general purposes, but shows no tendency to specialize itself or to adapt itself to the needs of any particular profession. It is almost totally devoid of technical words.

13. There are still remnants of the traditions of transportation to the American Colonies in the American underworld. I have in my possession some envelopes in which an old-time thief mailed me his letters; in the upper left-hand corner he usually wrote some synthetic name or his initials, followed by a jocular and ironic 'F.F.V.'

14. On this point Mr. Baker notes: 'There are, of course, certain terms peculiar to con-men, thieves, harlots, etc., but they are not of sufficient bulk to be worthy of the description group-slang.' He adds that it might be possible to divide this Australian underworld slang into three groups, all decidedly overlapping: 1. General criminal

in Australia a well defined underworld argot but it is by no means stabilized. The vastness of the country, its small population, and the very small present-day underworld group all combine to make the creation and preservation of a strictly criminal argot difficult.

As the population increased it concentrated in cities, especially in Melbourne and Sydney, from which Australia's most accomplished vulgate emerged, along with the *larrikin* or hoodlum, who in his scores made up the *pushes* or gangs—brutal, tough, villainous, and a brilliant user of slang. The great days for the larrikin were between 1880 and 1900, although his antecedents are much earlier and he still thrives exceedingly well. But in those twenty years he did amazing things to the language, coining hundreds of new terms which have bred into thousands and form an exceedingly large proportion of the indigenous and current slang. The *larrikin* and the *push* represent what is probably the greatest leveling influence in Australian life, the common ground on which argot, slang, and colloquialism have met and fused.

Rhyming argot is used in Australia, but not to any great extent, and rather by the populace as a whole than by the underworld. Because of the widespread impression to the contrary in the United States, I quote Mr. Baker verbatim:

> I don't know to what unkind stroke of destiny is due the reputation in the United States that the Australian crooks talk in rhyming slang. . . . Nothing could be farther from the truth than the assertion by G. Irwin (*American Tramp and Underworld Slang*, 1931, p. 20) that Australian users of slang and cant speak 'with an affected English accent' in 'rhythmic and colorful couplets.' I have yet to hear a genuine Australian crook who would bother himself to imitate an 'English' accent; and I am sure that he would be unable to speak in 'couplets' for the simple reason that his greatest failing is to clip and abbreviate. . . . For instance, the Cockney rhymester would use *frog and toad* for road; *plates of meat* for feet; *almond rocks* for socks. It is unlikely that the Australian would get past *down the frog* for down the road; *plates* for feet; *almonds* for socks, and so on.[15]

---

slang. 2. Prison slang. 3. The less well-known forms of larrikin slang. However, in none of this slang is the rhyming system prominent. He gives samples of Australian criminal argot, of which several follow: *dog*, a railroad detective; *steel-jockey* or *scaler*, a train-jumper; *smear*, to murder; *in the line*, under police observation; *seventeener*, a corpse; *dump*, a cache for stolen goods; *squirt*, a revolver; *peter-school*, a gambling den; *yike*, a row or argument; *jay, snack, dill, soda*, an easy victim; *chinkie, chow, pong, dink, pat, paddy, dingbat*, a Chinese; *lash*, a trick; *camp*, any lodgings; to *twist, touch* or *rib* (a person), to swindle or cheat him; *scone* or *hot-scone*, a detective (by rhyme upon John, a policeman), probably influenced by the Australian use of *to go hot-scone for a person*, to abuse him. Says Mr. Baker, 'Here are just a few more examples to show that our underworld has the beginnings of an argot of its own; but the majority of these expressions are not confined solely to crooks.'

15. Letter, May 16, 1942.

Certainly Mr. Baker's view of the situation is reflected in his recent *Dictionary of Australian Slang*,[16] which lists only about two dozen rhyming terms in a collection of over 3,000 slang items. I say 'about' two dozen because rhyming slang does not always appear as such, as Mr. Baker points out in the case of *amster* or *ampster,* a crook's confederate, also known as a *ram;* a rhyme was made *(amsterdam,* a *ram),* but shortly the phrase was cut back to *amster,* and the origin, as well as the fact that it was rhyming argot, is obscured.[17] Hence I may have missed a few terms which are, or were, rhyming argot. We are safe, I think, in estimating the concentration of rhymes in Mr. Baker's collection at well under 1%. My figures show a much higher incidence of this type of slang in certain localities here than do Mr. Baker's for Australia.[18]

Perhaps the best summary—and the only one, to my knowledge, by an Australian scholar—comes from Mr. Baker's most recent book.[19] Says he:

Reviewing the subject as a whole it can be said that rhyming slang has had much smaller currency in Australia than is generally realized. Australians are inclined to resist its use if only for the fact that it is a dull, unimaginative, foolish type of slang, and that there is little of the sharp, business-like nature of other Australianisms about it. What little authentic rhyming slang there is in this part of the world will usually be found in a disguised form. The periods of greatest popularity of rhyming slang in Australia have always coincided with wars. It first achieved note during the Boer War, then faded out and staged a come-back during World War No. 1. It has been revived during World War 2.

Now to turn to a specific analysis of the 'Australian' argot as found in the United States. Of the 352 terms included in this glossary, Mr. Baker finds that 314 are *not* used in Australia, and, to the best of his knowledge, have never had any currency there. Of the remaining thirty-eight terms, *only nine are definitely of Australian origin*[20] *and three have possible*

---

16. Melbourne, Robertson and Mullens, Limited, 1941, 84 pp.

17. Other instances from Australian slang are *Oscar* for cash, cut back from *Oscar Asche; knock-me* for billy (a tin pot), from *knock me silly; poddy* for two shillings and sixpence, from *poddy-calf* out of *half a caser* by an obscure rhyme on 'half'; *fiddley* for a pound note, from *fiddley-did,* a quid. *To have the jimmies* is to suffer from diarrhea, by an obscure rhyme on Jimmy Britts, a prizefighter, who toured Australia in the early years of the 20th century. These terms have not been encountered by this writer in the United States.

18. With all deference to Mr. Baker's scholarship, which is undoubtedly sound, we cannot rule out the possibility that he has as yet not tapped certain social areas where rhyming argot may be used.

19. *A Dictionary of the Australian Language,* prepared by commission of the Australian Government, and now in the press.

20. These terms are: *Captain Cook, cockie's clip, mad mick, Pat Malone, Sydney Harbor, Hawksbury Rivers, Cobar shower, Malee root,* and *Kennedy rot.* They will be amply annotated in the Glossary.

Australian origins. Of this group of thirty-eight, twenty-three (all of British origin) have been recorded at some time in Australia.[21]

Of the residue of 314 terms *not* used in Australia, Mr. Baker makes the following distribution:

> 75 have definitely been borrowed by the United States from England.[22]
> 34 have probably been borrowed by the United States from England.
> 34 may be either American or British in origin (definitely not Australian).
> 171 appear to have originated in the United States.[23]

Thus 340 out of the original 352 terms (or nearly 97%) are either American or British in origin. Only 12 (or slightly over 3%) are definitely or possibly of Australian origin. England has contributed 166 terms (or about 48%) of the total, and the United States 171, or about 49%.

In view of these figures, it would seem that the rhyming argot has been badly misnamed in the United States, for it appears to be anything but Australian in origin.[24] Once the system of forming this type of argot established itself in the United States,[25] it has grown by imitation until the imitative argot terms now outnumber those imported from Australia or England. It appears to be 'Australian' only in a trivial degree; it is infinitely more English (or Cockney) and still more is it indigenously American.[26] Because it is so firmly and widely established in non-standard

---

21. It should be noted that 32 of the total number of terms are found in Australia with different meanings, or with variant forms.

22. Of the total of 352 terms considered, 98 come definitely from British sources (75 of these being used in America and 23 used both in America and Australia), while 34 have possible and 34 have probable British origins.

23. Only 2 of the total of 171 terms apparently originating in America have been recorded in Australia. This is a strikingly small number in view of the known migration of criminals between the United States and Australia.

24. Says Mr. Baker on this point: 'The fault (in ascribing an Australian origin to this type of argot) is not that of American observers, but rather of Australians themselves or of people who did a hasty tour of these parts and then rushed off to write about it. The truth is, and as far as I can ascertain always has been, that while Australians have always used a little rhyming slang, it is certainly of insufficient bulk to be classed as an outstanding characteristic of our vernacular. The English—especially the Cockneys—are infinitely greater practitioners of rhyming slang than we are.'

25. The earliest example of rhyming argot in America which has come to my attention appeared in an early issue of the New York *Police Gazette* in the 1850's.

26. This is but a bare statement of an obvious conclusion in the light of the facts as collected. In interpreting these facts, certain problems arise to which I, frankly, do not have the answers: 1. In view of the distribution of so-called 'Australian' argot, how do we explain its concentration on the West Coast of the United States, and especially in San Francisco, the main port of entry from Australia? 2. In view of the fact that large numbers of British criminals were transported to Australia within relatively recent times, while on the other hand, the immigration of British criminals to America has been proportionally light, how did the rhyming system of argot arrive in the United States (and especially on the West Coast) without also taking root in Australia? 3. Whence arises the general belief among American criminals that this

usage, we may look for it to have an increasing influence upon the slang used by the public at large, a tendency which will doubtless be strengthened by the association of American soldiers with British and Australian troops who know and use some of the argot.

For reference to the following Glossary, Mr. Baker and I have agreed on the following symbols which will follow each entry:[27]

No. 1. The term is of Australian origin.
No. 2. The term is of English (probably Cockney) origin; *not* used in Australia.
No. 3. The term is used in Australia, but is not definitely No. 1 or No. 2.
    3a. Probably originally Australian.
    3b. Probably originally British.
    3c. Probably originally American.
No. 4. The term is used in Australia, but with different meaning, or in a variant form.
No. 5. The term is not used in Australia.
    5a. Origin uncertain, but probably American.
    5b. Origin uncertain, but probably British.
No. 6. Definitely of American origin, but recorded at some time or other in Australia.
No. 7. Definitely of British origin, but recorded at some time or other in Australia.

GLOSSARY[28]

A LA COMPLAIN. Rain. 2. *A la compain* in England, 1859.
ALL AFLOAT. A coat. 2. England, 1859.
ANDY McGINN. The chin. 5a.
APPLE AND BANANA. A piano. 5a or 5b.

APPLE PIES. The eyes. 5b.
ARTFUL DODGER. A lodger. 2. England, 1857.
ARTICHOKE RIPE. A pipe. 2. England, 1855. In Cockney slang, to smoke a pipe.
BACON AND EGGS. The legs. 3b.

---

system is of Australian origin? 4. Is it not possible that this type of argot may have gone 'underground' in Australia, as it has in America, with the result that it has not been tapped by conventional surveys and studies? With Americans widely distributed over the Orient and in Australia and Great Britain, it may be that some of them will see this study and find an opportunity to shed some light upon the questions raised above.

27. A digest of the distribution of terms in the Glossary based upon these symbols follows:

No. 1—9 terms	No. 5a—171
No. 2—75	No. 5b—34
No. 3a—3	No. 5a or 5b—34
No. 3b—2	No. 6—2
No. 3c—1	No. 7—23
No. 4—32	

28. The annotation 'England, 1859' following an entry indicates that it appeared in J. C. Hotten's *The Slang Dictionary* published in 1859, while 'England, 1857' refers to the term as printed in *The Vulgar Tongue* by 'Ducange Anglicus,' 1857; both are glossaries of British underworld cant. Other dates indicate the earliest known appearance of the term in either England or Australia and have been supplied by Mr. Baker from his own files. Little if any printed data is available on earliest appearances in the United States, although assiduous research in obscure or unpublished Americana in the late 19th or early 20th century might yield some information.

BAG OF FRUIT. A suit. 5a.

BAG OF NAILS. Anything confusing. 6. (Given by an informant as rhyming argot, but the rhyme cannot be found.) Recorded in Australia, 1895; in Farmer's *Dictionary of Americanisms*, 1889.

BALL AND BAT. A hat. 2. 1918.

BAND IN THE BOX. Pox (syphilis). 5a. Mr. Baker's classification is open to question since pox is seldom used in this sense in colloquial American; rather 5b.

BANG AND BIFF. The siff (syphilis). 5a.

BASIN CROP. A haircut. (Given as rhyming argot, but the rhyme cannot be found; perhaps clipped back.) 3a.

BEES AND HONEY. Money. Probably 5b. *Pot o' honey* in Cockney slang.

BEN FLAKE. A steak. England, 1857.

BIG BLOKE. Coke (cocaine). 5a.

BILLY BUTTON. Mutton. 2. England, 1857.

BILLY MUGGINS. Mutton. 5a. In Australian slang, a fool. 4.

BLOCK AND TACKLE. A shackle (leg-iron or handcuff). 5a or possibly 5b.

BOAT AND OAR. A whore. 5a.

BOB'S MY PAL. A gal (girl). 3b.

BOILED RAG. A hag. 5a. In Australian, a stiff shirt. 4.

BONNET SO BLUE. A stew. 2. England, 1859.

BONNY FAIR. Hair. 5a.

BO PEEP or LITTLE BO PEEP. Sleep. 2.

BOTANY BAY. In the hay (in bed). 5a.

BOTTLE AND GLASS. The buttocks. 2.

BOTTLE AND STOPPER. A copper (policeman). 5b.

BOTTLE OF SPRUCE. A deuce (card). 2. In England, also twopence, by rhyme on deuce.

BOWL OF CHALK. Talk. 5a.

BOY IN BLUE. Stew. 5b.

BRACE AND BITS. Teats. 5a or 5b.

BRANDY SNAP. A slap. 5a. In Australia, obsolete for a mark caused by a blow.

BREAD AND JAM. A tram. 2.

BROKEN MUG. A hug. 5a.

BROKEN OAR. A whore. 5a.

BROTHERS AND SISTERS. Whiskers. 5a.

BROWN BESS. Yes. 2. England, 1859.

BROWN JOE. No. 2. England, 1859.

BUBBLE AND SQUEAK. To speak. 2.

BUGS AND FLEAS. The knees. 5a or 5b.

BULL AND COW. A row. 2. England, 1859.

BULL'S AUNTS. Pants. 5a. In Australia, *bullants*. 4.

BUSHY PARK. A lark (good time). 2. England, 1859.

BUTTER FLAP. A cap. 2. England, 1859; now obs.

BY THE PECK. The neck. 5b.

CABBAGE HAT. A rat (informer). 5b, with possible Australian antecedents. *Cabbage tree* and *cabbage hat* may be remotely linked with Australia. The *cabbage tree hat* seems to have had its origin in Australia at the end of the 18th century; however, Mr. Baker notes that *rat* (informer) was originally English, so that the development into rhyming argot is probably American.

CABBAGE TREE. To flee. 5a or 5b, with possible Australian antecedents.

CALICO YARD. A guard. 5a. In Australia, a type of corral. 4.

CAPTAIN COOK. A look. 1 or 3a.

CASTLE RAG. A flag. 2. England, 1859, now obs.

CAT CUFF. A bluff. 5a. In Australia, a blow in boxing. 4.

CATHERINE HAYES. Long days. 5a. In Australia, a mixed drink. 4.

CATS AND KITTIES. Titties (breasts). 5a or 5b.

CHAIR AND CROSS. A horse. 5a. Version of *Charing Cross*.

CHALK FARM. The arm. 2. England, 1857.

CHARING CROSS. A horse. 2. England, 1857.

CHARLEY BECK. A check (usually worthless). 5a.

CHARLEY CHALK. Talk. 5a.

CHARLEY HORNER. The corner. 5a.

CHARLEY PRESCOT. The vest (waist-coat). 7. England, 1857.

CHARLEY ROCKS. Socks. 5a. In Australia *almonds*, from *almond rocks* (Cockney); rare.

CHARLEY ROLLAR. A dollar. 5a.

CHEESE AND KISSES. The Mrs. (one's wife). 3b.

CHEESE AND SPICES. Prices (the morning line on racehorses). 5a.

CHERRY RIPE. A pipe. 2. England, 1857.

CHESAPEAKE SHAD. Not bad. 5a.

CHEVY CHASE. The face. 2. England, 1857. Now obs. in England.

CHEWS AND MOLASSES. Glasses (spectacles). 5a.

CHIP AND CHASE. The face. 5a.

CHOPPER. A copper (policeman). 5a.

CHUCK A CHARLEY. A dollar. (Bonafide rhyming argot?) 5a. Australian, to throw a fit. 4.

CHUNK OF BEEF. A chief (boss). 3a. In Australia, clipped to *chunka* or *chunker*.

CINDER SHIFTER. A drifter. 5a. In Australia, a speedway driver.

CLINK AND BLANK. A bank. 5a.

CLUB AND STICK. A dick (detective). 5a.

COAST ABOUT. A roustabout. 5a.

COBAR SHOWER. A flower. 5a. This term is used in Australia, never to mean a flower but a dust-storm, from the small town of Cobar in New South Wales; *Bedourie shower* and *Darling shower* are used similarly.

COCKED HAT. A rat (informer). **5a.**

COCKIE'S CLIP. A dip (pickpocket). While this term is not used as rhyming argot in Australia, it unmistakably stems from there, where it means to shear a sheep. A *cockie* is a farmer, derived from *cockatoo;* it appears in such combinations as *cane cockie* (sugar grower), *cherry cockie, scrub cockie, cow cockie,* etc.

COLONIAL PUCK. Fornication. 5a.

COOKSHOP. A hockshop. (Bonafide rhyming argot?) 5a.

COW AND CALF. A laugh. 5a.

COWS AND KISSES. The Mrs. (one's wife). 2. England, 1857.

CRACK A BOO. To coo (make love). 5a. In Australia, to betray a secret or give way to one's feelings; rare. 4.

CRACK A CRY. To die. 5a.

CRACKERS AND TOAST. The post (racing). 5a.

CUP OF TEA. To see. 5a or 5b.

CUT AND SLICER. A dicer (hat). 5a.

DAISY ROOTS. Boots. 7. England, 1874.

DANNY TUCKER or DANNY RUCKER. Butter. 5a.

DERBY KELLEY. The belly. 5a.

DIME A POP. A cop. 5a.

DING DONG. A song. 7. England, 1859.

DINKY DIRT. A shirt. 5a. In England and Australia, *dicky dirt.* 4.

DIP SOUTH. The mouth. 5a or 5b. In Australia, *to dip South,* to search for money in one's pocket.

DUKE OF CORK. A talk; a walk. 2.

DUKE OF YORK. A talk; a walk. 2. England, 1859.

EAST AND SOUTH or NORTH AND SOUTH. The mouth. 5b. 1860.

EAST AND WEST. The vest. 5b.

FANNY BLAIR. The hair. 2. England, 1859.

FAR AND NEAR. Beer. 7.

FIDDLE AND FLUTE or FIDDLE. A suit of clothes. 5b.

FIELD OF WHEAT. A street. 2. 1900.

FIFTEEN AND SEVEN. Perfect (like heaven). 5a.

FIFTEEN AND TWO. A Jew. 5a.

FILET OF VEAL. A wheel. 5a.

FINE AND DANDY. Brandy. 7.

FINGER AND THUMB. Rum. 2. England, 1857.

FISH AND SHRIMP. A pimp. 5b.

FLEA AND LOUSE. A house (brothel). 2. England, 1859.

FLEAS AND ANTS. Pants. 5a or 5b.

FLOUNDER AND DAB. A taxicab or cab. 2. England, 1857.

FLY FLAT. A gat (gun). 5a. In England, a would-be sport; a wise-guy.

FORTY-FOUR. A whore. 5a.

FOWL ROOST. To boost (assist a pickpocket). 5a.

FRANCE AND SPAIN. Rain. 2. 1900.

FRANK AND HANK. A bank. 5a.

FRILLED GIZZARD. A lounge lizard. 5a.

FROG AND FEATHER. A leather (wallet). 5a.

FROG AND TOAD. A road. 7. England, 1859.

FROG A LOG. A dog. 5a or 5b.

FULL AS AN EGG. A slug in the head. (Bonafide rhyming argot?) 5a. In Australia, to be drunk. 4.

GARDEN GATE. A magistrate. 2. England, 1859.

GARLIC AND GLUE. Beef stew. 5a.

GAY AND FRISKY. Whisky. 7. 1900.

GERMAN BAND. The hand. 2. 1900.

GERMAN FLUTE. A boot. 2. England, 1857 (obs. in England).

GIGGLESTICK. A penis. 5a.

GINGER ALE. A jail. 5b.

GINGERBEERS. Tears. 5a or 5b.

GIRL AND BOY. A saveloy (sausage). 2. England, 1859.

GLORIOUS SINNER. Dinner. 2. England, 1859.

GOD FORBID. A kid (child). 2. 1900.

GOOSE AND DUCK. Fornication. 2. 1870.

GUNGAH DIN. The chin. 5b.

HAIR AND BRAIN. A chain. 5a.

HAIRY FLOAT. A coat. 5a.

HAIRY GOAT. The throat. 5a or 5b.

HALF A PECK. The neck. 5b.

HALF-AN-HOUR. Flour. 5a or 5b.

HALF-A-LICK. Sick. 5a.

HAMMER AND TACK. The back. 5a. In Australia, a road, by rhyme on *track*. 4.

HAPPY HOURS. Flowers. 5a.

HARD AND FLAT. A hat (derby). 5a.

HASH-ME-GANDY. Handy. 5a. In Australia, a type of stew. 4.

HAT AND CAP. The clap (gonorrhea). 5a.

HAWKSBURY RIVERS. The shivers. 1. In Australia, often cut back to *Hawksburies*.

HEAD AND TAIL. Jail. 5a.

HEAP OF COKE. A bloke (man). 2. 1910.

HEAVENLY BLISS. A kiss. 5b.

HERE AND THERE. A chair. 5b.

HICKORY DOCK. A clock. 5a or 5b.

HIGH STEPPER. Pepper. 2.

HIT AND MISS. Urine. 7.

HOLY GHOST. The post (racing). 5a.

HOOK A MUTTON. A button. 5a. In New Zealand, *to hook one's mutton* for to go away.

HOOT AND HOLLER. A dollar. 5a.

HOP TOAD. A road. 5a.

HOT HAY. The bay. 5a. Cf. *Botany Bay;* any possible connection?

HUSBAND AND WIFE. A knife. 5b.

I DECLARE. A chair. 5b.

I DESIRE. A fire. 2. 1900.

I DON'T CARE. A chair. 5b

IF AND AND. A band (music). 5b.

I'M AFLOAT. A boat. 2. England, 1859.

IN THE BOOK. A hook (thief). 5a.

IN THE SLEET. In the street. 5a or 5b.

IRISH KERBY. A derby (hat). 5a.

JACK AND JILL. A till. 2.

JACK DANDY. Brandy. 2. England, 1857.

JACK IN THE BOX. Socks. 2.

JACK RANDLE. A candle. 2. England, 1859. In England, *Jack Randall.*

JACK SCRATCH. A match. 5b.

JACK SHAY. To slay. 5a. In Australia, *Jackshea,* a tin quart-pot. 4.

JACK SPRAT. A brat (child). 2. In England, an undersized man or boy since the 16th century.

JERRYDIDDLE. A fiddle. 5a. In Australia, a drink on the house. 4.

JERRY McGINN. The chin. 5a.

JERSEY CITIES. Titties (breasts). 5a.

JEW CHUM. A bum (tramp). 5a. In Australia, an European Jewish refugee. 4.

JIG AND PRANCE. A dance. 5a or 5b.

JIMMY LOW. Go slow. 5a. In Australia, a folk-name for a type of tree. 4.

JOE BLAKE. A steak. 2. In Australia, a snake. 4.

JOE GOSS. The boss. 5a.

JOHNNY RAW. A saw; the jaw. 5a or 5b. In Australia, a *new chum* or immigrant.

JOHNNY RUMP. A pump. 5a.

JOHNNY RUSSELL. To bustle. 3c.

JOHNNY SKINNER. Dinner. 5a.

JOLLOPP. Stop. 5a.

KEITH AND PROCTOR. A doctor. 5a.

KELLEY NED. The head. 5a. (In Australia, *Ned Kelley* was a famous bushranger.)

KENNEDY ROT. A sot (drunkard). 5a. In Australia, a type of land scurvy named after a Queensland district.

KICK AND PRANCE. To dance. 5b.

KIDNEY PIE. The eye (not recorded in the plural). 5a or 5b. In Australia, insincere praise. 4.

KIDSTAKE. A fake. 5a. Plural, pretense, nonsense. 4.

KISS THE CROSS. The boss. 5a or 5b.

LAMB FRY. A necktie. 5a.

LAME DUCK. Fornication. 5a. In Australia, a scapegrace.

LARD AND PAIL. Jail. 5a.

LARRY HAPPY. Sappy (feebleminded). 5a. *Happy as Larry,* very happy. 4. 1900.

LARRY SIMON. A diamond. 5a.

LEAN AND LAKE. A steak. 5b.

LEAN AND LINGER. A finger. 5b.

LEAN AND LURCH. A church. 2. England, 1857.

LEG ROPE. Hope. 5a.

LOAF OF BREAD. The head. 7. 1900.

LORD LOVEL. A shovel. 2. England, 1857.

LUMP OF LEAD. The head. 7. England, 1857.

MACINTIRE AND HEATH. The teeth. 5a.

MAD MICK. A pick. 1. 1900.

MAD MILE. A smile. 5a.

MAGGIE MAHONE. A 'phone. 5a.

MAID'S ADORNING. Morning. 2. England, 1859.

MAIDSTONE JAILER. A tailor. 2. England, 1857.

MALLEE ROOT. A prostitute. 1. *Mallee* is an aboriginal word applied to a species of Eucalypt which covers a large area in Victoria known as 'The Mallee.'

MAN AND WIFE. A knife. 2. 1918.

MARY AND JOHNNIE. Marijuana (accidental rhyme in translation from Mexican Spanish?). 5a.

MINCE PIES. The eyes. 7. England, 1857.

MOAN AND WAIL. Jail. 5a.

MOTHER AND DAUGHTER. Water. 5b.

MUFFIN BAKER. A Quaker. 2. England, 1859.

MUMBLEY PEGS. The legs. 7.

NANCY PRANCE. A dance. 5a.

NEAR AND FAR. A bar. 2. 1910. A car. 5a or 5b.

NEAR AND THERE. A chair. 5a.

NEPTUNE'S DAUGHTER. Water. 5a.

NEW SOUTH. Big mouth. 5a. An abbreviation for New South Wales. 4.

NIAGARA FALLS. Balls; meat-balls; theater stalls. 2.

NICKLE AND DIME. Time. 5a.

NIGHT AND DAY. A play. 5b.

NITS AND LICES. Prices (racing). 5a.

NOAH'S ARK. A park. 2. *Nark* (a spoilsport). 4.

NORTH AND SOUTH. The mouth. 2. 1880.

NOSE AND CHIN. To win (a race). 2. 1860.

OCEAN WAVE. A shave. 2.

OH BY HECK. The neck. 5a.

OH MY DEAR. Beer. 7.

ONES AND TWOS. Shoes. 5b.

OSCAR HOCKS. Socks. 5a.

(To go) OVER THE STYLE. To stand trial. 5a.

PAIR OF BRACES. The races. 5b.

PAT MALONE. Alone. 1. (Rare.) Commonly clipped back to *on one's pat.*

PEACHES AND PEARS. The stairs. 5b.

PIG'S FACE. Lace. 5a.

PINT POT. A sot (drunkard). Possibly 5a, but adumbrated by Shakespeare's use of the term for a beer-seller.

PITCH THE PLOD. To plow the sod. 5a.

PLATES OF MEAT. Feet. 7. 1874.

PLOW THE DEEP. To sleep. 2. England, 1859.

PORT AND SHERRY. I'm jerry (wise). 5a.

POT AND PAN. A man. 7. 1870.

POT OF GLUE. A Jew. 5a or 5b.

POT OF JELLY. The belly. 5a.

POVERTY POINT. A joint. 5a. In Sydney, a meeting place for theatrical folk. 4.

PRIDE AND JOY. A boy. 2.

PUDDING AND PIE. The eye. 5b.

QUARTER POT. A sot (drunkard). 5a.

RATS AND MICE. Dice. 2. 1870.

RATTLE AND HISS. To urinate. 5a or 5b.

RAW AND RIPE. A pipe. 5b.

READ AND WRITE. To fight. 2. England, 1857.

READER AND WRITER. A fighter. 2.

RED HOT CINDER. A winder (window). 5a or 5b.

RED SHIRT. A skirt (woman). 5a.

RED STEER. A beer. 5a.

RIDE PLUSH. To hush. 5a.

RIPSEY ROUSERS. Trousers. 5a.

ROASTY ROAST. The post (racing). 5a.

ROARY O'MORE. The floor. 5a.

ROCKS AND BOULDERS. The shoulders. 2. 1900.

ROLLEY ROAR. The floor. 5a.

ROOTS. Boots. 7. 1874.

ROSES RED. A bed. 2.

ROUND THE HOUSES. Trousers. 7. England, 1859.

RUBBITY RUB. A tub. 5a. A 'pub,' usually clipped to *rubbity* or *rubby*. 4.

RUMBLE AND SHOCK. A knock. 5a.

RUMPTY DOLLAR. A holler (cry). 5a.

SANDY BLIGHT. Dead right; a type of ophthalmia. 4.

SATIN AND SILK. Milk. 5b.

SCARLET PIPS. The lips. 5a.

SCOTCH PEGS. Legs. 2. 1860.

SCREAM AND HOLLER. A dollar. 5a.

SEE THE SHINE. To give a dime. 5a.

SELDOM SEEN. A limousine. 5a.

SHERRY FLIPS. The lips. 5a.

SHIP IN SAIL. Ale. 2. England, 1857 (ship in full sail).

SHORT OF A SHEET. In the street. 5a. Stupid or mentally deficient. 4.

SHOVEL AND BROOM. A room. 5a or 5b.

SIGHS AND TEARS. The ears. 5a or 5b.

SILK AND TOP. A cop (policeman). 5a.

SILK AND TWINE. Wine. 5a.

SIMPLE SIMON. A diamond. 5a.

SIR WALTER SCOTT. A (chamber) pot. 5b. A pot of beer. 2. England, 1857.

SKY ROCKETS. The pockets. 2. 1879.

SKY THE WIPE. A hype (hypodermic). 5a.

SLICK AND SLEATH. The teeth. 5a.

SLIM DILLY. A filly. 5a. A girl. 4.

SLOOP OF WAR. A whore. 2. England, 1859.

SLUM OF SLOPS. Hops (tea). 5b. (In England *slops*, tea; *slum*, a chest, since c. 1860.)

SMACK IN THE EYE. Pie. 5a.

SMART AND SIMPLE. A dimple. 5a or 5b.

SMEAR AND SMUDGE. A judge. 5a or 5b.

SMOOTH AND COARSE. A horse. 5a.

SMOOTH AND ROUGH. On the cuff (credit). 5a.

SNOW AND RAIN. A train. 5a.

SONG AND DANCE. Pants. 5a.

SOUTH OF THE EQUATOR. An elevator. 5a.

SPANISH GUITAR. A cigar. 5a.

SPINNING TOP. A cop (policeman). 5a.

STAND AN ALE. Bail. 5a.

STICK SLINGERS. Fingers. 5a.

STORM AND STRIFE. One's wife. 7.

STORMY DICK. A penis. 5a.

STRING AND TWINE. Wine. 5a or 5b.

STRONG AND THIN. Gin. 5b.

SWEET MARGUERITE. A cigarette. 5a. (Bonafide rhyming argot?)

SWITCH AND BONE. A phone. 5a.

SYDNEY HARBOR. A barber. 1.

TAR AND FEATHER. The weather. 5a or 5b.

TARRY ROPE. A dope (fool). 5a. A waterfront prostitute. 4.

TEA AND TATTLE. A battle. 5b.

TEA AND TOAST. The post (racing). 5a.

TEARS AND CHEERS. The ears. 5a.

THIS AND THAT. A hat. 7.

THESE AND THOSE. The toes. 5b.

THREE OR FOUR. A door. 5a or 5b.

TICK-TACK. The track (racing). 5a or 5b. *Tic-tac*, signals to a bookmaker. 4.

TIDDLEDY WINK. A drink. 2.

TING-A-LING. A ring (finger). 5a.

TIP AND TAP. A cap. 5a.

TIT FOR TAT. A hat. 7.

TOAD IN A HOLE. A roll (money). 5a.

TOM TART. A fart. 5a. A girl. 4.

TOMMY DODD. A rod (gun). 5a.

TOMMY ROCKS. Socks. 5a.

TOM TUG. A mug (sucker). 5a.

TOTAL WRECK. A check. 7.

TRAP AND MOUSE. A house. 5a or 5b.

TOY. A boy. 5a.

TROT AND PACE. The face. 5a.

TURTLE DOVES. Gloves. 2. England, 1857.

TWIST AND TWIRL. A girl. 7.

TWO BY FOUR. A whore. 5a.

UNCLES AND AUNTS. Pants. 5a.

UPPER DECK. The neck. 5a or 5b.

UPPERS AND BENEATH. The teeth. 5a.

VERY BEST. The chest. 5a.

WEEPING WILLOW. A pillow. 2. 1900.

WHALE AND GALE. A jail. 5a.

WHAT AM. A ham. 5a.

WHIP AND SLASH or LASH. Mustache. 5a.

THE WINDS DO WHIRL. A girl. 5a.

WISH ME LUCK. To duck. 5b.

YOU KNOW. Snow (cocaine). 5a.

13

Marijuana Users and Their Lingo

This chapter represents some early observations on the development of a sub-culture of marijuana users and their relationship to the older subculture of hard drug users. At this time the number of users of marijuana was infinitely smaller than it is today, and the tendency was to ostracize them both from legitimate society and from the society of hard drug users. Perhaps it is significant that the general reader has little more accurate knowledge of the nature and effects of marijuana than he had more than thirty years ago. The use of marijuana, however, has increased a thousandfold in the dominant culture, with the general public leaning toward the position that light or occasional use of marijuana has little if any deleterious effect on the smoker. Meanwhile, at the other end of the spectrum some valuable medical uses for marijuana are being discovered but have not yet been generally recognized.

This paper is included largely because it represents a look at the subculture of the marijuana smoker not long after the passage of the Marijuana Tax Act (1937) which classified *cannabis* as a narcotic and made its sale and possession illegal. In reprinting this article, the words *addict* and *addiction* have been deleted and generally the words *user* and *use* substituted because of the change in the public attitude toward marijuana and the medical concept of addiction itself. Perhaps the chief point of interest in this article is the date at which it appeared (1946) and the social status of the marijuana user at that time.

The subculture of the marijuana user has rapidly and widely diffused, taking the language as well as the drug to the heart of the dominant culture. A later chapter will show clearly the nature and effect of this diffusion as well as the changes and additions to the argot of the marijuana user.

• • •

WITHIN the past few years a great deal of popular material has been printed about the effects of marijuana, much of which is highly colored. The use of marijuana, like the use of opiates of any kind, seems to be most common among individuals with noticeable emotional instability.

Medical men do not agree on its classification as a narcotic, or on its addicting qualities as compared to the derivatives of opium, though all agree that the users of marijuana (a species of *cannabis*), when denied the drug, suffer little of the withdrawal distress experienced by those addicted to the use of other narcotics. The current controversy in medical journals reflects this difference of professional opinion, ranging from the contention that marijuana when smoked has little if any true narcotic effect and that it may actually be a useful drug under certain circumstances, to the view that it is a very dangerous drug.

It is extremely difficult to evaluate the effects of this drug, for no case studies have been made on a large scale under normal living conditions. The LaGuardia report, made by a New York committee, tends to minimize the harmful effects of marijuana in comparison to opium derivatives; the studies made by the United States Army are applicable only to a particular situation; a recently published study of some 1,800 users of *cannabis sativa* in India seems to indicate that the drug may be extremely harmful and that it may be a factor leading to the commission of violent crimes. However, it is obvious that an adequate estimate of the potency of marijuana can be arrived at only as the result of studies of its use in relation to the entire life-pattern of the user.

This article is not intended to add to what has already been brought to light in the controversy over the dangers of marijuana but rather to discuss the behavior of users observed during the course of my research; a significant part of this behavior is the argot or lingo, which contrasts sharply with that used by addicts of opiates.

I am frankly skeptical regarding the highly touted aphrodisiac effects that marijuana is reputed to have on the unconditioned smoker, although some habitual or occasional users state that they like the drug because it reduces their inhibitions and gives them the feeling that they are sexually irresistible. I cannot help feeling that the effects of the drug are intensified by a psychological situation in which the smoker has been conditioned to expect and to experience these effects. When neophytes are being initiated into the mysteries of the drug, for instance, it becomes obvious that, without the liberal use of suggestion, the smoker would apparently feel little more euphoria or exhilaration than he might from the consumption of a whisky highball. The exaggerated merriment, the partly forced laughter, the affected ribaldry, all suggest that the experimenter is working rather hard at being a *tea-hound*. He is trying to behave as he thinks he should; he would be disappointed if he did not experience the sensations which he knows are associated with the drug. He wants to become a *viper*.

What is marijuana? It is simply commercial hemp which is a native weed in the southwest United States and Mexico, but which, as gangs who deal in it as a drug have demonstrated, can easily be cultivated anywhere in the country. It has a very bad name down in Asia Minor—hashish. The habit-forming drug is not contained in any quantity in the leaves, as is sometimes believed, but develops in late maturity in the female hemp flowers, just before the plant goes to seed. The flowers of the male plant do not produce *cannabin*. The ripe female flowering tops are stripped of their leaves and are then known to dealers and users as *potiguaya*. These pods are dried and crushed and are ready to pass into commerce as bulk marijuana, often mixed with tobacco or some other base to facilitate smoking.

This drug is known to the fraternity as *greefo, muggles, Mary Warner, fu, bo-bo bush, mezz, Indian hay, mutah, Texas tea*, etc. Cigarettes made from it are *reefers, sticks*, or *twists*. Users are *reefing-men, vipers*, or *tea-men;* those who habitually roll their own cigarettes for economy are *twisters*.

The standard price per cigarette seems to vary from fifteen to twenty-five cents—with a profit of about 1,000 percent for the manufacturer. Many dealers in the more highbrow dance spots sell a special variety for fifty cents a throw; it is whispered to the customer that they contain "an extra wallop," but they usually contain exactly the same ingredients as the cheaper type, but are sometimes distinguished by a brown wrapper instead of a white.

Marijuana is almost always inhaled in the form of smoke, though some users like to soak bits of the *potiguaya* in liquor. Smoking is known as *viping* or *sending*. Smokers use a somewhat different technique from that one would use in smoking an ordinary cigarette. The *reefer* is held in the center of the mouth and the lips on either side are drawn back to allow the entrance of considerable air as the user inhales. Since a good deal of the absorption appears to take place in the lungs, the more air one gets with the smoke, the more intense the effect is said to be. New recruits are usually "taught" to smoke by peddlers or other users, often by girls who get a commission on what they sell. All the effects are described in detail by the "teacher" in an atmosphere of voluptuous merriment, and the smoker is given every encouragement to say that he feels the effect of the drug. Soon the neophyte learns to get the reactions without much assistance, though it is to be noted that marijuana is almost always consumed in the company of the opposite sex.

Marijuana smoke smells somewhat like the interior of an ancient and unkempt coffee pot. The first symptom of euphoria is unrestrained laughter and a general atmosphere of good fellowship; dealers, I have noted, almost always attempt to establish this atmosphere artificially before the drug could have possibly had time to take effect. After two or three cigarettes the smoker feels a sense of well-being, his ego expands, and he exhibits some of the glow that frequently accompanies cases of very mild intoxication. If there is music available — and there always is — he feels a desire to dance. He may have the delusion that he is irresistible. His inhibitions break down (though most people who use it have few inhibitions left to break down) and he abandons himself to mutual erotic stimulation on the dance floor.

The relation of marijuana consumption to swing music is very interesting. Most users want swing music while they are on a jag; many swing musicians are users, and some popular composers and directors attribute much of their success to the rhythms released by the drug. Such songs as *Texas Tea Party, The Chant of the Weed, Smokin' Reefers, Reefer-Man, Viper's Moan, Viper's Drag,* and *Muggles* reflect, in a very thinly disguised manner, the close relation of drug-aroused sexual desire to swing music. How much of this sexual stimulation is due to the drug, how much to the music, how much to one's partner, and how much to the state of anticipation, which dominates the user's mind, is difficult to say.

The popular belief in marijuana as a powerful aphrodisiac persists; perhaps the fact that it does persist makes it a potent agent. Some time ago, a well-known health-fad magazine carried a rather flamboyant article in which a beautiful, innocent, completely unsuspecting virgin was solemnly pictured as smoking one cigarette at her escort's suggestion, whereupon she lapsed promptly into a voluptuous swoon, became putty in his hands, and demanded to see his etchings. I can't escape the cynical feeling that the young lady overestimated the excitive powers of marijuana. Although the drug does release inhibitions and may have some sexual implications, it isn't like turning on an electric switch. It takes time and practice to *vipe* satisfactorily.

Later stages of use, if the doses are timed properly, may be characterized by periods of depression following states of exaltation in which the user experiences fleeting sexual dreams and feels something of the power over time and space which opiate addicts associate with morphine euphoria. If smoking is continued, the user passes out cold. Some federal officials feel that the last trancelike state is the dangerous stage, for while in it users sometimes break up furniture, strip off their clothes and scream hysterically, or become extremely pugnacious. Afterward they conveniently remember nothing.

Naturally, the marijuana traffic produces many users and pseudo-users, although the users of the drug do not manifest many of the physiological, psychological, and social characteristics that are to be observed among those who are addicted to opiates. The marijuana habit is easy to spread, it is not so expensive as other forms of addiction, it has a certain romantic appeal, and youngsters are especially susceptible to it. The use of the drug is closely linked to the prostitution racket and many brothels and call houses supply marijuana cigarettes to both the girls and their patrons — at the usual price.

Prostitutes who deliberately smoke a *reefer* before a waiting customer in order to be able to "show him a better time" are of course only playing upon the illusions of gullible males as their profession has done from time immemorial. However, the only additional pleasure that the customer receives is that of paying for the *reefer.* The next step of course is selling the customer a smoke (or giving him one as a starter), and if he once establishes the link between *muggles* and sexual gratification, he is hooked — though hardly in the sense that he would be hooked on opium, morphine, heroin, or cocaine, for his system does not develop a tolerance to the drug (thereby obviating an increase in dosage), and there are no measurable withdrawal symptoms. Marijuana users are not as a rule accepted into the fraternity of full-fledged narcotic addicts, but are regarded as distinctly inferior in depravity.

Marijuana users are clannish, but not so much so as opiate addicts, who regard outsiders with suspicion and distrust exceeded only by the fear with which they look upon other addicts suspected of being *stool pigeons.* They are also suspicious, but seem to take their group-solidarity less seriously than do drug addicts — perhaps because deprivation of marijuana does not carry with it the connotation of severe withdrawal distress which it carries for users of opium, morphine, or heroin. It is infinitely easier, for instance, for a stranger to gain entrance to a *tea-pad* where marijuana is used than it is to be admitted to an opium den. But then there are more *tea-pads* than opium dens.

Like all groups operating outside the law, marijuana users have developed their own secret or semisecret argot, which differs sharply from that of opiate addicts. One of the most interesting of these differences is the fact that it overlaps the lingo of the jitterbug, jive, and swing groups and hence has a tendency to filter into respectable speech. While only a small proportion of so-called jitterbugs are *muggles* users, the jitterbug is thrown into direct contact with some users, and both jitterbug talk and the argot of the *vipers* have their linguistic roots well grounded in the fast life of the Harlem dives and brothels.

It appears to be true that excessive use of *cannabin,* the toxic element in marijuana, may eventually release subconscious impulses leading to the commission of violent crimes while the user is in a confused state, or in delirium. However, the same may be said regarding the excessive use of alcohol. As yet it is difficult to ascertain just how significant marijuana may be in the motivation of crime, although some criminals like to attribute their crimes to marijuana in the hope of securing leniency in court — and often they are not disappointed.

The danger of wholesale addiction among stable, legitimate people is, I think, overrated. Reports have come out repeatedly during the past several years which have set women's clubs agog with tales of so-called love cults in high schools; boys and girls of tender age, it is stated, engage in group orgies after having smoked themselves into a fine frenzy of desire. I seriously doubt that adolescent promiscuity is promoted to any extent by the group-use of marijuana, or that "love cults" among youngsters of high-school age exist in appreciable numbers outside the imaginations of the gullible. While such cults do exist in small numbers, as any psychiatrist or sociologist knows, they are most often attended strictly by the sophisticate.

More dangerous to the youth of the land — especially those in the large urban centers — is heroin (*witch-hazel, H., courage-pills* to the initiate), a powerful opiate to which they may be addicted by unscrupulous peddlers. This method of addiction receives relatively little publicity, presumably because it lacks the titillating element of sex. But it, along with morphine, accounts for many of the thieves, shoplifters, and pickpockets who support their habits by crime.

The conclusion to be drawn is that the use of marijuana, although less habit-forming than other narcotics, is nonetheless dangerous to the unstable type of person. It may serve as amusement for some thrill-seekers, but it is risky amusement, for the fact that one habitually seeks his entertainment in that form reveals a treacherous instability of personality which may lead merrily to the gutter, or worse.

14

The Argot of
the Three-Shell Game

The three-shell game is a classic short-con game which has been played in one form or another for centuries. Along with three-card monte, a similar game in which the victim tries to pick out the queen from three cards tossed on a board by the *inside man,* it is a prototype of all con games and parallels in miniature the three big-con games which have taken many millions of dollars from well-to-do-victims. While this subculture contributed thousands of good shell-game operators, only a few had the intelligence, the social abilities, and other skills necessary to become big-con operators. It is a fact, however, that a surprising proportion of successful big-con men started out on the shell game or three-card monte and then graduated to the big-con games.

The three-shell game contains the following essentials which, as we will see later, are the backbone of the three big-con games: the *wire,* the *rag,* and the *payoff.* First, there is a con mob which has the following division of labor: the *inside man* who operates the game; the *outside man* who controls the victim; one or more *ropers* who locate other victims and steer them to the game; several *shills* who are the poor man's prototype of the elegant *boost* used in the big-con games; and the employment of the *fix* which buys protection from the police.

Second, there is the device, which always includes the use of a location (the *store*), where the action takes place; here it is a small board with three shells and a sponge-rubber pea. This is the prototype of the elaborate big store, a fake brokerage house, or private gambling club used in the big-con games. Third, there is a *gaff* by which the victim thinks he has a *sure thing* enabling him to cheat the store. Inherent in the gaff is the reliable trick which enables the mob to cheat the sucker while he is trying to cheat them.

While circuses no longer carry the *grift,* including the shell game, this subculture persists and the game is still played by both locals and road men who follow state fairs, county fairs, carnivals, race tracks, or work in any place where a festive crowd gathers.

• • •

THERE ARE two distinct phases of argot indigenous to American circuses. The one, used by performers and employees, is really a sort of occupational jargon and has been frequently sampled by students of language. The other, comprising elements of several obscure criminal argots, is almost exclusively the property of the *circus-grifters* who keep themselves aloof from the other personnel, share their take with the management, and constitute a small, closely-knit social unit within most circuses. These men are specialists in many rackets, each of which has some individual argot of its own. Formerly, these *grifters* were standard equipment with all road shows; today some of the more progressive circuses have dispensed with the *grift* as being poor business policy. This study gives a sampling of the technical argot of the *three-shell man,* which in turn is only a minor aspect of the large body of the argot of the *circus-grifter* now under observation by the writer.

Everyone has seen the simple-looking little shell-game played at fairs, on circus lots, or on the backstretch at a big racetrack. In recent years, some magicians have studied it as a basis for parlor entertainment. It looks harmless enough—and usually is, except in the hands of specialized *grifters,* where it can take as much as several thousand dollars a day from a gullible public. It has in it many of the elements of the deadly *big-con,* and, so far as the psychological factors are concerned, is the great-grand-daddy of modern big-time confidence games. This relationship is borne out by the fact that a whole generation of first-rate *big-con* men, some of them unsurpassed, got their start on the *circus grift* and particularly on the three-shell game.

Historically this game is very old. We got it from England, where it appears in the 18th century as *thimble-rig,* played with three thimbles weighted in the top with solder. Some old-timers in this country still refer to three-shell operators as *thimble-riggers.* However, it was in the United States, during the late 19th and early 20th centuries that the game was fully developed as an adjunct to the very lucrative *circus grift.* Recently it has enjoyed a revival in the hands of old-timers who smell easy money; skilled mobs working in prosperous areas will easily gross from $200 to $400 per day, and it is a matter of record that Colonel Weaver, dean of the shell-men, once turned in over $4,000 to the Hagenback privilege-car at the end of one day's work; Kid Monahan is said to have once grossed $3,000 for second place.

Other topnotchers would include the following old-timers: Jerry Daly, one-time partner of the famed Soapy Smith and Ironfoot Johnson, and strongly affiliated with the John Robinson Circus, later a notorious *big-con* man and ultimately killed by Cuban Frank, fixer for the *big-con* in Havana; Kid Hunt (the Up and Down Kid), later on the *big-con;* Little Chappie (John) Lohr, of Freeport, Illinois, brother to Big Chappie whom he turned out, an expert at the *big-con* games; Knobby Clark, later a partner of Joe Furey and Bob Terry; Jack Hardaway, eventually sent to prison with the Blonger mob who were most competent at both the *rag* and the *pay-off;* Dan the Dude, later *big-con* fixer and proprietor of the world-famous hangout at 28 West 28th St.; Blind Tom from St. Joseph, Missouri, later a roper for the *pay-off;* Big Ed Burns of Chicago, later a skilled *mitt-man* and *short-con* operator; Mike Golden, for years the fixer in San Francisco, and partner of Jerry Mugivan, recently dead and already legendary; Sawdust Jack of St. Louis; Big Adams of San Francisco; Archie Fenton; the White Headed Kid; Beefsteak Bob; Kid Minor; Lum Clark; Frenchy Baker, later better known as a pickpocket; Red Brew, now probably working as a *big-con roper* in Mexico; Baker Tom; Johnny Barton, and a host of others. Men with the social and professional standing of Charley Gondorff and his brother Fred, the High-Ass Kid (Eugene Allen), the Indiana Wonder (Roy MacMullen), and Kid (Walter) McGinley, who married Anita Baldwin along with the Comstock millions, sometimes prefer not to recall their humble origins among the *flat-jointers* on the circus lot.

There are today two fairly well defined types of professional *shell-men* operating. The first are strictly 'circus' in that they prefer to work under the protection of a show and often cannot work successfully anywhere else; the second are more versatile and will work any place that a crowd gathers. However, both organize their mobs on the same basis, and the standard pattern is this: an *inside-man* (who appears to the public as the 'player' and ostensibly the sole operator of the game); an *outside-man,* posing as one of the crowd but really a *roper* who locates victims with money and steers them into the game; a *stick-handler,* who surreptitiously directs the synthetic 'play' which excites the victim's cupidity; and the *shills* or *sticks* (recruited locally and either paid small wages or promised some minor privileges with the show) who 'keep the game warm' between plays.

Most spectators assume that the basis of the shell-game is legerdemain or sleight-of-hand, and that the victim succumbs solely to optical illusion induced by the manual skill of the player; this belief is encouraged by most operators, who can be counted on to call attention to the old saw which says that the hand is faster than the eye. Incidentally, there are some 'exhibition players' and professional magicians who do strange and wonderful things with three walnut shells and a 'pea'; but these men do not and cannot take money professionally with the game. The *grifters* depend more upon the psychology of the confidence-game than upon spectacular skill and, contrary to popular belief, use a very limited number of plays, or variations on those plays. Because their techniques are not lightly divulged (I know of no publication which chronicles them) it is perhaps worth while to give here a brief and somewhat oversimplified description of how professionals use the game; many additional technical details will be found in the Glossary.

1. Equipment: A board about 12 by 18 inches, usually mounted on a tripod, but sometimes laid on any convenient rest. Three English walnut shells (or other substitutes) are weighted in the top with wax, clay, or putty to make them easier to handle. A small sphere of sponge-rubber completes the simple ensemble.

2. The mob: This organization has already been described above.

3. *The Convincer:* Once a victim is roped and steered to the game (which has been kept going meanwhile by the shills and a stray sucker here and there among the spectators) he is given a place just in front of the center of the board. The *inside-man* is very friendly and shows him the shells, giving out meanwhile an amusing patter which is known as *spieling the nuts.* He raises the right hand shell and catches the pea under the edge so that it shows in an obvious *peek;* then with a quick movement he pushes this shell forward, rolling the pea underneath. Immediately he makes two fake moves with the other two shells, pushing them into line with the first. 'Give me a bet on where the little pea is,' he says, and a *shill* bets $2.00 or $5.00. When the shells are turned up, the *shill* wins. The *mark* sees it is easy.

4. *The Runaround:* A repetition of the previous stage, except that the *inside-man* makes some elaborate passes with the shells, apparently changing the position of the two end shells with each other or with the center shell under the cover of lively chatter. But his speed is only apparent, for he allows the victim to see where the pea is all the time. 'Give me a bet,' says the *inside-man.* Meanwhile the *stick-handler* has surreptitiously

passed out money to the *shills* and one bets a $5.00 bill. He loses it by betting on the wrong shell. The *mark* sees him make this mistake and thinks he understands how it is done. Then all the *shills* bet their money fast to simulate action for the benefit of the *mark* as well as the crowd, which may furnish some suckers who join spontaneously into the betting. As fast as the *shills* win, the *stick-handler* takes the money from them and re-distributes it as necessary. This sort of play goes on until the mark is 'ripe'; then the *inside-man* turns to him and says, 'Can you follow it? Is your eye faster than my hand? In this game, the eye has to be faster than the hand. Can you pick it out? Go ahead, you don't have to bet. Just try it for fun. It won't cost you anything. Just for the fun this time.' Naturally, the *mark* can pick it out, for this play has been for his benefit. 'You have a good eye,' says the *inside-man*. 'Now do you want to try it for two, five, or ten?' Perhaps the *mark* bets right away; if not, two or three *shills* wave $5.00 and $10.00 bills. 'Here's a gentleman,' says the *inside-man,* who takes a $10.00 bet and *blows* it to the *shill*. If the sucker still hesitates (the best marks are often the cautious ones), the *outside-man* who has been right at his side during the play says, 'Didn't you see how he does it? Go ahead and take him.' So the *mark* bets $5.00 and loses it. The *boosters* come in to keep the game going and the *outside-man* whispers, 'You shouldn't have lost that bet. He always moves them the same way. Watch closely and take him the next time.' The *inside-man* then turns to the *mark* and makes some passes; the *outside-man* pulls out a large roll of money and makes sure that the *mark* sees it. The *mark* bets $10.00 and wins.

5. *The Count-down:* The *outside-man* now has his money in his hand and looks enviously at the *mark,* who has just received $20.00 from the *inside-man's* large bankroll. He bets $10.00 himself and loses. Turning to the *mark* he says, 'How the hell does he do it? I watched him and I was sure it was under that one.' The *mark* may then try to explain it to him, but the *outside-man* says to the *inside-man*, 'Just do that again, please.' Meanwhile he has put away his money. The *inside-man* moves the shells, and the *outside-man* says, 'There it is, I saw it. Hold that shell right there till I get my money out.' The *mark* holds the shell, for he saw it too. 'Ten dollars,' says the *outside-man*. 'If you think it's under that one,' says the *inside-man,* 'I'll just take you on. But not for $10. I'll bet you for your roll.' 'Fine,' says the *outside-man,* 'you can't scare me off,' and slaps down six $20.00 bills and a $10.00 bill. 'You're on,' says the *inside-man*. 'All right,' says the *outside-man,* 'cover my bet.' The *inside-man* peels off $130.00 and covers the bet. 'Now,' he says to the *mark*, 'turn that shell over for me.' The *mark* does this, the pea is there, and the *outside-man* wins $260. This prepares the *mark* for the kill.

The *outside-man*, pretty well pleased with himself, says to the *inside-man*, 'Want to try it again?' The *inside-man* does. He moves the shells again. The *outside-man* picks a shell, winks at the sucker, and puts his hand firmly on the shell. 'You held a winner for me,' he says, 'so I'll hold one for you.' The mark says 'O.K.' and reaches for his money, intending to place a $10.00 or $20.00 bet.

Meanwhile the *stick-handler* distracts the *inside-man's* attention momentarily. The *outside-man* nudges the *mark*, raises the shell slightly, and shows the *mark* that the pea is there. It is a sure-thing bet. The *inside-man* whirls on the *mark* and says, 'I'll match your roll dollar for dollar and take all you've got.' The *mark* takes him on, counts out all his money, has it covered, and turns the shell over. The pea is not there, for the *outside-man* has *copped* it when he gave the *mark* a *flash-peek*. So the *mark* is whipped, and the *shills* warm the game up for the next sucker.

In the event that the mark *chills* on this last play, or its equivalent, the *inside-man* kids him for being cautious, while the *outside-man* turns the shell over. The pea is there. That usually does the trick, and he is taken on the next play. This simple device is strikingly similar to the *prat-out* as used in the *big-con* games, and usually arouses the cupidity in even the most stubborn sucker.

Note that the sleight-of-hand involved in these plays is so simple that any high-school lad could master it with very little practise. It is the *cross-fire*, or patter, which really beats the *mark*. However, there is an alternative play which can be used if a *mark* cannot be taken on the *count-down*. It requires a little more dexterity.

6. *The Rudy:* The *inside-man* sets shell No. 2 on a *peek* so that the mark sees the pea under the edge. He moves it forward as in 'The Convincer,' and covers the pea. Then he takes his hands off shell No. 2 and never touches it again. He picks up both shells 1 and 3 to show that they are empty, then *passes* them around in a very obvious manner. The *mark* is sure the pea is still under No. 2, which it is. Then, increasing the speed of his *passing*, the *inside-man* strikes either No. 1 or No. 3 lightly against No. 2 in such a way that the pea shoots out from No. 2 under one of the other shells. The *passing* is well covered by *cross-fire*, and the *mark* never sees the shells touch; if the trick is properly done, he hardly hears them click. The *mark* is so sure that the pea is still under the center shell that he is then willing to bet, and loses.

Following is a transcript illustrating the usage of an old-time *three-shell man:*

When the rag hits town early in the morning, the fix goes up town to see the law, but he don't call (the game) the shells, as you know the hucks are made out of wood and there are four of them, one not in use, so that takes the chill out of the block-game.

If the patch says you can rip and tear, you can go the limit on anything. Rip and tear is snatch and grab. Then the dink spieler tells the stick-handler to get the boost lined up for the battle of the kid-show, which starts early in the afternoon. Then the stick-handler gets himself six good-looking sticks and tells them what to do and how to do it right. They never pay out jack to a booster, just fill them full of lemonade and popcorn and sometimes promise them a lay with one of the show girls, but that never happens. . . .

When the kid-show opens and the tip is large he spreads the store, and then he says, 'Boys, step up to this little shop and get some easy spending money for yourself.' Then the sticks and the handler move up by the joint and the spieler tells them, 'Watch the little sheep-turd, watch it keen-eyed, now watch which block it is under, now you, big boy, just for fun take any one you like.' The stick takes the center one and wins the first time, then the player says to him, 'Boy, you've got a keen eye, now take a chance for two, five, or ten and I'll pay even money for the right guess.' The handler fixes his mitt with a deuce and says, 'Take the center one,' and the stick cops two bucks and they all laugh, and the player says, 'Stand right where you're at and I'll give you another chance,' and the stick is fitted again with a deuce and told to take the center one, and the player just moves the end nut around and cops the bet and says, 'I fooled you that time.' The outside (man) says, 'He moved the block around while you was getting your money out.'

It goes this way for all the boost—two, five, or ten, just cop and blow, then the tip warms up to see how easy it is to pick out the pea. The player just keeps on grinding. Then some egg in the tip puts his hand in his kick and he (the *inside-man*) gives the office to the outside, who comes into the play. The outside makes a bet of five or ten or whatever the player says he will bet—blow a fin or cop a saw, all to the runaround. Then the mark is now warm, and the player says to the mark—if he don't go natural—he says to him, 'Now boy, I'll give you a chance as I'm loser and would like to catch even. Now stand right there and tell me which one it is under just for fun.' The mark says, 'That one in the center,' and the dealer says, 'Turn it over and see.' The egg turns it over and the pea is there. Now the egg is on for the blow. . . .

When a mark blows on a play, the player says (to the *outside-man*) to shade the store so the tip won't see the play. The outside-man bends over the store so the tip won't get ranked, as the tip thinks it knows where the pea is too, but it don't. When the store is shaded, you can't see what is going on, and the tip is just the same as before. . . .

Then they go back to the grind again, and keep the store hot by cop and blow, then they move around the tent for a new tip, or they might slough for a new show. You know, Doc, the way to win more money with the hucks is the grind, just keep on grinding for twos, fives, and tens, and at the end of a day you'll have a lot of jack. No fancy doings on the nuts, just the plain plays, and don't let the joint get tipped off. The outside-man is always on the watch for some egg in the tip who has got his duke in his kick, and he prats him in (at) the right place for the spieler to play for him. . . .

In some places a nut-joint wouldn't win a dime, and the other flat-joints would have a big day. What heats up a rag is the short and the dinks. As Colonel Weaver used to say, 'Ham, you could cook eggs in the air it is so hot around here. I'm packing in on this spot while I'm all together!' Big Whitey and the Colonel were the perfect dink-players. Very seldom would the town get warm. But if McGinley was playing the inside, or Kid Hunt, you would see plenty of smoke. Mac was rough in the slide and the push, but he would surely get the dough if it was around, and there was plenty of heat with it. . . .

GLOSSARY

ARM-BOARD. A small shell-board which can be clipped to the left wrist. The operator plays the shells one-handed. Used in making *sneak pitches*.

The BACK-HAND ROLL. A method of rolling the pea from the back of the hand to the palm or between fingers; it is rolled over little finger by pressure against table. Also the reverse from palm to back. Used to show hand 'empty.' Chiefly used by exhibition players.

BACK-HAND TURNOVER. Method of turning up shell to show it 'empty' while concealing pea between or under 3rd and 4th fingers. Exhibition players.

BACK-SHIFT. A type of *pass* which enables the player to conceal the pea on the back of his fingers after stealing it. Exhibition players.

BLOCKS. The hollowed-out wooden cubes used as a substitute for the more notorious walnut-shells. There are often four, with only three in use. Also *hucks, hinks, dinks, shells.* In England and Australia, *thimbles.*

To BLOW. To lose a bet. 'Cop a deuce and blow a fin on the runaround.'

BOODLED. In possession of a large amount of money; usually said of a sucker.

The BOOST. The *sticks* or *shills;* considered collectively.

To CHILL. For a victim to lose interest in the game, or to become suspicious.

To CLEAN, v.tr. 1. Said of the *sticks*, to take their winnings away as fast as they complete a play. 2. Said of a victim, to fleece him.

COME-THROUGH, n. Also *to come through*, v.i. A victim who has been trimmed and comes back with an officer in an effort to find and identify the *grifter* who trimmed him. Occasionally victims return from their home communities, or follow the show to the next stop with an officer. It is the *fixer's* responsibility to prevent such goings-on before they cause the show trouble. In very hot cases, all or part of the money taken is given back to the victim.

. . . the marks are after the sticks,

And Mr. Bates comes through,
And it's the possum-belly for you . . .

To COP. To win a bet. 'Let that tall stick cop a double-saw.'

The COUNT-DOWN. A type of play in which the victim is built up by seeing the *inside-man* take all the money the *outside-man* has; the victim thinks he sees how it was done, and when the *inside-man* wants to match his roll at even money, he takes the bet and loses. There are numerous variations of this play, one of which is described in the body of the article.

DINK-SPIELER. The *inside-man*, ostensibly the 'player' of the shell game, and the only one of the mob having any obvious connection with the game.

DOUBLE-DECKER. A play in which one shell is placed partly over another (the pea is under it). Then the lower shell is moved forward and the upper shell cops the pea as the lower shell is moved forward and to right.

To DRAW, v.t. For the *inside-man* to move a shell toward himself on the board.

To DUKE. 1. To slip a *stick* money to bet on the game. 'Duke him a saw and blow it.' 2. In the phrase *to duke (someone) in.* To place the sucker's hand on a shell and hold it, meanwhile building him up for a big bet. See *the count-down* in the body of the article. Also *to mitt (someone) in.*

FAKE-LOAD. A deceptive play in which the *inside-man* pretends to put the pea under a shell from the rear.

FAKE-STEAL. The reverse of a *fake-load;* the *inside-man* pretends to remove the pea from a shell from the rear.

FINGER-POSITION. The position of the *inside-man's* fingers on the shells during any given move. Exhibition players.

FINGER SUCKER STEAL. A move for the benefit of the *mark;* he is allowed to see the *inside-man* lift the pea between his fingers.

To FIX (ONE'S) MITT. Also *to fit (one's) mitt,* or *to fit the stick.* For the *handler* to slip a *stick* some money to bet. 'That is when the stick-handler fixes his mitt with a saw.' 'Fit him with a fin.'

FLASH. 1. n. A quick look at the pea under the shell, given the *mark* by the *outside-man* as he holds the shell for him; may also be given by the *inside-man* in some plays. Also *peek, flash-peek,* or *sucker-flash.* 2. v.tr. To intentionally reveal the position of the pea to the *mark.*

FLASH-PEEK. See *flash.*

To FRAME THE GAFF. See *to spread the store.*

FULL-PEEK. A good look which the *inside-man* permits the *mark* to get as the shells are moved; a better look than one would get in a *peek* or a *flash, q.v.*

To GO NATURAL. For a victim to respond to the play of the *sticks* and take a bet without further artificial stimulation. 'A mark might stand there looking the thing over and then go natural, that is, he'd make a bet without being boosted in the play.'

To GRIND. To play along steadily for small bets between the times when a lucrative sucker is being fleeced. 'You just keep on grinding, and that is called keeping the store hot.'

HALF-LIFT. A move which permits the *mark* to see under a shell.

To HEEL THE STICKS. To pass out money with which the shills are to bet as instructed.

To HOLD OUT. To secrete the pea in the hand while the *mark* believes it to be under a shell.

HUCKS. See *blocks.*

INSIDE-MAN. The operator of a *three-shell game.*

INSIDE-SHIFT. A play in which the *inside-man* secretly shifts the pea from a hiding place between two of his fingers to a new position between two others. Largely exhibition players.

JOINT. The *three-shell game.* 'Any flat-joint with a circus is called a store, and almost any crimpy business is called a joint.'

To KEEP THE STORE HOT. To simulate play with the *sticks* and with casual suckers from the crowd while the *outside-man* locates a good mark.

KICK-STEAL. A move in which the player flips the shell toward the *mark* for examination, but catches the pea between his fingers as the shell passes over it. Largely exhibition players.

KID-TOP. The sideshow tent, near which or inside which the *shell-man* traditionally makes his *pitch.* Many *circus-grifters* agree that the best spot on the lot is inside the animal tent, but the game is seldom played there.

LEFT-SIDE SUCKER-STEAL. A move in which anyone on the player's left is permitted to see the pea removed as the shell is moved forward.

LIFT. 1. n. A move raising the shell for a *flash.* 2. v.tr. To raise a shell for a *flash.*

LIFT-UP SUCKER-STEAL. A move in which the *inside-man* permits the *mark* to see the removal of the pea from the rear. Cf. *fake-steal.*

To LOAD THE PEA. To put it under a shell in preparation for a play. Cf. *to steal the pea.*

LOADING POSITION. A position from which the *inside-man* can put the pea under a shell unobserved.

LONG DOUGH. A considerable amount of money, usually in the possession of a mark. See *boodled.*

MARK. The victim or intended victim of the *shell-game.*

MENDER or MR. MENDER. See *patch.*

To MITT (SOMEONE) IN. See *to duke* 2.

MR. BATES. A sucker or *mark.* Probably borrowed from pickpockets.

OFFICE. 1. n. A signal passed between members of the mob, usually unobserved by spectators and players. This term is widely used by all types of organized criminals, with specialized forms adapted to various professions and to various individual mobs. 2. v. tr. To signal another person surreptitiously.

OKUS. A wallet. Also *poke* or *skin.* All terms probably borrowed from pickpockets.

To BE ON FOR THE BLOW. For a victim to be built up for a trimming. 'When a mark is on for the blow he sometimes puts his mitt in his kick, and then the outside moves in and either makes a cop or a blow . . .'

OUTSIDE-MAN or (The) OUTSIDE. The member of a *shell-mob* who locates promising suckers on the lot, steers them to the game, and assists in the play.

PASS. Any movement of the shells or the pea as a part of a play.

PATCH. The fixer for a circus, and especially for the *flat-joints* and *grifters.* These fixers make arrangements in advance with the local authorities, and handle hot individual cases personally if possible. Also *mender, Mr. Mender.* The fixer is usually paid by the circus management; sometimes he owns part or all of a *flat-joint* himself. In some cases he takes 10% of the proceeds of those *stores* (such as the *shell-game*) for which he fixes. The day's 'take' from the grift is turned in each night in the *privilege-car,* and divided thus: 60% of the gross to the management, who may pay the *fixer* his 10%; 20% to the *inside-man;* 20% to the *outside-man;* wages to the *stick-handler.*

PEA. The small rubber ball used in the *shell-game.* Also *pill.*

PEEK. See *flash.*

PILL. See *pea.*

To PRAT A MARK IN. To maneuver a *mark* into a position where he will play; to get a man *roped* by the *outside-man* up close to the board where he can be played. This term also probably borrowed from pickpockets, who use it in a slightly different sense; the *big-con* men borrowed it from the *flat-jointers,* and have applied both the word and the principle in the *big-con* games.

PRIVILEGE-CAR. A circus-car set aside for the use of the management, the *grifters* and other privileged characters. Drinks may be sold and gambling sponsored by the management. See *patch.* '. . . and many a grift was there. They damn nigh filled the Wallace privilege car. . . .'

To PUSH, v.tr. To move a shell forward on the board.

To PUT THE RAISE ON A MARK. To induce a victim to raise his bet after he thinks he knows which shell conceals the pea. 'This is just the same as poker. The inside-man forces him to go the limit,

say as much as he has. The outside-man says, "Take it, he's trying to bluff you, just take it and show him something . . ." '

RAG. A circus.

To RANK THE STORE. To inadvertently allow the crowd to see how a play works, or to arouse the crowd's suspicions that the *inside-man* is too smart for them. 'If you rank the store, the tip will be cold, and you will have to slough for another tip . . .'

The REACHOVER. A method of stimulating play and reviving interest in the game. So called because the *inside-man* reaches over the *sticks* into the crowd to make a bet.

RIGHT-SIDE SUCKER-STEAL. Same as *left-side steal,* but in reverse.

RIGHT TOWN. A city where the officials have been *fixed,* or can be *fixed.*

RIP AND TEAR. 1. adj. Openly rough or obvious tactics used in skinning a sucker. 2. Said of a spot or city which is strongly fixed, so that such tactics can be used. 'It was rip and tear in Toronto when Johnny Tolbert was the patch.' 3. v.i. To use rough tactics.

ROLL-FLASH. A type of play in which the *inside-man* deceives the *mark* by dropping the pea as if by accident as he *passes* the shells. It appears to go under one shell, but does not stay there as *inside-man* steals it.

The RUDY, also *rowdy.* A play sometimes used to take a stubborn victim who is known to have considerable money. Described in the body of the article. 'The rudy is seldom used. It's fancy stuff.'

The RUNAROUND. A simple, almost foolish type of play in which the *inside-man* moves one shell or the other around the center one, allowing a *shill* to win or lose on that play, in order to show the crowd how easy it is to play this game. 'You keep on playing the runaround until a fink takes a whack at it, but the inside-man knows when a mark is on the spring, and the outside comes into the play right away . . .'

To SHADE THE STORE. To protect the board from full view of the crowd at the moment the victim is fleeced; this is usually done by the *outside-man.* See *to take the chill out of a game.*

To SLOUGH, v.tr. or intr. To take down the game; to close it upon that spot and go with another show.

SNEAK-PITCH. A *shell-game* set up in a spot which is not protected, or where authorities have prohibited it.

SPIELER. The *inside-man.* Also *huck-spieler* or *dink-spieler.* This term was at one time used to mean the *inside-man* on the *big-con* games, reflecting the close relationship between *circus-grifters* and early confidence-men. Parenthetically, it was picked up by law-enforcement officers and is still almost universally used by them to refer to the *inside-man* in a big-con game; I have heard some of the best detectives in the country use it, although it is obsolete among *con-men* in this sense. In fact, the odds are that anyone using it, referring to the *big-con,* is, or has been, a detective.

To SPREAD THE STORE. To set up the *three-shell* board on the tripod and prepare to open the game. Also, *to frame the gaff.*

To SPRING, or To BE ON THE SPRING. For a mark to put his hand in his pocket, reach for his wallet, or otherwise give signs of wanting to bet. 'Move in on that mark in front of you, he's on the spring, and blow a saw.' The *office* is often passed in the phrase, 'That man's from Springfield.'

To STEAL, v.tr. To take the pea from under a shell; see *fake-steal, finger sucker-steal, left-side sucker-steal, right-side sucker-steal,* etc.

STICK-HANDLER. The member of the mob who hires the *sticks* at each stand, instructs them how to bet, and provides them with money for each bet. After each winning bet, the money is retrieved from the *stick* in such a way that the crowd never sees the transfer. The *stick-handler* takes his cues from the *inside-man;* these are often transmitted in humorous or surreptitious argot-phrases, and this constitutes one of the few situations among *grifters* where argot is openly used in the presence of the sucker for communication on a secret or semi-secret level. 'The inside-man offices the stick-handler just what to do for every play, and how much to cop or blow.'

STICKS. Local men recruited by the *stick-handler* to act as 'shills'; they stimulate the play and build up the larceny in the victim.

SUCKER-FLASH. See *flash.*

SUCKER-MOVE. A *pass* intended to arouse the cupidity in the mark.

To TAKE THE CHILL OUT OF A GAME. To keep down suspicion that the shell-game is crooked. 'When a mark is being trimmed, the store is always shaded by crowding around the store to protect it from the tip. This takes the chill out of the game.'

TIP. The crowd, either the general crowd on the circus lot, or the small group to which the *three-shell* man plays. Probably borrowed from pickpockets, among whom the usage is very old.

To WEED. 1. To supply a *shill* with money. 'Weed that stick a saw.' 2. To take money away from a shill once he has won. 'The stick-handler always weeds the sticks right away.'

15

The Argot of the Professional Dice Gambler

Originally, the glossary of this article was written for John Scarne's first book on gambling entitled *Scarne on Dice* (1945). Scarne was already a master at manipulating both cards and dice and, prior to that time, was barred from most of the casinos in the United States and the Caribbean. Today anyone who is familiar with gambling at all is aware of his incredible skill at manipulating the law of averages. Eventually he was employed by some of the largest and most prestigious casinos in the Southwest where his job was to detect those who tried to beat the house either from the inside or from the outside.

Subsequently, the editors of *The Annals of the American Academy of Political and Social Science* approached me for a study of some phase of gambling to be included in a special issue devoted entirely to gambling in America. At this time I not only updated the glossary, but I also added a substantial introduction which discussed in some detail the sociology and psychology of the gambler, especially the dice gambler. This puts the linguistic elements into some sociolinguistic perspective and discusses somewhat in depth the genesis of argots and the reasons for their social distribution. Because dice gambling is an ancient and stable phenomenon and because the game has changed little in the last thirty years, the argot recorded here is substantially that used today by the dice hustler. However, because of the systematic recruitment of patrons from all parts of the country to be flown on gambling junkets to Las Vegas and other centers, there has been considerable linguistic diffusion among gamblers who might be regarded as suckers rather than as hustlers. At the same time many of these sucker gamblers are unaware of the special senses of certain words used by the hustler. Nevertheless, the core of the argot remains the exclusive property of the skilled dice hustler who knows so well how to beat any dice game in which he participates either alone or with a partner.

• • •

Acknowledgments: My wife, Barbara S. Maurer, provided her expert assistance in drawing from my files the material for this study and in helping in fieldwork, verification, and editing. I am indebted to Mr. Everett Debaun, an inmate of a large Eastern Penitenitary and author of "The Theory and Practice of Armed Robbery," *Harpers Magazine* (February 1950), who did painstaking work of verifying this material against both his own rich experience and that of many others in prison. Clayton Rawson and John Scarne contributed generously their knowledge of techniques and their patience with a simple philologist; in a few instances I have used in this study direct quotations from Scarne's authoritative *Scarne on Dice,* which I trust will not be taken amiss, since I wrote, or helped to write, most of his glossarial material; at the same time, knowing that John Scarne is a perfectionist, I do not imply that he may be responsible for any of my mistakes. Stuart Flexner, Suzanne Resnick, Sylvia Widerschein, and other graduate students assisted on verification. I am also grateful to the professionals (all of whom by preference remain nameless) who have made available their own technology and experience on the level of fieldwork.

G AMBLING is inherent in American life. It came early to these shores with the Spanish and French adventurers; it was reinforced by the British garrisons in New England; it was the sport of the first families of Virginia, from aristocrats to thieves and debtors; it spilled over the edges of New Orleans and migrated up the Mississippi Valley to father a great midwestern underworld with concentrations in Memphis, St. Joseph, St. Louis, Kansas City, Chicago, Minneapolis, St. Paul, Cairo, Terre Haute, Louisville, Newport, Cincinnati, Youngstown, Pittsburgh. It followed the frontier, especially the gold rush, and settled down in swank splendor on the West Coast, with headquarters in Tijuana, San Diego, Reno, Los Angeles, San Francisco, and a score of other coastal cities. In fact, I do not know of any major American city that is not profoundly influenced both politically and economically by professional gambling interests.

IMPLICATIONS OF GAMBLING

In itself, gambling can hardly be considered criminal, although it is so classified in the statutes of most of the states and in some federal codes. Parenthetically, the professional gambler is a recognized and legitimate taxpayer under the Treasury Department's income tax program, with the craft of computing the gambler's net income long acknowledged by gambler and government alike.

Although gambling may not be criminal, its viciousness lies in the fact that it gradually corrupts city, state, and federal government agencies; it pays off regularly to political machines; it imports strong-arm men and gangsters to enforce its jurisdictions; it nominates and elects public officials; it constitutes a powerful and semilegitimate front for the underworld. On its heels come the harlot, the pimp, the pickpocket, the narcotics peddler, the safe-cracker, the stickup man, the blackmailer, the extortionist, the professional thief, the confidence man, the labor racketeer, the municipal fixer, the shakedown copper, the machine boss, the corrupt judge, and other paid protectors of crime less easily condoned than gambling.

Within our own times it has made household words of such proper names as Capone, Pendergast, Rothstein, Annenberg, Costello, and scores of others. At the same time it has commercialized the lust for easy money in millions of legitimate citizens, who are of interest in this study only as the suckers supporting a vast, lucrative, and highly organized industry operating almost exclusively under paid protection from the law.

Needless to say, there is no such thing as an "honest" professional gambler, although there are still a few gentlemen gamblers who rely on their phenomenal understanding of the game and a sort of sixth sense which makes cheating superfluous; but these men play for sport and not for a living. The professional gambler depends upon an edge, or advantage over the nonprofessional player.

Naturally, the mechanical devices by which the gambler cheats for his profit are legion, and the manual skills that he develops are often superb. It is not my objective to examine these devices or techniques in detail here, except insofar as they are reflected in the technical language used by professional gamblers. Sometimes the "edge" is not a deliberate cheating device, but rather a set percentage which the gambler must take from a total of the individuals with whom he plays; that is, a bookmaker must make a living. If he "dutches" his books, he cannot pay off his customers. Therefore, he combines some knowledge of mathematics with the genuine desire to improve the breed (which is said to motivate most race-track gamblers), and takes a rather steady percentage from all who place bets with him.

A similar situation exists in many established gambling houses, where all the gambling devices are set to yield an overall percentage for the house; this may range from, say, 13 percent on a crap table to 80 to 1 against the player on the slot machines. Often such houses do not consider themselves in any way dishonest but look upon this percentage as a normal profit comparable to that taken by any legitimate business, which, in a sense, it is. However, most of them maintain both the men and the equipment to separate any lucky sucker from large amounts of money he may win, and this separation may take place on the basis of either skill or violence.

Individual gamblers—those who do not work for the house but may work against other individuals or against the house—are of necessity skilled and seasoned sharpers who combine great manual skill with specially prepared equipment and a subtle knowledge of human psychology.

On the basis of personal honesty, gamblers vary as much as do ordinary individuals; but on the whole they appear to be more scrupulous in the payment of their debts and the maintenance of their credit than the average legitimate citizen, because the maintenance of a good reputation in this respect is an absolute necessity in the underworld. Some professional gamblers carefully cultivate and protect a reputation for high personal integrity. Naturally, this does not always carry over into their professional life.

THE PLACE OF THE GAMBLER IN THE UNDERWORLD

By underworld standards, the professional gambler ranks between the confidence man and the thief; that is, he is in the upper brackets of what is known as "the grift." Usually, successful gamblers combine some of the psychological skills of the confidence rackets with the manual skills of the thief, adapted, of course, to their particular racket; in fact, there is a good deal of overlapping between the con rackets and gambling, in that some of the best confidence men make their expenses when traveling about the world by operating as "deep-sea gamblers." Some professional gamblers, often those employed by reputable gambling houses, double as confidence men during either short-con or big-con touches, which are laid in the gambling house either with or without the knowledge of the management.

Sometimes, also, gamblers lean heavily toward respectability and operate as bookmakers in social areas which appear to be remote from the underworld. Others lean the other way, toward the occasional use of violence and maintain effective business connections with the so-called heavy rackets. Within the last ten years it has become the fashion in the underworld to avoid violence and to work more and more on an ostensibly respectable level; the word has gone out in most organizations, "Don't do anything spectacular."

This tendency toward gentility has paid off handsomely, with the result that we now support an underworld far more extensive and far more prosperous than anything that existed in the gangster days of the twenties. Protected gambling, of course, is the hub around which this underworld revolves.

ORGANIZATION

Gamblers operate primarily on two levels: as lone-wolf or individual gamblers, and as a mob. The free-lance or lone-wolf gambler is a survival of the old frontier days which produced some remarkably competent operators. Among dice gamblers today these men are known as hustlers. Usually they work alone — and against everyone else including other hustlers — but they may on occasion team up temporarily with a mob. The types of mob organization among all types of gamblers are multifarious.

The organized gambler works with a mob that ranges in number from two to twelve individuals, if we include all the steerers, tailers, paid policemen and others. In Detroit several years ago a grand jury discovered that more than a hundred public officials were in the employ of organized gamblers and sent them all to prison—much to the surprise of everyone. These were, of course, all auxiliary or accessory to mob operation.

In the mobs there is a rather sharp division of labor, with the steerer, roper, or outside man rooting out marks and steering them to the game, where the amount of money in evidence is calculated to arouse the native larceny in the sucker and prepare him for the kill. If the mob operates on the verge of the confidence rackets, the dealer, banker, or stickman may sometimes serve as an inside man; usually, he is simply a highly skilled technician. The cappers or shills win and lose during the play according to the instructions of the inside man, who directs their play in such a way as to produce the desired reactions on the part of the suckers. The play may occur anywhere, from a swank gambling house to a cheap hotel room.

Some mobs operate consistently in one city or one vicinity; others travel regular routes over the country (mitt mobs, smack teams, tat workers, and so forth). Some dealers travel from house to house on a sort of rotational schedule, being moved into certain localities for certain types of play, or occasionally to handle individual suckers who are known to be ready to play with large amounts of money. Some gambling houses are stable and enjoy a good reputation for fair play within the limits of the percentage they are known to take. These are really a form of semilegitimate business. Others are less savory, and change their personnel as frequently as possible in order to stimulate play and to allay suspicion which may fasten itself upon any of the house personnel.

Some houses are large, luxuriously furnished, and prosper under secure political protection. Others range down the scale to the corner drug store where controlled dice are used, or to the doorway bookmaker who is prepared to "go over the hill" when mathematics fails him.

Because of the high degree of organization among gamblers and because of the close dependence of the profession upon such nationally organized aids as wire service, form-sheet publication, or the manufacture of crooked gambling equipment, and because of the similar technical and social habits developed by gamblers, the gambling fraternity consists of a rather close-knit social group. This racket extends over the entire continent, even reaching abroad, while at the same time it penetrates every small community with enough money to interest a gambler.

THE FIX

Probably no other underworld group enjoys such universal and effective police protection as the professional gambler, especially since gambling has become an important industry with a tremendous national gross. For a nominal weekly payment, the gambler can operate in comparative safety from law enforcement agencies, from reform groups, from irate victims, and from non-paying competitors.

Sometimes the "fix" is a simple transaction between the gambler and the policeman on the beat; usually it is more subtle than that. In most cities there is a fixer (or several, one for each type of racket) who arranges in advance for a gambler to operate in that community. He collects an advance plus the regular weekly payment, plus campaign contributions, plus extra payments when "the heat" is turned on by reform groups, by honest enforcement officials naïve enough to think they can buck the machine, or by competitors trying to muscle in. Often this fixer is a person of both local and national prestige; almost never does he have open or ostensible connection with the rackets. Gone are the days when the corner saloon keeper acted as the fix for all the rackets in his neighborhood.

While some fixing is done on a goodwill basis, most of it is a cold commercial transaction by which a law violator buys immunity up to a certain point; after that, he buys assistance in the courts; if that fails, he buys leniency from an appeal judge; occasionally, when all fails, a gambler goes to prison. He is the exception, for a well-oiled machine operates in every community, in every state, in every congressional district, with the fixing done through very potent political channels. Some of it eventually goes to Washington.

In each community, however, the police department is the focal point of the fix, and every gambler must decide whether or not he wants armed and uniformed police for his business or against it. Usually he is a step ahead of even the most dishonest policeman, and fans the spark of larceny dormant in most gendarmes with a sheaf of notes calculated to build it instantly into a hot and consuming blaze. And so the gambler who in frontier days found himself driven from city to city by armed and irate citizens now basks in security and prosperity under the blessings of civilized government, which protects, to some degree, not only the gambler but all forms of organized crime with the exception of kidnapping.

THE DICE GAMBLER

There are many types of gambler operating on many different social levels in an infinite number of communities. Some make their living entirely as professionals, some are semiprofessionals, and others are strictly amateur. They gamble by all the means known to human kind. By no means are all of these underworld characters, for the desire to gamble cuts across all social strata. The point is that anyone who likes to gamble with dice can perhaps be called a dice gambler, and many an otherwise legitimate citizen studies and practices with the dice to learn to "control" them. Eventually he learns about crooked dice and how they are used. He may secure one of the catalogues from the several solid mail-order houses which prepare equipment. Sometimes he learns to use it properly, but more often it simply makes him a better mark for other gamblers, for the real quality of a gambler lies within himself and not in his equipment or even in his skills. One must have true grift sense, and what often appears to be an innate capacity for taking money from strangers.

There is something about criminal enterprise which breeds a special type of language, or argot. All rackets develop special modes of speech, and in the United States nearly all argot falls into two broad classes — that of the heavy rackets and that of the grift. Each of these broad areas comprises innumerable rackets, with the gambler ranking high within the grift. In turn, there are many gambling rackets, some of which, as has been indicated, overlap with the confidence games, and each of these gambling rackets develops a specialized argot of its own, retaining, at the same time, many elements in common with all gambling argot and with the parent argots of the grift. Since the line between the grift and the heavy rackets is not always a sharp one, there are also embedded in the speech of the dice gambler occasional elements shared in common with the heavy rackets, which usage reflects the ancient and multifarious connections which all criminal enterprises have.

GENESIS OF ARGOTS

The extent of the entire body of criminal argots is vast, and the motives underlying it obscure. Superficially, we might say that the growth of this phase of nonstandard and semisecret language springs from strong group rapport; from a reaction to outside forces, many of them hostile; from a desire for recognition or professional status; from a compensatory tendency to establish superiority; from the need for becoming established as one of the fraternity; from individual compulsions; from atavistic tendencies toward the animism of language and its control over the material world; and not least from the large variety of equipment and technology which go with the racket.

Certainly minimal is the popularly accepted theory that argots are used to conceal meaning from outsiders. While outsiders usually understand little if any of a criminal argot, the element of deception can hardly be called intentional, since argots are seldom spoken in the presence of outsiders, especially victims or potential victims. Usually argot is spoken freely and without inhibition only among the initiate, where it serves as a sort of union card. Some professionals in all fields shun the use of argot as *déclassé*; others cultivate it with great wit and originality. Some men speak only the argot of their specialty, either through pride or lack of experience in other rackets; some speak several argots fluently and have a peripheral knowledge of many more.

The argots are more than specialized forms of language; they reflect the way of life in each of the numerous criminal cultures and subcultures; they are the keys to attitudes, to evaluations of men and society, to modes of thinking, to social organization, to technology. Often they show the keenest sort of perceptive mechanisms and involve imagery that is sharp, clear, and cynical.

Argots are not the creation of dull minds, except insofar as barbaristic usage is picked up and used with unconscious irony. Underlying most argot is a body of vivid imagery and a current of humor which is not always apparent to the uninitiate. Parenthetically, the argots of criminal and semicriminal groups—those who live primarily by their wits—form a large and only partially explored matrix from which a heavy proportion of current slang is derived.

The argots of various types of gamblers differ from other argots in many ways, of course, but principally in that they are known in part by many nonprofessionals and noncriminals. Every person who gambles learns a little argot even though he may never penetrate beyond the sucker level, and though what he knows on this level may be improperly used or understood. People who gamble a great deal know quite a bit of it, and sometimes take pride in this usage, although they too are excluded from the inner circles of the hustlers, the dealers, the diemakers, the cardmarkers, the ropers, the inside men, the shills, the bookmakers, the numbers boys—in short, the professionals, where a large percentage of the new and fresh coinages first appear.

The main flow of argot seems to be out from this professional center to the semiprofessionals, to the legitimate gamblers, to all players, to the public at large. There are some back currents of course, with some usages working in toward the center; but in the main the legitimate language—in fact, the literary language—is constantly being bombarded with idiom from the professional groups. Some of it dies as soon as it emerges from the speech of specialists, but some of it persists until it is adopted by the standard language on many different levels.

SCOPE OF PRESENT STUDY

The speech of dice gamblers is typical of gamblers' argot, although of course it differs in content and imagery from other gambling argots. In this study I have held closely to usage indigenous to the fraternity and have on the whole excluded terms from related rackets and from other social or criminal groups, even though those terms may be current among dice gamblers. This is done to conserve space and to give a clear picture of gambling argot in a rather strict sense. However, I have included here and there single entries borrowed from other types of gambling or from other rackets, or words that have generalized or specialized as they emerged from the dice-gamblers' argot proper, and have so labeled these isolated examples that the reader may have one or two pertinent examples of each for reference.

Furthermore, this check list is not complete, since the dice gamblers are legion and since the behavior pattern of the individual as well as the type differs widely according to both social and geographical distribution. These variants in the pattern are naturally reflected in linguistic usage, which changes both extensionally and intensionally at a rate relatively rapid compared to standard printed American English. I have omitted the conventional slang of legitimate dice gamblers, since it can hardly be called argot. Therefore this survey, while conducted with great care, cannot claim to be either comprehensive or exhaustive. It represents an attempt to generalize on the basis of some years of experience with both the culture and the language patterns of the professional criminal.

GLOSSARY [1]

ACE: The number one on a die.

ACTION: (1) The betting between players. "There's plenty of action." (2) Fast play with the dice.

ADA FROM DECATUR: See EIGHTER FROM DECATUR.

ALONE: Playing against the house, usually used in reference to a cheater trying to beat the house by himself.

ANGLE: A method of playing or cheating. "He's got an angle that he thinks will give him the best of it."

ASS-ENGLISH: The actions of a shooter who believes that by various contortions and cabalistic actions he can influence the dice.

BACKER: The financer of the game, whether it be an individual or a house.

BACK OF THE LINE: The space on the layout where bets are placed after the come-out. See COME-OUT. "Bets are sometimes placed back of the line to get odds of 2–1 on 4."

BAGGAGE: (1) An observer of the game who does not play. (2) A member of a mob who does not win enough to pay his own way.

BAGGED: Cheated. Said of a house which has been beaten by an employee in collusion with a player.

BAG-JOB: A setup by which a house is beaten by an employee (a dealer or stickman) working in collusion with a cheater.

BANK: (1) The dealer in bank craps. (2) The house. (3) The house bank roll. "The bank is money used to pay off."

BANK CRAPS or BANKING CRAPS: A crap game played on a layout in which all bets are made against the house. Although the policy varies from house to house, usually the player either pays a direct fee for each wager or else accepts smaller odds, as specified on the table layout.

BANKING CRAPS: See BANK CRAPS.

BANKER: (1) A dealer who collects and pays off bets for the house. (2) A bank-roll man or money man.

BANK-ROLL MAN: (1) A person who finances a dice game. (2) One who acts as a cashier for a game, usually the dealer.

TO BAR A POINT: A type of bet which seems to vary from house to house. It involves barring certain combinations of numbers on the dice so that even though the shooter makes his point, if it is made through one of these combinations, he loses the bet. "Barring a point is strictly a proposition-bet laid on tens and fours, nothing else, at even money." "Some say the bet (bar-bet) is sometimes made on other points with the shooter giving odds, but I doubt it." "To bar a point is a sucker-bet. They wouldn't stand for it in the East." ". . . no bar-bets in bank-craps, only small games, or hulley-gulley games . . ."

BAR BET: Same as to BAR A POINT. (Hustler usage.)

BATTERY JOINT or BAT: A place where electric dice controlled by batteries or current are used. Also JUICE-JOINT.

BEEFER: A player who consistently complains when he loses

BEHIND THE SINK: Broke. (Probably a

---

[1] Because this study is predominantly sociological in interest, the linguistic elements have been minimized.

variant of BEHIND THE SIX, from faro bank.)

BEHIND THE DICE or BACK OF THE DICE: Said of the player who, having just lost the dice to the current shooter, has the privilege of fading in round-table games.

The BEST OF IT: An advantage accruing from chance, percentage, or dishonest techniques. "Even-up or six and eight gives the player the best of it."

To BET BOTH WAYS: To bet the dice either to win or lose. "The table has two-way action because the players can bet both ways."

BETS ON THE LINE: The cry of the stickman before the first roll, indicating that players must put their money on the line.

To BET THE DICE TO LOSE: To bet that the dice will not make a point, neither will they make seven or eleven on the first roll.

To BET THE DICE TO WIN: To bet that the dice will make a seven on the first roll or repeat the point before a seven is thrown.

To BET ON THE LINE or BET THE LINE: (1) To bet that the dice will win or that the shooter will make a pass. (2) To bet before the come-out that the shooter will win. See COME-OUT.

To BET THE HIGH SIDE or BET THE HIGH NUMBERS: To bet that the dice will show points 8, 9, 10, 11, 12. "Betting the high side isn't used in craps. Pertains to the game Under and Over Seven. The percentage on this bet in craps would be 16⅔, which makes it a sucker-bet. . . ." "He is mistaken. It (betting the high side) is a hustler's bet used in street games sometimes. Also sometimes used in casino craps where 6–5 odds go with the bet. Actual odds are 21–15 or 7–5. . . ."

To BET LEFT AND RIGHT: To bet with players beside one.

To BET ON ONE'S MUSCLE: To bet on credit without the money to repay losses.

To BET THE LOW SIDE or BET THE LOW NUMBERS: To bet that the dice will show points 2, 3, 4, 5, 6. Cf. to BET THE HIGH SIDE.

BIG DICK: Point ten in craps. Also BIG DICK FROM BOSTON; BIG DICK THE LADIES' FRIEND.

BIG EIGHT: Eight on the layout (usually drawn large).

BIG GAME: See BIG TABLE.

BIG SIX: Six on the layout. Cf. BIG EIGHT.

BIG TABLE: A dice table where the wagers or limits are large. Also BIG GAME.

BLANKET ROLL: A type of controlled roll, so called because it can best be made on a blanket or rug. Also PAD ROLL or EVEN ROLL.

To BLOW: (1) To lose a sum of money. "I seen I had the edge so I zinged it in, but either they was lucky or had the gaff working. Anyhow I blowed the B-R." (2) To become aware of cheating. "The sucker blowed the move"; or "The sucker blowed." (Generalized underworld usage, but much used by dice gamblers.)

To BLOW THE WHISTLE: To complain to the police; said of a sucker who has lost. (Somewhat generalized.)

BOARDS: The raised rail around a crap table against which the dice must be thrown. Also RAIL; CUSHION.

BOOK: (1) The man who collects the money and pays off bets. (2) The backer of the game. (3) The house bank roll.

BOUNCER: (1) The employee who keeps order in a gambling house. (2) A worthless check. (Somewhat generalized.)

BOUNCE SHOT: A control shot somewhat similar to a box shot except that it is not made off a cushion or backboard. The bottom die falls dead because of the impact of the top one which strikes it.

BOX: (1) The container on the crap table in which the stickman keeps the dice. Also used in other types of dice games. (2) The dealer's box, usually made of leather. Subject to various cheating devices and techniques.

BOX CARS: Two sixes on a pair of dice.

BOX-CAR NUMBERS: Large sums of money. "He's OK for a short tab but make sure you don't let him go into box-car numbers."

BOX-MAN: The houseman who sells chips or changes money at bank craps, usually exchanging new bills for old.

BOX NUMBERS: A space on the layout where each point number appears within a square or box. Cf. OFF NUMBERS.

To BOX NUMBERS: To bet on any number but the point by laying the money in the proper square on the layout.

BOX UP or BOX THEM UP: The cry of a player who wants to change dice. The stickman then mixes the dice in the bowl and the player takes a new pair.

BOX SHOT: A control shot whereby the shooter may control the fall of one die. The dice are thrown one atop the other. The bottom die strikes at the junction of playing surface and cushion and, being prevented from rolling over by the weight of the top die, rebounds from the cushion in a slide. Cf. GREEK SHOT.

To BREAK A GAME: For a player to force a game to its conclusion by winning all or most of the money. Indication that the game is broke or busted is sometimes given by turning the box upside down on the table.

BRICK: A die that has been shaved or cut so that, while its sides are planes, it is not a true cube. Also FLAT.

BROKE MONEY: A small sum of money, as $5 or $10, given to a broke player by the house.

BROWNIE: A buster. See BUSTERS; WHERE'S BUSTER BROWN?

The BRUSH or BRUSH-OFF: A technique of switching a buster for a legitimate die, employed as the player returns the die to the shooter. Cf. BUSTERS.

BUCK: A marker placed on a number to indicate the point in a house game.

BUCK FEVER: Fear of risking one's money. (Sucker word.)

To BUCK IT: To repeat the come-out number on the second roll.

To BUCK THE GAME: To bet against the house.

To BUCK THE LINE: To bet the dice to win.

BUM MOVE: (1) A suspicious action on the part of a player. (2) An error.

BUM RAP: A framed charge or conviction.

BUNDLE: A large roll of money.

To BURN THE DICE: For a houseman or another player to stop the dice before they have finished rolling, usually when a roll appears suspicious. It is not done in casino games except where one or both of the dice fail to reach the cush-

ion. It is sometimes done by a superstitious individual to change the player's luck. Cf. to GATE.

To BURN UP: Said of dice when a player is having a winning streak. Cf. HOT.

BUSTERS: A pair of mis-spotted dice. These are made in many combinations designed to turn up certain numbers. Either one or both may be switched into and out of the game as the situation demands. See TOPS.

To BUST IN AND OUT: To switch busters or tops into and out of a game.

BUST-OUT MAN: An accomplished manipulator of crooked dice whose specialty is switching the dice when necessary.

To CACKLE THE DICE: To pretend to shake the dice by making them rattle when actually they are being prevented from turning freely in the box.

CALIFORNIA or CALIFORNIA BET: A bet in which the player covers all the box numbers and takes back the winnings, though not the original bet after each throw.

CALIPERS: Dice that are true to one-thousandth of an inch or thereabouts. Also PERFECTS.

CANE: The croupier's stick (hickory, rattan, bamboo) used to retrieve the dice after each throw.

CAP: The gross take. "Expenses are taken off the cap." (Rare.)

CAP DICE or CAPPED DICE: Crooked dice which are covered on certain sides so that these are more resilient than the others. The dice tend to bounce off the worked sides.

CAP WORK or CAPPED WORK: See CAPPED DICE.

CASE DOUGH: One's last bit of money. (Probably borrowed from faro players.)

CASE NOTE: One's last bill, theoretically a $1 bill. (Probably from faro.)

CAUGHT UP: Said of a person who has lost his credit because it is known that he owes money which he cannot pay.

CENTER or CENTER BET, CENTER MONEY: The combined wagers of the shooter and the fader, as distinct from all other bets.

CHALKED: Widely known as a cheater.

To CHALK: To bar a player from an establishment or a particular game.

CHECKER: A houseman who checks steerers to see how many players they bring to a game.

To CHILL: To lose interest. (General underworld usage.)

CHIPPY: (1) A sucker. (2) An inexpert player.

To CHISEL: To place small bets, always with a favorable percentage.

CHISLER: A cheap, careful player who plays strictly for the best of it.

CHISELER'S TABLE: A table which will accept small bets and one at which the limit is not high. Also SMALL TABLE.

CHOPPER: The cutter in a dice game.

To CLACK: to knock the dice together inadvertently in the process of making a switch.

CLEAN: (1) to get rid of crooked dice or any incriminating objects. "He cleans himself of gaffs." (2) Free of incriminating objects, such as cheating devices or guns.

CLEANED: Broke. (General.)

CLEAN MOVE: Any cheating move cleverly executed.

CLOSED GAME: A game open only to certain players, often a private game between big-money men.

CLOSE TO THE BELLY or VEST: Cautiously. Said of a dice player who bets only when almost sure of winning. (Borrowed from cards.)

COCKED DICE: A dice throw which does not count, either because the dice roll off the table or because there is doubt as to which surface is uppermost.

COLD: Said of dice that are losing more often than winning.

COMBINATION: Numbers facing each other when the dice are held for certain controlled rolls, the pad roll and the drop shot.

To COME: To succeed in either repeating the number of one's second roll or making one's point before rolling a seven.

COME-BET: A bet that the shooter will either repeat the number of his second roll or make his point before rolling a seven. ". . . he'll throw a natural on the come-bet roll. . . ."

COME-ON: (1) Small bets given a sucker to build up his confidence prior to cheating him. (2) Any action designed to stimulate the sucker to get him into the game. (Generalized.)

COME-OUT: The first throw of the dice after a shooter's decision.

COMING OUT: A phase used by the stickman to signify the come-out. Usually an admonition for the bettors to get their bets down.

CONTROL SHOT: Any of a number of methods of throwing the dice whereby the shooter is able to control their fall, if not totally, a high proportion of the time. See DROP SHOT; GREEK SHOT; SPIN (THEM); WHIP SHOT.

To COP: To win. (Probably borrowed from the circus grift.)

To COPPER THE DICE: To bet the dice to lose. (Probably taken over from faro bank.)

COWBOY: A reckless gambler. Also HIGH-ROLLER.

CRAP: The numbers 2, 3, and 12 on dice. (Origin obscure, perhaps French.)

CRAP HUSTLER: A professional crapshooter who makes his money by betting where he can take a high percentage, by offering sucker bets, or by the use of cheating methods.

To CRAP OUT: To roll a 2, 3, or 12 on the first roll.

CRAPS: (1) A dice game, fully described by John Scarne and Clayton Rawson in *Scarne on Dice*. (2) The dice.

CRIB: A gambling house.

CROSS: The act of beating someone who is engaged in cheating. "Every gaff has its cross." "We gave him the cross."

CRUMB BUM: A small-time chiseler.

CRY ACT: The bewailing of imaginary losses; characteristic of hustlers.

CUP: A leather receptacle for shaking dice. Also BOX.

CUT: The percentage taken out by the house or the operator of a game.

To CUT UP BIG WINS: To reminisce; to talk over old times.

CUTTER: An operator who charges a player making one or more passes in an open game.

CUTTING GAME: A round-table or street game in which a percentage of the center is taken by the stickman after two or more consecutive passes.

DEAD HEAD or DEAD ONE: A person who is not playing, the implication being that he is broke.

To DEAL: To collect winnings and pay off losses in a crap game.

DEALER: The banker in a dice game.

DEUCE: Point two on the dice.

The DICE ARE OFF: Said of dice which are not true, either because they are cheap dice or because they are crooked.

DICE PICKER or DICE DETECTIVE (East): A houseman whose job is to pick up the dice that have fallen from the table. Also FLOOR MAN (West).

DIPSY: A hustler. (West).

DO: A win bet, meaning "bet they (the dice) do win." "Bet they do, bet they don't, bet they will, bet they won't."

DOCTOR: A signal or office, used by cheaters in the presence of suckers. "O.K., Doctor," sometimes in conjunction with a hand signal, informs the cheater that his move has been noticed by another cheater who will ride along with him, naturally expecting a share of the win. "Is the Doctor working?"

To DOG IT: To refuse to honor a wager or debt.

DON'T: A lose bet, meaning "bet they (the dice) don't win."

DON'T-COME or DON'T-PASS BET: A side bet in which the bettor wagers that the dice will lose, considering the next roll as the come-out. See COME-OUT.

DON'T-PASS LINE: A line on the layout where don't-come bets are placed.

DOORMAN: Anyone who admits players to a gambling room; part of his job is to look for weapons.

DOOR POPS: Crooked dice which roll seven or eleven predominantly. Some combinations include a three.

DRAG: A bettor who does not let his money ride.

To DRAG DOWN: To take back all or part of money won instead of letting it ride on the next roll of the dice.

DROP: The location where players are picked up (by housemen or steerers) and driven to the game.

DROP SHOT: See GREEK SHOT.

To be DROWNED: To lose heavily.

DRY: Broke.

To DUST (someone) OFF: (1) To flatter a player by telling him how smart he is. (2) To cheat a player out of his money. (Hustlers' usage.)

EDGE: An advantage.

EDGE WORK: Dice which have been altered (beveled) along the edges.

EIGHTER FROM DECATUR: Point eight in craps.

ENGLISH: The simultaneous sliding and spinning action of the dice characteristic of most control shots.

ENGLISH SHOT: A control shot, nearly always a drop shot.

EVEN ROLL: See BLANKET ROLL.

EVEN-UP: A bet or proposition that is fifty-fifty.

To FACE OFF: To place certain faces of the dice against each other as in certain control shots. This is done in shooting either from the hand or from the box.

To FADE: To cover all or part of the shooter's center wager.

FADER: The person who covers the shooter's center wager.

FADING GAME: See OPEN CRAPS.

FAT: Said of a person with a large bank roll.

FEVER: (1) The gambling habit. (2) Point five in craps.

FEVER IN THE SOUTH: Point five in craps.

FIELD: A space on the layout containing a group of numbers, 2, 3, 4, 9, 10, 11, 12, or 2, 3, 5, 9, 10.

FIELD BET: A bet that one of the "field numbers" will be thrown on the next roll.

FILL: Weight put into dice to favor certain combinations.

FILLS or FILLED WORK: Dice which have been loaded.

FINIF: Point five on dice.

FIRST FLOP DICE or FIRST POP DICE: A type of heavily loaded dice which tend to bring up the same number each time they are thrown. Used with a slick box or slick cup. Also SETTLERS.

FIX: (1) Arrangement with a politician or police official under which a gambling house operates. (2) The money paid.

FIXER: A person who has political connections through which he can secure the protection necessary to operate a gambling house.

The FIX IS IN: A situation in which protection is bought and paid for by gamblers; while this protection is not absolute, it enables gamblers to operate freely.

To FLAG: (1) To call or signal a confederate. (2) To bar a player from a game or establishment.

FLAT BET: A side bet made among players that the dice will or will not win.

FLAT: See BRICK.

FLOATING GAME: A game which is shifted from place to place in order to escape police detection or a raid by a holdup mob.

FLOATS: Crooked dice which have been hollowed out inside so that they are off balance. This type of work cannot be done on transparent dice which are now used in most games, so floats are almost obsolete.

FLOORMAN: (1) A houseman who acts as manager of a house. He is usually owner or part owner. (2) A houseman who watches both players and employees for cheating moves, who picks up dice that are dropped on the floor, etc.

FLUSH-SPOT DICE: Dice with spots flush with the surface, rather than indented as is customary.

To FREEZE OUT or SQUEEZE OUT: (1) To force a gambling house out of business. (2) To force a gambler out of a game.

FRISK ROOM: An anteroom in some gambling houses where players are searched immediately after they enter.

FRONT LINE: See PASS LINE.

FRONT MONEY: (1) Money used to make an impression on suckers. (2) Bankroll money.

FRONTS: Legitimate dice, or square dice.

FULL TABLE: A crowded dice table.

GAFF: (1) Any secret cheating device. (2) The method by which dice are altered.

GAFFS: Crooked dice of any kind.

GAG: See the HARD WAY.

GAG-BET: A bet that the point will be made with a pair.

GALLOPING DOMINOES or CUBES: A pair of dice. (Sucker word.)

To GATE: To stop the dice before they have finished rolling, usually when a roll appears suspicious; also done by superstitious gamblers on occasion to change the shooter's luck.

GETAWAY LAYOUT: A layout for craps which can be moved quickly and easily.

To GET BEHIND THE STICK: For a dealer or stickman to go to work—i.e., to open the game.

To GET ON THE STICK: To work at the crap table, either as dealer or stickman.

To GET OUT or GET WELL: To regain one's losses.

G. I. MARBLES: Dice. (Obsolescent.)

GIMMICK: (1) A cheating device. (2) A means whereby dice are gaffed, q.v.

To be GIVEN THE DOZENS: (1) To be shortchanged. (2) To be cursed and called names.

To GIVE (someone) THE ARM: (1) To strong-arm a man in order to take money away from him. (2) To fail to pay money owed.

To GIVE (someone) THE BUSINESS: (1) To harm or cheat someone. (2) To use crooked dice or cards. (3) To give someone a brush-off, that is, diplomatically refuse his request, allay his suspicions, etc.

To GIVE (someone) THE NEEDLE: To rib or tease someone.

To GO A MARKER: To advance funds to a player whose credit is good with the house.

To GO FOR IT: To be taken in by some crooked plan.

GOOD MAN: (1) A player with a large amount of money. (2) A good cheater.

To GO SOUTH or HEAD SOUTH: (1) To take one's money out of a crap game. (2) To steal the bankroll.

GRAVITY DICE: A type of loaded dice. Cf. FLOATS.

GREEK SHOT: A controlled cast of the dice. The dice are set one atop the other, with the desired faces up. They are then thrown with a whiplike motion which causes them to twirl rapidly. Dropped properly on a soft surface, they will fall dead without sliding or rolling. Also DROP SHOT.

To GRIND AWAY or GRIND: To bet slowly and steadily. Also to GRIND UP NICKELS AND DIMES; to GRIND UP A LIVING.

HAND: Collectively, the rolls between the shooter's taking up and losing the dice.

The HARD WAY: Making the points 4, 6, 8, or 10 in pairs, such as two 2's, 3's, 4's, etc. Also the GAG.

HARD-WAY BET: A bet that the point will be made with pairs. Also GAG-BET.

To HAVE A SIGN ON (one's) BACK: See CHALKED.

HEAD: The gross take. "Off the head means paid before expenses are deducted."

HEAD TO HEAD: Betting between two players.

The HEAT IS ON: Said of a situation in which a house has been closed because of unfavorable publicity, complaints by customers, or police shakedowns.

To HEDGE: To cover a wager with a compensating bet to avoid a loss or to break even.

HEEL: A cheap gambler.

HEELED: (1) Carrying a gun. (2) Carrying a large sum of money.

HEP or HIP: (1) Understanding a crooked game. (2) Understanding the proper odds on proposition bets.

HEP-GEE or HIP-GEE: A person who understands the angles of a game. Also HIPSTER.

HIGH CRAPS: Craps for big stakes. "When I was in the rocks I used to play a lot of high craps."

HIGH-ROLLER: See COWBOY.

The HIGH SIDE: Numbers 8, 9, 10, 11, 12 on a dice layout.

HILLBILLY CRAPS: A private or street crap game.

HIPSTER or HEPSTER: See HEP-GEE.

HIT: A pass in dice.

To HIT: To win.

HITS: Mis-spotted dice that do not throw seven.

To HIT AND RUN: To win quickly and withdraw from the game.

To HIT IT: To make a point.

To HOCUS: To alter fair dice to crooked dice.

HOLDOUT: A method of holding extra dice concealed in the hand. See PALM HOLDOUT; SOCKET HOLDOUT; SUCKER HOLDOUT.

HOLDOUT ARTIST: A gambler who conceals the full amount of his winnings from a partner or other members of the mob and pockets the difference.

To HOLD HEAVY: To be well supplied with money.

HOOK SHOT: See the HUDSON.

HOOP: A finger ring sometimes put into a crap game when the player is out of funds.

HOPTOADS: Crooked dice, in general. (East.)

HORSES: A type of mis-spotted dice. (Usage obsolete except in the catalogues.)

HOT: Said of dice when they continue to win. Cf. RED HOT; COLD; ICE-COLD.

HOT SHOT: A plunging bettor.

HOUSE: (1) The bank or proprietors of a game. (2) The bankroll. (3) Anything pertaining to the management.

HOW'S THE PLAY? or HOW'S THE ACTION? A question asked to learn whether or not there is lucrative play going on at the crap table.

The HUDSON: A type of controlled shot. This is a spin shot in which the dice are thrown so that they spin with the same face down rather than tumble.

HUSTLER: See CRAP HUSTLER.

ICE: Protection money.

ICE-COLD: Said of dice that are losing consistently. Cf. HOT.

INSIDE WORK: Any internal alteration of dice.

IN THE BLACK: Winning steadily.

IN THE CHIPS: Having a large amount of money.

IN THE CLEAR: (1) Free of debt. (2) Not wanted by the police.

IN THE HANDS OF THE PHILISTINES: Indebted to loan sharks or other gamblers.

IN THE RED: (1) Owing money. (2) Losing steadily.

JIMMY HICKS: Point six on dice.

JOE: See LITTLE JOE.

JOE GOSS: The proprietor of a gambling house or game. (From so-called Australian rhyming argot: Joe Goss, the boss.)

JOINT: Gambling house.

JONAH: (1) A superstitious player who tries to control his luck with phrases or gestures. See PRAYING JOHN. (2) One whose presence is thought to bring bad luck to others. (3) To try to influence the dice by words or gestures. (4) To appear to bring bad luck to some one.

JUICE: Electricity, especially as applied to control of dice.

JUICE-JOINT: A gambling house where electric dice are used.

JUMP SHOT: A control shot used in street games where the dice are thrown for some distance in the air.

To KILL ONE: To control one of the dice, particularly the bottom one.

To KNOCK or KNOCK A MARK: To reveal a cheating device to a sucker, thus discouraging his play.

KNOCKERS: See TAP DICE.

LADDERMAN: A person who watches both housemen and players in order to guard against trickery. So-called from the elevation where he stands to observe the game. Used only in large gambling houses.

LAGGED: Arrested.

LAYER: A consistently wrong bettor; that is, one who bets the dice to lose.

To LAY IT: To bet that the dice will lose.

To LAY IT ON or LAY IT DOWN: To bet heavily.

LAY IT ON THE GREEN: A phrase sometimes used by the houseman to indicate that the house will accept a check offered by a gambler. The green refers to the felt-topped table.

To LAY THE ODDS: To bet that the dice will lose.

LAYOUT: A diagram showing the odds and bets on the board or crap table.

LEGIT GAME: An honest game.

LEGIT GUY: A person without underworld connections, though not necessarily an honest man.

To LET IT RIDE: To place all the money won on a new wager.

LEVELS: Honest dice. Cf. PERFECTS; FRONTS; TOPS; EDGE WORK.

LIGHT: (1) Too low in funds to cover a bet. (2) Said of dice which are loaded so as to give a slight percentage to the shooter.

LIMIT: The maximum amount which can be wagered on any bet according to house rules.

LINE: See PASS LINE.

LITTLE JOE, JOE, or LITTLE DICK: Point four in craps.

LIVE ONE: A sucker with money. (Probably from the argot of the old-time circus grifter.)

LOAD: (1) A weight, sometimes consisting of mercury or gold, concealed under the spots, which causes the die to turn up a certain number more frequently than the law of averages would permit. (2) An unfavorable percentage. "When six-ace flats are riding, the field has a load instead of an edge."

LOADS: Loaded dice.

LOB or LOBBY GOW: A house employee who cleans, runs errands, etc. (Probably from the argot of the old-time opium smokers.)

LOOKING FOR ACTION: Seeking a gambling game.

LOOKOUT: An employee of the house who watches everyone and every action to spot cheating or trouble.

LOOSE TABLE: A table with only a few players.

LOP EAR: (1) A sucker, especially a stupid one. (2) An inexpert player.

LOW SIDE: On the dice layout, the numbers 2, 3, 4, 5, and 6.

LUGGER: A steerer for a crooked gambling house or game.

To MAKE A HIT: To win heavily.

MAIN: The shooter's original stake and its fade.

MARBLES: See ROLLERS.

MARK: A sucker.

MARKER: (1) An I.O.U. (2) A disc placed on the point number so as to indicate it. Also BUCK.

MASON: A person who will not take part with his money. Also STONEWALL.

MECHANIC: A gambler skilled at manipulating crooked dice.

MEMPHIS DOMINOES: Dice.

MICHIGAN BANKROLL: A large bank roll consisting of $1 bills topped by larger ones. Also MISH.

MISS or MISSOUT: A losing decision made by either rolling craps on the come-out or rolling a seven before a point number.

To MISS or MISS IT: To roll craps on the first roll or to roll a seven before the point number.

MISSES or MISSOUTS: Crooked dice which tend to lose more than legitimate dice.

MIS-SPOTS: Dice on which the standard sequence of numbers is altered. Also TOPS; TEES; TONYS; and others.

MONKEY: (1) One who complains to the police. (2) A timid person.

MONICKER: The house-mark on dice.

To MURDER: To win money easily, quickly, and in large amounts.

MUSCLE MAN: (1) A tough guy. (2) A person who tries to cut in on the profits from a gambling game. (3) One who plays on credit without the money to make good his losses.

NAILED: (1) Caught cheating. (2) Arrested.

NATURAL: A seven or eleven thrown on the come-out roll. Cf. COME-OUT.

NEVER GIVE A SUCKER AN EVEN BREAK or NEVER SMARTEN A SUCKER UP: A grifters' saying common among dice gamblers.

NICKEL GAME: A game in which correct odds are paid players. "Old John Winn brought the nickel game to Philly around 1910."

NICKEL MAN: The dealer of a nickel game. So called because he collects the five-cents-per-dollar charge for the house.

NINA or NINA FROM CAROLINA. Point nine in craps.

NINETY DAYS: Point nine in craps.

NO DICE: A roll which does not count, either because one of the dice has rolled off the table or is standing on edge, or because the shooter has not observed the rules.

NO GOOD UNDER FIRE: Said of a dice cheater who can manipulate the dice but becomes nervous when he is taking money away from someone.

NO LIMIT GAME: A game in which players may bet any amount they wish.

NUMBER: Any point. "He picked up the dice and throwed six numbers." (That is, made six passes.)

NUT: Expenses or overhead required to operate a crap game.

NUTMAN: (1) One who finances a game or gambling house. See BACKER. (2) See CRAP HUSTLER.

ODDS: The ratio of unfavorable chances to favorable chances.

OFFICE: Any secret signal used by gamblers.

OFF NUMBER: (1) Any number appearing on the dice except the point which the shooter is trying to make. (2) See BOX NUMBERS. (Called off numbers in private craps, and box numbers in bank craps.)

OK: Protection furnished by politicians permitting a game to operate; the "go-ahead" signal to open for business.

ONE DOWN: The stickman's cry when one die has fallen from the table.

ONE ROLL BET: A bet which is decided on the next roll.

To be ON THE ERIE: Attempting to overhear a conversation.

ON TAB: Gambling on credit.

OPEN CRAPS: A house game permitting side bets among the players.

OPEN LIMIT GAME: See NO LIMIT GAME.

To OPEN UP: (1) To start the game. (2) To divulge information.

OUT IN FRONT: Winning money at dice.

The OUTSIDE: Players as distinguished from employees of the house.

OUTSIDE MAN: (1) An employee of a gambling house who directs players to the house. Also LUGGER or STEERER. (2) Any player other than the stickman who switches in crooked dice.

OUTSIDE WORK: Any external altering of the dice.

OVERLAY: (1) A bet made by a player who cannot cover it with his bankroll. (2) A wager made at higher than "natural" odds. ". . . as even money on a six-eight whipsaw."

OVERS: Bets which have been overlooked; a sleeper. (Sucker word.)

OVER THE HUMP: A winner who is playing on the house's money.

PAD ROLL: See BLANKET ROLL.

PALM HOLDOUT: A means of concealing extra dice in the palm. A difficult and sometimes dangerous move. "The hand which has developed the necessary muscle to operate a palm holdout looks clumsy and large and is likely to create suspicion." (Not necessarily true, though believed by the speaker quoted.)

PASS: To roll either seven or eleven on the first roll or to make a point, any one winning for the shooter.

PASS LINE: A space on the layout where bets that the shooter will pass are placed.

PASSERS: Crooked dice that show a higher percentage of passes than do legitimate dice.

PAST THE BOX: A phrase used in some crooked games, meaning that the dice cannot be bounced against a nearby cushion. ". . . a rule is made that the dice must be thrown past the box. This is to give the stickman a chance to bust in."

PAY OFF: The collection of a bet.

PAY OFF ODDS: The odds at which a bet is paid off.

PEEK SHOT: See the HUDSON.

PEE WEE DICE: Very small dice, usually made of bone.

To PEE WEE: To throw the dice to determine the order in which players will shoot. Not done in banking games. Also to PINKY.

To PEG (a number): To place a marker on a number to indicate the point.

PERCENTAGE or P.C.: A favorable advantage obtained in many different ways—through offering less than true odds, through crooked dice, through controlled shots, or through a combination of these methods.

PERCENTAGE DICE: A general term for crooked dice which gradually build up a percentage in the cheater's favor. Cf. SURE POPS.

PERFECTS: Dice that are true to approximately one-thousandth of an inch.

PHOEBE: Point five in craps. Also FEVER IN THE SOUTH; WEST KENTUCKY (rare).

To PICK THE DICE: See to CACKLE THE DICE.

PIECE: A percentage or cut of gambling-house profits.

To PINKY: See to PEE WEE.

PLACE BET: A right point bet at bank craps. See POINT BET.

The PLAY: See ACTION.

POKER DICE: (1) A set of five dice used in shooting for the highest score. (2) A set of five dice engraved with replicas of face cards which are used to play dice with values of poker hands.

POINT: Any of the numbers 4, 5, 6, 8, 9, 10 which the shooter throws on the first roll and then tries to repeat before throwing a seven.

POINT BET: A bet at odds that the point will or will not be made.

POSING DICK: A gambler who likes to show off.

PRAYING JOHN: One who believes that the fall of the dice may be influenced by incantations, secret signals, etc. See JONAH.

PROPOSITION BET: (1) In private craps any bet except a point, an off number, or a flat bet. (2) A combination bet favored by hustlers.

To PULL DOWN: See to DRAG DOWN.

To PUT THE BEE ON: Variant of the phrase to PUT THE BITE ON; that is, to attempt to borrow money, usually from a fellow gambler.

To PUT THE EARS ON: To attempt to make a controlled shot. (Possibly transferred from cards, where a crimp may be called an ear.)

To PUT THE FINGER ON (someone): To file a complaint with the police; to identify someone.

To PUT THE HEAT ON: (1) To apply pressure on someone. (2) To cause a raid on or police investigation of a gambling house. (3) Police raids to force payments for protection.

To PUT THE HORNS ON: To give a player bad luck by changing positions at the table, altering a bet, or using any other device involving superstition.

QUEER: Counterfeit money, sometimes passed into circulation through gambling games.

QUININE: Point nine in craps.

RAIL: See BOARDS.

The RAP: A fine or prison term taken by an employee or a gambler.

RATS or RATS AND MICE: Dice in general. (Clipped form of the rhyming argot.)

RAZOR EDGES: Dice cut perfectly square. They are preferred in many gambling houses because they show up wear more easily and because they are more difficult for the holdout man to manipulate.

RED HOT: Said of dice that are winning steadily.

To RIDE WITH THE SHOOTER: (1) For the house to let its cut on a round-table game remain as part of the center bet. This is usually done only on request by players who have even or "lucky" money in the center. If the shooter passes, the house then collects a double cut. (2) To let a bet ride; to parlay a bet.

RIGHT BETTOR or PLAYER: A player who bets the dice to win.

To RING IN: (1) To introduce crooked dice surreptitiously into the game. (2) To force someone in on another's plans.

To have a RING IN ONE'S NOSE: To lose heavily.

To have a RING IN SOMEONE ELSE'S NOSE: To be able to beat him at will.

To RIP: To swtch dice.

RIPE or RIPE FOR A TAKE: Ready for fleecing or for a "touch."

ROCK: A tightfisted player who refuses to lend money or to make foolish bets. Also STONEWALL JACKSON.

ROCKS: Money.

To ROLL: To cast the dice.

ROLLERS: Dice (often crooked, though not necessarily so) which have rounded corners. The advantage of honest rollers is the fact that they may make control shots more difficult.

ROLLING BONES: (1) Dice, so called from the old-time dice which were made of ivory or bone. (2) Gambling with dice.

ROLLING FULL BLOOM: (1) A phrase describing fast play with the dice. (2) A phrase applied to a place that is operating wide open under police protection.

To ROPE: (1) To cheat. (2) See LUGGER.

ROSCOE: A pistol.

To ROUGH IT UP: To bet heavily, thus livening up the tempo of the game.

ROUNDS or ROUNDERS: Ball-cornered dice. See ROLLERS.

ROUND-TABLE GAME: A game in which players bet among themselves.

RUBBER: Worthless. Said of a check.

To RUMBLE: To excite a mark's suspicion. Used in the transitive only. Intransitive use restricted to TUMBLE; that is, you *rumble* a mark, but a mark *tumbles*.

SACKS: A term used by gamblers to indicate that everything is "in the bag."

SCORE: (1) To win. (2) The amount won.

To SCORE A BIG TOUCH: To fleece a player of a large amount of money.

SCRATCH: Cash, as distinct from other assets.

SEND IN: A plunging bet.

To SEND IT IN: To make a large wager, especially to parlay one's winnings in the hope of breaking the game.

To SET THE COMBINATION: To arrange the dice properly in the hand for a controlled shot.

SETTLERS: See FIRST FLOP DICE.

SEVEN-ELEVEN: A new start given a broke player by other gamblers; done only in small or street games.

To SEVEN OUT: To roll a seven when rolling for a point number. Cf. CRAP OUT.

SHAPE: A crooked die that has been altered so that it is not a true cube. Shapes are made in many different ways, some slightly concave or convex, etc.

To SHARK: To use a control shot. (Sucker word.)

SHARPSHOOTER: A hustler.

SHILLS: Housemen who pose as players to stimulate the play.

SHORTSTOP: A small bettor; a chiseler.

SHOOTER: The player who rolls the dice.

SHOT: (1) The rolls until a single decision is arrived at. (2) A means of controlling the fall of honest dice. (3) One who can control the fall of the dice.

SHY: Owing money.

SHYLOCK: A loan shark.

SICE: The point and the number six.

SINGLE-O: Working alone, usually said of hustlers.

SIX-ACE FLATS: A pair of crooked dice whose six and ace sides have a larger area than tht others, so that they tend to throw missouts.

SIXTY DAYS: Point six in craps.

To SLAMBANG: To clip patrons or other players with cheating methods.

SLEEPER: A wager or part of a wager overlooked by the winner. (Probably borrowed from faro-bank.)

SLICK BOX or CUP: A leather dice box with a polished interior to facilitate rolling out the dice without altering their position. A cheating device.

SLICK DICE: Crooked dice which have some sides polished so that they are smoother than the remaining sides. "Slick dice are seldom used, since they must be thrown on cloth to be effective and the P.C. is weak."

To SLOUGH or SLOUGH UP: (1) To compel the closing of a game or house. (2) To close a game.

SLUG: The small metallic weight used to load dice.

SMALL TABLE: See CHISELER'S TABLES.

SNAKE EYES: A one-spot showing on both dice.

SNEAK GAME: A game operating without police protection.

SOCKET HOLDOUT: The space between the base of the thumb and the forefinger.

SPELL: A consistent winning or losing streak. (HOT SPELL; COLD SPELL.)

To SPIN (them): To control dice by spinning them across the playing surface with the desired faces up in such a fashion that they appear to have been given a fair roll. Cf. WHIP SHOT; GREEK SHOT.

SPLITTER: A crooked die which is substituted for one of a pair of crooked dice in the play so that it splits the combination; that is, changes passers to missouts, etc. Cf. BUSTERS.

To SPRING: (1) To pay the check. (2) To get someone released from custody. (3) To get out of jail. (4) To take out one's money or wallet.

To SQUARE A BEEF: To take care of a complaint, either by returning part of the money or by talking the victim out of legal action.

The SQUEEZE: (1) Any kind of device applied to increase the favorable percentage for the house. (2) The control operating a cheating device.

SQUEEZES: Flats which have been made, not by shaving off certain surfaces, but by squeezing them in a vise.

STAND: The platform on which the lookout sits to observe the game.

STAND-OFF: A situation in which there it no decision; that is, everyone gets his money back or all bets are off.

STAND-UP GUY: A trustworthy person.

STEERER: An individual who persuades customers to patronize a certain gambling house, which is usually crooked.

STEER JOINT: A crooked gambling house, usually employing steerers to bring in suckers.

STICK: (1) A crap stick. See CANE. (2) A house employee who acts as a player. A SHILL.

STICKMAN: A croupier at a dice table.

STIFF: (1) An unlucky player. (2) A losing number.

STONEWALL or STONEWALL JACKSON: A tightwad. Cf. MASON; ROCK.

STORE DICE: Cheap dice that are not true.

STREAK: Consistent winning or losing at dice. Cf. SPELL.

STRONG: Said of crooked dice which give the player a heavy percentage over legitimate dice.

STRYCHNINE: Point nine in craps.

To be STUCK: To be losing at dice.

STUFFED: Having plenty of money.

SUCKER BET: A bet that provides the operator with a high percentage.

SUCKER HOLDOUT: Dice retained in the curled little finger are said to be in the sucker holdout. Possibly so called because it is easy to detect, since this move requires that the hand be held in a cramped and unnatural position.

SUCTION DICE: Crooked dice with one concave surface each. The concave faces have a tendency to come up more frequently, since they cling slightly to the surface.

To be SUNK: See drowned.

SURE POPS: Heavily loaded dice. Cf. PERCENTAGE DICE.

SURETHING BOYS: Gamblers. So called because they always have an edge on the law of averages. Also used ironically to refer to gamblers who always want or think they have a system or device which is infallible.

To SWITCH: To substitute one object (such as a crooked die) for another (such as a legitimate die). Cf. BUST IN.

The TAKE: The receipts of a gambling house.

To TAKE: (1) To accept bribe money. (2) To cheat.

To TAKE A BATH: To lose heavily or to go broke.

To TAKE IT: To bet the dice to win by making the odds.

To TAKE IT OFF THE TOP: To pay out money from the gross receipts before any division of profits is made.

To TAKE THE ODDS: (1) To accept a bet to lose at odds. Cf. to LAY THE ODDS.

TAKE-OFF: The percentage taken by the house.

TAKE-OFF GAME: A cutting game.

TAKE YOUR BEST SHOT: Phrase applied to a game among cheaters in which all use their crooked devices and all are aware of the techniques being used.

To TAIL: To follow someone.

TAP DICE or TAPPERS: Loaded dice containing a shifting mercury load which can be changed (by tapping) to percentage dice and back to square dice.

TAP OUT: (1) The last wager. (2) To go broke.

To TAP (someone) OUT: (1) To bet the exact amount of money which the other player has. (2) To force a game to its conclusion by winning all the money.

TAT: (1) A mis-spotted die bearing only high numbers, which is used in a short con game. (2) The short con game making use of this die.

TATS: Dice, especially crooked dice.

TEES: Mis-spotted dice. See TOPS.

To TELEGRAPH: To betray a cheating move prior to executing it, usually by some unconscious or clumsy movement.

THERE'S WORK DOWN: An expression signifying that crooked dice are being used.

THEY HIT: The cry of the right bettor on making a bet.

THEY MISS: The cry of the wrong bettor on making a bet.

THEY'RE BURNING UP: Said of dice which are consistently winning for the shooter.

TIN: A police officer, referring to the badge.

TONY: A word or signal meaning mis-spotted dice. "Is Tony here tonight?"

TONYS: See TOPS.

The TOP: Gross receipts of a game or gambling house.

To TOP IN: To switch tops into a game.

TOPS: Mis-spotted dice on which some numbers are repeated. Usually made with identical numbers on opposite sides so that an observer does not see more than one of any number on the three sides within his field of vision.

TOPS AND BOTTOMS: See TOPS.

TOUCH: (1) A loan. (2) A score. (3) To borrow money.

TOWN'S DRIED UP: An expression applied to a town where there is not much money circulating.

TREY: Number three on dice.

TRIP BOX: A type of dealer's box with a leather rim inside to turn the dice over as they come out. Used to discourage attempts to control dice within the box.

TRIP DICE: Crooked dice utilizing rough sides and edges to bring up certain numbers. Cf. SLICK DICE.

To TUMBLE: To become aware that cheating methods are being used. See RUMBLE.

TUMBLERS: See ROLLERS.

TWO-NUMBER BET: A bet that a specified two numbers will or will not be thrown before a seven on the next roll.

UP JUMPED THE DEVIL: The cry of the stickman when the shooter seeking a point sevens out.

VELVET: Money that has been won or secured in some illegitimate fashion.

VIGGERISH or VIGORISH: (1) The percentage taken by a gambling house, which may be overt or hidden by altering the odds in favor of the house. Usually 3 to 5 per cent. (2) See BROKE MONEY (used around New York).

WEIGHT: The pace of the game.

WHERE'S BUSTER BROWN? An expression informing stickmen to switch crooked dice into or out of the game. (Used only around suckers.)

WHIPSAW BET: A bet that the shooter will or will not make either the point or its complement before he throws a seven.

To be WHIPSAWED: To lose two or more bets on a single roll, as in the case of a shooter who makes a come-bet and sevens out without having made either his shot or come-bet.

WHIP SHOT: A difficult control shot in which one die is controlled. It spins sliding from the hand and is aimed to strike the side rail at a short angle, throwing it against the end rail, also at a short angle, from which it rebounds, still in its spinning slide, with the desired face up. Cf. TO SPIN.

WINDOW'S OPEN: An expression used by cheaters signifying that switching of dice is being done ineptly and that the alternate die or pair of dice can be seen in the player's hand.

WINNERS: Crooked dice that tend to make more than the usual number of passes.

The WIRE: A signal used between gamblers.

WIRE JOINT: An establishment where electric dice and layout are used.

WON'T SPRING: Phrase applied to a person who will not gamble or take a chance, or who will not treat anyone else. See SPRING (4).

WOOD or DEAD WOOD: Hangers-on, non-players, or gamblers without money.

WORK or WORKS: (1) Crooked dice. (2) The method of making dice crooked.

The WORST OF IT: A disadvantage. Cf. the BEST OF IT.

WRONG BETTOR or WRONG PLAYER: A player who bets the dice to lose.

The X or to HAVE THE X (on): (1) To control gambling in a town. (2) To be able to beat another player consistently.

ZING or to ZING IT IN: To bet heavily, particularly to parlay one's winnings.

16

The Argot
of the Racetrack

It is perhaps an anomaly that, in a highly industrialized country, horse racing is the most popular vehicle for gambling, involving more bettors and a larger *handle* than any other single sport. Although I do not have at hand current figures on attendance at pari-mutuel tracks and pari-mutuel handles, the paid admissions must run close to fifty million annually and the gross handle in the billions. Off-track betting through bookmakers is proportionately big business, and it is well known in the underworld that the profits from syndicate gambling—largely illegal—are used to finance the ever-expanding drug traffic.

As in all other forms of gambling, the terminology generates among insiders and gradually filters out to some extent among the suckers who constitute the bulk of the bettors. Contributing to the language of this subculture are four separate and very different satellite groups: 1) the gamblers, largely illegal; 2) the breeders and trainers, predominantly legitimate; 3) the jockeys and stable personnel, who are more interested in purses and horses than in the gambling, though they do bet; and 4) the handicappers, form sheet writers, and sportswriters, who constitute a liaison between those on the inside and the betting public. These writers serve as a conduit for some of the specialized language that filters into use in the dominant culture.

Although this study is fairly complete, it has been updated in several respects since its first appearance in 1951, but the addenda—running to some 350 entries, many of them concentrated in the bookmaking area—have not been brought into shape for publication. On the whole, this argot shows considerable stability. Those changes that occur reflect changes in custom, in gambling laws, in the rulings of various racing commissions and governing boards, fluctuations in the popularity of various kinds of betting, and the personnel involved in both the legitimate racing business and the vastly expanding off-track bookmaking. While some bookmakers are as reliable as any legitimate businessman, there has been, in the last thirty years, a heavy influx of syndicate figures into this phase of the subculture. In fact, one might say that it is difficult today for a bookmaker to operate without some interference by the big syndicates. How far this influence may penetrate the other more legitimate aspects of racing such as the breeding and training of horses is obscure. However, it is obvious that horseracing has come a long way from the "ancient sport of kings."

• • •

HORSERACING came early to America from England.[1] It was more than a sport among the gentry; it became a functional part of agricultural life in the colonies. Belmont Track, established near the first American racetrack (Newmarket, 1665), has, for more than a century and a half, set the pattern for American racing. Although racing has long been carried on under the guise of "improving the breed," it has been throughout the centuries one of the most attractive of all gambling devices. In England it was very well developed by the beginning of the eighteenth century, though at that time it was largely the sport of the nobility. Very early in colonial America, racing stock was imported and bred, and so-called race-paths appeared in many of the colonies, with notable concentrations in New York, Virginia, and Kentucky. In many American cities horses were raced in the main streets; in fact, within the memory of living citizens of Louisville, Kentucky, certain streets were cleared for racing of an informal type.

With the development of county and state fairs during the nineteenth century, larger racetracks were established on a permanent basis and, where large urban populations made it profitable, racetracks were constructed just outside many large American cities. Today there are more than eighty-five of these major commercial racetracks, as well as hundreds of smaller tracks at

1. Although I am, of course, indebted to many people in the preparation of this study, and I appreciate the interest of many informants who are not named here, special acknowledgements are due the following: to Judge Charles Price and to Mr. Robert Leopold of Louisville, both deceased, for their assistance in getting this project under way; to Mr. Bill Ladd and Mr. Joseph Landau of the Louisville *Courier-Journal* for their interest, especially in the early phases of this study; to Mr. Morris Bein of the University of Louisville for his suggestions and advice; to Mr. Stuart Flexner of New York City for his thorough checking of my racing files and, in addition, his valuable conferences with bookmakers; to Mr. Robert White, now in the armed services, for his close work both on the files and in reading the early drafts of the manuscript; to Mr. Robert O'Hara of the University of Louisville, for undertaking at Churchill Downs a verification of all field-work done up to 1951, which provided a pre-publication check of the greatest value; to Mr. Ted Johnson, a pre-medical student at the University of Louisville, for making "dry-runs" on various betting systems studied; to Mr. Everett DeBaun of Rutherford, New Jersey, for reading the manuscript in the light of his own very extensive experience with non-standard language; to Miss Varena Gilpin of Cincinnati, Ohio, and Mrs. Mary Shipley of Louisville for their patience in the preparation of several drafts of manuscript; to Mrs. Mary Danser of Wilmington, Delaware, for her valuable assistance in proofreading both manuscript and galleyproofs.

There are undoubtedly errors, omissions, and oversights in a survey covering a field so broad and so diverse as the language of racing; for these mistakes the author takes full responsibility.

To the University of Louisville an acknowledgement is due for financial assistance in the preparation of the manuscript.

county fairgrounds and other rural gathering places. Racing is still a seasonal sport, with the major circuits being open for several weeks during the best weather conditions, and the season varying from North to South. The minor circuits operate on a much less regular schedule, but conduct racing somewhere during all the open weather. Modern motorized vans make it possible to transport horses easily from track to track; jockeys, trainers, and stablehands travel a regular circuit; the great breeding farms, formerly concentrated in Kentucky, and still to some extent so concentrated, have spread out to other states where the centralization of industrial wealth has made it fashionable to maintain large stables for the breeding and training of racehorses. Kentucky still dominates, however, both in the number and the quality of racehorses produced. From the earliest times, good English and Irish breeding stock was imported, and still is.

Although it is still possible for small owners, breeders, and trainers to operate on an individual basis, racing has, in the second quarter of the twentieth century, become a millionaire's game. The great racing stables, bidding competitively for breeders and trainers as well as for horses, are gradually acquiring a monopoly both on stock and on the services of experts. (Citation: a six-year-old, owned by Calumet Farms, won $1,085,760 in purses up to July 1951; and Bewitch, his stablemate, is at present the greatest money-winning mare in racing history.) The jockeys, formerly lightweight farm-hands (often black) are now highly specialized athletes in a position to command handsome prices for yearly contracts. Gambling, once handled on a gentlemanly man-to-man basis, passed into the hands of the professional bookmaker at the track and, when the tracks saw the opportunity to increase their take from the customer, was put on a mechanized basis. Most if not all important tracks in the United States today have outlawed bookmaking and take bets through the pari-mutuel machines. Racing has become a gigantic spectator sport with some 20,000,000 fans attending annually (most of whom know nothing about horses except the price) and betting more than two billion dollars a year; while racing makes heroic efforts to clear itself of the influence of the professional gambling interests, the racketeers continuously try to muscle in, as they do in most sports, both amateur and professional. As this is being written, for instance, the Boston *American* carries a story regarding a nationwide tie-up between gangsters and jockeys, and the Thoroughbred Racing Protective Bureau is investigating what appears to be a jockey ring operating at most tracks, tied in with gambling syndicates of national scope. At the same time, in my opinion, racing today is relatively cleaner and better regulated than it ever has been in all its history.

When the bookmaker was ruled off the tracks, he opened his establishment in every community near a track; in fact, bookmakers were well established in most cities even before pari-mutuels took over. With the extension of special wire service by Western Union and the Bell Telephone Company, it was possible for every town and hamlet, however remote from the track, to have its own bookmaker where local citizens could wager on horses they never saw and never wanted to see. Meanwhile, puritan elements in our society— opposed to the cavaliers who liked gambling—wrote laws that made a crime out of what had been formerly a harmless rural pastime.

Although modern gambling is not always criminal, the professional gambler is usually affiliated with the underworld, even where gambling is legalized. However, in many communities where gambling is illegal, it is at the same time both respectable and fashionable. It is a paradox of modern morality that the pari-mutuel machine is accepted in most states as legal, but the bookmaker is not; it is likewise a fine point of gambling ethics which requires that all bookmakers close up shop during the season when pari-mutuels operate in any community.

Big-time gambling, usually protected by the police, is organized about the bookmaker on a scale which surpasses in scope anything in the annals of modern crime. While this is not the place to analyze the social problems incident to racketeer-controlled gambling, anyone who is not already aware of the details can rapidly become so by reading reports of the recent Kefauver Committee; these investigations have only scratched the surface. It is obvious that racing constitutes the core of the highly organized gambling syndicates which, in turn, partially control most large municipal governments in the United States. Influence generated on a party-machine level extends not only to state politics, but appears to go directly to Washington. Therefore, horse-betting interests exert an influence on both local and national politics which is out of all proportion to the importance we might expect it to have in a contemporary industrial culture. The effects of the recently enacted federal tax on gamblers and gambling profits are not yet discernible.

It is inevitable that such a large specialized industry as racing, together with its peripheral criminal and semicriminal gambling interests, should develop a specialized language. While we are probably not justified in calling this language a criminal argot, since many aspects of the business are quite legal, it certainly deserves a place among the major nonstandard fountainheads which constantly freshen the literary language. On the one hand, it is firmly rooted in the agricultural and rural traditions of the country; and on the other, it is sharply current. Some of it goes back to British usage of the seventeenth and eighteenth centuries; much more of it is indigenous and American in origin. Although it may lack the antiquarian value sometimes attached to dialect words and phrases, it does constitute a large block of nonstandard language which is neither occupational nor regional, but which is and has been, from the seventeenth century down, an integral part of American speech.

Within this phase of the American language there are discernible speech elements emanating from at least four social groups, with some peripheral usage extending into other social areas. First, and probably most important, there are the words and phrases used by those people who gamble on the races; these generally originate within the tightly organized professional gambling groups, then spread gradually to the ordinary citizen who likes to go to the races or place a bet with his local bookie. Often these terms are unmistakably criminal argot and may be derivative from or related to the argot of dice or card gamblers. Everyone who bets on horses at all learns a little of this argot, even though he may never penetrate beyond the sucker level.

Second, there is the usage characteristic of breeders and trainers; this is agricultural in origin and reflects a traditional culture-pattern in no way criminal; some of the most substantial people to be found anywhere are interested in the breeding and training of racehorses. These persons may bet heavily on horses but do not make gambling a profession.

Third, there is the usage characteristic of those who come into direct contact with horses before, during, or after racing. This group comprises jockeys and stable-hands largely, though it may overlap to include some trainers and breeders. In a racing stable at Keeneland in Kentucky, for instance, it is not unusual to hear the brogue of an imported Irish groom mingled with the urban accent of a second-generation Italo-American jockey and the rural speech of an American black. To these people, a thoroughbred racer is obviously and unequivocally the finest and most useful product of modern civilization. Although this group gambles consistently on the horses, that interest is not primary, for they literally live with horses during most of their working lives.

Fourth, there is the printed language used by handicappers, form-sheet writers, and newspaper reporters. This is a form of journalese which influences the language of the millions of racetrack fans more, perhaps, than any of the other language-levels, though it to some extent includes elements of all the other three. There are, incidentally, some fifty specialized racing publications, not including the sports sections of daily newspapers. The *Daily Racing Form* alone documented some 20,000 horse races in 1950; it is published in eight cities and has a daily circulation of about 150,000. This particular form maintains its respectability by recognizing only those tracks approved by the New York Jockey Club.

Regionally, this nonstandard usage cannot be limited, for it extends to a considerable element of the population wherever racing or racebetting is practiced. Its extent can hardly be accurately reflected by the isogloss used on dialect maps to indicate the distribution of speech-forms characteristic of the household and the occupational usage of the farming community, since the isogloss has not as yet been adapted to include the social structure of language. The language of racing, then, is not a dialect, properly speaking, although its pronunciation follows well established dialect patterns; it spreads out over the entire country, but is current only among certain social groups (often remarkably divergent) in each speech community. It has both a spoken and a printed form, with printed usage appearing daily in racing forms and newspapers, reflecting verbal and somewhat affected use of the argot by millions of fans who otherwise would have little opportunity to get a firsthand knowledge of it.

No historical considerations can be taken up here, although these could be studied with considerable profit. My purpose is to survey current usage and to list a characteristic sampling of the terms indigenous to racing and gambling thereon; occasionally terms from other areas such as veterinary medicine, farming, or riding terms in general, are included in view of their close identification with racing. Because of the circuits traveled by racing people and because of the syndicated nature of the gambling interests, there does not appear to be so much regional variation as one finds in other argots; however, when such variations are known, they are indicated.

Two important phases of racing have been omitted from this survey; these are steeple chasing and harness racing. Occasional terms from these forms of racing are mentioned but only when they appear in the language commonly associated with flat racing; such overlappings usually occur because either horses or jockeys, or both, participate in more than one form of racing, or because all forms of racing share in common certain basic phraseology. Both steeple chasing and harness racing are omitted because they would extend this study considerably, although both are rich in racing tradition. Steeple chasing is especially so, and the present steeple chases retain more of the older colonial flavor than any other type of racing; they are usually held on private estates or at county fairgrounds; there are gentlemen riders as well as professional jockeys, and usually, even at present, there are professional bookmakers on the grounds. The crowds attending differ from the racing fans at the large urban tracks in that most of them not only know horses but are accomplished horsemen and horsewomen. The annual steeple chases held at Fair Hill, Cecil County, Maryland, on the estate of William K. du Pont are famous, and the course there is comparable to the one at Aintree, England. Good examples of other community-sponsored racing are Radnor, Pennsylvania, where gentleman riders compete exclusively in both steeple chasing and flat racing, and Rose Tree, Pennsylvania, the site of what is probably the oldest hunt club in the United States, where both gentleman riders and professionals compete in both steeple chases and flat racing, with bookmakers in attendance. In this type of racing the element of rural sport is still prominent, and in many such community-sponsored race meets ordinary farmers who like horses ride their own mounts in competition with society riders.

In addition, this survey omits, in general, the terminology of the specialized criminal rackets which go with racing, mainly the bigtime confidence games as well as numerous short-con games. These, along with their argots, have been treated in detail in my book *The Big Con*.

The following glossary, therefore, should not be regarded as either exhaustive in scope or final in form.[2] It represents a sampling of the more or less technical language associated with racing and with race gambling. The fieldwork was done intermittently over a period of more than ten years, during which time I was simultaneously working in several other social areas where argots flourish; this experience provided valuable perspective, in terms of both linguistics and culture. In treating the terminology, I have made every effort to be concise without sacrificing finer shades of meaning; as a result, the cross-referencing[3] is perhaps more extensive than that normally encountered in standard lexicography.

2. A number of terms have been omitted either because they are widely known and used colloquially outside of the racing fraternity or because they are variants of or closely related to terms listed and defined.

3. In the cross-referencing, it should be noted that the terms following *also* are synonyms or approximate equivalents of the entry, although it is often necessary to define these terms separately to catch slight variations in meaning. The terms following *see* are entries under which the reader will find additional information bearing on the entry being defined, or on closely related items. The terms following *cf.* are antonyms or phrases involving concepts diametrically opposed to those covered in the entry. The fact that so much of racetrack talk is idiomatic requires the extensive use of phrases or word combinations with a combined meaning which cannot be rendered by defining the words separately. No attempt has been made to record the subtle uses of stress and of inflection bordering on pitch, since this is not primarily a phonetic study and since regional and social speech-patterns vary; an illustration of one phase of this problem can be seen under the entry *out to show*. In general, hyphenated forms have been avoided, except where they are standard usage, or where they seem necessary to carry meaning.

The reader will note that there are a few phrases in which the prepositions *in, off,* and *out* are so definitely a part of the idiom that the phrase is listed under the preposition which introduces it, such as *in the minus pool, off-time,* and *on the nut.* Furthermore, there are some nouns which are used characteristically with the definite or indefinite article, such as *a man from Kokomo, the pack, a country mile, the field,* etc. In a small number of cases the article is entered after the noun or the noun phrase.

ACROSS THE BOARD. phr. To bet, usually the same amount of money, on a horse to win, place, and show. Also *through the board.* Cf. *parlay, quinella.*

ADDED MONEY. n. Money added by the track to the nomination, entry, registration fees, etc., paid by the owner to enter a horse in a race, and used to make up the winner's purse. The added money goes to increase purses for the second, third, and sometimes the fourth horse in the race. Cf. *stake (race), purse.*

AIR. v.i. To win easily. "He aired by twenty."

AIRING. 1. part. Running easily, especially in a workout. Not used to refer to actual racing. 2. n. A light workout. 3. n. An easy pace. See *breeze, blow out.* Cf. *cool a horse out, trials, railbird, set down, free pace.*

ALL ALONE. phr. 1. Ahead by several lengths. 2. Exercising alone. See *with his*

mouth wide open, with plenty to spare, finish on the chinstrap, on top, breeze, on the Bill Daley.

ALLOWANCE RACE. n. A type of race in which a horse is "allowed" weight off for his previous failures. The nature of the conditions for these races may vary widely, but a typical condition book entry might read thus: "For three-year-olds. Non-winners of $750 twice since June 1 allowed 5 pounds; non-winners of $1000 once since June 1 allowed 8 pounds; maidens allowed 12 pounds." See *weight.* Cf. *weight for age, clerk of the scales, track handicapper, condition book, apprentice allowance.*

ALSO ELIGIBLE. phr. A horse that is not drawn in the requisite number of starters but that may get a chance to start provided enough withdrawals are made to include him within the limited number of starters.

After the first drawing, only the first, second, and third may be eligible. See *preferred list, eligible, entry, enter, scratch, declare.*

APPEAR. v.i. 1. Of a horse: to come to the post. 2. To finish second in a race (rare). Also *place* (1).

APPRENTICE. n. A rider who has not won 40 races in the past year and has never won a total of 100 races. See *bug, bug boy, apprentice allowance.*

APPRENTICE ALLOWANCE. n. An allowance in poundage which varies according to the rules of the racing commission. Most apprentice jockeys are allowed to carry five pounds less than the standard requirements until one year after they win their first race. Then they "lose their bug," become full-fledged professionals, and carry regulation weights. * Indicates bookmaker's code for apprentice allowance of five pounds; ** indicates seven pounds; *** indicates ten pounds. See *bug, bug boy, weight.*

AROUND THE BEND. phr. Said of horses entering or about the enter the stretch. See *turn, bend, stretch.*

AROUND THE PARK. phr. 1. Describes a morning workout over one lap of the entire course. 2. Describes a race over the full course. (Sports writers) See *airing, breeze, blow out.*

AT HOME IN THE GOING. phr. Said of a horse that is running on a track perfectly suited to his style. The condition of the track on the day of a race often determines the winner. See *fast track, rate.* Cf. *spot* (1), *cold dope, sloppy track, mudder.*

ATTACK OF THE SLOWS. phr. An imaginary disease from which a racehorse is said to be suffering when he bogs down during a race (humorous). See *untrack (himself), speed jam, in the can, back up, hang,* some with specialized meanings.

AT THE POST. phr. Said of horses that have reached the starting gate. See *start* (1), *appear.* Cf. *starter, post parade, bad starter, Bahr stall gate, standing start, walk up start.*

AUSTRALIAN BARRIER. n. A mechanical starting device designed to get the horses off to an even start. Now obsolescent except in England and Australia. Cf. *wire to wire, post parade, bad starter, beat the gate, Bahr stall gate, standing start, walk up start.*

B. abbrev. Form sheet code for blinkers.

BACK DOWN. v.t. To lower the approximate odds on a horse by a heavy volume of wagering. "John's Joy was *backed down* to 3-5." Cf. *mutuel, pool.*

BACK UP. 1. v.i. Of a horse: to weaken sufficiently during a race so that other horses take his lead away from him. Also *dog* (2), *hang, beheaded, quitter,* with specialized meanings. Cf. *attack of the slows, collar, doesn't bend.* 2. v.t. Of a jockey: to rein a horse in until he regains stride.

BAD POST ACTOR. phr. See *bad starter.*

BAD STARTER. n. A horse whose nervousness, unruliness, or other temperamental qualities make him a problem at the post. Thus, regardless of his ability or his relative merit in a particular race, he is a somewhat unreliable and uncertain factor in the betting. However, the fact that a horse is a *bad starter* does not necessarily mean that he will get off to a bad start in a race. See *rank, bad post actor, dwell.* Cf. *Australian barrier, post parade, Bahr stall gate.*

BAHR STALL GATE. phr. One type of starting gate. Even though the term "leaving the barrier" is frequently heard, it is really an anachronism, for most modern tracks use more convenient and accurate mobile starting gates which provide individual stalls.

BALL or MEAT BALL. n. A composite of different cathartics administered to a horse. Also, *physic ball.*

BANG TAIL. n. A racehorse, originating from the obsolete practice of tail-bobbing. Also *beagle, beetle, dog, gee gee, goat, hide, jobbie, lob, meat eater, oat burner, oat muncher, oil burner, plater, plodder, stiff,* and many other terms not included.

BAR PLATE. n. A shoe with a metal connection running across the heel.

BARRIER. n. A starting gate. Cf. *wire to wire, Australian barrier, walk up start.*

BASTARD PLATE. n. A type of heavy racehorse shoe that protrudes over the rear of the hoof. See *plate.*

BAT. n. 1. The whip used by the jockey. Also *leather, stick.* See *go to bat.* 2. A *battery.*

BATTERY. n. A small electric hand battery used to sting a horse in the stretch. A jockey caught using one is almost certain to be ruled off the track for life. See *buzzer.*

BATTLE THE IRON MEN. phr. 1. To bet on horses through the pari-mutuel machines. Also *play the mutes*. 2. To bet money through the mutuels on one horse in order to raise the price on another (bookmakers).

BEAGLE. n. A derogatory term for a racehorse. See *bang tail*.

BEAK. n. A horse's nose. Usually used in expressing a win bet. "Give me two tickets right on the *beak*." Also "Playmay won by a *beak*." See *nostril, bet on his nose*.

BEAR IN or OUT. phr. The tendency of a horse to swing either toward or away from the inner rail, especially in the last turn. See *get him a drink of water, lug out, overland route, turn* (*wide*), *rail runner, run wide, lug in*.

BEAT THE BUSHES. phr. To race a horse in the smaller, cheaper circuits because he shows up well in that type of company but is not sufficiently good to maintain himself in bigtime racing. See *leaky roof circuit, overnighter*.

BEAT THE FAVORITE. phr. A game played by most two-dollar bettors who will not bet on a hot favorite but prefer to pick a long shot to beat the favorite. This game improves the play at bookies and evens up the odds.

BEAT THE GATE. phr. 1. Of a horse: to get the jump, to get away a split second ahead of the other horses, just before the gate is sprung. 2. Of a horse: to make a speedy getaway, thus gaining an immediate advantage. Man o' War was noted for this ability. Cf. *Australian barrier, gate* (1), *wire to wire, bolt, break, wheel*.

BEETLE. n. A derogatory term for a horse. See *bang tail*.

BEEZER. n. See *beak*.

BEND. n. The curve in a racetrack, usually that which precedes the finish stretch or straightaway. See *around the bend*.

BEST BET. n. In the opinion of a dopester or a bettor, the horse most likely to win. See *sure thing, chalk horse, finger horse, dead to the pan, factor, good thing, hot stuff, kick in the pants, lock, odds on* (*favorite*).

BEST COMPANY. n. A flexible term varying in meaning according to the position in which a horse finishes a race. Thus if a certain horse wins, *best company* consists of the horses finishing second, third, and fourth. If the horse places, *best company* includes those horses finishing first, third, and

fourth. If the horse shows, *best company* includes those horses finishing first, second, and fourth. If the horse is unplaced, *best company* consists of those horses which win, place, and show. See *unplaced*. Cf. *best times*.

BEST OF THE OTHERS. phr. The horse that ran the best race of the horses not already referred to under *best company*.

BEST TIMES. n. The fastest recent records of listed entries for the same distance as the scheduled race. See *best company, comparative times*.

BET ON HIS NOSE. phr. See *beak*.

BET TAKER. n. The one who receives the money bet and gives the bettor a bet ticket at a bookmaking establishment.

BETTING BAROMETER. n. 1. The official odds board at a racetrack where pari-mutuel machines are used. The odds on all horses are changing continuously in proportion to the amount of money being wagered. (sportswriters). Also *ouija board*. (Newspaper parlance) Cf. *best bet, track odds, book, brackets, price*. 2. The totalizer used to compute odds.

BETTING RING. n. 1. The section of the track where wagers are made. 2. A betting group that has inside information (usually jockeys). See *boat race*.

The BIG APPLE. n. Bigtime racing, especially New York racing, which has built up a tradition of offering high purses, excellent tracks, and fine horses. Cf. *leaky roof circuit*.

BIG BOY. n. Jockey.

BIG HORSE. n. 1. From the spectator's point of view, a favorite, especially in any big race like the Preakness or the Derby. 2. From the owner's point of view, one that consistently wins large purses, especially prizes over and above the regular purse. Also *big train, oil burner, champion*. See *best bet*. Cf. *stake* (*horse*), *oat burner, claimer*.

BIG TRAIN. n. See *big horse*. Used in an affectionate manner in describing a great horse, e.g.: Equipose was often spoken of as the "*big train*." Note similar reference to great baseball players.

BILL DALEY. n. See *on the Bill Daley*.

BLANKET FINISH. n. A close heat, one in which the lead horses could figuratively be covered with a blanket. See *photo finish*.

BLEEDER. n. A horse that suffers bleeding at the nose as a result of racing or working out.

BLINKERS. n. A hood restricting a horse's vision preventing him from indulging in bad racing habits such as crowding the rail or swinging wide. Also used on horses that shy when other horses run at them. Also *goggles, French blinkers, blister, rogue's badge, cup blinkers.*

BLISTER. v.t. 1. To put a compound on a horse's skin causing excessive counterirritation. 2. Of a jockey: to use the whip (journalese). Cf. *bear in or out.* 3. n. (pl.) See *blinkers.*

BLOCK HEEL. n. A type of racehorse shoe. See *plate.*

BLOOMER. n. A horse that makes an excellent showing in the morning workout but cannot run well in a race. Also *morning glory.*

BLOW OUT. 1. v.t. To ease the pace of a horse gradually after a workout. "You can *blow out* that horse now." Also *cool out.* 2. v.i. Of a horse: to work out in training. Cf. *trials, railbird, set down.*

BLUE BOOK. n. A sheet containing the day's entries, the morning odds, and handicappings. This is one of many such sheets and happens to have a bluish tint to it. Cf. *finger sheet, scratch sheet, morning line.*

BOARDMAN. n. A man, in a book, who writes the race results on a blackboard or paper wall-sheet. See *tickerman.*

BOAT RACE. n. A fixed race, usually manipulated by the jockeys who agree before the race to let a long shot win. They then place bets away from the track, on the winning horse. See *jockey ring, betting ring, getaway day.*

BOLT. v.i. 1. To lose stride or falter during a race; to alter course drastically during the running of a race, usually to the inside or outside rail. Cf. *front runner, in the rut, quitter, stretch runner, chop his stride.* 2. To make a weak or bad start in a race (sportswriters). See *bad starter, trouble maker, rank, wheel.* Cf. *beat the gate.*

BOOK or BOOKIE. n. 1. A place where bets are taken; not to be confused with pari-mutuels. See *layer.* Cf. *clearing house, dutch-book, joint* (2), *oral betting.* 2. A person who takes bets on horses but is not officially connected with any track. See *bet taker.*

BOOKIE JOINT. n. A handbook location.

BOOKING ODDS. n. Although most books offer track odds, a few employ a handicapper who makes the odds for the book. This practice is losing favor. Track odds on two-dollar bets are paid in most places, and other odds figured at 20-8-4; 60 and 100-1 on parlay or daily doubles. See *house odds, oral betting, pari-mutuel betting, limit.*

BOOT. v.t. Of a jockey: to apply spurs or heels to a horse. See *sting a horse, spark a horse, urge, boot a horse home, crawl down (on a horse),* each with specialized meaning.

BOOT A HORSE HOME. phr. Of a jockey: to win a race. "Arcaro *booted* Time Supply *home* in the fifth." See *boot.*

BOWED TENDON. n. Lameness, frequently suffered by racehorses; caused by separation of a sheaf of leg tendon from the bone. Also a tear or stretch in the leader between the ankle and the knee.

BOY. n. 1. A jockey. See *big boy, pilot, punk.* 2. Any minor employee of a racing stable such as an exercise boy or swipe.

BRACKETS. n. The parentheses used in a racing form to indicate that a horse has won any particular race. See *earn brackets.*

BREAK. 1. v.i. See *start.* 2. v.t. To prepare a horse or break him to being ridden.

BREAKAGE. n. *Breaks.*

BREAK A MAIDEN or ONE'S MAIDEN. phr. 1. Of an apprentice jockey: to ride his first winner. 2. Of a horse: to win his first race. See *maiden, cherry, bug boy.*

BREAK HIS CHERRY. phr. To win his first race, said of either a jockey or a horse.

BREAK IN or BREAK OUT. v.i. 1. Of a horse: to veer out of line as he gets away from the barrier. Also *wheel.* Cf. *bear in or out.* 2. (BREAK OUT only) For a horse to sweat noticeably.

BREAK IN THE AIR. phr. Of a horse: to leap into the air instead of forward at the break from the gate, thereby losing some distance as well as traction in his second stride. Cf. *break in or break out, bad starter, bolt.*

BREAKS. n. The odd cents really due the bettor but retained by the racetrack. Pari-mutuel machines calculate the returns due the bettor to the single cent and the breaks accrue when a horse pays, for instance, $7.28 for $2.00; most mutuel tracks "pay to the dime" or "to the twenty cents" and in this case the track would retain the eight odd cents.

BREAK WATCHES. phr. Of a horse: to be exceptionally fast in the morning workouts, where he is being clocked by numerous unofficial observers—trainers, newspapermen, rival owners, bookies. Cf. *railbird, morning glory.*

BREEZE. n. 1. An easy pace at which horses are worked. See *drive, free pace, blow out, set down.* 2. A race easily won. Also *canter* (3), *click, dead to the pan, draw clear, go away, lock* (1), *cop, gallop, be in* (3), *with his mouth wide open, with plenty to spare, finish on the chinstrap, on top, shoo in* (2), *boat race, finish strongly, hold the race safe, outfinish,* with somewhat specialized meanings.

BREEZE IN. n. A race in which the winner takes the lead and holds it easily; one in which there is no doubt about the winner. Also *breeze* (1), *breeze through, on the Bill Daley.*

BREEZE THROUGH. v.i. To take the lead easily and hold it to win. See *breeze* (2), *breeze in, hold the race safe.* Cf. *wear down.*

BRIDGE JUMPERS. n. Conservative bettors who consistently play favorites and complain pitifully when they lose. "The infield lake was full of *bridge jumpers* tonight" would imply that few favorites won on that particular day.

BROKEN DOWN. adj. Said of a horse injured in a workout or a race; usually implies a ruptured tendon or a broken bone.

BUCKED SHINS. n. An inflammation, common to young racehorses, caused by concussion about the shins.

BUG. n. Apprentice allowance, so called from the asterisk in racing forms.

BUG BOY. n. An apprentice jockey. See *apprentice allowance.*

BUNCH. n. A roll of money. "He bet the *bunch* on Little Egypt." Also *iron men, kale, negotiable grass, jack, monkey, lush green, sucker money, sugar, wad, sucrose, clover.* "To bet the bunch" has an alliterative quality that is especially attractive to bettors.

BURNING PACE. n. See *chasing pace, burn up the ground.*

BURN UP THE GROUND. phr. To race at a terrific speed. See *chasing pace.*

BUSINESSMAN. n. 1. A jockey who may be persuaded to *pull a horse.* Also *strong arm.* 2. A smart operator generally, not necessarily illegal; anyone who is out for himself.

BUY THE RACK. phr. To purchase several combinations of daily double tickets.

BUZZER. n. See *battery.*

CALIFORNIA HARROW. n. A device for sifting out the under-surface of a racetrack and smoothing over the top at the same time, a process that keeps the track much faster than would be possible otherwise. Good tracks are expensive to build and maintain, and they are worked carefully, even between races. See *fast track.*

CALL. 1. v.t. At books, the races are broadcast partially by means of Western Union wire service and a caller. The numbers of the first 3 or 4 leading horses are called 4 or 5 times during the race. Example: "Off Kentucky at '05 . . . the quarter; 3 by a length, 7 by a half and 8 by a length . . half, 3 by a half, 7 by a length and 8 . . . stretch; 3 by a half, 7 by a length and number 8 . . . close fit at Kentucky . . . waiting on the photo . . . 2 was closing fast . . . at Kentucky winner number 7, second number 3, show horse number 2 . . . o.k. Kentucky at 3, t-h-r-e-e, 7, s-e-v-en, and 2, t-w-o. Running time 1:15 and 2. Run down coming Kentucky . . . 7.30, 5.20 and 4 dollars; 4.80, 3.60, and 2.80 on the bottom . . . next post Kentucky at 3:30." 2. n. This is the complete call or running of a race. Each time the numbers of the first several horses are given it is a *call.* There is the *quarter call, stretch call,* etc. Also any horse that is among the first few and whose name is called (as number 8 in the example) is said to have got a *call.*

CALLER. n. The bookie's employee who calls the races as they are run. See *call.* Cf. *boardman, chart caller.*

CALL ON A HORSE. phr. See *urge.*

CAMPAIGN or CAMPAIGN A STABLE. v.t. 1. To operate a racing stable as a business; to train and race horses. "James Fox *campaigned* six head at New Orleans last week." See *beat the bushes, circuit.* 2. To follow the seasons at various tracks.

CAMPAIGNER. n. 1. A horse that races the year round. 2. A horse that races under all types of track conditions and carries all degrees of weight. Not necessarily a stake horse or champion. 3. A steady horse.

CANTER. 1. n. A slow gallop. 2. n. A race that is won easily. Also *breeze* (2). 3. v.i. To run easily, not necessarily in a race. Cf. *finish strongly*.

CAN'T MISS. phr. A phrase used to refer to a horse that looks very promising; a set phrase among tipsters and touts. See *best bet, sure thing, double X*.

CAPPED HOCK. n. A swelling of the hock often resulting from shipping bruises.

CARD. n. See *program*.

CARRY THE SILKS. phr. To ride for a particular owner; each stable has its own combination of colors which is exhibited in the *silks* (jackets, caps, etc.) worn by jockeys. See *colors, silks*.

CHALK EATER. n. A gambler who consistently plays favorites. The term derives from the custom of writing odds on a blackboard, with the bookmaker heavily chalking favorites. See *chalk horse, bridge jumpers*.

CHALK HORSE. n. A horse that is conceded by most of the so-called experts to have the advantage in a certain race. Sportswriters compute the horse's chances to win, place, or show on the basis of past performance, running time, distance to be run, weight to be carried, age of the horse, pedigree, reputation of the owner. However, *chalk horses* seldom pay a very high return; the great number of bets placed on them forces the odds down. Bookmakers and form writers use a triangular symbol (Δ) to indicate a *chalk horse* in any particular race; the next time he is entered in a race with other horses, his odds may be high and he will not be a *chalk horse*. However, only horses that are rather consistently favorites are termed *chalk horses*. See *best bet, cold dope, winning favorites, favorite, big horse*.

CHALLENGE. v.t. Of a horse: to close in on the leader or leaders, especially in the stretch. Also *make a bid, make a move, move up, drive, go up front, close*, with somewhat specialized meanings. See *drive, get to the winner, work his way up*.

CHAMPION. See *big horse*.

CHARMED CIRCLE (SECTOR). n. The circle before the judges' stand where the winning horse is taken and his owner or a representative is presented with the trophy, if any (sportswriters). See *get the nod*.

CHART or CHART BOOK. n. A list of a horse's past performance. See *finger sheet, blue book, form sheet*.

CHART CALLER. n. *Racing Form* employee who records the margins between horses' positions during the running of the race for official publication.

CHASING PACE. n. A fast pace set by a challenger, usually at the beginning of the race. Also *burning pace*. Cf. *breeze* (1).

CHERRY. n. A horse that has not yet won a race. See *maiden, break a maiden*.

CHOP or CHOP HIS STRIDE. v. or phr. Of a horse: to shorten his stride. This may be the result of training soreness or may be a natural trait of the horse.

CHOPPY. adj. A short, choppy stride as contrasted to a long, smooth one. See *chop his stride*.

CHUTE. n. An auxiliary straight piece of track entering the elliptical track at any given point. Its function is to eliminate the need for starting a race on the turn. See *nursery chute, straightaway*.

CIRCUIT. n. A group of tracks located in one area which cooperate in arranging their racing dates so that horses can move from one track to another throughout the season without making any unnecessary long trips. See *campaign, beat the bushes, leaky roof circuit*.

CITY BLOCK. n. A wide margin. Also (a) *country mile*. Cf. *best bet, double X, sure thing*.

CLAIMER. n. A horse that is run consistently in claiming races. Cf. *big horse, cup horse, stake* (*horse*), *plater*.

CLAIMING PRICE. n. The price, set by the track, at which a horse may be claimed. If the owner agrees to race at this price, he accepts it for his horse if it is claimed. If he refuses, he must forfeit his purse, provided the horse is in the money. Racing rules governing claiming differ in different states; for instance, in Kentucky a horse may be claimed only by a man who had a horse in the same race.

CLAIMING RACE. n. See *claiming price*.

CLASS. n. The type of competition as judged on speed, previous claiming price, and weight carried over a specified distance.

CLASS OF THE RACE. phr. The horse in any

race which has run with the best horses, won the most money, has the best past performance, etc. Also *best bet.*

CLEAN BOOK. n. 1. A bookie, or booking establishment, which need not fear the authorities. A book that has the fix in. 2. A bookie who has a clean reputation. One who will not welsh. See *book.*

CLEARING HOUSE. n. A large organization that has many books under its control. It finances books, and gives them 25 percent to 33 percent of the net profit. See *book, lay off.*

CLERK OF THE SCALES. phr. An employee of a track who weighs the tack and the jockeys before and after a race to see that they have the proper weight. Cf. *allowance race, apprentice allowance.*

CLICK. v.i. To win. See *breeze* (2).

CLIMB. v.i. 1. Of a horse: to have difficulty getting a foothold, especially at the start. This is often due to the condition of the track which allows the ground to break from under the horse's hooves. Also *break in the air.* Cf. *fast track, break, dwell.* 2. To run with a high gait, sometimes caused by bad shoes.

CLOCK. v.t. To time a horse, usually unofficially. See *railbird, timer.*

CLOCKER. n. 1. An unofficial observer, usually a handicapper, bookie, or tip writer, who times horses in a morning workout. 2. An official representative observing for a form sheet, newspaper, etc. See *railbird, timer, time* (1), *Ingersol Willie.*

CLOSE. v.i. 1. To increase the pace or to gain on the challengers in the stretch or near the finish. See *challenge.* 2. (Used only with *at*) Phrase referring to the last approximate odds flashed on the mutuel board before the race is run. "Mountain Roar *closed* at 9-1." Cf. *open up at, back down.* 3. (Used only with *fast*) Of a horse to finish very fast; to show a great deal of reserve strength.

CLOSE FIT. n. A race that is won by a close margin. See *locked in stride.*

CLOSING STRIDES. n. The last few paces of a race; the finish.

CLOTHES. n. A horse blanket.

CLOVER. n. Money. See *bunch.*

CLUBHOUSE. n. At a racetrack, the most elaborate, expensive section of the spectator area, equipped with fancy bars and restau-

rants, and usually opposite the finish line.

CLUBHOUSE TURN. n. The track turn nearest the clubhouse.

CO-FAVORITE.n See *split choice.*

COLD DOPE. n. 1. Racing information based on actual facts; statistics on past performance and observations during the morning workout. Cf. *chalk horse, handicapper, form, dope, at home in the going.* 2. Inside information, or pseudoconfidential information.

COLD HORSE. n. 1. A horse whose owner has no intention of winning the race. See *pull a horse.* 2. A horse that seems likely to win. See *best bet, cold dope.*

COLLAR. v.t. 1. Of a horse: to overtake another horse and run neck and neck. 2. To win by a neck. Cf. *nostril.*

COLORS. n. 1. The silk jackets and caps worn by jockeys. 2. The uniform of a jockey. See *silks.*

COME BACK MONEY. n. Money wired into the track at the last minute by out-of-town bookmakers to cover bets placed with these books earlier. See *lay-off man, dynamite.*

COME DOWN LIKE TRAINED PIGS. phr. Of horses: to win, place, and show just as the track commentators had predicted. To finish according to form or according to the way a bettor has picked them.

COME HOME EARLY. phr. To win a race. Used most commonly in the imperative, where it is an order from the trainer or owner to the jockey; it means "go to the front and stay there." See *get the orders.*

COME IN HOME FREE. phr. Of a horse: to win a race easily. See *breeze* (2).

COME ON MAN. n. A tout's accomplice who takes the tout's information and places a bet or claims to have won heavily on the tout's information. He helps find likely suckers and sets them up for the tout. Also *go ahead man.* See *tipster, tout.*

COME THROUGH. v.i. To improve position by coming up through the pack. See *collar.* Cf. *pocket.*

COMMISSION BET. n. A large bet that is split up among a number of gamblers or layers, then placed through an agent in small amounts which do not attract attention and therefore do not affect the odds unfavorably. See *come back money, dump, dutch a book.*

COMMISSIONER. n. 1. An agent who places bets, especially *commission bet*. See *book*. 2. A bookmaker at a steeple chase.

COMPARATIVE TIMES. n. The relative speeds of various tracks, as determined by past track records. See *cold dope* (1). Cf. *fast track, best times*.

CONDITION BOOK. n. A booklet that lists all the conditions of races, purses, and qualifications at a certain meeting; usually reissued officially every ten days. Cf. *form, tip sheet*.

CONDITION RACE. n. A race made up of horses with specified requirements or conditions. Not now so popular as formerly.

CONTRACT RIDER or CONTRACTOR. n. A jockey who has a contract to ride for a single stable.

COOL A HORSE OUT. phr. To walk a horse about under the shed after a race; this is done to cool his blood down gradually so that he will not be susceptible to stiffness or colds. Cf. *blow out*.

COOLER. n. 1. A light blanket thrown over a horse during the cooling-out process. 2. A horse that is not trying to win.

COOL OUT. v.t. To soothe a bettor who has lost (touts, bookies, and con men).

COP. v.t. or v.i. To win a race. See *breeze* (2).

A COUNTRY MILE. n. See *city block*.

COUP. 1. v.t. To win a bet, usually a large one. "We should *coup* this race." 2. n. A large winning, often in the phrase "to make a *coup*." Cf. *dynamite, tip*.

COW KICK. 1. v.i. Of a horse: to kick forward and out to one side with the hind leg. 2. n. Such a kick.

CRACK DOWN. v.i. Of a jockey: to try hard to win.

CRAWL DOWN or CRAWL DOWN ON. v.t. or phr. Of a jockey: to push a horse to his utmost in order to get a final burst of speed out of him. Usually done without the whip. "Roberts *crawled down on* Night Bandit when he hit the stretch." See *boot*. Cf. *elbow ride*.

CROSSFIRE. 1. v.i. Of a horse: to clip his back and/or front hooves together while running. 2. n. Talk between two touts or con men for the benefit of a sucker.

CROWD. v.t. or v.i. To jostle a horse or jockey in an effort to gain an advantage in racing position either at the start or during the race, usually used with *against* in referring to horses in motion. Thus: "Blue Bon was *crowded* at the post" (before the race) and "Blue Bon was *crowded against* the rail" (during the race).

CUFF A BET. phr. See *dutch a book* (2).

CUP BLINKERS. n. A type of blinkers which permits the horse to see only straight ahead. See *blinkers*.

CUP HORSE. n. A horse that distinguishes himself as a distance runner in races of over a mile. Cf. *claimer, big horse, campaigner*.

CUPPY TRACK. n. A track that is in apparently fast condition but which forms cups or a slightly hummocky surface as the horses run over it. This condition reduces the speed. Cf. *fast track*.

CUP RACE. n. 1. A race in which a trophy goes to the winner, usually in addition to the purse. 2. Any big race, such as The Oaks or The Derby.

CUSHION. n. The surface of the track. See *fast track, slow track, muddy track, sloppy track, mudder, heavy track, mud runner*.

DAILY DOUBLE(S). n. A betting pool that pays off on combinations of any two races which the track designates. The odds are usually high and the winner sometimes takes several thousands of dollars for his two-dollar investment. The *daily double* includes two of the first races on a program, varying from track to track. See *parlay, quinella*.

DARK HORSE. n. 1. A horse that is generally conceded to be a poor risk to bet on but which may surprise and win. May or may not be a *long shot*. Also *eagle bird, sleeper*. 2. A horse worked out before the official timer arrives at the track.

DEAD. adj. 1. Describes a horse that has very little chance of winning against his competitors in a certain race; a horse that is racing out of his class; sometimes described as "not here" or as "being out." See *overmatched*. 2. Describes a horse that makes no effort to win.

DEAD TO THE PAN. phr. "Pomp Rita is *dead to the pan* in the 8th." See *best bet*.

DEAD TRACK, n. 1. A track that appears fast but lacks resilience; this condition makes for noticeably slow time on an ordinarily fast track. See *fast track, cuppy track*. 2. A track that is slow or muddy. See *deep footing, muddy track, cushion*.

DEAD WEIGHT. n. Leaden weights carried under the saddle flaps if the jockey is too light to meet the weight requirements of the race. Cf. *feather, clerk of the scales, handicap.*

DECLARE. v.t. To nominate a horse for a race in which he does not run; predominant form *declared*, used to indicate that the horse did not run. See *scratch.*

DEEP FOOTING. n. A muddy or sloppy track. Also *heavy track, sloppy track.* Cf. *fast track, slow track.*

DERBY. A race for three-year-olds only. In contrast to a sweepstakes race where the winner gets the entire purse, the track retains a certain part of the purse for place, show, and even fourth position. A 1¹/₄ mile race.

DICKEY LEGGED. adj. Said of an unsound horse with bad legs, usually one that throws his weight on the outside edges of his hooves.

DISQUALIFY. v.t. or v.i. Of a horse: to finish in the money but to be refused official notice of this fact (or to be reduced to a lower position) because of some violation of the racing rules. See *finger horse* (2).

DO BUSINESS. phr. To engage a jockey to *pull a horse.* See *business man.*

DOESN'T BEND. phr. Of a horse: to retain his lead and win, used only in the negative. "A horse that doesn't quit is a horse that *doesn't bend.*" Cf. *quitter.*

DOG. 1. n. A cheap horse. See *bang tail.* 2. v.i. Of a horse: to fall behind or slacken his pace. Always used with *it.* "He *dogged it* in the last furlong." See *back up.*

DOG RACE. n. A race in which cheap claiming platers compete.

DON ALONZO. n. A horse that sulks; so called from the old racehorse Don Alonzo, a sulker. Obsolescent.

DOPE. n. 1. Information on a race; tips. See *cold dope.* 2. Narcotics used to stimulate horses.

DOUBLE(S). n. Same as *daily double(s).*

DOUBLE X. n. 1. On some programs, a good mud runner, marked XX. 2. A *best bet.*

DRAW CLEAR. v.i. Of a horse: to finish a race with plenty of speed still in reserve. (Predominant form a part. phr. as in "Charlie J. won drawing clear.") Also *go away, finish on the chinstrap.* See *breeze* (2).

DRAW OUT. v.i. To increase speed, usually without punishment from the whip or spurs.

DRIVE. 1. n. See *stretch.* 2. v.i. Of a horse: to extend himself to his full power, especially in the stretch. See *challenge.* Cf. *breeze* (1).

DROP BACK. v.i. See *dog* (2). Cf. *draw clear.*

DROP DOWN. v.i. Of a horse: to run with cheaper horses than he is accustomed to meeting, especially in claiming races. See *best company.* Cf. *in too deep, system.*

DRUGSTORE HANDICAP. n. Any race in which drugs are used to stimulate horses or in some cases to deaden the pain in bad feet. See *hophead, dust a horse, boat race.*

DUMP. v.t. To bet heavily on a horse at the last minute before starting time. This money is usually bet in town or away from the mutuels to keep the odds up. See *commission bet.* Cf. *dutch a book, past post, come back money.*

DUST A HORSE. phr. 1. To give a horse any narcotic or drug before a race. This term usually implies the use of cocaine. See *boat race, drugstore handicap, hophead.* 2. To go to the front or to leave dust in the face of the horse behind.

DUTCH A BOOK. phr. 1. Of a bookie: to accept bets in such a proportion that he will lose, no matter which horse wins the race. 2. Of a group of men: purposely to force a bookie out of business by betting so that the book inevitably loses, or consistently to past post the same book, which can be dangerous. Also *cuff a bet.* See *dutch book, past post.*

DUTCH BOOK. n. A bookie who consistently loses money because of his own lack of foresight, business acumen, or grift sense. See *book, dutch a book, take a run-out powder, tip run.*

DWELL. v.i. Of a horse: to get away slowly at the start. See *break, climb, break in the air.*

DYNAMITE. n. Money that one book bets with another to cover bets he does not wish to keep. This money sometimes passes on in other lay-off bets and comes back to the original bookie to his disadvantage. Hence *come-back money.* See *lay-off money.*

DYNAMITER. n. 1. A gambler who is engineering a *coup.* 2. A bookie using *dynamite.*

EAGLE BIRD. n. 1. A horse with a better chance of getting into the money than his odds indicate. A good long shot. See *dark horse, sleeper.* Cf. *overlay.* 2. A horse with more money bet on him at the books than at the track.

EARLY SPEED. n. A brief display of speed on the part of a horse early in a race, after which he falls back into the pack. Also *flash of speed.*

EARLY STAGES. n. Approximately the first half of a race or less. See *later stages.*

EARN BRACKETS. phr. 1. To win. The phrase is derived from the parentheses used in the racing form to indicate that a horse has won any particular race. See *brackets.* 2. To be listed in first place on the official track bulletin board. See *betting barometer.*

EASY RACE. n. 1. A race won without too much effort. See *breeze* (2). 2. A race on which a book wins heavily.

EDISON. n. See *battery.* Obsolescent.

EDUCATED CURRENCY. n. Bets that are placed on a horse as a result of supposedly authentic information. Also *smart money.* See *tip, dope.*

ELBOW RIDE. n. A deceptive riding technique by which the jockey seems to be using his hands to urge his horse but is only waving his elbows. Cf. *pull a horse.*

ELIGIBLE. n. A horse that meets the requirements to run in a specific race. Also *appear* (2), *eligible.*

END BRED. adj. Colloquial variant of *inbred.*

ENTER. v.t. or v.i. To name a horse to compete in a certain race. Also *nomination.* 2. To pay the entry fee in a given race.

ENTRY. n. 1. A horse whose owner has signed for that horse to participate in a specified race. 2. Two or more horses (usually from the same stable but not necessarily so) run as one entry, that is, the odds on both horses are the same. A single mutuel ticket equals a ticket on both horses, and if either horse is in the money, the ticket may be cashed at full value. Horses in an entry are usually designated as 1 and 1A on the program.

EQUIVS. n. The equivalent odds to $1 posted officially by the track and covering the entries on the race immediately preceding. These odds are based only on bets placed through the pari-mutuels. "If odds are 10-1 then equivs are $11." Cf. *booking odds, house odds.*

EXCUSE. v.t. To withdraw a horse from a race after the official scratch time (with the judges' permission). *Excused* the predominant form. See *declare, scratch.*

EXERCISE BOY. n. One who rides horses during the workout.

EXPECTING. part. For a handbook to be expecting a raid (humorously punning on expecting as used with pregnancy). "You guys better not hang around, I'm *expecting.*"

EXTENDED. part. For a horse to be traveling with full power and speed, especially in the stretch. See *drive, all alone, wire to wire, early speed.*

FACTOR. n. 1. A horse that has a fair chance to win a race. Also *best bet.* 2. When a horse is referred to as "a *factor* from the start," the implication is that he has held his own in third or fourth position and might at any time have made a bid for a position in the money; he is one of the three or four best horses in the race.

FAKE START. n. A type of start in which the horses begin running before signaled by the starter. Rare since the prevalence of the modern automatic starting gate. (Still used in harness racing.)

FARRIER. n. A blacksmith at a racetrack. Once standard usage but now obsolete except among racehorse and saddle horse people.

FAST TRACK. n. A track which is dry and in such condition that horses are able to make their best time. Cf. *sloppy track, mudder.*

FAVORITE. n. A horse with a very good chance to win. Hence, a horse with low odds. Also *best bet.* See *chalk horse, sure thing.*

FEATHER. n. A very light jockey. "That horse has a *feather* up." Cf. *dead weight.*

The FIELD. n. 1. Horses (all long shots) that are grouped together as an entry because of the shortage of betting capacities of pari-mutuels. 2. Those horses that do not finish in the money. See *pack.* 3. The entire group of horses in a race.

FILL HIM UP. phr. See *have a bucketful.*

FINGER HORSE. n. 1. A favorite. The designation probably originated from the fact that one of the morning line sheets (called a *finger sheet*) indicates its handicapper's choice by the symbol of a finger opposite the name of the horse. Cf. *morning line, finger sheet, scratch sheet.* 2. A horse cited for infraction of the racing rules (rare).

FINGER SHEET. n. See *scratch sheet.*

FINISH ON THE CHINSTRAP. phr. Of a horse: to win easily; to finish under restraint. Also *breeze* (2).

FINISH STRONGLY. phr. Of a horse: to finish a race while trying but not having spent his strength. See *breeze* (2).

FIRE. v.t. To treat a horse's shins by puncturing the skin with a hot iron or an electric needle. 2. To cauterize an injury.

FIRST TODAY AND LAST TOMORROW. phr. See *hot and cold.*

FIT. 1. n. The finish of a race. 2. v.i. To finish a race. "Big Ping always gets off to a slow start but he *fits* fast." 3. adj. Of a horse: to be in its best racing condition. 4. adj. Said of a horse that has been held in during training and is to be let out in a certain race. Also *ready.* See *sleeper, dark horse, full of run* (1), *work a horse by lantern, spot* (1), *tight.*

FLAG DOWN. v.t. To wave an object at the exercise boy to inform him that he is working the horse too fast.

FLAG WAVER. n. A horse that flicks his tail up and down while running.

FLASH. n. The late changes in betting as shown by the figures on the approximate odds board. Cf. *equivs, booking odds.* 2. See *flash of speed.*

FLASH OF SPEED or FLASH. phr. or n. A brief display of speed on the part of a horse early in the race. Also *early speed.*

FLAT RACING. n. A term used to avoid confusing running races with harness racing. See *harness racing.*

FOLD UP. v.i. 1. To drop behind in a race and go definitely out of the running. See *bolt* (2). 2. To stop riding a horse out. "He folded up his horse on the eighth pole."

FOOTING. n. The surface of the track. Also *cushion.* See *deep footing, turf.*

FORM. n. 1. A daily form sheet published by dopesters. These forms, costing 25 cents, are more reliable than the tipsheets that are hawked at the track. In the form, the bettor is given the information and computes his choice from these data. Form sheet gamblers consider themselves more scientific than those who bet by hunches, tips, etc. See *cold dope, finger sheet, tip sheet, form sheet.* 2. The condition of a horse. See *fit* (1).

FORM REVERSAL. n. A term indicating that a horse has reversed his past performance record temporarily.

FORM SHEET. n. 1. The *Daily Racing Form,* published daily except Sunday, carrying entrants and past performance records of all horses at the major tracks in the United States, as well as race results, selections, news about racing and racing personalities. 2. Any racing publication such as the *Cincinnati Record* or the *Racing Record.*

FORM SHEET CODE. n. A standard code used by form sheets and newspapers to indicate various tracks. These names are listed in full here because the code is not translated in the various racing publications. This list includes only tracks reported to be operating as of April 1951:

1.	AC	Agua Caliente
2.	AD	Arlington Downs
3.	AGM	Agawam Track
4.	ALA	Alamo Downs
5.	AP	Arlington Park
6.	AQU	Aqueduct Track
7.	AUR	Aurora
8.	BB	Blue Bonnets Track
9.	BEL	Belmont Park
10.	BEU	Beulah Park
11.	BLR	Bel Air Track
12.	BM	Bay Meadows
13.	BP	Brookline Park
14	BR	Brookline Track
15.	CAN	Canfield Track
16.	CD	Churchill Downs
17.	CF	Cumberland Fair
18.	CHIN	Chinook Track
19.	CLA	Columbia Downs
20.	CLW	Colwood Park
21.	CP	Connaught Park
22.	CRD	Cranwood Park
23.	CT	Charlestown Park
24.	DAL	Dallas Track
25.	DAY	Dayton Track
26.	DEL	Delaware Track
27.	DET	Detroit Track
28.	DEV	Devonshire Track
29.	DM	Del Monte Track
30.	DOR	Dorval Park
31.	DP	Dade Park
32.	DUF	Dufferin Park
33.	ED	Epsom Downs
34.	EMP	Empire City
35.	FE	Fort Erie Track
36.	FG	Fair Grounds Track
37.	FP	Fairmont Park
38.	FRA	Fraiming Track

39.	GRM	Gresham Park
40.	HAG	Hagerstown Track
41.	HAM	Hamilton Track
42.	HAV	Havana, Cuba
43.	HAW	Hawthorne Track
44.	HdG	Havre de Grace
45.	HLA	Hialeah Park Track
46.	HO	Hamilton, Ohio
47.	HP	Hazel Park Track
48.	JAM	Jamaica
49.	JP	Jefferson Park
50.	KEE	Keeneland Track
51.	KGS	King's Park Track
52.	LAN	Lancaster Track
53.	LAT	Latonia Track
54.	LB	Long Beach
55.	LEX	Lexington Track
56.	LF	Lincoln Fields Track
57.	LGA	Longacres Track
58.	LP	Landsdowne Park Track
59.	LRL	Laurel Track
60.	MAR	Marlboro Track
61.	MR	Mount Royal Track
62.	NAR	Narragansett Track
63.	OP	Oakland Park
64.	PLA	Playfair Park
65.	POM	Pomona Track
66.	PP	Polo Park
67.	QP	Queens Park
68.	RD	River Downs Track
69.	RKM	Rockingham Park
70.	RP	Riverside Park
71.	SA	Santa Anita Park
72.	SAR	Saratoga
73.	SPT	Sportsmans Park
74.	STN	Stanford Park
75.	SUF	Suffolk Downs
76.	TAN	Tanforan Track
77.	TDN	Thistle Down Park
78.	THF	Thorncliffe Park
79.	TIM	Timonium Track
80.	TRP	Tropical Park
81.	UH	United Hunts
82.	VP	Victoria Park
83.	WAS	Washington Park
84.	WDB	Woodbine Park
85.	WER	Whittier Park
86.	WIL	Willows Park

Most other data pertinent to the calculation of odds appear in form sheets and handicappers' columns in code or abbreviation. Many individual items are listed under separate entries, such as *G.*, *M.*, *P.P.*, *S*, ***, *bug*, etc.

FOUL, TO CLAIM. phr. When a jockey charges that his horse has been the victim of illegal tactics, the results remain unofficial until the stewards allow or disallow his claim. Predominant form, *foul claimed.* "In the 6th race, *foul claimed.* No results." On those tracks controlled by G. E. Widener, the British term *objection* is used. See *entry, set back, set down, inquiry, official.*

FRACTIONALS. n. The time recorded by a clocker for the quarter mile and half mile in a three-quarter mile workout. Thus: "He did $^3/_8$ furlong in $33^1/_5$, three quarters in $1:16^3/_5$, and worked out the mile in 2:02 handily."

FREEMARTIN. n. The filly of a pair of twins.

FREE PACE. n. See *breeze* (1).

FRENCH BLINKERS. n. A type of colored blinker which restricts a horse's vision selectively. See *blinkers.* Sometimes called *French cups.*

FROM FLAG FALL TO FINISH. phr. (Journalese) See *wire to wire.*

FRONT RUNNER. n. A horse that runs his best only when he is well in the lead. Cf. *bolt* (2), *quitter.*

FULL OF RUN. phr. 1. Of a horse: to be in good form. See *fit* (1). 2. To have plenty of strength in reserve; hence, to win easily. Also *finish on the chinstrap.*

FURLONG. n. $^1/_8$ mile.

FUTURITY. n. A race (often $^5/_8$ mile) for two-year-olds exclusively, in which the horse must be entered before it is foaled. See *derby, preferred list, purse.*

GALLOP or GALLOP HOME. v.i. or phr. See *breeze.*

GAP. n. 1. A lead of one horse's length or more. See *length.* 2. The gateway leading to the track.

GARRISON FINISH. n. A fast driving finish named after a jockey who was famed for holding his horse back until the last minute and then letting him out to win, thus preserving all his strength for the final drive. 2. Any close finish.

GATE. n. 1. The starting barrier behind which horses are lined up for the start. See *Australian barrier.* 2. Any starting line. Also *wire.* See *beat the gate, go to the post.*

GEARED. adj. Said of a horse in best form. Obsolescent. See *ready.*

GEE GEE. n. A racehorse. See *bang tail.*

GENTLEMAN RIDER. n. 1. An amateur rider who participates in society races or in so-called gentlemen's cup races. 2. A rider in a steeple chase. 3. An owner who rides his own horse or drives it in harness racing.

GET A RING IN ONE'S NOSE. phr. To lose everything by betting. "I can't pay you now because I *got a ring in my nose.*" Also *get taken.*

GETAWAY DAY. n. The last day of a racing meet. Proverbially the best day to have a *boat race.*

GET HIM A DRINK OF WATER. phr. The expression applied to a jockey who allows his horse to run toward the outside rail, usually applied to the last turn when the natural tendency of the horse is to swing wide. Also *bear out, lug out, turn (wide).* Cf. *lay a horse on the rail, inside, outside.*

GET OUT. v.i. 1. Of a gambler: to win and recoup his previous losses and hence "*get out* of the hole." The usual phrase is "If my horse comes in, I'll *get out.*" 2. v.i. To *bear out,* referring to a horse. "This horse *gets out.*"

GET SOMEONE ON A SLOW BOAT. phr. To take one for all his money through sucker bets. "I'd like to *get him on a slow boat.*" Cf. *get a ring in one's nose.*

GET TAKEN or TOOK. phr. 1. To lose a bet. See *get a ring in one's nose.* 2. By implication, to be cheated or imposed on while betting. See *pad the (iron) ring, store.*

GET THE ENTIRE POT. phr. Of a horse: to win easily; refers rather to the purse than to bets placed on a horse. See *gallop, breeze* (2).

GET THE JUMP. phr. See *beat the gate.*

GET THE NOD. phr. To win a race; theoretically, to receive acknowledgment from the judges by a nod. See *charmed circle.*

GET THE ORDERS. phr. Of a jockey: to be told in the paddock immediately before the race that he is expected to win; owners and handlers determine whether or not a horse is to be a contender for the money, and a jockey usually carries out the orders he gets if he is able to do so. Also *come home early.*

GET THE WORKS. phr. Of a horse: to be poorly ridden in a race; to have his good points hidden by the jockey because of either incompetence or a willingness to have the horse lose. See *boat race.*

GET TO THE WINNER. phr. When a horse is moving up in the stretch and making a strong challenge for first place, he is said to be *getting to the winner.* Usually used of horses that place. "Wax improved his position steadily and was *getting to the winner* in

the last sixteenth." See *challenge, withstand.*

GET WELL. v.i. To recoup a betting loss.

GET YOUR DOUBLES IN. phr. A phrase heard in books. This call goes up about 11 o'clock when the first races are starting in the East and is a warning to those daily double players that they must hurry and get their daily double bets on; it means that the day's work and business are about to begin.

GIVE HIM HIS HEAD. phr. See *let him go.*

GIVEN THE MEET. phr. Of a jockey: to be banned from racing during the entire racing meet. See *set down.*

GO AHEAD MAN. n. A tout's accomplice. See *come on man.*

GOAT. n. See *bang tail.*

GO AWAY. v.i. Of a horse: to win easily. See *draw clear, breeze* (2).

GO DOWN MAN. n. A person who, when a bookie is raided, claims to own the book and is therefore taken and fined instead of the real owner. Thus the real owner's name is kept off the police records; and if the same book is raided again, since another *go down man* will be taken in, no extra fine or sentence will be incurred. Also used as *go in man, walk in man, walk down man, stand in man.*

GOGGLES. n. Blinkers.

GOING. verbal n. 1. Track conditions. 2. Competition or breaks in a race.

GOING AWAY. phr. Of a horse: to win a race while he is still increasing his lead. See *breeze* (2), *handily.*

GOO. n. Mud or a muddy track. Also *deep footing.* See *track condition.*

GOOD DAY AND GOOD TRACK. phr. A phrase used relative to track records and comparative times established on various tracks. No two tracks are exactly the same speed, even under similar conditions; hence by examining the past track records for all distances from half a mile up to a mile and a quarter, a dopester can calculate with some accuracy the time of a horse whose past performance record he has at hand, assuming *a good day and good track.* See *track condition.*

GOOD FEELER. n. A lively, spry horse; one showing some promise. Also *hopeful.*

GOOD THING. n. 1. A horse that is considered by gamblers to be an easy winner before the race, especially if the odds on him are

high. See *lock, mortal lock, kick in, best bet.*
2. A hot tip.

GOOD TRACK. n. A track that has a little water on it, owing to a heavy dew or light rain, or that is drying out and has only a little water left on it.

GO TO BAT. phr. Of a jockey: to use his whip, especially in the stretch. See *bat, shaking up, draw out, rouse, hustling tactics, put to the punishment, strongly handled, straighten out* (2), *hand ride* (1).

GO TO THE FRONT. phr. Of a jockey: to force his mount out toward the lead; to take an advanced position. Also *challenge.* See *go to bat, hand ride.*

GO TO THE POST. phr. To line up in the starting gate preparatory to starting a race. See *gate, post parade.*

GRAB. v.t. Of an owner or jockey: to win a purse with a long shot. See *dark horse, outsider.*

GRAB HIMSELF. phr. Of a horse: to catch his front leg with his hind foot, as War Admiral did in one Belmont race. Sometimes this throws a horse, sometimes causes him to lose stride.

GREEN. adj. Applied to horses that are inexperienced in actual racing. Cf. *cherry;* also can apply to people.

GRIFTER. n. 1. A track fan or gambler who makes only safe bets. Cf. *piker* (2), *boat race.* 2. A professional horse player, thief, or short-con man who follows the races. Also applied to professional gamblers and big-con men. Also *hustler.*

GROCERIES. n. 1. Feed. 2. Money used for the necessities of life like food, shelter, and women (whimsical or humorous).

GROOM. n. 1. The person who leads the horse from the stable to the paddock (Southern usage, esp. Florida). 2. The man who cares for the horse in the stable.

GUINEA. n. 1. A rub-down man for racehorses. 2. A black employed at the stables. Also *boy* (2), *swipe, groom.*

GUMBO. n. See *goo.*

GUN FROM THE GATE. phr. A fast-starting horse.

GUNNING. part. Getting all possible speed out of a horse, not necessarily with whip or battery. Said of the jockey.

HACK DRIVER. n. A derisive term for a jockey. See *boy* (1).

HALTER MAN. n. One who claims another's horse in a *claiming race.*

HANDICAP. n. 1. A race in which the better horses are given more weight to handicap them. 2. Any big race; now all races are made fairly even because of the distribution of lead weights; therefore, in effect all races are handicaps. 3. v.t. To try to pick the winner of a race by means of past performance, etc.

HANDICAPPER. n. 1. A writer or commentator who predicts race results from past performance. See *track handicapper, chalk horse.* 2. The track official who puts weight on the horses.

HANDILY. adv. 1. Easily, applied to the way a horse runs or wins. 2. Without being whipped or driven during a race or workout. See *breeze, handy work, going away.*

HANDLE. n. 1. The total money bet by all the fans on one race. "The *handle* for the 5th was at least $30,000." 2. The total money bet for a meeting, or entire year. Cf. *track odds, booking odds, pool.*

HAND RIDE. v.t. 1. To lift a horse's head at the beginning of his stride, thereby lengthening his stride. Such tactics call for strong hands and expert timing. 2. To ride a horse "by hand" rather than by spurs and whip; bringing out the best in a horse by crossing the reins high up on his neck and literally riding him by hand. An experienced jockey who has perfected this technique can do remarkable things with a horse in the stretch without recourse to punishment. Cf. *go to bat, heavy-headed horse, handy work, let out a wrap.*

HANDY WORK. n. A workout in which a horse is not pushed or driven. "He did three quarters in 1:15 in a *handy work.*" Also *breeze* (1). See *hand ride.*

HANG. v.i. 1. Of a horse: to fail to gain ground in the stretch. Also *bolt* (2). See *drive.* 2. To keep up with the leaders or to maintain a slim lead to the finish.

HARDBOOT. n. 1. A horse breeder from the Kentucky hills or from Tennessee; so called because in the old days his boots hardened from the mud and water through which they had traveled. 2. An old-time, experienced breeder. See *racetracker, wrinkleneck.*

HARNESS RACING. n. As contrasted to running races, racing with harness and a sulky. See *flat racing, steeple chase.*

HARROW. n. See *California harrow.*

HAVE A BUCKETFUL. phr. A horse that has been fed just before a race to cut his wind and decrease his chance of winning is said *to have a bucketful.* Also *fill him up.* See *hophead, sponge a horse, boat race.*

HAVE A PULL IN THE WEIGHTS. phr. Any horse carrying less weight in ratio to age than any competitor. See *track handicapper.*

HAVE ONE IN HIS BOOT. phr. Of a jockey: to carry in his boot a betting ticket on his mount. Often the ticket is given the jockey by a gambler who thinks it brings luck.

HAVE THE FIX IN. phr. 1. To make an agreement that a race has been *fixed* for a certain horse. See *boat race.* 2. To purchase police protection for gambling.

HAWTHORNE START. n. See *standing start.*

Be HEADED. v.t. To be overtaken. "Gay Secret *was headed* in the stretch by Jimpin." See *drop back.*

HEAD OF THE STRETCH. phr. See *lane.*

HEAT. n. Any one of several races run on one day. See *stanza, spasm.*

HEAVY-HEADED HORSE. n. A horse that is difficult to hand ride, especially one with strong neck muscles or one that runs with its head low. See *hand ride, hold him in.*

HEAVY SHOES. n. Heavy training plates for a horse's hooves.

HEAVY STEEL TRAILER. n. A type of racehorse shoe. See *plate.*

HEAVY TRACK. n. A track that has passed beyond the sloppy stage; the worst possible track condition for most horses. See *track condition.* Cf. *fast track.*

HERDER. n. 1. A jockey who maneuvers his horse in front of the pack. 2. A horse that crosses to the inside at the start, forcing the pack to bunch.

HIDE. n. See *bang tail.*

HIGH ON A HORSE. phr. To back a horse heavily; to be confident that he will run in the money. See *fit* (1), *sleeper.*

HIGH SCHOOL HORSE. n. A horse that often wins when the price is high on him; the implication is that he is able to read the approximate odds board.

HOLD A HORSE IN RESERVE. phr. Of a jockey: to hold a horse in so that he will have additional stamina for the final stretch. Not to be confused with *pull a horse.*

HOLD HIM BACK. phr. To prevent a horse from winning. Usually this is done when the owner is waiting until the odds are better.

HOLD HIM IN. phr. 1. Of a jockey: to force his horse to run behind at the beginning of a race so as to reserve speed for the finish. See *Garrison finish.* 2. Of a jockey: to force his horse to stay near the inside rail at the turns. See *turn (wide), on the rail.*

HOLDOVER. n. Winning tickets that can be cashed at a book, but that the gambler does not collect until later. These tickets, or the money they are worth, are held at the book overnight. See *outstanding ticket.*

HOLD THE BOOK ON A JOCKEY. phr. To act as a jockey's booking agent. See *jockey agent.*

HOLD THE RACE SAFE. phr. To gain a safe lead and hold it. See *breeze* (2).

HOOP. n. The color ring around a jockey's sleeve or body. See *colors, silks.*

HOPEFUL. n. See *good feeler.*

HOPHEAD. n. A horse that has been given a drug before a race to alter his speed. See *boat race, drugstore handicap, dust a horse, tea.*

HOT AND COLD. phr. Of a horse: to run erratically; to run a fine race one day and a bad one the next. Also *first today and last tomorrow.* See *form reversal.*

HOT HORSE. n. 1. A horse that is stimulated by drugs. 2. A horse that, although not normally a favorite, has been touted until odds drop very low.

HOT STUFF. n. 1. A good tip. See *best bet, sure thing.* 2. A "sure" winner. See *double X, sure thing.*

HOT WALKER. n. An exercise boy who walks a horse after a race or workout. See *blow out, cool a horse out.*

HOUSE ODDS. n. The odds given by a bookmaker who has a handicapper and so gives odds independent of track odds. Largely supplanted by the practice of giving standard bookmaker's odds, which may approximate track odds. See *limit.*

HURDLE RACE. n. A steeple chase.

HUSTLED or HARD HUSTLED. v.t. 1. Of a horse: to be pushed by his competitors into a pace that he has difficulty withstanding. See *wear down.* 2. Of a horse: to be ridden hard

by his jockey; to get the whip and spurs. See
go to bat, hustling tactics.

HUSTLER. n. 1. A *tout.* 2. A *grifter.*

HUSTLING TACTICS. n. The tricks that a
jockey knows to force speed out of a horse or
to put his competitors at a disadvantage.

IF COME BET or COMING BET. n. A type
of bet providing that if the gambler wins on
one horse, a specified amount of the winnings is automatically placed on another
horse in another race: if the first horse loses,
there is no money coming back to the gambler, and so no bet is made on the second
horse. See *parlay.*

IMPOST. n. The amount of weight carried by
any horse in a race.

Be IN. v.i. 1. To be entered in a race. Also *pit.*
2. Of a horse: to finish a race. 3. Of a horse
or an entry: to be regarded as a "sure" winner. "Gee Gee *is in* for the sixth." See *breeze*
(2), *sure thing, double X, best bet.*

Be IN BANDAGES. phr. Of a horse: to wear
leg bandages to brace and strengthen his legs
during racing and working out.

INDEX NUMBER. n. The code number used
when consulting the form sheet regarding
the past performance of a horse. See *form.*

INFIELD. n. The section of ground enclosed
by the racetrack proper.

INFORMATION. n. Statistics or rumors con-
cerning the condition of a horse or his
chances in a race. There are many types of
information sold, some of them verging on
confidence games.

INGERSOL WILLIE. n. The official clocker
at the morning workouts. See *clocker.*

Be IN GOOD or BAD COMPANY. phr. To
compete with; to race against. Cf. *cold
dope.*

IN HIGH. phr. At top speed.

Be IN LINE. phr. 1. Of a horse: to be second,
third, etc., as a betting favorite. See *chalk
horse.* 2. Of a horse: to command odds in
approximate agreement with those assigned
by the handicapper or track commentators.

INQUIRY. n. When the word *inquiry* is
flashed on the pari-mutuel board, it indicates that the judges are investigating the
race results. See *foul, set down.*

IN SHAPE. phr. 1. Of a horse: to show up well
in the workouts; to look promising. 2. Of a
horse that has been held in by his handlers or
owners until track conditions, competitors,

etc., all seem favorable: to be ready to be let
out to try for the money. Coming from some
stablemen this phrase is equivalent to a good
tip. Also *fit, ready.*

INSIDE. 1. n. The part of the track close to
the inside rail. 2. prep. Between a horse and
the inside rail. "Lady Swift came up *inside*
Quibble." Cf. *on the rail, outside.*

IN THE CAN. phr. Not trying to win or not
intended to win. Cf. *attack of the slows.*

IN THE MINUS POOL. phr. Said of a track
that loses money on a race. Big gamblers will
often bet huge amounts on solid horses such
as Citation or Armed and cause *minus pools.*
Small gamblers never cause *minus pools*
since many $2.00 bettors will try to beat the
favorite.

IN THE MONEY. phr. 1. Said of a horse that
finishes first, second, or third. See *win.* 2.
Said of a gambler who has a bet placed on a
horse that wins, places, or shows. See *bet on
his nose.*

IN THE PINK. phr. See *fit.*

IN THE POOL. phr. 1. To be short of money.
2. To have something go wrong. "If that
business deal flops I'll be *in the pool.*" In this
sense the term is a generalization of *in the
minus pool.*

IN THE RUT. phr. A racing position from
which a horse has little or no chance to make
a challenge. See *pocket.* Cf. *bolt* (2).

IN TOO DEEP. phr. Of a horse: to be entered
in a race with competitors far better than he
is. Also *out of his class.* Cf. *drop down, system.*

INTO THE LANE. phr. When horses round
the last turn and are just entering the
stretch, they are said to be coming *into the
lane.*

IRON MEN. n. Pari-mutuel machines (obsolescent except in such phrases as "to battle
the *iron men*").

IRONS. n. Stirrups.

JACK. See *bunch.*

JAM. 1. v.i. Of horses: to crowd together in a
race, especially in the stretch. 2. n. The result of such crowding. See *speed jam, crowd,
pocket.*

JAUNT. n. 1. A race. 2. An unimportant
race. See *stanza.*

JERK. v.t. Of a jockey: to pull a horse in deliberately to keep him from winning. Also *pull
a horse.* See *boat race.*

JOBBIE. n. A race horse. See *bang tail.*

JOCK. n. A jockey, a professional rider.

JOCKEY AGENT. n. A booking agent who secures the services of jockeys for owners. Most of the better class owners employ jockeys under contract by the year and pay them good salaries. See *hold the book on a jockey.*

JOCKEY RING. n. A group of jockeys banded together to promote *boat races.*

JOCKEYS' ROOM. n. Quarters in which jockeys change their clothes and leave their tack.

JOG. v.i. 1. See *breeze.* 2. A horse's gait in which its legs move in diagonal pairs.

JOINT. n. 1. A racetrack. 2. An illegal betting establishment; one that has no connection with the track. Also *store.* Cf. *book, dutch book, track odds, battery.*

JUDGES. n. Stewards, timers and those who place horses at the finish, as well as patrol judges who are stationed at intervals around the track to observe the race and spot fouls. Predominant form, plural.

JUICE. n. Protection money paid police by gamblers, bookies, and others (West Coast).

JUMP. n. 1. The start of a race. Cf. *Australian barrier.* 2. A jocular form of address (vocative) around race tracks.

JUMPER. n. A race horse that has been trained for steeple chases. Also *leaper, timber topper.* See *suicide club.*

KALE. n. See *bunch.*

KEEP A HORSE STRAIGHT IN THE STRETCH. phr. To ride in the proper lane; to avoid crowding the other horses in the stretch. When a jockey is fined or penalized for not *keeping his horse straight in the stretch,* the implication is that he used foul tactics. Often the jockey is not responsible for his mount's swerving. See *crowd, break in* or *break out, foul.*

KICK IN, KICK IN THE ASS, KICK IN THE PANTS. phr. A horse that is heavily touted to win a race easily. Also *shoo in, breeze.* See *boot a horse home, best bet, sure thing, double X.*

KILLING PACE. n. See *chasing pace.*

LANE. n. The stretch, especially the far end of it. Also *head of the stretch.* See *drive.*

LATE GOOD THING. phr. 1. A horse on which the betting increases noticeably just at post time, often as the result of a circulating tip. 2. A last-minute tip.

LATER STAGES. n. The second half of a race, whatever the length. Often applied to the stretch. Cf. *early stages.*

LATE SCRATCH. n. A horse that is withdrawn just before the beginning of a race. See *excuse.*

LAY A HORSE ON THE RAIL. phr. Of a jockey: to hold a horse close to the inside rail, thus securing the most advantageous racing position. See *pole, inside, overland route, save ground, straighten out.*

LAYER. n. A bookmaker. See *book.*

LAY OFF. n. Money that one bookie gives to another to cover bets which he does not wish to hold. Also *dynamite.* See *book, lay-off man.*

LAY-OFF MAN. n. Sometimes a bookmaker gets jittery about certain horses on which he has already laid bets. He may then give sufficient money to cover his possible losses, or part of them, to an accomplice who visits other bookmakers or tracks and places it as advantageously as possible: This accomplice is called a *lay-off man;* most big bookies employ him regularly on a salary basis. See *come back money, pad the (iron) ring.*

LEAD PONY. n. A saddle horse (not a pony in the orthodox sense of the word) which is used to lead the racehorses out of the paddock to the post parade; also used to handle and quiet fractious horses.

LEAKY ROOF CIRCUIT. phr. Small-time racing; either tracks that do not use the highest quality horses and offer smaller purses, or tracks that have a circumference of under one mile, or both. See *beat the bushes, overnighter.*

LEAPER. n. A steeple chaser. See *jumper.*

LEATHER. n. 1. The whip. See *bat.* 2. Strap connecting stirrups to saddle.

LEGGED UP. phr. See *fit.*

LEG LOCKING. phr. Of a jockey: to ride close to another in the race and place his leg in front of the other's leg, in such a manner as to hold him back. Such procedure is, of course, illegal.

LENGTH. n. The length of a horse, approximately 8 feet. Distance between horses is referred to in lengths.

LET HIM GO (RUN, or OUT). phr. Of a jockey: to allow his mount to run at his greatest speed. See *give him his head.*

LET OUT A WRAP. phr. Of a jockey: to loosen his grip on a horse that has been running under restraints; equivalent to getting a voluntary burst of speed out of a horse, for the horse will forge ahead as soon as he is taken from under restraint. See *hand ride, go to bat, under wraps.*

LEVEL. v.i. To try to win.

LIKE A PRICE or LOOK FOR A PRICE. phr. Of an owner or handler: to hold a horse in unless the odds are long; this is usually done by men who bet on their own horses. "Sand Bag won't win in the fifth; his stable *likes a price,* and he is running at even money." See *fit, in shape.*

LIKE THE TRACK. phr. 1. This phrase indicates that a horse has a good record at the racetrack where he is running. 2. That he runs best on a track in a specified condition. See *at home in the going.*

LIMIT. n. Arbitrary odds set by a bookmaker as the highest he will pay, regardless of what a long shot may pay at the track. These odds are fairly universal. The old and the new limits follow:

Old Limit	New Limit as of 1948
to win 15-1	to win 20-1
to place 6-1	to place 8-1
to show 3-1	to show 4-1
on a parlay 40-1	on a parlay 60-1
	on a daily double 100-1

See *house odds, booking odds.*

LOAFER. n. A horse that has ability but that must be pushed continually. See *sleeper* (2), *dark horse.*

LOB. n. 1. A horse that is deliberately pulled to keep him out of the money. 2. A horse that never makes a very impressive showing. 3. A horse that is not intended to win; one that is in the race for the conditioning and to give his owners some idea of his prospects. Often a maiden running with more experienced horses. See *fit.*

LOCK or MORTAL LOCK. n. 1. A race to be won easily; a "cinch" for a certain horse. See *breeze* (2). 2. A "sure thing" bet. See *best bet, sure thing.* 3. By implication, a fixed race. See *boat race.*

LOCKED IN STRIDE. phr. When two horses come down the stretch like a team, in step, and usually headed for dead heat finish, they are said to be *locked in stride.* This is one of the most beautiful sights in racing.

LONG SHOT. n. A horse that pays high odds. See *dark horse.*

LOOK FOR A PRICE. phr. See *like a price.*

LOOK GOOD ENOUGH TO EAT. phr. Of a horse: to look promising. See *hopeful.*

LOOKING OUT OF THE WINDOW. phr. When a gambler has bet on a horse consistently without winning, then bets against him or fails to bet at all on the day the horse wins, he is said to be *looking out of the window.* Cf. *system.*

LOSE ONE'S MAIDEN. phr. To win one's first race. Said of horses as well as jockeys. Also *break his cherry.*

LOUSE BOOK. n. 1. A small-time booking establishment. Usually a book that will take 10- and 25-cent bets. Often located in poorer neighborhoods or around high schools where there may be many small gamblers who bet often but not much at a time. 2. A bookie who runs a small book. These men are looked down upon by the bigger bookies.

LUG IN. 1. v.i. Of a horse or a jockey: to work in toward the rail during a race. See *inside, lug out.* 2. v.t. To bring suckers into a book or store.

LUG OUT. v.i. or v.t. To bear toward the outer rail. See *lug in, outside.*

LUSH GREEN. n. Money. See *bunch.*

MAIDEN. n. 1. A horse that has never won a race. 2. A race for horses making their first start. 3. The quality (in a jockey or a horse) of never having won a race. Also *cherry.* See *break a maiden.*

MAIN LINE. n. The place where the largest number of mutuel machines are located at a track. Adapted from older usage describing the line-up of bookies at the track. See *one for the end book.*

MAKE A BID. phr. Of a horse: to try to pass the leaders in a race; to attempt to take the lead. Usually applies to such an effort in the stretch. See *challenge, make a move.*

MAKE A (AN OLD-TIME) KILLING. phr. To win with a good long shot. Also *grab.*

MAKE A MOVE. phr. 1. Of a horse: to maneuver into a more favorable racing position. 2. Of a jockey: to get a burst of speed out of his mount. 3. Of a jockey: to attempt to take over the lead at any time during the race. See *challenge, go to bat, let him go, move up.*

A MAN IN KOKOMO. phr. A trainer, owner, or tout who has wired persons in other cities to bet money on certain horses; such a tip is generally credited to *a man in Kokomo* regardless of his actual location. 2. Anyone whose name is to be kept a secret. See *tout*.

MATCH RACE. n. A race for certain specified horses. Often a special event between two horses.

MEAT EATER. n. A horse that quits or is not game; a horse without spirit. See *bang tail*.

MEET. n. The period of days over which races are run, excluding Sundays. See *season*.

MIDNIGHT HANDICAP. n. A race whose outcome is decided the night before it is run (humorous usage). See *boat race*.

MONEY FROM HOME. phr. 1. Any easy money. 2. The proceeds of a bet made with a sucker. Hence, also *sucker money*.

MONEY RIDER. n. 1. A jockey who rides better with a ticket on his own mount. 2. A well-known jockey who has many mounts.

MONKEY. n. A $100 bet.

MONKEY CROUCH. n. The jockey's position in certain riding techniques.

MORNING GLORY. n. A horse that works out well but races poorly in competition. See *bloomer*.

MORNING LINE. n. A list of probable odds posted or published in the morning before races run in the afternoon. These odds are computed by the track handicapper and serve as a basis for much of the betting that takes place before official and exact odds are available. See *handicapper, track odds*.

MORNING SHEET. n. See *scratch sheet*.

MORTAL LOCK. n. A "sure thing." See *lock*.

MOVE UP. v.i. Of a horse: to challenge for a place in the lead; to improve racing position. See *challenge, make a move* (1), *get to the winner, work his way up*.

MUDDER. n. See *mud runner*.

MUDDY TRACK. n. A track that has a soft surface as a result of heavy rain; one on which the mud splatters as the horses run. See *fast track, good track, slow track, sloppy track, heavy track, mudder, mud runner, cushion*.

MUD RUNNER. n. A horse that performs well on a muddy or slow track. In the *Daily Racing Form* the following symbols are used: *, fair mud runner; x, good mud runner; ⊗, superior mud runner.

MUTES or MUTS. n. The pari-mutuel betting machines. Also *iron men*.

MUTUEL POOL. n. The entire amount of money bet through the machines after the track has taken its percentage. See *take out, pari-mutuel betting, pool*.

NAME. v.i. (used only in the passive and usually with *for*). To be entered in a race. "Phar-Mond is *named* for the fifth at Churchill" means that Phar-Mond has been entered in the fifth race at Churchill Downs. See *nominations*.

NECK. n. Less than half a length; a horse winning by this measure is said to have *won by a neck*. Less than a neck is a *head, nose,* or *whisker* progressively. See *nostril*.

NECK AND NECK. phr. Two or more horses running abreast, usually at the finish. See *locked in stride*.

NECK THE HORSE. phr. Of a jockey: to lie extremely low on his mount; to bend down as close over the horse's neck as possible.

NEGOTIABLE GRASS. n. Money (journalese). See *bunch*.

NERVE. v.t. To deaden the pain in a horse's legs by removal of nerve tissue. Most commonly used in the past or past participle Cf. *drugstore handicap*.

NICKEL. adj. A deprecatory word applied to anything that is of inferior quality or that is unsuccessful. "That nickel nag ran out on me." "He always bets those *nickel* tips."

NIGHTCAP. n. 1. The last race of the day. 2. A laxative given a horse so as to tire him out for tomorrow's race.

NIGHT RIDER. n. One who sneaks a horse out of his stall at night and tires him so that he cannot do his best in the next day's race. Cf. *work a horse by lantern*.

NINE OF HEARTS. phr. A horse that has no chance to win. See *in the can*.

NOMINATIONS. n. Horses named for a certain stake race. For certain famous stake races like the Kentucky Derby, there may be several hundred nominations, but the day before the race only a dozen or so accept, that is, actually become entries. See *stake (race), eligible*.

NOSE. n. Literally the tip of the horse's nose. Any very narrow margin by which one horse surpasses another at the finish; that part of a horse that must pass his competitor before he can win; hence to *bet on the nose*. See *neck, length*.

NO SNOW ON YOUR SHOES. phr. Trustworthy. Literally, the person has no snow on his shoes because he has been in the book long enough for it to have melted; therefore he cannot have any advance information and can be trusted not to "past post" the book. May be related to *snowshoe*, an old-time word for policeman or detective.

NOSTRIL. n. An even smaller margin between horses than *nose*; usually jocular or ironic. See *beak, beezer, collar, neck.*

NOW AND THEN (THENER). phr. A horse that tries sometimes, and sometimes does not try.

NURSERY CHUTE. n. A $^3/_8$ mile chute such as used at Hialeah track. Nursery chutes are used, as the name indicates, exclusively for two-year-olds, especially in the earlier part of the year. See *chute.*

NUT. n. 1. Losses at betting. See *on the nut.* 2. A bankroll. "To get a *nut*" means to acquire a bankroll. 3. Expenses involved in bookmaking or grifting.

NUTS. n. Horses picked as winners by the form sheets; also *favorite.* See *play the nuts.*

OAT MUNCHER (BURNER). n. 1. A horse that does not pay for his feed with his winnings. 2. Any worthless horse. See *bang tail.*

OBJECTIONS. n. See *foul.*

ODDS ON (FAVORITE). n. A horse that is so universally conceded the advantage in a race that no one will bet even money on him. See *chalk horse.*

OFF. 1. adv. Of a horse: to be slower than the other horses in a race. If the horses have run $^3/_4$ mile in 1:14$^1/_5$ and one horse has run it in 1:15, then that horse is $^4/_5$ second *off* (time). 2. adv. In motion at the beginning of a race, as "They're *off!*" 3. n. The difference between the time for running a race and the record time. 4. adj. (Used with *time*) The exact time at which the race starts. "The *off* time of the third race was 3:03." This information is given to prevent the book from being past posted.

OFF BELL. n. 1. A gong that is rung at the track just before the start of each race to indicate that no more bets may be placed on horses in that race. 2. The bell that rings when the horses break from the gate.

OFF CONDITION. phr. Said of a slow or muddy track. See *track condition.*

OFFICIAL. 1. adj. Race results that the track stewards have passed as being all right, meaning that they consider the race to have been fairly won. Then the word *official* is flashed on the pari-mutuel board in the infield. 2. n. Any track employee with authority.

OFFICIAL BOOKING ODDS. n. Odds that differ from the track odds in that they are set by the bookmaker. These odds fluctuate; an average was formerly taken and all bettors were paid off on the average price. Because of the ill feeling this caused among gamblers, most books now pay track odds (up to 20/1). See *track odds, limit.*

OFF SIDE. n. The right side of a horse.

OFF THE PACE. phr. Of a horse: to be running behind the challengers in a race, perhaps conserving his strength for the drive. See *under restraint, hold a horse in reserve.*

OFF TIME. n. See *off* (3). Cf. *post time.*

OIL BURNER. n. 1. A cheap plater. 2. A fast horse. See *bang tail.*

OIL IN THE CAN. phr. A horse that the backer believes to be a sure winner. See *chalk horse, system, best bet.*

ON EDGE. phr. 1. In top form. 2. Of a horse: to be nervous or excited before a race.

ONE FOR THE BOY. phr. A betting ticket bought by the owner, trainer, or a gambler on the horse that the jockey is riding. This ticket is given to the jockey to give him more interest in winning the race. In some states the jockeys are not allowed to bet at all. In most states the jockey is not allowed to bet against himself. Even the practice mentioned above is frowned upon by track officials. See *have one in his boot.*

ONE FOR THE END BOOK. phr. 1. A bad race run by a horse that has been consistently good. There is a humorous reference to the days when bookmakers lined up, with the newcomer taking a place at the end of the line where there is a preponderance of bad bets. See *main line, book.* 2. By extension, anything out of the ordinary, unusual, or notable, sometimes incredible. This phrase, cut to "here's *one for the book*" has enjoyed wide usage and various plausible folk etymologies.

ON THE BILL DALEY. phr. Of a jockey: to take the lead at the start and keep his horse out in front of the rest all the way to the finish. Also *wire to wire.*

ON THE GROUND. phr. Of a jockey: to be suspended (never disqualified). A horse may be disqualified because of an action that is not a fault of the jockey. In such cases, the judges decide as to the jockey's guilt. Often, despite disqualification, the jockey is not set down. On the other hand, a jockey may be set down without a disqualification of the horse. Usually in big races a foul of a minor nature may be overlooked in regard to the disqualification of the horse; yet after that race the jockey may be suspended for a certain period. Also *set down*.

ON THE HEAD END. phr. Of a horse: to be leading or taking the lead. "Saunders put the horse *on the head end*." See *make a move, drive*.

ON THE NUT. phr. To lose heavily at betting. See *get a ring in one's nose, play the nuts, nut*.

ON THE RAIL. phr. Of a horse: to run next to the inside rail of the track (the shortest route). See *inside*.

ON TOP. phr. Of a horse: to be in the lead at any point in a race. See *breeze* (2).

OPEN THE MEETING (MEET). phr. Of a horse: to win the first race on the program. "Syriac *opened the meeting* at Belmont."

OPEN UP AT. phr. 1. Of a horse: to command certain odds the first time odds are flashed on the mutuel or totalizator board (racetrack proper). 2. To command certain odds in the *morning line*. Cf. *close* (3), *tote board*.

ORAL BETTING. n. 1. Legal betting formerly carried on at the track by bookmakers, in contrast to pari-mutuel betting (obsolescent). 2. Betting carried on at books where track odds are not given. At such a place, the book may have friends to whom he gives better odds than customers who do not regularly patronize him. See *booking odds, track odds*.

OUIJA BOARD. n. The official approximate odds board at a racetrack. Usually manually operated. Also *betting barometer*.

OUT. 1. n. A race. 2. adj. Entered to run in a race. 3. adj. or adv. Unplaced, or out of the money.

Be OUT. v.i. To have no chance of winning. Also *dead, overmatched*.

OUTFINISH. v.t. To leave a competitor behind late in the stretch or at the finish. See *breeze* (2).

OUT FOR AN AIRING. phr. 1. Said of a horse that is entered in a race for the experi-

ence; one that is not intended to win. See *lob*. 2. Taking a light workout.

OUT OF (THE CHUTE). phr. 1. A term indicating that the horses in a race that started in the chute have left the chute and are now running on the track proper. See *chute, straightaway*.

OUT OF HIS CLASS. phr. Said of a horse running with horses much better than those he is accustomed to run with. See *in too deep*.

OUT OF LINE. phr. A horse is said to be *out of line* when he commands odds that, in the opinion of commentators, are either too light or too heavy, usually too heavy. Cf. *in line*.

OUT OF THE RUNNING. phr. Definitely not a *factor*.

OUTSIDE. n. 1. The middle of the track, away from the inside rail. 2. The part of the track between the middle and the outside rail. See *get him a drink of water, run wide*. Cf. *inside*.

OUTSIDER. n. 1. The longest shot in a race. 2. Any long shot.

OUTSTANDING TICKET. n. A ticket that the gambler has won on but not yet redeemed. See *holdover*.

OUTSTAY. v.t. To be able to equal the speed of one's nearest competitors long enough to defeat them. See *wear down, outfinish*.

OUTSTAY THE FIELD. phr. Of a horse: to take the lead and hold it until the finish. See *wire to wire, on the Bill Daley, shake off*.

OUT TO SHOW. phr. 1. A phrase indicating that a horse will not pay any return if he shows. This is usually announced before the race and the original $2.00 investment is returned to the bettor. In four-horse races no show tickets are sold through the pari-mutuels; thus a price is laid against the winner, as, for instance, $4.00 to win, $3.20 to place, and *out to show*. Bookmakers, away from the track or at tracks where there is oral betting may figure that it will be impossible to break even or profit on show money regardless of how many horses are entered; they may then lay a horse at "even, 1–3, and *out*." Distinguished from sense 2 by stressing the *out*. 2. A phrase indicating that a trainer, owner, or jockey is intending to bring his horse in third. Distinguished from sense 1 by a shift in stress to the word *show*.

OVERDUE. adj. Used to describe a horse that has not won for some time. Some gamblers go on the theory that horses win in cycles; they wait until a horse is *overdue*, then place a bet on him in every race he runs, covering each day's losses with a heavier bet the following day. See *fit, sleeper, system*.

OVERLAND ROUTE. n. A horse that races wide around the track is said to have taken the *overland route*. See *lay a horse on the rail, get him a drink of water*.

OVERLAY. v.t. To quote odds that are generally considered too high. See *underlay, booking odds, dutch a book, oral betting*.

OVERMATCHED. adj. When a horse runs against a field of admittedly superior horses, he is said to be *overmatched*. Also *dead*.

OVERNIGHTER. n. 1. A horse that does well in so-called overnight handicaps. 2. A horse that shows up well in cheap company.

OVERNIGHT HANDICAP. n. A race for which entries may be made through the entry box as late as the day preceding the race, in contrast to those races for which entries must be named some time in advance. Hence, a cheaper race in which first-class entries are seldom made. See *overnighter, leaky roof circuit, beat the bushes*.

OVERWEIGHT. n. or adj. Weight carried by a horse in excess of the amount assigned him by the handicapper, usually because the jockey has been unable to train down to his usual weight. "In the second race, Abby B., *overweight* one and a half pounds." See *weight*.

OWNER'S HANDICAP. phr. A race in which the owners of the entries designate the weight their entry will carry (obsolescent).

PACE. n. The rate of speed being made by the leading horse. See *killing pace, off the pace*.

The PACK. n. 1. Those horses not in the lead. 2. Horses with high odds, bet as an entry because of their small chance of being in the money. See *field*.

PADDOCK. n. 1. The enclosure where horses are saddled. 2. The small railed enclosure under or behind the stands where the horses entered in each race are paraded immediately beforehand. See *post parade*.

PADDOCK JUDGE. n. The track official who is responsible for getting the jockeys up on their mounts on time, for seeing that all the horses reach the post at the time set, and for identifying the horses in each race. He must know every racehorse in his section of the country — and as many as possible from other sections — by sight in order to prevent running horses under false names and qualifications. Cf. *placing judges, ringer*.

PAD THE (IRON) RING. phr. To change the odds in favor of a horse one is backing by laying smaller bets on his competitors at the track. Thus a man who has what he considers very reliable information on a horse may bet large sums of money on him through bookmakers away from the track; then, just before the starting bell, he may bet $1,000 on each horse in the race except his own. This sudden influx of money will make a noticeable change in the machine odds, perhaps forcing the odds on a horse from 8-5 to 5-1, and assuring him a neat profit when he collects from the bookmakers. See *lay-off man*.

PAGODA. n. The judges' stand at a track.

PAGODA CZARS. n. The official judges at a racetrack (journalese). See *pagoda*.

PARI-MUTUEL (MUTUEL) BETTING. n. Legal betting worked out on a mathematical basis. The pari-mutuel machines add up all the money bet to win, to place, and to show in each race and calculate the return on each horse. The use of machines gives the gambler more protection against unethical betting practices, provides constant and accurate information on odds, and guarantees payment. See *take out, track odds, betting barometer*.

PARI-MUTUELS. n. Machines used by racetracks for the purpose of figuring odds automatically, and in many cases for the automatic issuance of tickets.

PARLAY. n. A type of bet in which the gambler picks two or more horses in different races; he places a bet on the first horse with the understanding with the bookie that if it wins, all of the money shall automatically be put on the second horse. If the second horse wins and the gambler puts all of his winnings on a third horse, he has a three-horse parlay, etc. Parlays may be made on win, place, or show positions. See *if come bet*.

PAST POST. v.t. To place a bet on a horse that has just won a race. To do this the gambler must obtain the race result before the bookie does (by using walkie-talkies, etc.)

PATH. n. The better portion of the track. Usually used in reference to a muddy or sloppy track when referring to the driest portion next to the rail.

PAY TO THE DIME or TO THE TWENTY CENTS. phr. See *breaks*.

PEEP. v.i. Of a horse: to finish in third place; *show*, "High Diver *peeped* for me yesterday."

PEEPHOLE. n. The third place at the finish. See *peep*.

PHOTO or PHOTO FINISH. n. A close finish in which the results must be determined by a photograph. Such a picture is automatically taken by a timing device at the finish of each race. See *picture*.

PHYSIC BALL. n. See *ball* or *meat ball*.

PICK UP. v.t. To note the time a horse makes in the morning workouts. "Joe, *pick up* Time Supply at the half-mile post." Also *clock*, *time*, with specialized meanings. Cf. *railbird*.

PICTURE. n. A photo finish. "Our Delight won in a *picture*." See *photo finish*.

PIG. n. A horse that quits. See *bang tail*.

PIKER. n. A small-time gambler. See *bridge jumpers*.

PILOT. n. A jockey, especially an excellent jockey. See *boy*.

PIN A HORSE'S EARS BACK. phr. To get the very best out of a horse; to push him to the limit. From the practice of pinning ears to start a balky horse; not literally used on race horses. See *make a move, urge, crawl down on (a horse), hand ride*.

PINCH. v.t. Of a horse: to cut in front of another, especially on the turns, thus gaining a more advantageous racing position. If the horse cuts in toward the rail more sharply than necessary, thereby blocking the horse being passed, the judges can call a *foul*. See *crowd, jam*.

PINS or UNDERPINNINGS. n. A horse's legs.

PIT. v.i. or v.t. To enter a horse in a race. See *be in* (1), *entry*.

Be PITCHED. phr. Of a horse: to be entered against better competitors than he has been accustomed to meeting. See *in too deep, system, out of his class*.

PLACE. 1. v.i. Of a horse: to come in second. Cf. *bet on the nose, show*. 2. n. The location of a bookie; a bookie's establishment.

PLACING JUDGES. n. Usually referred to as *judges*. The track officials who decide the results of the races. See *paddock judge, official*.

PLANT. n. A racetrack.

PLATE. n. A racehorse shoe, much thinner and smaller than the ordinary shoe for saddle horses. There are many different kinds of shoes in use, all made by hand and fitted to the indiviual peculiarities of the horse that is to wear them. Several of the more popular types are toed plate, a shoe with a sharp projecting toe; block heel, one with the ends of the shoe turned up behind; bastard plate or heavy steel trailer, types that protrude beyond the hoof in the rear.

PLATER. n. 1. A cheap racehorse. See *bang tail*. 2. A term of deprecation applied to any horse that does not perform as well as his backer had hoped.

PLAY THE FAVORITES. phr. Of a gambler: to bet on the favorites consistently, hoping that the law of averages will operate in his favor.

PLAY THE MUTS (MUTES). phr. To bet on horses through the pari-mutuel machines. Also *battle the iron men*.

PLAY THE NUTS. phr. To follow the advice of the form sheets in betting; to avoid long shots. Also *play the favorites, stay in line*. See *best bet*.

PLODDER. n. A horse that is steady but not brilliant. See *bang tail*.

POCKET. 1. v.t. Of jockeys: to surround a horse while racing and block him off with their own mounts; in this way a good horse may be forced out of the money. See *crowd*. 2. n. The close quarters described under 1.

POLE. n. 1. The inside rail. See *lay a horse on the rail*. 2. Any one of the sixteen vertical posts that mark a mile racetrack off into equal parts.

POLICEMAN. n. A "stooge" horse entered in a claiming race in those states where an owner, in order to claim another man's horse, must have one of his own entered in the same race. Of course, the *policeman* is not a valuable horse. See *claiming race, ringer*.

PONY. n. 1. A racehorse. See *bang tail*. 2. Any horse that is used around a racetrack for other purposes than racing, lead ponies, etc.

POOL. n. The total amount of money bet on a race through the pari-mutuel machines. Cf. *breaks*.

POOLROOM. n. See *store*.

POSITION. n. A word indicating that a horse is first, second, etc., at a specified time or on a specified section of track.

POST. n. 1. The place from which horses begin a race. 2. See *pole* (2).

POST PARADE. n. 1. The act of parading the horses in front of the stands before racing. 2. The procession of horses to the post.

POST POSITION. n. (usually abbreviated to P.P.) The number of the stall gate from which a horse starts. The horse in the stall gate closest to the inside rail has post position 1, the next has P.P. 2, etc.

POST TIME. n. 1. The time at which horses reach the post. No bets are accepted after *post time*, which is officially confirmed. 2. The time schedule on a racing card. The *post time* for each race is designated before the races begin, but may differ from *off time*.

PREFERRED LIST. n. A list of horses that have been excluded from previous races which they have tried to enter because too many were already entered. These horses take precedence over new entries in making up the programs for future races. See *eligible, entry*.

PRESS A BET. phr. To increase a bet with a bookie.

PRICE. n. A term of rather loose usage referring to the equivalent odds to $1 which a horse is calculated to pay.

PROGRAM. n. 1. An official publication issued by the individual track listing names of horses appearing in each race, their owners, trainers, jockeys, weight carried, equipment, conditions of the races, etc. 2. The day's racing, considered collectively.

PROSPECTIVE STARTERS. n. Candidates for entry into a race. See *entry*.

PULL A HORSE. phr. Of a jockey: to hold a horse back deliberately to prevent his doing his best. Not to be confused with *holding a horse in* to reserve his strength for the drive. Also *do business*. See *business man, strong arm, jerk (a horse)*.

Be PULLED UP. phr. Of a horse: to be forced to stop during a race because of an injury or accident. Cf. *pull a horse*.

PUNK. n. A deprecatory term for a mediocre jockey. See *boy, pilot*.

PURSE. n. 1. The total amount of money awarded to the first several horses finishing a race. The amount of money that one of the first several horses wins. See *stake (race)*.

PUT A HORSE OVER. phr. Of a jockey ring, owner, or gambler: to fix a race.

PUT TO THE PUNISHMENT. phr. Of a horse: to receive the whip, spurs, or battery, applied severely. See *go to bat, buzzer, pin a horse's ears back*.

QUARTER. n. 1. A quarter of a mile, usually referring to the first quarter of a race. 2. A quarter of a second. 3. A *quarter horse*. 4. The first phase of any race regardless of its length.

QUARTER CRACK. n. The separation between outer and inner walls of the hoof near the heel, caused by a bruise or stepping on a stone. It is painful and causes lameness.

QUARTER HORSE. n. A horse that shows up well in short races; not to be confused with the saddle-type of the same name. Also *sprinter*. Cf. *cup horse*.

QUARTER POLE. n. Strictly speaking, any one of the four poles marking off quarter-mile intervals around the track; usually refers to the last or three-quarter pole just before the finish. See *quarter, pole*.

QUINELLA. n. A betting arrangement in which the gambler selects the first two horses to finish the race. The ticket does not pay unless the horses picked finish 1–2. Such tickets pay higher odds than a win ticket alone. Bookmakers only. See *parlay*.

QUITTER. n. 1. A horse that lacks sufficient wind to finish a race well. See *run out* (2), *run up an alley*. 2. A horse that cannot run well out in front of the field. This type of horse is usually held back during the early stages of the race so that one or two horses are always ahead of him until the finish.

RACE FORWARDLY. phr. To show promise, especially in the early stages of a race. Also *show early foot*. See *breeze* (2).

RACETRACKER. n. A professional who makes his living by caring for racehorses or moving from track to track in some capacity with the racing season. See *hardboot*.

RACE WIDE. phr. Of a horse: to run in the middle of the track instead of competing for a place on the rail. Often enough there are excellent reasons to *race a horse wide*. Lack of interference from other horses, and the possibility that the "outer" part of the track may be faster than the rail position are both good reasons. See *bear out.*

RACING FORM or DAILY RACING FORM. n. A racing publication issued from Chicago. See *form sheet.*

RACING SECRETARY. n. The track official who sets the conditions under which horses may enter specific races. He also handles details such as accepting nominations.

RAILBIRD. n. An amateur clocker who follows the morning workouts and keeps a close check on the performance of various horses. Railbirds may be observed at any large track in the early morning hours, equipped with stop watches and notebooks, keeping careful records of the horses they are studying. See *clocker.* Cf. *blow out* (2), *break watches, clock, timer.*

RAIL RUNNER. n. A horse that performs best near the inner rail.

RANK. adj. Of a horse: to be unruly at the starting post. See *bad starter, bolt* (1).

RATE. v.t. Of a jockey: to judge his horse's capabilities shrewdly so that he may keep up with the field and at the same time reserve enough stamina for the stretch; to hold a horse back until he has an opportunity to make a challlenge. See *at home in the going.* Cf. *hold him in.*

READY. adj. Fit, in good shape, primed for a race; in a *spot.*

READY FOR PATTING. phr. Of a horse that has been in training: to be judged fit for racing; a rather loose equivalent for *fit.*

RECORD. n. 1. The fastest time in which a race over a certain course has been run. 2. Past performance record. 3. The *Daily Racing Record,* a journal on racing.

RED BOARD. n. A red signal displayed by the judges to indicate a dead heat; or, after the numbers of the horses and jockeys have been posted in the order in which they have been in the money, to indicate a disqualification. See *set down.*

RESULT(S). n. 1. The list of names of the first four finishing horses and the prices paid by the horses in the money. "The *results* are:

Say Blue	$10.80:6.40:4.20
My Boy	4.80:4.60
Yippit	3.80
Wumpum	. . . ."

2. The sequence in which the horses finish. See *run down.*

RIDDEN OUT. phr. 1. Of a horse: to be skillfully ridden so that he has just spent his power at the end of a race. When a horse is said to have won *ridden out,* the implication is that he was rated perfectly by his rider. 2. Of a horse: to finish a race exhausted. 3. Said of a horse that wins without being subjected to punishment but still not eased up. See *hand ride.*

RIDE WITH. phr. To bet on a horse (and thus to ride with it in spirit).

RIGHT. adj. Ready to win. See *fit, ready for patting.*

RIGHT NUMBERS (PRICE). n. Odds that please the stable owning or backing a horse. "Leros will win today if he gets the *right numbers.*" See *like a price.*

RINGER. n. A horse that runs a race under an assumed name, either that of another horse or a false one; thus a good horse is substituted for a lesser one, thereby giving high odds on a good horse. Lip tattooing has made this practice rare.

ROGUE'S BADGE. phr. Blinkers.

ROUSE v.t. To punish a horse in order to get an added burst of speed. See *go to bat.*

ROUTER. n. A horse that likes to race over a long distance; a distance runner.

ROUT RACE. n. A race over a course of more than a mile, usually run by so-called *cup horses.* However, many cheap races are run over courses from one mile to $2^1/2$ miles.

RUB THE BOARD. phr. Of a bookmaker: to lay his own odds to get a sudden volume of play on a single horse; this may force him to lay an entirely new line of prices. See *booking odds.*

RULED OFF. phr. Barred from a track. When racing privileges are taken away from an individual, usually a clause is included to the effect that he will not be allowed to enter tracks in addition to the one from which he was barred.

RUN DOWN. phr. The current change of odds in a booking establishment, caused by fluctuations of opinion or by a flurry of betting.

RUN DOWN SHEET. n. A printed list provided for the patrons of the book. It contains the day's entries and the morning-line odds and is used by the gambler to keep track of the fluctuations in odds. See *scratch sheet, morning sheet, finger sheet, blue book.*

RUN IN SPOTS. phr. Of a horse: to show a flash of speed for perhaps a furlong, then falter, then make a strong finish; to run in form inconsistently. May be used in reference to a single race or in reference to continued performance over a period of time.

RUN OUT. 1. n. The final odds on winners at non-mutuel tracks (obsolescent). 2. v.i. Of a horse: to finish out of the money. See *field, pack*. 3. v.i. Of a horse: to run away from the inside rail. 4. v.i. Of a book: to leave town without paying off. See *take a run-out powder*.

RUN OUT BIT. n. A bit designed to keep horses from running wide.

RUN UP AN ALLEY. phr. To fail to win, place, or show; to be entirely out of the money. See *run out* (2). Cf. *quitter* (1).

RUN WIDE. v.i. Of a horse: to fail to stay near the inside rail at a turn. See *bear out*. Cf. *inside, outside, hold him in*.

S. n. Form sheet code for spurs or use of the spurs.

SADDLE. v.t. To train a horse for racing.

SADDLE CLOTH. n. The cloth placed between the saddle and the horse; the post position of the horse is printed on this cloth.

SALIVA TEST. n. A test made by the official race veterinarian to see whether the horse has been doped. Doping of horses other than with novocaine is relatively rare in modern racing. See *dust a horse*.

SAVAGE. v.t. Of a horse: to attempt to bite another horse during the running of a race.

SAVE GROUND. phr. 1. To restrain a horse skillfully. See *hold him in reserve*. 2. To maneuver a horse as close to the rail as possible during a race. To race with a minimum of crisscrossing and jockeying. See *lay a horse on the rail*.

SAWBUCK. n. 1. A ten-dollar bill. 2. Sometimes, by implication, a ten-dollar bet placed with a bookie rather than at the track (obsolescent). See *book*.

SCHOOL. v.t. To train a racehorse how to act at the barrier, in the paddock, and on the track; the entire course of breaking and training a horse. See *fit, ready for patting*.

SCHOOLING. verbal n. The training of a horse for racing.

SCORE A DOUBLE. phr. 1. Of a jockey: To ride two winners on the same day. 2. Of a stable: to enter two winners in one day.

SCRATCH. v.t. or v.i. To withdraw a horse after it has been officially entered in a race.

SCRATCH SHEET. n. A printed list of the day's race entries and the morning odds, usually found at booking establishments. Also *blue book, finger sheet, morning sheet*.

SCRATCH TIME. n. The time, usually 3:30 A.M., by which all withdrawals must be in the hands of track officials; after *scratch time*, all withdrawals must have the approval of the judges or the permission of the stewards. See *scratch, excuse*.

SEASON. n. The period of time during which a racetrack is in operation; dates are assigned the different tracks by the racing commission, which considers the number of Sundays and holidays included in the period, the length of time requested, and the requests of neighboring tracks. Also *meet*.

SEAT. n. The manner in which a jockey sits his horse.

SEND. v.t. 1. Of a trainer or owner: to enter a horse in a race. See *be in* (1), *name*. 2. Attempt to get your horse to an early lead, referring to jockeys. 3. Attempt to win a race, referring to trainer. "We're sending him today."

SERVICE. n. Wire service to bookmakers, usually supplied by Western Union or the Bell Telephone Company. Tickers or teletype machines have been supplied by Western Union; switchboards and phone sets are often installed by skilled technicians who do not represent any company.

SET BACK. phr. To disqualify a horse for interfering with other horses or running wide on the turn. The horse may be disqualified but the jockey not set down if the judges feel that the horse offended in spite of honest efforts to control him. See *foul, set down*. Cf. *suspended*.

SET DOWN. v.t. 1. To give a horse a hard, fast workout. 2. To suspend a jockey. See *foul*.

SHAKE DOWN. v.t. To search a jockey for illegal battery at starting gate or jockey's quarters or to search a trainer's quarters for illegal medications.

SHAKE OFF. v.t. Of a jockey: to push his horse enough to outdistance his nearest competitors. See *wear down*.

SHAKING UP. phr. A severe application of spurs and whip. See *go to bat*.

SHED, (BETTING). n. 1. The long open building at a track where the official and legal betting is carried on. See *pari-mutuel betting*. 2. shed only. A barn or stable rented to owners at the track.

SHED ROW. n. The row of barns along the backstretch of a racetrack.

SHEET. n. Generally, any racing publication. See *form sheet, finger sheet*.

SHOO IN. 1. n. A fixed race. See *boat race*. 2. n. An easy race. See *breeze* (2). 3. v.t. To allow an inferior horse to win, as heard in the phrase "to *shoo* a horse *in*," the implication being that the other jockeys, by agreement, get behind a picked horse and chase him across the finish line.

SHOW. v.i. Of a horse to finish third; also *peep*.

SHOW EARLY FOOT. phr. To *race forwardly*.

SHOW THE WAY. phr. Of a horse: to take and hold a lead over the rest of the field. See *make a move, wire to wire, on the Bill Daley*.

SHUFFLE. v.i. Of a jockey: to hand ride and urge a horse with his heels simultaneously.

SHUT OFF. v.t. Of a horse: to be cut off by another horse crossing in front of him. See *herder*.

SILKS. n. Colors worn by a jockey. Each stable has its own combination of colors, which are shown by the silk shirts, scarves, and caps worn by the jockeys. See *carry the silks, colors*.

SLEEPER. n. 1. A horse that has been highly trained in secret and is slipped into a race. The owner thus has an excellent long shot. See *dark horse, fit*. 2. A horse that appears to be erratic in his running, usually showing poorly but occasionally running a brilliant race. See *loafer*.

SLOPPY TRACK. n. A track that is wet on the surface but solid under the water. Faster than a *muddy track*.

SLOW TRACK. n. A wet track that is drying; a condition between good and muddy but usually not so fast as a sloppy track.

SMART MONEY. n. See *educated currency*.

SNOW SHOE. n. A policeman or detective, especially one in a book. See *no snow on your shoes*.

SNUG. v.t. Of a jockey: to restrain a horse until things look favorable for a drive. See *reserve, hold him in*. Cf. *pull a horse*.

SOLID HORSE. n. A horse that runs among the best in his class.

SPARK A HORSE. phr. To use a hand battery to get added speed out of a horse in the stretch. Also *sting a horse*. See *buzzer, go to bat*.

SPASM. n A single race on a program. See *stanza*.

SPECS. n. Blinkers.

SPEED JAM. n. When a horse is outrun , he is humorously said "to have been caught in a *speed jam*."

SPEED RATING. n. 1. An estimation of the speed a horse is making on a given track. In this sense the term refers to a mental estimate by the jockey who is riding, either in the morning workout or in actual racing. Some jockeys have developed this time sense to an uncanny degree and can bring a horse around the track in any time within the horse's range which the trainer may call. Some good jockeys employ this time sense to great advantage, during a race, keeping in mind the various shifts in speed and position, and holding the horse sufficiently in reserve to give him a strong finish; many of them say that the calculations are automatic and unconscious. See *reserve, Garrison finish*. 2. See *best times*. Applied to horses, with reference to the speed made. 3. See *comparative times*. Applied to tracks.

SPLINTS. n. Boney growth, usually between the knee and ankle, often caused by a bruise or kick.

SPLIT CHOICE. n. When two horses are posted at the lowest prices on the board, and both at the same odds, they are said to constitute a split choice. Also *co-favorites*.

SPONGE A HORSE. phr. To insert a sponge into a horse's nostril in order to cut off part of his wind. The sponge is removed immediately after the race and leaves no trace. See *boat race, have a bucketfull*.

SPOT. n. 1. A rather loose term referring to the combination of circumstances including track conditions, jockey, competition, etc., which influences a horse's chance to run in the money. See *at home in the going, fit*. 2. An opportunity to win heavily on a bet.

SPOT PLAYER (BETTOR). n. 1. A gambler who bets only occasionally. 2. A gambler who does not bet steadily but bets only on "hot tips."

SPOTTER. n. An accomplice who works with a crooked gambler; one who locates prospects for the gambler. See *tout, come on man, go ahead man.* Among confidence men called a *roper* or *outside man.*

SPRINT. n. A race over a distance of less than a mile.

SPRINTER. n. A horse that races best over a short distance.

STABLE. n. A group of horses raced by a single person or group, not necessarily all running from the same stable or even at the same track.

STABLE TOGETHER. phr. Of two owners or handlers; to share one of the large stables at a racetrack.

STAKE (RACE). n. A race to be run on a specified date in which the owner of each entry pays a set amount to enter and a fixed amount to allow his horse to start. These fees accumulate to form an additional fund which goes to the winner, over and above the purse put up by the track.

STALL WALKER. n. A horse with a compulsive nervous vice of circling its stall.

STANDING START. n. A type of start in which the horses line up exactly at the pole marking the distance they are to run and break at the starter's command, as is done at Hawthorne track. No starting gate is used. Also *Hawthorne start.* Some tracks using this type of start allow the horses to start twenty yards behind the pole and time them from the pole. Cf. *Australian barrier, walk up start.*

STANZA. n. A single race on a program. Also *spasm, heat.*

START. 1. v.i. or v.t. Of a horse: duly entered in a race and participating in it. 2. n. The first split second of a race as the horses leave the starting gate.

STARTER. n. 1. Any horse that runs (starts) in a race. 2. The track official whose job it is to see that the race is begun evenly. See *off.*

STAY IN LINE. phr. See *play the nuts.*

STEEPLE CHASE. n. A race over obstacles such as hedges and water jumps. See *suicide club.* Cf. *flat racing.*

STEWARDS. n. The appointed track officials who supervise the enforcement of rules at a race meeting. See *official.*

STICK. n. See *bat.*

STIFF. n. 1. A horse that is *pulled.* Also *lob*

(1). 2. A horse entered in a race but not intended to win. Also *lob* (2). 3. Any worthless or cheap horse. Also *plater.* See *bang tail.*

STING A HORSE. phr. See *spark a horse, buzzer.*

STOOPER. n. A hanger-on at racetracks who makes his living by picking up and checking all discarded betting tickets, then cashing redeemable tickets at the window. See *outstanding ticket.*

Be STOPPED. 1. phr. Of a horse: to weaken or slow up during a race. See *attack of the slows.* 2. v. To tamper with a horse so as to cause him to lose. 3. v. To get shut off in running a race.

STORE. n. 1. A handbook located away from the racetrack. Sometimes used with the implication that the place is unusually crooked. 2. Among con men, a simulated book used by confidence mobs for the *pay-off.* Also *poolroom.*

STRAIGHTAWAY. n. 1. See *stretch.* 2. See *chute.*

STRAIGHTEN OUT. v.t. or v.i. 1. Of a horse: to deliver all the speed he has in the stretch. See *breeze* (2). 2. Of a jockey: to force the final burst of speed out of a horse. See *go to bat.* 3. Of a horse: to return to the rail after racing wide. See *lay a horse on the rail.*

STRETCH. n. 1. To a spectator, the last bend before the finish line. 2. To a jockey, the straight part of the track between the last bend and the finish line.

STRETCH RUNNER. n. A horse that runs fastest in the stretch. See *Garrison finish.*

STRING. n. A group of horses under one owner or trainer. Also *stable.*

STRONG ARM. n. A jockey who will *pull a horse.* Also *business man.*

STRONGLY HANDLED. phr. To be ridden under severe urging from spurs and whip. See *go to bat.*

SUBSTITUTE RACE. n. A race scheduled on the program to replace a race that has been withdrawn because of lack of entries or too many scratches.

SUCKER MONEY. n. The proceeds of questionable bets. Money taken from naive or inexperienced gamblers. See *money from home.*

SUCROSE. n. Money. See *bunch.*

SUGAR. n. Money. See *bunch.*

SUICIDE CLUB. n. A jockey who rides in stee-
plechases is said to belong to the *suicide club*
because of the great number of casualties in
that sport. See *jumper*.

SULKER. n. A surly, temperamental horse.

SURE THING. n. A horse that a gambler believes "can't lose"; often used ironically. See
best bet, double X.

SUSPENDED. adj. Ruled off a track. See *set
down*.

SWEAT THE BRASS. phr. To campaign a
horse steadily over long periods of time without giving him any rest periods.

SWERVE. v.i. Of a horse: to fail to run
straight on the track; usually refers to a tir-
ing horse. See *keep a horse straight in the
stretch, run out, break in* or *break out*.

SWIPE. n. 1. A stable boy. See *boy* (2). 2. A
groom.

SYSTEM.* n. Any arrangement by which a
gambler tries to determine the results of a
race in advance. Systems are usually based
on some attempt at rational analysis of the
factors that enter into the performance of a
horse and are not to be confused with
"hunches" of a more or less superstitious nature; some systems, however, border closely
on the superstitious. Here are several sample
systems: if a horse wins by five lengths in his
last race, money is "out on his nose" for the
next three races; that is, he is not bet to win.
If a horse has very recently been entered in
cheaper races, he is a good bet. For instance,
if he has been running in races with a $3500
purse and is entered in one with a $2500
purse, he will probably run well against

cheaper company. If a horse bearing a certain number wins a race, it is not advisable
to bet on any other horses that day which
bear the same number. If favorites win the
first three races, one's bets should be shifted
to a long shot. Some gamblers figure their
bets scientifically on the basis of past performance; they calculate about when a certain
horse is "due" and keep betting on him until
he wins—if he does. Each time they lose,
they increase their bet to cover their previous
losses. This is known as *doubling* or *pyr-
amiding*. Some gamblers follow jockeys
rather than horses and bet on the jockeys
who have a long record of wins to their credit. A handicapper friend reports at least one
authentic instance of a gambler who uses an
astrological system on the birth dates of the
horses. Perhaps the most scientific system is
of the type put out by Bert Collyer, in which
ratings are made up from all the factors involved in the past performance of a horse
and a mathematical formula is evolved
which can be used to calculate his probable
chances against any other horses in the field.
There are many varieties of this system, each
with its particular name, such as "Systol-
ogy." The three most representative systems
used by gamblers today are: 1. The Post Position System. This system is based primarily
on the speed of the horse. If a fast horse is in
the number one, two, or three post position,
he is bet on. 2. Consensus and Progressive
Betting. The gambler takes the horses
picked by the consensus of handicappers and
pick sheets and bets progressively on these se-

*From these results a general concept of the reliability of systems in general can be formed.
However, most gamblers will not reveal a system that they believe is profitable.

	System	Bet	Won	Lost	No. of horses bet on	Wins	%
I	Post Position	$ 60	$17		30	8	26.6
II	Repeater System	$ 50		$ 22.80	25	3	12.0
III	Consensus and Progressive Betting System	$378		$119.60	41	11	26.8
IV	Bet on a long shot which has won its last race	$ 22		$ 22	11	0	00.0
V	Bet all defeated favorites to win	$ 36		$ 14.20	18	3	16.6
VI	Bet the horse with highest speed rating to win	$ 60		$ 28.90	30	6	20.0
VII	Bet a horse to win when he has lost three races but won the fourth	$ 36		$ 4.80	18	4	22.2

lections, i.e., if the first horse does not win, four dollars is bet on the second selection, six on the third, etc. 3. Bet All Defeated Favorites to Win. If a horse was a favorite in its last race and lost that race, bet it to win.

SYSTEM HORSE. n. A horse that a gambler has selected to win according to a peculiar system which he depends upon. Usually every horse in the race is being selected by someone as a *system horse,* and someone has implicit faith in each entry as the horse that will eventually pay big money. See *system.*

TAB. 1. v.t. To follow the record of a particular horse. 2. v.i. To win a race.

TACK. n. A jockey's equipment for racing, including saddle, bridle, crop.

TACK ROOM. n. A room or closet where riding equipment is kept. See *tack.*

TAKE. v.t. To win money in gambling. "I *took* him for 200 fish yesterday."

TAKE A HORSE BACK. phr. To restrain a horse that is in the lead and save him for the stretch. See *hold a horse in reserve.*

TAKE A RUN-OUT POWDER. phr. Of a bookmaker: to disappear without paying off his obligations; to welsh. See *run out.*

TAKE COMMAND. phr. Of a horse: to take the lead. See *make a move.*

TAKE DOWN THE NUMBERS or TAKE THE NUMBERS DOWN. phr. 1. To remove a jockey's number from the results board after he has been posted as being in the money. This is usually done to indicate that he has been guilty of illegal tactics and is accompanied by a red signal. See *red board.* 2. By extension, to fail at anything; to receive a setback; to be disappointed. "I thought I was all set for a job with Bradley, but they *took my number down.*"

TAKEN (TOOK), GET (BE). phr. To lose money gambling. "I *got taken* for 50 bucks." "He *got took* at the track."

TAKE OUT. n. The percentage retained by the track from the total amount of money bet through the pari-mutuel machines on any single race. The take out is usually 8, 10, 12, or 15 percent. This does not include the "breakage" which the track gets. See *take, breaks.*

T.C. abbrev. Formsheet code for turf course. See *turf race.*

TEA. n. Drugs, usually cocaine or strychnine,

with which a horse may be stimulated before a race. See *hophead.*

TENDERFOOT. n. A horse that runs well on a soft or muddy track. See *cushion, at home in the going.*

THREAT. n. The next best horse, considering the favorite first. A possible winner.

THREE-HORSE PARLAY. n. See *parlay.*

THROUGH THE BOARD. phr. Indicates the placing of three bets, usually of the same size, on one horse; one to win, one to place, and one to show. "Put five *through the board* on Eternal Reward." See *across the board.*

TICKERMAN. n. The man who calls off the race results from a ticker in a book that uses ticker service. See *boardman.*

TICKET. n. A betting receipt, whether from the mutuels or from a bookie.

TIGHT. adj. 1. Fit to run, in good condition. 2. Close quarters during the running of a race.

TIMBER TOPPER. n. A horse used in steeple chases. See *suicide club.*

TIME. v.t. 1. To take an official measurement of the time horses make on the track. See *clock.* 2. See *pick up.*

TIMER. n. The official who records time made by a horse in a race. Cf. *clocker* (1).

TIP. n. Information on how a horse will run in a race. Usually tips are unreliable, especially if they come from a professional tipster or tout. Cf. *best bet, coup.*

TIP RUN. n. A group of bets all placed on one horse or on one entry because of authentic information that has seeped out of the training stable, or out of a jockey ring. These bets are usually placed with books so that they will not run the odds down at the track and reveal that a certain horse is being heavily backed. When these bets are cashed, the bookmakers refer to them as a *tip run.* Such an unexpected run often bankrupts small bookies. See *tip, dutch run.*

TIP SHEET. n. A small printed handbill listing the opinions of some self-styled expert on what the best bets in each race will be. These handbills are hawked at racetracks. See *scratch sheet.* Cf. *condition book, tip, form.*

TIPSTER. n. One who writes tip sheets. A kind of *tout.* See *tip.*

TOED PLATE. n. A type of racehorse shoe. See *plate*.

TOP. n. On an oval track, the beginning of the stretch, usually the home stretch. See *stretch*.

TOP FORM. n. A horse's best running condition.

TOP HORSE. n. The best horse in a stable.

TOP RIDER. n. 1. A first-class jockey. See *boy, contract rider*. 2. The best rider a particular stable has.

TOPWEIGHT. n. The horse in a race carrying the most weight.

TOTE BOARD or TOTALIZATOR. n. The electric board in the infield which keeps the gamblers informed of the changes in odds. The word *tote* is replacing the older *pari-mutuel*. Examples of this are *tote prices* for pari-mutuel prices, *tote tickets* for pari-mutuel tickets, etc. See *betting barometer, pari-mutuels*.

TOUT [taUt]. n. One who claims to have inside information on racehorses. Touts seldom have reliable information but resort to all sorts of trickery to obtain an outright payment in advance or a commission on winnings. Some touts work in pairs as short-con or even big-con men. Also *hustler*. See *tip*.

TOWN DOLLARS. n. Money bet with a bookie in town rather than at the track.

TRACK CONDITION. n. The condition of the track proper, due to the weather. The track may be — in order of decreasing fastness — fast, good, slow, sloppy, heavy, or muddy. A sloppy track is faster than a muddy one because the water is on top and has not yet seeped in to make the track sticky.

TRACK HANDICAPPER. n. A track official who sets the weights for the horses, makes up the programs, determines which horses shall appear, sets up the condition book, etc. See *weight for age, condition book, handicapper*.

TRACK ODDS. n. The odds paid on bets at the track; pari-mutuel odds. Cf. *booking odds*.

TRACK RECORD. n. The best time made by a horse over a certain distance on a certain track. See *record*.

TRAILER. n. A weak horse; one that seldom gets into the money. See *sleeper* (2), *loafer*.

TRAINER. n. One who supervises the care and training of racehorses. A trainer may or may not handle horses for more than one owner at a time.

TRAVEL IN STRAW. phr. 1. Of a stable hand: to travel from one track to another in a truck or freight car with the horses. 2. To earn one's transportation from one city to another by posing or working as an employee of the stable shipping the horses.

TRIALS. n. The morning workouts. See *blow out* (2), *railbird*.

TROUBLE MAKER. n. A temperamental horse that gives trouble at the post or during the race. Trouble makers are often arbitrarily given the outside position at the post. Also *rank*. See *bad starter*.

TRY A HORSE. phr. 1. Of a jockey: to run his horse alongside a challenger during a race to see what chance there is of passing him. See *make a move*. 2. To test a horse's quality by racing him without necessarily intending to win in order to run him again and/or bet on him.

TRYING. part. Said of a horse giving his best effort.

TUB. v.t. To treat a horse's injured or inflamed leg by soaking it in hot water, usually with epsom salts added.

TUCK UP. v.i. Of the muscles around the flanks of a racehorse: to draw up after a stiff workout.

TURF. 1. n. The surface of the track. See *track condition*. The grass of the infield. 2. adj. Synonymous with racing as a sport; *turf club, turf information*.

TURF RACE. n. A race run on the soft green of the infield. Such a race supposedly gives the mudders an advantage. The track on the inside of the rail is called a *turf course* (*t.c.* in the racing form).

TURN. n. On an oval track, the two curves at either end of the track. The single word *turn* usually refers to the curve leading into the home stretch. *Far turn* is used to designate the curve preceding the backstretch. Also *bend*.

TWILIGHT HANDICAP. n. The last race on a program. See *stanza, drugstore handicap, boat race*.

TWO-YEAR-OLD. n. A horse that has seen two New Year's Days, even though he may be actually only a year and one day old. Race-horses have their birthdays on January 1; a yearling has seen one, and a two-year-old arrives at two on the second January 1 of his life.

UNDER A DRIVE. phr. Of a horse: to receive strong urging from his jockey in an effort to get all possible speed out of him. See *drive, urge.*

UNDERCOVER. adv. Worked out and trained secretly. See *dark horse* (2).

UNDERLAY. v.t. To lay booking odds that are lower than conditions warrant. See *overlay.*

UNDERPINNINGS. n. See *pins.*

UNDER RESTRAINT. phr. Said of a horse whose power is being conserved by the jockey. Not to be confused with *pulling a horse.* See *hold a horse in reserve.*

UNDER WRAPS. phr. 1. Of a horse: to be running easily without extending himself. See *breeze* (1). 2. Of horse: to be entered in a race for the experience, one in which the owners have no intention of pushing him to get into the money. See *let out a wrap, lob* (3).

UNPLACED. adj. 1. Describes a horse that does not run in the money. 2. Describes a horse that runs fourth. See *best company.*

UNTRACK (HIMSELF). v. reflexive only. Of a horse: to show a burst of speed. Conversely, a horse that cannot *untrack himself* is floundering in the going. Usually used in a humorous sense.

UP. adv. When a jockey is contracted to ride a horse, he is said to be *up.*

URGE. v.t. Of a jockey: to try to force a horse ahead with every means at his command — spurs, whip, voice.

USED UP. adj. Without sufficient reserve to make a showing in the stretch. Cf. *Garrison finish.*

WAD. n. Money. See *bunch.*

WALK UP START. phr. A method of starting a race in which all the horses walk up to a given point and break at the starter's command. See *standing start, Australian barrier.*

WARMING (WARM) UP. phr. Galloping a horse between the stable and paddock or the paddock and post to get him warm and supple for the race. Some horses run better after a stiff *warm up,* other just tire.

WARNING BELL. n. A signal made to warn that it is time to saddle the horses entered in the next race.

WEAR DOWN. v.t. 1. Of a horse: to inch up on his nearest competitors, which exert themselves to the utmost to retain their lead, and finally fall behind. 2. Of a horse: to exhibit superior stamina, especially before entering the stretch; thus he *wears down* his competitors by keeping just far enough ahead so that they extend themselves fully and have insufficient power left for the drive. Also *withstand, outstay, shake off, work his (her) way up,* with somewhat specialized meanings. Cf. *breeze through.*

WEBFOOT. n. A horse that runs well in the mud. Also *mudder.* See *cushion, at home in the going.*

WEIGHING IN. phr. The procedure of weighing jockeys and their tack before and after a race to see that they are carrying the required weight.

WEIGHT. n. The amount of poundage each horse must carry in a race; it is determined arbitrarily by each racing commission and varies from track to track. Some commissions work out a graduated scale of poundage which increases gradually for each month of a horse's age. See *allowance race, apprentice allowance, clerk of the scales, overweight.*

WEIGHT FOR AGE. phr. A race the conditions for which specify that each horse carry the weight assigned to a horse of his age by the condition book. This type of race differs from the others in that the track handicapper does not assign weights arbitrarily according to his judgment of the horse. See *track handicapper, condition book.*

WELL IN HAND. phr. For a horse to be admirably handled by his jockey during a race. When a jockey has a horse *well in hand,* the implication is that he knows his mount's limitations perfectly, that he weighs all the strong and weak points of his competition, etc. See *at home in the going, call on a horse.*

WELL UP. adj. or adv. Of a horse: to be in the lead or near the lead during a race. See *make a move, wire to wire.*

WHEEL. v.i. Of a horse: to veer suddenly to right or left just after he leaves the starting gate. Also *break in* or *break out.* See *beat the gate, swerve, break in the air, bolt* (1).

WHEEL OFF. v.t. To run, usually with the idea of time involved, as *to wheel off* a mile in so much time. The implication is that the horse is performing nicely. Use is generally in connection with a workout.

WIDENING. part. Said of a horse opening a gap between himself and other horses.

WIN. v.i. or v.t. 1. Of a horse: to come in first. See *bet on his nose, place, show.* 2. Among racetrack gamblers, the present tense is universally used for *won* in standard English. "I *win* $23.40 in the seventh."

WINDOW. n. The place at which betting tickets are purchased. At the track always qualified by prefixing the size of bet accepted there. See *shed.*

WINNING FAVORITES. n. Those favorites that have won on a given track or in a given meet. The ratio is usually expressed in percentages, and is important in figuring odds. Thus, in 1950 the track at Detroit might show the percentage of favorites winning, .34, Hawthorne; .37, Beulah Park; .41, etc. Predominant form plural.

WIRE. n. 1. The finish line, a wire stretched across the track. 2. The starting line or barrier. At most tracks a mechanical barrier or other starting mechanism has replaced the older wire, but the word persists. See *Australian barrier.*

WIRE FAILED. clause. A cry that the bookie or his caller yells when the Western Union wire or telephone wire fails, and hence service is momentarily discontinued. Since certain people have been known to make the service fail purposely so as to be able to hold up race results and past post the book, the cry *"wire failed at* Chicago" would mean that no more bets will be taken on the races at Chicago until service is resumed. Some-times if a book does not wish to accept any more bets on a certain horse or race, he will give the cry and stop the betting.

WIRE TO WIRE. phr. From start to finish of a race; usually refers to a horse that takes the lead at the post and keeps it until the finish. Also *on the Bill Daley.*

WITH HIS MOUTH WIDE OPEN. phr. When a horse wins easily, he is said to do it *with his mouth wide open*; the implication is that he has not extended himself. Also *with plenty to spare.* See *breeze* (2), *going away.*

WITHIN STRIKING DISTANCE. phr. For a horse to be close enough to the leaders, in a strategic position to make an effective challenge. See *well up.*

WITH PLENTY TO SPARE. phr. See *with his mouth wide open.*

WITHSTAND. v.t. Of a horse: to resist a competitor's efforts to *wear him down.* Also *outstay.*

WORK A HORSE BY LANTERN. phr. To train a horse just at daybreak before clockers and railbirds have assembled. This is done to conceal his true form from the public, especially when an owner wants to bet heavily on a horse whose past performance has not been impressive. Horses are ordinarily worked from about 5:00 to 7:30 or 8:00 a.m.

WORK HIS WAY UP. phr. Of a horse: to improve its racing position; to pass or outmaneuver his nearest competitors. See *challenge, wear down, move up.*

WORKOUT BOY. n. One who exercises horses.

WORRY. v.t. Of a jockey: to ride a horse. "How many do you *worry* today?"

WOUND UP. adj. In top form.

WRINKLENECK. n. An old timer at racing or handling horses. See *racetracker, hardboot.*

17

The Argot
of Pickpockets

This study is based on the linguistic field notes collected preparatory to the writing of the book *Whiz-Mob: A Correlation of the Technical Argot of Pickpockets with Their Behavior Pattern* (1955). Although this book deals in great detail with the relationship of language to behavior, a glossary was not included. Much of the material in this volume was taken directly from tape recordings in which pickpockets discussed or described their craft.

The pickpockets who cooperated in this study were selected from the top echelons of the racket using two basic criteria: 1) the reputation that pickpockets have among their peers; and 2) the ratings given pickpockets by highly specialized pickpocket detectives in large urban areas. For this reason the book — and consequently the present glossary — is slightly weighted toward the viewpoint of the *class cannon*. Detailed study of lower-class pickpockets would yield a different picture together with many variants in the argot since these gentry do not have the sharp analytical approach that *class cannons* have toward their craft, the sucker, and the law. Terms concerned with the nontechnical language of pickpockets have been largely omitted.

This argot is of some interest because of the ancient nature of the craft. In fact, Renaissance painters such as Romanino depicted mobs in action with techniques similar to those used today. Technology has had little influence on the craft since the main elements are digital and bodily skills plus sound *grift sense* on the part of each thief. As long as money or valuables are carried on the person these skills are effective. It is also interesting to note that some of the terms date back to sixteenth- and seventeenth-century writers like Robert Greene (*Cony Catching Tracts*) and Thomas Dekker (*Belman of London; Lanthorne and Candlelight*) as well as several others.

Incidentally, the rate of illiteracy is high among pickpockets. Even the good ones, if they can read at all, limit themselves to deciphering the racing form, the betting slips, and the newspaper headlines. For instance, Dago Foley, one of the best in the business, could count money but could not read a word. He *turned out* a young man who could read and write and made him his partner on the road, thus partially compensating for his own deficiency.

Foley was a veritable sartorial dude and his appearance gave no hint of his illiteracy. It is a common observation by other types of criminals that pickpockets have their brains in their fingertips.

ACCORDIAN POKE. n. phr. Old-style folded wallet with many compartments. Usually *cordeen poke* or simply *cordeen.*

ACE. n. Single dollar bill. See *Michigan bankroll.*

ACTION. n. 1. The movements and activity leading up to, including, and following the act of picking a pocket. 2. A single step in the process of picking a pocket. 3. The day-to-day activities of a mob. 4. Any illegal or questionable activity such as gambling or prostitution.

AIRTIGHT. adj. Fixed; safe for thievery (in reference to a town in which those who pay off are protected and those who do not are prosecuted, often for crimes they did not commit).

AIRTIGHT FIX. n. phr. A fix that is completely safe.

ANCHOR. n. 1. A guard or catch on a tiepin (which prevents it from being removed easily). 2. A safety pin or other device used to close a pocket or to hold bills or a wallet in the clothing.

ANCHORED. adj. Held in place with an *anchor.*

The ARM. n. 1. A direct assault upon a victim during which his wallet is removed. 2. A stranglehold applied to a victim from behind (restricted to *muggers* and/or *clout and lam* workers).

BACK. n. The shoulders, used by a *stall* to maneuver a victim into position.

BACKSTOP. n. A *stall* who works directly behind the mark (especially the Chicago area). Used by older pickpockets.

BAD FALL n. phr. An arrest in which the *rapper* (victim who prefers charges) is determined, and the fix does not hold. Compare *shakedown.*

BAIL PIECE. n. phr. A deed or security that can be put up as a bond in case of arrest. Also *colat.*

BALL BUSTERS. n. phr. Thieves who work in pairs, one of whom grabs the testicles of the mark and squeezes while the other removes the victim's wallet (*clout and lam* procedure). Also *ballocks workers, bollix workers.*

BALLOCKS WORKERS. n. phr. See *ball busters.*

BANG. v.t. 1. To steal an object from the person. 2. To steal by separating the stolen item from a chain. 3. To open a purse by twisting the knob clasps (*moll buzzers*).

BANG A HANGER. v. phr. To steal or pick a woman's purse.

BANG A PROP. v. phr. To steal a man's tiepin.

BANG A SOUPER. v. phr. To twist a pocket watch off a chain.

BANG-UP. adj. phr. Accomplished; displaying excellent technique, as *bang-up tool, bang-up stall,* etc.

BANNER SCORE. n. phr. The largest score taken during a specific period (East Coast). West Coast: *red one, darb.*

BASKET SETTING. n. phr. Jeweler's term used to describe a particular stone mounting of a ring.

BAT AWAY. v. phr. For a mob to work industriously and cooperatively.

BATES or JOHN BATES. n. A middle aged victim.

BATTED OUT. v. phr. To be arrested in the act of picking a pocket.

BEAD ROPE. n. phr. A pearl necklace.

BEAT. 1. v.t. To take a victim's wallet or valuables (implies overcoming the various obstacles posed by the mark, his clothing, his wallet, etc.). 2. v.t. To avoid conviction, as to *beat a rap.* 3. n. The circuit that a pickpocket works in the course of a day.

BEAT THE DONICKER. v. phr. Old-timer's trick to avoid paying for a train ticket by hiding in the car toilet stall.

BEBOP LINGO. n. phr. Name given by white pickpockets to argot spoken by black pickpockets.

BEE. n. 1. One-dollar bill, from *bumblebee.* 2. The act of theft. See *put the bee on.*

BEEF. 1. v.i. To complain to the police or publicly about a theft. Also to *yell.* 2. n. Such a complaint; cut back from rhyming argot: *hot beef* (a thief).

BEEFER. n. A victim or witness who complains about a theft.

BEEF GUN. v. phr. To complain about a

thief, usually a pickpocket. Also *beef whiz.*

BEEF WHIZ. v. phr. See *beef gun.*

BEHIND. adv. In connection with any organization, exposition, show, etc. (as to *grift behind the big top*).

BELONG. v.i. 1. When a pickpocket feels that the wallet or object is in his control, it *belongs* to him, even though it may still be in the mark's possession. 2. A particular area controlled by local pickpockets is said to *belong* to them. See also to *own.*

BENNY. n. A full-sized overcoat; cut back from *Benjamin.*

BE THERE. v. phr. For a mark to have a large bankroll or wallet filled with money.

BIG ONE. n. phr. A wallet that contains many bills, regardless of denomination; a wallet that a thief believes will contain much money.

BIG TIME. n. The upper echelons of a racket.

BIG TIME IT. v. phr. To spend freely and extravagantly.

BILL. n. See *C note.*

BING. v. t. Variant of *bang* (*moll buzzers*).

BING A HANGER. v. phr. To open and rifle a woman's handbag.

BIT. n. 1. A jail sentence, usually brief. 2. The portion of the take that belongs to each mob member.

BLIND STEER. n. phr. A wallet that does not contain much money.

BLOCK. 1. n. A pocket watch, as in the phrase for watch and chain, *block and tackle.* 2. n. Body movement and placement used by a *stall* to set the victim up to be robbed. 3. v.t. To perform such an action.

BLOW. v.i. For the mark to discover that his pocket has been picked or is being picked.

BLOW (ONE'S) MOXIE. v. phr. To lose the confidence and courage necessary to be a competent pickpocket, perhaps because of repeated arrests or inactivity while imprisoned.

BLOW (SOMEONE) OFF. v. phr. To leave or get rid of (a robbed victim).

BLUTE. n. A newspaper carried by the *tool* or a *stall* to obscure the activities of the *tool.*

BOARDING-HOUSE DECEIVER. n. phr. A cheap suitcase carried by a grifter as one of his props.

BOFFMAN. n. A thief who applies force to the victim in a theft involving direct violence. Also *mugger, muscle man.*

BOLLIX WORKERS. n. phr. See *ball busters.*

BOOB. n. Any place of incarceration (clipped back from *booby hatch*).

BOODLE. n. A fake bankroll, often carried by gamblers or other grifters, consisting largely of one-dollar bills covered by a few *coarse ones* (large bills). Sometimes stage money is used.

BOOK. n. Old-timer's name for a billfold, clipped back from *pocketbook* (archaic).

BOON MOB. n. phr. A pickpocket mob made up of blacks.

BOOST. 1. v.t. or v.i. To shoplift. 2. n. The shoplifting racket.

BOOSTER. n. A shoplifter.

BOXCAR TOOL. n. phr. A derogatory description indicating that a man is a bum (usually used by one pickpocket describing another).

BREAK. 1. v.i. To stop work, either to rest, to divide the take, to eat, or to take narcotics. 2. n. The departure of a crowd from an athletic event, auditorium, etc.; the time when pickpockets go to work.

BREECHES. n. Old-time term for side pockets of pants.

BRIDGE. n. Variant of britch (East Coast).

BRIDGE SCORE. n. phr. See *britch score.*

BRING. v.t. To get a wallet or roll of money into position where it can be removed from the pocket.

BRING A MARK OUT. v. phr. To accompany a victim out of a bank or other public place where he has just shown or acquired a large amount of money in such a way as to insure a successful theft. Also to *take out.*

BRING (SOMEONE) OUT. v. phr. 1. See *bring a mark out.* 2. To sponsor the entrance of a youngster to the racket. Also *turn out.*

BRITCH. n. Side pocket in a pair of trousers. Usually *right britch* or *left britch.*

BRITCH JERVE. n. phr. A pants pocket in which a watch and chain are kept.

BRITCH KICKS. n. phr. Side pants pockets.

BRITCH SCORE. n. phr. A wallet or money stolen from the side pocket of a pair of pants.

BRITCH TOOL or BRITCH WORKER. n. phr. Specialist in side-pants pocket-picking.

BRUSH (SOMEONE) OFF FOR. v. phr. To rob a victim.

BUCK. n. A Catholic priest — a prime victim when he is traveling abroad with nuns.

BUCKET. n. A city or county jail. Also *can, joint.*

BUGGY TOOL. n. phr. An unpredictable or unreliable pickpocket.

BULL. n. A policeman in uniform.

BUM RAP. n. phr. A false charge of theft. Also *wrong rap.*

BUNDLE (OF SCRATCH). n. A roll of money. See also *knipple, nipple.*

BURGLAR COPPER. n. phr. A plainclothesman who is always looking for known pickpockets to *shake down* by threatening them with arrest. Compare *shake artist.*

BURN. v.t. 1. To cheat. 2. To *burn a touch*— for one mob member to take more than his share of the proceeds.

BURNED UP. adj. phr. Said of a locality that has been hit so many times that thieves cannot operate safely.

BURNER. n. A pickpocket who divides the take unequally or cheats another member.

BURR HEAD MOB. n. phr. A mob of black pickpockets. Also *shine mob.*

BUSINESS or A PIECE OF BUSINESS. n. or n. phr. A theft, speaking professionally.

(TO DO) BUSINESS. v. phr. 1. To arrive at an understanding with the police or with a victim. 2. To engage in plea bargaining.

BUST. 1. v.t. To arrest. 2. n. An arrest.

BUST OUT. v. phr. To enter a mob; said of a new member who has had some experience and just joined a working mob.

BUTTON. n. A detective's badge, which may be carried by a mob member to use in *cooling out* a victim who has caught the *tool* in the act (East Coast). Also *buzzer.*

BUTTONS. n. A uniformed police officer.

BUY. n. A purchase of narcotics.

BUY THROUGH. v. phr. To avoid working in a particular town; in other words, the mob buys a train ticket straight through.

BUZZER. n. A detective's badge (West Coast). See also *button.*

BY THE THROAT. prep. phr. Under the control of an angry victim.

CAMERA EYE. n. phr. A detective with a remarkable memory for faces, names, and physical descriptions. Sometimes this becomes the given name of a particular detective, such as Camera Eye Wilkerson.

CAN. n. See *bucket.*

CANNON. n. A pickpocket. Derived from Yiddish *gonif* (thief) which yields *gun*, which in turn is amplified to *cannon.* More often applied to *tools* than to *stalls.* Among blacks it appears as *big shot* cut to *shot.*

CANNON BROAD. n. phr. A good woman pickpocket.

CANNON MOB. n. phr. A good team of pickpockets.

CANNON MOLL. n. phr. A good woman pickpocket.

CAREFUL TOOL. n. phr. A very gentle, cautious, and expert *tool.*

CARNIVAL BUM. n. phr. A pickpocket working at a circus or carnival. Also *carnival cootie, carnival louse, sure-thing grafter.*

CARNIVAL COOTIE. n. phr. See *carnival bum.*

CARNIVAL GRIFT. n. phr. Thieves or thievery connected with the carnival.

CARNIVAL GRIFTER. See *carnival bum.*

CARNIVAL LOUSE. See *carnival bum.*

CARRY BRIEF CASES. v. phr. To carry stolen items for sale or personal use.

CARRY OUT, CARRY (SOMEONE) OUT. v. phr. To employ a method of beating hotel bills in which one person (who may have stayed only one night) carries out the luggage of another, who has stayed a longer time.

CASE. 1. n. A legal case that cannot be easily fixed. 2. v.t. To follow a victim after a theft to make sure he does not notice the loss. 3. v.t. To survey a situation before performing a theft.

CAT-EYE or CAT'S-EYE. n. phr. A diamond with a yellowish cast.

CATHOLIC. n. A pickpocket; implies a solid type (rare; old term).

CAUTIOUS TOOL. See *careful tool.*

CENTER BRITCH. See *center britch tool.*

CENTER BRITCH TOOL. n. phr. A pimp or a pickpocket turned pimp temporarily. So-called because certain *tools* specialize in certain pockets (e.g., *left britch tool*). The *center britch* exists only in metaphor (a highly insulting term). Also *center britch worker.*

CENTER BRITCH WORKER. n. phr. See *center britch tool.*

CENTER FIELD. n. phr. See *center fielder.*

CENTER FIELDER. n. phr. A pickpocket who always wants his share of the loot but is reluctant to make close contact with the victim; he works in *center field.* Also *mile-away* or *sneeze-shy.*

CHAIN. n. A chain or other device attached to a wallet to prevent theft. Also *string*.

CHILL. v.t. To ignore another thief, especially when he is broke.

CHINAMAN (or CHINO) ON (ONE'S) BACK. n. phr. A narcotic habit.

CHIP. n. A diamond weighing less than twenty-five points (current use among jewelers).

CHIPPY or CHIPPY AROUND. v.i. To use narcotics occasionally; often precedes a habit (from prostitutes' argot).

CHOKE. n. A necktie or scarf from which a pin may be stolen.

CHOP UP OLD TOUCHES. 1. v. phr. To recall old exploits or discuss technique. Also *chop them up, cut up old ones, punch guff* or *gun*. 2. v. phr. To hold a conversation with a friend.

CHUMP. n. A victim, a sucker. Also found in such combinations as *honest chump, square chump*, etc. Not as derogatory as *sucker*.

CHUTES. n. Subways or the subway system (Chicago).

CIRCULATION. n. Professional availability. Used with *in* or *out of*.

CIRCUS GRIFT. n. phr. 1. The various grift operations at a circus. 2. Circus thievery or thieves, especially pickpockets.

CIRCUS GRIFTERS. n. phr. Grifters associated with a circus; considered superior to *carnival grifters*.

CLASS CANNON. n. phr. An accomplished pickpocket, especially one who observes the professional code of ethics.

CLASS MOB. n. phr. A highly regarded mob of pickpockets, composed of *class cannons*.

CLAW. n. The member of a pickpocket mob who does the actual stealing; the one who does the *pinching* or *digging*. Also *hook, mechanic, tool, wire* (rarely used; British term).

CLAW (SOMEONE) DOWN. v. phr. To arrest.

CLEAN. adj. 1. Empty, as of a wallet or pocket. 2. Anything that does not yield what is expected, such as a *clean* crowd. 3. Without any recent arrests or charges pending.

CLEAN THE POKE. v. phr. 1. For one mob member to steal from the total take. Compare *weed*. 2. See *turn over*.

CLIP. v.t. To victimize, especially by picking pockets.

CLOUT. v.t. To steal.

CLOUT AND LAM. adj. phr. Said of an act of theft from the person which is performed ineptly or with disregard for whether the victim realizes the theft. See *rip and tear, root and toot, snatch and grab*.

CLOWN. n. A small-town policeman, sheriff, or constable.

C NOTE. n. phr. A one-hundred-dollar bill. Also *bill*.

COARSE ONES. n. phr. Large bills (used in preparing a *boodle*).

COAT JERVE. n. phr. A small pocket either on the inside or the outside of the coat; sometimes called a *ticket pocket*.

COAT PIT. n. phr. Inside coat pocket.

COATTAIL. n. phr. Outside pocket of a suit coat.

C.O.D. adj. Broke or in bad financial straits.

COIN ROLLERS. n. phr. Hustlers or thieves who rob patrons in pay toilets, often distracting the victim by rolling a large coin from one toilet stall to another under the partition.

COLAT. n. Valuables upon which money can be raised quickly if necessary; from collateral.

COLD. adj. Empty; valueless.

COLD POKE. n. phr. Wallet without anything of value in it.

COME. v.i. To leave the victim's pocket. Said of an object that is stolen.

COME AWAY WITH IT. v. phr. To steal from the person. Also *come away with*.

COME DOWN ON. v. phr. To lay hold of; said when the victim grabs the pickpocket.

COME OFF. 1. n. phr. The lifting of the victim's wallet. 2. n. phr. A large gathering of people. 3. v. phr. To make a successful theft.

COME' ON. n. phr. The victim.

COME THROUGH. 1. v. phr. For the *stall* to shoulder the mark so that he bumps into the *tool*. 2. n. phr. A signal that the *stall* is going to bump the mark into the *tool*.

COME WITH IT or COME UP WITH IT. v. phr. To remove an object from the person of the mark.

CON. n. The branch of the grift in which the victim is separated from his money while trying to cheat someone else. Some pickpockets make use of a crude and minimal con element.

CONNECTION. n. 1. Source of narcotics or other contraband. 2. A fixer. 3. The channels through which the fix is made.

COOL OFF or COOL OUT. v. phr. 1. To make amends (usually restitution) with a victim who has discovered a theft. 2. To live away from the rackets for a certain time.

COOZIE STASH. n. phr. Female version of *kiester plant*. 2. Usually adapted for the female anatomy.

COP. 1. v.t. To get or take anything, especially a wallet. 2. v.i. To accept a bribe. 3. n. Something stolen. 4. n. A policeman.

COP A PLEA. v. phr. To plead guilty to a lesser charge rather than contest a more serious one. Also *cop out*.

COP A SHORT. v. phr. To catch a streetcar, bus, subway, or local train.

COP OUT. See *cop a plea*.

COP-OUT ROOM. n. phr. Police interrogation room; sometimes a conference room for attorneys.

COPPER. n. A police officer, in or out of uniform.

COP THE SCORE. v. phr. For the *stall* to receive stolen money from the *tool*.

COP THE SHORT. v. phr. For a conductor to accept a reduced fare paid in cash from a professional.

CORDEEN or CORDEEN POKE. n. See *accordion poke*.

COUSIN. n. 1. An easy mark. 2. Person who holds *fall dough* for a thief.

COVERED. adj. Under police surveillance.

COZEN. n. Sucker or victim (archaic).

CRACK. 1. n. The opening of a pocket. 2. n. An attempt at theft. 3. v.t. To succeed at theft from the pocket. 4. v.i. To speak.

CRAPPER HUSTLERS. n. phr. See *coin rollers*.

CROAKER. n. Physician.

CROSS FIRE. n. phr. Rapid dialogue between two grifters intended to trick the mark into compliance. Not to be confused with *offices*.

CROW. n. Imitation merchandise.

CRUMB THE PLAY. v. phr. To arouse the suspicions of the intended victim: to *rumble*.

CRUSH. n. A heavy crowd. See also *tip*.

CRY COP or CRY COPPER. v. phr. See *beef gun*.

CURDLE. v.i. To go bad. Said of the fix or any other arrangement.

CUSH. n. Money.

CUT. n. A shared portion of anything, especially the score.

CUT INTO (SOMEONE). v. phr. To engage a victim professionally, either by talking or by closing with him physically.

CUT OFF. v. phr. To remove a wallet from a chain.

CUT (IT) UP. v. phr. To divide the day's proceeds.

CUT UP OLD ONES. v. phr. To gossip over old times. Also *cut them up, cut up the scores, cut up touches*. See also *punch guff*.

DANGLER. n. A charm or pendant.

DARB. n. See *banner score*.

DAY. n. The date of a particular local festivity (Midwestern origin). Especially important to road mobs.

DAY'S WORK. n. phr. Temporary work in a mob.

DEAD. adj. Empty. Usually said of a wallet.

DEAD SKINS. n. phr. Wallets stripped of valuables.

DEAD TO RIGHTS. adv. phr. In the very act. Also *dead bang, dead right*.

DECLARE (IN) or (OUT). v. phr. To state whether or not a thief wishes to participate in a theft or a particular sort of theft, with consequent involvement of his *fall dough*.

DIBBY or DIB. n. Watch pocket (East Coast). See *britch jerve*.

DICK. n. A police detective.

DIG or DIG IN. v.i. To ply the pickpocket trade with skill and industry; to go to work in a crowd. Also to *dive*.

DING. v.t. 1. To throw (a wallet) onto the ground under duress. 2. To discard (an empty wallet).

DING THE DEAD ONES. v. phr. To throw away emptied wallets.

DIP. n. Pickpocket; used by old-timers. Folk etymology from German *Dieb*.

DIPSY. n. 1. Device used to hold a pocket closed. 2. A warrant or detainer. Also *reader*.

DIVE. v.i. See *dig*.

DIVER. n. A *tool* (archaic).

DO A BIT. v. phr. To serve a prison sentence.

DOINGS or DOIN'S. n. The gathering of a festive crowd. Compare *day*.

DONICKER. n. A toilet or restroom.

DONICKER HUSTLERS or DONICKER WORKERS. n. phr. See *coin rollers*.

DOORMAT THIEF. n. phr. Small-time thief.

DO THE MENDING. v. phr. To arrange the fix.

DOUBLE DUKE FRAME. n. phr. A frame used by a *four-handed mob* with one *stall* in front, one on each side, and the *tool* behind.

DOUBLE SAW. n. phr. A twenty-dollar bill.

DOWNSTAIRS. n. The lower pockets on a vest (rare).

DRAW A BLANK. v. phr. To be disappointed; especially to steal an empty wallet.

DRIBS AND DRABS. n. phr. Slim pickings from many scores.

DROP. v.t. To lose a member of a mob through arrest.

DROP IT. v. phr. See *ding* (the poke).

DUCKET. n. A ticket; sometimes a race ticket (circus usage origin).

DUKE. 1. n. The hand. 2. v.t. To give or pass from one pickpocket to another.

DUKE (SOMEONE) IN. v. phr. 1. To accept someone as a mob member. 2. To give someone his share of the *knock up*.

DUKE MAN. n. phr. The *stall* that obscures the movements of the *tool*'s hand from passersby. See *shade the duke*.

DUST. v.t. To strike repeatedly but not with full force, as with a blackjack.

DYNAMITE. adj. First-rate.

DYNAMITER. n. A *tool* who likes *rip and tear* techniques. Sometimes a strong-arm man.

EASY. adj. Presenting no difficulty in theft; said of a victim.

EASY SCORE. n. phr. A theft that presents little difficulty.

EGG. n. A male victim up to age thirty-five. Compare *Bates*.

EGYPTIAN SETTING. n. phr. A solid mounting of a gem which may conceal an imperfection (jeweler's term).

END. n. A share (in the take).

The EYE. n. The Pinkerton agency; a Pinkerton operative.

FALL. n. An arrest.

FALL DOUGH. n. phr. Money saved to be used in case of arrest or trouble with the law.

FAN. v.t. To run the hands lightly over the clothing of a prospective victim in order to locate valuables or money, usually done by the *tool*.

FAN THE IMPRESSION. v. phr. For the victim to feel for his wallet or valuables in order to reassure himself.

FAT. adj. 1. Working profitably (said of the mob). 2. Carrying valuable possessions (said of the victim).

FAT ONE. n. phr. A wallet with a good deal of cash in it.

FENCE. n. A receiver of stolen goods (archaic among pickpockets).

FILL IN. 1. v.i. To work temporarily with another mob; to substitute for another man. 2. v.t. To permit a pickpocket to work as a new member in a mob. 3. n. A substitute taken on by the mob when they have *dropped a man*.

FIN. n. 1. A five-dollar bill. 2. The hand.

FINDER. n. See *steerer*.

FINGER. v.t. To identify (someone accused of a crime).

FINK. 1. adj. Damaged or worthless, as a *fink* stone. 2. An informer.

FISH EYE. n. phr. An imitation diamond stud or pin.

FITTED FOR ALL GRIFT. v. phr. Willing and able to accept the fix for grifting crimes; said of police officials.

FIT THE FUR. v. phr. See *fit the mitt*.

FIT THE MITT. v. phr. To supply the fix directly to a pickpocket detective (used by old-timers).

FIX. v.t. To forestall action by the law, either by paying off the police beforehand or the victim after apprehension.

The FIX. n. An arrangement, used by all criminals in one form or another, by which protection is bought from the law or other persons with influence. A prearrangement with the police or any politician is the commonest form; it operates much like life insurance. The pickpocket usually operates under this type of fix, but if arrested while grifting *on his own*, he bribes the arresting officer if possible. If not, he tries the victim. Failing here, he submits to arrest, then buys political influence, has the case *nol-prossed* or repeatedly continued until the victim tires of appearing. Or he may plead guilty on the promise of a suspended sentence. If all such efforts fail, as they rarely do, he will *take the fence*, that is forfeit his bail and later (if he values his freedom) reimburses the bondsman. Relatively few pickpockets get punishment in proportion to their criminal acts; the police record of any known pickpocket shows a great number of arrests and few convictions, which speaks for the efficacy of the fix.

FIX A BANG. v. phr. To take a shot of narcotics. Also *take a bang*.

FIX A BEEF. v. phr. To squelch a complaint from a victim.

FIXER. n. One who sells or deals in political influence for the benefit of professional criminals.

FIX MONEY. n. phr. See *fix*.

FLASH. 1. n. A fleeting glance at something (often money); also *flash peek*. 2. v.t. To show something for an instant.

FLATFOOT. n. A uniformed policeman (archaic).

FLING IT. v. phr. See *ding* (1).

FLOATER. n. 1. A pickpocket with no stable relationships who travels from town to town. 2. A sworn warrant for the arrest of a thief.

FLOP. n. 1. A person sleeping in a public place. 2. The pickpocket's room or apartment.

FLOP WORKER or FLOPHOUSE WORKER. n. phr. A thief who specializes in sleeping victims.

FLY. adj. Smart, crafty, or intelligent.

FLY COP. n. phr. Small-town policeman (archaic), used ironically.

FLYER. n. A police circular listing wanted criminals giving photos, fingerprints, and other descriptions.

FOB. n. See *britch jerve*.

FOB WORKERS. n. phr. Oldtime pickpockets who stole valuables, coins, and watches from *fobs* (archaic).

FOLDER MAN. See *steerer*.

FOLDERS. n. Timetables for railroad trains, buses, etc.

FORK. v.t. To pick a pocket with the index and middle fingers, using them as pincers.

FORTY-SECOND STREET THIEF. n. phr. A pickpocket who can only work in a particular locality or area. Also *home guard* or *one-spot hustler*.

FOUR-HANDED. adj. phr. With four members.

FRAME. 1. n. The position in which a victim is placed by a *stall* so that the *tool* can rob him. 2. v.t. To place in a frame. 3. v.t. The act of positioning a mark so that he can be robbed.

FRESH MONEY. n. phr. Money that comes in regularly, as opposed to savings.

FROG. n. A Frenchman.

FRONT. 1. n. The clothing the thief wears and therefore the impression that he conveys. 2. n. A watch and chain (archaic). 3. v.t. For a *tool* to work facing the victim. 4. v.i. To serve as a cover for an illicit operation.

FRONT MAN. n. phr. A *stall* who works in front of a victim.

FRONT WORKER. n. phr. A *tool* who can work facing the victim.

FUR or FUZZ. n. A policeman, especially a plainclothes detective. See *fuzzy tail*.

FUZZY TAIL. n. phr. Cat (archaic). By extension, a cop, as in *fuzz*.

G. n. A thousand dollars (from gamblers).

GAG. n. An indeterminate sentence.

GAG TOWNS. n. phr. Towns where the authorities are strict with pickpockets.

GANDER (AROUND). v.i. To walk around preliminary to action.

GET (ONE'S) DUKE (or MITT) DOWN. v. phr. 1. For the *tool* to reach for a wallet or valuables in a pocket. 2. To work as a *tool* as opposed to a *stall*.

GET OFF THE NUT. v. phr. To steal enough money to account for working expenses, including the fix.

GET-ON. n. A bus or trolley stop; especially one used by pickpockets for thefts.

GILLIGAN HITCH. n. phr. A stranglehold (West Coast). *Clout and lam* tactic also used by police.

GIVE (SOMEONE) A DAY'S WORK. v. phr. To *fill in* an operator temporarily.

GIVE (SOMEONE) THE MARY. v. phr. To steal someone's wallet by using force (*clout and lam* or *muggers*).

GIVE UP. v. phr. To pay shakedown money.

GIVE UP (ONE'S) KISSER. v. phr. To allow the victim to see the pickpocket's face while working.

GLOMMED. v.t. Arrested (mostly past participial usage in passive voice).

GO DOWN or GET DOWN. v. phr. To enter the pocket.

GO DOWNSTAIRS WITH IT. See *ding* (1).

GO FOR. v. phr. To care for an arrested mob member with funds for the fix and/or legal aid.

GOING-OUT MEET. n. phr. The gathering of the mob members on the street before working.

GONIF. n. Yiddish for thief.

GOOD FRONT. n. phr. An acceptable and prosperous appearance.

GOOD MAN. n. phr. A skilled, dilligent, and trustworthy operator.

GOOD' PEOPLE. n. phr. Any old-timer, especially one who has *packed it in*. Used in the singular: "He's good people."

GO OUT. v. phr. To pick pockets.

GO TO THE FLOOR WITH IT. v. phr. See *ding* (1).

GOULASH JOINT. n. phr. Inexpensive restaurant frequented by pickpockets.

GRAB (SOMEONE) RIGHT. v. phr. To catch or arrest during the act of theft.

GRAFTER. n. An old-time term for pickpocket or thief. An earlier form of *grifter*. Compare O. Henry's "The Gentle Grafter."

GRAPEVINE. n. Underworld communication system.

GREASE. v.t. To bribe.

GREASER. n. Mexican or Latin American.

GREASY. adj. 1. Measly. 2. Well worn (said of money).

GRIFT. n. 1. That branch of criminal activities that separates the victim from his money by stealth, deception, manual skill, or other means not employing violence. Opposed to the *heavy rackets*. 2. n. When used by pickpockets, their racket. 3. v.i. To pick pockets. 4. v.i. To work at any racket on the grift.

GRIFTER. n. A criminal on the grift.

GRIFT GUTS. n. phr. The courage to operate on the grift.

GRIFT JUGS. v. phr. To pick the pockets of victims who are leaving or entering a bank.

GRIFT KNOW. n. phr. The complex of sensitivities and abilities which makes a good grifter. Also *grift sense*.

GRIFT ON (ONE'S) OWN. v. phr. To work without the protection of the fix. Also *grift on the sneak*.

GRIFT RIGHT. v. phr. To work under the protection of a fix arranged in advance.

GRIFT SENSE. See *grift know*.

GRIFT WITH A SHADE or GRIFT WITH THE PRO. v. phr. To operate with protection.

GRIFT WITH A SHADE ON (ONE'S) TAIL. v. phr. To pick pockets followed by a fixed detective who will intervene if the *tool* is discovered.

GRIFT WITH A SQUEALER. v. phr. To pick pockets with an infant on one's arm. Used by female pickpockets.

GRIND IT UP. v. phr. To make little money while picking many pockets.

GRIND UP NICKELS AND DIMES. See *grind it up*.

GUN. n. Thief or pickpocket, clipped back from Yiddish *gonif* (thief). Archaic, but common in various combinations. Also *gunner* (rare).

GUN MOB. n. phr. A team of pickpockets.

GUN MOLL. n. phr. A woman pickpocket. Contrary to popular belief, "gun" has nothing to do with firearms.

GUN PIT. n. phr. A shoulder holster for a pistol.

GUN TIP. n. phr. A crowd ripe to be worked by pickpockets (rare).

GUN TURN. n. phr. A turn at the game of faro which reveals two fives. The phrase comes from the humorous saying "Two fives together, what the mark has in his leather."

GUZZLED. v.t. Arrested (past participle; rare in other forms).

HACK. n. Prison guard. Also *screw, shack*.

HALF A C. n. phr. A fifty-dollar bill.

HALF-ASSED PICKPOCKET. n. phr. An unskilled, part-time pickpocket.

HALL OF FAME. n. phr. A rogues' gallery or collection of photos of known criminals; the police mug book.

HANDLE. v.t. To make a successful theft from the person.

HANGER. n. 1. A woman's handbag, especially one with a shoulder strap. 2. An easy score; one that figuratively hangs partly out of the pocket. Also *kick-in-the-ass, kick-out, pop-up*.

HANGER BINGER. n. phr. Thief who steals from handbags or a purse snatcher.

HANGOUT. n. Place of gathering for thieves, frequently enjoying immunity from the police.

HARNESS BULL or HARNESS COPPER. n. phr. A uniformed policeman.

HAT DUCKET. n. phr. The hat slip passed out by conductors when tickets are taken up. Traveling pickpockets lift these to avoid paying fares.

HAVE (SOMEONE) RIGHT. v. phr. To have applied the fix to the person under discussion.

HEAT. n. 1. Pressure from the public or

police headquarters to crack down on criminals. 2. A pistol.

HEAVY. 1. adj. Pertaining to the heavy rackets. 2. adj. Armed or violent. 3. n. A criminal on the heavy rackets.

The HEAVY. n. The heavy rackets, especially in the phrase *on the heavy.*

HEAVY GEE. n. phr. A criminal on the heavy rackets. Also *heavy man, heavy operator, heavy worker.*

HEAVY ONE. n. phr. A full wallet.

HEAVY OPERATOR. See *heavy gee.*

HEAVY RACKETS. n. phr. Those criminal activities that use force or the threat of force to separate the victim from his valuables. Compare *grift.*

HEAVY WORKER. See *heavy gee.*

The HEEL. n. A specialized theft performed by a *heel thief*; a skilled grifter who can steal money from a cashier's till in a bank or other institution.

HEEL PLANT. n. phr. A hiding place for money, narcotics, etc., inside a rubber heel.

HEEL SCORE or HEEL TOUCH. n. phr. A score taken by means of the *heel.*

HEIST MOB. n. phr. In pickpocket parlance, same as *clout and lam mob*; otherwise stick-up gang.

HIDE. See *poke.*

HIDEAWAY. n. A town or resort area where a thief can relax and live between periods of activity with little fear of arrest. Also *lay-off spot.*

HIGH-JACKER. n. phr. A pickpocket using rough techniques.

HIP. adj. Smart or suspicious; said of a victim who is *rumbled.*

HIP (A SUCKER). v.t. To arouse (a victim's) suspicions.

HIT AND RUN. See *clout and lam.*

HIT THE GATE. v. phr. To leave the penitentiary.

HOCUS or HOCUS POCUS. n. See *poke.*

The HOLE. n. A subway.

HOLLER COPPER. v. phr. See *cry cop.*

HOME FREE. adj. phr. Safe from prosecution.

HOME GUARD. n. phr. See *local.*

HOOK. 1. n. A *tool.* 2. v.t. To steal (valuables from the person).

HOOKED. adj. Habituated or addicted.

HOOKS. n. The hands.

HOOSIER. n. A farmer or rural person.

HOOSIER GRIFT. n. phr. Work at a county fair or carnival.

HOPSCOTCH. v.i. 1. To travel about the country with no regular route. 2. To work a trolley or subway line, frequently changing cars.

HOT. adj. 1. Dangerous for pickpockets or other criminals (said of a place or area). 2. Illicit or stolen. 3. Wanted by the police.

HOT SPOT. n. phr. A place hazardous to work.

HOT THIMBLE. n. phr. A stolen watch (archaic).

HUMP. n. The *stall*'s back and shoulders, used to control the movements of a victim.

HUNGRY. adj. Always working; avaricious.

HUNGRY MOB. n. phr. An aggressive mob that is always working hard.

HUNKY. n. A foreigner, usually a Hungarian or Central European.

The HURDY GURDY. n. The cutting apart of the clothing of pickpockets by police to discover if they have any money hidden there. Once done in Council Bluffs, Iowa, but now archaic.

HUSTLE. 1. n. A racket. 2. n. Any occupation. 3. v.i. To work (at an illegal occupation).

HUSTLE BEHIND A SHADE. v. phr. See *grift with a shade.*

HUSTLER. n. Anyone with a *racket*, as a prostitute, dice hustler, etc.

HUSTLE THE FLOPS. v. phr. To steal from sleeping persons, especially on skid row.

HUSTLE WITH A BRAT. v. phr. See *grift with a squealer.*

HUSTLE WITH A SHADE. v. phr. See *grift with a shade.*

HUSTLE WITH PRO. v. phr. See *grift with a shade.*

The HYPE. n. A short-change racket sometimes used by pickpockets or their women.

ICE. n. 1. Jewelry. 2. Fix money.

IMPRESSION. n. The outline of an object contained in a pocket.

IN. prep. Having access to the fix.

IN or IN WITH. prep. 1. Willing to take part in a crime. 2. Full participation in a mob including the involvement of *fall dough.*

IN AND IN. prep. phr. An arrangement made in advance by mob members whereby any member may declare himself in with one touch and out with another. For example, a

Catholic pickpocket might declare himself out when a priest is robbed while a Jewish pickpocket might declare himself *in*. A member who has declared himself *in* shares in the touch even though he may not participate, though his *fall dough* is involved in the event of an arrest. A member who declares himself out does not share in the profits nor does he risk his *fall dough*. The entire arrangement is often referred to as "in and in and out and out." Restricted to *class cannons*.

IN (ONE'S) SEAMS. prep. phr. Set aside for hard times or for use as *fall dough*; said of money.

INSIDER. n. 1. An inside coat pocket. 2. A hidden pocket in a vest lining. 3. In one's possession (as in "How would you like to have that in your insider?").

INSURANCE MAN'S POKE. n. phr. A long oversized wallet carried in the inside suit coat pocket.

IN WITH THE GRAVY. adv. phr. See *in and in*.

IN WITH THE GRIEF. adv. phr. See *in and in*.

IN WITH THE PINCHES. adv. phr. See *in and in*.

IN WITH THE POKES. adv. phr. See *in and in*.

IOWA TWEEZER or IOWA TWEEZER POKE. n. phr. A small purse with a square steel frame that snaps shut with clasps.

IRON-BOUND IN. n. phr. A secure arrangement with police officials or politicians. See *airtight fix*.

IT'S OFF. v. phr. An *office* from the *tool* to the *stall* indicating that the *tool* has the wallet, allowing the *stall* or *stalls* to proceed to the next mark. Often indicated by a sharp intake of breath causing a barely audible high-pitched chirp.

JACKET. n. A police record; referring to the folder in which an individual's record — sometimes called a *yellow sheet* — is filed.

JACK GAGGERS. n. phr. Thieves who steal from workers who are paid large sums seasonally such as lumberjacks. Also *jack hustlers, jack rollers, jack sneaks*.

JERVE [dʒarv]. n. A watch pocket in the trousers or vest. Also *fob*.

JIG. n. A black.

JIG MOB. n. phr. A team of black pickpock-

ets. Some mobs are all white, some are all black, and some are mixed.

JIG TOOL. n. phr. A black pickpocket.

JOHN. n. A potential victim.

JOIN OUT. v. phr. To become a member of a pickpocket mob.

JOIN OUT THE ODDS. v. phr. To have one's girlfriend work as a prostitute during hard times.

JOINT. n. 1. A place of business. 2. A prison or penitentiary.

JOSEPH. adj. Variant of *Joe Hep* (in the know) as in "Who's going to put him Joseph?"

JOSTLE. 1. n. A technique for throwing a potential victim off balance, which is a mark of poor technique (police term, rarely used by pickpockets). 2. v.t. To employ such a technique.

JUG. n. A bank.

JUG GRIFT. n. phr. Stealing from patrons as they emerge from banks (*class cannons*).

JUG MOB. n. phr. A team of pickpockets that specializes in the *jug grift*.

JUG SCORE. n. phr. Money taken from a victim who has just left a bank. Also *jug touch*.

JUNKER MOBS. n. phr. Pickpocket teams in which all members are addicts.

JUNK MONEY. n. phr. Money set aside for narcotics.

KASHN. n. A synonym for *cousin* (1), perhaps from the Yiddish.

KAYDUCER. n. A conductor on a train, streetcar, etc.

KEEP THE MEET. v. phr. To come together at a prearranged time and place to work as a mob. Meets are timed precisely.

KETTLE. n. The gold case of a large old-fashioned pocket watch. See *souper*.

KICK. n. A pocket, usually in the coat or pants.

KICK-IN-THE-ASS. n. phr. See *hanger*.

KICK-OUT. n. phr. See *hanger*.

KICKS. n. Usually pockets, but also sometimes shoes.

KIESTER. n. 1. A suitcase. 2. The buttocks or hips. Also *prat*.

KIESTER KICK. n. phr. A hip pocket.

KIESTER MARK. n. phr. A victim carrying a suitcase or bundles.

KIESTER PLANT. n. phr. 1. A hidden compartment in a suitcase for storing valuables, false identification, etc. 2. A metal or plastic tube containing money or drugs and secreted in the rectum. Compare *coozie stash.*

KINKY KAYDUCER. n. phr. A conductor who is willing to *cop the short.*

KIP. n. 1. A room or apartment. 2. A bed or sleeping place.

KISSED IN WITH A MOB. part. phr. Accepted as a member of a *whiz mob.* Passive use only.

KISSER. n. The face, especially as recognized by the mark.

KISS THE DOG. v. phr. To work face-to-face with the victim while working from the front. Usually said of a *tool.*

KNIPPLE or NIPPLE. n. A roll of bills (East Coast usage). Probably from Yiddish *knippel.*

KNOCK. v.t. To criticize, especially applied to any racket, particularly one's own.

KNOCK (A MARK). v.t. To arouse the suspicions of a victim or a potential victim.

KNOCKABOUT MOB. n. phr. A team of pickpockets which works anywhere, with no specialty or any restricted territory.

KNOCK OFF. v. phr. To arrest.

KNOCK UP. 1. v. phr. To gather money together, usually by stealing. 2. n. phr. The day's total take.

LAG. v.t. To arrest.

LARCENY SENSE. See *grift sense.*

The LAW. n. Any police officer.

LAY DEAD. v. phr. To be professionally inactive temporarily, usually by hiding out. See also *cool off.*

LAYING DOWN. p. part. For a wallet to be lying crosswise in the *prat kick,* requiring the *tool* to *top* it before removing. Also *crossed poke, lying down, on its side.*

LAY IT ON THE LINE. v. phr. To spend money extravagantly.

LAY' OFF SPOT. n. phr. A safe location where pickpockets under indictment or *on the lam* can stay without fear of arrest.

LEATHER. n. A wallet, even one that is not made of leather.

LEFT BRITCH (or BRIDGE). n. phr. Left-side pants pocket.

LEFT BRITCH SCORE. n. phr. A successful theft from the left-side pants pocket.

LEFT PRAT. n. phr. The left hip pocket.

LEFT TAIL. n. phr. The left-side pocket of a suit coat.

LET (SOMEONE) GEE (or GO). v. phr. To release a victim from a frame so the mark can be *put up* again, or because the *play* has been *ranked.*

LET IT GO. v. phr. To release an object being stolen from the person because of difficulty in removing it.

LIGHTNING TOOL. n. phr. A *tool* who works quickly and with great dexterity, seldom *rumbling* the mark; a *class cannon.* Also *electric tool, live wire.*

LINE. n. An area, sometimes limited to a single street, where pickpockets operate. Also *spot.*

LINED UP. p. part. phr. Paraded before police and witnesses for identification.

LINE' UP. n. phr. A display of recently arrested suspects at a police station for the purpose of identification by police or victims.

LIVE CANNON. n. phr. A police term distinguishing a pickpocket who steals from moving victims from other types of pickpockets such as *lush busters* or *purse snatchers* (East Coast).

LIVE WIRE. n. phr. See *lightning tool.*

LOADED DOWN. p. part. phr. Carrying a large sum of money (refers to a mark). Also *loaded up.*

LOAD THEM IN. v. phr. To frame victims moving through a crowded passageway, entry, or public conveyance. Compare *unload.*

LOAD THEM ON. v. phr. To work in a crowd boarding a boat, train, or other conveyance.

LOCAL. n. A pickpocket who works exclusively in one city or district and will not travel. Also *home guard, local talent.*

LOCAL MOB. n. phr. A mob of *local* pickpockets.

LOCATE. v.i. See *touch* (3).

LONE WOLF. n. phr. A *tool,* usually skilled and intelligent, who works alone. Also *single-o tool.*

LOOK BAD. v. phr. To look shabby, a decided disadvantage in an occupation where so much depends on personal appearance. To *look good* or *sharp* means to present a prosperous, natty appearance.

LOUSE. n. 1. A stool pigeon. 2. See *carnival louse.*

LUSH BUSTER. n. phr. A thief who steals from drunks but does not use any of the subtle techniques of the pickpocket. Also *lush hunter, lush roller, lush worker.*

246 Language of the Underworld

LYING DOWN. part. phr. See *laying down.*

MAIN DRAG. n. phr. The chief street of a city.

MAIN-LINE SHOT. n. phr. An injection of a drug made directly into a vein. There is a heavy use of addict's lingo because of the prevalence of addiction.

MAKE v.t. 1. To recognize someone. 2. To successfully accomplish something (especially a theft). 3. To arrive at (as to *make a tip*).

MAKE A BEAT. v. phr. To accomplish a theft.

MAKE A FRAME. v. phr. See *frame.*

MAKE A FUZZ. v. phr. To realize the presence of a policeman.

MAKE A GET. v. phr. To escape or get away from the scene of a theft.

MAKE A MAN (or THIEF) ON HIS MERITS. v. phr. To recognize a person as a thief from his appearance alone. Although some pickpockets claim this is possible, police rely on memory of faces and photographs to make arrests that would indicate such an ability.

MAKE A PLAY. v. phr. To attempt a theft.

MAKE A TIP. v. phr. To reach a crowd of potential victims.

MAKESHIFT MOB. n. phr. A temporary mob, often assembled on the spur of the moment, of variable quality. Also *pickup, pickup mob.*

MAKE THE CENTER BRITCH. v. phr. 1. To be a *center britch tool.* 2. To have sex with a woman.

MARK. n. A victim or intended victim.

MARY ELLEN HUSTLERS (or WORKERS). n. phr. Pickpockets who employ an unorthodox style of stalling whereby the victim, often slightly drunk, is approached in a friendly manner, *fanned,* and given a sexual proposition which may be either heterosexual or homosexual in nature. While the *stall* or *stalls* — who may be male and/or female — have the mark occupied, the *tool makes the score.*

MECHANIC. n. A *tool,* especially a very skillful one. This term is used widely for comparably skilled operators in several rackets.

MEET. n. 1. The gathering of mob members at a specific time and place in the morning before beginning work or at some other time of the day. At the *morning meet* or *going-out meet* the day's itinerary and other details are planned out. Usually, the day's take is divided during a final meet at day's end. 2. Any engagement or appointment.

MICHIGAN BANKROLL. n. phr. 1. A few bills wrapped around a roll of paper or stage money to simulate a large bankroll. Also *boodle.* 2. A big roll of one-dollar bills (*aces*) with a bill of larger denomination wrapped around it. Also *mish.*

MIDDLE BRITCH. n. See *center britch.*

MILE-AWAY. n. phr. A pickpocket who is overly cautious about getting close to the victim. Also *center fielder, playing safety first, sneeze-shy.*

MISH. n. See *Michigan bankroll.*

MISS MEETS. v. phr. For a member of the mob to fail to show up at the *going-out meet* more or less habitually and without a valid excuse. In a *class mob,* this is grounds for *dropping* or *declaring out* the offender. Normally, illness or some other valid reason for absence does not prevent the member from being *in* for his share of the day's proceeds.

MITT. 1. n. The hand. 2. v.t. To take in the hand. 3. v.t. To pass something from one person to another.

MOB. n. An organized group of two or more pickpockets. Formerly most mobs consisted of four, five, or even more members — two *tools* and several *stalls.* Now most are *three-handed,* with one *tool* and two *stalls,* but some are *two-handed.*

MOB IT UP. v. phr. To become a member of a mob of pickpockets. Also *join out.*

MOCKY. n. A Jew (pejorative).

MOCKY JEW MOB or MOCKY MOB. n. phr. A Jewish pickpocket mob, often made up of immigrants.

MOLL. n. A woman, especially one on the rackets (archaic).

MOLL BUZZER. n. phr. A pickpocket, either a man or a woman, who specializes in robbing from women. Pejorative when applied to a male.

MOLL MOB. n. phr. 1. A group of *moll buzzers.* 2. A group of women pickpockets.

MOLL WHIZ. n. phr. A woman pickpocket. Also *gun moll.*

MONEY GETTER. n. phr. A diligent and industrious operator, especially a *class cannon,* who likes to live high. Compare *money hungry.*

MONEY HUNGRY. adj. phr. Said of a pickpocket who thinks only of stealing and hoarding money.

MONICKER. n. An underworld nickname given to a pickpocket by other members of the profession. Aliases change rapidly, but *monickers* are permanent.

MONKEY. n. A Chinese (West Coast).

MORNING DAY. n. phr. A day on which the best conditions for picking pockets are in the morning (West Coast).

MORNING MEET. n. See *meet*.

MUG. 1. v.t. To put a stranglehold on a victim from behind so that he can be robbed. *Lush buster* technique. 2. n. The face.

MUG BOOK. n. phr. See *rogues' gallery*.

MUGGED. p. part. Photographed, usually at the time of an arrest.

MUGGER. n. One who *mugs*. See *boffman*.

MURDERER'S PUSH GRIFT. n. phr. 1. An ideal situation for using rough techniques while picking pockets such as a large crowd entering a sports arena. 2. The rough, fast work appropriate to this sort of crowd.

MUSCLE MAN. n. See *boffman*.

MUZZLE AROUND (SINGLE-O). v. phr. To pick pockets without the aid of a *stall* or con federate. A whimsical application derived from *muzzlers* (nonpickpockets who molest women sexually in a crowd).

MUZZLER. n. See *muzzle around*.

NAIL v.t. 1. To pick a pocket successfully. Usually appears as "to nail a sucker." Also to *nick*. 2. To arrest.

NAILED. p. part. 1. Said of a wallet or bankroll that is fastened with a safety pin or other device. 2. Said of a sucker who is robbed.

NAILED DOWN. p. part. phr. See *nailed* (1).

NERVOUS MARK. n. phr. A fidgety or suspicious victim.

NICE SCORE. n. phr. A large single theft.

NICK. v.t. See *nail* (1).

NIGGER HEAD. n. phr. A flawed diamond (jeweler's term).

NIPPERS. n. Small metal clippers used to cut off or *nip* valuables that are fastened by a pin or light chain.

NIPPLE. n. See *knipple*.

NOTCHERY. n. A brothel.

NOTE. n. 1. A sum of money, especially one paid as a bribe or for protection. 2. A hundred-dollar bill, clipped from *C note*.

NUT. n. Overhead expenses; the cost of travel, living, the fix, etc. See *on the nut*.

NUT MONEY. n. phr. Money set aside for expenses.

OAKUS or OKUS. n. See *poke*. Probably from "hocus" as in the ancient bogus Latin phrase *hocus pocus dominocus*.

OBIE. n. A post office, derived from O.B., an office box.

The ODDS. n. 1. See *join out the odds*. 2. A pistol.

OFF. adj. Completed successfully (said of a theft). See *it's off*.

OFFICE. 1. n. A signal, either verbal or kinesic, used to attract attention or direct the actions of an accomplice. 2. v.t. To signal in such a manner.

OFF THE CAP. prep. phr. Expenses or other sums subtracted from the common *knockup* before it is divided are said to come *off the cap*. Also *off the head, off the top*.

OLD COUNTRY GUN. n. phr. A European pickpocket, either an immigrant or a traveler.

OLD COUNTRY MOB. n. phr. A group of European pickpockets, either immigrants or visitors. Their methods and organization differ somewhat from native groups.

OLD MINE STONE. n. phr. A gem, especially a diamond, cut in an old-fashioned design that reduces its value (jeweler's term).

ONE FOR THE (END) BOOK. n. phr. An extraordinary experience. From old-time racetrack bookies.

ONE-SPOT HUSTLER. n. phr. See *Forty-second Street thief*.

ON FIRE. adj. phr. Extremely dangerous for *working*—said of either a person or a place. See *hot*.

ONION. n. An old-fashioned pocket watch (archaic).

ON ITS FEET. adj. phr. Said of a wallet that has the fold at the top or bottom of the pocket and is therefore easier to remove. Compare *laying down*.

ON ITS SIDE. prep. phr. See *laying down*.

ON (ONE'S) RECORD. prep. phr. For a policeman to deal with a thief on the basis of the thief's previous reputation; the use of the *yellow sheet*.

ON THE BLOCKS. adj./adv. phr. 1. Soliciting as a street prostitute. Also *on the turf*. 2. Free or recently released from prison.

ON THE BOOST. adj./adv. phr. Working as a shoplifter.

ON THE CANNON. adj./adv. phr. Working as a pickpocket. Also *on the dip, on the grift, on the hustle, on the whiz.*

ON THE HEIST. adj./adv. phr. To be engaged in an act of theft employing violence. Said of *heavy gees.*

ON THE HUSTLE. prep. phr. See *on the cannon.*

ON THE NUT. adj./adv. phr. 1. Paid out for overhead. 2. Working on an advance or on credit.

ON THE RACKETS. adj./adv. phr. Said of any operating professional criminal.

ON THE ROAD. adj./adv. phr. Traveling from town to town in order to work as a pickpocket. See *road man.*

ON THE SHAKE. adj./adv. phr. Said of detectives who seek out known thieves in order to extort money from them.

ON THE SNEAK. adj./adv. phr. Engaged in thievery without having made prior arrangements with the law.

ON THE TAKE. adj. phr. Willing to accept bribes.

ON THE TEAR. adj./adv. phr. Working diligently as a pickpocket.

ON THE TURF. prep. phr. See *on the blocks.*

ON THE WHIZ. prep. phr. See *on the cannon.*

OPERATE. v.i. To slit a pocket with a razor blade so that the contents may be stolen. Also to *perform an operation.* Frowned upon by *class cannons.*

ORGANIZED MOB. n. phr. A working unit of pickpockets whose duties are specialized according to a strict division of labor, who work under the fix and who carry enough *fall dough* to get them out of any ordinary scrape.

OUT. adv. See *prat out, prat (someone) out.*

OUT AND OUT. adj. phr. On one's own. See *in and in.*

OUTFIT. n. 1. A watch and chain. Compare *red outfit* and *white outfit.* 2. A mob of pickpockets. 3. Hypodermic equipment.

OUT OF. adv. phr. Operating from, as in "out of Philly."

OWN. v.t. 1. To work undisturbed with exclusive rights at a particular locality, usually by arrangement with local authorities. 2. Said of a wallet that has been successfully *topped* by a tool but not yet taken.

OX TONGUE. n. phr. A long tubular pouch used by some rural men for carrying large sums of money.

PACK IT IN. v. phr. To call an end to.

PACK THE RACKET IN. v. phr. 1. To quit for the day. 2. To quit active participation in thievery, permanently or temporarily.

PANCAKE POKE. n. phr. A flat round purse fastened with a clasp.

PANTHER. n. A shakedown policeman or avaricious fixer (archaic).

PANTS POCKET WORKER. n. phr. Police term for a pickpocket.

PAPER. n. A stolen check or valuable paper which may be turned to profit by an experienced operator. Also *stiff.*

PAPPY, OLD PAPPY, PAP. n. An elderly man; may imply that he has money.

PASS THE POKE. v. phr. (For the *tool*) to hand a stolen wallet (to a *stall*).

PASS THE SHEET. v. phr. To solicit funds for a pickpocket who is broke or in jail. Sometimes each contributor records his name and amount on a sheet of paper with a view to reimbursement.

PASSUP. n. The ignoring of the presence or activity of pickpockets by the law, usually because the fix is in.

PATCH POCKET. n. phr. A pocket on a woman's suit or sweater.

PAY' OFF. 1. n. The fix. 2. n. A bribe given to a victim to insure that he will drop or not press charges. 3. v. phr. To give money to the police, a victim, or a witness in order to forestall arrest or prosecution.

PAY (SOMEONE) OFF IN THE DARK. v. phr. To cheat someone.

PEA SOUP TIP. n. phr. A cheap crowd; one not worth working.

PENITENTIARY GRIFT. n. phr. A crowd in which everyone is standing still.

PERFORM AN OPERATION. v. phr. See *operate.*

PETTY LARCENY BUM. n. phr. A small-time thief who is afraid to take risks.

PICKUP or PICKUP MOB. n. phr. See *makeshift mob.*

PIECE. n. 1. An article of jewelry worth taking. 2. A piece of paper money. 3. A pistol.

PINCH. 1. n. An arrest. 2. v.t. To arrest. 3. v.t. To remove by grasping an object between the thumb and index or middle finger.

PINCH A POKE. v. phr. See *pinch* (3).

PINK or PINKY. n. A Pinkerton detective.

PIT. n. 1. An inside coat pocket. 2. A shoulder holster worn inside the coat or under the shirt.

PIT SCORE. n. phr. A theft from an inside coat pocket.

PLANT. 1. n. A place of concealment for money or valuables, often on or about the person. 2. n. A frame-up. 3. v.t. To conceal (about the person). 4. v.i. To lie in wait for someone.

PLANT (ONE'S) PRAT. v. phr. To place one's buttocks against a victim to help put him in a frame.

PLAY. n. 1. An attempt to victimize someone, as in to *make a play for*. 2. The action of picking a pocket.

PLAY SAFETY FIRST. v. phr. See *mileaway*.

PLAY THE RATTLERS. v. phr. To work by traveling on trains, both *loading them on* and *unloading them*. Also *railroad grift*, *work the rattlers*.

P.O. n. A post office, the standard meeting place for newly arriving pickpockets or those separated during a day's work.

POCKETBOOK SNATCHER. n. phr. Derogatory term used by one pickpocket to describe another. Implies *clout and lam* tactics.

POCKET GALLERY. n. phr. A pocket-sized book containing photos and/or descriptions of known criminals and circulated among policemen. See also *rogues' gallery*.

POKE. n. A wallet. Originally this referred to a long sacklike pocket purse fastened at the top with a clasp or a drawstring. Also *hide*, *hocus*, *leather*, *oakus*, *okus*, *and skin*.

POKE GLOMMER. n. phr. A clumsy operator.

POLLY. n. A politician, particularly when his association with the fix is implied.

POP-UP. n. phr. See *hanger*.

PRAT. n. 1. A hip pocket; short for *prat kick*. Usually appears as *left prat* or *right prat*. 2. The hips and buttocks. See *prat (someone) in*.

PRAT DIGGER. n. phr. A *tool* whose forte is hip pockets. Also *prat worker*.

PRAT (SOMEONE) IN. v. phr. To maneuver the victim into position closer to the *tool* so that he can be victimized. To *prat out* means to move an interfering pedestrian from between the *tool* and the intended victim, or to separate the victim from the *tool* after a theft. The term springs from the use of the buttocks and hips to maneuver the other person, who is often unaware of the interference.

PRAT KICK. n. phr. See *prat*.

PRAT POKE. n. phr. A wallet carried in the hip pocket.

PRAT SCORE. n. phr. A successful theft from a victim's hip pocket.

PRAT WORKER. n. phr. See *prat digger*.

PRESS. n. See *tip*.

PRINTED. past. part. Fingerprinted by police authorities.

PRO. n. See *grift with the pro*.

PRODUCE. v.i. To be active and successful in picking pockets.

PRODUCER. n. A *tool* who is diligent and businesslike in picking pockets.

PROP. n. A man's tiepin (archaic).

PROTECTION. n. The active or tacit approval of illegal activities by police officials.

PUNCH GUFF. v. phr. To discuss previous experiences in a professional career; to tell stories. See *cut up old ones*. Also *punch gun*, *punch whiz*.

PUNK. n. 1. A young man or boy with criminal potential; often in the phrase *punk kid*. 2. An obnoxious young pickpocket.

PUSH. n. See *tip*.

PUSH GRIFT. n. phr. Work in a tightly packed, excited crowd where technical finesse is often not required.

PUT (SOMEONE) AWAY. v. phr. To arrest someone.

PUT (ONE'S) DUKE DOWN. v. phr. 1. To enter the pocket with one's hand. 2. To engage in picking pockets. 3. To *reef a kick*.

PUT (ONE'S) HUMP UP. v. phr. 1. To act as a *stall*. 2. To use the back to control the motions of a victim. Also *put (one's) back up*.

PUT THE BEE ON. v. phr. To defraud or *sting*.

PUT THE FINGER ON. v. phr. To identify a person to someone else, especially to identify a criminal to the police.

PUT THE SHAKE ON. v. phr. See *shakedown*. Also *shake (someone) down*.

PUT THE TAIL ON. v. phr. See *tail*.

PUT ' UP or PUT-UP TOUCH. n. phr. A victim who is robbed on the advice of an informant.

PUT UP FOR. v. phr. See *put (one's) hump up*.

PUT UP FOR THE MARK. v. phr. See *frame* (3).

RACKET. n. 1. A specific division of the underworld in which practitioners of a given crime are specialists in that crime. 2. A criminal *hustle*. 3. Any occupation or profession (whimsical).

RAG. n. 1. The generic term for paper money (used rarely). 2. A circus or any large tent show that pickpockets sometimes follow because of the crowds it attracts.

RAILROAD GRIFT. n. The somewhat outdated practice of whiz mobs working trains, especially city-to-city trains.

RANK. 1. v.t. The foiling of a play by one of the mob members. 2. n. A suspicious reaction from a sucker or a bystander.

RAPPER. n. A victim who presses charges against a pickpocket.

RATIONS. n. The supply of drugs needed by an individual or a mob (if drugs are used) in a given time period.

RAT STOP. n. phr. A railroad station or layover point where freight trains stop.

RATTLER. n. A railroad train.

RAUST. n. A verbal *office* given to a *stall* by a *tool* indicating that the *stall* is to brush against the mark.

RAUST AND COME THROUGH. n. phr. A verbal *office* given by the *tool* to the *stall* indicating that the *stall* should brush against the mark as he (the *stall*) comes back toward the *tool*.

RAW. adj. Stale or out of practice in one's profession.

READER. n. 1. A descriptive circular listing fugitives or persons suspected of participating in organized crime. 2. A warrant, especially an "arrest and hold" warrant. See *dipsy*.

REBEL. n. Anyone from the South. Also used as adjective.

RED-NECK. n. phr. A mark that is a laborer; a working man. See *working stiff*.

RED ONE. n. phr. The biggest individual score taken in one day (Midwestern or Western usage). See *banner score, darb*.

RED OUTFIT. n. phr. A yellow gold watch case. Compare *white outfit*.

REEF. 1. v.t. To extract a *leather* from a pocket by hooking one's index finger just inside the slit of the pocket, taking up a pleat in the lining between the fingers, thus forcing the *poke* out of the pocket by the mark's own movements. 2. n. The act of reefing. 3. n. A pleat.

REEF A KICK. v. phr. To use the reefing method to steal a roll of bills; done only by *class cannons*.

RICHARD. n. A plainclothes detective. See *dick*.

RIDGE. n. Gold coins (archaic).

RIGHT. adj. A general term with multiple and very loose usage in the underworld, with meanings shifting to fit the necessities of pickpocket usage. The pickpocket takes *right falls* (is arrested for a crime he actually committed); he gets a *right rap* (a sentence for such a crime); he *rights up* (bribes) *right coppers* (who are susceptible to the fix), after which the pickpocket says he has them *right*. He may be able to *right the case* (buy off the victim or the officials) even though he was *grabbed right* (caught red-handed) in a *right town* or *right spot* (where there is a well-established system of fixing for criminals). This term with its antonym *wrong* is treated in some detail in *The American Confidence Man* and in *Whiz Mob*.

RIGHT BRITCH (or BRIDGE). n. phr. The right-side pants pocket.

RIGHT COATTAIL. n. phr. The right-side pocket of a sportscoat, suit coat, or topcoat.

RIGHT COPPER. n. phr. A policeman susceptible to the fix.

RIGHTEOUS. adj. Applied to a mark who is determined to gain a conviction of a pickpocket.

RIGHT FUZZ. n. phr. A *right copper*.

RIGHT PINCH. n. phr. An arrest for a score the pickpocket really *took off*.

RIGHT PRAT. n. phr. The right hip pocket.

RIGHT RAP. n. phr. *Right pinch*.

RIGHT TAIL. n. phr. The right-side pocket of a suit coat.

RIG-OUT. n. A situation that signals a frame-up.

RING IN or RING OUT. v.i. To dress like the other people in a crowd; to be inconspicuous by dressing to resemble others.

RIP (IT) or RIP OFF. v.t. To take a wallet by main force or skill, especially when the wallet is torn from the mark's pocket.

RIP AND TEAR. adj. phr. Rough or hasty as

pertaining to thieving or grifting technique. See *clout and lam.*

RIP AND TEAR MOB. n. phr. A whiz mob that employs rip and tear techniques while picking pockets.

RIP THE TIP. v. phr. For a mob to steal rapidly and efficiently in a concentration of people.

ROAD MAN. n. phr. A pickpocket who travels from town to town.

ROAD MOB. n. phr. A traveling troupe of pickpockets who follow an itinerary, in contrast to those who work one city or a limited locality.

ROAD WORK. n. phr. Traveling work performed by a *road man* or *road mob.*

ROGUES' GALLERY. n. 1. A handbook used by pickpocket squad detectives which contains pictures and/or descriptions of all known pickpockets; *pocket gallery.* 2. The large collection of mug shots kept in detective headquarters.

ROOT AND TOOT. v. phr. 1. To work skillfully and with enthusiasm. 2. To work hastily and roughly. See *clout and lam.*

ROOT RIGHT IN. v. phr. To join in smoothly; for a mob to work smoothly and profitably together.

ROPE. n. A pearl necklace.

ROUGH TOOL. n. phr. A determined but unskilled *tool.*

ROUGH WORK. n. phr. The act of picking pockets openly and without finesse.

ROUND. v.i. To turn around, especially if the act is accompanied by a suspicious stare.

RUFUS. n. A bumpkin.

RUMBLE. v.t. To make the mark aware that he is being victimized.

SACK. n. A side coat pocket.

SAFE AS KELSEY. adj. phr. Conservative; not inclined toward taking unnecessary risks. Euphemism for "safe as Kelsey's nuts."

SAW, SAWBUCK. n. A ten-dollar bill.

SCAT. n. Whiskey.

SCATTER. n. A saloon, especially one used as a thieves' hangout.

SCHMECKER. n. A narcotic addict.

SCORE. 1. n. A single theft or proceeds of a theft. 2. v.t. To complete a theft.

SCORE COMES OFF. The accomplishing of a theft.

SCRATCH. n. 1. A roll of bills. 2. Money, especially paper money.

SCRATCH PUSHER. n. phr. A clerk, as in a hotel or business; from *scratch* for pen (forger's argot).

SCREW. n. 1. A prison guard (prison argot). 2. A key.

SEAMS. n. The lining of clothing where *fall dough* is often hidden.

SENSATIONAL PUNK. n. phr. A novice pickpocket who brags about his scores in an obnoxious manner; often these exploits are fictional.

SETTLED. p. part. Sent to prison.

SETUP. n. The situation wherein a pickpocket sees a victim put money into his pocket or is told the victim has done so. Used in *jug touches.*

SHACK. n. 1. A subway guard or platform man. 2. Any railroad employee except a railroad detective. 3. A prison guard.

SHADE. 1. n. A newspaper, topcoat, or other object to conceal the operations of the *tool.* 2. n. By extension, any protective or concealing device or expedient. 3. v.t. To conceal something from observation; hence, to protect. To *shade the duke* indicates that a *stall* interposes his body, coat, or other object carried for the purpose of hiding the *tool's* activities from bystanders.

SHAG. adj. Worthless or low grade.

SHAKE. 1. n. The process of extorting a bribe under the threat of arrest or of extorting money under any word of threat. 2. v.t. To throw someone off the track; to give someone the slip.

SHAKE A RAP. v. phr. To arrange with police for withdrawal of charges after the pickpocket has been arrested and arraigned.

SHAKE ARTIST. n. phr. A policeman expert in extorting money from pickpockets.

SHAKEDOWN. n. Extortion, especially on the part of a member of the police pickpocket detail.

SHAKE MOB. n. phr. 1. A police detail that practices extorting money from pickpockets. 2. A whiz mob that poses as police and does the same thing.

SHAM. n. A verbal *office* that warns members of a mob that the police are approaching. Cut back from Yiddish *shamus.*

SHAMAS, SHAMUS. n. 1. Police in general. 2. A particular policeman.

SHARP. adj. 1. Professionally accomplished. 2. Well dressed.

SHARP UP. v.i. To rehearse or perfect one's professional techniques.

SHED. n. A railway station.

SHEET. n. 1. A list of contributors to a defense fund for any thief in good standing who has taken a particularly rough rap or a wrong one. This sheet may be a piece of paper setting forth the purpose of the fund and carrying the names of those who subscribe; or it may be imaginary in that some friend circulates through the hangouts and solicits subscriptions. These are often considered loans, and high-class thieves conscientiously repay them. See also *pass the sheet*. 2. A newspaper or magazine used to *shade the duke*.

SHINE. n. A Negro.

SHINE CANNON. n. phr. A black pickpocket.

SHINE MOB. See *burr head mob*.

SHORT. n. A streetcar.

SHORT RIDER. n. phr. A commuter or local resident shunned by local pickpockets under the terms of the fix.

SHOT. n. A skilled black *tool*; a *shine cannon*.

SHOW UP. n. 1. A meet. 2. A police line-up where victims identify suspects.

SIDE KICK. n. phr. An outside coat pocket.

SIDE MONEY. n. phr. Money taken from sources outside one's regular profession.

SINGLE-HANDED. adj./adv. phr. Alone; working by oneself as a *single-o cannon*.

SINK. v.t. To withhold all or part of another's share of the take; a cardinal sin among pickpockets.

SIT ON A BEEF. v. phr. For a pickpocket to await the disposal of charges against him; usually he does not work during this period.

SIXER. n. A six-month sentence.

SKIN. 1. See *poke*. 2. n. A shirt. 3. v.t. To remove the contents of a stolen wallet and then dispose of it. 4. v.t. To touch the victim inadvertently or to allow him to feel the movement in his pocket or pocket-lining. Compare *reef*. 5. v.t. To avoid payment of a bill or to get something for nothing.

SLANG. n. A watch chain (archaic).

SLANT. n. An opportunity for the *tool* to get at the victim's pockets.

SLAVE. n. A person, usually from the dominant culture, who works legitimately for a living.

SLAVE GRIFT. n. phr. The act of working in a crowd of people with pay envelopes; also work in any gathering of working people. The term indicates contempt for those who work for a living.

SLING. n. A watch and chain.

SLIT. n. The break between the tails of a man's overcoat.

SLOUGH. v.t. To throw away or get rid of, especially empty wallets.

SLUM. n. 1. Jewelry of any kind. 2. Worthless or false jewelry. 3. Food in jail or in prison.

SMART TOWN. n. phr. A town that is known to be hard on pickpockets, or where pickpockets are racketeered by police; a *wrong town*.

SMASH. n. Silver coins; change.

SNATCH AND GRAB. adv. phr. See *rip and tear*.

SNATCH SCORE. n. phr. A type of theft in which the *stall* shoulders the victim into the *tool* with a somewhat violent contact, whereby the *tool* lifts the wallet on impact. Used by *rough mobs* or unskilled pickpockets.

SNEAK TOOL. n. phr. A *tool* that picks pockets without the aid of *stalls*. He may work in a mob but still relies more on his skill than upon the efforts of his confederates.

SNEEZE. v.t. To arrest, usually used in the part participle form. Sometimes used as a noun.

SNEEZE-SHY. adj. phr. See *mile-away*.

SOCK. 1. n. Any device in which money is carried on the person; sometimes actually the foot covering. 2. v.t. Usually to *sock away*, which is to ply one's grifting trade diligently.

SOFT. n. Paper money.

SOFT MARK or SOFT TOUCH. n. phr. A person easily victimized.

SOLO CANNON. n. phr. A *single-o worker*.

SOUPER. n. A watch; derived from *kettle*.

SOUPER AND SLANG. n. A watch and chain.

SPEAR. v.t. To extract a wallet between the middle and index fingers. Also to *fork*.

SPECIAL. n. A Japanese, considered a soft touch by pickpockets (West Coast).

SPICK. n. A Latino, Mexican, or Chicano. Also *spik*.

SPICK MOB. n. phr. A troupe of Latin pickpockets.

SPIKE. n. A safety pin or other fastening device for closing a pocket or fastening a money bag or other receptacle to the clothing.

SPLIT. 1. n. Percentage of the proceeds from a theft. 2. v.t. To divide the take. 3. v.i. To leave precipitously.

SPLIT OUT. 1. v.i. To separate oneself from the mob or from a group. 2. v.t. To separate a member of the mob from the persons immediately surrounding him in a crowd and enable him to leave the scene; usually done to remove an accomplice upon whom suspicion has fallen or to save a member from apprehension. 3. n. The swift scattering of a mob of pickpockets from apprehension. 3. n. The swift scattering of a mob of pickpockets when trouble occurs. 4. n. The act of *splitting out* an accomplice.

SPOT. n. A locality, especially a grifting place; for pickpockets, a bus stop or subway station.

SPRING. v.t. 1. To secure one's release from jail. 2. To *split out*.

SPRING MONEY. n. phr. *Fall dough.*

SQUARE A BEEF. v. phr. To arrange for the withdrawal of charges, usually through a return of all or part of the loot to the victim, or through the efforts of the local fixer.

SQUARE JOHN. 1. n. A member of the dominant culture; a noncriminal type. 2. adj. Anything suggesting the dominant culture, such as a *square John* idea.

SQUARE PINCH. n. phr. An arrest for an offense in which the pickpocket is caught in the act of committing the crime.

SQUARES. n. Occasional criminals who have no tie with an organized professional racket. Members of the dominant culture who have committed crimes and have been sent to prison.

STALL. 1. n. The member of a mob who puts the victim in position and holds him there while the *tool* robs him. With a good *stall,* the mark is unaware of what is happening. 2. v.t. To place the victim in a frame so he can be robbed. The frame varies with the location of the wallet.

STAND FOR THE PINCH. v. phr. To *take the rap* voluntarily when arrested or to substitute for someone else who has been arrested.

STASH. 1. n. Money. 2. v.t. To conceal something, especially paper money so that it can be used at a later time.

STEM. n. The street.

STEM COURT. n. phr. The practice of arresting, trying, convicting, and securing a fine from a pickpocket all in the course of a few minutes, usually on the street; a form of the *shakedown.*

STICK. 1. n. A *stall.* 2. v.t. or v.i. To act as a *stall.* 3. v.t. To place the victim in a desired position and hold them there long enough for the *tool* to do his work. 4. v. imper. STICK! An *office* spoken in an undertone or a whisper indicating that the mark is to be held just as he is.

STICK A MARK DOWN. v. phr. For the *stall* to hold a victim firmly.

STICKER. n. A warrant for arrest or a detainer.

STIFF. 1. n. A check, possibly so-called because checks are worthless to pickpockets. 2. n. A newspaper used to shield the movements of the hand during operations. Also a *blute.*

STING. 1. n. A successful thieving act, especially picking a pocket. 2. v.t. To complete a theft.

STIR. n. Prison or jail.

STONE. n. A man's tiepin that has a diamond setting.

STRAPHANGER. n. A pickpocket who tries to avoid his share of the work; one who is not very diligent.

STRIDES. n. Trousers.

STRING. n. A chain attached to a wallet used to secure it to the clothing.

STRONG. adj. Analogous to "depth" in the sense that it reflects the relative force or strength in which a mob is operating, indicating the number of members in a mob.

STUCK. v.t. Victimized; especially to have victimized a mark.

SUCKER. n. A victim or potential victim. Also *apple, chump, egg, mark.*

SUCKER TOWN. n. phr. A town where there is no fix; therefore, once arrested, it may be impossible to *beat the rap* or, at best, very expensive to buy oneself out of trouble.

SUCKER TROUBLE. n. Trouble resulting from arousing suspicions of a victim, although such difficulty does not necessarily imply arrest.

SUMMER CANNON. n. phr. A pickpocket who cannot score on a victim wearing a topcoat; these *tools* often work as *stalls* in the winter or go south where the clothing is lighter.

SUMMERTIME TOOL. n. phr. A *summer cannon.*

SUPER. n. Pickpocket spelling of *souper.*

SURE-THING GRAFTER. n. phr. A mean, cautious, petty thief; one who takes no risks and plays for small scores. Mostly applied to carnival flat joint guys and therefore somewhat archaic.

SWAMP. 1. v.t. To use very rough and open stalling techniques, such as obviously jostling, bumping, or crowding victims. 2. v.t. To be arrested.

SWING. v.t. or v.i. To execute a theft; to make away with it.

SWING UNDERNEATH WITH IT. v. phr. To conceal an object that is being shoplifted under a skirt (woman) or overcoat (man).

TAIL. 1. v.t. To follow. 2. n. The person who does the following. 3. n. Term used by East Coast black pickpockets to indicate the side pocket of a suit coat.

TAIL PIT. n. phr. *Coattail* (black terminology).

TAKE. 1. v.t. or v.i. To be susceptible to bribery; said of a police officer. 2. v.t. To victimize; to pick a mark's pockets. 3. n. The proceeds of grifting or hustling for a given time period.

TAKE A BANG. v. phr. To inject drugs directly into the vein; to fix.

TAKE A FALL. v. phr. To be arrested.

TAKE A MARK OUT. v. phr. To follow a victim known to have money or valuables on his person: especially to follow him out of a bank, ticket office, etc. Also *bring (someone) out, take (someone) out.*

TAKE A POWDER. v. phr. To jump bail. Also *take a fence, take it on the á.d.* (for Arthur Duffy, a dancer), *take it on the lam, take it on the heel and toe.*

TAKE A RAP. v. phr. See *stand for the pinch.*

TAKE A SCORE. v. phr. To get a wallet or roll of money into one's possession; to complete a theft.

TAKE OFF. v.t. To steal.

TAKE OUT. See *bring a mark out.*

TAKE THE FENCE. v. phr. See *take a powder.*

TEAM. n. A whiz mob, especially a two-handed mob.

TEAR-OFF KIDS. n. phr. A *rip and tear* mob.

THIEVES' BLOOD. n. phr. Literally, the blood of a pickpocket, which is believed to be passed from one generation to the next; thus, a thief whose relatives, especially his mother or father, were thieves has stealing in him genetically and is therefore more likely to be a successful thief himself (pickpocket lore).

THIEVING CON. n. phr. A railroad conductor, bus driver, or interurban conductor who permits pickpockets to work his run for a fee. See *kayducer, kinky kayducer.*

THIEVING COPPER. n. phr. A policeman who can be fixed; a *right copper.*

THIMBLE. n. A watch; an *onion.*

THIN OUT. v.i. To dwindle in size, as a crowd dispersing.

THIRD RAIL. n. phr. A pickpocket who works the subways during rush hours.

THIRD RAIL MOB. n. phr. A pickpocket mob that works subways.

THREE ESSES. n. phr. Short for shit, shine, and shave—the usual excuses for being late for a *meet.*

THREE-HANDED MOB. n. phr. A pickpocket troupe with two *stalls* and one *tool.*

THROAT. See *by the throat.*

THROW A NIGHT. v. phr. To have a party or raffle to help raise funds for a pickpocket who has been beset by undue financial difficulties such as an unusually high fine or legal fees.

THROW IT. See *ding* (a poke).

THROW (ONE'S) MOB. v. phr. For a pickpocket to betray other members of his troupe to the police or to leave a confederate in the hands of the police without offering to help him.

THROW THE HUMP. v. phr. For a *stall* to work the victim advantageously to the *tool;* usually this is done with the hips, back, and/or elbows, but not always.

THROW THE MITT. v. phr. To work; to pick pockets.

TIFFANY SETTING. n. phr. A ring with the stone held by prongs (jeweler's term).

TIP. n. A crowd or the event at which the crowd has assembled.

TIP OFF. v.t. To give confidential information to someone or about someone.

TIP OFF THE RACKET. v. phr. To tell someone how pickpockets operate.

TOG. n. An overcoat or topcoat used to distract the victim or to conceal the action of the *tool*. Sometimes also expanded to include raincoats, sweaters, or other garments so used. May also refer to clothing worn by a victim.

TOG PIT. n. phr. An inside breast pocket in a topcoat.

TOG TAIL. n. phr. An outside topcoat pocket.

TOO HOT. adj. phr. A situation where there are many complaints being registered by victims with the fix *curdling* as a consequence.

TOOL. n. A pickpocket who commits the theft as opposed to the *stall*, who prepares the victim for the *tool's* attention. Also *hook*, *wire*.

TOP. 1. n. The total take for the day, as in *off the top* (*cap*). 2. v.t. To turn a wallet on end before removing it. 3. v.t. To *reef a score* close enough to the pocket opening for it to be *forked* out.

TOP BRIDGE or TOP BRITCH. n. phr. A side pocket in trousers so made that the opening of the pocket is parallel or almost parallel to the belt.

TOUCH. 1. n. A single theft; the act of stealing a wallet. 2. v.t. To steal money from someone. 3. v.t. To feel or *fan* a prospective victim so as to locate his wallet or money; usually done by the *tool*. Sometimes *touch up*. Also *locate*.

TRAP. n. Any place where payment is required to enter through a turnstile and exiting must be accomplished by riding out, as on a subway.

TRIBE. n. A group of pickpockets.

TRICK. n. A professional act; a theft.

TRIM. v.t. To steal from.

TROUPE. n. A pickpocket mob; the term is usually used by police.

TUMBLE. 1. n. A suspicion; an inkling that all is not well. 2. n. An arrest. 3. v.t. To suspect. 4. v.t. To arrest.

TURN. v.t. To count the money taken from the day's work or from several wallets.

TURN (INTO). v.t. For a *stall* to maneuver a victim into a position where the *tool* can work effectively.

TURN OUT. 1. v.t. To initiate someone into the rackets; to start a novice out with a grifting mob. 2. v.t. To take up the racket or enter it as a professional. 3. n. Release from the custody of the police.

TURN OVER. v.t. To examine anything, especially a wallet, to see how much money it contains.

TURN TURTLE. v. phr. To become a stool pigeon.

TWEEZER or TWEEZER POKE. n. A pocketbook or pocket wallet that is fastened with small clasps.

TWIST. n. A woman, especially a woman pickpocket. From *twist and twirl* (Australian rhyming argot for girl).

TWIST MOB. See *moll mob*.

TWO-HANDED JUG MOB. n. phr. A team of pickpockets who work outside a bank.

TWO-HANDED MOB. n. phr. Two pickpockets working together—a *tool* and a *stall*.

UNLOAD. v.t. 1. To dispose of wallets or purses that have been emptied of their contents. *Class cannons* put these emptied objects in a mailbox; hence, the victims often have them returned by police since they still contain identification—and often other materials the victims are glad to have returned. *Rip and tear mobs* throw them anywhere. 2. To pick the pockets of a crowd streaming from an exit or alighting from a train, bus, etc.

UNSLOUGH. n. An office indicating that the front man is to unbutton the victim's overcoat or raincoat so that the *tool* can get into his pockets.

UPTOWN BRITCH. n. phr. A front pants pocket.

VEST INSIDER. n. phr. The inside pocket of a vest.

VEST JERVE. n. phr. An outside vest pocket.

VEST KICK. n. phr. A pocket in a vest.

VISE. n. The frame in which the victim is held while being robbed, especially a very light frame where he is held helpless for the instant necessary for the *tool* to work. Marks are not conscious of a good vise.

WEAR THE GLOVES. v. phr. To avoid taking a fair share of the risk.

WEED. 1. v.t. To remove money from a stolen wallet, often while the wallet is still in the victim's possession. 2. v.t. For a member of a mob to remove surreptitiously money from a wallet while it is being handled and before the common *knock up* is divided. Considered very unethical, especially by those who are not clever enough to do it.

WHISKERS. 1. n. Any federal official. 2. n. A federal check.

WHISKERS STIFFS. n. Government checks.

WHITE OUTFIT. n. phr. A watch and chain made of white gold or silver.

WHIZ. n. A pickpocket or the profession of picking pockets. Probably from *wizard* but cut back to *wiz* by folk etymology and then to *whiz* by dialectal variation.

WHIZ COPPER. n. A pickpocket detective.

WHIZ DETAIL. n. phr. The pickpocket squad of a police force.

WHIZ MOB. n. A mob of pickpockets.

WHIZ MOLL. n. A woman pickpocket.

WHIZZER. n. A pickpocket.

WILD TOOL. n. phr. A *tool* that is not too careful about rumbling his victim, although this does not mean that he is not a skilled pickpocket. A *wild tool* will try any method to secure the score.

WINNER. n. A successful operator.

WIPE. n. A handkerchief, clipped from *wiper*.

WIPER KICK. n. phr. The outside breast pocket.

WIRE. n. A *tool*. The member of the mob that does the stealing.

WORK. 1. v.i. To be active professionally; to ply a criminal craft. 2. v.t. To grift a specific locality or steal from certain persons, as to *work a get-on, work a right spot, work a tip.* 3. n. The actual business of lifting the wallet from the pocket.

WORK BEHIND THE BIG TOP. v. phr. To work the circus grift.

WORK BLIND. 1. v. phr. To work without the protection of the fix. 2. v. phr. To work with no predetermined plan or thought about which suckers should be victimized. This is often done to build up the *working nut.*

WORKING NUT. n. phr. The expenses connected with grifting; overhead. Also the *nut.*

WORKING RIGHT. v. phr. Operating with the cooperation of the police. See *doing business, grifting right.*

WORKING STIFF. n. phr. Anyone who works legitimately for a living; implies blue-collar status usually.

WORKING WITH AN EDGE. v. phr. Working with the cooperation or protection of the law. Also *hustling with pro* (East Coast), *working with a shade* (Midwest), *working with the odds.*

WORK ON THE SNEAK. v. phr. To work without the protection of the fix or other advance arrangements.

WORK (SOMEONE) OVER. v.t. To beat someone up; especially for a policeman to assault a pickpocket.

WORKS. n. 1. Someone *on the rackets.* 2. The law, specifically a policeman, usually a plainclothesman.

WRONG. adj. 1. When applied to a policeman or police protection it indicates that the fix is not established or secure. A *wrong copper* is one who will not take a bribe or cooperate with police who have an arrangement with the thieves; a *wrong town* is one where the fix is not dependable, or where it does not operate. 2. When applied to a person, especially one on the whiz, it implies that the individual is a stool pigeon. 3. When applied to being arrested or sentenced, it implies that the charge is false or not deserved; a *wrong pinch* is one for a crime the thief did not commit; a *wrong rap* is an undeserved or trumped-up charge for which the pickpocket is held.

X. n. Any exclusive arrangement giving an individual or mob certain privileges such as an arrangement with authorities to permit a mob to work a certain area or to steal from certain types of individuals within that area.

YELL. v.i. To complain or to file a formal complaint with the law; to *beef gun.*

18

The Argot of the Criminal Narcotic Addict

This material is taken from the fourth edition of *Narcotics and Narcotic Addiction* (1973) which Victor H. Vogel and I first conceived in 1951 as a possible avenue of information to the general public. Dr. Vogel had considerable clinical experience with drug addicts, and for several years I had been doing sociolinguistic research work among addicts who supported themselves by crime.

In 1952 we began work on this book, largely as a response to an upsurge in drug abuse, especially among the young people, the like of which had not been recorded in the history of Western culture. That time now seems far removed for in those days it was not fashionable to admit that there was a drug problem in the United States; nor was it respectable to delineate this problem in a book comprehensible to any educated reader. The full powers of repression within the establishment were brought to bear on us to prevent publication—at times even reaching the point of harassment. The United States Public Health Service reprimanded Dr. Vogel for referring to drug abuse as an "epidemic," and the Bureau of Narcotics was determined to keep all technical knowledge of drug abuse in a classified category, their assumption being that to inform people about drug abuse was to encourage it on an even wider scale. The philosophy at that time seemed to be that if we spent enough money for enforcement and said as little as possible about the problem, it might go away.

In the ensuing years, as we all know, the problem has not gone away. The subculture of drug users has expanded and engulfed multitudes of people in the dominant culture. Not only have users increased a thousandfold, but powerful new drugs like LSD, PCB, DMT, methadone, and the methamphetamines have given new and sinister dimensions to drug abuse.

It is the earmark of our culture to deal with problems on the basis of law, and while many problems yield to this approach, the drug problem has remained singularly recalcitrant. The reason for this is that we have attempted to handle drug abuse in terms of legal controls, with severe penalties falling on the victims of the drug and largely bypassing the powerful syndicates who grow rich on the traffic. Meanwhile, we appear to have learned little from experience.

The section of this book which deals with the argot of addicts does so in a broad sense by including data on both the language and behavior patterns of a rapidly diffusing subculture. All the material included here has been collected over the period from 1935 to 1973, and during this period the argot was continuously sampled in various large centers of addiction at Lexington, Kentucky, Fort Worth, Texas, and Corona, California, where many users were gathered from all sections of the country. I do not know of any other argot that has been subjected to study over a similar period of time and comparable geographic spread. Therefore, this chapter contains a good deal of information about argots: their genesis, the social and linguistic forces that spur their growth, their diffusion into the dominant culture, and the cycles through which specialized languages pass in the subculture. This diffusion of the narcotic subculture is still actively progressing.

• • •

THE SOCIAL ASPECTS OF ARGOT FORMATION

IT IS BASIC to human social organization that whenever people are closely associated, they develop certain special aspects of language, often on several different levels. Most trades and occupations, for instance, carry with them a specialized vocabulary which not only is useful in the performance and perpetuation of the work pattern, but gives status to the worker. Thus printers, sailors, railroaders, physicians, etc., develop a sort of occupational language which is functional as well as social in its nature. In addition to vocabulary, many other aspects of language are specialized to the group, such as intonation pattern, stress pattern, voice quality, et cetera. Furthermore, a whole series of body and facial movements accompany speech and amplify it significantly. These kinesic gestures are correlated with language in ways that are not yet fully understood.

Sometimes these specialized linguistic phenomena are associated with religion or sacred ritual, and, among primitive peoples, we may find the language used by warriors on the warpath, or the language used by priests or medicine men, considered as sacred and often kept completely secret from the outgroup. The presence of these sacred languages among Stone Age people shows us that this tendency in language is very very old, and perhaps fundamental to human society.

When we go into the underworld we find that the forces which motivate the formation and use of secret or semi-secret languages are intensified. First, legitimate society is organized against the professional criminal, who may experience both social and economic ostracism during his entire lifetime. Professional criminals, on the other hand, have formed a counter organization in order to protect themselves as best they can from the pressures of legitimate society expressed through the law.

Second, because the criminal organization is much tighter than the organization of the legitimate world, it is extremely powerful, and part of its power emanates from the close-knit structure made possible by the fact that all criminals share certain habits, certain stigmata and certain security problems in common. Within some occupational groups, this group solidarity is greater than in others, but in all groups it is observable to some degree, and finds expression not only in mannerisms, beliefs and customs, but most characteristically in the use of language. Speech patterns reflect the behavior patterns of the group, as well as the traditions and group subculture, insofar as this rudimentary culture differentiates the criminal group from legitimate society on the one hand, and from other criminal groups on the other. To a greater or lesser degree the language of the group is semi secret; it is, in effect, a union card, for it is difficult for an outsider to know and use the argot like a professional. These argots are keys to the behavior patterns as well as the techniques used by various specialized criminal groups.

Third, the modern underworld is composed of four or five major social and occupational divisions, within which there are literally hundreds of specific criminal activities. A professional criminal is usually identified loosely with one of the social divisions and speaks the idiom common to that division, in addition, of course, to standard English, on whatever level he would normally use it. Furthermore, he knows and uses the specialized vocabulary of the specific racket or rackets with which he makes his living. These aspects of language in the underworld are called argots, and a confidence man, for instance, would speak the general argot of the *grift,* with special reference to the *big con* or the *short con;* he might further specialize his vocabulary according to the individual con games which he consistently practices. Some widely experienced operators will know and use several argots, and have a peripheral knowledge of several more, but these individuals are increasingly rare.

We now know that each of the many subdivisions of professional criminals constitutes what we might call a subculture or micro system, which is a cultural entity differing both in behavior pattern and language from the dominant culture. Some of these subcultures are almost outside the dominant culture and have little in common with it—as, for instance, the gypsies. Others, like the confidence rackets, share many cultural indices with the dominant culture, and simulate the behavior of successful business men so well that good big con men are usually accepted in very respectable financial circles; they have to be to operate. While we do not know exactly how subcultures begin, we suspect that language is a strong factor in their origin and survival.

When a professional criminal learns his occupation, as, for instance, thievery, with specialization as a pickpocket, he starts with the very specialized techniques of pocket picking in terms of a specific language. More than that, he constantly thinks of his occupation in terms of that language and discusses his work with other pickpockets in terms of their common language. In other words, his entire occupational frame of reference is both technical and linguistic, and the language is fundamental not only to the perpetuation of the craft of thievery but to its practice.

Last, a professional criminal usually takes great pride in his craft. He identifies himself with it very closely and rationalizes its importance in the underworld and his importance within the group in a way which is satisfying to his own sense of self-importance. To each individual, a knowledge of the language of his own craft, as well as perhaps that of several others, is a mark of status in the underworld. Also, it furnishes identification and provides him with recognition. Among people who live and work constantly under a legal, social and perhaps moral stigma, this element of recognition is very important.

Thus we see that the formation of specialized argots within the underworld is a natural phenomenon, and we know from having explored many of the highly specialized rackets, together with their appropriate argots, that a vast body of secret and semisecret language is used by people in the underworld. As yet it is imperfectly explored, and its relationship to the legitimate language has not been fully charted. However, we have observed that professional criminals operating in a certain technical and social area developed a specialized argot, while nonprofessional or occasional criminals performing similar criminal acts as individuals do not know or develop a specialized language pattern. For instance, a professional killer or *torpedo* for a racket mob will know and use the argot of his profession fluently; a psychopathic murderer who might well have committed more murders in a lifetime than the professional killer will not develop any standardized language pattern in connection with murder. A bank teller might indeed embezzle more money over a period of years than a competent professional *heel thief* would steal (and both would take it from behind the cashier's window), yet the embezzler would have no knowledge of the argot spoken by the thief, nor would he form an argot to be used in speaking or thinking about his own criminal activities. An individual forger will never develop an argot on his own, but professional passers of forged checks have a well-defined argot, though they almost always work alone. While legitimate gamblers have some slang (largely borrowed from professionals), those who gamble professionally in the underworld have a large and highly developed argot.

We now know that the so-called *underworld* is nothing more than an aggregate of criminal subcultures, all parasitic on the dominant culture and each distinct from the others to a variable degree. Each of these subcultures has its own characteristic behavior pattern, including mores, technology, modes of defense against the dominant culture, attitudes toward professional crime, bi-sexuality, etc. Language is one of the most significant of these subcultural indices.

Argots, then, are a reflection of social structure. They are learned and transmitted and used within organized groups in the practice of a criminal profession. They are indeed the earmark of the professional. They are used almost entirely within the in-group and are spoken almost exclusively in the presence of other members of that group. Contrary to popular belief, argots are seldom used to deceive victims, to mystify noncriminals or to fool the police. In fact, they are seldom used at all in the presence of outsiders.

Because argots reflect the way of life within the group, and the way of life within many professional criminal groups is insecure and sometimes dramatic, the language pattern of those groups is often vivid and salty. For thousands of years the argots of professional criminals in many languages have constituted a fresh source of vivid phraseology which is used to enrich the standard languages spoken and written by noncriminals. As far back as the *Satyricon* of Petronius, for instance, we find that much of the author's freshness stems from his lively use of the argots of the Roman underworld. In the Golden Age of Spanish literature, it was fashionable for writers, some of them great, to affect the usage of thieves, vagabonds and swindlers; this custom was carried so far that today much of the writing of an author like Francisco de Quevedo defies exact translation; in fact, during the seventeenth century, a whole literary genre, the picaresque novel, concerned itself with the adventures of thieves, written in what passed for a reasonable facsimile of their own language. This school of writing was popular not only in Spain, but all over Europe. Shakespeare borrowed freely from the underworld argots of his day, and other Elizabethans, like Thomas Dekker, acquired a very accurate firsthand knowledge of criminal argots. Such masters as Defoe, Fielding, Smollett and Sterne flavored their literary vocabularies not only with older underworld terms, but with contemporary eighteenth century argot phrases which were strong and colorful. Today, most popular slang is borrowed or discarded from the underworld, but the closed corporation of modern bigtime crime makes current argots less accessible to modern writers than were the argots of the Renaissance, when it was fashionable for gentlemen and writers to rub shoulders with rogues.

However, it is only within recent years that linguists have realized the importance and the extent of the contribution which criminal groups make to standard usage in all civilized languages. Naturally, when words and phrases from criminal groups become widely used by outsiders, those words are usually replaced by others known only within the profession, so that criminal argots are often less stable than standard language, with a high birth rate of words balanced by a high death rate within the ingroups, and a relatively low survival rate compared to standard language.

These birth, death and survival rates are also influenced by the fact that most criminal argots are not generally written, and almost never printed. Argots live principally in the minds and on the tongues of individual speakers, and the turnover in terminology is frequently very great, especially among those argots which, through contact with legitimate people, become known outside the ingroup. Some criminal argots, however, remain surprisingly stable, with a portion of the vocabulary becoming almost traditional. While in this study we are mainly concerned with words, or lexical elements, it should be noted that argots differ from the standard language in some aspects of structure, and especially in intonation, pitch and juncture. These are now being investigated in the argots used by professionals.

The importance of a study of argots has been recognized only recently, with the realization among psychologists, anthropologists and linguists that the language of any group is one of the most reliable keys to the culture pattern; and, since this culture pattern is not so obvious or so easily observed as the life pattern of the groups which do not operate outside the law, a knowledge of the argot is not only useful in penetrating the ingroups, but is essential to understanding the motives, the techniques and the attitudes of the professional criminal.

A study of these linguistic phenomena implies a simultaneous anthropological study of the subcultures in the same depth with which some primitive cultures have been studied. At present, we can only make some generalizations about them with some degree of validity.

First, subcultures and specialized linguistic phenomena seem to arise spontaneously and simultaneously; language seems to lie at the heart of their cultural genesis. They develop against the background of a dominant culture already highly sophisticated in handling symbols, and this tends to shape the subcultures into entities of special symbolism, all of which tends to nurture a heightened sense of group identity.

Second, subcultures really begin to expand and intensify and differentiate when pressures from the dominant culture are generated. In fact, it appears that, without some of these pressures, subcultures become abortive or tend to atrophy. There must be a threat from the dominant culture—or from other subcultures—and this threat intensifies the internal pressures already at work. The language indigenous to the subculture tends to intensify the attitudes, values and technology which characterize the group. The development of techniques, especially those which may be a threat to the dominant culture, may be disapproved or suppressed, which excites increased linguistic activity, usually accompanied by an intensification of internal cohesive forces and an increased emphasis on secrecy.

This special language or argot is a strong influence toward homogeneity; through it, group identity is further developed, and, as the subculture becomes stronger, it tends to pull away from the dominant culture, becoming more aware of itself as its communication system becomes more versatile. It comes to believe what it hears, and is more positive in what it says. The behavior pattern shapes itself ever closer to what the group says it is and what its acts prove it to be.

Third, when the dominant culture senses the presence of a criminal subculture, it tends to draw away, and this dichotomy increases the differentiation, which process is speeded up as social distance becomes more and more obvious.

It is not accidental that the dominant culture usually first becomes aware of an emerging criminal subculture through the leakage of terms and idioms from this group. At first these new expressions provoke humor, derision and some curiosity in the dominant culture. As soon as it becomes apparent that they have linked with them a hostile and even sinister behavior pattern, the dominant culture manifests first fear, then hostility. The dominant culture may counterattack with suppressive measures—usually enacting a new law or the shoring up of an old one—for society has a firm belief that a new law, and preferably a very stiff one, will take care of everything. Increased pressure provokes stronger resistance, and there is now a minor power struggle in the making. By this time, the subculture has structured a set of laws of its own—often more severe and more rigorously enforced than those of the dominant culture—and has no intention of accepting the laws of the dominant culture. However, we of the dominant culture still cling to the myth that we can convert professional criminals into law-abiding citizens if we only apply enough law, enough psychiatry, or both.

Last, we might note that this hostility between the dominant culture and various criminal subcultures has characterized the growth of American civilization. Indeed, there have been times in our history—and this by no means excludes the present—when highly organized criminal subcultures have taken over entire communities and even large cities. When these subcultures maintain an exclusive membership, a tight code of enforcement and the utilization of pressures from the dominant culture to strengthen their own subsystem, they become formidable indeed. Such a group is the modern Mafia, which is well nigh untouchable. Sometimes these subcultures have been battled, in the past often in bloody fashion, by vigilante-type splinter groups from the dominant culture, with very little real law involved in the struggle. Sometimes, also, the dominant culture has been dismayed when the very people who subdued the criminal subcultures (which are usually only driven out, not exterminated or effectively subdued) turned out to be mere exploiters of these groups for their own profit after the furor died down. This is the cycle of so-called "reform" governments on the local level in the United States.

ARGOTS AND THE NARCOTIC ADDICT

Narcotic addicts fall into two main groups. First, there are those legitimate people who become addicted but who do not resort to organized crime to support their habits. They do not secure their drugs from underworld sources or habitually associate with underworld characters. These people have no knowledge of the argot of the underworld narcotic addict, and modify or utilize colloquial or medical terminology when they think of or discuss the use of drugs. A second larger group of addicts inhabits the underworld, lives by a criminal profession, secures its drugs from underworld dealers or peddlers and associates with other addicts. These addicts know and use the argot of the underworld addict. It is with this group that we are particularly concerned.

It is important to note that addiction is very common in some underworld professions and rare in others, that it is acceptable in some professions, even highly respectable ones (from the underworld point of view) and not acceptable in others. For example, among professional thieves the incidence of narcotic addiction is very high, and addiction is socially acceptable among most thieves, especially pickpockets and shoplifters. The authors estimate addiction among thieves at between 60 and 70 per cent, depending upon the type of thievery. On the other hand, among stick up mobs, bank robbers, payroll bandits, etc., the incidence of narcotic addiction is very low, and addiction is looked upon as a sign of weakness and unreliability.

We should also note that different groups of professional criminals have differing attitudes toward the use of various drugs. Old-time safecrackers, for example, accepted the smoking of opium as a gentleman's vice, and this toleration of the use of opium is still found in some of the higher brackets among the underworld, noticeably among big time professional gamblers and big time confidence men. These same groups, and especially the old-timers in these groups, tended to reject the use of the needle along with morphine, heroin, etc., although some of them accepted the needle as a substitute for the pipe only because the smoking of opium while traveling was too cumbersome and too dangerous. There is also a tendency at the present time for those criminal groups who accept the use of narcotics by needle to look down upon those who use narcotics by other methods, or those who use other types of drugs. A mob of professional thieves who use morphine, for instance, would not accept a marijuana user on a level of equality; in fact, they would distrust him completely and would probably refuse to recognize marijuana as a drug of addiction. Among modern heroin users, however, this pattern is changing, since so many of them started with marijuana and consequently carry over into heroin addiction their earlier argot usage connected with marijuana. In a sense, they have "corrupted" the argot of the users of hard drugs by needle in something of the same manner that needle addicts corrupted the argot of the old-time opium smoker.

Among underworld addicts, the use of various drugs, then, carries with it varying status in different groups, with opium smoking still remaining the almost inaccessible preference of the aristocrats of the underworld. Furthermore, among some underworld groups, the size of the habit is an important index to status, with those who support large habits feeling more important and receiving more recognition than those who have small habits, this recognition being more common among professionals in the lower brackets. This differentiation is in part influenced by economic considerations, since, with drugs at the present high prices, a professional who can support a large habit must *ipso facto* be sufficiently successful at his profession. However, among opium smokers, the support of a small regular habit is considered a gentleman's privilege, but at the same time, successful big time criminals do not as a rule regard overindulgence in opium as a mark of distinction; in fact, quite the reverse. The opium addict who can hold his habit down to a reasonable level is considered *smart*. The same thing is true of alcohol, for it implies a high degree of self-control. *Big-con* men, for example, almost never drink while they are working.

Also in the underworld a distinction is made between the individual who supports a narcotic habit as a luxury which interferes to a small extent or not at all with the practice of his profession, and the one who works at a criminal profession for the sole purpose of supporting a habit. Usually, the latter type tends to degenerate in his profession, to lose status among his associates and to go downhill rapidly.

Professional criminals who use narcotics have a tendency to work together; thus, a nonaddict may work temporarily with a mob whose members are addicted, but he will probably not enjoy this association, nor will a nonaddict mob accept without reservations a member who is addicted, despite his skill or special abilities. Temporary or fill in work would be an exception. This acceptance or rejection, while partly based on moral and social reasons, is primarily a result of the physical limitations which addiction places upon an individual. An addict must maintain regular contact with sources of supply; he must withdraw from his work at very regular time intervals in order to take drugs, which may appear to others to be an unsavory and time consuming process; the transportation of drugs and equipment may be difficult among traveling mobs; and the possession of these articles constitutes a safety hazard for the rest of the mob, since drugs and equipment for using them might cause the arrest of a mob or involve the entire mob in difficulties not connected with the usual hazards of their work. Furthermore, among nonaddict criminals, the taking of narcotics is often looked upon as distasteful, and nonaddicted professionals have a tendency to distrust addicts; however, addicts work rather well together in mobs since their problems are the same, and since they have all accepted the phenomenon of addiction. Thus a pickpocket mob will stop work at certain intervals to take narcotics, one member of the mob may do the purchasing of narcotics for the entire mob, and needles and accessories someimes are shared, though a certain class of addicts prefer not to share this equipment.

In addition to associations on the road or in the course of a criminal occupation, narcotic addicts have a tendency to gather in taverns, restaurants, saloons and other places where it is convenient to meet. Sometimes these establishments supply drugs, or someone living near them can be contacted in order to secure drugs. Also, addicts sometimes congregate in the places where drugs are supplied to users. Some addicts cannot use the needle themselves or prefer not to, and require the services of an attendant to make the injection.

Where opium is smoked, a chef (either professional or amateur) is always available to cook the pills for the smokers. In these establishments (usually referred to in literature as *opium dens* but known to the addicts as *hop joints* or *lay down joints*), conversation is lively, and addicts enjoy associating with their friends. Among opium smokers, especially where the smoking is done in groups, conversation is a notable concomitant to smoking; the general sense of well-being and mental relaxation tends to stimulate conversation. This tendency to converse, often on a high intellectual level, has been noted by noncriminal opium smokers—such as the artists and writers of Paris and other Bohemian centers—but seems to be notably absent among needle addicts, who like to coast and enjoy the drug subjectively.

At these meeting places, addicts confer and gossip freely, and here the argot is coined and transmitted. Since many of these addicts are in trouble with the law rather frequently, they carry the argot into the jails and eventually into the prisons.

In both these institutions, addicts have a tendency to congregate and to connive in order to secure drugs, a procedure which is not too difficult in most correctional institutions if the addict or his friends outside have any money. In prisons, the argot of the narcotic addict is recognized as different from the argot of the other professional groups, and the association of addicts in prisons tends to stimulate the production and use of argot.

Within the past few years, the close fraternity of addiction (which was previously tightly closed to outsiders) has been invaded by literally thousands of newcomers, many of them youngsters under twenty-one who, twenty years ago, could never have penetrated the underworld circles where they now circulate freely. While underworld opiate addicts formerly excluded the *weed heads* or marijuana users from their company, the marijuana traffic has now become vast and immensely profitable; furthermore, young marijuana smokers can become opiate addicts almost overnight. Years ago, most drug addicts were over thirty, and a juvenile addict had yet to be encountered. All this activity has not only introduced a vast new class of addicts, but has also disturbed the argot. Phraseology which, forty years ago, was standard and well stabilized to opium smokers or needle addicts, is now used in all sorts of new and unorthodox ways by the younger generation of addicts; furthermore, the drastic changes in the bootleg market and in the drugs available, as well as in the rackets adopted by addicts to support their habits, have forced the incorporation of many new terms and the corruption of many older ones. The conservative, sometimes dignified and intelligent opium smoker has given way to an increasing number of cool needle pushers and marijuana smokers who are not only playing havoc with the drugs of addiction, but with the argot as well. Consequently, one hears some surprising adaptations and applications of what was formerly a fairly stable argot.

Also, among addicts there is a very close relationship between argot usage and the psychic and physical effect of drugs. As addicts verbalize their reactions to drugs, they also reinforce the effect which these drugs have on them, and the association of certain terms with specific experiences tends to create an associative pattern which undoubtedly plays a part in the satisfaction which the addict gets from the use of the argot. Many terms in the argot describe vividly and graphically not only the effects which drugs or abstinence from drugs produce, but also, by use of metaphor and suggestion, relate the sensations derived from drugs to other physical and emotional sensations, notably those connected with sex.

Although many underworld people are strongly inclined to be gregarious, addicts are especially so; as soon as two or more gather, the conversation turns to drugs, which may be consumed simultaneously with the visiting and gossiping that goes on among the users.

This tendency to give drugs a prominent place in the conversation increases noticeably when addicts gather in places where drugs are not readily available, such as a prison, a narcotic hospital or jail, where the talk of narcotics is continuous and intense.

Historically, the argot of the narcotic addict is interesting for several reasons. First of all, it seems to spring from the language used by opium smokers; some old-time smokers have retained the basic argot, much of it Chinese or Oriental in origin, which they learned thirty or forty years ago; however, as pipe smokers were forced by circumstances to take up the needle and substitute morphine or heroin for opium, a good deal of the pipe smokers' argot was adapted to the use of narcotics injected hypodermically. Now many younger addicts are quite unaware that much of their argot is derived from the opium traffic. Also, marijuana smoking on a large scale is relatively new in the United States; marijuana apparently entered through New Orleans about 1910. It became obvious as a problem about 1935, and its use has since expanded tremendously, so that there are now more marijuana smokers than all other types of narcotic addicts combined. For a time the users of opiate drugs refused to accept marijuana smokers into the fraternity, and the argot of marijuana smokers was looked upon with contempt by opiate addicts. Now, however, with many young marijuana smokers turning to heroin, the argot of the marijuana smoker is no longer so distinct a phenomenon, and much of it is being accepted into the general argot of the narcotic addict.

It is probable that the smoking of marijuana has been carried on in the United States from colonial days to the present, though on a very small scale and in isolated communities. The impetus which brought about the present popularity of marijuana in the last few years seems to have come from Mexico, Central America and Cuba. Because of the close association between swing or rock music and the consumption of marijuana, the marijuana smoker has not only adopted much of the slang and argot characteristic of rock music, but has contributed heavily to it. Some of it also comes from the black-and-tan joints, the tea pads and the brothels of such large metropolitan centers as Los Angeles, San Francisco, San Antonio, New Orleans, Memphis, Louisville, St. Louis, Chicago, Cleveland, Pittsburgh and New York. The important centers in the evolution of the slang of popular music, however, have been New Orleans, Chicago and New York. Furthermore, many youngsters are quite familiar with the language of the musician including some of the argot of the marijuana smoker, and use it freely even though they are not smokers.

The argot of the marijuana smoker, then, is somewhat different from the argot of opiate users in character, imagery, connotation and in the life pattern reflected. Compared to the argot of opiate users it appears to the authors to reflect the very different type of person who uses marijuana, the marijuana user usually being young, naive and unseasoned while the opiate addicts, especially the old-timers, are cynical, sharp-witted, mature and rich in life experience. Especially among the ranks of the opium smokers there are some brilliant minds to whom the carefully turned phrase and the meaningful metaphor are very important.

To some extent, the argot of the addict is affected by the kind of drug he consumes and the method by which he takes it. For instance, addicts who sniff cocaine or heroin may have very little knowledge of the argot of the needle addict—until their increased tolerance forces them to substitute injection for sniffing; if they continue to take cocaine or heroin by inhalation indefinitely (a very unusual circumstance), they might never become aware of the argot of the needle addict; however, most needle addicts are familiar with the phraseology of those who sniff drugs, since large numbers of needle addicts were formerly inhalers. Users of drugs like Benzedrine and the barbiturates may never become familiar with the argot of the opiate addicts unless they are thrown with these addicts in intimate association. Even so, users of Benzedrine are looked upon by opiate addicts in much the same light as are marijuana smokers. Perhaps they are even less acceptable to the fraternity than users of marijuana. Also, it is noticeable that the users of barbiturates and Benzedrine have contributed very little to the argot of narcotic addiction. Neither have the addicts who take drugs by mouth been very active in developing the argot, with the possible exception of opium addicts, who eat opium or drink it in solution; these addicts usually know the argot of opiate addiction and use it, largely because sooner or later they go to the needle themselves.

The argot used by narcotic addicts, then, reflects rather vividly the way of life of the addict—the ecstasy of narcotics, the necessity for escape from the world of reality, the compensatory effect of drugs upon the inadequate personality, the constant preoccupation with the needle as a symbol, the eventual exclusion of all other motives for living and the complete preoccupation with the necessity for securing drugs. There is also the ever present evidence of the substitution of drugs for sexual activity. A study of this argot has already proved of value to psychoanalysts, psychiatrists and sociologists, since through the argot the addict unwittingly reveals a considerable portion of the unconscious which is preoccupied with addiction.

On the whole, relatively little of the argot of the underworld addict passes into general usage while it is currently popular in criminal circles, although, as time goes by, a rather large body of archaic or obsolescent argot finds its way into the language of the dominant culture. As new terms appear, the ones which they replace often are discarded, sometimes because they are already beginning to be used by squares. A great number of terms, however, seem to remain in the argot for a long time and do not seep out into the dominant culture. Much of the argot which does get out develops meanings somewhat different from those used within the addict subculture. However, the argot used by underworld addicts is definitely expanding in size, and it is still obscure to the outsider. Therefore, a rather comprehensive glossary of words and phrases associated with addiction is appended.

Several points should be made regarding this material, which has been collected from practically all regions of the United States where addiction is at all common. It represents the usage of literally hundreds of addicts, although it is unlikely that any one addict would know all the terms included, since no single addict is familiar either with all geographical regions or all the social classes from which the usage has been collected. Certain subcultures are open to some addicts, closed to others; from these subcultures, only the terms used by these criminals *as addicts* have been included, since otherwise the whole of these specialized languages would have to be treated. However, with the proliferation of addicts into some subcultures from which they were largely excluded fifteen or twenty years ago, even in the marginal status which they now have, some of the words from these specialized subcultures are beginning to appear in the general usage of addicts. Also, only a small portion of the data collected on each word can be included here because of the need for condensation.

Readers with a linguistic background who use this material will note immediately that there is an apparent inconsistency in the forms used in each main entry. This is deliberate, since many terms have incomplete paradigms, with the form listed usually being the most common, or in some cases, the only form used. For example, some terms occur only in the plural, others only or mostly in a participial form. Verbs defined as infinitives usually have a complete, or hypothetically complete, set of paradigms. Many idioms have a variable usage, and only one or two illustrations are given from the many recorded.

Cross-referencing is somewhat irregular, since many items which are near synonyms but have slight differences in meaning nccd to be linked together for the general reader. There has been a rather close cross-referencing of terms intimately connected with drugs and addiction, since that is the main concern of this book, while terms less closely associated with addiction are not cross-referenced or rather loosely treated in this respect. The spelling is somewhat arbitrary, since most of the words are taken from verbal usage and must be rendered in graphics according to the best judgment of the writers. There simply is no authority to consult in this connection, for the great bulk of this linguistic material was first put into print by Dr. Maurer, who always reserves the privilege of altering spelling in the light of new information, usually of an etymological nature. For example, one term for marijuana was first recorded as *greefo* or *griffo,* until its probable relationship to Mexican Spanish *potación de guaya* (drink of grief) was noted, after which the variant *griefo* was added. *Potación de guaya* (marijuana pods soaked in wine or brandy) is an old Mexican term, incidentally also probably the source of the very modern *pot* for marijuana to be smoked. Addicts are seldom if ever aware of these etymological connections.

It will be noted that the qualification *obsolescent* appears after a number of terms. This means only that a number of informants have expressed the idea that a given term is out of date, or not so much used as more popular ones, or the informant indicated that he knows the word but does not use it himself. However, the situation with regard to obsolescence varies dramatically from area to area, with a word which is already old-fashioned in one area being at the height of popularity in another. Sometimes these popular words are new contributions; more often they are simply older terms rediscovered and used in original senses, or given new meanings. Often these words are modifications or corruptions of older terms which the current generation regard as new only because they have never heard the older form. And so, while obsolescence is a kind of cyclical phenomenon, it is rare that a word can be labeled truly obsolete, for about the time that label is applied, it is almost certain to pop up in another area or among a different class of addicts; it has merely been kept alive in some obscure circles which have not been currently studied. It is notable that, thirty or thirty-five years ago, younger addicts

learned the argot from their elders and imitated it rather carefully; today, because of the preponderance of younger addicts, the
older ones seem to go along with the language currently in use
in order to maintain status and identity within the subculture.
In general, a movement of terms from East to West has been
observed, although there are many exceptions to this, and new
words tend to generate and reach popularity in any center where
a number of addicts congregate. However, it is a common experience to find that a new term on the East Coast is unknown on the
West Coast, and by the time it reaches the West Coast—if it does
—it may well be obsolescent in the East. At the same time, one
can observe terms used on the West Coast, or from the Chicago
or Detroit areas, which are unknown in the East, though eventually they may appear there.

Phonologically, there is little to say about the argot of addicts
at the present time, largely because this phase is difficult to study,
and because the evidence is far from complete. However, we
might oversimplify a bit and say that the phonology of addicts
tends to follow that of the geographical regional dialect as well
as the social level to which they are indigenous. At the same time,
there are some paralinguistic and kinesic factors which, though
very subtle, seem to be almost universal among American underworld addicts, who readily recognize one another by these means,
even though they may be hard put to it to explain exactly and
specifically how they do this. A trained observer, however, can,
after sufficient experience with addicts, readily isolate and identify some of these.

While this glossary is by no means complete, pains have been
taken to see that it is representative. Consequently, there is a
sprinkling of terms from the institutional argot of narcotics hospitals, jails and prisons which, several years ago, would not have
been characteristic. Also there are some terms for the hustle or
small-time racket by which the addict supports his habit; often
these are modifications, corruptions or improper applications of
terms already established in other rackets, for they have been
hastily adapted by young addicts who have had no real experience in the rackets proper before drugs forced them into some
form of criminal activity. There are also a number of terms which

originated or were adapted by black addicts, reflecting not only the preponderance of addiction among blacks but also the widespread tendency of the argot of the black addict to proliferate all aspects of the drug subculture. An extension of this is seen in the tendency of the dominant culture to borrow heavily from the phraseology of the ghetto.

REFERENCES

Note: There are no references to previously published material in Chapter 10 because the authors felt that it was desirable to include a fresh study of the argot, based on field-work done during 1965-66. However, the following titles are relevant to any consideration of the argot, at least in an historical sense, because of the obscure nature of addicts' usage and in the light of the widespread changes which have taken place in that usage within the past decade.

1. BERREY, LESTER V., and VAN DEN BARK, MELVIN: *The American Thesaurus of Slang.* New York, Thomas Y. Crowell, 1942. (Contains some data on the argot of addicts, very loosely edited, based on the work of D. W. Maurer, with acknowledgments in the fifth and subsequent printings.)

2. COWDRY, F. V. JR., and GOTTSCHALK, L. A.: *The Language of the Narcotic Addict.* The United States Public Health Service Hospital, Fort Worth, Texas, 1948.

3. GOLDIN, HYMAN E., O'LEARY, FRANK, and LIPSIUS, MORRIS: *Dictionary of American Underworld Lingo.* New York, Twayne Publishers, 1950. (Contains some sound data on the usage of addicts, especially in prisons.)

4. MAURER, DAVID W.: Junker lingo: A by-product of underworld argot. *American Speech, 8:2,* April, 1933.

5. MAURER, DAVID W.: The argot of the underworld narcotic addict, Part I. *American Speech, 11:2,* April, 1936. Reprinted by the United States Public Health Service, 1936.

6. MAURER, DAVID W.: Addenda to addicts' argot. *American Speech, 11: 3,* October, 1936.

7. MAURER, DAVID W.: The argot of the underworld narcotic addict, Part II. *American Speech, 13:3,* October, 1938. Reprinted by The United States Public Health Service, 1938.

8. MAURER, DAVID W.: *The Big Con: The Story of the Confidence Man and the Confidence Game.* New York, Bobbs-Merrill, 1940. (Contains notes on the use of narcotics among confidence men and consequent reflection in their argot.)

9. MAURER, DAVID W.: The argot of forgery. *American Speech, 16:4,*

December, 1941. (Contains notes on addiction among forgers and passers of forged checks.)

10. MAURER, DAVID W.: Speech of the narcotic underworld. *The American Mercury, 62:*266, February, 1946.

11. MAURER, DAVID W.: Marijuana addicts and their lingo. *The American Mercury, 63:*275, November, 1946.

12. MAURER, DAVID W.: *The Technical Argot of the Pickpocket and Its Relation to the Culture-Pattern.* A paper presented before the Modern Language Association, Detroit, Michigan, December, 1947. (Contains notes on the use of drugs among thieves and pickpockets, with consequent reflection in the argot. Also, *Whiz Mob: A Correlation of the Technical Argot of Pickpockets With Their Behavior-Pattern.* Publication No. 24 (Book) of the American Dialect Society, 1955. Publication No. 31, 1959 contains a word-finder list for the above book. Trade edition, New Haven, College and University Press Services, Inc., 1964, 216.

13. MAURER, DAVID W.: *The Argot of the Criminal Narcotic Addict.* A paper presented before the Foreign Language Conference, The University of Kentucky, April 25, 1952.

14. MAURER, DAVID W.: *Reflections of the Behavior-Pattern in the Argot of Underworld Narcotic Addicts.* A paper presented before The American Dialect Society at the convention of The Modern Language Association, Boston, December 29, 1952.

15. PARTRIDGE, ERIC: *A Dictionary of the Underworld, British and American.* New York, Macmillan, 1950. (Contains data on the usage of addicts, rather loosely edited, based on the work of D. W. Maurer, with acknowledgments in the second American edition.)

16. PROVOST MARSHAL GENERAL'S SCHOOL: *Glossary of Colloquial Terms Used by Narcotic Addicts, and Commercial Preparations Containing Narcotic Drugs.* (Vol. II of *Narcotics and Other Drugs.*) Camp Gordon, Ga., 1952. (Argot materials contributed by D. W. Maurer.)

GLOSSARY

ab or **abb.** An abscess which forms at the site of injection on needle addicts, largely as a result of impure drugs or unsterile needles.

Addicts are sometimes literally covered with draining sores. Barbiturates also produce abscesses. Also, *Raspberry, cave.*

"The worst abs I ever saw were caused by yen shee, cooked and shot in the line or in the skin." "Yen shee will not cause an ab if shot in a vein or deep in muscle. Worst abs are caused by Nembutal when the vein is missed."

Abe. A five dollar bill. Also *Lincoln, nickel, fin,* etc.

Acapulco gold. A reputedly potent variety of dark brown marijuana from Mexico. See *muggles.*

Acapulco red. A reputedly good grade of reddish brown marijuana from Mexico. See *muggles.*

ace. 1. A one-year sentence. Also *bullet.* "He laid an ace on me for that score." 2. One of anything. 3. Or *ace note.* A one dollar bill.

acid. Lysergic acid diethylamide (LSD-25), a powerful psychomimetic drug, produced synthetically, which duplicates in a highly concentrated form the same hallucinogenic agent found in peyote, mescaline and psilocybin. It appears on the contraband market in the form of powder, liquid in ampules and sugar lumps on which a drop of the concentrated drug has been deposited. Much used by amateur experimenters, but of little or no interest to opiate addicts. See text for a detailed discussion.

acid dropper. One who uses LSD. Also *acid head.*

acid head. A user of LSD. Also *acid dropper.*

acid test. The experience involved in taking LSD. A common phrase among users is, "Can you pass the acid test?" (meaning, Can you take the psychological consequences of using this drug? Have you been initiated to it?)

action. 1. The selling of narcotics. 2. Anything pertaining to criminal activities. "All the action is going on at Pete's pad" (meaning *planning*). See also *happenings, skams.*

all lit up or **lit up.** To be under the influence of narcotics; to be obviously experiencing the euphoria immediately following an intravenous injection. Usually restricted to needle addicts, especially *speed ball* shooters. Also *coasting, floating, hitting the gow, hitting the stuff, in high, on stuff, on the gow, picked up,* some with specialized meanings.

"He was racing his motor and all lit up too." "Their eyes shine and stay lit up. . . ." Commonly used by squares to refer to anybody under influence of anything. Not commonly used by West Coast addicts. See *geed up, ripped, smashed, wired up, charged, zonked, stoned, loaded, knocked out.*

amp. A 1 cc Methedrine ampule, legitimate.

angel dust. Finely chopped or powdered marijuana for smoking or inhaling. 2. Heroin, morphine and cocaine mixed for injection or inhalation.

around the turn. For an addict who is *kicking the habit* to have passed through the worst of the withdrawal syndrome, which reaches its maximum intensity in from thirty-six to seventy-two hours from the last regular injection. Also *over the hump, reach the pitch.* Present-day addicts without habits so severe as in former years often use it to refer to the last day of withdrawal. "Doc, give me a pick up and it'll put me around the turn."

artillery. The outfit used to inject drugs hypodermically, that is, usually, a medicine dropper fitted with a hollow needle. Specialized to needle addicts. Also *Bay State, emergency gun, gun, hype, joint, Luer, nail, needle, works,* some with specialized meaning. ". . . it (a needle) is referred to as a spike usually, and a dropper is a dripper. Put them together and you have artillery."

ask for the cotton. 1. To ask for another addict's filtering cotton in order to squeeze out the residue for a very small shot. An indication that the addict is broke and out of drugs. "He was around T.O. asking for the cotton a few weeks ago." 2. By extension, to dislike a person. "I wouldn't ask that bum for the cotton."

aspirin smoke. Cigarette tobacco mixed with crushed aspirin and consumed along with a carbonated drink.

attitude, show an attitude, have an attitude, etc. Hostile or aloof and uncooperative. Common in ghetto, prison, and institution usage, often shortened to *'tude.* "I pegged him for a lame with an attitude. . . ."

away. Incarcerated.

away from the habit. To be *off drugs.* Also *to break the habit, to be off, to catch up, to fold up, on the up and up, washed up, cleaned up.*

back up. 1. To allow the blood to come back into the glass (dropper or glass syringe) during a vein shot. See *register, jack off, booting.* "He always liked to back up a shot three or four times." 2. To refuse to make a connection because of suspicion that the addict (or the peddler) may be a stool pigeon. Also to *blow the meet.* 3. To fold up or back away from something.

bad. Intensely good. One of many reversal-of-value terms in ghetto usage. See *up tight.*

bad scene. Any situation where trouble is a likely result, with drugs or otherwise. See *bummer, bad trip.*

bad trip. 1. An unpleasant experience, sometimes psychotic, from taking LSD. Sometimes used of other drugs. 2. By extension, any unpleasant experience. See *bummer.*

bag. 1. A quantity of drugs packaged in small paper or cellophane parcels, *e.g.* five dollar bags. Also *balloon,* though a *balloon* is usually a condom or small rubber balloon. See *bindle.* 2. To put in a classification as convict, thief, con man, etc. 3. Personal taste, occupation, hobby, etc. "Dropping acid isn't my bag."

bale. One pound or ½ kilo of marijuana. (Dealers.)

ball. (Transitive and intransitive.) To have sexual intercourse.

balloon. A quantity of drugs packaged in small paper, cellophane or rubber parcels. See *bindle*.

bambalache. Marijuana (New York). See *muggles*.

bamboo. An opium pipe. Specialized to opium smokers. Obsolescent. Also *gong, gonger, dream stick, hop stick, joy stick, saxophone, stem, stick, yen chung, crock, gongola, log.* "Seems like I can't get my habit off this morning. Let's have another crack at that bamboo. . . ."

bang. 1. An injection of narcotics, usually taken intravenously, but may refer also to subcutaneous injections. Restricted to needle addicts, and usually means morphine, heroin or cocaine or a combination. Also *bang in the arm, fix up, geezer, jolt, pop, shot, bird's eye, skin shot, vein shot, speed ball, jab,* with specialized meanings. All these terms indicate a ration of drug prepared for injection, as contrasted to a *bindle, check, deck,* etc., which indicate units of drug as they are sold retail. "I'll loan you a bang till you score. . . ." 2. The thrill or drive experienced immediately after a vein shot; euphoria. Restricted to needle addicts. Also *bing, boot, drive, jab off, kick* or *kicks, belt, buzz, flash, charge.* "I took four shots of that flea powder and couldn't get no bang out of it." "Yeah, I noticed I didn't get the right bang out of that last shot myself." 3. The lift or exhilaration experienced from taking drugs in any manner. "Now I'm on horse, I can't get no bang out of muggles any more." 4. To inject narcotics, especially in the vein, but may refer to *skin shooting* also. Also to *shoot,* to *get with it.* See *bang in the arm.*

bang in the arm. Usually shortened to *bang.* An injection of narcotics. Obsolescent. See *bang* 1. "A bang in the arm and we'll be dead ready for that tip tonight."

barb freak. A user of barbiturates, usually combined with alcohol.

barbs. Barbiturates.

Bay State. A standard medical hypodermic syringe, usually of glass with metal reenforcement, using a plunger and screw type needle. Derived from the trade name of the syringe. Seldom used by underworld addicts. Also *Luer* (for a standard syringe). "She wouldn't use anything but a Bay State to fix, but I liked a dripper. . . ."

bean. A Benzedrine tablet or capsule. See *benny.*

bean head. One who takes pills, especially *bennies, q.v.*

bean trip. Intoxication from ingesting Benzedrine; a *benny jag.*

bear claw. The shape of a calcium carbonate crystal formed on marijuana in an identification test. Spread to addicts' usage from the technical language of the toxicological laboratory.

bear down on (one). For a habit to come on, especially the early withdrawal symptoms. See *habit.*

beat. 1. To cheat. 2. Sick for lack of drugs. 3. Down and out. 4. To rob. See *knock off* 4.

beat a till. To steal from a cash register. See *till tapping.*

beat the gong. To smoke opium. See *hit the gong, kick the gong.*

beat the rap or **beat the beef.** To be acquitted of a charge.

bee that stings. A drug habit, especially one coming on; *a monkey on my back.* See *habit.*

bees and honey. Money. From "Australian" rhyming argot, in which the meaning rhymes with the second element in the phrase and is filled in by the one who hears it. *E.g.,* "twist and twirl" means "girl."

beetlebrow. An aggressive female homosexual.

behind stuff. Using heroin.

belly habit. A drug habit satisfied by taking drugs orally. See *mouth habit.*

belt. 1. The euphoria following an injection of narcotics. See *bang* 2. 2. A shot, or a quantity of drugs to be injected. "Gimme a belt of stuff."

bending and bowing. To be under the influence of narcotics. Obsolescent. See *high, all lit up.*

benny. Benzedrine (amphetamine) in tablets, capsules or inhalers. Also *whites, crosses, beans, blancas* (Mexican), referring to capsules, *Catholic aspirin,* referring to tablets.

benny jag. Intoxication from ingesting Benzedrine. Also *wired on whites, bean trip, white scene.* See *benny.*

Bernice, Burnese, Bernies. Crystallized cocaine used either for inhaling or for mixing with morphine or heroin in the form of hypodermic injections. Sold in papers or capsules. Also, *C, Corine, Carrie, coke, Cecil, Cholly, happy dust, heaven dust, dust, snow, star dust,* and other similar terms beginning with *C.*

". . . soon as I get Bernice we'll go for a ride."

big man. The brains behind a dope ring; the one who seldom takes the rap. Most traffic in narcotics is controlled by gangsters of a vicious type, often with sound political connections. The *big man* wholesales drugs to dealers and for peddlers, and may racketeer them for protection and the privilege of selling. *Big men* are usually not addicted.

bindle. A quantity of narcotics (usually restricted to morphine, heroin and cocaine) prepared for sale, as contrasted to a *ration,* which is prepared for injection. Both *bindles* and *rations* vary widely in size and strength. Also *cap, card, check, cigarette paper, cube, deck, O., O.Z., piece, balloon, half load, load, bundle, bag,* with specialized meanings. ". . . and this connection had bindles for five dollars, ten dollars and twenty dollars, good H, too."

bing. An injection of drugs. Also *bingo, bird's eye, fix, gee, go, jab, pop, load, penitentiary shot, pick up, pin shot, geez* or *geezer, point shot, prod, prop,* with specialized meanings. See *bang.*

bird cage hype. A down and out underworld addict, probably so called because he often lives in a *bird cage joint* or flophouse where the cots are separated by chicken wire. There is also a saying that a down and out addict "has a bird cage on one foot and a boxing glove on the other." "He's just a bird cage hype stemming his score dough." Obsolescent. Current popular term, *gutter hype.*

bird's eye. 1. A half size or small ration of narcotics. "A bird's eye is generally what a junker takes in his first bang after being on vacation for a while. . . ." 2. A small pill of opium, especially opium prepared for smoking. This is the smallest size. The next in sequence are *buttons* and *high hats.* 3. A very small quantity of drugs.

"When Whitey bought the cap I took just a tiny bit—a bird's eye— and gave the rest to him." 4. A small quantity of narcotic solution held in the *joint* for another addict to take; equivalent to "butt's" on a cigarette. "Save me two or three points of that for a bird's eye." Also *taste, lightweight taste.*

bit. A short prison sentence. *Jolt, stuff.*

bitch or **the bitch.** The death penalty or life imprisonment. Also used for a long sentence given to a habitual criminal. Clipped back from *habitch*, in turn clipped from habitual.

biz or **business.** 1. An outfit (*joint* and *spoon*) for taking drugs hypodermically. Also *factory, joint, layout, machinery, works,* etc. See *artillery.* "Have you got the business? I'm sick." 2. The hypodermic needle as separate from the syringe. Also *harpoon, point, tom cat,* with specialized meanings. "Let me use the business." 3. Narcotics in general. See *junk.* "What I want is the business." 4. The "third degree" administered by the police. "Everyone gets the business from those dicks in Cincy." 5. Death or a beating given a stool pigeon. "They finally gave that rat from Chi the business." 6. As *B.I.Z.* To emphasize the action, with each letter pronounced separately. "That dude is really taking care of the B.I.Z." (He is being successful in criminal activity.) 7. The end of anything. 8. Bad or fake dope. See *blank.*

black and white. A policeman.

Black Beauty. A capsule of mixed amphetamines and barbiturates. Also *black widow.*

black mollies. Barbiturates. (Ghetto usage.)

black shit. Smoking opium. See *black stuff.*

black stuff. 1. Opium prepared for smoking, as contrasted to crude gum. Also *gee yen, hop, gum, mud, pen yen, san lo, tar, black shit, yen shee, ah pen yen, dai yen, fi doo nie, hok for, sook nie, li yuen, gee, gonger 3, lem kee,* with specialized meanings. 2. Laudanum is now being called *black stuff* by extension. 3. Concentrated paregoric cooked down for injection. 4. Dark brown heroin that comes from Mexico.

black widow. See *Black Beauty.*

blackjack. Paregoric which has been cooked down to be injected in a concentrated form. See *P.G.*

blancas. Benzedrine tablets (Mexican).

blank. 1. A quantity of bad or fake dope. Also *turkey, sugar, flea powder, talcum powder, queer 5, business 8.* 2. An individual who is nothing especially as far as the rackets are concerned.

blasted. Under the influence of drugs. More intense than *stoned, q.v.*

block. 1. A *cube* of morphine as sold by the can (or ounce). "It comes 120 to 130 blocks to the ounce." 2. Crude bootleg morphine. 3. A kilo (2½ lb.) of bulk marijuana.

block buster. See *yen shee baby.*

bloomer girls or **bloomer broads.** Shoplifters who wear specially constructed underwear in which stolen articles are concealed. See *hustling drawers.*

blow. To inhale narcotics in powder form, usually heroin, though cocaine was formerly popular taken by sniffing it up the nose, usually from the back of the hand. Narcotics in tablet form are crushed between two coins before inhaling. ". . . when I could get a dozen heroin tablets for fifty cents, I'd blow one just before I went on (the stage) and one as soon as my act was over. . . ." "You know Slim. Well, he first started blowing C around a layout." Also *horn, snort.* 2. To smoke marijuana, as to *blow weed.*

blow a pill. To smoke opium.

blow a shot. To waste drugs by missing a vein, or because of a break or malfunction of the equipment. Restricted to needle addicts. ". . . never seen it fail. On short stuff I'll always blow a shot." Also *skin* or *skin the punk.* 2. To spill the solution.

blow the meet. To fail to keep an appointment, usually because of suspicion on the part of either addict or peddler. ". . . considered high treason for a peddler to blow a meet, he will lose his customers quick . . . it's bad for the addict, too." "It takes a pinch or its equal to make me blow a meet." Also *hang him up, blow the scene.*

blow the mind. To produce psychological and sensory experiences by use of a hallucinogenic or "consciousness expanding" drug. See *mind-blower.*

blow the scene. 1. To fail to keep an appointment, especially for the sale or purchase of narcotics. Also *hang (someone) up, blow the meet.* 2. To flee; to leave precipitously.

blow weed. To smoke marijuana.

blue angel. Sodium amytal. Also *blue birds, blue heaven.*

blue grass. To obtain a commitment to the Lexington Hospital under certain conditions. If an addict breaks those conditions, he usually serves a year in jail. This term is now loosely applied to similar situations elsewhere, although the practice is not much used now in Kentucky. Used as adjective, noun, or verb. "If you leave Lexington, the Kentucky authorities will place a charge against you for drug addiction unless you recommit yourself and stay until you're pronounced cured. This is called a blue grass commitment."

blue heaven. Sodium Amytal in capsules. Also *blue birds, blues, jack up.*

blue velvet. 1. Sodium Amytal. See *blue birds, blue heaven.* 2. Pyribenzamine.

blue birds or **blues.** Sodium Amytal in capsules. Also *blue heaven, blues, jack up.*

boat sailed or **boat's in.** Said when narcotics are successfully smuggled into prison. See *drive* 4.

bo bo bush. Marijuana. See *muggles.*

body trip. A drug experience with mainly physical effects. Especially used of *speed, q.v.*

bogart. To take more than one's share, usually by violence.

bogus beef. See *meat ball rap.*

bogus smack. See *blank.*

bogus trip. False information regarding drugs or peddlers.

bombita. An amphetamine capsule; from Mexican Spanish for "little bomb."

bonaroo. 1. Good narcotics, uncut or cut only a little; the best. 2. Wearing starched, pressed clothing in a prison or a narcotics hospital. "That dude was looking bonaroo when he flashed at the board (parole board)."

bonche. A group of marijuana smokers. Also *cofradia* (Cuba and New York City).

bonita. Mexican Spanish, slang term for milk sugar, which is used to adulterate heroin.

boo gee. The *gee rag* used to make a tight connection between syringe and needle. Probably a variant or corruption of the medical term *boogie*. Rare. Also *geep, boat, collar*. See *gee rag* 2.

book. The maximum penalty, usually in the phrase, "He threw the book at me," "He gave me the book." Also *stuck it to me* (West Coast).

boomer. An addict who moves frequently. Borrowed from the lingo of the old-time railroaders, meaning a railroader who drifted from job to job, working a while at each, or riding freights when he had no work. *Cf.* German *bummeler, bummel-zug,* etc. Also *globe trotter, drifter, floater, boot and shoe*.

boost. 1. To shoplift. Probably the most common way of supporting a habit, excepting prostitution. The noun form is often recorded in such idioms as *rooting on the boost, on the boost, working the boost*. 2. See *boost* 3.

booster. A professional shoplifter, male or female.

booster stick. 1. A cigarette of treated marijuana, reputedly potent. Also *gold leaf special*. 2. An ordinary cigarette, the tip of which is dipped in a concentrated essence of marijuana preserved in alcohol. It is lit, blown out when it flames, and inhaled.

boosting drawers. See *hustling drawers*.

boot. 1. Euphoria following injection See *bang, belt, flash, gassed, stoned*. 2. The *gee rag* used to make a tight connection between needle and dropper. 3. To back blood into the dropper, allow it to mix with the drug, then shoot it back. Also *verification shot*.

boot and shoe. 1. Down and out, as applied to an underworld addict. Probably derived from the bizarre garb worn by some addicts, especially those who make a living by begging or panhandling. "The boot and shoe junkies made that joint a hangout, so it was really hot." The plural is sometimes used with adverbial function. "All hypes eventually go boots and shoes." Also *bird cage hype, broker*.

booter. One who uses *boot shots*. See *boot* 3.

boots on. In the know, informed. Recorded as *have (one's) boots on, keep (one's) boots on,* etc. "Tell Joe to put his boots on, to wise up."

boss. Wonderful or choice. Also *righteous, groovy, solid, out of sight, something else, too much, (the) end*.

boss habit. A very heavy habit.

bottoms. A male homosexual who is the passive receptor in pederasty. Also *sissy, stuff, sex punk, rap and bag it, queen pussy, boy girl*.

bow sow. Narcotics. West Coast, obsolescent.

box. 1. A record player. 2. The vagina. 3. A carton of cigarettes. 4. Radio. 5. Television. 6. A safe.

box of L. 100 ampules of Methedrine in a pharmacist's box.

boy. Heroin. See *Racehorse Charlie*.

boy girl. 1. See *bottoms*. 2. A person who adopts the mannerisms of the opposite sex.

brace and bits. The breasts. From "Australian" rhyming argot.

bread. Money.

break the habit or **break.** 1. To go *off drugs.* See *kick* the *habit.* "I have to break the habit for I have a State case coming up." 2. To suffer severe localized withdrawal distress. An opium smoker may say, "I always break the habit in my stomach."

Breckenridge green. A reputedly low grade marijuana from central Kentucky. See *muggles.*

brick gum or **brick.** 1. Crude opium after it is cooked into smoking opium or prepared opium. "Sometimes it comes in bricks weighing a pound, and sometimes in odd-shaped lumps." "Used to get brick gum for $40.00 to $60.00 a pound; now it's $300.00 to $450.-000." 2. *Brick* (only). A kilo of marijuana (2½ lb.).

bricked. Having a more intense drug experience than when *stoned, q.v.* (stimulant users).

bring up. To distend the vein into which the *shot* will be injected by holding up the circulation with a cord or tourniquet, simultaneously massaging the skin over the vein toward the tourniquet. Also *tie off,* which is more popular on the West Coast.

britch. A pocket, especially a side pants pocket. Borrowed from pickpockets who seldom use *britch* alone, but rather *right britch* or *left britch,* and then only for side pants pockets.

Brody. 1. A feigned "fit" or spasm staged by an addict to elicit sympathy and perhaps a ration of narcotics from a physician. Obsolescent. Also *cartwheel, circus, wingding, figure eight, twister, toss out, meter, Duffy, bitch,* as in *pitch a bitch.* "He threw a Brody for the croaker and scored for some stuff." 2. A long chance, derived from the dive of Steve Brody from Brooklyn Bridge. ". . . an awful Brody he took, but he made a clean get."

broker. A down and out addict. See *boot and shoe.*

brown eye. Coitus *per anum.*

brownies. Pastries often made for marijuana drug parties.

buffalo. A five-year sentence. Obsolescent. Also *nickel, fin.*

bug. 1. To inject an irritant such as kerosene or the creosote disinfectant often used in jails into the muscles or beneath the skin to produce a swelling or abscess; used to solicit narcotics from a doctor. "That time seven guys bugged themselves and got junk for a while, also a rest. . . ." 2. To annoy someone, especially a guard in a prison or jail. "Steve had two speeds, slow and slower. He'd slip into slower to bug the hack." 3. To tap a telephone line. 4. An abcess or sore, self-inflicted and used to solicit narcotics from physicians. Probably derived from the *bugs* or sores cultivated by oldtime beggars.

build up the habit or **a habit.** To increase one's tolerance to narcotics by gradually increasing the dosage, usually inevitable with opiates. "A guy can buld up one hell of a habit using Dilaudid before he realizes it." Also *strung out, hooked, got a thing going.*

bull. 1. A policeman. Also *the man, the heat, screw, black and white, hudda* (Mexican). 2. An aggressive female homesexual, clipped from *bulldyker,* sometimes rendered *as bulldagger, q.v.*

bull horrors. The delusions often experienced by cocaine addicts; part of the anxiety complex produced by the drug and sometimes reinforced by paranoid tendencies in the user. Policemen (*bulls*) and detectives often figure prominently in these delusions, hence the term, "Monty had the bull horrors bad. . . ."

bull jive. 1. Marijuana heavily cut with tea, catnip or other impurities. 2. Inaccurate or exaggerated speech (ghetto usage).

bullet. A currently popular expression for one year sentence, supplanting *ace* on the West Coast.

bum beef or **bum steer.** False complaint or information, which is usually given deliberately to the police.

bum kick. Boring, unpleasant.

bum rap. An arrest or conviction for a crime the man actually did not commit, as distinguished from denying it. See *rap 2, rap partner, rap sheet.*

bum steer. False or unreliable information about drugs or peddlers. "You gave me a bum steer, Jack, about that joint. . . ." Also *bogus trip, bum wire, jive.*

bum trip. See *bad trip.*

bum wire. False information regarding peddlers or drugs.

bummer. 1. A *bad trip, q.v.* 2. Generalized to anything boring or unpleasant.

bundle. 1. A quantity of narcotics for sale. Variant of *bindle.* 2. A sum of cash, especially a roll.

bunk habit. 1. The desire to hang about where opium is being smoked; actually, a mild opium habit can be contracted from continually breathing smoke-filled air. See *bunk yen, lamp habit.* 3. "His girl don't smoke but she has a bunk habit." 2. An opium habit (smoking). 3. A tendency to sleep a great deal; used to refer to ad-

dicts of any kind by extension. "They ought to call her The Pajama Kid; she has an awful bunk habit."

bunk yen. 1. A small opium habit requiring only two or three pills to satisfy. Also *bunk habit 2, lamp habit 3.* ". . . well, he only had a bunk yen, but he would get so sick. . . ." 2. The slight addiction acquired from breathing the smoke-filled air in a *lay down joint* or in a room where opium is regularly smoked. Also *bunk habit 1.* "I used to let the pup lay down with us, and he finally got a bunk yen. . . ." (Many West Coast prostitutes formerly had Pekingese or other lap dogs who were obviously addicted.) "Some Chinese broads did not smoke, but had a bunk yen just from cheffing. . . ."

burn. 1. To cheat. 2. To cheat or steal from someone. 3. To sell bad or fake drugs. "I burnt that poop butt. I sold him some Ajax." 4. The initial exhiliration following the injection of opiates. See *jaboff.*

burned out. A sclerotic condition of the veins resulting from abscesses and continued puncturing. Also *up and down the lines.* ". . . had to go to the skin, all his lines are burned out." See *soul searching, up and down the lines.*

Burnese. Variant of *Bernice, q.v.*

burr. Crystalline formation in heroin under microscopic test. Adapted from toxicological testing.

bush. Marijuana.

business. See *biz.*

bust. 1. To arrest or be arrested. See *put away, down, nailed, clouted, snatched, rousted, knocked off, knocked out.* 2. To catch someone redhanded. "I knew I'd bust Jimmy dipping if I left the snack on the table."

bust the mainline. To inject narcotics intravenously. Also *to shoot, to take it in the vein, to take it main, hit the sewer, send it home, geeze* or *geez.*
From my dropper I'll shake the dust
From my spike I'll scrape the rust, And my old main line I'll bust. . . .

busted on a buzzer. See *meat ball rap.*

butch. See *bull.* 2. A *butch* is not necessarily a *bull*, however. She may simply be the active lesbian partner.

butch game. 1. An ultimatum to cooperate or suffer heavy penalty. Also *murder game.* 2. The technique used by a lesbian prostitute beating her trick for money without going through with the sexual act.

button. 1. A pill of smoking opium, in size between a *bird's eye* and a *high hat.* See *bird's eye.* 2. A nodule of peyote, not addicting, but used experimentally and in Indian religious ceremonies.

buy. 1. A narcotic peddler. 2. A purchase of narcotics.

buy money. The money used to purchase drugs. See *connection dough.*

buzzer. 1. A homosexual. 2. A prison guard. 3. An enforcement officer's badge. "We got his leather that had his buzzer in it."

buzzing. Beginning to have a drug experience. "Are you buzzing yet?"

C. Cocaine. See *Bernice.*

C. Vol. An addict who has been committed to the USPHS Hospital by a county court in Kentucky.

He usually volunteers for such commitment.

call. The initial exhilaration following the injection of opiates. See *jaboff.*

Cam or **Cambodian red.** A reddish-brown variety of marijuana of Cambodian origin. See *muggles.*

Cambodia trip weed. A reputedly potent black variety of marijuana of Cambodian origin. See *muggles.*

canary. A nembutal capsule. See *yellow jacket.*

candy. 1. Barbiturates. 2. A term for opiate drugs, now being revived with a general application. 3. Cocaine or Benzedrine.

candy a J. To treat a marijuana cigarette with another drug, such as heroin, to increase the potency of its effect. Cut back from *candy a joint.*

candy man. A *connection, q.v.*

canned stuff. Commercial smoking opium, usually put up in tins, as *li yuen* (No. 1 quality), *low foo kee 2, lem kee 3* and *san lo 4.*

cannon. An expert pickpocket; one with "class."

cap. 1. A capsule containing a drug, usually heroin or cocaine. The contents vary widely in both quantity and strength according to the source. Today, addicts measure both their purchases and their habits by the number of *caps* bought or taken per day. Seldom applied to morphine. Often used also to indicate barbiturates. See *paper.* 2. A person's head or mind. "That nic nac's cap is wide open, like he's howling at the moon." 3. Or *cap up.* To transfer drugs (usually heroin) from a loose bulk form to individual capsules for retail sale.

"I like to cap it on a big mirror as that way you don't lose a bit."

card. A *bindle* of opium sold (usually in a *hop joint*) ready for smoking. About four to six *fun* of prepared opium is weighed out on a card—often a playing card—and the chef or the smoker rolls the *pills* from this supply. "We laid down in the joint together, then she ordered four cards of hop. . . ." "Playing cards are used, except the ace of spades." Street peddlers (now rare) use blue or red cellophane envelopes about two inches square.

carpet. See *Murphy.*

carry. 1. For a given amount of narcotics to support an addict, or prevent withdrawal signs, for a specified length of time. "It takes at least a grain and a half to carry me four hours." "Six pills don't carry me all day." 2. A *plant* of drugs, secreted on the person to be used only in case of arrest; sometimes called *Miss Carrie.*

cartwheel. A feigned illness or "fit." Restricted to needle addicts and notably used by circus and carnival grifters who use drugs. Obsolescent. See *Brody.* "All you had to do in those little burgs was turn a couple of cartwheels and some croaker would fix you."

cat. 1. A person, especially a young Negro who has a *hustle* to support his habit. 2. A cat nap. 3. A destitute person who sleeps in a different place each night. 4. Generalized to refer to anyone.

cat nap. To get small (and very welcome) snatches of sleep during the withdrawal period.

catch up or **be caught up.** To be *off drugs.* Rare. Obsolescent. "Yeah, he's all caught up now."

Catholic aspirin. An amphetamine, so called because of the cross-shaped scoring on the tablet. See *crosses.*

cave. An abscess at the site of injection. The reference seems to be not to the cavity, but to the fact that the vein "caves in" at this spot. See *cave digging.*

cave digging. Searching among caved-in veins for one which can be used for injection.

Cecil. Cocaine. See *Bernice.*

cement. Wholesale illicit narcotics as they pass into contraband channels. Restricted to *big men* or wholesalers of the New York area. Not used by addicts.

cement arm. Heavy deposits of sclerotic tissue over the veins. Obsolescent, giving way to *dirty arm, needle tracks, tracks, service stripes.*

change. A short jail or prison sentence.

changes. Adjustments, especially as *being put through the changes* in prison or hospital prison life.

channel. A vein or *main line* into which drugs are injected. Also *sewer, home;* when referring specifically to the cubital area, *ditch* or *pit.*

charged or **overcharged.** 1. Stupefied or drowsy as a result of taking too much of a drug. This state may range from mild drowsiness to complete unconsciousness, or sometimes fatal narcosis. See *play the nod, O.D., overjolt, zipped, out of sight, gowed.* 2. **Charged** only. Under the influence of narcotics.

Charley. Cocaine.

Charley Coke. A cocaine addict (restricted to New York and New England). Obsolescent. "That boy you met last night, he never smoked, he is just a Charley Coke, and there aren't many left."

Charley Cotton. One of the mythical Cotton Brothers, C., H. and M. Cotton. See *cotton, Cotton Brothers, rinsings.* "He's strictly a Charley Cotton man. . . ."

chase the dragon. To inhale heroin fumes through a paper tube or straw from a foil trough held over a flame (Hong Kong).

che chees. The breasts.

cheater. 1. An attendant in a *joint* who is skillful at mulcting the addict of his *shot* as it is administered. He does this by putting a bit of cotton inside the medicine dropper bulb so that he can draw most of the shot up into the bulb and keep it there, injecting only a small portion into the customer. Some *cheaters* steal much of the shot for themselves by pinching up a bit of skin, then running the needle through it and into their own thumbs or fingers. The customer feels the needle enter, but does not get much of the drug (Chicago, Detroit and vicinity). Also *burn artist.* "Georgie the Rat could palm a cotton and cheat more gow than eight guys could steal the money to buy. He was a cheater and no mistake." 2. Any dice or card *hustler.*

check. A *bindle* of narcotics, usually heroin or cocaine. See *bindle.* ". . . and she said, 'Hon, get two toys of grease and three checks of C on your way home.' "

cheeo. Marijuana seeds to be chewed.

chef. 1. The attendant in a *hop joint.* He warms the pipe and rolls the pills for the smokers. He may be a professional supplied by the house, or, on private parties, a smoker who has the necessary skill to officiate. Also *cook* or *cooker.* "A chef can't always cook opium from gum to prepared." 2. The act of rolling and cooking pills. "In my time I've been called on to chef for some fairly important people."

chemical. Any synthetic drug; also specialized to any nonopiate drug (loose usage, high school).

Chicago green. A reputedly potent grade of marijuana. See *muggles.*

Chicago leprosy. Multiple abscesses.

chicharra. The communal cigar or cigarette (sometimes wrapped in a cornhusk) made of tobacco and marijuana combined, used by Latin American smokers (New York City).

chicken shit beef. See *meat ball rap.*

chicken shit habit. A relatively small drug habit; one which is satisfied with a small quantity of drugs. Distinguished from a *chippy habit,* which is irregular. Also *light-weight nothing.*

chill. 1. To make someone fearful. 2. To give someone the cold shoulder. Also *shine him on, freeze, play the shoulder.*

Chinaman on my back or **monkey on my back.** 1. Suffering abstinence symptoms. 2. Supporting a drug habit.

Chinese needle work. A euphemistic expression for using or dealing in narcotics, especially opium. "He has a store in Frisco, now, sells jewelry and novelties and Chinese needle work. . . ."

chingadera. The outfit or *fit* used for injecting drugs (Mexican-American usage). See *artillery.*

Chino. A Chinese. While some (mainly *li yuen*) of the opium traffic in North America is still in control of the Chinese, and especially the *tongs, q.v.,* they seldom deal in other forms of narcotics, and the older generation refuse to take drugs by needle. Most Chinese who deal in opium are also addicts. The bulk of smoking opium in the United States today is controlled by Mexicans, and is sold in cans or *tins*. "You can never tell about a Chino, what he is thinking. . . ."

chipping. Using drugs irregularly, as a *chippy*. See *chippy habit, pleasure user.*

chippy. 1. One who uses drugs irregularly and is not yet physically dependent. See *hype*. 2. A prostitute.

chippy habit. A small irregular habit which precedes almost inevitable addiction. Also *coffee-and habit, ice cream habit, cotton habit, three-day habit, hit and miss habit, weekend habit, pleasure user, Saturday night habit, chicken shit habit,* with specialized meanings.

Christmas roll. An assortment of barbiturates, so called because of the variety of colored capsules. Also *rainbow roll.*

Christmas trees. Tuinal capsules.

Chuck habit, chuck horrors, or chuckers. The ravenous appetite for food which an addict develops after he goes through the withdrawal illness. "I don't get the chuck habit like I use to. But still, I do feel it for a few days. . . ." See *grease* 6, *root.*

cigarette paper. A *bindle* of heroin, today mostly in prisons or jails, put up in a folded cigarette paper. On the street heroin is not sold anymore in cigarette papers, but in capsules, cellophane or a *balloon*. ". . . so you could ask for a cigarette paper anywhere and no fear of being fingered for stuff. . . ."

circus. A feigned spasm or "fit." Obsolescent. See *Brody.*

clean. 1. Away from the habit. Also *straight, squared up, hang it up, put it down.* 2. To remove seeds, stems, and other impurities from marijuana, especially through a screen; also to pulverize seeds and stems to match their consistency with that of the crushed leaves.

clip. 1. To steal. 2. To arrest.

clip joint. 1. Any place where *hustlers* and prostitutes hang out. 2. A known crooked gambling house.

cloud nine. See *in high.*

clout. To steal, especially as a shoplifter. Many, if not most, underworld addicts support their habits by thievery of one kind or another. "Right then they went out to clout a new front for Alabam." Also *boost, gaffel, sneeze.*

coasting. 1. The sensation of euphoria following the use of a drug. Used of all drugs except cocaine. See *in high, floating.* "That day, when the phone rang, I was just laying there coasting and getting my kicks." Also *grooving, tripping, T.V. action.* 2. Serving an easy prison sentence.

coffee-and habit. A form of *chippy habit, q.v.* The inference is that it is no habit at all. Probably taken from the phrase *coffee-and pimp,* one who gets only enough from his girl to buy doughnuts and coffee (pronounced coffee-ann).

cofradia. A group of users smoking marijuana. Also *bonche* (Cuba and New York City) .

coin. 1. Money. 2. A perforated silver coin covering an ordinary tobacco pipe for opium smoking.

coke. Cocaine. See *C.* "Just a little

coke is the thing to use with tincture of opium, then it requires no cooking or burning the alky off, just drop the coke in and shoot it."

coke and crystal. Parties at which addicts drink beer or gin and sniff cocaine.

Coke-time. A break from other activities for addicts to take drugs, originally cocaine. Analogous to a coffee break.

cokie or **coke head.** A cocaine addict. Rare; addicts who take cocaine straight are uncommon today, but once were prevalent. Obsolescent.

cokomo or **Kokomo.** A cocaine user. Obsolescent.

cold. More reserved than *cool.*

cold turkey. Treatment for addiction (withdrawal) in jails, hospitals, etc. where addicts are taken off drugs suddenly without the tapering-off process always desired by addicts. "It's something to kick the habit cold turkey. . . ." "I'll never forget the first cold turkey kick I went through. . . ." See *kick cold.*

collar. 1. The small piece of paper, thread or rubber used to make an airtight connection between dropper and needle. Also *gaff, shoulder, jacket, jeep* or *geep.* See *gee rag.* 2. To arrest.

come down. 1. For drug-induced euphoria to subside. 2. Or *comedown.* Any deflating experience or disappointment. 3. Effect of a depressant drug.

con. 1. To make contact with a *peddler.* 2. With *for* indicates that someone else is buying narcotics for an addict. "I just got there and he was conning for me." 3. The confidence element in any small-time racket.

connect. 1. To make contact with a peddler. Also *score.* 2. With *for* indicates that someone else is buying narcotics for an addict. "When I was so hot, he was connecting for me. . . ." Also *score for, con for.*

connection. 1. A generalized underworld term for getting anything —usually with the implication of illicit traffic; the person who controls, sells or obtains certain items. "To cop the short you gotta see that heavy set kayducer (conductor). He's the connection." 2. In the narcotics rackets, specialized to mean a fairly important figure near the top; a big dealer or wholesaler. "Jeez, I never see five ounces of stuff. You'll have to see the connection." 3. Used by some addicts to mean a peddler, physician or anyone through whom or from whom narcotics are obtained. "Sometimes Bill used to jump 500 miles across country to see the connection and get junk for the mob." Also *the man,* in all three senses.

connection dough. The price of a *bindle* of narcotics. Also *buy money, score dough.* "He's nuts, planted his connection dough and can't find the plant."

conned. 1. To be the victim of a small time confidence game. 2. To be persuaded .

contact high. 1. The emotional contagion of jazz musicians who are *on* may be picked up by a musician who has not used drugs. 2. One who has not smoked marijuana but is nevertheless *high* from the smoke in the room is said to have *contact high.* See *bunk habit.*

cook. 1. An individual who knows how to cook up raw gum opium for prepared smoking opium.

Sometimes a *chef* can do this, but by no means always. "A cook is most always a chef, but a chef isn't always a cook." 2. Sometimes used interchangeably with *chef, q.v.* (West Coast).

cook a pill. To prepare a small quantity of opium for smoking; usually done by the *chef,* but may be done by the smoker. The sticky opium is manipulated on the *yen hok* over the flame and worked on the top of the bowl or some other flat, hard surface. For full description, see text. Usually the *pills* are smoked immediately, but may be prepared in advance. "He used to cook a few extra pills so I could take some yen poks along on the road."

cook it up. To prepare heroin (or other opiates) for injection by heating it in a *cooking spoon* or other *cooker* held over a small flame, such as a match or a cigarette lighter. The drug is dissolved in a very small quantity of water.

cooker. 1. The receptacle, usually a spoon with a handle bent back, a small bottle cap with a wire handle or a little glass vial, used to boil the narcotic solution before it is injected. "Never leave your cooker dirty and in sight. People are so nosey." 2. Or *cook.* The *chef* in a *hop joint* who prepares the *pills* and *cooks* them for the smoker.

cookie. A *chef, q.v.* Restricted to Chinese or Chinese-Americans of the older generation.

cooking spoon. Variant of *cooker, q.v.*

cool. 1. A vague term of approval, now being supplanted by *groovie* or *groovy,* with the same meaning. 2. Reserved.

cool it. 1. To remain reserved or quiet under pressure. 2. To take it easy, relax, stop any activity. 3. To take drugs, but conceal the effects from others. 4. To go silent and aloof, usually in anger. Also *freeze, dummy up, lighten up, hang tough.*

coozie stash. Drugs hidden in the vagina, usually in a condom or *balloon.* See *stash.*

cop. 1. To obtain. "Do you dig spending all your time trying to cop?" 2. To steal or rob. 3. To buy drugs for someone else.

cop a fix. To obtain a ration of narcotics.

cop a peek. To get the *lay* of the *joint* to be *knocked off;* to *case* the *outfit.* (Used by addicts who have progressed to robbery or burglary.)

cop a pill. To smoke opium; the act of inhaling one's smoke. "Let's cop a few more pills before we go. . . ."

cop a sneak. To sneak away, to escape by running or walking away.

cop man. 1. A narcotics dealer. 2. A middle man in the narcotics sale. 3. A *fence* who will buy stolen goods.

cop out. 1. To retreat from reality, as by drug use. 2. To refuse responsibility, to quit. 3. To plead guilty.

cop (someone's) rap. To steal someone's thunder; to complete an enterprise begun by another, thus depriving him of any rewards or acclaim.

cop-out. 1. A retreat from reality; an act of betrayal by refusal to participate. 2. One who cannot bear competition.

copper. 1. A policeman. 2. *Good time* in prison.

cotics. Drugs in general, especially those of the opiate series and cocaine; *white stuff,* including principally morphine, heroin and cocaine. Also *junk, Miss Emma, gow, M., G.O.M., God's Medicine, horse, courage pills, C., skamas,* some with specialized meanings. Any kind of narcotics used by confirmed addicts, excluding marijuana smokers and barbiturate users. "They got three grand and a kiester full of cotics."

cotton. The small wisp of cotton placed in the cooking spoon and used as a filter when the solution is drawn up into the needle. See *cotton shooter.* "Save your cottons, boy. We may be in for a panic."

Cotton brothers. 1. Narcotics. (H., M. and C. Cotton.) "Are the Cotton brothers in town?" might mean "How is the drug situation here?" 2. The cottons used by addicts to filter drugs before injecting, and often reused by addicts who are broke. See *cotton shooter.*

cotton habit. A small irregular habit which an addict may support by begging or retrieving *cottons, q.v.* See *chippy habit.*

cotton shooter. A down and out addict who hangs around other addicts and begs or picks up the *cottons* used to filter drugs. The *cottons* are soaked for the *narcotic* residue they contain. Some addicts use them over and over. ". . . one cotton would knock out the average junker today." "Did you ever see so many characters around T.O. (Toledo, Ohio) on the pling (begging) for cottons?" "Cotton Bob took a geezer of cottons that had soured and bumped himself off. The pistols thought he had an O.D."

cotton tail route. Suicide.
> *Toes turned up, ass full of cotton,*
> *Long gone, but not forgotten.*

See *Dutch route.*

count a man out. 1. To short change a person. 2. To fail to *cut someone in* on the score. 3. To leave someone out of a *caper* because he's not safe.

courage pills. Heroin in tablet form, usually ⅛ to ½ grain. Obsolescent as argot, but used by *squares.*

cracking shorts. Breaking into cars to support a habit.

crank handle. A voluntary patient in a prison or narcotics hospital. Also *self-starter, stem winder, winder, hitchhiker, Mr. Fish.*

crash. To return to reality from a drug-induced euphoria. Often boomerangs into a state of depression.

crazy. Very good. Also *groovie, righteous, boss, too much, George, way out, cool, out of sight, something else, insane, far out.*

creep. A disgusting person. Also *lame, jerk, rumdum, low rider, poop butt, nic nac, punk, gunsel, rumkin.*

creep on the cash register. See *heel, till tipping.*

crib. 1. One's home or apartment. 2. A house of prostitution. Also *flat, pad, notch house.* 3. A hypochondriac with many persistent symptoms.

croaker. An addict's term for physician; also in general underworld usage, especially for a prison or jail doctor. "All that croaker will give you is salts or cc. pills." Also *horse doctor, vet.* See *ice tong doctor.*

croaker on the make. See *ice tong doctor.*

crock. 1. An opium pipe. See *bamboo.* 2. The bowl of an opium pipe. Obsolescent. 3. A person who talks foolishly or senselessly. Also *loose, cap's loose, talking trash.*

crocked out. An addict who has committed suicide.

cross-country hype. See *R.F.D. junker.*

crosses. *Benny* pills, Benzedrine tablets, marked with a scored cross; also *Catholic aspirin.*

crutch. A split match or twig used to hold a short marijuana cigarette butt. See *roach clip.*

crystallized. Having taken too much Methedrine. Also *overamped.*

crystals. Methedrine.

cube. 1. Crude bootleg morphine in the wholesale trade. 2. A small cube (3 or 4 grains) sold in ounce cans which contain 120 to 140 such morphine cubes. Currently, 1-grain cubes are more common. The large ones are sometimes called sugar lump cubes. "Pushers shaved these cubes to a uniform size and wrapped them in tinfoil and sold them for $.50 to $1.00 each when a can of M was $25.00."

cure. 1. The length of time volunteers are required to stay in the USPHS Hospital, to be released as hospital treatment is completed. 2. To treat bulk marijuana with sugar and/or alcohol to produce a milder smoke.

curtains. 1. The end of anything. 2. An arrest. Also *end gate, the business, snatched, nailed,* etc. 3. A life sentence or the death penalty.

cut. To adulterate drugs, usually with sugar of milk. Modern bootleg heroin for instance may be cut from five to ten times before it reaches the consumer. "This flea powder passed through fifty hands, and everybody must have cut it."

cut (someone) in. A specialized form of general underworld usage. Addicts use the term to mean sharing a purchase made by someone else with the purchaser. See *connect, score.* "He is getting cut in by four different people that I know of, so he must have stuff. . . ."

cut (someone) loose. 1. To release. 2. To exclude someone from the *action;* to refuse to associate with him. Also *freeze on, shine on.* 3. Among established professional thieves, working on an "in and in" and "out and out" basis, to agree to exclude one member of the mob from any given theft, at the same time removing his *fall dough* from jeopardy should an arrest be made and excluding him from any share in the proceeds.

cut out. To leave a certain place.

cutered pill. A strong, unpalatable smoke obtained when the bowl of the pipe is too hot or when too much *yen shee* has accumulated. Sometimes caused by too much poorly reworked *yen shee* in the opium or by an inexperienced cook who does not take it off right. Also *green pill.* "Nothing has the foul taste of a cutered pill or the heavenly taste of a good one."

cutting up. Cutting the wrists in the hope of getting drugs. One phase of a *Brody, q.v.*

D.C. commitment. A person committed to the Lexington Hospital from Washington, D.C., usually required to do a *cure.*

dabble. To indulge irregularly in

narcotics. Now widely used by *squares*. See *chippy habit, chipping*.

daisy. A male homosexual. Also *sissy, queen, sex punk,* etc.

deadwood. Arrested with narcotics on the person, or in the automobile or room of the addict (or peddler) (West and Southwest). "Glommed, eh?" "Yeah, deadwood, too." Obsolescent, except among old-timers. Current popular terms, *dead bang, dead bust.*

dealer. 1. Anyone who buys or sells stolen goods or contraband. 2. A wholesale dealer in narcotics. 3. A peddler. Also *the man.*

dealer's hand. A method of *holding* a paper of heroin, used by peddlers. A rubber band around the wrist or the finger is used to flip the paper away if arrest is imminent.

deck. 1. A *bindle* of morphine, cocaine or heroin. Now more commonly *paper* or *balloon.* 2. Rarely used to refer to smoking opium. See *bindle.*

deuce. 1. A two-year sentence. 2. Two of anything.

dex. Dexedrine, proprietary name of an amphetamine. Also *Dexy.*

diambista. Marijuana (Cuba, Central America, New York City).

diet pills. Amphetamines used in diet control.

dig. To understand or appreciate; to be *hip* or *hep.* "You dig working day and night trying to cop?"

digits. The *numbers racket.*

dime. 1. A ten-year sentence. 2. Ten dollars. 3. Ten of anything. 4. Or *dime bag, dime paper.* A ten dollar packet of drugs. Also *sawbuck, sawsky.*

ding. Marijuana. See *muggles.*

dingus, deazingus, dinghizen. The medicine dropper, the bulb, the needle or any part of the *works,* or the entire assembly. A loose, general term, synonymous with *phystaris.* See *artillery. Deazingus* taken from a carnival grifter's usage and an example of *cezearney,* an argot based on phonetic distortion.

dip or **dip artist.** A pickpocket who works with a mob; to professional pickpockets, a *tool, wire* or *hook. Dip* is not much used any more by pickpockets, but has been adopted by some addicts not very familiar with *the whiz.*

dirt. Heroin. See *shit.*

dirty. 1. Possessing or transporting drugs. 2. Having sclerotic or scarred veins from injecting drugs. See *cement arm.*

dirty jacket. A bad police record. Also *bad rap sheet, snitch sheet.*

ditch. The cubital area of the arm, a favored spot for injections. Also *pit* (West Coast).

do. 1. To use drugs. The paradigm is virtually complete. "Does he do morphine or heroin?" "I've done mescaline a few times." "They were doing speed when I was there." 2. Any deviant sexual act performed on one person by another. Especially prevalent among heroin users.

do popper. A needle addict. Obsolescent. See *needle fiend* 2.

dog it. To malinger or loaf on the job. 2. To run from a fight.

dolly. Methadone, or dolophin.

domino. 1. To complete any action, as, "Did you domino?" (meaning did you *score?* were you able to purchase drugs? etc.). 2. To achieve sexual gratification in prison or out. "What kind of machinery is she? Did you domino?"

dope. 1. Narcotics. 2. Information. 3.

To drug. This term, like *dope fiend,* tends to be taboo among addicts, though they use both pejoratively.

dope hop. A prison term for drug addicts, mostly used by guards, turn keys and police. "Where is the dope hop tier? On the flats like it used to be?"

do-right people. Nonaddicts, or legitimate people as contrasted to underworld characters. Also *square apple, Joe lunch pail, lame.* Sometimes heard as *do-right John,* but rare among underworld addicts. Obsolescent. "Should get this kite out Sunday through one of the do-right people." "Don't crack now, that character is a do-right John."

doublcheader. Two marijuana cigarettes smoked simultaneously in the belief that euphoria is increased.

down. 1. Incarcerated, *put away, busted.* 2. Under the influence of a depressant drug. 3. Back to normal after the use of euphoric or hallucinogenic drugs.

downers. 1. Tranquilizers, depressant drugs, barbiturates. See *uppers.* 2. Unpleasant experiences. See *bum trip.*

(the) dozens. 1. Playing *the dozens* is a verbal activity common among young ghetto males. More or less formulaic insults, usually of mothers and other relatives, are exchanged in an effort to make the opponent lose his *cool.* (2. and 3. are probably derived from 1.) 2. Gossip, especially about one's parents or close relatives. Also *to play the dozens,* to gossip or run someone down. 3. Low rating or cursing someone violently, especially about his mother.

Dr. White. A code word for narcotics, especially *white stuff.* Obsolescent. "Dr. White is a grand old man. . . ."

drag. Anything which is boring or unpleasant. Also *bummer, bum kick, hum bug, rank.*

dream stick. An opium pipe. See *bamboo.* Also *stick* or *stem.*

drifter. An addict who has no permanent base of operations.

dripper. See *dropper.*

drive. 1. Euphoria. See *bang* 2. "I like the drive I get from H; suits me better." Also *buzz, flash, charge.* 2. To force a person to *pull a caper* against his will. 3. To put a woman out to work as a prostitute. "I have to drive that bitch to get her on the track." 4. To smuggle drugs into prison. Also *drive in.* "The man is going to drive in tonight so be on the point.

drive in. See *drive* 4. ". . . expect Mr. B to drive in this week and I'm anxious."

drop. 1. To arrest with the merchandise, usually as *to get the drop on.* 2. To sell or deliver, as a *light-weight pusher* or delivery man. "I'm dropping smack for Sam." 3. To ingest, especially LSD, but also any drug which can be taken by mouth. "I dropped some acid there with some friends." See *dropping.* 4. Widely used for *fence.* "Joe was a good drop until the heat was put on him." 5. Place of concealment. "Do you know of a good drop for this trash?"

dropped. Arrested. Also *busted, nailed, snatched.*

dropper or **dripper.** The inevitable medicine dropper used by needle addicts to make a *joint, q.v.* "The dropper is the thing for a mainliner. It's easier to manipulate.

dropping or **dropping rainbows.** Taking drugs by mouth. This may include LSD and all forms of addicting drugs in capsules, tablets or solution in water or alcohol. Also *scarfing,* or *scoffing, pill dropping.*

drugstore stuff. 1. Barbiturates or amphetamines as distinct from heroin. 2. Legitimate drugs (usually opiates) as distinct from bootleg drugs.

drum. A dormitory, usually in a prison or hospital.

dry spell. A period of abstinence from drugs, usually due to police pressure or *heat.*

duck. See *gopher, Hoosier fiend.*

ducking and dodging. Wanted by the law.

dude. A garishly, often expensively dressed male, frequently a pimp or *connection.* Formerly ghetto usage, now often generalized to mean any male. Also widely recorded in southern dialect usage.

Duffy. 1. A feigned fit staged to obtain narcotics. See *Brody* 1. 2. Sometimes recorded as *Arthur Duffy.* Escape by running away. Also recorded as *on the Duffy, on the A.D., on the Arthur, to take a Duffy,* etc.

dugout. 1. An addict (or nonaddict) who eats all the time; especially applicable to one whose appetite increases strongly following withdrawal. See *chuck horrors.* 2. An addict who has reached the bottom, especially one of the *boot and shoe* class. One who is, as the saying goes, "lame, lazy and crazy," or "sick, lazy and lame." 3. A. playful expression, as "Why, you old dugout." Also *dug, Douglas, garbage freak,* in all three senses.

duke. 1. The hand. 2. To hand. 3. With *in.* To include someone in a *caper* or a deal. 4. with *out.* To exclude someone from a *caper* or a deal. May include fighting with him. "I had to duke that lame out the other day."

dummy. Bad or fake dope, passed as genuine in the traffic. "Caught selling dummies. . . ." Also *turkey, blank, the business, jaloney, flea powder, dust, bogus smack, sugar.*

dummy up. 1. To refuse to give information. Also *freeze, play the clam, play the exhaust, put it down, play the iggie* (for ignore or ignorant). 2. To take it easy, quiet down.

Dutch route. Suicide. Also *Gillette way out, crack out, cotton tail route.*

dyke. A woman taking the masculine role in a lesbian act; clipped from *bulldyker,* sometimes recorded as *bulldagger.*

dynamite. 1. Bootleg drugs which are strong or not very highly *cut.* "That stuff he pushes is dynamite. . . ." 2. A knockout dose concealed in narcotics, often a *hot shot.* 3. Someone who is *wrong* or who may be a stool pigeon.

easy rider. A pimp, especially a good one. Now much generalized as a result of the movie *Easy Rider.*

easy time or **doing easy time.** A prison sentence that is served smoothly and without difficulty; one in which the time does not drag too heavily. Also *having a ball, laying back and doing it, coasting, jailing it.*

eater. An addict who takes drugs by mouth. See *belly habit, scoff.*

eighth or **eighth piece.** About one gram or approximately 60 grains of *white stuff,* usually morphine. May also apply to commercial heroin, as ⅛ oz. containing about 2 per cent pure heroin. "I had about an eighth left when I came in off the road."

embroidery. 1. A term like *Chinese needle work* for opium or smoker's supplies. 2. Black scars, or *tracks* from injections, also known as *service stripes.*

emergency gun. An improvised *joint* or *works* made from a medicine dropper and a safety pin, nail, sewing machine needle, etc. The skin is punctured with the sharp point and the solution injected into the flesh or under the skin. It is makeshift, usually used in jails or prisons, and is not to be confused with a conventional *joint, q.v.* Also *fake, gaffus, the thing, makeshift gun.*

emsel. Morphine. Obsolescent. See *M.*

end. 1. The best, as "That's the end." 2. On the West Coast, *end* in various combinations means just the opposite of *end* 1, *i.e.,* the worst, the finish, etc.

end gate. 1. The end of anything. 2. A maximum penalty such as life imprisonment.

ends. Money.

engine. 1. The opium smokers' *layout, q.v.* 2. The *works* for other narcotics. "I've got the engine but no smack or cotics."

eye opener. The first *shot* of the day, taken on awakening. Also *morning shot, wake up* or *wakeup shot, get up.* "To wake up without an eye opener has only happened to me twice in all the time I've been on junk."

factory. 1. A needle addict's *layout* for injecting narcotics. "Get out the factory, the doctor is here." 2.

A wholesale distributing depot for peddlers where *caps* are filled. "I wouldn't go around that factory for all the gow in china." 3. A homosexual. "That factory is tops and bottoms" (two-way).

fag. A pimp. Not to be confused with the general slang *fag* (a homosexual), clipped from *faggot.*

fake, fakus or **fake a loo.** 1. The medicine dropper for a needle addict's *layout.* ". . . just get the fake out and let's fix. . . ."2. See *ice tong doctor.*

fall. 1. To be arrested. See *bust* 2, *take a fall.* 2. To receive a prison sentence.

fall dough. Money held in reserve, often by another person, to be used in event of arrest.

fall out. 1. To experience the effect of a drug. 2. To experience intense emotion, surprise, or disbelief (ghetto usage). "When he said that, I nearly fell out laughing."

fed. A federal agent, usually a narcotics agent. Also *the man, narco.*

feed (one's) head. To ingest drugs orally.

feel the (my, his, etc.) habit coming on. To experience the early symptoms of withdrawal; to need drugs. Also *hurting, it's bearing down on me, to feel a thing coming on, get a righteous thing going.*

fence. A person or establishment dealing in stolen goods. Also *drop* 3.

fiend. A disparaging term used by addicts for an addict who has lost control to the point where he cannot plan his dose schedule. He uses all of the drugs he can get and has no other interests besides drugs. Also *hog, pig, junk, freak. Fiend* is used only in anger. This is basically a *square* term clipped from *dope fiend.*

figure eight. See *Brody.*

fin. 1. A five-year sentence. Also *buffalo, nickel.* 2. A five dollar bill.

finger or **finger of stuff.** 1. A rubber finger stall or condom filled with narcotics and swallowed or concealed in the rectum. Also *keyster (or kiester) plant, stall.* 2. *Finger* only. The act of pointing an addict out to the police for an arrest. "I know the finger came right out of that joint. . . ."

finif or **finski.** A five dollar bill. (Variants of *fin.*)

fink. A stool pigeon; an untrustworthy person. Also *wrong, no good, rat, snitch.*

fire or **fire up.** 1. To inject narcotics hypodermically. Also to *geez, bang, fix, get with it.* See *bang.* 2. *Fire up* only. To light or begin smoking marijuana or hashish.

fire plug. A large opium pill. Also *high hat.* Also applied to a large *yen pok* taken away to eat later. "He took off about eight pills, but four of them were fire plugs."

fish. 1. A voluntary patient or prisoner addict. See *Mr. Fish.* 2. A new arrival in jail. 3. Greenhorn, sucker. 4. A pimp. Cut back from *fish and shrimp.* "Steve is a righteous fish. He has four ponies (prostitutes) on the track."

fistaris or **fisstaris.** Also *phystaris.* A currently popular word meaning about anything, especially anything connected with narcotics. "Hand me the fisstaris" might mean the needle, the dropper, the cord—or even a cigarette or matches. "Button up before you show your fistaris" might mean shut your mouth before you show

your ignorance, or close your fly before you expose yourself.

fit. A hypodermic *outfit.*

fix and flash. See *jolt.*

fix or **fix up.** 1. A ration of narcotics; specifically, the amount it requires to *fix* a particular habit. "He just couldn't spare me a fix up." 2. To inject drugs. "We can fix in the can." 3. *Fix* only. Money, influence, or other means of getting charges reduced or dropped; usually occurs as *the fix.* See *fixer.* Derived from usage of professional criminals.

fixed up. The state of balance achieved by an addict after he takes a *fix up.*

fixer. A lawyer or politician who can intervene to get charges reduced or dropped.

flake out. 1. To quit, pass out, fold up from drug use. 2. To abstain from something. Specialized from military usage.

flash. 1. Euphoria following injection of narcotics. See *belt.* One addict of long experience describes the sensations immediately following injection as follows: "Codeine gives a severe burn, turning the skin ruby red, and is painful. Morphine is a tingle or flash. Heroin gives a flush but no burn. Gum opium (in solution) gives a slight flash without the tingle, and more of a thumping or pounding sensation. With Nembutal one gets a black out, the vision going from yellow to blackish green, to black all in a matter of seconds. Paregoric gives a dull flush, not a flash and no tingle." 2. To vomit, as a phase of withdrawal.

flashback. A *trip* which sometimes occurs even though a person has not just taken a drug, especially for an LSD user.

flea powder. Highly diluted narcotics, especially heroin.

flip. 1. To inform. 2. To change one's routine. "I've got to flip; my habit's out of sight." 3. Or *flip out.* To become mentally unbalanced from the use of a drug, usually LSD or the amphetamines.

flip over. 1. To go off narcotics (usually temporarily). 2. To go homosexual. Also to *turn around.*

flipped. 1. Knocked out by chloral hydrate or some other drug, usually given an addict or user in order to render him unconscious. Sometimes used in connection with *rolling* or robbing addicts. 2. Or *flipped out.* Mentally unbalanced from the use of a drug, especially LSD or amphetamines.

flippy. Stimulating or exciting to one who is under the influence of a drug. See *freaky.*

floater. 1. A vagrant. 2. A particle of blood in the butt of the needle which, when dried, is difficult to remove.

floating. Under the influence of narcotics. See *coasting.*

fluke. An unjust conviction, a *bum rap.*

fly. Sophisticated yet carefree; wise in the ways of the underworld.

fold up. 1. To stop taking narcotics. See *to be away from the habit.* 2. To stop selling narcotics. "When George was guzzled, all the pushers had to fold up. . . ."

football. A type of encapsulated amphetamine (blue, purple, or red), or mescaline (yellow or brown).

frame or **frame for.** 1. To prepare or lay the groundwork for obtaining narcotics by deceiving a physician. 2. To pretend illness in order to get narcotics. "He would frame for a croaker and score for a bang." See *Brody.* 3. **Frame** (alone). A very slender or "skinny" prostitute.

freak. 1. An addict who enjoys playing with the needle, same as *needle fiend.* 2. A sexual deviate. 3. See *nic nac, weird, buzzer* 1. 4. A person whose appearance and habits emulate drug, youth and music subcultures. 5. A fan or devotee of anything, for example, a Jesus freak.

freak out. 1. To be intensely affected, sometimes to the point of mental imbalance, by something. "He dropped too much acid and really freaked out." 2. Also *freakout.* A drug party or other exhilarating experience. 3. A *bad trip, q.v.*

freaky. 1. Unusual, bizarre. 2. Especially stimulating to someone under the influence of drugs.

free loader. A down and out addict. Also *gutter hype, 24 karat poop butt, low rider.* See *boot and shoe.*

freebies. 1. Persons not addicted to drugs. 2. Anything free. 3. Rations of drugs given or sold on credit to beginning addicts.

freeze or **freeze on.** 1. To ignore, disregard, or refuse to acknowledge a person. "You'd better freeze on that snitch—he'll get you busted." 2. To refuse to give information.

fruit merchant. A homosexual. Also *fairy, sissy, punk, gunzel, stuff, works, queen, factory, nic nac.*

fu. Marijuana. See *muggles.*

fucked or **fucked up.** *Stoned, q.v.*

fuete. A needle. From Cuban Spanish for "whip." See *spike, artillery.* (New York, Miami areas.)

fun. (Pronounced *foon* in the Midwest and West, *foong* or *fong* in New York and the East.) Singular and plural forms identical. A unit of measure applied to opium; 5:79 grains. Most prepared opium is sold and used by the *fun* rather than by the grain. "The toys usually contained 10 to 12 fun."

fur. See *fuzz.*

fuzz or **fuzzy.** A detective. Cut back from *fuzzy tail.* Now generalized to any law enforcement officer. Also *fur.*

G.O.M. Literally, God's own medicine, a phrase borrowed from medicine.

gaffel. 1. To shoplift or steal. 2. To arrest.

gaffus. See *emergency gun.*

gang bang. Sexual intercourse by several males in succession with the same female, or group intercourse with several partners of both sexes. See *train.*

gap. 1. To yawn and salivate, the first signs of withdrawal distress. "About then she was feeling rough and starting to gap." 2. The female genitalia.

gapper. An addict in need of drugs. "The joint was full of gappers, a hot spot to stop at. . . ."

garbage. Inferior heroin. See *flea powder.*

garbage freak. See *dugout.*

gassed. Experiencing euphoria following injection.

gauge or gage. Marijuana. See *muggles.*

gay. Homosexual.

gazer. 1. A Federal narcotic agent. Also *whiskers, uncle* (New York and vicinity). "Watch that gazer at the corner table." 2. A pervert who likes to window-shop sexually; often specialized to *doodle gazers, kiester gazers,* etc. May or may not be homosexual. A man who shops in a crowd by touching women intimately is a *muzzler.*

gear. A sexually perverted person, usually a male.

gee (pronounced to rhyme with Mc-Gee). 1. Prepared smoking opium, probably from Hindustani *ghee,* though derivation from the *g* used as an abbreviation for *gow,* etc. is also "possible. 2. A person, as, "he's a right gee." Probably from guy.

gee chee. 1. A Negro from the Sea Islands. 2. Any bright skinned Negro, as contrasted to "high yellow."

gee fat. The *yen shee* which forms inside the pipe stem after opium is smoked. Probably a variant of *gee yen.* "There was at least 50 fun of gee fat in that old pipe."

gee rag or **gee.** 1. The small square of cloth with a hole in the center, used to make a tight connection between the shank of the bowl and the stem of an opium pipe. "The gee rag is about half the size of a woman's small wipe—about three inches." 2. Sometimes loosely used for the paper, thread or rubber used to make a tight connection between needle and dropper, properly known as a *collar, gaff, boot* or *geep.*

gee stick. An opium pipe. Obsolescent.

gee yen. Opium which precipitates in small quantities of thin or nearly liquid gum in the stem of the pipe. It is sometimes retrieved with a hot wire and reworked for selling or smoking. "They had about a half a pound of yen shee and gee yen to go in that batch."

geed up. 1. A down and out addict. See *boot and shoe.* 2. More generally, by extension, any person or thing or place which is undesirable, broken or out of order. "That was a geed-up joint. . . ."

geep or **jeep.** The *gee rag, q.v.* Also *boot, collar, boo gee.*

geetis or **geetus.** Money. Also *bread, scratch, green, lettuce, bees and honey,* etc.

geez. 1. An injection of drugs. 2. To inject drugs.

geezer. A *shot* of narcotics injected hypodermically, especially a small shot. Also *geez.* See *vein shot, bang.*

George. Very good.

George Smack. See *McCoy.*

get a finger wave. The process of having the rectum searched for drugs.

get a thing going or **have a thing going.** To build up a big habit. "I saw Jake the other day and he's got a thing going."

get in the wind. 1. To leave a place, sometimes in haste. 2. To become emotionally detached; to be at loose ends.

get it together. 1. To accomplish something, especially come to terms with one's own feelings, desires, etc. 2. To have sex.

get next to. 1. To upset someone's defenses. 2. To become emotionally involved, to anger. 3. To get in with police by acting as a stool pigeon. 4. To establish a good *connection,* especially with a physician or druggist.

get off on. To take drugs regularly; probably an extension of *to get the yen* or *habit off.* "At that time I was getting off on H and speed balls."

get or **be on the point.** See *play the point.*

get straight. See *get the habit off.*

get the bitch. To be convicted under a habitual criminal act.

get (the) habit off. To satisfy the desire for drugs at the regular time when abstinence symptoms are about to be felt or are felt slightly. "Seems like I can't get my habit off this morning." Also *get straight, get (the) yen off.*

get the works. 1. To receive punishment, especially in prison or jail. 2. To be killed or beaten up.

get up. 1. The first shot of the day. 2. The last day of a prison sentence. "I've got four days and a get up."

get up steam. To drink whiskey, followed by an intravenous shot of morphine, heroin or mixed cocaine and heroin. ". . . they would get up steam, take a drink and then fire up. . . ." Addicts disagree on this, as on many other aspects of drug use. "You *must* fix first. There is no quicker way to commit suicide than to take a big drink of whiskey, then take a shot of morphine or opium."

get (one's) yen off. 1. To satisfy a need for drugs; to take drugs. "I'll be seeing you when I get my yen off—and it will take several fixes to get *my* yen off" (note from an addict doing a two-year sentence). 2. Indulging in any pastime (or vice). "Charley is down at the corner getting his yen off" (meaning Charley is down there betting on the horses). 3. Sometimes used to apply to the substitution of any drug one can get for the drug of choice; often shortened to *get off on, q.v.*

get with it. To inject narcotics intravenously. See *bang.*

getting a righteous thing going. Experiencing early withdrawal symptoms. See *feel the habit coming on.*

gig. 1. A job or method of making money. 2. A *high* to pill droppers. "Get a gig on."

giggle weed. 1. Marijuana. 2. Marijuana combined with wine.

Gillette way out. Suicide.

girl. Cocaine.

give (someone) head. To perform oral sex, a common deviance among drug abusers.

give (someone his) wings. To administer drugs to someone, especially heroin. Also to teach someone to use drugs.

give (someone) some skin. To shake hands. Also *give (someone) five.*

give the chatter. To talk or answer questions of the authorities. Also transitive, as *give (someone) the chatter.* Also to give them a *grade B movie script.*

giving birth. Expelling the hard fecal matter inevitably resulting from the use of opiates. Also known as *giving birth to a duster* or *to a block buster.* This usage seems to be used largely by old-timers who have used opium. See *yen shee baby.*

giving up backs. Being initiated into homosexual practices, usually specifically anal intercourse.

glass. Methedrine in ampules.

globe trotter. One who moves frequently.

glom. 1. To steal. 2. To take drugs. 3. To take more than one's share, to be *on the muscle.* Also to *bogart.*

go. 1. A *bindle* or quantity of narcotics, often indicated by the price—a two dollar *go* is less than a five dollar *go.* Also, *cap, package, balloon* or *deck.* "I was giving him quite a play at five bucks a go." 2. A connection, "I had a good go with Joe."

go by. 1. A refusal to recognize an acquaintance. ". . . if not wanted or disliked, they get the go by." 2. Refusal by a peddler to recog-

nize an addict or to deal with one whose reputation he does not trust. "He didn't think anybody was hep to that business in St. Louis, but that's why he got the go by." See to *chill.*

go in the sewer. To inject narcotics intravenously. See *bang.*

go in the skin. To inject drugs subcutaneously. "I'm in a hurry, Jack. Go in the skin with that one. . . ."

go on a sleigh ride. To inhale cocaine, with the consequent exhilaration. Related to *snow* for cocaine. Also *snow ride,* both obsolescent.

go over the hill. To escape by runing away. Also *pull a rabbit,* take a *rabbit parole.*

go up. To experience drug-induced euphoria.

go up the manure chute. To perform coitus per anum.

God's medicine. Morphine. The phrase is credited to Sir William Osler. "Yes, it's God's medicine, for if there were any better, it would be kept in heaven for the angels to use."

going downhill. Past the halfway point in a prison sentence. Also *over the hump.*

going up the dirt road. Coitus *per anum.* Also *bust your brown, round eye,* etc.

gold leaf special. A marijuana cigarette which is (theoretically) more potent and sold at a premium. Usually a *booster stick* or cigarette of treated marijuana. See *stick* 2.

gone. See *in high.*

gong or **gonger.** 1. An opium pipe. See *bamboo.* "You bring the gong, the rest of the layout is here. . . ." 2. *Gonger* (only). An opium smoker. ". . . used to be a gonger, but squared up. . . ." 3. Opium or opium derivatives. "Any gonger around L.A.?" See *kick the gong.*

good time. The time allotted on a sentence for working in an industry and/or obeying the rules. Also *copper, stuff.*

goods. Narcotics, especially as they are bought and sold. Used by addicts or dealers in letters, phone calls or telegrams. Also *merchandise.* "Ship goods to Dayton, Ohio, same address."

goof artist or **goofer.** One who uses *goof balls,* inhales glue or gasoline, drinks cough syrup, such as Cosanyl, terpin hydrate, Cheracol.

goof ball. 1. A barbiturate capsule. 2. An addict who uses barbiturates. "He's a goof ball." "Them goof ball artists are really pitiful." 3. One of any kind of drug capsule, not restricted to barbiturates.

goofed up. 1. Intoxicated on marijuana; also used by heroin addicts (youngsters) who carry the usage over from marijuana. 2. Somewhat stupefied from taking too much drugs. See *gowed.*

goofer. 1. A barbiturate addict. 2. Sometimes used by youngsters to indicate an addict to heroin and cocaine in combination with barbiturates. 3. Generalized to mean any addict who takes drugs (especially barbiturates or amphetamines) by mouth; may include glue sniffers, gasoline inhalers and drinkers of cough syrup containing drugs. The implication is that he really doesn't have a *habit* of any size.

goofing. 1. Enjoying euphoria; used especially by youngsters who combine heroin with barbiturates or cocaine. "I was in a movie house

goofing when they picked me up." 2. Applied to youngsters who mix barbiturates with wine and hence are *goofing off* or *fouling up.*

gopher. 1. One who accepts unpleasant circumstances apathetically "Yes, I'd call a gopher a 'lame,' a 'trick,' a 'chump,' or a 'duck.' 2. One who 'goes for' drugs for someone else. (To go for.) See *lobby gow.*

got it beat. 1. To have passed through the most severe abstinence symptoms. 2. To have served half or more of a prison sentence. "I've got it beat" or "I'm going downhill."

gow. 1. Narcotics in general, especially those used hypodermically. Probably of Chinese origin and originally used for opium, but no longer so restricted. Obsolescent, being supplanted by *smack, schmeck, stuff,* although modern heroin users do not include morphine or opium. 2. To ream out the bowl of the opium pipe with the *yen shee gow.* ". . . gow the bowl, trim the lamp and fill it, too. . . ."

gow head. Originally an opium addict, but now generalized to include all types of addict except marijuana and barbiturate users. However, old-timers still use it to refer to opium users. "Doc, you put it your way and I'll put it mine. A gow head goes for the gow shee. Eats at the Y. Peeps in the heater. Goes for furburgers. Correct me if I'm wrong."

gowed. Having taken more narcotics than needed to satisfy a habit, and consequently being in a state of stupor or intoxication. (Past participle form only generally used.) "One pop in the main line and he's gowed." Also *dosed, out of sight, zipped, overamped, O.D.'d,* though the last term may mean seriously knocked out or killed by an overdose.

gowster. 1. A needle addict. 2. An opium smoker. Old-timers still like to restrict this term to opium users. "He's a gowster and won't go for the spike."

grade B movie script. See *give the chatter.*

grapevine. The system by which messages and other items circulate in prisons; the person-to-person contacts which lead an addict to a peddler. Usage of this term in the underworld is mostly whimsical: "Where did you get that lump?" "Why, Officer, I picked it off the grapevine." Also *trolley* in some prisons. *Grapevine* is also applied to the very effective communication system used by criminals outside prisons.

grass. Marijuana. Also *pot, weed, gage* and many others. See *muggles.*

grasshopper. A marijuana addict. See *reefer man.*

grease. 1. Prepared smoking opium. See *black stuff.* 2. To flatter. 3. Flattery. 4. To bribe. 5. A lawyer or politician who can intervene to get charges dropped or reduced; in effect, a *fixer* with political influence. See *juice.* 6. To eat ravenously after withdrawal. Also *root.* See *chuck habit.*

grease ball. 1. On the East Coast, an Italian. 2. On the West Coast, a Mexican, often *greaser.* Both are fighting words.

green ashes. Improperly or incompletely combusted opium; opium ash or *yen shee* from which some smoking opium may be retrieved by reworking. Obsolescent.

green hype. See *J.C.L.*

green mud. Smoking opium not cooked long enough or improperly prepared. Better for *shooting* than for smoking.

green pill. An improperly cooked pill of opium. See *cutered pill.*

green score. Profit made by passing counterfeit money.

griefo or **greefo.** Marijuana. "Smoking griefo is my idea of nothing to do." Much used in Texas and the Midwest. Sometimes recorded as *griffa.*

grift. The nonviolent rackets, as contrasted with the *heavy rackets.* Usually refers to a confidence mob working the *short con games.* Also pickpockets, some types of gamblers. "He played the grift at the 12th Street shed."

grocery boy. 1. An addict who has drugs but wants food. 2. An addict who has developed the *chuck habit, q.v.*

groove with junk. To be *high.*

groovie or **groovy.** Very good.

grooving. Experiencing euphoria following the use of drugs. Also *coasting, tripping.*

guinea. 1. An Italian. 2. A Creole. 3. A bright-skinned Negro.

gum. 1. Gum opium swallowed in small pieces broken off a larger brick or ball. A solution is sometimes used intravenously by needle addicts. 2. The raw *mud* from which smoking pills or *yen poks* (for swallowing) are made. Today it is sold in *papers* of 7 to 10 *fun* at $10.00, or 25 *fun* at $20.00 or $25.00.

gun. 1. An addict's hypodermic outfit. See *artillery.* 2. A pickpocket. 3. To look at closely.

gunk. Morphine. See *M.*

gunzel, guntzel, gunsel, gonsil. 1. A

disgusting person. 2. A male homosexual.

gutter or **gutter hype.** A deprecatory term used of and by *boot and shoe* addicts to indicate a down and out user; also applied to alcoholics who take *pleasure shots.* ". . . you know he's a gutter and can't hit a line. . . ."

guzzled. Arrested. Also *busted, batted out, glommed, glued, sneezed, snatched in the neck, paid off in gold, gaffeled, clouted, rousted, nailed,* etc.

H. Heroin. Also indicated by any words in which H is initial or conspicuous. Also *courage pills, horse, witch hazel, stuff, shit, junk, q.v.* Obsolescent.

habit. The need for a drug (especially opiates) as indicated by physical and emotional dependence. This term used with a great variety of shades of meaning: "My habit's coming on"; "I've got one hell of a habit"; "I traveled all day with a habit"; "That's a chicken shit habit"; etc. Also *run,* as "I've got a six-month run," and *strung out* as "I've been all strung out for a year."

hacks and croakers. The staff at the Lexington Hospital (guards, doctors, attendants, etc.). Names for guards in other places are legion —*hooligan, screw, the man, the buzzer, nix crackin-Jimmy Bracken,* etc.

half or **half piece.** Half an ounce of *white stuff, q.v.* See *piece, O.Z.* "Junkers usually say 'half' these days and the 'piece' in 'half piece' is understood."

hancty. Conceited.

hang it up. 1. To be away from the habit. 2. See *lay it down.*

hang (someone) up. To fail to keep an appointment for the exchange of narcotics. Also *blow the meet, blow the scene.*

hang tough. 1. Take it easy, quiet down, stop. 2. To *chill, q.v.*

hang up. 1. To abstain from using or selling drugs. Also to be *clean,* to *straighten out,* etc. 2. Or *hang-up.* Generalized to a mental block.

hanging paper. Passing worthless checks, usually on a mass production basis.

happenings. Action, planning of activities, criminal and narcotic. Also *skam.*

happy dust. Cocaine, especially cocaine used for inhaling. The trend is to regard this term as *square,* with addicts holding to *Cecil, coke, snow, crystals* or just plain *C.*

hard stuff. Any drug which produces physiological dependence. Also sometimes applied to DMT or any highly concentrated drug.

hard time. To be unhappy under confinement, as to *do hard time.* This includes convicts who have lost their *copper* through disciplinary problems. Also *tough time.*

harpoon. The hollow needle used with a *joint.* "I can get you cut in if you dig up a harpoon." Also *spike, silver serpent, pin machine, tom cat, fisstaris,* etc., with specialized meanings.

Harry or **hairy.** Heroin (West Coast). See *H.*

hash. 1. **Gum hashish.** 2. A concentrated essence of the hemp plant made by chopping it up and boiling it down.

hassle or **the hassle.** 1. The straight world of the nonaddict. 2. *hassle* (only). Police harassment, especially of drug users.

have a ball. To serve a smooth and easy prison sentence.

have a Chinaman (or **a monkey**) **on (one's) back.** To feel the need of drugs strongly; to experience the early stages of withdrawal distress. See *sick.* "When I woke up I sure had a Chinaman on my back. . . ." Chinese addicts sometimes say, "Your grandma die?" when they see the running eyes and nose in early withdrawal. Other phrases are, *"I'm hurting," "I'm up tight," "I'm sick,"* which are recognized by any addict or peddler.

have a habit. To need drugs; to be addicted. See *sick.* This term now losing favor with addicts who prefer *strung out, long run* and other euphemisms.

have a yen. 1. To feel the first symptoms of needing a *shot* or a smoke of opium. 2. To desire anything Obsolescent, giving way to *coming down, hurting,* etc. See have *a Chinaman on (one's) back.*

have something going. To be engaged in some illegal enterprise.

hawk. A guard in a federal prison. Obsolescent. "Hawk was very seldom used in my time, except by guys chopping up old scores."

head. A user of drugs, especially hallucinogens. See *hop head.*

head and body trip. A drug experience which has both psychological and physiological effects.

heat. Police pressure. 2. A police officer or narcotic agent.

heater. The female genitals.

heaven dust. Cocaine, especially as inhaled. Whimsical or "square" phrase.

heavenly blues. Morning glory seeds which have hallucinogenic effects.

heaves. 1. The vomiting and gastric discomfort accompanying withdrawal. See *twister* 3. 2. The vomiting usually following the first shot of heroin taken by a beginner.

heaves and squirts. Vomiting and diarrhea accompanying withdrawal.

heavy. 1. Intelligent, educated very serious, or important. 2. One who uses firearms or force in his *racket.* 3. A safecracker. 4. A violent person.

heeb. A Jew. Also *mocky, rabbi, skinless, popcorn,* etc.

heel. 1. To steal in a sneak thief manner. 2. A specialized type of highly skilled thief, especially a *bank heel.*

heist. 1. To rob. 2. To lift someone's *plant, q.v.*

hemp. *Cannabis sativa* or *Cannabis indica.* The plant, the flowering tops or pods used in marijuana. See *muggles.*

he's in. Said of anyone regularly using narcotics.

high. 1. Variant of *in high, q.v.* Also *gassed, stoned, zonked, tripping, loaded,* etc. 2. The maximum euphoria experienced by *pill droppers* or those who take drugs by mouth. "I get my high in about thirty minutes." "I seldom get my highs anymore."

high hat. 1. A large drug habit. 2. A large pill of smoking opium. See *bird's eye* 2. 3. A tall opium lamp, or, the shade thereof. Obsolescent. "High hat lamps were used around some old-time lay down joints."

highsiding. See *stepping high* 3.

hip or **hep.** To be aware of; to know. To be wise in the ways of the underworld. This is an old argot term which has enjoyed several cycles of popularity. It was originally recorded as *Joe Hep* in 1938 among grifters who remembered using it in the 1890's. Some old-timers still use *Joe* as a verb. "Let me Joe you to that, Doc."

hippie. Antiestablishment person characterized by bizarre and disreputable appearance and association with various musical cults.

hipster. 1. A *finger man* who cases a joint to be *knocked over*. 2. Among *squares* or part-time users of drugs, one who is much preoccupied with jazz and jazz musicians.

hit. 1. To succeed at anything. "Did you hit?" 2. To purchase narcotics. "Right after that he went on downtown and H. and R." (He *hit and ran,* i.e., bought drugs from the peddler and left town.) 3. For narcotics to *register;* for the user to feel euphoria. "Did that shot hit yet?" 4. To get a hypodermic needle into a vein. "You know he's a gutter and can't hit a line." 5. To borrow or attempt to borrow (especially narcotics). "Just now, did he hit you for stuff?" See *score.* 6. As a noun, a *toke* or *tote* of marijuana, or one lungful of its smoke. See *toke, tote.*

hit and miss habit. A small, irregular drug habit. "A guy with a hit and miss habit don't have half the trouble kicking."

hit on. 1. To make a proposition, especially to proposition for sexual activities, either homo or hetero- 2. To ask for something, to "put the bum on" someone. Also *put the lug on, put the bee on,* etc.

hit spike. A makeshift hypodermic needle. See *artillery.*

hit the gong. 1. To smoke opium in a group or party. Not used to refer to smoking alone. Also *hit the pipe, kick the gong, roll the log,* *beat the gong.* "We would phone the Chino then and see if it was OK to kick the gong at Charlie's place." 2. Recently adapted by marijuana smokers in the same sense. "Weed smokers say 'kick the gong,' too.

hit the gow. 1. To be addicted. "I hear Annie is hitting the gow again after all these years. . . ." 2. The act of taking narcotics. (Used largely by police officers and others who come into contact with addicts.) See *hooked.* 3. To an old-timer, to smoke opium.

hit the sewer. To inject narcotics intravenously. Also *go in the sewer.* See *main line.*

hit the stuff. Meanings and usage the same as to *hit the gow* except that currently this phrase is much used by police officers. See *hooked.*

hitch. A prison sentence. Also *bit, jolt, fall, skam,* etc.

hitchhiker. A voluntary patient in a narcotics hospital. See *C. Vol.*

hocus. Morphine prescribed in solution by physicians who believed it could not be resold for addict use in this form. Obsolescent. "In T.O. (Toledo, Ohio), the croakers all wrote for hocus for a while and stuff sold for so much a dripper."

hog. See *fiend.*

hold. 1 (Transitive only.) To support a habit. See *carry.* "That stuff won't hold me at all." 2. (Intransitive only.) To have drugs for sale, especially on one's person. "Yeah, I'm holding, but I can't let him have much."

(the) hole. Solitary confinement. Also *(the) slab.*

home. The vein into which drugs are injected. See *main line.*

homey. A person from the same home town.

hook. See *yen hok.*

hook shop. A house of prostitution. Also *shop, house, crib, joint, notch joint, pad, scatter, spread,* etc. Because of the widespread tendency for addicts to become pimps, many terms from the *broad rackets* are infiltrating addict usage. These include words for various kinds of brothels, types of prostitute, the genitalia and various kinds of sex acts.

hooked. Addicted to narcotics. Also *on the gow, hitting the gow, on stuff, hitting the stuff, on junk, got a run going, hitting, strung out,* etc.

hooker. 1. Notice that one is wanted by the law. 2. A prostitute.

hooligan. A prison guard. See *hacks.*

Hoosier fiend. 1. An inexperienced addict; a yokel who doesn't realize he is *hooked.* 2. Any addict who is not of the underworld; a business or professional man. "She filled in with that Hoosier fiend; they say he has plenty of scratch." Also *square hype, trick, duck,* in both senses.

hop. 1. Opium for smoking. 2. Narcotics for injection or inhalation. Nonsmokers use the term to mean any kind of drugs which will satisfy their habit, or any drug they are using at the time.

hop head. A narcotic addict. See *hype.* Restricted to opiate users in addict usage, but encountered increasingly among *squares* to mean any drug user.

hop joint. A place where opium (or other drugs) are sold and/or consumed. An "opium den" to *squares.* If opium is smoked there it is also a *lay down joint, q.v.*

hop layout. An opium smoker's out-

fit, including pipes, stems, bowls, lamp, suey pow, etc. "Blowed a fine hop layout in 1927."

hop stick. 1. An opium pipe. See *bamboo.* 2. Sometimes the *stem* only as contrasted to the *bowl.*

hop toy or **toy.** A small container (metal salve box, English walnut shell, etc.) for smoking opium. (Sometimes needle addicts buy opium and use it in place of *white stuff* in a panic.) See *toy.* A toy usually contains about 25 *fun* of opium. "I had to score for hop toy since the heat's been on."

horn. To sniff cocaine or heroin. Also *snort, blow.* See *joy powder.*

horse. Heroin. A term much used by the younger generation of addicts. See *Racehorse Charlie, snort.*

horse doctor. Prison or jail doctor. Also *vet, croaker.*

hot. The condition of being wanted by the law. Also *smoking, dead, in the freezer, on ice, no action* and many others.

hot money. 1. Stolen or counterfeit money. 2. Money (with serial numbers recorded) which is given to informers by narcotics agents for purposes of proof of sale.

hot shot. Cyanide or other poison concealed in narcotics to kill a troublesome addict, or to remove a stool pigeon. Sometimes very strong, uncut heroin is used. The *hot shot* kills the addict in contrast to *flipping him* or *taking him* with knockout drugs. "I hear that Mike got a hot shot in New Orleans." Also called a *ten cent pistol.*

hot spot. 1. The place to which a victim is brought for the purpose of defrauding him. 2. The state of being uncomfortable or anxious, such as *sick* user experiences when he is without a *connection.*

3. A place with the police staked out.

hot stuff. Stolen *merchandise.* 2. Bad narcotics. See *turkey.*

hots. 1. Meals. 2. Among pickpockets and short con men, a place or person which may involve *heat* if they work. For example, a bus or train depot today; a plainclothesman picked as a victim, etc.

hudda. A policeman (Mexican-American usage).

hummer. A fake arrest on any pretense which will permit a search, such as a traffic violation. "I was busted on a hummer."

humming gee bowl. The bowl of an opium pipe made, according to legend, from a piece of the human skull. Obsolescent. *Humming gee bowls were made in China by a certain clan or family. . . .*

hung up. 1. Dependent on narcotics, addicted. 2. Generalized to mean obsessed with anything. See *hang-up.* 3. Having a rigid personality, inhibited. See *up tight* 2.

hurting. Experiencing early symptoms of withdrawal. Also *in trouble.*

hustle. 1. To obtain money by illegal means such as shoplifting, pickpocketing, pimping, con games, prostitution or other *rackets* commonly worked by addicts. 2. The *racket* or *hustle* by which an addict supports his habit. Also *stick.*

hustling drawers. Specially made underwear, worn by women shoplifters, in which stolen goods can be concealed. The incidence of addiction is high among shoplifters. Also *boosting drawers.*

hype. 1. An addict, especially a needle addict. Also *junker, gowster, hop head, joy popper,* etc. "The fuzz didn't know Al was a

hype. . . ." 2. The entire *works* used to inject narcotics. See *artillery.* 3. The hypodermic needle considered separately from the syringe. 4. Or **hypo.** A placebo or nonnarcotic injection sometimes given addicts during withdrawal for its psychological effect. Largely institutional usage. "A hypo will take those butterflies out of your stomach."

(the) hype. 1. A *short-change racket* much used by addicts. Also called *laying the note.* "Papa Cole was a real specialist on the hype." 2. To swindle someone with this racket. "Sometimes we'd let our bankroll run down, and then we'd turn ourselves over and come up with a couple of ones. Two bumblebees will get you a deuce, and with that we'd hype till we had a five or two. Then we could hype for a saw. With a saw, we'd hype for a twenty, and be right back in business again."

hypo smecker, smacker or **smecker.** A needle addict. The short form usually used nowadays. Formerly, this term differentiated smokers from needle addicts and probably dates from the 1920s when many smokers were taking to *white stuff. Smeck,* probably from German or Yiddish *schmecken,* is an old term for opium. "Many a hypo smecker would be a smoker today if he had his choice."

ice cream habit. A small, irregular habit. See *chippy habit.* "Hit him with an aspirin tablet and a wet towel; he only had an ice cream habit to begin with."

ice tong doctor or **ice tong croaker.** A physician with a shady reputation; one who will perform abortions or sell narcotics. Obsolescent. Also *ice water croaker,* *fake, fakaloo, taker, right croaker, croaker on the make, solid M.D.*

ice water cure. See *iron cure.*

ice water John. A cold-hearted doctor at Lexington or Ft. Worth; one who will not give additional drugs during withdrawal.

idiot juice. Nutmeg and water mixed for intoxication, largely used in prisons.

idiot pills. Barbiturates.

in action. Actively selling narcotics. Also *doing business, turning, operating.*

in flight. Very high on Methedrine. See *in orbit.*

in front of the gun. To peddle narcotics, usually with the understanding that the peddler "takes the rap" if caught and protects the dealers or *big men* for whom he works; a specialization of the general underworld phrase meaning the same thing. Ex-addicts just out of prison (not a hospital) are actively recruited by big *dealers,* who use this type of *pusher* ruthlessly for two or three months. Many of them are content if they can get drugs and make good money for as much as six months before going up again. "Just out of stir, and there he is in front of the gun."

in high or **high.** At the peak of euphoria from morphine, heroin or cocaine injected intravenously or in the skin. Giving way to the more popular *stoned, loaded, gone, (on) cloud* 9. See *coasting.* "She was sure in high when I saw her."

in on the know. In the know, *hip, q.v.*

in orbit. Having taken exactly the right amount of a drug, especially heroin, amphetamine, Methedrine. See *in flight.*

in paper. Said of narcotics smuggled into a penal institution. The powdered drug *(white stuff)* is, for instance, folded into very thin tin foil, placed inside a split postcard, and pressed flat with a hot iron. There are various other methods, such as concealing Dilaudid (crushed) under postage stamps or the flaps of sealed envelopes.

in the sack. 1. In bed. 2. The situation when a peddler has made a sale to a government agent and is sure to be arrested. Also *in hock, dead.*

in trouble. Short of drugs; experiencing early withdrawal distress. "I'm in trouble. Bring over a gram." Also *hurting.*

Indian hay. Marijuana. See *muggles.*

insane. Very good.

iron cure. The cold turkey treatment used in many jails and prisons where the addict *kicks the habit* out on the floor of his cell. Also *steel and concrete cure, iron bound cure, ice water cure.* See *quarry cure.*

iron house. A city jail. Most other underworld terms *(can, joint, band house,* etc.) are also used by addicts. "I can't recall hearing *iron house* in England or Canada, but I have talked to a few fellows who have."

J. A marijuana cigarette. Cut back from *joint* 5, *q.v.* See also *reefer.*

J.C.L. or **Johnny come lately.** A beginning addict, or one who has not yet established a regular habit; one who has not been on drugs long (adapted from old-time circus usage.) Also *1972 model* or *1973 model* (using the current year to indicate recency). Also *shirt tail hype, green hype, lame hype,* or *lame.* See *student.*

J-pipe. A pipe for smoking marijuana, especially *roaches, q.v.* See also *toke, tote.*

jab. 1. An injection of drugs, with consequent euphoria. The problem here is to hit a vein, especially when shooting in the buttocks, since the vein is not *brought up,* and since the addict must guess at its exact location. For this reason addicts who *jab* and miss are called *jabbers* or *jab artists.* Those few who can hit a vein regularly are called *whizzes, sharp shooters, the greatest.* See *bang, jaboff.* "I like to take a jab under my left shirt tail. . . ." 2. To inject drugs.

jab artist. See *jab.*

jab pop or **jab poppo.** Drugs injected hypodermically. "I used to know a flat jointer (carnival) who would say,

J.P., that's not a justice of the peace,
Who will marry you or worse,
It's not jab poppo with its bitter curse,
It's Jack pot, with all the money in my purse. . . ."

jabber. 1. A needle addict.

A jabber he was
And a jabber he'll be
Till the day he's planted
'Neath the old apple tree. . . .

2. An addict who has trouble hitting the vein. See *jab.*

jaboff. The extreme exhilaration or euphoria immediately following intravenous injection; often described as resembling a prolonged sexual orgasm. Also *flash, burn, rush, call.* "You know, he wanted a jaboff every time he fixed, and finally took one that killed him."

jack a fix. A deliberately prolonged *verification* shot. Also, *jack off shot.* Also called *jacking off a fix.*

jack off. To allow the blood to come back into the glass during a vein shot. Also *booting.* See *verification shot.*

jack roller. One who robs drunks. Formerly, restricted to getting lumberjacks just out of the timber drunk and rolling them; now generalized.

jack up. Sodium Amytal.

jacket. 1. See *collar.* 2. A police record, from the folder or filing envelope in which it is kept. A *dirty jacket* is a bad police record.

jacking off a fix. See *jack a fix.*

jailhouse pimp. See *playboy.*

jailhouse romance. A romantic attachment between inmates, either heterosexual or homosexual. See *playboy.*

jailing it. Serving an easy prison sentence. Also *coasting, have a ball.*

jaloney. Bad or fake dope. See *turkey, hot shot.*

jam. 1. Trouble with the law; a case in court. ". . . finally squared that jam with five C notes." 2. To leave the *scene.*

jammed up. Overdosed with drugs.

jap. A hair straightener made of lye, potato peelings, and oil or grease. Much used by Negroes in prison. Also *strap, strap Johnson* or *konk.*

Jasper. An aggressive female homosexual. Also *butch, bull, sergeant, beetle brow.*

jeep. See *collar.*

jeff. To be obsequious, especially Negroes in relation to whites.

jenny barn or **ginny barn.** The dormitories for females at the USPHS hospital.

jerk simple. Mentally disturbed as a result of masturbation; a mythical condition probably originating in popular folklore.

jerker. See *leapers.*

jive. To be insincere or fickle.

jive talk. Insincere, fickle or "double talk."

jobbed. Framed or arrested by entrapment techniques.

John. 1. Any male, usually not of the underworld, or not addicted. 2. A customer for a prostitute addict. Also *trick*.

joint. 1. The *needle, dropper* and *connection;* the complete outfit with which to take drugs hypodermically, in contrast to a regulation hypodermic syringe. See *artillery*. 2. A prison. 3. A place of questionable reputation. 4. The penis. 5. Marijuana, or a marijuana cigarette. 6. A place to be robbed or burglarized.

jolly beans. Amphetamines.

jolt. 1. A *shot* of narcotics taken either in the vein or in the skin, but usually the former. "Let me try a jolt of that H." 2. A strong feeling of euphoria, or *drive. Fix and flash* is a popular synonym. "I get an awful jolt out of powdered Dilaudid that I don't get out of tablets." 3. A prison sentence or term. Also *stuff* 2.

Jones. 1. A drug habit, especially a large one. 2. A variable term used widely by Negroes as a greeting.

joy pop. See *joy popper*. A common rationalization is often heard: "I don't use; I just joy pop."

joy popper. A person, not a confirmed addict, who takes an occasional injection of narcotics; however joy popping is usually the beginning of permanent addiction. See *hype*. "They all think they can take just one joy pop, but it's the first one that hooks you. . . ."

joy powder. Heroin inhaled from a hollow quill or straw. Originally a quill toothpick was used; today a soda straw is used, or even a small paper tube. Any such device is called a *horn*.

joy smoke. Marijuana. See *muggles*.

joy stick. 1. An opium pipe. See *bamboo*. 2. A marijuana cigarette.

jug. 1. To tease. 2. A city jail or a holdover. 3. A 10 cc. multidose vial of Methedrine.

juice. 1. Political pull, connections with the *fixer*. Also *grease* 5. "If we get busted in Frisco, I have plenty juice there to fix the caper." 2. Bribe money. See *grease* 2, 3. Alcoholic beverages, especially when combined with drugs. See *juice freak*.

juice freak. 1. One who prefers alcohol to drugs. 2. One who uses alcohol to reenforce the effect of drugs.

juice joint. A type of hangout selling fruit juice for drug users, especially of the hallucinogens.

jumpy Stevie. See *leapers*.

junk. 1. Narcotics in general—any habit forming derivative of opium, including all new pain-killers (some synthetic) that are habit forming such as Dolophine, Demerol, Dilaudid, Pantopon. 2. Any specific kind of drugs except barbiturates and marijuana; the opiate series, with some exceptions. To very old-timers, this meant anything but opium. See *cotics*.

> *Even C is junk.*
> *Gum opium is junk.*
> *Grease is junk.*
> *Yen shee is junk.*

junk freak. See *fiend*.

junk hog. 1. An addict who takes more drugs than he needs to *hold* him, or who takes his *shots* oftener than necessary. A term of contempt. If applied to a female, the term is usually *pig*. 2. Sometimes used in a friendly or kidding way toward someone taking an extra *shot.*

junker or **junkie.** A narcotic addict, especially a user of *white stuff.* This term seems to have been originally applied to addicts who sniffed drugs—cocaine especially. See *hype.*

K.Y. or **Ky.** The Lexington Hospital.

keek or **kook.** See *needle fiend.*

keen cat. See *slick.*

keep the meet. For addict and peddler to meet so the addict can buy drugs. Addicts are traditionally punctual, peddlers traditionally late; the reason—self-preservation on the part of the peddler. See *blow the meet.*

key. 1. A volunteer addict patient. This term is probably related to *crank handle, stem winder, self-starter,* etc., with similar meanings in various narcotics hospitals. 2. From *kilo,* one kilogram, usually of marijuana. See *brick* 2. Also refers to uncut heroin.

keyster or **kiester plant.** A finger stall or condom used to conceal drugs in the rectum. "In Canadian prisons they are cylinders made of metal or wood . . . you must always keep your valuables in this keyster plant, for that is the only hiding place that is not searched—ever. . . ."

khai. A mixture of residue of smoked opium, morphine base, and aspirin. The fumes are inhaled from a metal container held over an open flame. (Indochina).

kick. 1. Euphoria. See *bang.* 2. To suffer abstinence symptoms. 3. A pocket. 4. Any form of preoccupation, as movie *kick,* etc.

kick back. 1. The addict's almost inevitable return to narcotics after having *kicked the habit.* "You know he'll kick back. . . ." 2. Re-

turn of stolen goods. 3. A portion or percentage of the take paid for cooperation or protection.

kick cold. Treatment in which the addict is taken off drugs suddenly. See *cold turkey.*

kick freak. See *joy popper.*

kick the gong or **gonger.** 1. To smoke opium, especially in a group. See *hit the gong, beat the gong, roll the log.* Obsolescent, except among oldtimers. 2. To smoke marijuana in groups. See *party.*

kick the habit or **kick.** To undergo the withdrawal syndrome, either with the aid of drugs (tapering off) or suddenly and without drugs (cold turkey). Also to *break the habit.*

kicked out in the snow. Stoned on drugs.

kiester. The rectum, a common hiding place for drugs, especially in prison where such a stash is called a *kiester plant* or *keyster plant.*

kiester stab. Coitus *per anum.*

kiester stash. See *keyster plant.*

kilo. One kilogram (2.2 pounds), usually of marijuana. See *brick* 2, *key* 2.

king kong. Home-made gin, especially in prisons.

kipping. 1. Sleeping after having passed the crisis of withdrawal. "I've got around the turn but still not *kipping.*" 2. Sleeping normally. An old underworld term.

kite. An unauthorized letter, smuggled in or out of prison.

knock off. 1. To stop. Also *freeze, hang it up, cool it, lighten it up.* 2. To arrest. Also *busted, rousted, sneezed,* etc. 3. To kill someone. Also *snuff, give (someone) a hot shot.* 4. To rob a person or place;

knock off a score. Also *pull a job, beat a joint.*

knocked out. Under the influence of narcotics. Also *gassed, stoned, out of sight, loaded, zonked, smashed, tore up, ripped* and many others. See *all lit up.*

knocker. Anyone who actively criticizes addicts; usually an underworld character who works with addicts or is around them. "There is a saying among junkers: 'a knocker will eventually get hooked.'" "He went the way of all knockers, he's hooked."

knockers. 1. The testicles. 2. A woman's breasts.

konk. 1. A mixture of lye, grease and potato peelings used by Negroes to straighten hair. Also *Jap.* 2. Or **konk out.** To go unconscious, as from an overdose of narcotics.

kook. See *needle fiend.*

lamb. The passive receptor in a homosexual relationship (usually pederasty). Also *gunzel, guntzel, gonsil, punk, brat, daisy.*

lame. 1. A dull person. Cut back from *lame brain.* 2. A disgusting person; an inexperienced addict. 3. In ghetto usage, any nonmember of an in group, especially drug users.

lamp habit. 1. An excessive desire for opium; a large habit. "He has to produce, with his broad, the horses and a lamp habit. . . ." 2. By extension, any large habit. "Does he have a habit? I'll say, a lamp habit." 3. A slight opium habit acquired from inhaling the fumes where opium is smoked. See *bunk habit.* "He won't have a tough time kicking, he only had a lamp habit."

later for that. A laconic phrase meaning "Never mind."

laugh and scratch. 1. To take drugs *(white stuff)*, especially intravenously. There is a prickling or itching reaction, especially if the addict has been off drugs for a time. "He had a laughing and scratching good time last night. . . ." 2. Extended to the use of marijuana, which often produces uncontrollable laughter, but no itching.

laughing grass. Marijuana. See *muggles.*

lay. 1. A place to be robbed. 2. The plan of a robbery or crime. 3. A place to smoke opium; a *hop joint.* See *lay down.* 4. The act of smoking opium. "How's chances for a lay?" 5. The privilege of smoking in a *hop joint.* "They didn't charge much for a lay at Ty Lane's place." 6. A *shot* of narcotics, not restricted to opium users.

And there's that lay of M.
My good old pipe and stem,
Good God how I love them. . . .
"We'll have to pack in for a lay before long."

lay down. 1. The act of smoking opium. 2. The price of smoking opium, but only in such a phrase as "What's the lay down here?," which is really elliptical, with *price of a* understood. "What do you get for a lay down?"

lay down joint. A place where opium is sold and smoked. See *hop joint.*

lay in the cut. 1. To secretly observe or reconnoiter. 2. To have sexual intercourse.

lay it down. To avoid something or let it alone. Also *hang it up.* "He thought he could take a couple of fixes and lay it down."

lay the house. To perform sexually in a group. Largely among hallucinogen users.

lay the note. To *short-change* a person by means of *the hype,* which is a kind of *short con* game.

laying back and doing it. Serving an easy prison sentence. Also *coasting 2, having a ball,* etc.

laying paper. Passing checks.

laying queer. See *pushing queer.*

layout. 1. The outfit of an opium smoker, varying in quality from cheap to very elaborate and expensive. Basic elements are *stems, bowls, yen hok, yen shee gow, suey pow, lamp, lamp trimmer, yen shee can,* peanut or vegetable oil for the lamp, etc.

> *Ten thousand hop layouts, all inlaid with pearl,*
> *Every hop head fiend will bring along his girl. . . .*

2. The hypodermic needle, spoon, cotton, etc.

leaf gum, leaf or **leaf hop.** Crude opium before it is prepared for smoking. So called because it is often wrapped in dried poppy leaves. See *black stuff.*

leak. 1. To disclose information. 2. A person with a slack jaw; one who talks too much.

leapers. Users of cocaine who reach an advanced stage where jerky movements resemble St. Vitus dance.

leaping and stinking. Under the influence of drugs. See *high.* Obsolescent. "An old-timer once told me leaping and stinking comes from a junkie being high on coke and stinking from want of M. . . ." "A sick addict throws off the most offensive odor imaginable. As you probably know, many addicts are caught at the border because of this. I have heard of dogs being used to locate them."

leaps. A state of extreme anxiety with delusions, sometimes paranoid, resulting from continued use of co-caine. This state may vary from the ludicrous to homicidal mania. "After three or four days with Cecil he had a mild case of the leaps. . . ." "This is the stage where one sees bugs on (his) body and will draw blood getting them off."

lem kee. Chinese "brand" name for prepared smoking opium. Probably, like *li yuen,* etc., based on the family name of Chinese opium merchants. These terms have now generalized, losing their former family associations. See *black stuff.* Also *rooster brand, li yuen.*

lemon. Bad or fake dope. See *turkey.*

lemon bowl or **orange bowl.** A hollowed-out half orange or lemon fitted to the bowl of an opium pipe like a cover; used when the bowl gets hot, or to avoid changing bowls. "Make a lemon bowl and we can cop a few more."

lemon squeezer. The vagina, especially among hallucinogen users.

lemonade. Very poor narcotics, usually very highly diluted heroin.

lent or **lint.** Japanese morphine in fibrous form; introduced into contraband trade about 1936, but never available in great supply. Many American addicts never knew about it. "It's true most lent was used on the West Coast; junkies who used it say it was powerful."

lick up a tab. To take a tablet or capsule of a drug.

lid. A commercial measure of marijuana equal to about one ounce or 50 cigarettes.

lie on your hip or **lay on the hip.** To smoke opium, which is done lying on the side with the head resting on another smoker's hip or, more exactly, in the hollow just above the hip bone. "Want to lay on the hip tonight?"

(the) life. The world of the *hustlers.* Also *(the) swinging life, (the) groovie life, (the) living end.*

lift. To progress from milder to stronger drugs. "Now he's lifted from grass to H."

light green. A grade of marijuana.

light up. To smoke marijuana.

light-weight chipper. An occasional user with a very small habit. See *chippy habit.*

light-weight nothing. A small drug habit. "That lame's got a light-weight nothing going and thinks he's righteous strung out."

lighten up. Take it easy, quiet down, stop.

Lincoln. A five dollar bill. Also an *Abe, fin, finik, finski, nickel.*

line. See *main line.*

line shot. An injection into the vein. See *mainline, bang* 2.

lip the dripper. To suck the air out of the medicine dropper before taking a shot; the common test is to make it stick by vacuum to the lip or tongue tip. "Needle pushers always lip the dripper, and smokers lip the pipsky too, bowl and stem, then both together."

Lipton tea. 1. Poor quality drugs, especially heroin heavily cut. The implication is that it is as mild as tea. 2. See *Mickey Finn* 1, where it is a euphemisms.

lit. Variant of *all lit up.*
> *After I do this bit*
> *In my old Morris chair I'll sit*
> *Oh, Gee! how I'll get lit. . . .*

li yuen. High quality smoking opium; originally a trade name for a brand of prepared smoking opium imported from China. See *lem kee.*

load. 1. Among needle addicts, the usual ration of drugs. "Got a load for this gun?" 2. Among opium smokers, more than the usual number of pills. "Boy, what a load he had on."

loaded. Under the influence of drugs. See *in high.*

lobby girl or **lobby shopper.** A prostitute who solicits in hotels.

lobby gow or **lob.** A hanger-on around a hop joint; usually an addict who runs errands or acts as a *connector.* "That old man was a lobby gow for the combination." "He's harmless, just a lob."

loco weed. Marijuana.

log. An opium pipe. See *bamboo.*

long run. An acute need of drugs. "On that Saturday morning, she had a long run I remember."

long-tailed rat. A stool pigeon of the lowest order. Also *ring tail* or *ring tail skunk.* "That long-tailed rat has lived much too long. . . ."

looking dap or **looking boss.** Well dressed, sharp.

louse. A stool pigeon. Also *rat, long-tailed rat, finger, finger gee, mouse,* etc. "Yeah, that louse works for the city and the feds."

love drug. Methedrine, taken intravenously; so called because of its physiological effect.

love weed. Marijuana. See *muggles.*

low rider. Down and out addict. Also *free loader, 24 karat poop butt, gutter hype.*

LSD. Lysergic acid diethylamide. A few years ago this term was known only to a limited number of researchers and psychiatrists; now it is a common argot term widely used among those who deal in contraband drugs. See *acid.*

Luer. A glass syringe (standard medical equipment) for giving hypodermic injection. Differs from a *Bay State, q.v.* in that the needle slips on a *Luer,* but screws on a

Bay State; the plunger on the *Luer* is solid. Most "square" addicts use a standard hypodermic syringe. See *Yale, spike.*

lug. 1. A person. 2. The ear (obsolescent), which survives in the phrase to *put the lug on (someone)* (meaning to "bend his ear" or beg narcotics from him).

M. Morphine. Also *junk, cube, lent, white stuff, white angel, God's medicine, Miss Emma, emsel, gunk, uffi, unkie, sweet Jesus, Miss Morph, etc.,* with specialized meanings.

machinery. The equipment for taking drugs by needle. See *artillery.*

mack man. One who *hustles,* especially a pimp. Also *fish* 4.

mahoska or **hoska.** Any kind of narcotics especially heroin (East Coast, particularly New York City).

main. In the vein, as applied to intravenous injection, and distinguishing this from *skin shooting.* "Man, I take it main. . . ."

main line or **line.** 1. The vein, usually in the crook of the elbow or instep, into which the needle addict injects narcotics. When these large veins become sclerotic, addicts, may use others in any part of the body where they are accessible. "A main line bang gives me action right now." 2. **Main line** (only). To inject drugs into the vein. "I can main line that 10-8-20 and not tell it from H." 3. An addict who *vein shoots.* "She was strictly a main line broad and it took her an hour to fix."

mainliner or **main line shooter.** A vein shooter. See *bang, bang in the arm.* "I don't think a main liner has the aches and pains kicking a habit that a skin shooter does."

make. 1. To obtain something. "He went out to make a croaker" (obtain drugs from a physician). "That Texas mob was trying to make old Sam" (obtain his drugs by theft). 2. To detect. "The captain would gun hell out of (look hard at) the line trying to make (detect) the cons (prisoners) who were fixed (who had taken a shot)." 3. To be fingerprinted and photographed after an arrest. 4. To arrive, as in the phrase *make the scene.*

make a hype pitch. To work a *short-change racket.* See *(the) hype.*

make a spread. 1. To set out the equipment for taking drugs; hence to prepare for a period of indulgence; often refers to addicts who gather together for a spree or to take their regular *shots.* Also *spread the joint.* "Make a spread, Mike's all right." 2. To cohabit with a girl, or set up such a proposal.

make bush. To escape from prison.

make the drive. To smuggle narcotics into prison. See *boat sailed.*

mama die? A set phrase probably originating among West Coast Chinese, euphemistically recognizing early withdrawal distress, especially the tears. The next step is probably a purchase of drugs. See *monkey on my back.*

(the) man. 1. A policeman. 2. A narcotics dealer or *connection.* 3. The dominant culture personified. 4. Any person in authority, probably the original term from which the others derived.

manicure. To trim the top leaves and flowering tops from the hemp plant to make marijuana cigarettes. Also *sift,* especially where screens are used to separate the seeds, which, if smoked, produce a violent headache. See *clean* 2.

manita. Milk sugar used to adulterate heroin. (Largely Harlem usage).

marcia. A water pipe used to smoke marijuana (South America). May be encountered in New York City; reported by Wolff in Brazil, and described as resembling the nargile or African water pipe used for smoking hashish; a hookah. In the Americas, the smoke may be drawn through wine or soda water.

margin man. A drug runner or smuggler who transports drugs in wholesale quantities between the *big men* and the dealers. "Margin men are usually non-addicts, so the term is rarely used among addicts." Also *straight man, runner, mule.*

mark. The victim of any *racket or hustle;* a sucker. An old term, but getting competition from *trick, q.v.* among addicts.

Mary Jane. Marijuana. See *muggles.*

Mary Warner. A variant of marijuana. Obsolescent. See *muggles.*

matchbox nickel, also matchbox, short nickel. A measure of retail marijuana, the amount held in a penny matchbox.

McCoy. 1. Medicinal drugs in contrast to bootleg drugs. Obsolescent. 2. Any drug with a high narcotic content; usually refers to bootleg drugs today. Also *righteous stuff, George, smack.*

meat ball rap. An adverse behavior report of a mild offense, or any relatively insignificant charge. Also *chicken shit beef, busted on a buzzer.* See *gunzel.*

medicine. 1. To the opiate user, any drugs of the opiate series; cocaine is usually excluded, also often codeine. 2. Cod liver oil with prepared opium, *yen shee,* morphine or heroin added. The cod liver oil disguises the drug and prevents its recognition by casual inspection. This preparation is carried on the road by opium smokers instead of a *layout* and, taken by mouth, *holds* the addict until he can smoke again. Other liquids are also used. 3. Any drug taken temporarily to sustain a habit while the drug of choice is unavailable.

meet. An appointment arranged between addict and peddler; a specialized sense of the general underworld usage. ". . . had a meet at the PO (post office) at 10, but he didn't show."

merchandise. Narcotics, especially in wholesale quantities. See *goods.*

mescaline. A hallucinogenic drug, either that derived from the mescal cactus or its synthetic equivalent.

meter. See *Brody, throw a meter.*

meth. 1. Methamphetamine hydrochloride. 2. Methadone.

methadone or **methadon.** A synthetic opiate. Earlier known as *amedone* and *10-8-20.*

mezz. Marijuana. See *muggles.*

Mick. To give a victim a *Mickey Finn, q.v.*

Mickey Finn or **Mickey.** 1. Chloral hydrate in a drink to knock out a victim. Also, euphemistically, *Lipton tea.* 2. A powerful physic such as croton oil, slipped into a whiskey to make the victim sick or to drive him away from a hangout. ". . . slip him a Mickey and slough the donicker on him" (lock him out of the toilet room). "Just Mickey. Finn got lost."

mind-blower. 1. A hallucinogenic drug. 2. By extension, any experience which has a strong psychological or sensory effect. See *blow the mind.*

mind-fuck. To initiate someone into the use of a drug, usually LSD, for the pleasure of experienced users who are spectators.

Miss Carrie. A *plant* of drugs, secreted on the person in case of arrest. So called because it "carries" the addict if his supply is interrupted. See *stash*.

Miss Emma. Morphine. A variant of *M*. See *cotics*.

Miss Morph. Morphine. Obsolescent.

mitt me, Slim, the ship is in. A kind of set phrase indicating that the *connection* has arrived.

mocky or **mockie.**   A Jew. Also *popcorn*.

mojo. 1. Narcotics of any kind in contraband trade, but usually signifies morphine, heroin or cocaine. Largely used by Negroes. "Bud, you got any mojo?" 2. Among Negroes, a good luck charm; *Toby*.

moll. A girl on the petty rackets. A very old term, *e.g.* Moll Flanders, Moll Cutpurse, etc.

moll buzzer. One who specializes in robbing women by snatching handbags. Not a true pickpocket. Also *prowl rat*.

monkey on my back. 1. Early abstinence symptoms. Also *hurting, Chinaman on my back, mama die?*, etc. 2. A drug habit.

monkeyman. An obsequious person, especially a Negro in relation to whites. Also *weasel, sucker, brown nose, Jeff,* etc.

mooter. Marijuana. Also recorded as *mota* or *moota*.

morning shot. The first shot of the day. See *wake up*.

mouse. 1. A stool pigeon. See *louse*. "The difference between a rat (long-tailed) and a mouse is, the mouse will not finger his own mother. . . ." 2. A young prostitute, just starting out, or a girl ripe to be recruited into the *racket*.

mouth habit. A drug habit which is satisfied by taking drugs orally. Also *belly habit, scarfing, scoffing, pill dropping*. "Most all pipe smokers who went to the needle went by way of the mouth habit first—after the pipe, that is."

Mr. Broadshoulders. A social worker. Also occurs as **Miss Broadshoulders** for a female social worker.

Mr. Fish or **fish.** 1. A newcomer in any penal institution, including jails. 2. A voluntary patient in a federal hospital for narcotic addicts. Obsolescent. Now called *winders, selfstarters,* or *crank handles, keys,* though *fish* is still used in some places.

Mr. Twenty-six. A needle. See *spike, Yale, artillery*.

mud. Prepared opium before it is rolled to be cooked for smoking. In emergencies opium in solution is sometimes used by morphine or heroin addicts for intravenous injections instead of the *white stuff* preferred by needle addicts. This is a cumbersome process, resorted to only in great necessity.

mug. 1. The face. 2. To be photographed. 3. To rob by strong arm techniques.

mugger. A small-time strong arm operator; one who *puts the arm on* anyone on the street. May be loosely extended to include *moll buzzers*.

muggled or **muggled up.** Under the influence of marijuana. ". . . we were muggled up. . . ."

muggles. 1. Crude dried marijuana before it is rolled into cigarettes. See *griefo, hemp, Indian hay, Mary Jane, Mary Warner, mess,* *mez, mutah, tea, Texas tea, viper's weed, weed, bambalache, fu, bo bo bush, ding, joy smoke, laughing grass, love weed, sweet Lucy, root, rope, Chicago green, grass, Acapulco gold, Acapulco red, Breckenridge green, Cam, Cambodia trip weed,* etc. Some of these terms also indicate rolled cigarettes. 2. Marijuana cigarettes. "What is the tag on muggles?" "Bale or stick?" (by the pound or by the cigarette).

mule. See *margin man.*

murder game. An ultimatum to cooperate or suffer a heavy penalty; pressure used either by the authorities or the underworld.

Murphy. One type of short con game worked on a *mark* who is looking for a prostitute. In the West, sometimes called *(the) carpet* or *(the) post.*

muscle relaxer. A barbiturate, tranquilizer, or *downer.*

mutah or **mooter.** Marijuana. See *muggles.*

nail. 1. The hollow needle, considered separately; especially the needle exclusive of the shank. 2. Anything sharp enough to take a *pin shot* with; a nail, safety pin, sewing machine needle, etc.

nailed. Arrested.

narcos or **narks.** Narcotics detectives, especially federal agents. Also recorded in the singular (*narco* and *nark*). See *fuzz, (the) man.*

narcotic bulls or **narcotic coppers.** Federal narcotic officers.

needle. 1. The entire outfit for injecting narcotics (East Coast and West Coast). See *artillery.* 2. The hollow needle alone (South, Southwest, and Midwest). 3. *White stuff* taken intravenously, as contrasted to opium. "He used to smoke, but went to the needle."

needle fiend or **needle freak.** 1. A drug addict who uses the needle. Also *needle pusher.* Obsolescent. 2. An addict who gets pleasure from dallying with the needle, often pricking his flesh or inserting an empty needle for the psychological effect. "Needle fiends are addicts off the drug who like to jab themselves with needles or give themselves injections of water."

needle habit. 1. A habit which is satisfied by hypodermic injections. 2. The habit described under *needle fiend* 2.

Needle Park. To New York addicts, upper Broadway and Sherman Square.

needle pusher. An addict who takes drugs hypodermically, usually *white stuff.* See *needle fiend* 1.

needle sharing. Use of the same equipment by several people for injecting drugs. The practice has obvious sexual implications, and is a major source for the transmission of hepatitis and syphilis. See *needle fiend.*

needle shy. A state of phobia against the use of the hypodermic needle; often encountered among beginners, and sometimes among confirmed addicts. "Go ahead and shoot her, she's needle shy. . . ."

needle trouble. Mechanical difficulties in making an injection; usually caused by clogging, breakage, leakage of air, etc. "You never have needle trouble when you have plenty of time." See *floater.*

needle yen. 1. A desire for narcotics taken hypodermically. Obsolescent. "Two drinks of whiskey and she had a needle yen." 2. A masochistic desire to dally with the needle, as described under *needle fiend.* 2. Rare. "There is a word used to describe people with a needle yen."

nic nac or **nick nack, knick knack.** 1. A homosexual "He'll nic nac for monkeys" (he'll participate in any perversion in any way). See *freak*. 2. A disgusting person. See *creep*.

nickel. 1. A five-year sentence. See *buffalo*. 2. A five dollar paper of heroin. 3. A five dollar bill. Also *Abe, fin, Lincoln,* etc. 4. A five dollar purchase of marijuana. See *matchbox nickel*.

nickel bag. A five dollar bag of heroin.

nimby or **nimbie.** A Nembutal capsule. Also *yellow jacket, canary, goofer*.

nodding. Dozing as a result of drug use. Also *coasting, sailing, floating,* with slight differences in connotation.

nose burner or **nose warmer.** The butt end of a marijuana cigarette.

notch joint. A house of prostitution. See *crib*.

nut. 1. To ignore or disregard. 2. Nutmeg; occasionally inhaled or drunk in solution by someone attempting to become euphoric; a prison substitute for drugs. More often drunk in solution. See *idiot juice*. 3. A psychotic. 4. The cost of maintaining a habit. "My nut ran me about a double sawski ($20) a day." 5. The expenses involved in any *racket*, such as living expenses, *fix money*, transportation, etc. "We can always clear $200 a week apiece, over and above the nut."

nut city. A mythical place in which anyone feigning insanity is said to live.

O.D. 1. An overdose of narcotics. This may simply put the addict into a stupor temporarily, or it may be fatal. There are several folk remedies for the severely *O.D.'d* addict—among them instant coffee or a stiff salt solution injected intravenously for heroin overdose. See text for the medical antidotes for various drugs of addiction. 2. Officer of the day in prisons or hospitals.

off or **off drugs.** 1. To be temporarily free from the *habit*. Also *clean, straightened up, squared up, turned over*. "It can be done. I know quite a few who have been off for years." "Every addict has a desire to be off drugs, sooner or later." 2. *Off* (only). To steal something. "Why didn't you off that ring?"

off the wall. An abrupt change of subject in conversation. "Why do you come off the wall when we're getting down to business?"

oil burning habit. A large habit; perhaps related to *oil burner*, from race track argot, perhaps a variant of *lamp habit* 1, 2, *q.v.* The lamp used in opium smoking burns peanut oil. Now extended to include all "hard" drugs. "Not too many junkies are capable of supporting an oil burning habit. . . ."

oil head. An alcoholic or drinker of alcoholic beverages. See *juice freak*.

old Steve. Morphine, heroin or cocaine. Obsolescent.

on. 1. To be using drugs regularly, as contrasted to *chipping*. "They can't make up their minds to be on or be off, so the feds step in and make the decision." Probably related to *turn on, turn (someone) on*. Formerly, *on drugs* was often encountered, but this phrase is disappearing. 2. To be honest, dependable, trustworthy.

Probably derived from the gambling phrase, "you're on" and unrelated to sense 1, although identical in form, and used mostly in regard to transactions in drugs. "That deal don't sound on to me." "It don't have to be on.'" "I'm on with Pete. You can't touch him."

on ice. 1. In jail. 2. To lie low or go off a *racket* temporarily, usually due to police surveillance, or a police stakeout in the neighborhood. 3. Wanted by the law. Also *dead, no action, in the freezer, ducking and dodging,* etc.

on the bricks. Free on bond or released from custody. Also *to hit the street, in biz, in circulation, out of the cooler* and many others.

on the gow or **on gow.** 1. Addicted to narcotics. "We were three handed, all on the gow." 2. May be used to indicate an addict under the immediate influence of opiates. Rare. Originally an opium smoker's term and now seldom encountered, though *gowed up (overcharged)* is still in use.

on the ground. Not incarcerated, out of prison. See *on the bricks.*

on the mojo or **on mojo.** Addicted, largely refers to *white stuff* users (Negro usage, mainly).

on the nod. A state of near stupor achieved by an addict who has just taken a stiff shot or a little too much.

on the point. To stare fixedly into space for a long interval as a result of taking Methedrine. Not to be confused with *play the point, q.v.*

on the send or **to have someone on the send.** 1. To obtain drugs through a runner or intermediary who makes the *connection* for a fee or a share of the drugs. Also

on the tracks. "We had three different people on the send at the same time." 2. To send a confederate for bond money. 3. To send a *mark* home for more money with which to play a confidence game.

on the shorts. 1. Low on drugs. 2. Low on cash to buy drugs. See *short.*

on the streets. 1. Out of prison. Also *on the ground, on the bricks.* 2. Looking for a *connection* to purchase drugs. 3. Jobless and homeless, at loose ends. 4. Working as a prostitute.

on the stuff or **on stuff.** Addicted to narcotics, usually indicating *white stuff.* "The whole mob was on stuff."

on the track. See *on the send.*

on the up and up. 1. To be *away from the habit.* "He packed it in and he's on the up and up." 2. To be trustworthy or *right.* "You can deal, he's on the up and up."

on the way down. Past the peak of a euphoric or hallucinogenic drug experience.

on the white scene. Under the influence of Benzedrine or cocaine.

operating. Actively selling narcotics.

orange bowl. 1. See *lemon bowl.* 2. A half orange scraped out and used for a shade for an emergency opium lamp shade. "Use a small condensed milk can for the oil and half an orange scraped out for a shade, punch a few air holes, and you have a fine little lamp.

orange wedge. A potent form of LSD.

out in the cold again. Out of prison. See *on the ground, on the bricks.*

out of sight. 1. Beyond comprehension. 2. Impossible. 3. Stupefied as a result of having taken too much of a drug. See *gowed*. 4. An extreme in any direction, expressing all reactions from high approval to total rejection.

outfit. 1. Equipment used for administering drugs. 2. The vagina, especially as it is involved in the concealment and transport of drugs.

over the hump. 1. See *around the turn*. "You'll soon be over the hump." 2. To build up a state of euphoria until a maximum of pleasure is reached. "I'm over the hump now; "I'll have a good bang of that M." 3. To have passed the halfway point in serving a prison sentence. Also *going downhill*.

overamped. Having taken too much Methedrine.

over-and-unders. Stimulants and depressants, amphetamines and barbiturates. See *uppers, downers*.

overcharged. Having taken more narcotics than necessary to *get the habit off*. "That day I went to work (thieving) overcharged, so anything could happen." See *gowed, charged*.

overjolt. Too much of a drug taken at one time. See *O.D., overcharged, gowed*.

O.Z. Ounce of narcotics, especially morphine, but may be applied to heroin, cocaine, opium and even marijuana, when it is handled in wholesale or large-scale transactions. Rare. Individual addicts of thirty years ago frequently bought an ounce of hard drugs at a time, but this is now a thing of the past, except on a wholesale level. See *piece, half piece*.

P.G. Paregoric. Also *P.O.*, rarely. Contains nearly two grains of opium per fluid ounce. Addicts drink it or refine it for injection by vaporizing the camphor, alcohol, etc. by cooking it down *(blackjack)* or by chilling it to separate the camphor and then boiling off the alcohol. Recently, on the East Coast, many addicts have begun to inject straight paregoric into the vein in large doses—as much as 20 cc. "I think pipe smokers were the first to drink P.G. to hold them." "The camphor in P.G. will become solid if you place it on ice."

P.O. 1. A parole or probation officer. 2. Paregoric. Rare. See *P.G.*

pack your keyster. To place a condom filled with drugs in the rectum or vagina. See *coozie stash*.

pad. 1. Home or apartment. 2. A bed. 3. House of prostitution or, more commonly, a room used for prostitution purposes. Sometimes this also means the place of sale or use of drugs, especially marijuana.

paddie. A white person, especially used by Negroes.

paid off in gold. Arrested by a federal officer who flashes his gold badge. Sometimes used as an ironical way of describing a purchase by an agent who "pays" for it by showing his badge. Obsolescent. "Shorty was paid off in gold that night. . . ."

panic. 1. A shortage of drugs in a certain locality. "There was a real panic in Memphis after that. . . ." 2. Failure of an addict to secure drugs, either because he cannot make a *connection* or because he has no money. "The panic is on with me right now, Jack."

panic man. An addict who is short of drugs or unable to secure them. Obsolescent.

paper. 1. A *bindle* of narcotics put

up by folding the powder in paper or cellophane so that all ends are folded in. "There are five dollar papers, ten dollar papers and so on." 2. A small package of prepared opium put up in oiled paper. "A paper of hop." "A paper of grease." See *nickel paper, dime paper.*

paper fiend. One who uses the paper *strips (q.v.)* inside inhalers as a source of amphetamine.

paper hanging. Passing forged checks systematically as a *racket* or *hustle.*

party. 1. As a noun, a social occasion for group drug use, especially LSD or marijuana. 2. As a verb, to participate in such use. See *socialize.* "We had some good grass and spent the week partying."

passing queer. See *pushing queer.*

past Monday. Extreme. Obsolescent.

pat down. To search a person. Also *skam 3.*

peak. The high point of euphoria or hallucination in a drug experience.

peddler. A retail dealer in narcotics; sometimes not addicted, but usually supporting his own habit by selling. "Shorty is a peddler and a square." See *pusher, the man, connection.*

peg. 1. The police. 2. To recognize. See *make.* 3. To stare steadily at someone. "When you peg a lame, you're playing the hinge."

pen and death. An indeterminate sentence.

pen yen. Opium. A term used mostly around *hop joints* and in conversation with Chinese in pidgin English. "You catchem pen yen, me yen shee quay. . . ."

penitentiary shot or **pen shot.** 1. Variant of *pin shot, point shot, q.v.* "A few more pen shots and

he's through." 2. A small shot due to scarcity or cost. Epsom salts is often added to *boost the kick,* or so some addicts believe.

period hitter. An occasional user. See *chippy habit.*

peter. 1. Knockout drops, especially chloral hydrate. Probably by extension from the *peter man's* term for nitroglycerine used to crack safes, which is *pete* or *peter.* 2. The *racket* of robbing people (addicts, drunks, customers of a prostitute, etc.) by the use of chloral hydrate. "They take off a lot of cash on the peter."

phystaris. See *fisstaris.*

pick up. 1. A shot of narcotics, usually given another addict as a gift or favor. See *bang.* Also *taste,* meaning a shot to hold an addict until he can *score.* "He sure was sick when I saw him, so hell, I gave him a pick up." 2. An arrest on a charge which is usually dropped, the idea being to get the addict into custody for questioning. See *hummer.*

pick (someone) up. To provide narcotics, clothes, money, etc. for an addict who is broke. "I know Ernie picked him up three different times coming out of stir."

picked up. Under the immediate influence of narcotics; feeling euphoria. "He said, 'You are picked up right now with a line shot.'" See *bang.*

piddle or **pital.** A hospital or sanatorium where a drug addict may be treated. See *pogie.* "There are piddles that are pogies, too. Then there are pogies that are not piddles, and there are piddles that are not pogies—do I make myself clear?"

piece. 1. An ounce of narcotics, especially morphine, heroin or cocaine. Formerly, addicts or groups of addicts often bought a *piece* and divided it up or rationed it over several weeks. Within the past three to ten years, purchases of this size by individuals are rare, but are still made in the wholesale trade. Today, an "ounce" must be suspected of dilution or reduction by one means or another. Medical or pharmaceutical morphine may be sold pure; heroin never. "You know, Shorty was guzzled (arrested) with forty pieces (ounces) in a kiester (suitcase)." See *O.Z.* 2. A pistol (largely teenage gangsters).

pig. 1. See *fiend.* 2. A female addict who takes more drugs than she needs to *hold* her. See *junk hog.* 3. A derogatory term for law enforcement officers, often generalized to any authority figure, such as a teacher, parent or employer.

pill. 1. A ration of opium, prepared for smoking. 2. (Plural). Used to distinguish prescription drugs from bootleg drugs. "Let me have a few pills" means that the addict wants to borrow or buy morphine. Dilaudid or Pantopon, *not* heroin. 3. By extension, also usually plural, the amphetamines or barbiturates, even though some of them are in capsules.

pill popper or **dropper.** A user whose drugs of choice are in the form of tablets or capsules.

pimp. One who lives from the earnings of a prostitute. Among addicts, both are usually using drugs, though not always. Often one *pimp* has several girls working for him. Many addicts without much criminal experience drift into the *broad racket* because it is one of the most obvious ways to support a *habit.*

When the pimp is also the *connection,* he has a high degree of control over the girl. Also *tail towel checker, fish, fish and shrimp,* etc.

pin. 1. To act as a lookout. 2. The hollow needle used with a *joint.* 3. The safety pin, nail or other sharp object used to take a *pin shot, q.v.*

pin man. A lookout.

pin shot. An injection of drugs made with a safety pin or other sharp instrument, and a medicine dropper. The pin is put into the flesh and left for a while to assure an opening, then the dropper is placed over the opening and the shot slowly forced in. Sometimes the dropper is actually pushed into the opening. Also *penitentiary shot.* "Pin shots are the accepted way of taking stuff in most stirs."

pinned. Said of an opiate addict's eyes when the pupils constrict noticeably after a shot. From "pin pointed." This condition has recently assumed great significance among addicts with the introduction of the Nalline test, which reverses the constriction in the eyes of opiate users, causing measurable dilation.

pipe. An opium smoker. Obsolescent.

pipe fiend. An opium smoker. Obsolescent. The word "fiend," while it survives in such phrases as *needle fiend, pipe fiend,* etc., is not much used by addicts, and the term *dope fiend* is almost taboo.

pipe smoker. An opium addict who uses a pipe. "That guy you saw me with last night was a pipe smoker for years, but he finally went to the needle."

pit. See *ditch.*

pitch. 1. To retail narcotics in small

quantities. Also *to push, to shove, to shove shorts, to push shorts,* with somewhat specialized meanings. "He's pitching now for Louie on 14th Street." 2. To manifest, as *to pitch a toss out, to pitch a wing ding,* etc. (meaning to put on an act or feign sickness for drugs). 3. The role of the male partner in the homosexual relation. "The butch pitches, (the) queen pussy catches."

plant. 1. Narcotics hidden away, either on the person or secreted in a hiding place. "At that time I had a plant of about 50 Dilaudid tablets in my fly (trousers)." "My plant was in the toilet room." 2. To smuggle narcotics into jail by concealing them on an individual and causing him to be arrested. "We could always count on Sam to plant a few bindles on some crumb bum. . . ." 3. A hiding place for narcotics, on or off the person, in jail or outside. "They had a plant in the radio that would hold a piece of stuff." See *stash.*

play around. 1. To begin to take *pleasure shots* now and then and cultivate a *chippy habit.* Also *dabble.*

play the clam. To refuse to give information. Also *play the exhaust, play the iggie, put it down* 2.

play the exhaust. See *play the clam.*

play the iggie. To pretend ignorance in order not to give information. See *play the clam.*

play the nod, on the nod or **to get the scratch and the nod.** See *charged.* "We sat around punching gun (chewing the rag, shooting the breeze) till he started playing the nod."

play the point. To act as a lookout. Also *get (or be) on the point.*

play the shoulder. See *chill.*

playboy. A prisoner who forms a romantic attachment for another inmate. Also *jailhouse pimp, romancer, player.*

pleasure jolt. An occasional *shot* taken by someone who is not a confirmed addict. Usually taken subcutaneously, but may be intravenous. See *chipping.*

pleasure shooter or **pleasure user.** An individual who takes an occasional *shot;* one who *dabbles* or develops a *chippy habit.*

pleasure smoker. One who smokes irregularly and does not become thoroughly addicted. A genuine *pleasure smoker* is not merely *playing around;* he smokes at will over a period of years without developing a full-fledged habit. Restricted to old time opium smokers. "I'd give anything to be a pleasure smoker."

pod. Marijuana, the top of the female plant containing concentrated resin.

pogie. A workhouse, or poor farm or a certain type of free hospital where minor offenders are sometimes sent and where down and out addicts can spend the winter, either as voluntary residents or prisoners. See *piddle.* "I told him, 'If you feel so bad, why don't you get into some pogie?' "

point. 1. The hollow needle used with a *joint.* "Haven't you got a point stashed (hidden) around here somewhere?" 2. Any substitute for this needle, especially a sewing machine needle. See *tom cat.*

point shot. 1. A type of injection taken when a hypodermic needle has been broken and cannot be replaced. The point of the needle is inserted into the vein or under the skin and the glass shank of a medicine dropper slipped over it so that the solution can pass into the blood when the bulb is pressed. Distinguished from *pin shot*. 2. An injection taken with a substitute for the hollow needle, especially a sewing machine needle from power sewing machines used in prisons. See *tom cat, pin shot*.

poison. 1. A *wrong gee;* a stool pigeon. "Watch out for that little guy, he's poison." 2. A *knocker, q.v.* "Don't let his wife hear you, she's poison." 3. The opiate drugs and cocaine; *white stuff*. 4. A physician who will not sell drugs or prescriptions to addicts. Obsolescent.

poison act. The Harrison Narcotic Act, including its various amendments and revisions.

policy. The numbers *racket*.

polluted. See *high, in high*. Obsolescent.

pop. 1. A shot of narcotics. See *bang*. 2. To arrest. 3. To inject drugs, especially in the skin.

pop stick. A homemade opium pipe.

popcorn. See *mockey*.

post. See *Murphy*.

pot head. See *reefer man*.

potaguaya or **pot.** Crude marijuana, especially the flowering tops; the seed pods of the hemp after the leaves have been stripped, sometimes soaked in wine or liquor (New York City). See *muggles*.

pound. 1. A five-year sentence. 2. Marijuana in bulk, theoretically a pound by weight. Sales (wholesale) are commonly made in units of a pound, half pound, kilo, half kilo and can (about 8 oz.). Sales practices vary in different areas.

powder. 1. To leave or run out. 2. Bad narcotics. Also *turkey, blank*.

powdered bread. Money which has been dusted with luminous powder so that it can be traced under fluorescent light.

pratt or **prat.** A hip pocket. From the pickpocket argot *prat kick*.

pretty people. Homosexuals, especially males.

Procter and Gamble. Euphemism for paregoric *(P.G.)*. One of several terms which coincidentally match the older abbreviation in initial letters. See *P.G.*

prod or **prop.** 1. A shot or bang of narcotics; the use of the needle. Obsolescent. "She was always on the prod." 2. **Prod** (only). Activity. "Harry is always on the prod. I mean on the hustle." "The narcos are really on the prod around here, rousting, making life miserable when they can't catch you dead bang." 3. The penis.

prowl rat. A thief or mugger who robs women on the street, especially prostitutes. Also *moll buzzer*, though these terms are not exactly synonymous.

prowling the mustard pot. Coitus per anum (largely institutional).

psychedelic. 1. Colorful, bizarre, sensorily intense, as a result of hallucinogenic drugs or imitation of their effects. 2. Also *the psychedelics*. The drugs which produce such a state, LSD, mescaline, peyote, etc.

puff. To smoke opium. Much used in Canada. Also *to roll the log, q.v.*

pull a job. To commit a crime. Also *knock off a score, beat a joint*, etc.

pull a rabbit. To escape by running away.

pull one's coat or **sleeve.** 1. To enlighten someone. 2. To stop one from doing something foolish.

punk. A male homosexual who practices pederasty. "Punks are different from queens or fags. They're penitentiary made."

purring or **purring like a cat.** Said of an addict who has taken just the right amount of drug to make him *high* (East Coast and South to Florida). See *floating, coasting, in high.*

push or **push shorts.** To peddle narcotics; to retail them in small quantities as a sub-agent or small-time peddler. Usually restricted to *white stuff*, but has been encountered rarely to include small retailers of opium (Detroit and vicinity). "When did you start to push?" Also *hold, stick, deal, swing.*

pusher. A narcotics seller, one who works the streets.

pushing queer. Passing counterfeit money. Also *laying queer, passing queer, passing green.*

put in a shot against him. To write an adverse behavior report on a prisoner. See *A.B.C., gunzel.*

put (it) in writing or **in paper.** The act of concealing narcotics between the split halves of post cards or other paper, or saturating a letter with drugs in solution. "Morphine can't be satched. Heroin is O.K. in paper, then ironed." "Chinese in Frisco used to wear large work shoes with the strings and the tongue satched with hop. Some types of leather belts were used too."

put it down. 1. To go off drugs. 2. See *play the clam.*

put the arm on. To strong-arm a person. Also occurs as *arm*, as, "They tried to arm that punk." Also *roust, mug* 3.

put the bee on. The act of begging narcotics. See *hit on* 2.

put the croaker on the send. See *Brody, frame* 2.

put the finger on. 1. To arrest. 2. To inform on. 3. To signal a friend for anything needed at the moment—a gun, knife, car, etc.

put the heat on. 1. To interrogate. 2. To inform on someone. 3. For the police to stake a place out.

put the lug on. See *hit on* 2.

put the shiv on. To threaten with a knife.

quarry cure. One form of *cold turkey* treatment in which addicts are worked in the stone quarry while they are *kicking the habit.* Restricted to the Chicago Bridewell and to addicts who have done time there. Obsolescent. "Iron Jaw of the quarry cure was the reincarnation of all the masters of cruelty since the Spanish Inquisition." "Obsolescent my ass! Ever hear of Big O'Rourke and his quarry cure built around the rock crusher in K.C.?"

quarter piece. A quarter of an ounce of morphine, heroin or cocaine. A very common unit of sales for heroin, though of course the strength varies. See *piece, O.Z.*

queen pussy. Passive receptor in the male homosexual act.

queer. 1. A sex pervert. 2. Counterfeit money. 3. To disillusion or inform. 4. To sell (someone) highly diluted or fake narcotics. 5. Or **queer stuff.** Diluted or fake narcotics. "Queer stuff is flea powder, crap." See *turkey, blank.*

quit. To leave, especially a *joint* or *pad* when it gets "hot."

rabbi. A Jew. See *mocky.*

rabbit parole. Escape by running away.

Racehorse Charlie. Heroin and, rarely, cocaine. Possibly influenced by an old brand name for heroin, "White Horse," no longer in existence. Also suggested association with the racetrack and drugged horses—though cocaine and strcyhnine, not heroin, are usually used at the track. Note the very popular term used by younger addicts for heroin—horse. "Doc, I've known many hypes with Racehorse Charlie as a monicker, but never knew why. Thanks."

rainbow roll. An assortment of vari-colored barbiturates, popular among addicts on the West Coast.

rap. 1. To converse with or speak to. 2. An arrest or conviction, usually the latter. See *bum rap.* 3. (With **to**). To recognize someone. "I was there but he didn't rap to me." "He won't rap to you here unless you raise for him."

rap partner. 1. A close friend in whom one confides. 2. The partner in crime who serves the sentence or takes the responsibility when arrested. This happens when one man has a minor record (implying a lighter sentence), when one has an easier case to "beat" than the other or when one is forced to take the rap for the other.

rap sheet. One's prison record or *jacket, q.v.*

raspberry. An abscess at the site of injection. Also *ab, cave.*

rat. 1. A stool pigeon. See *long-tailed rat.* "A rat used to have two chances of survival—a bum chance and no chance at all. Nowadays it's different. . . ." See *ring tail, wrong, fink,* etc. 2. To act as an informer or stool pigeon; to *stool.* See *rat row.*

rat row. The cells or section of a prison where informers are segregated for their own safety. Also *snitch joint.*

rayfield. 1. Unusual jeopardy for quick gain; a crime involving considerable risk. 2. To take more than one's share, usually by violence or a threat of violence. 3. Any crime involving violence.

reach the pitch. To pass the crisis in withdrawal. See *around the turn.*

reader. 1. A prescription for drugs; *to make a croaker for a reader* is to persuade a physician to write a prescription for narcotics. Also *script.* 2. A warrant for arrest.

reader with a tail. A prescription for narcotics, often an illicit one, which is being traced by narcotics agents. ". . . been scoring in that burg for over a year, same croaker, but that last reader had a tail. . . ." Also *script with a tail.*

red bird. A Seconal capsule. Also *red devil.*

red devil. See *red bird.*

red gunyon. Pulverized hemp seed pods or gum hashish smoked in a water pipe.

reefer. A marijuana cigarette.

reefer man. A marijuana smoker. Also *tea man, viper, grasshopper, stick man, pot head,* etc.

register. 1. For an addict to assure himself that he has hit the vein by applying a slight suction to the *dropper* and watching for the blood to show in the glass before injecting the *shot.* See *to back up* 1, *verification shot.* "He was very careful, and registered that shot as if it was his last one, and it was—a hot one." 2. For a shot to *register* by showing blood in the *dropper,* indicating that the vein is punctured.

rehash. 1. To try something again. "Do you want to rehash the croaker?" (that is, Do you want to see if he will give you another *shot?*). 2. The act of repeating something. "Will Charlie go for a rehash, do you think?" 3. To reuse the *cottons*. See *cotton, cotton shooter*.

R.F.D. junker, R.F.D. gowster, dopey dope head, floater, cross-country hype. An itinerant addict who depends for his drugs upon small town or country doctors. Obsolescent. "I believe the R.F.D. dope heads have the best go. . . ."

rifle range or **shooting gallery.** The withdrawal ward of a narcotics hospital.

right croaker. A physician or dentist who will, out of sympathy or for financial gain, sell drugs or prescriptions to addicts. Reputable physicians often supply drugs because of the trickery of the addict, which is described in the text. "I'd say that the croakers who really deal—the right croakers—are very much in the minority." "There is only one right croaker in town." Also *swinging croaker*.

right guy. A narcotic addict who will not inform when arrested. Also *solid, stone righteous*.

righteous. 1. Wonderful or choice. 2. Very, or the equivalent, as an intensive.

righteous scoffer. One who eats ravenously after withdrawal. Also a *dug out, Douglas*.

righteous stuff. See *McCoy*.

ring tail. A stool pigeon. See *rat*.

rinsings. The residue of solution remaining in the cotton after an addict fills the *joint*. A little water is usually drawn into the glass to rinse the *joint,* and this may be shot into a little ball of cotton and saved, especially by *skin shooters; vein shooters* cannot save it long because it usually contains some blood. "They shoot the rinsings into a ball of cotton, and over a period of a year can save quite a bit of stuff." See *cotton, cotton shooter*.

ripped. 1. See *geed up* 3. 2. Or **ripped off.** Stolen.

roach. The end of a marijuana cigarette. Also *nose burner, butt, nose warmer,* etc.

roach clip. A holder for smoking the butt ends *(roaches)* of marijuana cigarettes. May be a simple paper clip or toothpick, or very ornate, made of brass or gold; the most common is an ordinary pin.

roadie. A friend or traveling companion (ghetto usage).

(the) Robe. Robitussin, a codeine cough syrup.

rod. 1. A gun. 2. The penis.

roll a pill. 1. To prepare opium for smoking; usually done by *tching* the pill on the pipe bowl with the *yen hok,* and sometimes smoothing the pill afterward on the heel of the hand. 2. By extension, to roll a marijuana cigarette. Also *roll a stick*.

roll a stick. See *roll a pill* 2.

roll of reds. Ten Seconal capsules sold in a roll.

roll stuff. 1. To transport narcotics in wholesale quantities. 2. To deal in or sell narcotics wholesale, as distinguished from peddling or dealing in small quantities.

roll the log. To smoke opium. See *hit the gong*. Rare, obsolescent.

romancer. See *playboy*.

rooster brand. A cheap brand of commercial smoking opium.

root or **root on the derrick.** 1. To steal from stores, or shoplift, especially to support a habit. See *clout*. "We went down the valley three handed, rooting on the derrick." 2. Or **root** (only). Marijuana. 3. Or **root** (only). To eat ravenously. See *chuck habit.*

rope. Marijuana. So called because when smoked it smells of burning hemp. Obsolescent.

Roscoe. A pistol.

rosenbloom or **rosebud.** A swollen rectum, the result of expelling the hard fecal matter which follows opiate use.

round eye. 1. The anus. 2. Pederasty.

roust. 1. See *sneezed.* 2. See *put the arm on.*

rub. To search a person, as by an officer. See *pat down.*

rumble. 1. Sexual intercourse. 2. An encounter with the law. 3. A fight, especially among teenage gangs.

rumdum. 1. A disgusting person. Also *rumkin.* 2. An alcoholic in the later stages.

rumpsty dumpsty. Anal intercourse. Also *giving up backs, q.v.*

run. 1. See *habit.* "I've got a six-months' run." 2. A binge of intravenous amphetamine use.

run it down. To explain.

run (it) through the greaser. To subject something to change.

runner. See *margin man.*

rush. The first exciting euphoria from injecting opiates; also used of other milder drugs. See *flash 1, jaboff.*

S.S. 1. A *skin shot, q.v.* 2. A suspended sentence.

sack. Bed. Also *kip.*

saddle and bridle. An opium smoker's *layout, q.v.* Obsolescent.

sail. For a physician to give or sell drugs to an addict. See *turn.* "He went sailing for twenty tabs."

Sam. 1. Uncle Sam, *i.e.,* the federal government. 2. A widely used greeting in a sort of formula, with variations. "What's doing, Sam, what's the flimflam?"

San Francisco bomb. A combination of heroin, cocaine and LSD.

san lo. A cheap grade of smoking opium made from *dog* with *yen shee* added and the whole mixture reworked. Sometimes recorded as *sam lo.* "If the original gum was good, the san lo would be almost as good as the first cooking." "Been smoking san lo down at Ty Ling's and I could hardly tell the difference." "The first smoking is hop. The second is yen shee. The third is san lo."

sand. 1. Sugar, especially in prisons. 2. A jail term.

satch. A method of concealing narcotics or smuggling them into jails. Part of the garment (usually the shirttail) is soaked in a saturated solution of drugs (white stuff), dried and the drug later dissolved for injection. See *put (it) in writing.*

satchel. A girl.

satchel habit. A weakness for a girl; "carrying the torch."

Saturday night habit. See *chippy habit.*

sawbuck. A ten dollar bill. Also *saw, sawski, dime.*

sawski. See *sawbuck.*

saxophone. An opium pipe or opium *layout,* sometimes carried in a case. Obsolescent. "Did you check the saxophone at the shed?" *(Layouts* were often checked at railway stations, check rooms, etc.)

scene. Any place, event or happening. Usually in such combinations as *on the scene, make the scene, blow the scene,* etc.

schmeck, smeck or **smack.** Narcotics. From Yiddish or German *schmecken.*

schmecker or **smecker.** An addict.

scoff. To eat a drug or take it by mouth. Usually used when there is some compulsion which prevents taking the drug in the usual way. Formerly used in referring to a regular *mouth habit.* Now generalized to taking drugs by mouth for any reason. "We scoffed the forty tables between us just before we got snatched. . . ." When arrest is imminent, addicts often swallow all they have with them. See *scarf, drop pills, scoff stuff.*

scoff stuff. To think or daydream about *dropping pills.* When addicts are *away from the habit,* they spend much time thinking and talking about taking drugs. This is especially true in prisons.

scorch. To abuse someone verbally and very severely; to play the *dozens, q.v.*

score or **score a connection.** 1. To purchase drugs from a peddler. Also *cop.* 1. Also used as a noun, meaning the purchase. 2. To secure drugs by any means—theft prescription, etc. *Score* common in the Midwest, South, Southwest and West. *Score a connection* more common on the East Coast. 3. To hit the vein with a needle. 4. Or **score** (only). To take money on any *racket* or *hustle.*

score dough. The price needed to buy drugs. Also *connection dough.*

score for a connection. 1. To secure drugs in quantity from a *connection* or *T-man.* 2. May also be used to mean arranging a purchase for one's connection, on a wholesale level. Rare.

scratch. Paper money.

scratcher. 1. A forger. From *scratch,* a pen, originally a quill pen. 2. A low-class addict, or one who is down and out. "That cotton scratcher is always on my back."

screw. 1. A prison guard. 2. To run out on the police. 3. A policeman or detective. "Nix cracken, Jimmy Bracken, the screw is on the Erie."

script. A prescription for narcotics. See *reader.*

script with a tail. See *reader with a tail.*

seccy or **seggy.** Seconal. See *red devil.*

seeds. 1. Morning glory seeds used as mild psychedelic drugs. 2. Seeds, stems and other impurities in marijuana.

self-starter. A voluntary patient. See *crank handle.*

send. 1. The pleasurable effects of smoking marijuana. "I take a half a cap of horse and two red birds and drink a glass of milk and it really sends me" (teenager speaking). 2. To smoke marijuana. A technique is used whereby air is drawn in at both corners of the mouth when the smoker puffs on the cigarette. This provides extra oxygen in the lungs when the smoke is inhaled. "You don't smoke it like a regular cigarette —you send it."

send it home. To inject narcotics intravenously.

sergeant. An especially masculine-mannered lesbian. See *Jasper.*

service stripes. Black or blue scars from injections. Also *tracks.*

set or **set of works.** Instruments for administering narcotics hypodermically.

set up. 1. The arrest of a *pusher* or *dealer* by the police, usually brought about by an informer making a purchase. 2. To inform on. "Tracy set me up to the narcos to protect himself."

sewer. The vein into which drugs

are injected. "If I miss the sewer, then the geezer is wasted."

sex punk. The passive or "feminine" partner in a male homosexual act.

shades. Tinted glasses. Also *fades, cheaters* (not necessarily tinted), *fakes,* etc.

Shadow. An undercover agent formerly working in the Leavenworth Annex. Widely known and feared by addicts. "Another character was called The Shadow; his name was Hobson, and he was a thorn in old dopey's side in the Annex. . . ." "I knew Hobbie well. The shakedown was about his only duty."

shakedown. 1. To search. 2. A search of the cell or the person. 3. Blackmail. 4. A form of pressure sometimes exerted by addicts on peddlers, mostly *squares.* The addict tells the peddler that he has hidden some heroin in the peddler's *pad,* and threatens to *finger* him to the narcotics officers if the addict's supply is not regularly available. The *connection* never knows for sure whether the addict has done this or not, but does not dare take a chance. "Texas and Oklahoma were notorious for the shakedown. It works."

shakedown bust. See *sneezed.*

shank. A knife. Also *shiv, blade,* etc. Mexican-Americans often use *fila,* from the fact that in prison knives are ground out from a file.

sharp. Dapper in appearance, as in *sharp threads.* Also extended as a general term of approbation.

sharp shooter. See *jab.*

shave. Te reduce the size of morphine cubes by shaving the flat sides with a razor blade. This is done when drugs pass from dealer to dealer or to addicts buying by the can or the cube. Restricted to morphine; other drugs are *cut, q.v.* ". . . out of a can, he would shave at least a dram of stuff."

sheep. A passive pederast. Also *lamb,* if he is a young boy. Both these are very old hobo terms.

sheet writer or **sheet artist.** An agent for the *numbers racket* (policy).

shine (him) on. 1. To ignore someone. See *chill.* 2. To threaten or intimidate someone.

shirt tail hype. See *J.C.L.*

shit. 1. Heroin. 2. To smokers who do not use heroin, marijuana.

shiv. A knife. See *shank.*

shoes (or boots) laced up tight. To be well informed. Also occurs as to have your *boots on.* "Tell Joe to put his boots on" ("Tell Joe to 'wise' up").

shoot. Take narcotics by needle, either subcutaneously or intravenously. See *bang* 4. ". . . Oh shoot no more the main lines, Oh shoot no more today. . . ." "If I ever shoot again, 1 belong in jail."

shoot an angle. See *shoot the curve.* Also occurs as *shoot the angles.*

shoot (him) down. To write an adverse behavior report on a prisoner. See *A.B.C.*

shoot gravy. To reheat a *boot shot* after a vein is missed and reinject the mixture of blood, water and drug. An addict who is very short on heroin may do this if his needle clogs or breaks and the shot cools before he can make repairs.

shoot the curve. To connive in prison to secure certain privileges, sometimes including the use of drugs. "One of those curves he shoots is going to hit him right in the schnozzola. . . ." Also recorded as *shoot a curve, shoot the curves.*

shoot yen shee. To inject a solution of any form of opium, but especially that made from *yen shee, gee yen* or the residue accumulated in a *gee rag.* Injected intravenously, it satisfies an opium or morphine habit temporarily; injected under the skin, it usually causes an abscess. Most addicts resort to it only when there is a *panic.* "In the old days, you could compare hypes who shot *yen shee* with the lushes who drank derail or canned heat; however, if *yen shee* were obtainable today, a lot more junkies would shoot it." "Old Chinese smokers saved their yen shee to give the working class Chinos. Now it sells for five or six bills a tael, if you can get it at all."

shooting gallery. 1. The withdrawal ward of a prison or hospital. 2. A place where an addict can go and use a needle to inject his drugs either free or for a fee. "All his friends . . . stream in, and the place turns into a shooting gallery."

shooting up. Injecting drugs, usually heroin. See *bang* 4.

shop. A house of prostitution, or a room used for this purpose. Probably cut back from *hook shop,* an old word in the *broad rackets.*

short. 1. A small quantity of drugs sold by a peddler. See *push shorts.* 2. A quantity of drugs (including the *short can* or *short toy* of opium) which has been shaved, cut or tampered with. 3. Having only a short period of confinement left on a sentence. See *on the shorts,* which is related.

short can, short toy, or **shorty.** A can of opium which has been tamp-

ered with so as to contain less than represented. See *short piece.*

short change racket, or **(the) hype.** 1. A small-time swindle worked by one or two operators on clerks or cashiers; a small purchase is made, a large bill is offered in payment, and the clerk confused into giving more change than his customer has coming. Mostly the *hype* takes $5.00 out of a $10 bill or $10 out of a $20 bill. 2. To short-change someone by this racket. Anyone working this racket professionally is *on the hype.* Also *make a hype pitch.* This racket has several other names, including *(the) sting, (the) note, laying the note, (the) flue,* with slight variations in meaning. All these terms are old-time *grifters'* argot.

short con. Any of numerous confidence games which are played for the amount of money the victim has on his person, as contrasted to the *big-con* games, which involve more sophisticated methods, *the send* and much larger amounts of money. Many addicts try their hands at various of the simpler *short-con* games; few addicts are found among the *big-con* operators, though *big-con* men use *short-con* games to carry them between *touches.*

short go. A small or weak *shot;* the implication is that the peddler has not given the addict his money's worth. This is a universal complaint among modern addicts. See *bird's eye, go.* "He is pushing an awful short go for a fin."

short heist. A crime such as child molestation that is offensive to other criminals or addicts (prison or institutional usage).

short piece. A quantity of narcotics,

usually an O.Z., which has been shaved or otherwise reduced. See *short can.* "He specialized in short pieces and taking the first count on everybody. . . ."

shot. 1. An adverse behavior report. See *shoot (him) down.* 2. A Negro pickpocket. A variant of *cannon,* a first-class white pickpocket. 3. A big operator in illicit business, especially narcotics. Probably cut back from *big shot.* 4. An injection of narcotics. See *shot in the arm.*

shot or **shot in the arm.** An injection of narcotics, either subcutaneous or intravenous. Nowadays usually shortened to *shot.* See *bang, vein shot, skin shot.*

shot up. 1. Under the influence of drugs. See *high, in high.* 2. Said of an addict with multiple abscesses.

shoulder. 1. See *collar.* 2. To refuse to have anything to do with someone. See *play the shoulder.*

shove. To peddle or retail drugs. See *pitch.* "He used to shove for me. . . ."

shove shorts. See *pitch, push shorts.*

shoving it. See *shooting up.*

shuck. 1. To feign or pretend. 2. To loaf. 3. To converse. 4. To throw a *wing ding, q.v.*

shy. To prepare a pill of opium for smoking. See *tchi.*

sick. 1. To manifest withdrawal distress, for a description of which see *panic man.* Many addicts are *sick* even when they are not actually deprived of drugs or *kicking the habit;* as each injection wears off, they have a mild attack of withdrawal symptoms, which disappears as soon as they take narcotics. The term sick is often specialized to the early morning craving which conditioned addicts

like to satisfy before they arise. Also *to feel the habit coming on, to have a habit, to have a yen, to have a monkey (or a Chinaman) on one's back, to gap.* "He took that extra bang even though he knew he'd be sick in the morning." 2. Mentally ill.

sift. See *manicure.*

signify. See *wedge.*

silly putty, also **silo.** Psilocybin.

silver serpent. See *harpoon.*

sissy. Passive receptor in the male homosexual act. Also *stuff, sex punk, queen pussy, bottoms.*

situation. A local drug subculture, often a college campus, and especially with regard to the availability of drugs. See *scene.*

sixty-nine. Mutual oral-genital contact, either homosexual or heterosexual.

sizzling. Wanted very badly by the police.

skag. Heroin.

skam. 1. Action, happenings, planning of narcotic or criminal activities. 2. A prison sentence. 3. To search someone. Also *pat down.*

skamas. 1. Smoking opium. See *brick, cotics.* 2. Drugs in general. "Skamas is an old time word; seems like the Hebes (Hebrews) use it the most, along with smack or smeck. . . ."

Skid Row. Convalescent ward at the USPHS Hospital, Lexington.

skin or **skin the punk.** To miss the vein and *blow a shot.*

skin shot. An injection of narcotics beneath the skin. Some addicts prefer subcutaneous injection, and stay on it for years; for others it is only a prelude to *vein shooting.* Some *vein shooters* use it to *hold* them during a *panic.* "A skin shot will last you longer."

skinless. A Jew, or Jewish.

skinner. 1. A *skin shot, q.v.* 2. One who uses *skin shots* regularly.

sky rocket. A pocket. One of numerous examples of so-called Australian rhyming argot which are beginning to infiltrate addict usage.

(the) slab. See *(the) hole.*

slam. A city jail. To be *slammed* is to be in jail.

sleepers. Barbiturates. Used by *squares* or young addicts just initiated.

slick. 1. Opportunistic. Also *swift.* 2. Sophisticated. Also *swift.*

smashed. Under the influence of narcotics. Also *geed up, ripped, wired up, charged, zonked, stoned, loaded.*

smeck or **smack.** 1. A *bindle* of drugs, especially a card of opium. "He's O.K., a C-note in the seams and smeck in the plant." 2. Generalized to include all drugs. From Yiddish or German *schmecken.*

smecker. A narcotic addict; sometimes still means an opium user. Now giving way to the variant *smacker* and generalized in meaning.

smell it up. See *sniff, snort, horn.*

smoke. A marijuana cigarette. See *J, joint, reefer.*

smoke that off. 1. To examine something; to be interested in someone or something; to check it out. "Smoke that broad off. She looks good." 2. To do something easily or deftly. See *smoke the habit off* 4.

smoke the habit off. 1. For an opium smoker who has been on the road (thieves, confidence men, etc.) and subsisting on *yen shee suey* or *yen poks,* to return to the pipe for a time. "When we get to Boston we can smoke our habits off." 2. Applied also to regular morning or night smoke. 3. By extension to needle addicts, to return to customary injections of drugs after a period of shortage or using drugs by mouth. 4. Currently, a trend is noted to apply this phrase to a very weak or mild habit, as "I could smoke this one off," or "I could sleep that habit off."

snatch. 1. A woman. 2. The female genitals. 3. To grab a woman's purse and run away. See *moll buzzer.* 4. To arrest.

snatched or **snatched in the neck.** Arrested. See *bust.*

sneeze. 1. To steal or shoplift. 2. See *sneezed.*

sneeze it out. To kick the habit; cold turkey. So-called because withdrawal may be accompanied by or followed by violent sneezing. A guard may say to an addict who begs for drugs in prison, "You shot it in, now sneeze it out." Sometimes the sneezing follows withdrawal and continues into the convalescent period.

sneezed or **sneezed down.** For an addict to be arrested or held without charges (and without drugs) in order to persuade him to supply information to the law. Obsolescent. **Sneezed** (alone) still used commonly for "arrested." This usage stems from the fact that as soon as an addict is deprived of drugs, he begins to sneeze. "Well, he was sneezed down for seven days, but he didn't sing. . . ."

sniff. To inhale narcotics, specifically cocaine. Also *to snort, to horn,* now largely applied to heroin. "Pipe smokers sniffed quite a bit of C in the old days." See *joy powder.*

sniffer or **snifter.** An addict who

takes drugs by inhalation. Restricted to cocaine or heroin. "Yeah, those boys are both sniffers. They're needle shy."

snitch joint. A dorm or wing for informers in prison. Also *rat row*.

snort. To take cocaine or heroin by inhalation, usually from the back of the hand, sometimes through a paper tube. See *sniff*. Also *horn*.

snow. Cocaine. Obsolete among underworld addicts, but still used by police officers and the public. "C was always something else besides snow. We'd call it Corine or Cecil, as all the fuzz referred to junk as snow. . . ."

snowbird. 1. A cocaine user. Now obsolete among addicts, but still used journalistically. "You could tell he was a snowbird." 2. Current usage on the West Coast, an "Anglo" or Caucasian who associates with Mexican-Americans.

socializing. Gathering together, especially with *roadies*, and particularly for using drugs in a group. See *party*.

sol. Solitary confinement. This usually implies that the prisoner is "on a diet"—bread and water—with one slice in the morning, two slices at noon, and three slices in the evening. "Guys in sol could always get a little cough syrup (codeine terpinhydrate) from the croaker in a cup and would put it on bread. This was when it was piss and punk for seven days at a stretch."

solid. Okay, fine, all right.

solid M.D. A physician who will write *script*. See *ice tong doctor*.

solitary cure. See *iron cure*.

something for the head. Hallucinogenic drugs.

soul searching. The vein shooter's constant search for veins he can use.

sound or **sound on.** 1. To insult, especially by references to relatives, physical attributes, or poverty (ghetto usage). See *(the) dozens*. 2. **Sound** (only). To feel out a sucker. 3. As a noun, any one of the numerous traditional insults.

spaced (out). Experiencing the effects of a drug. Sometimes generalized to describe anyone with erratic or eccentric behavior, whether a drug user or not.

speed. Amphetamines, especially methedrine.

speed demon, speed freak. A methedrine user.

speedball. 1. An injection of morphine or heroin mixed with cocaine. "I'd like two speedballs for a wake up. . . ." See *whiz bang*. 2. An injection of heroin combined with amphetamine for a smoother effect. 3. Seconal and wine taken by mouth. "These J.C.L.'s speak of two reds and a glass of wine as a speedball. What's this world coming to, Doc?"

spike. 1. The hollow needle used with a *dropper* to make a regulation *joint*. Also often *ikespay* or *speezike*, standardized in a sort of pig-Latin. Also *Mr. 26, fuete, Yale*. 2. The nail, pin or other substitute used to make an *emergency gun*.

splash. See *flash 1, rush*.

split. To leave a place, sometimes in haste.

splivvy or **spivvy.** To be well dressed or sharp.

spoon or **cooking spoon.** 1. See *cooker*. "Some wag once called junkies the 'knights of the bended spoon' and it stuck." 2. A small quantity of heroin, usually about 1/32 oz. of retail heroin.

sporting life. The life of the *hustlers*. Also *the life, q.v.*

spot for (someone). To act as a lookout for an addict while he takes a *shot* in a public place or in a prison where a guard may see him. "I want this chair to spot for Jim while he fixes. . . ." Also *play the point* or *get on the point.*

spread the joint. See *make a spread.* "Give him room to spread the joint so we can fix."

square. 1. A member of the dominant culture. 2. Anybody who is disliked or stupid. 3. Any nonuser of drugs. Probably cut back from *square apple* or *square John*, which is the older term.

square apple. A non-addict. See *do right people.* "Watch your chatter, the gee with Joe is a square apple."

square business. The truth.

square John or **square.** A non-addict. See *do right people.* "How did he get in Narco? I thought he was a square John."

squared up. See *away from the habit.*

squawk. To inform or complain.

squeal. To inform.

stable. The community of girls who prostitute for one pimp. Sometimes these girls know each other, sometimes not. Also *stake bag.* The pimp may also use *crib, flat, joint, pad* as an equivalent, even though the girls may not all live there.

stall. See *finger.*

star dust. Cocaine, Journalistic usage. See *white stuff, Bernice.*

stasch or **stash.** Variant of *satch.* Probably a hybrid word resulting from a combination of *sach* or *satch* (from saturate) with *cache.*

A concealed plant of narcotics, usually one which an addict keeps as a last resort in case of arrest. The variety of these plants is limited only by the ingenuity of the addict. The most popular one in jails is a blotter or a piece of cloth—often one of the garments —soaked in a saturated solution and dried. But there are many others. See *finger of stuff, keyster.* "You can put your stuff in my stasch."

steel and concrete cure. See *iron cure, quarry cure 1.*

> *We must slap them in the hole,*
> *On the concrete let them roll.*
> *That will fix them, Dr. H——,*
> *You've said it, Dr. K——.*

"The steel and concrete cure is the only cure I recommend for stool pigeons."

stem. 1. An opium pipe. 2. The bamboo stem of a pipe. There is a Chinese belief that if the pipe is broken in and smoked by a man, the stem (bamboo) will split if it is smoked by a menstruating woman. See *bamboo.*

stem winder or **winder.** A voluntary patient. See *Mr. Fish.*

stepping high. 1. See *high, in high.* "He was stepping high every time I saw him." 2. Operating a profitable *racket* or *hustle.* 3. Pretending to be a big-time operator. Also *highsiding.*

stevie. Hallucinations experienced by marijuana users. "A real seal named Cleo, with a shark's head, once ate my arm and leg off, a bite at a time, smiling all the while."

stick. 1. A homemade or makeshift opium pipe made of a bottle and rubber hose. Obsolescent. See *bamboo.* 2. A marijuana cigarette. 3. A one-year prison sentence. 4. Occupation or way of making money, as, "His stick is boosting." The equivalent of *racket* or *hustle*.

stick it to (someone). For a court to give the maximum penalty.

stick man. See *reefer man.*

stir. Prison. Also *joint, trap, pen, hatch, frame,* etc.

stir bugs. See *stir simple.*

stir simple. Mentally disturbed as a result of confinement. Also *stir bugs* (most common), *psycho, flipped his lid, blew his top, jerk simple, stir happy,* etc., with various shades of meaning.

stomach habit. The habit of eating opium or drinking it in solution, an obsolescent form of *mouth habit,* and used only by old-time pipe smokers. Also *belly habit.* See *scoff, scoffer.* "The old hop heads used to refer to a mouth habit as a stomach habit."

stone. A prefix element meaning confirmed or totally given over to something, as "he's stone police," "he's stone crazy."

stoned. 1. Under the influence of narcotics. 2. Drunk on alcohol, or a combination of alcohol with barbiturates or amphetamines.

stool. 1. A stool pigeon, used by officers to catch addicts or peddlers. *Stoolie* is often used by the law. Also *rat, fink,* etc. "It's supposed to be right guys who are stools that cause all the grief." 2. To act as a stool pigeon. See *rat* in various combinations. "He has been ready to stool on someone for years, never had enough pressure put on him before."

stool pigeon. A government informer; an addict or peddler used to trap others. "A good dick is one who knows how to handle stool pigeons." "In the old days you could make book that a stool pigeon wouldn't live six months." See *rat* in various combinations.

store. The female genitals.

STP. A hallucinogenic amphetamine, dimethoxymethamphetamine. The initials are reputed to stand for Serenity, Tranquility and Peace.

straight. Said of an addict who has had the proper *ration* to make him feel normal. See *bang, fix, gowed.*

straight man. See *margin man.*

straighten out. See *hang up* 1.

strap or **strap Johnson.** See *Jap.*

street people. Groups on many urban streets who beg, sing, and idle. They are often *hippies, q.v.,* runaways and traffickers in narcotics and other contraband.

streeter. A hoodlum-type addict.

strip. 1. A letter. 2. The impregnated paper or fiber from inside an amphetamine inhaler, used as a stimulant.

strung. Addicted. See *strung out.*

strung out. To be severely addicted. "I've been all strung out for a year now."

stud. 1. A male, especially a male Negro. 2. An aggressive female homosexual. Also called a *stud broad, boss broad,* etc.

stud broad. The masculine partner in a lesbian combination. Also occasionally recorded as meaning any girl or woman.

student. A beginning addict who has not yet established a regular habit, or who has difficulty establishing one. See *J.C.L.* "He's a student now, but he'll get squared away. . . ." This term appeared long before the use of drugs spread to actual students in high school or college and is now very popular.

stuff. 1. A generalized term for narcotics, especially *white stuff.* "That word 'stuff' is in use again everywhere. A few years ago you seldom heard it." "To the new generation, only heroin is stuff" See *junk.* 2. A prison term. "I started in San Quentin and finished my stuff in Chino." 3. A passive homosexual. See *sissy.*

suede. A Negro. Also *stud, spook, blood,* etc.

suey pow. A small sponge, cloth, or powder puff dampened and used to clean and cool the bowl of an opium pipe. Part of the *layout.* "She threw him on the suey pow and stabbed him with the yen shee gow. . . ."

sugar. 1. Narcotics. 2. Inferior or fake drugs. "He sold me sugar." *Sugar* seems to have been used for drugs well before cutting with sugar of milk became common. See *sugar lump cubes,* which were and are pure medical morphine, though they are no longer so common in the contraband traffic.

sugar cube or **sugar lump.** A *ration* of LSD as it is sold on the illicit market in the form of a lump of sugar containing a drop of the drug.

sugar habit. A light narcotic habit, so called from the heavy sugar of milk content in much of the heroin sold today.

sugar lump cubes. Large cubes of bulk morphine. See *cube.*

Sunday popper. An occasional user of narcotics. See *hype, chippy.*

sunshine or **yellow sunshine.** LSD or any other potent hallucinogen.

Sweet Jesus. Morphine. See *M.*

Sweet Lucy. 1. The resinous gum of marijuana (hemp) dissolved in wine. See *muggles, potaguaya.* 2. Muscatel wine, often used by alcoholics (wine heads) or for consumption with barbiturates.

sweet lumps of lead. See *sugar lump cubes.*

Sweet Morpheus. Morphine. See *Sweet Jesus.*

sweet stuff. 1. Narcotics, especially *white stuff.* Obsolescent. Used somewhat around jails and prisons, but there was a conflict with the several other and unrelated meanings of the term. 2. A homosexual.

swift. See *slick.*

swing. To peddle narcotics. See *push.*

swinging croaker. See *swing, right croaker, sail, turn.*

sympathizer. A social worker. Also *rabbi, preacher, chaplain, Mr.* (or *Miss*) *Broadshoulders.*

syrup. Dark brown heroin of Mexican origin. Heroin ranges from almost white through tan to dark brown.

T or **T man.** 1. A *big man, q.v.* Now more widely used than *big man.* It indicates *the top.* 2. A federal agent, especially a treasury agent or *narco,* as contrasted to an FBI man.

tabs. 1. 5 mg methedrine tablets. 2. Any drug in tablet or even capsule form.

tail towel checker. A pimp.

take. 1. To rob an addict or peddler known to be carrying a quantity of drugs. Knockout drops are sometimes used. The form most frequently encountered is the past participle. "I hear Sam was taken for ten OZ last night." 2. The proceeds of a racket.

take a fall. See *take a tumble, fall.*

take a sweep or **take a sweep with both barrels.** To inhale cocaine or heroin. Rare. Obsolescent. *Pass the quill, I want to take sweep.* The *quill* refers to the older custom of inhaling drugs, especially cocaine, from a soda straw, paper tube or hollow quill toothpick. The smoke from heroin is also sometimes inhaled by putting the dry powder in a tinfoil trough, heating it with a cigarette lighter and passing the smoking drug underneath the nostrils.

take a trip. To use LSD, which is frequently taken in groups where experienced users like to observe the reactions of novices who have never had the drug before. See *trip.*

take a tumble. To be arrested. See *fall.*

take it in the line. To inject narcotics intravenously. See *bang* 4; *shoot.*

take it main. To inject drugs intravenously. See *shoot.* "Take it main, that's the way to put the test to it."

take off. 1. To smoke, as opium. "He took off about eight pills. . . ." 2. To take a shot of narcotics. "I just took off about an hour ago. . . ." 3. To rob a place, especially of narcotics. "I'm going to take off that croaker's office tonight."

take off artist. A type of strong arm man who preys on addicts and robs *connections, peddlers,* etc.

take the rope. To commit suicide by hanging. See *Gillette route.*

talcum powder. Inferior or fake narcotics. See *flea powder.*

tar. Smoking opium. Obsolescent. "Any tar around the Big Apple these days?"

taste. A small ration of narcotics. Also *bird's eye.* "Save me a lightweight taste for a get up."

tchi or **shy.** To roll a pill of opium preparatory to smoking. "This hop is like li yuen, it tchis (or shies) to a golden brown."

tea or **Texas tea.** Marijuana. See *muggles.* "Get some tea for Johnny's gal."

tea man. A marijuana user. Obsolescent. See *reefer man.*

teenybopper. A teenager or younger person, usually female, who imitates *hippies, q.v.*

tell it to the chaplain. To inform. See *rat.*

ten cent pistol. A *hot shot* or a heavy overdose sold to an informer with other capsules or *papers* and undistinguishable from the standard purchase.

that's all she wrote. There is nothing more; that is the end. Apparently originated in the Lexington Hospital around 1935-38.

THC. Tetrahydrocannabinol, a synthetic marijuana.

thin dirties. Diarrhea accompanying withdrawal.

thin hips. An old-time opium smoker, the folk belief being that lying on one side to smoke makes the hips small. While it has been observed that most old-time opium smokers tend to be slender, especially about the middle, this condition probably stems from the tendency to neglect food. When these men go *off drugs* for a time, they tend to gain weight, losing it again when they go back on opium. "Old Charlie there is the original thin hips. . . ."

thing. 1. See *emergency gun.* 2. Favorite drug, occupation, hobby. See *bag* 3.

three-day habit. 1. See *chippy habit.* 2. A *habit* which has not been satisfied for three days, by which time withdrawal distress is acute. Also *hung up, beat, hurting.* "Been beat for three days. And that three-day habit is getting tough."

throw a meter. See *Brody*. Rare, obsolescent. "He would throw a meter just to keep in practice."

tie up. 1. To distend a vein with a tourniquet preparatory to taking a *vein shot*. "Tie me up, will you?" 2. To block something or interfere with someone. "Don't do anything to tie up the connection."

tight. Intimate.

till tipping or **tapping.** Stealing from a cash register. Also *creeping*. See *heel*, which is a specialty among a certain class of thieves called *heels*, or *bank heels* if they operate through a cashier's window.

tin. 1. A tobacco can of marijuana. 2. Sealed or canned smoking opium.

tip. 1. A gang. 2. A crowd. 3. To inform. 4. To expose oneself, or someone or something. "Joe tipped his mitt by talking too much." "I looked at the spindle and tipped the gaff."

tired. Disgusted, quiet, ready to stop the action.

toby. Any good luck charm carried, especially by Negroes—a copper disc, piece of wire, rabbit's foot, etc. Also *mojo*.

tom cat. A sewing machine, especially one in prison. 2. The needle from a power sewing machine, often used in making a *pen shot*, *q.v.* "All those guys from the West Coast rather use a tom cat." Also *point*, *q.v.*

tong. A secret Chinese fraternal organization, such as the Hip Sings, On Leongs, etc. At one time in control of the opium traffic in the U.S. and still active therein.

too much. A superlative used to denote the utmost. Giving way to terms like *righteous* on the West Coast and *the end* in the East.

tools. Instruments for administering narcotics hypodermically. Obsolescent. See *artillery*.

top sarge. A very aggressive female homosexual. Also *sergeant, jasper,* etc.

tops. A male homosexual who practices fellatio.

tops and bottoms. A male homosexual who will practice his perversion orally and anally.

torpedo. 1. A drink (usually whiskey) containing chloral hydrate. See *Mickey Finn, knockout drops.* 2. To beg money by getting sympathy. 3. A gunman used by a *mob* to execute informers or other undesirables.

torture chamber. A jail or prison where an addict cannot secure drugs. "Most stirs in Canada are real torture chambers."

toss out. 1. A pretended fit or illness. See *Brody.* "He always pulls a toss out too fast." 2. A means used by *boot and shoe* addicts to beg money on the street by getting sympathy. "He is a toss out artist, gets him twenty bucks a day."

total body orgasm. Addict's description of the effect of intravenous heroin use.

tote. A pipe with a small bowl, often very ornate, used for smoking marijuana. Also, the amount of marijuana held by such a pipe. Also *toke, toak.*

touch. See *score* 4.

tough time. See *hard time.*

toy. A small box of opium, or for containing opium. Small tin salve boxes are sometimes used; also half-shells from English walnuts are referred to as *toys* when filled with opium. *Toys* are put up usually to contain 5, 6 or 12 *fun* of smoking opium. In some areas like California, a toy contains 25 *fun,* in others 20 *fun.* Smaller quantities are put up in *papers,* *q.v.*

tracks. Supravenous scars. See *service stripes.*

train. Sexual intercourse with more than one partner. See *gang bang.* "She was on the train last night."

train arrived. Narcotics successfully smuggled into prison. Also *drive boat sailed,* etc.

trained nurse. Narcotics (*white stuff* usually), especially drugs smuggled to an addict to "take care of him" while in prison or jail.

> Funny as it may seem,
> See the prints upon my arm,
> They were put there by fingers, deft,
> Of my trained nurse, Miss Morphine.

trap. Prison.

tray. 1. A quantity of narcotics on the retail level. 2. Or **trey.** Three of anything, as a three-year sentence.

treat. See *candy a J.*

tremble. 1. To ogle the female patients in the hospital. 2. To commit an adverse act, which may be discovered.

trick. 1. A person who is willing or looking for sexual gratification. 2. A victim of one of the rackets. 3. The sexual act performed to obtain money for drugs. Usually occurs as *"turn a trick."* 4. Any foolish person. 5. Any customer serviced by a prostitute. A girl refers to him as *"my trick,"* and from this usage comes such phrases as *trick hype,* meaning a "square" addict, or one only partly or very recently addicted.

trick bag. 1. The mythical place for victims, as, "He is in the trick bag." 2. Someone pretending to be too stupid to follow orders.

trick hype. See *Hoosier fiend, trick* 5.

trip. 1. The experience of taking LSD or another hallucinogen. 2. As a verb, to have such an experience.

trip conductor or **guide.** An experienced user who abstains from use to help others, especially at an LSD *party.* Borrowed from psychiatry.

trip out. See *freak out* 1.

tripper. A user of hallucinogens, especially LSD.

tripping. Experiencing euphoria following the use of drugs. Now specializing to LSD users. See *high.*

tripping double header. Using more than one drug at a time.

trolley. 1. The secret channels through which narcotics and other articles are distributed inside prisons; sometimes an actual string or wire passing from cell to cell. "In a Canadian stir, the trolley was a string of plaited shoelaces and reached from No. 1 cell on the No. 3 gallery to the 33 cell on No. 1 gallery and it was called the telegraph, French pronunciation. . . ." 2. A low-type female *hustler.*

turkey. A *bindle* of bad narcotics, or a capsule containing only sugar or chalk. "Got a second turkey before we scored, but it was sure bonaroo stuff." See *blank.*

turn. To consent to sell drugs to an addict, applied to peddlers mostly, but also used of physicians. "That outfit won't turn to me; I'm on the cuff (credit) for two bills ($200.00) now. . . ." "He'll turn if you know somebody."

turn around. 1. To reform or go off drugs. 2. To confess. 3. To put somebody in jeopardy. 4. To upset someone. 5. To *flip over* or go homosexual.

turn a trick. 1. To prostitute. "My frame will have to turn a trick before we can score." 2. To cheat.

turn in or **turn up.** 1. To point out an addict or peddler to the law, with the implication that an arrest takes place. "The same broad turned him in before. . . ." 2. The arrest resulting from the act of a stool pigeon. "He had a turn up this month a year ago."

turn on. 1. To inject drugs by needle. 2. To introduce someone to drug use. "Nobody ever turned me on. I turned myself on, just from being in the life."

turn over. To abstain from using or selling drugs. See *off drugs.*

TV action. Euphoria from drugs. See *high.*

twist. 1. A marijuana cigarette. 2. A girl, from Australian rhyming argot: *twist and twirl.* "I had a twist who hustled her Kelseys with every trick. She was a nympho."

twisted. Under the influence of narcotics.

twister. 1. A feigned illness or "fit" for the purpose of getting drugs. See *Brody.* "I threw a twister, but it cut me a duster." 2. An addict expert at this trick. "See Joe, he's the twister for the outfit." 3. A fit of violent retching or the vomiting of blood and mucus during withdrawal. Also *heaves.* "His habit was one twister after another. . . ." 4. A marijuana user.

uffi or **uhffi.** Morphine. Rare (New York City and Detroit areas). See *M.*

Uncle. 1. A federal narcotic agent, or any federal officer. "Blow, bub, Uncle is everywhere tonight. . . ." 2. The federal government. "No use spending big dough for a mouthpiece when Uncle has you. . . ." See *Sam* 1.

under the gun. 1. To be under observation by the police. See *on ice* 2. 2. To be taking a long chance, as having a pusher who sells for his *connection* just to support his own habit.

unkie. Morphine (New York City and Detroit areas). See *M.*

unwind. To relax by taking drugs; especially used by jazz musicians.

up and down the lines. Having ruined the veins by repeated puncturing. The phrase reflects the *vein shooter's* constant hunt for veins he can use. See *burned out.*

up tight. 1. Out of money. 2. To be in an uncomfortable position, as out of drugs, *sick* or in fear of being picked up by the police. 3. To be in a very good position or situation. An example of the reversal of value of many terms in some subcultures, as *bad* to mean "good" and *shit* to mean "heroin" in the ghetto vernacular.

uppers. Stimulant drugs, amphetamines, as opposed to *downers, q.v.*

uptown connection. A big-time peddler. See *connection.*

user. See *gow head.*

V.S. A vein shot, the opposite of *S.S.* for *skin shot.*

vein shooter. An addict who uses drugs intravenously (*white stuff*, barbiturates and, on occasion, opium).

vein shot. An intravenous injection of narcotics. "I remember his first vein shot knocked him kicking."

verification shot. 1. An injection during or before which a little blood is drawn up into the needle to make sure it is in the vein. See *back up, register, boot shot, booting.* 2. A shot of narcotics taken to test its strength or quality. "After a couple of OZ are bought by a mob, the first round of shots before the stuff is chopped up are called verification shots."

vet. A prison or jail physician. See *croaker.*

vipe. To smoke marijuana. See *muggles, send.*

viper. See *reefer man.*

viper's weed. Marijuana. See *muggles.*

wake up or **get up.** The first shot of the day, taken the first thing in the morning; a must for a *strungout* user. "If I didn't save a *wake up,* I'd be up tight." Also *morning shot.*

warped. Experiencing the effects of a drug. See *high.*

washed up or **cleaned up.** 1. Temporarily off drugs, as when an addict is out on bond. See *away from the habit.* 2. To be forced to go off drugs for a long time, as when in prison, etc.

waste. To kill a person. "Some day we'll have to waste that fink."

wasted. 1. Under the influence of narcotics, especially when unconscious. See *gowed.* 2. Arrested as a *peddler.*

way out. 1. Incomprehensible. 2. The best. Also *far out.*

Weasel. An undercover agent formerly in Atlanta Penitentiary. Widely known for his ability to sense that a man was using or getting narcotics. "Never knew the Weasel, but his name was Head and of his exploits I've heard plenty. . . ." "Mr Head or

The Weasel would stand in the chow line and dog eye each con. Knees and Elbows Jr. at the Annex (Leavenworth) got his start the same way."

wedge. To manipulate people by playing the opinion of one person in authority against the opinion of another (largely institutional usage).

wedge. To manipulate people by playing the opinion of one person in authority against the opinion of another (largely institutional usage). On the street this may be referred to as *signifying.*

weed. Marijuana. See *muggles.* "I don't like weed, the taste, the effect or the weed heads that use it."

weed head. A marijuana smoker.

weekend habit. A small, irregular habit which may be indulged over weekends. A kind of *chippy habit, q.v.* "An exaddict can't have a weekend habit but two weekends. . . ."

what did you knock over? What brought you here? (refers to a prison, jail or hospital). Other common phrases: "What's your rap?" "What's your beef?" "What did you fall for?"

wheels. A car.

where it's at. Where the action is, whether drugs, sex, money, or whatever.

whips and jingles or **jangles.** The symptoms of withdrawal, especially in the early stages.

whiskers. 1. A federal narcotic agent. "Second guy from the left at the bar is whiskers." 2. Any federal officer. 3. The federal government. "Whiskers just returned a true bill against George and his old lady. . . ."

white angel. 1. A nurse or other attendant in an institution who can be bribed or persuaded to obtain narcotics for an addict. Obsolescent. 2. Morphine. "A white angel is one tablet or cube of morphine scored for in jail. . . ."

white goddess. Morphine. See *Sweet Jesus, white angel* 2.

white nurse. A general term loosely used to cover cocaine, morphine, or heroin; more often morphine.

white scene. A state of advanced intoxication from ingesting amphetamines; a *benny jag.*

white stuff. 1. Morphine, heroin, cocaine, Dilaudid. 2. Any drug which can be injected by an addict. 3. A cotton field or, by extension, penal labor or chain gang labor. There is a saying among underworld addicts: "You mustn't fall in Dixie, for white stuff will flip a junker" (meaning that an addict shouldn't get arrested in the South, for he can't stand penal labor). "Since I did that bit in Arkansas I can see a blade of white stuff for half a mile." "A *blade* of white stuff? A boll. . . ."

whites. Benzedrine tablets. See *benny.*

whiz bang. A mixed *shot,* usually morphine or heroin with cocaine. See *speed ball.* Rare, in this idiom, but the mixed *shot* is very common. "My favorite whiz bang is tincture of opium and C."

whizzes. See *jab.*

winder. A voluntary patient. Probably originated at Lexington, and not widely used elsewhere. Also *crank handle* and many other terms. See *Mr. Fish.*

wing ding. A feigned attack or "fit." See *Brody.* "Then he threw a wing ding in the bath house to cover up the get."

wired on whites. See *benny jag.*

wired up. Under the influence of narcotics.

with it. Also *on top of it.* Belonging to the in group, for instance, drug users. Adapted from old-time circus usage.

wolf. An aggressor in a homosexual affair.

wolf ticket. Harassment, as being *sold a wolf ticket,* is to be picked on. Here *wolf* does not necessarily have homosexual connotations.

works. 1. Instruments for administering narcotics hypodermically. See *artillery.* 2. A government agent or undercover man. 3. A sexual pervert.

write scrip. For a physician to supply an addict regularly with drugs. An old term among addicts. See *right croaker.* "He started to write scrip in '29, and now he has a gold pen and a Packard, and he's still writing scrip. . . ."

write up. To write an adverse behavior report on a prisoner. Also to *shoot (someone) down, put in a shot against (someone).* See *A.B.C.*

writing. 1. Porous paper, saturated with a drug in solution, on which a letter is written to a prisoner. See *satch.* "Big Nose Tommy got some writing today; you're invited." 2. Said of a doctor who is writing prescriptions for addicts.

wrong. Untrustworthy. Usually means just the opposite of *right* from the speaker's point of view. Thus a *right* town has the fix for certain *rackets* while a *wrong* town does not; a *wrong* copper cannot be *fixed,* while a *right* one can.

Yale. A needle, from one brand of standard commercial hypodermic needle. See *spike, Luer.*

year. A dollar bill. Also *ace*.

yellow jacket. A capsule of Nembutal. Also *nimbie*.

yen. 1. A desire for narcotics, even though an addict may not be using drugs at the time. 2. The need for narcotics which recurs regularly with an addict using drugs. 3. By extension, a desire for anything. Originally used by pipe smokers, but now generalized.

yen hok. 1. The steel needle-like instrument on which an opium pill is made or shaped. Also *hook*. 2. A tall, slender person, usually an addict.

yen pok. 1. The pill of opium after it is cooked. 2. A pill which is taken away by the smoker to swallow in place of a smoke. "An opium pill is always an opium pill until it is removed (from the *joint*) to be taken by mouth, then it is referred to as a yen pok." "Fix me a couple of high hats for yen poks." "I used to wrap yen poks in cigarette papers to take to work. . . ." "Usually made of yen shee or sam lo. . . ."

yen shee. The residue of opium which forms inside the bowl of the pipe; it is removed with the *yen shee gow* and used to mix with more gum to prepare more smoking opium. It is very concentrated. In solution, it is known as *medicine* or *yen shee suey*, and is carried on the road when smoking is difficult or impossible. Some addicts eat *yen shee;* others mix it with alcohol as a drink. Mostly mixed with cod liver oil, peanut oil or cottonseed oil. Rarely used today.

yen shee baby. The difficult bowel movements from severe constipation which accompanies addiction. "Wrap it up in a towel and it'll live—it's a yen shee baby."

yen shee boy. Possibly a variant of *yen shee quoi*. An opium addict, especially one who eats *yen shee, q.v.* "In the old days there were many addicts, male and female, who used strictly yen shee. Most pipe smokers would give it away when hop was plentiful."

yen shee gow. The scraper (sometimes made from a brass door key) which is used to cut the yen shee out of the inside of the hollow pipe bowl. These scrapers are widely variant in form, but generally resemble the letter Z with an extra angle for a handle. "We often made a yen shee gow out of a shoe hook . . . for button shoes, that is." Rare except among old-time opium smokers.

yen shee kwoi. Also recorded as "quoi," "quoy" or "quay." An opium smoker. "Me yen shee quoi, you got pen yen?" "My little colored gal would holler upstairs, 'Elnay, you know yen shee quay?' She was being secretive, or so she thought."

yen shee suey. See *yen shee.* "Ng king had the best yen shee suey in San Francisco. Also the best string of smoking bottles."

yesca. Marijuana. See *muggles*.

yet low, yet lo. The second or third ashes of opium; *yen shee* which has been reworked several times, like *san lo* or *sam lo*. See *yen shee*.

yummies or **yum-yums.** Any kind of drug, especially used by teenagers.

zipped. Under the influence of drugs. See *high, in high*.

zonked. Under the influence of narcotics. See *high, in high*.

zoom off. To experience the initial effects of a drug, especially opiates and hallucinogens. See *flash* 1, *rush*.

Addenda

AH PEN YEN. See *black stuff*.

BAD RAP SHEET. See *dirty jacket*.

BATTED. See *guzzled*.

BINGO. See *bing*.

BOOT SHOT. See *verification shot*.

BURN ARTIST. See *cheater*.

BUST YOUR BROWN. See *going up the dirt road*.

CAP'S LOOSE. See *crock* (3).

CLEANED UP. See *washed up*.

DAI YEN. See *black stuff*.

DIRTY ARM. See *cement arm*.

DOUGLAS. See *dugout*.

DUG. See *dugout*.

FADES. See *shades*.

FI DOO NIE. See *black stuff*.

GIVE (SOMEONE) FIVE. See *give (someone) some skin*.

GLUED. See *guzzled*.

GOT A THING GOING. See *build up the habit*.

The GROOVIE LIFE. See *(the) life*.

HIT THE PIPE. See *hit the gong*.

HOK FOR. See *black stuff*.

HUM BUG. See *drag*.

JOE LUNCH PAIL. See *do-right people*.

KIESTER. 2. A suitcase.

The LIVING END. See *(the) life*.

LOOSE. See *crock* (3).

MESS. See *muggles*.

ON TOP OF IT. See *with it*.

OUT OF THE COOLER. See *on the bricks*.

PLAYER. 1. See *playboy*. 2. *pimp*.

QUEEN. See *daisy*.

RANK. See *drag*.

RAP AND BAG IT. See *bottoms*.

RUMKIN. See *creep*.

SCARF. See *dropping*.

SNITCH SHEET. See *dirty jacket*.

SOK NIE. See *black stuff*.

SQUARE HYPE. See *Hoosier fiend*.

STAKE BAG. See *stable*.

STICK IT TO (SOMEONE). See *book*.

STIR HAPPY. See *stir simple*.

The SWINGING LIFE. See *(the) life*.

TALKING TRASH. See *crock* (3).

TIE OFF. See *tie up*.

TOKE (TOAK). See *hit*.

TWENTY-FOUR KARAT POOP BUTT. See *free loader*.

WEIRD. See *freak*.

WITCH HAZEL. See *H*.

YEN CHUNG. See *bamboo*.

19

The Argot
of Confidence Men

In the 1930s I noted and rather thoroughly explored the subcultures of the big-con and short-con operators. *The Big Con* appeared in 1940 and was simply a book-length expansion of the results of this exploration. In order to make the material more readable, most of it was presented in narrative form, synthesized from a large quantity of field data collected over a period of several years. To my knowledge, there has been no other extended exploration in this field, though a brief description of the *wire* appears in the work of the pioneer criminologist Edwin Sutherland (*The Professional Thief,* 1937).

Of some assistance to me was Colonel Philip Van Cise of Denver, Colorado, who prosecuted the infamous Blonger mob which operated largely on one big-con game, the *rag* (*Fighting the Underworld,* 1936). In this and subsequent editions I have also acknowledged the kind personal assistance of postal inspector Herbert N. Graham, who during his lifetime captured more confidence men than the entire FBI at the time. He made a lifetime career of running down con men and assisted me in the identification of many when this was needed. He was known in the underworld as the "Galloping Ghost," largely because of his great foot-speed and a frosted lens in his glasses concealing a blinded eye. He was also called "Old Poison" because of his deadly attacks on big-con rackets. In addition, I should thank my longtime friend the late Captain Danny Campion of the New York Police Department. He headed the con squad there for a number of years and, previous to that, headed the pickpocket squad as a lieutenant. He had access to many victims of con games who often did not understand how they had been *trimmed,* but from their accounts we were able to get some understanding of the many variations to be found in these games. He was also to put me in contact with a number of excellent professionals who might be in jail, on bail, or had temporarily or permanently *packed the racket in.* Furthermore, the late Dr. Victor H. Vogel, while medical officer in charge of the Lexington Narcotics Hospital, assisted me while I was working there by calling to my attention occasional confidence men who might serve, voluntarily and anonymously, as informants while they were inmates. I also had the expert assistance of a number of successful big-con operators who took a special interest in the collection of material for this study.

The assistance of neither Graham nor Campion could be acknowledged in 1940 since both were prohibited by their departments from contributing openly to any form of published material. I acknowledged their assistance in the 1974 edition, from which this material is taken, entitled *The American Confidence Man.* Both of these men were what I call scholar detectives because they read everything in their field and had a good understanding of the relation of the argot to behavior in the subcultures. Indeed, they used it functionally. I mention them here not only to render credit long overdue but also to indicate that there are a few police officers who can assist in the collection of argot materials, though this type of officer is very rarely encountered. Most law enforcement officers seem to have a limited and sometimes inaccurate concept of argots and can often be spotted by professional criminals on the basis of their argot usage. The real penetration of criminal organizations is usually done by undercover men who are not police officers but a sophisticated form of stoolpigeon. These people are often valuable sources for language study since they are natives of the criminal subcultures. They are difficult to contact, however, since there is great pressure on the police to protect their identities in order to discourage retaliation.

Con men, it should be mentioned, are almost entirely nonviolent, at least toward their victims, and they owe much of their prestige in the underworld to their use of intelligence instead of muscle. As far back as Harman and Dekker, short-con men have been near the top of the criminal hierarchy, a position that big-con men still occupy today. Within the last few years in the dominant culture there has been an academic and journalistic interest in the terms *con, con man,* and *con game* which have been very loosely applied to any fraud or cheating device. While these terms have diffused, they have not carried the specific argot meanings with them. Deception, while present, is not the essential ingredient; rather, it is the presence of larceny on the part of the victim. In addition, there is an extensive technical knowledge on which the successful operation of a professional con game depends.

• • •

E VERY professional criminal subculture has its own distinctive argot. This is true not only of modern criminals, who have streamlined crime and put it on a big-time basis, but also of professional criminals in all times and in all countries. Denizens of the Roman underworld had their argot, some of which we can read in writers like Petronius. With the growth of cities in Europe and the subsequent invasion of criminal subcultures from the Near East during the late Middle Ages, professional criminals spread throughout the Continent; in fact, Martin Luther edited the first glossary of their argot, which had been compiled in Latin during and after a number of criminal trials in Switzerland. As these professionals (including, among other groups, the "wandering Jews" and the Gypsies) migrated around, they introduced criminal techniques and principles new to Europe, but already very ancient.

Germany, France, Spain, Scandinavia, Russia, and Italy were all well infested, as Renaissance writing as well as Renaissance art testify. In fact, in Spain during the sixteenth and seventeenth centuries, the *picaro*, or professional grifter, became a kind of national hero; many of the best writers of Spain learned to use his argot, and it was fashionable to write serious literature heavily studded with argot, or in straight argot. Cervantes, Mateo Aleman (whose lengthy novel *Guzman de Alfarache* went through thirty editions in six years as well as translation into other languages), Vincente Espinel, Francisco de Quevedo, and a hundred others wrote fluently in the argot. As a result, it is well-nigh impossible today to translate many passages in Quevedo's novels.

England, too, was invaded by the migrating subcultures, and soon had a home-grown crop of her own. Shakespeare and his contemporaries were well acquainted with these criminal groups, who left an indelible linguistic mark on English literature. From England, as well as from France and Spain, they moved to the New World (Mateo Aleman, incidentally, migrated to Mexico, probably as a printer, along with another famous Spanish writer, Juan Ruíz de Alarcon, in 1608), where conditions were ideal for tightly knit criminal subcultures to flourish. The ultimate result is the formidably organized underworld of modern times, which spreads over much of both American continents. The subculture of the confidence rackets was an integral part of this long-continued migration, which is not yet finished, for there are still short-con men and a few big-con men who speak English with a foreign accent, not to mention some top-notch big-con men who speak with a British accent in America. Although most argots spoken in the United States today are based on the structure of English, many of them still carry a residue of foreign words and phrases.

Professional crime is nothing more than the way of life in a criminal subculture, highly organized and parasitic on the dominant culture. And the so-called underworld is nothing more than an aggregation of many and various subcultures. Criminal argots are the languages indigenous to these subcultures, and they reflect the behavior pattern of the groups which use them. Each subculture has its own argot, conforming to a large system of argot formation which is now becoming evident in the American underworld. Men and women working rackets which stem from intimately related subcultures tend to speak similar argots; those working rackets from less closely related subcultures speak argots with less in common. This pattern holds true over a very wide social and geographical range of professional criminal activity which might include at one end the Mafia and at the other the rural Southern moonshiner.

All organized professionals speak at least one argot fluently—that of their own racket, which is based in turn on that of the subculture to which they belong. Thus, among the literally hundreds of rackets practiced today, the argots used by some are closely related, while those used by others are widely divergent. The knowledge of the argot is the mark of the professional, a union card so to speak, and criminals recruited from outside find that it takes them several years to master it adequately. Some professionals understand and even use more than one argot, but these are usually argots derived from related subcultures; rarely one encounters a man who has a good knowledge of two or more argots derivative from widely variant sources. Usually these are old-timers who had an unusual opportunity to grow up in contact with more than one group. These men are passing rapidly, however, and the modern generation tends toward specialization of a kind. In fact, youngsters on the rackets today hardly know that there are argots other than the one they naturally speak, whatever that may be.

In addition to the argot, all professionals have some knowledge of the language native to the country where they live and work—in this case, colloquial American English. Often—though not always—the effectiveness with which they use the official language depends upon how much they need it in the course of their criminal activities. Thus pickpockets, who have little need for the official language, tend to think and speak almost exclusively within the confines of the argot; to some, standard English is virtually a foreign tongue which is maddeningly used in form sheets and other basic literature. Many native-born pickpockets are illiterate, and this has included some of the best I know. There are many who still speak a foreign language—on the appropriate level—and know only a few words and phrases in English. If they have been working with American mobs, they have picked up a little American argot; if not, they pick up a few useful words and phrases wherever they are exposed to them. But if they continue to work as a mob of foreign-born, they still use Spanish or French or Polish or Russian, for in the business of picking pockets, the less said to the mark, the better. On the con rackets, of course, it is necessary not only to speak English fluently, but to use it on a level acceptable in the social areas where con men must work. In addition to an extensive argot, then, the big-con men almost always have an impressive command of both spoken and written English. They are among the most articulate of all professional criminals. They cannot, like the pickpocket, allow their brains to accumulate in their fingertips.

Is argot indigenous to crime? What about the rare but very intelligent and spectacularly competent lone-wolf jewel thief, swindler, blackmailer? What about those members of the dominant culture gone wrong? The answer is that argots are not indigenous to all crime, but are used only by organized criminals who are members of, affiliated with, or inducted into a criminal or semi-criminal subculture. The lone-wolf type of thief would not know or use argots unless (as is seldom the case) he has connections with the subculture. The legitimate citizen gone wrong and given, say, to embezzling, will not develop an argot in connection with his criminal activities, regardless of how long or how much he embezzles. On the other hand, the criminal narcotic addict, who belongs to the addict's subculture, almost surely, if he is to have a racket and secure contraband drugs, knows and uses an argot; the medical addict (say a patient suffering from a slow, painful disease, or the nurse who filches morphine from a hospital or a patient) will never even know that there is an argot which goes with addiction, let alone develop one.

Why do argots develop? There are several reasons, perhaps the most widely accepted of which is that criminals must have a secret language in order to conceal their plans from their victims or from the police. In a few cases — such as flat-jointers, three-card monte men, and some other short-con workers — criminals do use them in a very limited way to confuse or deceive their victims. But it should be emphasized that this kind of usage is minimal and limited. Most professionals speak argot only among themselves. They are amused at the idea that crooks are supposed to deceive people with their lingo, for the mere fact that to speak argot in public would mark them as underworld characters.

It is a fact that argots are largely unintelligible to the layman, but I think that we cannot assume that they are a deliberate protective device invented by criminals. We might as well assume that, because the technical language used by railroaders or fighter pilots or physicians or tobacco auctioneers is not readily understood by outsiders, it was created to deceive the public. Argot is indigenous to organized, professional crime; secrecy is a very minor motive for its formation and use, although it is true that, once a word from the argot becomes known and used outside the subculture, another word takes its place.

There are other and, I believe, much more pertinent reasons why argots are indigenous to criminal subcultures and the rackets derived from them. Incidentally, most of these reasons are not realized by the ordinary criminal, although the very intelligent ones may become analytical about it. First, criminal groups live and work outside the law and consequently count very little on it for protection — unless it is protection bought and paid for. Therefore, very strong internal pressures develop to consolidate the subculture, pressures which are in turn intensified by the outside pressures just referred to. There is a very strong sense of camaraderie among members of the subculture — including, in emergencies, even individuals or groups who dislike each other — and a highly developed group solidarity which is further increased by internal organization as well as by external pressures from the dominant culture and its laws and from other predatory subcultures. A common argot serves as a binder for members of the "in group" and expresses the powerful fraternal spirit which prevails among them.

Second, each specific profession or racket develops a feeling of mutual exclusiveness among its members. This feeling springs not only from their common cultural background but from these facts: their *turning out,* or induction to the racket, is the same; they face identical technical problems which must be solved with certain known tools and techniques; and certain professional codes or "ethics" must be observed if the mob is to prosper. Most professionals become skilled craftsmen in their fields, and the same factors which operate among legitimate craftsmen activate the creation and use of special language among criminals.

Last, many concepts exist for which there are no terms in the vocabulary of the ordinary citizen. This is particularly true since every thought pattern, every technique, every attitude, every aspect of organization, and most of the tools and devices ranging from pick-locks to nitroglycerin are focused against the dominant culture. It is quite natural that criminals should create, borrow, or adapt words to meet these needs, and that, since the criminal subcultures are continuous throughout history, many of these concepts and the words for them should accumulate in the argot.

At the same time, different attitudes toward argots prevail among different criminal groups. *Class cannons* (high-class pickpockets), for instance, work all day largely out of verbal communication with each other and have a strong belief that, if possible, a professional should not talk to suckers; but they are very talkative among themselves and love to cut up touches in the argot when they are in private. *Peter gees* (safecrackers) are typically silent as individuals, but they have a very well-developed argot which they appear to dust off and use among themselves on special occasions. Because the profession has dwindled during the past twenty years, owing to heavy federal prosecution for bank-blowing, it seemed for a while that this argot was moving toward extinction; however, a new crop of safecrackers is appearing, many of them *turned out* in prison by top-notch old-timers, and the profession is now reviving along with the argot, though the youngsters often work with a crudity which must shame their mentors. Criminal narcotic addicts, in general shunned by nonaddicted criminals, are extremely clannish, and when they are together talk or *jive* constantly about the one subject which obsesses them — drugs and their effects. Prostitutes create little argot of their own but borrow freely from other groups; their limited creativity is probably a result of their generally low intelligence, for it takes sharp minds to make lively argot. Grifters, and especially confidence men, like to talk and tell merry tales among themselves; in private they seem to compensate for the fact that they must use conventional English in their work, for they indulge in the fluent use of an argot which is highly developed. In general, all professionals take a certain pride in their command of the argot, and frequently they judge strangers immediately on the basis of its use. Almost universally, however, they restrict its use to their own culture or to friends whom they trust.

Of all criminals, confidence men probably have the most extensive and colorful argot. They not only number among their ranks some of the most brilliant of professional criminals, but the minds of confidence men have a peculiar nimbleness which makes them particularly adept at coining and using argot. They derive a pleasure which is genuinely creative from toying with language. They love to talk and they have markedly original minds, minds which are singularly agile and which see and express rather grotesque relationships in terms of the flickering, vastly connotative metaphor which characterizes their argot.

The lingo of confidence men is one of the most extensive in the underworld. The large number of technical situations which arise in the course of confidence games makes for a very complete technical vocabulary which covers many different types of games, the nature of the victims, standard situations within the games, etc. Con men are continually studying to improve their games, all of which makes for a rapid enlargement of the technical vocabulary. Furthermore, the fact that con men are recruited largely from other branches of the grift means they they bring with them methods, techniques, and attitudes which require argot for expression; this fact also links the argot of con men closely with the general argot of the grift.

But con men, as contrasted to other professional criminals, have creative imagination. Their proclivity for coining and using argot extends much beyond the necessary technical vocabulary. They like to express all life-situations in argot, to give their sense of humor free play, to revolt against conventional language. Thus they have a large stock of words and idioms for expressing ideas connected with travel, love-making, the creature comforts including food, drink, clothing, etc., recreation, money, people, the law, social relationships, etc. In fact, if con men find it necessary or convenient to discuss any topic for long, they will soon have an argot vocabulary pertaining to that particular subject. And one may rest assured that they will use good rich, roistering, ribald words which will radiate connotations for the initiate.

Closely related to the phenomenon of argot formation—in fact, one aspect of it—is the use of *monickers,* many of which have already been used in referring to individual confidence men. Relatively few criminals are known in the underworld by their real names; in many cases their closest friends know little of their family connections. Often professionals abandon their original family names and assume others. All of them work under numerous aliases and many have no criminal records under the names by which they are commonly known in the underworld. These underworld nicknames (known as monickers) usually stick to a professional criminal throughout life; they are genuine and cannot be shaken off like a mere name. However, not all con men bear monickers; those who do often carry them over from some other criminal occupation which they followed before becoming con men.

The monicker, like the names used by primitive peoples, is vastly connotative and becomes even more suggestive when one knows the circumstances which lead to its acquisition. Sometimes it reflects some striking physical characteristic of the bearer, as, for instance, the Bow-legged Lip, who had the misfortune to be both bow-legged and hare-lipped, the High Ass Kid, who was quite long-legged, the Square-faced Kid, Nigger Mike of swarthy complexion, and Crooked-arm Smitty, whose crippled arm resulted from jumping through a window in his early thieving days. The Narrow Gage Kid's height was just the distance between the rails of a narrow-gage railway.

Some monickers commemorate a personal exploit or recall some personal idiosyncrasy or former occupation. The Yenshee Kid chewed yenshee (gum opium); the Postal Kid was once a messenger boy; the Brass Kid peddled cheap jewelry; the Yellow Kid sold cheap watches with a story that they were stolen property; Brickyard Jimmy was once assigned to work in a prison brickyard during a brief reprieve from grifting.

Other monickers only designate the home town of a con man or the city in which he was turned out as, for example, the Ripley Kid, the Harmony Kid, the Honey Grove Kid, the Big and Little Alabama Kids, the Indiana Wonder, Glouster Jack, Kid Niles, and many others.

The con men who have monickers have often acquired them in other branches of the grift and carry them over into the big con which, incidentally, is not so rich in colorful monickers as are many other rackets. I should like to include here such pungent monickers as the Collars and Cuffs Kid, Proud of His Tail, the Narrow-minded Kid, the Money from Home Kid, Slew-foot Wilson, the Squirrel-toothed Kid, the Harum-scarum Kid, the Gash Kid, the Seldom-seen Kid, the Molasses-face Kid, and many others, but the talents of these gentry lie in other fields.

By whatever manner the monicker is acquired, it fits the personality of the bearer well and is often the only permanent name a grifter has; once it is applied and accepted, it becomes one of his few permanent possessions. It is tagged to him for life.

In the Glossary, no attempt has been made to present a complete list of con argot; a sizable volume would result if that were attempted. Rather, a representative section of con argot has been selected in order to clarify the argot which it has been necessary to use in the previous chapters, and at the same time, to give the reader some idea of the general nature of confidence argots. Both big-con and short-con argots are represented, for it is impossible to separate them; short-con workers may not know any big-con argot, but most of the outstanding big-con workers know and use some short-con argot along with the big-con lingo.

ADDICT. A mark who believes so firmly in a sure-thing investment that he comes back again and again. See *to knock (a mark)*.

APPLE. 1. See *mark*. 2. Any person.

The AUTOGRAPH. A short-con game in which the mark is induced to sign his autograph to a piece of paper which is later converted into a negotiable check.

BANK. A faro-bank game.

To BANKROLL. 1. For the insideman to finance an outsideman with expense money. 2. See *faro bank* (2).

The BAT. See *the gold brick*.

BATES, MR. BATES, or JOHN BATES. See *mark*.

To BEAT THE DONICKER. For two confidence men to ride the trains on one ticket by keeping one concealed in the washroom while tickets are being collected. Also *to play the runaround*.

To BEEF. For a mark to complain to the police.

To BEEF GUN. For a victim to complain that his pockets have been picked.

BEHIND THE SIX. See *chick*.

The BEST OF IT. 1. A prearranged method of cheating which will ostensibly allow the mark to profit by dishonest means. "All marks crave the best of it." 2. A cinch; a sure thing.

The BIG BLOCK. The second touch taken from a mark. Restricted to the rag. Cf. *the little block.*

BIG CON. Any big-time confidence game in which a mark is put on the send for his money, as contrasted to the short con where the touch is limited to the amount the mark has with him. There are three recognized big-con games: the wire, the pay-off, and the rag. However, competent confidence men often put the send into short-con games, especially the smack and the tip, with very good results. Touches on the big con range from $10,000 up. Cf. *short con.*

The BIG MITT. A short-con game played against a store with insidemen and ropers. The victim is enticed into the store, drawn into a crooked poker game, and is cold-decked on his own deal. See *the tear-up, big store, (huge) duke.*

The BIG STORE. An establishment against which big-con men play their victims. For the wire and the payoff, it is set up like a poolroom which takes race bets. For the rag, it is set up to resemble a broker's office. Stores are set up with a careful attention to detail because they must seem bona fide. After each play, the store is taken down and all equipment stored away in charge of the manager. See also *store.*

The BILK. A short-con swindle worked on a brothel madam. Similar to *lay the flue.*

To BILL (THEM) IN. For swindlers to induce marks to enter a swindling establishment (short con).

BLOCK GAME. The three-shell game played with small hollow boxes, weighted on the top. Also *the blocks, the boxes, the dinks, the hinks, the nuts, the peeks, the shells.*

To BLOW. 1. v.t. To allow a mark to win some money in a confidence game. "Blow a fin on the runaround" (short con). 2. v.t. To lose. "I blew my okus." 3. v.t. To realize.

"The mark never blowed it was a gaff." 4. v.i. To leave. "Let's blow." 5. or BLOW OFF. v.t. To separate the mark from the insideman or get him out of the big store after he has been fleeced. See *the cackle-bladder.*

BLUTE. A newspaper, especially fake clippings from a newspaper which are used in big-con games.

BOARDING-HOUSE DECEIVER. A cheap suitcase which is often left empty in a hotel when the grifter leaves without paying his bill.

BOARD-MARKER. The clerk in a big store who marks up the fake stock quotations or fake race results.

BOAT-RIDER. A professional gambler who rides the ocean liners and frequently ropes for confidence games. Also *deep-sea gambler.*

To BOBBLE. To excite a mark's suspicions, especially while short changing him (short con).

BOODLE. 1. A bankroll made up to resemble the mark's money (short con). 2. On the big con, a fake bankroll of small bills made up to pass for, say, $100,000. Also *B.R.*

BOOKMAKER. The manager of a payoff store. See *manager.*

The BOOST. 1. The shills used in big-con games. 2. Shoplifting.

The BOXES. See *the block game.*

B.R. See *boodle.*

BRACE (or BRACED) GAME. A crooked gambling game.

The BREAKDOWN. The stage in big-con games where the operators find out exactly how much money the mark can raise.

BROAD. 1. A railroad ticket. 2. A playing card.

The BROADS. Three-card monte. "Little Chappie Lohr used to steer against the broads for Farmer Brown." See *open monte, closed monte.*

BRUSH ONE'S TAIL OFF. To avoid or lose someone who is following.

BULLDOG'S NOSE. A carbonated drink or highball in which cigar ashes have been dissolved.

BUMBLEBEE. A one-dollar bill. Also *push-note, case-note* (the hype).

BUM RAP. A conviction on a trumped-up charge.

The BUTTON. 1. One method of blowing a

mark off after he has been fleeced. A fake detective raids the con men and arrests them. The mark is allowed to talk his way out. Cf. *the cackle-bladder, the tear-up.* 2. A type of short-con swindle in which the mark and the roper are accused by the insideman posing as a detective of passing counterfeit money. The insideman pretends suspicion and takes their money to "headquarters" for examination. Cf. *the shake with the button.*

C or The C. 1. The con, or confidence games. "He's on the C now." 2. The mark's confidence. "The insideman always has the mark's C."

The CACKLE-BLADDER. A method of blowing off recalcitrant or dangerous marks after they have been fleeced. The insideman shoots the roper with blank cartridges on the pretense that the roper has ruined both the mark and the insideman. He then hands the mark the gun, while the roper spurts blood on the mark from a rubber bladder he holds in his mouth. The mark flees, thinking he is an accessory to murder. The insideman keeps in touch with him for some time and sends him to various cities on the pretext of avoiding arrest (big con). Cf. *to cool a mark out.*

CANADIAN BUILD-UP. A hypester's racket in which he takes $50 out of $100 when change is made.

CANNON. A pickpocket. Also *gun, whiz, dip,* etc.

CAP. Expenses connected with roping and fleecing a mark, especially the roper's expenses while he is on the road. See *to cut up the score.* Also *the nut.*

The CARRIE WATSON. The best; anything or anyone of high quality or high attainments. From the old Carrie Watson House in Chicago.

C-GEE. A confidence man (big con).

CHICK or CHICANE. Short of money. Also *behind the six.*

To CHILL. 1. For a mark to lose interest in a con game. 2. To refuse to recognize someone. 3. To stack a deck of cards (gambling and short-con games).

CHUMP. See *mark.*

To CLEAN. To strip, as to strip the equipment out of the store.

To CLEAR THE BOOK. For the police to attempt to pin several unsolved crimes on a known criminal.

CLOSED MONTE. A monte game played in a store, with ropers and an insideman. Now obsolete. See *three-card monte.*

C-NOTE. A $100 bill.

COARSE ONES. Large bills used to impress the mark in a big store (big con).

The COLD POKE. A mock game played on gun molls for a joke. A young grifter points out an old grifter as a wealthy old gentleman and connives with the girl to steal his wallet. Meanwhile, the old man has substituted for his full wallet one filled with paper and often furnished with ribald verses. Just as the girl slips away with the wallet, the old man *beefs gun,* and a hue and cry is raised after the girl. Cf. *the engineer's daughter, the tish.*

To COME HOT. To take a con touch when the victim realizes he is swindled. See *the payoff against the wall.*

To COME OFF. To be consummated, as a theft or the cheating of a sucker.

COME-ON. 1. See *mark.* 2. A mark who has been put on the send and is returning to be fleeced.

COME-THROUGH. A fleeced mark who refuses to be blown off and follows confidence men in attempts to have them arrested.

CONFIDENCE GAME or CON GAME. Any type of swindle in which the mark is allowed to profit by dishonest means, then is induced to make a large investment and is fleeced.

CON MOB. 1. On the big con, the personnel of the big store; strictly speaking, the insideman, the manager or bookmaker, and the staff of ropers and shills. 2. On the short con, an insideman, his ropers and handlers. Also *mob.*

CONNECTION. 1. A source for purchasing illegal drugs. 2. Any person cooperating with criminals or dealing in contraband.

CONSIDERATION. A straight fee paid the boost in stores where they do not work on a percentage basis.

CONVINCER. The cash which the mark is permitted to win before he is given the big play.

To COOL (A MARK) OUT. To pacify a mark after he has been fleeced. Most marks are kept under perfect control by the insideman. Cf. *the cackle-bladder, the button, to blow* (5), *the tear-up.*

To COP. 1. v. To take money from a mark, in contrast to *blow* (1). 2. v. To take, as to cop a peek, etc. 3. n. The money which a mark is allowed to win.

To COP A HEEL. To run away. Also *to light a rag, to take a powder*. Cf. *to cop*.

COPPER ON and COPPER OFF. A crooked system for beating the faro bank from the outside, worked by a mob of four—one of whom keeps the cases. The case-keeper, by means of a hair and a swivel attachment, removes the copper from a bet which he sees is going to win, thus keeping the mob from losing its money.

To COP THE SHORT. For a railroad conductor to accept half fare from grifters, few of whom ever pay full fare on any transportation system. "A kinky kayducer will always cop the short."

COSE. A nickel.

The COUNT AND READ. A short-con swindle in which a mark's money is examined, presumably for counterfeit bills or for premium notes, and he is fleeced by the *slide* (*q.v.*).

The COUNTESS. Mrs. Maurer. Also *the raggle*.

To Be COUPLED IN THE BETTING. For con men to work together. Also *to run as an entry*.

To CRACK OUT OF TURN. 1. For one member of a con mob to miss his cue and speak his lines in the wrong place. Big-con games are rehearsed like plays, and each man must know his part perfectly. See *to rank a joint*. 2. To butt in, or offer unwanted advice.

The CROSS. A short-con game in which the mark loses his money betting on the roper's ability to beat a third man at dice. Five square dice are used, and the mark is played for in a saloon which is right.

CROSS FIRE. 1. In short-con games, a conversation in argot between the insideman and the outsideman to deceive the mark and any bystanders. 2. In big-con games, where no argot is used, conversation between the insideman and the other members of the mob for the mark's benefit. "It's really the cross fire that beats the mark." When secret signals must be given in big-con games, they are made in the form of offices (*q.v.*).

CROW. Fake or cheap. Also *snider*.

To CURDLE. For anything, especially the fix, to go wrong.

CUSH. Money. For other specific terms relating to money, see *ridge, meg, deemer, cose, push-note, fin, sawbuck, double saw, half a C, C-note, G-note, coarse ones, soft ones*.

CUSHIONS. 1. A passenger train. 2. The day coaches, as contrasted to Pullman coaches. 3. Reserved seats at a circus (short con).

To CUT IN. 1. v.i. To break into a conversation; to accost a mark. 2. v.t. To share the profit of a con game with an outsider, as for instance someone who furnishes the names of lucrative marks.

To CUT INTO. To set a sucker up for a con game.

To CUT UP THE OLD SCORES. To gather together and talk over old times. Also *to punch the guff*.

To CUT UP THE SCORE. To divide the profits of a con game. In big-con games the lay is usually as follows: The insideman takes 55 percent of the score, out of which he pays the manager 10 percent of the total, gives each of the ten or twelve shills 1 percent of the total, pays the bank at least 5 percent, and takes care of the fix. The outsideman takes 45 percent of the total, out of which he pays all expenses incidental to roping.

DEEMER. A ten-cent piece.

DEEP-SEA GAMBLER. See *boat-rider*.

DINKS. See *block game*.

DIP. A pickpocket. This word, still used by old-timers, is not much used by young pickpockets. From Yiddish *dieb*.

DOLLAR STORE. An early form of the present-day big store originated by Ben Marks at Cheyenne, Wyoming, during the building of the Union Pacific Railway. The dollar store displayed valuable articles priced at one dollar in order to bring in marks, who were played for with short-con games.

DOUBLE SAW. A $20 bill.

The DOUBLE TRAYS. A short-con game in which the mark is roped and agrees to help fleece a gambling house with misspotted dice (double trays). However, a pair of loaded *and* misspotted dice is slipped in to replace the originals, and the mark is fleeced.

DROP-IN. Something which is easy; easy money. So called because a fat mark may sometimes *drop in* to a confidence game without being steered.

The DUCATS. A short-con game played with five business cards. The roper connives with the mark to put a pencil mark on one card which will enable him to draw the right one and beat the insideman. But the cards are turned end for end and a duplicate pencil mark on a nonwinning card misleads the mark. Also *the tickets.*

The DUKE or HUGE DUKE. A form of the big mitt played on railroad trains without a store. A mob of three collects marks and fleeces them one at a time in a compartment or stateroom. Probably coined by Eddie Mines, noted duke player and big-con roper. See *the big mitt.*

EAR-WIGGER. Anyone who tries to overhear a conversation. Also *wiggin's.*

EGG. See *mark.*

The ELECTRIC BAR. A swindle worked at a saloon bar with a magnetized plate and dice with metal spots so arranged as to turn up the desired numbers when the current is on.

END. 1. A share of the score which is due each grifter who participates. 2. A portion of the score taken as a bribe by the law. See *have (someone) right.*

The ENGINEER'S DAUGHTER. A mock con game played by con men for a conceited grifter. A grifter's wife or girl poses as the *engineer's daughter.* The point-out is played for the victim, who finally manages to get on intimate terms with the engineer's daughter. Another con man dressed as an engineer bursts into the apartment, brandishing a pistol. The victim collects what clothing he can and rushes out into the street, where he is welcomed by all the grifters who happen to be in town. Peculiar to resort cities, like Hot Springs, Arkansas. Cf. *the cold poke, the tish.*

EXCESS BAGGAGE. A grifter who is incapable of discharging his duties with the mob.

EXPENSING. The process of getting payments from a mark who believes he was hiring telegraph operators to tap wires and get race results in advance for him. Obsolete except among old-timers (short con).

The FAKE. 1. A short-con game practiced by news butchers on trains. The prospective customer buys a cheap book for two dollars because he thinks he sees a five-dollar bill protruding from it. 2. Also *Fakus* or *Mr. Fakus.* Any cheating mechanism used in short-con games, especially on gambling devices and flatjoints.

To FALL. To be indicted and convicted of a criminal offense.

FARO BANK. 1. n. A gambling game formerly much used by con men in which the players bet on the order in which the cards will be drawn from a dealing box. See *the last turn.* 2. v. To take a mark's money by allowing him to win and lose, always losing more than he wins. Also *to bankroll.*

To FEED THE HOTEL (or STORE). For hypesters to cheat the hotel when they check out.

FIGHT STORE. An early form of the modern big store in which the roper connived with the mark to beat the insideman through betting on a fixed prize fight. Similar swindles were worked through the foot-race and wrestle stores.

FIN. A five-dollar bill.

To FIND THE LEATHER. See *the poke.*

FINGER-EGG. See *to put the finger on.*

FINK. See *mark.*

The FIRST COUNT. The total score from a con touch, the implication being that the insideman has cheated the other members of the mob. "The first count is always the best."

FISH. See *push-note* (1).

FITTED EVENT. The *fixed race* upon which the mark is induced to bet. See *the payoff.*

FITTED MITT. A bribed official.

To FIT THE MITT. To bribe an official. See *to have (someone) right.*

The FIX. Cooperation bought from the police by a fixer. "The fix is in." See *to have (someone) right.*

FIXER. A local man employed by grifters to fix the law.

FLAT JOINT. A form of short-con swindle with many variations. Used extensively with circuses, fairs, etc.

The FLOP. A short-con racket sometimes worked by con men when they are short of money. Also *the hype, the sting.* Not to be confused with *the slide, the push,* and *the boodle,* which work on a different principle and are restricted largely to short-con workers and circus grifters.

FLUE. The envelope in which money is placed in any big-con or short-con game.

FLYER. A warrant for arrest sent out simultaneously in all large cities.

FLY GEE. An outsider who understands confidence games, or who thinks he does.

The FOOT RACE. A pay-off game now obsolete which preceded the modern big-con games. The outsideman posed as the disgruntled secretary of a millionaire (the insideman) who fancied runners and bet heavily on them. The secretary offered to double-cross his employer, fix the race, and share the profits with the mark. The racer who was *fixed* to win collapsed, a "doctor" pronounced him dead, and the mark lost heavily.

FORTY-SOME-ODD. A pistol. Also *the odds*. See *the cackle-bladder*.

TO FRAME (THE GAFF or THE JOINT). To set up the big store.

G-NOTE. A $1,000 bill, used in making up the *boodle* (big con).

GAFF. See *joint*.

To GET A HARD-ON. To reach for a pistol.

The GIVE-AWAY. See *the high-pitch*.

The GOLD BRICK. An obsolete con game in which a sucker bought what appeared to be a genuine gold brick from a farmer or Indian. Also *the bat*.

To GO ROUND THE HORN. For an arrested suspect to be transferred rapidly from one police station to another to prevent his attorney from serving a habeas corpus writ.

GRAPEVINE, or THE VINE. The underground communications system used by all professional criminals.

GREEN-GOODS RACKET. See *the spud*.

GRIFT. 1. n. A racket or criminal profession. Often used where grifter would not be used in a strict sense. "I've been on the grift all my life." 2. n. A group of criminal professions which employ skill rather than violence. "All those boys were on the grift." 3. v. To work any profession included in the grift. See *grifter*.

GRIFTER. In the strict sense, one who lives by his wits, as contrasted to the heavy men, who use violence.

GRIND-SHOW. A short-term, repeating show on a circus or carnival lot.

To GUIDE. See *to rope*.

GUN. From *gonif*. See *cannon*.

GUN MOLL. A thief-girl, especially a female pickpocket. The term has no connection with guns or with killings—as is sometimes suggested in the newspapers—but comes from Yiddish *gonif*, thief.

HALF A C. A fifty-dollar bill.

HANDLER. The accomplice in a short-con game who directs the betting of the shills (short con). Roughly comparable to the manager in the big con.

To HAVE SMALLPOX. To be wanted on a warrant; *smallpox* is said to be *catching* because anyone in the company of the wanted man may be arrested also.

To HAVE (SOMEONE) RIGHT. To buy protection from an official. "The Postal Kid had the chief right for years." Also used of cities, banks, etc.: "The Yellow Kid had Rochester, Minnesota, right at that time." Also *to fix, to fit the mitt, to take*.

The HEAD OF THE JOINT or TOP OF THE JOINT. The total amount taken in a single confidence touch. "Sometimes the nut comes off the head of the joint." Also *the top of the score*.

HEAT. Trouble, especially pressure from the law or tension created by a beefing mark.

HEAVY GEE. A professional on the heavy rackets, usually a safeblower.

HEAVY RACKETS. Those rackets involving violence or threat of violence, as contrasted to the grift. See *grift*.

HEEL GRIFTER. A cheap, small-time grifter. See *grifter*.

The HIGH PITCH. A short-con game involving the sale of cheap merchandise, the price of which is refunded by the operators, who then sell worthless goods at a high price and drive away. Also *the give-away*.

HOME GUARD. 1. A victim who lives in the city where the store is located. 2. A local grifter, as contrasted to an itinerant one.

To HOPSCOTCH. To go on the road with a confidence game (largely short con).

HOT SCORE. Proceeds from a con game or theft in which the sucker immediately realizes he has been taken.

The HOT SEAT. A British version of the American *wipe* in which the victim is convinced that he has been commissioned to deliver a large sum of money to the pope. In reality he takes a parcel of newspaper, while the money he has posted as security is kept by the swindlers.

The HYPE or HIPE. See *the flop*.

INSIDEMAN. 1. (Big con.) The member of a

con mob who stays near the big store and receives the mark whom the roper brings. Insidemen are highly specialized workers; they must have a superb knowledge of psychology to keep the mark under perfect control during the days or weeks while he is being fleeced. See *to cut up the score*. 2. (Short con.) The one who operates the game by which the marks are fleeced, as the three-shell game.

JACKET. 1. An entry in the police records which may stand against a criminal if he is picked up on another charge. So called from the folder or *jacket* in which the entry is filed. 2. A tip-off, or a witness to a crime who may testify later. "We got a jacket on that one."

JOE HEP or HEP. Smart, or wise to what is happening. Probably ironically so called from one Joe Hep, the proprietor of a saloon in Chicago where grifters had their headquarters.

To JOIN OUT THE ODDS. To turn pimp.

JOINT. 1. A place of business (legitimate). 2. A gambling house, big store, or other establishment where marks are trimmed. Also *gaff*. See *big store*. 3. The score from a confidence game. See *the head of the joint*.

JUG or JAY. A bank.

KICK. A pocket.

To KICK BACK. To return part or all of a touch.

KICKING HAND. The member of a mitt mob who has a set line of cross fire, grumbling, and protesting because he loses. See *big mitt*.

KIP or KIPPER. 1. A room, especially a hotel room; the place one lives. 2. A bed.

To KNOCK (A MARK). To convince a mark that he is being swindled. "There's a mark born every minute, and five to trim him and five to knock him." Usually the term is used ironically, for all con men know that a good mark literally cannot be knocked. "That fink craved the tat and you couldn't knock him." See *mark*.

KNOCK-OFF. An arrest.

LAGGED. Sent to prison.

LAMSTER. One who is wanted by the law.

LARCENY. A tendency to steal; *thieves' blood*.

The LAST TURN. A faro-bank con game in which the dealer agrees to tip off the mark to the last turn, on which the betting is very

heavy. The mark loses steadily during the early part of the game and thus finds it impossible to recoup on the last turn. "After the mob finished with G— R—, they turned him over to us and we gave him the last turn for $50,000." See *faro bank*.

To LAY THE FLUE. To work a short-con swindle in which money is put into an envelope (flue) in the victim's presence, then removed through a slit. Another version swindles a merchant who changes a twenty-dollar bill and retains an envelope which he believes to contain twenty dollars. See *the switch*. Cf. *the bilk, the cold poke, the poke (2), the tish*.

To LIGHT A RAG. See *to cop a heel*.

The LITTLE BLOCK. The first touch taken from a mark. Restricted to the rag. Cf. *the big block*.

LITTLE CON. An older term for *short con*.

LONG-TAILED RAT. See *stool pigeon*.

LOOKOUT. A member of the con mob who serves as doorman for the big store.

LOP-EARED. Stupid. Used in reference to a victim so stupid that he cannot see his own advantage in a con game, sometimes so stupid that he cannot be trimmed. See *mark*. Cf. *to knock a mark*.

To LUG. To steer a mark for a confidence game.

LUGGER. See *outsideman*.

To MAKE. To see or recognize.

To MAKE A MAN ON HIS MERITS. Theoretically, for a detective to be able to pick up a grifter even though he does not know him; to recognize that he is a grifter from his manners and general appearance. "Camera-eye McCarthy is the only dick in the country who can really make a man on his merits." Actually, there probably are no such detectives.

The MANAGER. The member of a con mob who has charge of the big store. See *bookmaker* (big con only). Cf. *handler*.

MARK. 1. A victim, or intended victim. Also *apple, Bates, egg, fink, John Bates, Mr. Bates, savage, winchell, chump*. 2. A term of disdain and opprobrium, applied to anyone. For specialized meanings, see *addict, come-on, come-through, lop-eared*.

MEG. A one-cent piece, used in the smack.

MICKEY FINN. Confidence men use the term to denote a very fast physic given by the bartender to cocky grifters after the toilet doors have been locked.

MILL'S LOCK. A sure thing.

To MITT A MAN IN. To get a mark to bet a stack of checks placed before him, or to bet them for him, to get him into a mitt game (short con). See *big mitt.*

MOB. See *con mob.*

The MONEY BOX. A swindle in which the mark is induced to purchased a machine which he thinks will make genuine paper money (short con).

MONICKER. An underworld nickname.

MOUSE. See *stool pigeon.*

MUDKICKER. A prostitute.

MUGGED. Photographed for the rogues' gallery.

The MUSH. A short-con game played at the ball parks. The operator poses as a bookmaker, takes money for bets, then raises his umbrella (the mush) and disappears into the maze of umbrellas on the bleachers.

NUT. See *cap, to cut up the score.*

The NUTS. See *block game.*

The ODDS. 1. See *forty-some-odd.* 2. A woman, especially one who does or will support her man through prostitution.

The OFFICE. 1. On the big con, a cluck with the tongue or a velar fricative used as a signal among members of the mob while the mark is being played. Also, a similar sound made on the street when a con man does not want other grifters to recognize him. 2. Any private signal, as with the eyes or hands.

OPEN MONTE. Three-card monte played outside, as contrasted to closed monte. See *three-card monte.*

OUTSIDEMAN. The member of the con mob who locates the mark, brings him to the store, and assists in fleecing him. Also *lugger, roper.*

PACK IT IN or PACK THE RACKET IN. To leave the grift for some legitimate form of business.

To PAD THE CAP or PAD THE NUT. For a roper to falsify his expense account (big con). See *to cut up the score.*

PANEL STORE. A brothel where marks are robbed.

PAPER. A check or other negotiable document.

PAYOFF. A big-con man.

The PAYOFF. The most lucrative of all big-con games, with touches running from $10,000 up, with those of $100,000 being common. It operates on the principal that a wealthy mark is induced to believe that he has been taken into a deal whereby a large racing syndicate is to be swindled. At first he plays with money furnished by the confidence men, then is put on the send for all the cash he can raise, fleeced, and blown off. The pay off (invented in 1906) evolved from the *short-pay at the track* (*q.v.*) and was fully developed by 1910, when the big stores appeared in many of the larger cities. See *big con.*

THE PAYOFF AGAINST THE WALL. A type of the payoff which is played without a store, boosters, pros, etc. Good confidence men can take off a touch this way, but it always *comes hot* (*q.v.*) and facilities for cooling the mark out are lacking.

The PEEKS. See *block game.*

PETER. A safe.

PICKUP GUY. A "wise" outsider who hangs around a monte or shell game hoping to beat the operators at their own game (short con). Cf. *fly gee.*

The PIGEON. See *the short deck.*

To PLAY THE C. 1. To get a mark's confidence. "I'll play the C for that old pappy." 2. To operate a confidence game.

To PLAY THE CHILL. To ignore someone. "We'll play the chill for him."

To PLAY THE HINGE or WORK THE HINGE. To look behind. "Don't play the hinge or you may get sneezed for it."

To PLAY THE RUNAROUND. See *to beat the donicker.*

PLINGER. A street beggar.

POGY O'BRIEN. A grifter who will not pay his debts.

POINT-OUT. 1. A method of tying up a mark for the big-con games. The outsideman points out the insideman as a former acquaintance who has very good connections in racing or investments. 2. An agent who locates prospective marks for a roper on a percentage basis.

The POKE. 1. A method of tying up the mark for the payoff or the rag. The outsideman and the mark find a pocketbook containing a large amount of money, a code cipher, and newspaper clippings describing the owner's phenomenal success in either gambling or races or in stock-market investments, and race tickets or stock receipts (big con). Also *to find the leather*. 2. A short-con game in which the mark and the outsideman find a wallet full of money. The mark is induced to raise a fund equal to the amount in the wallet to show his good faith. When he gets the pocketbook, it contains only scraps of newspaper.

The PRAT-OUT. See *the shut-out*.

To PUNCH THE GUFF. See *to cut up old scores*.

The PUSH. A type of short-change racket.

PUSH-NOTE. 1. A one-dollar bill. Also *bumblebee, case note, seed, fish*. 2. A person who resembles someone else. "He was a push-note for John W. Gates." Also *stand-in*. Cf. *to put (someone) away*.

To PUT (SOMEONE) AWAY. For a confidence man to pose as some prominent person whom he resembles or to point out an accomplice as some prominent person.

To PUT (ONE'S) HUMP UP. To stall for a pickpocket mob; that is, to use the hips to jockey the victim into position and distract his attention while his pockets are picked. Also *to stall, to prat (a mark) in*.

To PUT THE BITE ON. To try to borrow money.

To PUT THE FINGER ON. To turn a criminal over to the police; to act as a stool pigeon.

To PUT THE MARK UP. For a roper to locate a good prospective mark, especially in line at a railroad ticket office. Some ropers (especially for the tip) have agents who put up marks for them in advance and are paid a commission.

To PUT THE MUG ON (A MARK). To put a stranglehold on a mark who grows obstreperous after he has been fleeced. Cf. *the cackle-bladder*.

To PUT THE SHIV IN THE TOUCH. See *to cut up the score*.

The QUILL. Genuine. Cf. *crow*.

The RAG. An intricate big-con game very similar to the payoff, except that stocks are used instead of races. The insideman poses as an agent for a broker's syndicate which is trying to break the bucket shops. The mark profits on several investments, is sent for a large sum of money, and is fleeced. See *big con*.

RAGGLE. An attractive young girl.

RAGS. Clothing.

To RAISE. To signal by raising the hat.

To RAISE A MARK. To force a mark in a confidence game to raise his price by bluffing, as in poker. "I was playing the hinks, and I raised a mark that had a C-note in his seams. He blowed it on the runaround."

To RANK A JOINT. For a grifter to make a mistake while a mark is being played for, thus revealing that the confidence game is crooked. If the mark sees the mistake and realizes what is happening, the store is then ranked. See *to crack out of turn*.

RAT. See *stool pigeon*.

RATIONS. The amount of narcotics which will sustain an addict without withdrawal symptoms.

RIBBING HAND. The member of a mitt mob who has a set line of humorous talk which he keeps going while the mark is being fleeced. He distracts the mark's attention from the still hand, who holds the winning cards. The ribbing hand is usually a large man, the still hand a small man. See *the big mitt*.

To RIDE IN (A MARK). To rope a mark and bring him to the store. See *to steer against a store*.

RIDGE. Metal money.

RIGHT. 1. As in "right territory," territory protected by the fix. 2. As in "right copper," one who will accept a bribe. 3. As in "right guy," one who is trustworthy, especially one in sympathy with criminals. Cf. *wrong*.

To RIP AND TEAR. To grift without restriction in a protected or "airtight" area.

The ROCKS. A short-con diamond swindle in which the mark is shown "stolen" diamonds and invited to have a jeweler evaluate them. The ones submitted are good, the rest are paste.

To ROLL. To rob someone, especially a drunk. Largely used of prostitutes.

ROOTING ON THE BOOST. Working as a shoplifter.

ROOTING ON THE CANNON. Working as a pickpocket.

To ROPE. To secure a mark for a confidence game. Also *to lug, to steer against a store, to guide*.

ROPER. See *outsideman*.

To RUMBLE. To excite a mark's suspicions. Cf. *to knock (a mark)*.

SAVAGE. See *mark*.

SAWBUCK or SAW. A ten-dollar bill.

SCAT. Whiskey.

SCATTER. A saloon.

The SCORE. See *touch*.

SEED. See *push-note* (1).

The SEND. The stage in big-con games at which the mark is sent home for a large amount of money.

SEND STORE. Any type of store which plays for a mark and sends him home for his money (short con and circus grift). Not to be confused with *big store*.

To SEW A MAN UP. 1. To caution a mark, who has just been beaten with a shortchange racket (but doesn't know it), against pickpockets, then sew his wallet in his pocket with needle and thread carried for the purpose (short con). 2. To make any arrangements necessary to prevent the mark from causing trouble after he has been fleeced (big con). See *to cool a mark out*.

The SHAKE. 1. A shakedown; extortion of money from criminals by officers. 2. See *the shake with the button*.

The SHAKE WITH THE BUTTON. A short-con swindle in which the mark and the operators are arrested for gambling on the street and "shaken down" by a fake officer.

SHED. 1. The railroad station. 2. Loosely, any terminal, as a bus station.

SHEET WRITER. A minor employee in a big store usually the clerk who takes the bets.

SHILL or SHILLABER. An accomplice who plays a confidence game so that the mark sees him win. Many con games use shills, but in the big con the shills are frequently professional confidence men who dress and act the parts of men high in the financial world.

The SHIV. A short-con game played with a knife, the blades of which can be locked at will. Cf. *the slough*.

SHORT CON. As contrasted to the big con, those games which generally operate without the send. Also *little con*.

The SHORT DECK. A short-con game operated by a man who drops one card out of a deck he has offered to sell a mark very cheaply. They argue over whether or not it is a full deck, then bet. The mark thinks the deck is short one card, but the operator produces a full deck. Also *the pigeon*.

The SHORT PAY AT THE TRACKS. A crude, short-con version of the payoff, played by racetrack touts without a store, etc. See *the payoff*.

SHORT RIDER. A mark who lives close to the city in which a big store is located. Big-con men usually agree with the fixer to avoid fleecing all local residents and short riders.

The SHUT-OUT. One stage in playing for a mark in a big store. For instance, in the payoff, the mark goes to the window to make a bet, but is "shut out" by members of the boost who are all betting huge sums of money. By the time the mark gets to the window, the announcer says, "They're off," and betting is closed. The mark hears the race called precisely as the con men had predicted and resolves to get his bet down on the next race at all costs (big con). Also the *prat-out*.

The SINGLE-HAND CON. A short-con game played by one man who picks up an old gentleman on a train, shows him a large check, gets his confidence, borrows a sum of money with the check as security, and leaves the victim to watch the baggage.

To SIT IN (WITH A MARK). For a roper to feel a mark out with regard to a con game, then signal his partner to come in on the deal (short con).

The SLICK BOX. A controlled dice game played with a roper and shills. The mark is fleeced by a skilled manipulator who controls the dice by means of a box shellacked inside (short con).

The SLIDE. A sleight-of-hand maneuver by which some bills are "weeded" out of a sheaf while they are being handled or counted.

The SLOUGH. A short-con game similar to the shiv, except that a small padlock is used.

To SLOUGH. To lock.

The SMACK. An intricate short-con game based on matching pennies. Big-con men often apply the principles of big-con work to it and take off scores of thousands of dollars. See *big con*.

SMOKED GLASS. A glass of beer into which heavy cigar smoke has been blown through a straw.

SNEEZED. Arrested.

SOAP GAME. A short-con game in which the grifter appears to wrap up a twenty-dollar bill with each cake of soap he is selling. It is worked with shills and cross fire. Said to have been invented by the notorious Soapy Smith.

SOFT ONES. Old bills used by a shortchange artist to make up his *boodle* (short con).

SPIELER. 1. The front man who herds the crowd into any circus or carnival show, such as a freak show. 2. A police word for the insideman on the big-con.

To SPIEL THE NUTS. To play the shell game under cover of a brisk *cross fire*.

The SPUD. A swindle in which the con man convinces the mark that he can buy real money from a man who has stolen plates from the government. Also *green-goods racket*.

SQUARE PAPER. An honest person, usually a legitimate person.

SQUEEZE. A dishonest device for controlling a mechanical gambling game (short con).

To STAND A RAP FOR (SOMEONE). To resemble someone closely. Cf. *to put (some-one) away*.

STAND-IN. See *push-note* (2).

STARTER. A crooked dealer in a gambling house.

To STASH. To hide something.

To STEER AGAINST A STORE. To rope marks for any con game using a store.

STICK. A shill, especially one used in a short-con game. See *shill, the boost*.

To STICK UP. For detectives to question a grifter, then release him.

STILL HAND. The member of a mitt mob who holds the winning hand. See *ribbing hand, the big mitt*.

The STING. 1. See *the hype*. 2. The point in a confidence game where a mark's money is taken.

To STING. To take a mark's money. "We'll sting coming into St. Louis."

STIR. Prison.

STOOL PIGEON. A police informer. See *rat, fink*. Also *long-tailed rat, mouse*, and many other uncomplimentary names.

STORE. Any establishment against which short-con games like the mitt or monte are played. Cf. *the big store*.

The STRAP. A short-con game played with a coiled strap, one coil of which the mark tries to catch with a pencil.

To STREET. To get a mark out of a store.

STRONG JOINT. A flat joint which is heavily gaffed.

SUBWAY DEALER. A cardplayer who deals from the bottom of the deck.

SUCKER BROAD. A woman who is dishonest and unreliable, but who is not of the underworld. Cf. *gun moll*.

SUCKER FEEL-OUT. The constant questioning to which the mark subjects the outside-man while the former is tied up. "He's got me waxy with that sucker feel-out."

SUCKER GAMBLING HOUSE. A gambling house not run by professionals. Sucker is used for anything not strictly professional. See *sucker word*.

SUCKER WORD. An argot word used or mis-used by outsiders, and hence not generally used by professionals. For example, *stool pigeon* or *plugger* used for shill.

The SWINGING BALL. A *strong joint* in which the sucker tries to knock over ten-pins with a ball which swings from a pivot.

The SWITCH. The sleight of hand by which one object is substituted for another, used in *the wipe, the poke* (2), and other short-con games.

To SWITCH. To transfer a mark's confidence from the roper to the insideman.

To TAB. To make note of.

TAILER. The armed grifter who keeps tab on the mark while he is not with the con men. See *con mob*.

To TAKE or TAKE HIS END. To accept bribe money. Applied to anyone who is fixed. See *to have (someone) right*.

To TAKE A POWDER. See *to cop a heel*.

The TALE. A British swindle played at the racetrack. An Englishman pays the con man for a lost bet, even though he did not instruct the con man to make it. Cannot be played in America owing to the difference in sporting ethics.

The TAT. 1. A crooked dice swindle worked by grifters in nightclubs. The mark is allowed to find a die (sometimes made from a sugar cube) and is inveigled into a betting game. The tat is substituted for the square die when the operator throws, and the mark is fleeced. Also *up and down Broadway*. 2. A crooked die made with fives and sixes on all sides. It is otherwise a duplicate of the one which the mark finds.

TAW. A bankroll.

T.B. Literally, total blank; no score. "That savage from Omaha was a T.B." Also *twenty-eight*.

To TEAR (SOMEONE) OFF. To cheat one's partner of part of his share of a touch.

The TEAR-UP. A method of *blowing* a mark, especially with the mitt and the duke. The roper tears up the check covering the victim's losses, saying that the man did not understand the play. This check is a duplicate, and when the victim returns home, he discovers that the original check has been cashed.

TELL BOX. A faro dealer's crooked dealing box.

To TELL THE TALE. 1. For the insideman to tell the mark the story of his illicit dealings (big con). 2. To tell any story to a prospective victim (short con).

THREE-CARD MONTE. The well-known card swindle, worked with insideman, outsideman, and shills (short con). Cf. *closed monte, open monte.*

The TICKETS. See *the ducats.*

TIE-UP. 1. The process of keeping the outsideman constantly with the mark while he is being played (big con). 2. A mark who is being played (big con).

TIGER. A faro bank. To "twist the tiger's tail," to play the faro bank.

To TIGHTEN UP (A MARK). For the insideman to give the mark a convincing talk just before he is sent home for his money (big con).

TIN MITTENS. A fixer. By implication, one who likes to hear the coin clank in his hand.

TIP. A crowd of people.

The TIP. A short-con game sometimes worked by big-con men. The roper offers to help the mark fleece the insideman by tipping off his hand in a poker game. He is allowed to win a convincer and is then faro-banked out of his money. See *big con.*

The TISH. A mock con game used with women. A con man puts a large bill in a woman's stocking with the admonition that she will be sorry if she takes it out before morning. She takes it out at the earliest opportunity, only to find that it has turned to tissue paper. Cf. *the engineer's daughter, the cold poke, the switch.*

TOOL. The member of a pickpocket mob who does the actual stealing. Also *wire,* not to be confused with *the wire,* one of the big-con games.

TOP OF THE JOINT or TOP OF THE SCORE. See *the head of the joint.*

TOUCH. The money taken from a mark. Also *the score.*

TRANSPIRE. A short-con game in which the mark is led to bet on the meaning of the word *transpire,* which the outsideman uses to mean *perspire.*

To TURN OUT. 1. v.t. To train a grifter in some special line of work. "Old John Russell turned out the Yenshee Kid when he was only fifteen." 2. v.i. For a grifter to start on the rackets.

TWENTY-EIGHT. Based on the superstition that 28 is an unlucky number on a roulette wheel. See *T.B.*

TWIST. A woman or girl, usually one in the rackets or connected with the underworld. From the Australian *twist-and-twirl.*

UP AND DOWN BROADWAY. See *the tat.*

To WEED. To extract surreptitiously one or more bills when handling a wallet or a roll of money.

WEIGHT. Psychological persuasion used by a grifter.

To WHIP. To walk.

WHIZ. A pickpocket.

WIGGINS. See *ear-wigger.*

WINCHELL. A mark. Also used in such combinations as *willing winchell, winning winchell.*

The WIPE. A short-con game worked largely with blacks and Gypsies. The victim is induced to put a large sum of money into a handkerchief, which is tied up and put away. The switch is put in and the mark finds that his money has turned into newspaper cuttings. Cf. *the poke* (2). See *the switch.*

WIRE. See *tool.*

The WIRE. A big-con game in which the insideman (passing as a Western Union official) convinces the mark that he can delay the race results going to the bookmakers long enough for the mark to place a bet after the race is run. The roper makes a mistake, and the mark loses. Cf. *the rag, the payoff.*

WIRE-TAPPING. An obsolete short-con game from which *the wire* developed.

WORK. Any kind of illegal activity.

WRESTLE STORE. See *fight store.*

WRONG. 1. As in "wrong town," one not protected by the fix. 2. As in "wrong copper," one who cannot be bribed. 3. As in "wrong guy," one who is untrustworthy, especially a stool pigeon. Cf. *right.*

YELLOW. A telegram, especially a fake telegram used in the payoff and the rag.

20

The Argot
of the Moonshiner

This material on the sociolinguistic aspects of moonshiners' speech was included in the book *Kentucky Moonshine* (1974). I first investigated this argot in 1949 and published a preliminary study of it in *American Speech* (May 1949), followed by "The Liquid Capitalists" (*Reporter* [April 11, 1950]), so that this study of the argot represents an accumulation of materials and a refinement of concepts over a twenty-five-year period. There is some information on the argot's historical relationship to Northern English and Scotch Irish, on the influence of the influx of urban racketeers during prohibition, and on the close relationship of the speech patterns to the craft itself. Preceding chapters of *Kentucky Moonshine* give a clear, complete, and authentic account of the position of illicit whiskey-making in American history and especially in Kentucky history. The subject, interestingly enough, has been so taboo in Kentucky that the mention of the legitimate manufacturing of whiskey is minimized if not neglected from early histories on down to the fine historical studies of Professor Thomas D. Clark, while references to moonshine are conspicuously minimal in any history.

With over ninety of the 120 counties in Kentucky being "dry," it can easily be seen that this is a sensitive political subject even today. The mention of moonshine whiskey itself is under strong taboo in rural Kentucky; so much so that when it is introduced into a home by an outsider, whether a Kentuckian or not, the reference is likely to produce an embarrassed silence regardless of the family's "wet" or "dry" persuasion. Psychological factors underlying this taboo — political protection, religious affiliation, social status, etc. — are too complex to discuss here but are taken up in detail in *Kentucky Moonshine*.

• • •

ALL subcultures tend to develop some specialized linguistic characteristics that set their members apart from the general cultural matrix to which they belong. When this subculture operates outside the law, this linguistic phenomenon is called *argot*. Some of the social and psychological forces that stimulate differential linguistic development can be very simply stated. First, there is a dichotomy with the dominant culture, with the subculture being quite aware—sometimes over a period of centuries—of its minority status. Second the subculture differs from the dominant culture in some (though never all) behavioral indices. For instance, often there is within the subculture one or more occupations that are exclusive and somewhat secretive. There are differences in ethics and moral values. The status of women may vary from that in the dominant culture, as well as concepts of time and territoriality. Patterns of association and interaction are sometimes different from those of the dominant culture. There is a strong sense of the "in-group."

When the subculture is a criminal one, there is hostility toward the dominant culture, hostility that is reciprocated and often expressed in terms of laws designed to control the subculture. In turn, this suppression causes the subculture to strengthen its internal security and to further differentiate itself from the dominant culture. Without some external pressure, criminal subcultures do not develop beyond the rudimentary or abortive stage. The threat from the dominant culture intensifies the internal forces already at work and tends to accentuate the values, attitudes, and techniques of the subgroup, at the same time fostering disparagement of those outside; the special aspects of their language reflect these forces. Improvements in criminal technology intensify this linguistic activity, often with the emphasis on secrecy. The gap between culture and subculture widens. As a criminal subculture becomes more aware of its functional identity, a self-image is generated that must be bolstered by word and deed, and the argot becomes a prime factor not only in the transmission of criminal techniques, but in triggering criminal behavior as well. This glorified self-image may be confused with reality, while the argot constantly serves to enhance prestige and to gratify ego-expansion.

Professional criminal subcultures are consistently parasitic, and agglutinate against the matrix of a legitimate society already vastly experienced in symbolizing its values through language.[1] The subgroups tend to draw words and phrases from the contiguous language, rather than creating many neologisms, and to give these established words new and special meanings. This makes for group solidarity, mutual recognition, and a sense of exclusiveness. It is significant that criminal subcultures seem to evolve against such a body of specialized language, and that both the subculture and the argot proliferate in response to the interplay of the forces mentioned above. I have examined this phenomenon in detail in various other studies bearing on specific subcultures of professional criminals.

While the moonshiners commit their crimes against the law rather than against persons or property, they nevertheless constitute a criminal subculture

---

1. For portions of this phraseology I am indebted to a young sociologist who used it in a paper on microsystems and macrosystems delivered before a sociological conference in the late 1960s. His paper is not available and I regret that I am now unable to identify him by name.

with many of the characteristics thereof. This subculture was made criminal by law, however, and not by any vicious or vindictive behavior. It is interesting in that its criminal activity is largely confined to violation of the liquor laws; in most other respects it blends with a conservative agricultural society. This compatibility between the law violators and legitimate agricultural life prevailed in both England and America for nearly 300 years. Almost always, moreover, this society, on a local level, in general approves of moonshining and tends to protect the violators who live there as long as they cooperate with those in political power.

In addition to the factors already mentioned, the subculture of the moonshiner in Appalachia has a long history of breaking European laws considered unjust. Scotsmen and Irishmen had no scruples about evading taxes levied by the British crown long before it began to tax illicit whiskey. They were specialists in poaching and smuggling, and the strong "Geneva waters" (later called gin) from the Continent was just one of the products they imported duty-free. In fact, the word moonshine referred to any smuggled goods, and then to smuggled liquor, well before it was particularized to strong drink made illegally at home. The Scotch and Irish found many an English farmer in Northumberland, as well as English seamen out of Glasgow and Belfast, who liked to play the smuggler's game. The stock that migrated to Appalachia already had generations of experience at expert law violation, heavily concentrated in the area of the making and transporting of liquor. In fact, they made and drank it long before it was taxed.

This stock brought to America something that most criminal subcultures do not have—a genuine and ancient mystique. In Scotland and Ireland the process of fermentation of grain had been a part of sacred Gaelic fertility rites since long before the Romans occupied Britain. A thousand years later, after the alchemists introduced the still from Arabia, the making of alcohol was surrounded with an aura of magic and mystery that characterized the highly secret activities of alchemy. In colonial America and the Caribbean, where slaves were used in some areas as still labor, perhaps touches of African magic were incorporated. Primitive animistic beliefs, which we would refer to today as superstitions, still permeate the subculture, and remnants of them linger as the carefully guarded trade secrets of portions of the modern legitimate distilling industry.

This heritage probably intensified the social and psychological factors that account for the development of a semisecret argot. Today the speech patterns of the moonshine subculture are indistinguishable from those of the immediate geographical area to which it is indigenous; phonologically and syntactically there is nothing to set a moonshiner off from others in the broad agricultural community. These patterns have been recorded very precisely by many linguistic researchers, notably those of the *Linguistic Atlas of the United States and Canada*. However, the moonshiner has had something else: a lexicon associated with his craft known to all members of the subculture almost exclusively. It is notable that, among the literally thousands of dialect terms collected by linguistic geographers, very few words and phrases from this argot appear. In very recent years, however, linguistic diffusion seems to have begun, old taboos seem to have weakened, and within the past two years some terms from the moonshine subculture have begun to appear in various forms of "country" music that exploit the Appalachian culture in general. Previously a small amount of the argot had appeared in fiction.

The content of this lexicon is rather a mixed bag. One might expect that the technical language used by Appalachian moonshiners would go back to Scotch-Irish sources dating from the eighteenth century. It is probable that some of it does, and that these elements were dialectal or nonstandard at the time. It is also possible that some of the vocabulary used by moonshiners in the United States dates back beyond the eighteenth century. In other words, the craft may have evolved along two lines, overlapping to some extent, but with one line following ancient folk traditions—ultimately illicit—and the other developing with the standard industrial distilling activities—largely legal—that arose in Great Britain during this period. Undoubtedly early Continental technological influences were strong in this development. This situation might well be paralleled today in Kentucky, where moonshining persists as a craft in the hands of people using older folk methods, while the modern legal industry has grown up in the same area, inheriting some of the ancient folklore, but increasingly dominated by scientific technology.

All this is speculation, based on a rather superficial examination of notes taken in the field. The entire language of distilling, both licit and illicit, in both the United States and Great Britain, deserves to be studied in depth. Such a study might well untangle these threads and give us a documented picture of the diachronic elements involved. The connections to Scotch-Irish and even Gaelic dialects are obscure; at the same time the relationship of the moonshiner's language to that of standard legal distilling is looser and less specific than we might expect.

During the eighteenth century legal distilling in Europe reached a rather sophisticated level. I have consulted some of the rather specialized works dealing with this period, notably the exhaustive *Practical Treatise on Brewing, Distilling, and Rectification* by R. Shannon, M.D. (London, 1805). This voluminous work describes traditional practices standardized during the previous century, includes precise diagrams of equipment, and cites as well the technical language used in England, Scotland, Ireland, the West Indies, and on the Continent. There has been relatively little transference of this language to the idiom of modern Kentucky moonshiners. In fact, modern moonshiners seem to share only some basic rudiments of terminology for methods and equipment, such as *worm, coil, malt, mash, mash tub, vat, double, double back, backings, beer, beer cap*. Apparently lost to American moonshiners is the bulk of the older vernacular, some of it smelling of the colorful terminology of alchemy.

Two other influences on the moonshiners' image should be mentioned. The first of these is the terminology used in modern legal distilling, especially in the smaller distilleries where tradition lingers heavily. Even this influence is not so strong as we might expect, in view of the commercial distilleries' proximity to moonshine areas and the fact that many moonshiners have at one time been employed as still labor. Some terms are of course borrowed, but more typical perhaps is what happened in the case of such a device as the dephlegmator. The moonshiners observed the dephlegmator working, made a crude replica of their own, rejected the technical term as too fancy, and produced their own name for it, which was *puker,* with a derivative transitive verb *to puke,* as in "You get the fire a mite too hot and you puke the still." The American moonshiner seems to have most frequently adapted nontechnical dialect words already familiar and created neosemanticisms in preference to adopting a more technical vocabulary in connection with his craft.

The second influence is what we might loosely call "the underworld" of Prohibition days; during this time, many moonshiners came into contact with urban gangsters. Since most of these contacts were with rum-runners, a few terms from this subculture were adopted, largely in the transportation end of the industry.

Following is a glossary of terms found among Kentucky moonshiners. While it is not complete, it has been carefully prepared and gives an overview of the terms presently used in the manufacture, sale, and distribution of illicit whiskey in large quantities. It should be noted that there is also a somewhat smaller and partially overlapping vocabulary used by bootleggers, of whom there appears to be at least one in every sizable Kentucky community; these terms have been largely omitted except where they overlap the usage of moonshiners.

ALKY. n. 1. Illegal beverage alcohol. Not in general use among moonshiners, but used by bootleggers and wholesalers who distribute illegal liquor. 2. A grade of moonshine which, although of poor quality, is high-proof stuff to be cut by an equal amount of water. Used especially by those operators with experience during Prohibition.

ALKY COLUMN. n. A crude but effective column still for making illicit whiskey on a large scale. Mostly found in large, urban areas where syndicates control illicit liquor. Unknown to rural moonshiners.

BACKER. n. A third person or associated party who owns and/or finances moonshine operations.

BACKINGS or BACKINS. n. Low-proof liquor, not containing enough alcohol to be considered whiskey. Usually low-proof distillate near the end of a run. ". . . about a gallon backins left in the thumper." Compare *singlings.*

BEAD. 1. n. The little bubbles that form along the meniscus of liquor when shaken in a bottle, allowing an experienced moonshiner to judge the proof and quality of the liquor with great accuracy. "This stuff holds a good bead." 2. v.i. To form bubbles and hold them around the surface periphery, as liquor tends to do. "This don't bead so good."

BEADING OIL. n. Oil added to low-proof liquor to make the bead appear as if the liquor were 100 proof. This practice, a survival from Prohibition days, is frowned upon by both moonshiners and bootleggers. "When the bootleggers get it, they'll slip a little beading oil in it and two parts water."

BEER. n. Fermented mash, either grain or sugar. "That beer's working off good." Also called *still-beer*.

BEER STILL. n. The still in which the beer is cooked to separate the spirits (low-proof alcohol) from the residue. In some areas this same still is then used to redistill the spirits to make whiskey. "We just got one more charge of beer. You put it in the beer still while I. . . ."

BIG FELLOW. n. A federal law-enforcement officer. In Central Kentucky, moonshiners make little distinction between branches of the law, largely because all enforcement officers wear rough clothes instead of uniforms when making raids. "We best pull out. The big fellows was by here today." Also called *Feds, the law, marshal, prohi, revenoo.*

BLUBBER. n. The froth created when moonshine and beading oil are shaken in a temping bottle.

BOILER. n. An enclosed vessel in which water is boiled to generate steam for a steam still. It may be anything from an old oil drum, with crude fittings, to a standard upright, factory-made steam boiler with gauges, fittings, safety devices, etc. ". . . boiler blowed up and kilt three of 'em."

BOX. n. See *fermenter.*

BREAK. v.i. Used of the distillate. To drop to a low proof, indicating that the beer is becoming exhausted in the still. The moonshiner often says that the liquor "breaks at the worm" or "breaks at the coil" since he becomes aware of the drop of proof at this point.

BREAK UP. v.t. To sift the scalded mass of meal through a coarse screen (usually hardware cloth) in order to remove the lumps. Part of the mashing operation. "Tomorrow we'll break up them barrels and set in." "We got to break up that scalded meal."

BULLDOG. v.t. To heat used barrels by setting them against a large oil drum in which a fire is built in order to sweat out the whiskey that has soaked into the barrel staves. In some areas a slower process involves setting closed barrels in hot sunlight. ". . . bulldog them barrels and get ten gallons of likker." Also *dog, sweat.*

BURNER. n. A kerosene or gasoline heating unit for cooking mash or distilling liquor. Usually used with steam stills. "That old burner roars till I can't hear what you're saying."

CAN. n. 1. In the southern mountains, a half-gallon fruit jar. Also called *glass can.* 2. In other districts, a five- to ten-gallon wood-covered metal container. Also called *jacket* or *jacket can.* 3. A GI or jerry can (a postwar addition); one of the army's five-gallon gasoline cans adapted to distilling needs. While the "glass can" and "jacket can" are usually used only to hold liquor, the GI cans may be set aside for kerosene or gasoline. However, large shipments of liquor are often made exclusively in GI cans. "Only time I was ever caught. . . . Had ten jacket cans." "Set that can of likker over here."

CAP. n. 1. The cover, usually of copper, that is placed over the opening in the top of the still through which vapor passes via the connections to the condenser. "You put the cap on and I'll put the paste to her." 2. The frothy formation on the top of the vat of fermenting beer that finally clears away, settling through the beer. "It ain't ready to run. The cap ain't broke."

CATCH-CAN. n. The receptacle that receives the distillate from the terminal of the flake-stand. Usually a five-gallon can or bucket.

CHARGE. 1. n. One filling of the still from the fermenter vats. "We only lacked one charge of being through." "We can run a charge an hour." 2. v.t. To fill the still with beer.

CHIPS. n. Oak chips added to liquor to give it color and congeners in one method of quick aging. Usually done in kegs or barrels. "We can throw a handful of chips in that and get more for it." See also *quick aging.* Compare *needling.*

CLEAR. v.i. Used of the cap of meal on top of the fermenter. To break and settle to the bottom, leaving the beer relatively clear. "Quick as that beer clears, we'll run it."

COFFIN STILL. n. A small still designed to fit over two burners of a gasoline or kerosene stove.

COIL. n. A type of condenser, usually made of twenty to forty feet of copper tubing coiled within a barrel of cold water. "That coil's sixty foot long." Also called *worm.* See also *condenser.* Compare *straight-condenser.*

COLLAR. n. The copper band or ring connecting the cap and the still.

CONDENSER. n. Copper tubing used to condense alcohol vapor. Sometimes one tube enclosed within another of larger diameter. "That condenser acts like they ain't no baffles in it." See also *coil, straight-condenser.*

CONNECTIONS. n. The copper parts that join the still or still-cap to the thump-keg, and the thump-keg to the condenser. "The connections are what's hard to make."

COOKER. n. 1. The beer still proper. 2. A tank or box used to precook beer.

COPPER. n. 1. See *still-pot.* 2. See *condenser.* 3. Any copper part of the moonshiner's equipment. "Pull out the copper and leave the rest be."

CORN LIQUOR. n. 1. Among moonshiners, used to mean liquor made with some corn, usually from one peck to one bushel per barrel of mash, the balance of which is sugar or, more rarely, some other grain. 2. In selling, used to mean liquor made from pure (100 percent) corn, which is rare indeed. Also called "straight corn." 3. Any untaxed moonshine liquor. Intonation often reflects the degree to which corn is actually used. "You got any corn likker?" "This ain't sugar likker, this is corn likker." "Shore, that's corn likker." Compare *sugar liquor.*

CRASH CAR. n. 1. A junker that can be abandoned in an emergency. 2. Widely used in Prohibition, days, now rare in Kentucky, an escort car that follows or precedes a liquor transporter for purposes of protection.

DOCK. n. A term used in Lyon and Trigg counties, Kentucky, for the still equipment. "They's two docks over on Stinking Crick."

DOG. v.t. See *bulldog.*

DOG HEAD. n. A large viscous bubble that forms in the still just before the cap is sealed.

DOGGINS. n. Liquor obtained from used barrels by the process of bulldogging.

DOUBLE or DOUBLE BACK. v. To remash at the same place, in the same vats, using the slops from the preceding distillation as a part of the mash. "We doubled back and made a good run." Also *mash back.*

DOUBLER. n. A processing keg, placed between the still and the flakestand, that redistills the liquor by using the heat of the vapor itself, thus eliminating the need to distill twice or use separate stills. "Listen to that old doubler chuckle." Also called *thumper, thump-keg.*

DOUBLINGS. n. (*plural only*). The complete cycle that is made by running fermented beer through a still, extracting the alcohol, and doubling or mashing back. "Yeah, we made ten doublings at that place."

FAINTS. n. 1. Low-proof distillate that comes through the condenser at the end of a run. Also called *tailings.* Sometimes applied to weak *first shots.* 2. Heated slops used for setting mash.

FEDS. n. Officers of the Alcohol Tax Unit. "Yeah, the Feds got Bill and Luke." Also called *revenoo, marshal, prohi, the law.* See also *big fellow.*

FERMENTER. n. A container in which the mash is set to ferment: 1. *Tub,* often made of half barrels or square wooden vats. 2. *Box,* a rectangular vat made from heavy boards bolted or nailed together. "That was a real set—six big boxes bubbling with beer."

FIELD A BOND. v. phr. To make, fill, or get bond when arrested. Origin of this idiom is obscure. "Bill could help us field a bond." "If I can't field a bond, I'll rot in this damned place."

FILTER. 1. n. A strainer, usually of felt, though sometimes of other material, used to remove foreign matter or cloudiness from liquor. "Get that filter off the bush. This stuff's cloudy." 2. v.t. To strain the distillate. "You filter what's in the catch-can."

FIRE IN THE HOLE! interj. Local warning cry, especially on Coe Ridge in Cumberland County, Kentucky, and elsewhere near the Tennessee line, heard immediately after word has spread that the "law's in." Called in a high-pitched, far-carrying yodel, it is necessary to know the words in order to understand them. Adapted from the coal mines, where it is used to indicate that the fuse has been lit and a powder charge is about to explode. (In parts of Tennessee, especially in Cooke County, dynamite charges are set off as alarms; the explosions rocket through the valleys, reverberating for many seconds.)

FIRST SHOTS. n. The initial distillate which emerges from the flakestand as the stilling process begins. This liquor is high in esters, aldehydes, and fusel oil that make it undrinkable. "This 'ere still yet runnin' first shots." Also called *heads, foreshorts.*

FLAKE or FLAKESTAND. n. The container,

filled with cold water, in which the con
denser is immersed so that the alcohol vapor
will condense. Usually a barrel or a drum.

FORESHOTS. n. See *first shots.*

FURNACE. n. A base made of fieldstone,
clay, or mortar that houses the fire under a
pot still, or under the boiler of a steam still.

GET PROBATE. v. phr. To be placed on probation. Because there is no jail sentence involved, the defendant is considered by the
community to have "beaten the case." Conviction on a moonshine charge carries no
stigma, incidentally, in moonshining areas,
most of which are "dry" by local option.
"Naw, they never convicted Lem. He got
probate."

GLASS CAN. n. See *can.*

GOOSE EYE. n. A perfect bead, indicating
100 proof.

GO ROUND. 1. v.i. To distill and remash all
of one's fermenters in sequence. Big-time operators consider it wise to run only a short
time at one location and then move the still.
The length of time is expressed not in days,
but in *go rounds.* ". . . hell, we went round
six times at that old spring." "Maybe we kin
go round once more before we run out." 2.
n. See *doublings.*

GUARD. n. The individual who gives warning
in case of a raid. In some areas, distinction is
made between the lookout, who gives the
warning, and the guard whose job is to put
up a fight. Carefully spaced shotgun blasts
are universally employed throughout Kentucky as a warning.

HEADS. n. See *first shots.*

HEATER or HEATER-BOX. n. Found only
on large stills, a box into which beer is
poured or pumped to be preheated. It uses
heat from the liquor vapor to serve double
duty as both dephlegmator and precooker.
Heater-boxes occur in a wide variety of sizes,
shapes, locations, and connections with a
still. "Pump some beer in the heater-box,
Joe." Also called *preheater.*

HIGH SHOTS. n. Very high-proof liquor
which must be cut with water or backings to
100 proof.

HORNY-MAN. n. Federal agent, a euphemism for devil.

HORSE-BLANKET WHISKEY. n. A crude
form of liquor made by covering a boiling
kettle of beer with a heavy, folded horse-
blanket. When the blanket is heavy with
condensed moisture, two men twist it to ex-
trude the liquor. The process is then repeated. This technique is not approved by
first-class moonshiners.

JACKET or JACKET CAN. n. See *can.*

KEROSENE LIQUOR. n. Liquor contam-
inated by kerosene. A teaspoon of kerosene
in a one thousand-gallon vat of beer will
cause all the liquor to taste of kerosene.
When kerosene is used to fire the boiler in a
large steam still operation, the moonshiner
must be extremely careful to wash his hands
after filling the pressure tank, and not allow
any of his supply bags to lean against a kerosene drum when hauling them to the still
site. "Kerosene likker . . . sold me a pint of
kerosene likker."

KICK or KICKER. n. Any form of nitrate
added to mash with the intent of increasing
the yield.

The LAW. n. See *Feds.*

LIME. v.t. To whitewash the inside of the fermenters to reduce contamination. "We got
to lime them boxes."

LOOKOUT. n See *guard.*

LOW WINES. n. The low-proof liquor produced by the first distillation; the first run of
the still.

MALT CORN, CORN MALT, or SPROUT-
ING MALT CORN. n. Universally used in
the eastern Kentucky mountains, made by
burying a sack of corn under damp leaves
until the corn has sprouted, then grinding
the sprouted grain. Used principally by
small operators. Large operators buy barley
malt in larger quantities. "Yeah, I got a
gunny sack of malt corn sprouted."

MARSHALL. n. See *Feds.*

MASH. 1. n. The mixture in the vats prior to
or during fermentation. 2. v.t. To prepare
ingredients for fermentation.

MASHING IN. v.i. 1. To put the ingredients
in the vats for fermentation. 2. To begin the
process of whiskey making. "We've got to
finish mashing in before noon." See also
mash.

MASH BACK. v.i. See *double back.*

MASH-FLOOR. n. A platform built adjacent
to the vats (usually over a creek) on which
the operator stands to stir the mash. "You
ain't got a thing on me. I never set my foot
on the mash-floor."

MASH-STICK. n. A hardwood stick $1\frac{1}{2}$ or 2 inches in diameter and from 5 to 8 feet long, pierced through at the lower end by several small sticks of different lengths. Used to stir mash to assure maximum conversion.

MIDDLINGS. n. A kind of livestock feed often used by moonshiners as a substitute for grain. ". . . used middlings because we didn't have no meal."

MUD, MUD IN, or MUD UP. v.t. To build up the still furnace and smokestack with masonry. "You mud up the stack." "You mud it for me."

NEEDLING. gerund. A method of quick aging, used by some moonshiners, whereby an electric needle is inserted in the keg. The beneficial effects are questionable. "That ain't aged likker, it's needled."

OUTFIT. n. See *still.*

PASTE. n. A thick mixture of flour, rye, or meal, and water, used for sealing joints in the still connections to prevent the escape of vapor.

POT. n. 1. A pot still with all its accessories. 2. Variant of *still-pot.*

POT STILL. n. See *still.*

POUR UP. v.t. To distribute moonshine (after it has been temped to 100 proof) into containers for distribution.

PREHEATER. n. See *heater.*

PRESSURE TANK. n. The container that supplies kerosene under pressure either to the burner under the still, or to a steam boiler. It is usually pumped with an ordinary tire pump or with an air compressor. "Pump up that pressure tank before the burner quits."

PROHI [pronounced prohai]. 1. n. See *Feds.* 2. adj. Federal or law enforcement. "Them goddam, low-down sonuvabitch prohi bastards. . . ."

PROOF. n. A term borrowed from legitimate distilling to indicate the percentage of alcohol in any distillate. One hundred proof distillate is 50 percent alcohol.

PUKE. v.t. To allow the still to boil over into the connections. This often necessitates dismantling the still and cleaning out the connections, the thump-keg, and the condenser. "Don't throw no more wood on that fire, you'll puke the still."

PUKER. n. A primitive dephlegmator between the still and the thump-keg that returns any boiled-over mash to the still, there-by preventing it from contaminating the distillate.

PULL OUT. v.i. 1. To take the still out of the furnace or stack, and hide or remove it. This is often done when operators suspect that the still has been reported. Also *pull the still.* 2. To quit stilling at that particular spot. 3. To remove all the most expensive equipment, especially the copper, and leave the location. "We got to pull out before he reports on us."

PULL THE FIRE. v. phr. To remove the fire under the still (in pot-type operations) in order to stop the beer from boiling. The pot can then be emptied and refilled without danger from scalding steam. In copper pot operations, the fire must be pulled every time the charge is changed. The fire must also be pulled at the end of each operation or day of operation and carefully put out or scattered on the naked ground as a precaution against forest fires. "That's what takes the time, pullin' the fire every time you change a charge."

PULL THE STILL. v. phr. See *pull out.*

QUICK AGING. gerund. Any method of giving color to liquor quickly and, of course, artificially. "That likker ain't old. It's just been quick aged." See also *chips, needling.*

QUILL. n. A straw used to sample beer in the vats. Still-beer is considered at its best for drinking just before distillation; however, it is drunk at almost every stage after it has begun to ferment. Passersby often slip in to sample it, although this practice is discouraged. "Hand me that quill. I'm fixing to drink some beer out of this barrel."

RACE. n. The chase to escape law enforcement officers. It may be either by car or on foot. Such a chase is quite common, since federal officers seldom shoot first at violators of the liquor law. "Me and the law had a race." "I shore give the law a race yesterday."

RAISE YEAST. v. phr. To grow one's own yeast rather than buy it. There are interesting legends regarding the proper method of catching the "wild yeast" to get a start. In eastern Kentucky many moonshiners think they do not use yeast. They keep their fermentation going by using some old mash in each new batch, but do not know why. "We never bought no yeast. We raised our own yeast."

RELAY ARM. n. The connection between the relay barrel and the still through which heated beer is piped.

RELAY BARREL or KEG. n. A large-scale puker combined with a preheater arrangement for preheating beer and charging the still. Seldom used in Kentucky.

REPORT or REPORT ON. v. To inform the law of a liquor violation. "He reported on me." Also *to turn in, to turn up.*

REVENOO, REVENEUER, or REVENOO-ER. n. See *Feds.*

RIG. n. See *still.*

RUN. 1. v. To distill a batch of fermented beer. 2. v. To transport whiskey. 3. n. A cycle of whiskey.

RUN OUT or RUN (IT) OUT. v. To finish distillation of the beer on hand and cease operation, either temporarily or permanently. "We're gonna run out and quit." "This set's hot, but we may have time to run it out." "When we run out, we'll move up the creek."

SCALD. v.t. In corn or part-corn operations, to cook the meal in preparation for making mash.

SCORCHED LIQUOR. n. Liquor made from mash that has been allowed to burn at the bottom of the fermenter, or meal that has burned in the still-pot while being scalded. "This tastes like it's scorched likker."

SCREEN. n. A frame covered with coarse, wire netting through which scalded mash is sometimes worked to remove lumps.

SET. 1. n. See *still.* 2. v.t. To scald mash and prepare it for fermentation. 3. v.t. To prepare the equipment and place the mash in the vats for fermentation. 4. v.t. To establish a still. Used intransitively in phrases like "to set up" and "to set in." "We got set in one Sunday and run a month."

SETTLE. v. See *clear.* "The cap ain't broke up, let 'er settle."

SHACK. n. 1. A makeshift shed in which the still is sometimes set. ". . . built a shack over the shine." 2. The storage shed for materials and supplies at a still.

SHINE. n. A moonshine still.

SIGN. n. 1. Tracks. 2. Evidence of moonshine traffic.

SINGLINGS. n. Low-proof liquor that does not contain enough alcohol to be considered whiskey. This liquor has been run through the still only once in cases where two stills or two distilling operations are used. Also applied to the condensate in the thump-keg. "That ain't likker, that's jest singlin's." Compare *backings.*

SLOP or SLOPS. n. Exhausted still-beer.

SLOP MASH. n. Mash to which the stillage from the previous distillation has been added in order to get the benefit of whatever alcohol is left in the slop. This procedure usually follows the first mashing. "We ought to get a better turn-out from slop mash." See also *mash.*

SOUR MASH. n. Mash made by scalding meal with hot slops, in contrast to *sweet mash,* which is made by scalding the meal with fresh water.

SPENT BEER or SPENT MASH. n. Beer, hot from the still, from which the alcohol has been exhausted. This is either discarded or used to set a new tier of fermenters.

SPLO. n. Cheap low-grade whiskey.

STACK. 1. n. The rocks or bricks built around the still in pot operations, and the boiler in steam operations. "This still ain't been outa the stack for a month." 2. v.t. To set the still or the boiler up in masonry so that a fire can be applied. "You stack the still while I get the . . ." See also *mud.*

STASH. n. A cache of raw materials or liquor, usually not at the still site. "We got ninety gallon left in the stash."

STEAM STILL. n. See *still.*

STILL. n. The pot or container in which the beer is distilled to make whiskey. 1. In *pot* operations, a small copper container. "We got us a fifty-gallon copper pot." 2. In *steam* operations, a large vat, usually made of silo staves, but sometimes of metal. "That's a steamer. The still will hold five hundred gallons of beer."

STILL-BEER. n. Variant of *beer.*

STILL-POT. n. The metal body of the still in which the beer is cooked. ". . . old still-pot's about burnt up."

STRAIGHT-CONDENSER. n. A straight piece of copper tubing laid in a trough of cold running water and used to condense alcohol vapor. Not common. Compare *coil.*

STRAIGHT CORN. n. See *corn liquor.*

SUGAR JACK. n. One hundred proof whiskey made from sugar without the addition of corn, except for a small amount to start and maintain fermentation.

SUGAR LIQUOR. n. Liquor made from sugar. "This ain't no good. It's sugar likker." Compare *corn liquor*.

SUGAR MASH. n. A sugar solution, sometimes mixed with a small amount of cornmeal, set to ferment into beer.

SWAB. n. A long, hickory sapling, well frayed at one end and used along with the mashstick to keep mash from sticking and scorching in the still. Sometimes to better get at the mash, a rag is tied to the end of the stick.

SWEAT. v.t. See *bulldog*.

SWEET MASH. n. See *sour mash*.

TAILINGS. n. See *faints*.

TAKE THE WORD. v. phr. To spread the alarm of a pending raid. The signal may consist of two spaced gunshots. Often moonshiners send a runner with the message; "the word" of a stranger's approach travels with incredible rapidity. "Yeah, he took the word, else they'd got ketched Friday." "We took the word just in time to git gone."

TEMP. v.t. To test the bead on liquor by shaking it in a bottle in order to ascertain whether or not the liquor must be "tempered" by the addition of water or backings. If the liquor does not hold a bead, higher proof distillate must be added.

TEMPING BOTTLE. n. A bottle in which a sample of liquor is placed and shaken to test the formation of the bead, indicating the proof of the liquor. "Here, take that temping bottle and see how this stuff beads."

THUMPER or THUMP-KEG. n. See *doubler*. The term derives from the putt-putt thumping noise caused by steam in the keg.

TROUBLE. n. An arrest for liquor law violation. "Yeah, he's been in trouble before."

TUB. n. See *fermenter*.

TURN-OUT. n. Yield of whiskey per amount of corn or sugar used. "What turn-out did you get—ten gallons to the bag?" "We ain't gettin' no turn-out."

VAT. n. See *fermenter*.

VAT PLUG. n. The plug in the drain hole of a fermenter. "Pull that vat plug and wash that box out."

WATER MASH. n. The first mash made in a stilling operation; since there is no spent stillage available, it is mixed with water. "We never got much turn-out on the water mash." See also *mash*.

WEED-MONKEY or WEED-MULE. n. The old car or truck used to haul supplies to the still site and to transport liquor. Mostly Tennessee usage. "Take that old weed-monkey and go get the meal."

WHISKEY STILL. n. A small auxiliary still (in addition to the beer still) used sometimes for rectifying low wines. "This little pot is big enough for a whiskey still."

WORM. n. See *coil*.

WORT. n. A mixture of malt, water, and sugar used as an infusion in still-beer to promote fermentation.

EPILOGUE

Social Dialects as a
Key to Cultural Dynamics

Why study social dialects? Having read this far, the reader might naturally be asking this question. Perhaps a brief answer might serve to put this area of the study of American language into perspective alongside the other, more generally recognized aspects of linguistics.

Language is one of the most important of human developments, and research into the nature of social dialects, including argots, is just one aspect of the large-scale investigation into the many different phases of language in general which involves ideas of human behavior, social structure, and that ever-mysterious phenomenon — human thought. That is, social dialectology comprises just one phase of general linguistic research which may help us understand the nature of human interaction better.

Since social dialects are essentially cultural phenomena, any discussion of them might logically include some remarks on the culture within which they are spoken. In the United States, the middle class is presumed to be the ideal cultural median. It is here where we find a certain degree of comfortable living, considerable conformity of beliefs, agreement on political concepts, and commonly held attitudes toward economics, education, social responsibility, the relation of man to man, man to government, and man to God. The history of our immigrant waves has been a struggle to enter this middle class, which is uniquely accessible to anyone who can qualify financially. Education and race are secondary criteria in a society where upward mobility is the ideal. Thus, the middle class is subject to the constant freshening and flexibility which stems from the absorption of recruits from many occupational and ethnic groups and subcultures.

The proliferation of the middle class into the power structure, however, has given rise to certain myths which are sometimes confused with reality: that life there is all good; that economic status is the mark of intelligence; that beliefs there are infallible, the mores not to be improved upon, the educational methods superior, philosophy perfect, and the citizens therein inferior to none elsewhere — which takes in a great deal of territory. The general assumption is that the middle class is the dominant culture. Actually, however, the dominant or mainstream culture is comprised of a number of subcultures, none of which share identical patterns of cultural indices, but all of which share certain subdivisions thereof. Through this sharing the middle class attains its dominance in the power structure, maintains itself, and gives the illusion of homogeneity.

Of course, a heavy degree of conformity comes with participation in the bounties of middle-class life, and the consequent sacrifice of true individualism is the price that most people gladly pay for enjoying the emoluments of this life. With a plethora of creature comforts, economic security, political power, unlimited educational, industrial, and professional opportunities, to mention only a few of the accruing benefits, it has been only natural for the middle class to grow somewhat self-satisfied. This has always happened on a smaller scale in European cultures too, but until recent years there has been an elite caste above the middle class—the aristocracy—which served, and still does to some extent, as the final arbiter.

Nevertheless, on this side of the Atlantic the middle class appears to be the dominant culture. It makes the laws, collects the taxes, controls the educational system, exerts police power, sponsors industry and business, regulates the lives of our citizens, and, without doubt, controls the destiny of our nation. Linguistically, all this is important, for the hypothetical class-dialect of the middle class constitutes the model for so-called standard English. By that I mean the English taught in the schools and legitimized in written or printed form. Unfortunately, the teaching of English, like much of American education, is still geared, to some extent, to obsolete eighteenth-century educational theories. The nature of standard English (whatever that actually is) depends upon the textbooks used in the schools, and these texts hark back to the guidebooks to language etiquette written in England in the eighteenth century. These guidebooks, originally meant to be shortcuts to social acceptance, imitated the usage of the aristocracy as recorded by former tutors in upper-class families. They were replete with curious standards of correctness, dubious etymologies, arbitrary rules of pronunciation, and superimposed grammatical concepts, all of which have too little relationship to the English language spoken and written in America today. Largely ignored are the very sound findings of historical linguistics, descriptive linguistics, modern syntactic approaches, and the more recent observations in sociolinguistics which are readily available, but to which only passing lip service is paid in most contemporary school textbooks. Here conformity takes its real toll, for millions of youngsters are theoretically imbued with facility in standard English, only to find themselves confused in the face of the actual usage they encounter outside the classroom. While the teaching of English should ideally free the imagination, the excessive dependence on textbook English tends to limit and stultify the thinking processes. There is every reason to teach English with an emphasis on precision of diction, originality of thought, and facility in clear and vigorous expression. This, however, is obviously not being done effectively in either the public schools or the universities where the teachers are educated. Some fifty years ago, H. L. Mencken warned that the "schoolmarm" (male or female) was inadequate and even dangerous as a custodian of the language. Subsequent events tend to validate his indictment.

But this tendency toward teaching an "official" language is analogous to Castilian in Spain, Parisian in France, Hoch Deutsch in Germany, the King's English in Britain, and so on. The King's English, for instance, attained theoretical perfection, epitomized in Fowler's *The King's English,* which relegated any English spoken elsewhere to third-rate colonial status. However, along with the decline of the British Empire has come the development of independent power structures within the individual former colonies themselves. In the United States, for example, the general public finds British English and the King's English increasingly irrelevant, though this trend has not yet become fully recognized by English departments throughout America. In many universities, technology appears to be rapidly cannibalizing the humanities. Fortunately, a number of first-class writers—from Chaucer to Joyce and Hemingway—have not hesitated to write in the English language they heard about them, textbook restrictions be damned.

Furthermore, underneath the apparent solidarity of the middle class and its "standard" English lies a web of multicultural divisions based on the behavioral patterns of the groups who share, to a limited extent, in the cultural indices of the dominant culture. When pressures (economic, social, political, ethnic) exert themselves, the older matrices of the subcultures surface, engendering salient linguistic and social hostility. For example, recently gasoline and diesel fuel shortages and prices excesses have exerted extreme pressure on the independent truck drivers, who, in response, coalesced into a counterpressure group violently opposed to the power structure, though most of the involved truckers share enough cultural indices with the dominant culture to claim legitimate membership therein. A similar phenomenon has been noted among farmers and other special-interest groups, including some big oil companies at the other end of the economic spectrum.

Moreover, an expansion of the current energy crisis may possibly sever the fragile bonds which tie many subcultures to the dominant culture, cause them to tighten their own internal security, and thereby fragment the dominant culture into a situation conceivably bordering on anarchy. The stronger bonds are those within the subcultures, and they are the ones that emerge when pressure is applied. Thus, the dominant culture is really extremely vulnerable. Undoubtedly the time has come to discard the myth that America is a giant melting pot producing a standard human amalgam and accept the fact that we are a multicultural society held together by rather tenuous cultural indices, or subdivisions thereof, which tend to disintegrate under extreme pressure. Energy shortages represent only one source of pressure from special-interest groups whose demands threaten the unanimity of Congress itself. Other pressures, not yet clearly visible, are surely waiting in the wings.

If the values of the dominant culture were unified and supreme, we would have a monolithic society. But this we do not have. In the last analysis literally hundreds of subcultures must be considered. Some of these are totally within the dominant culture; some are partly within it and partly outside; and a few, like the Gypsies, are mainly outside, and seem to prefer it that way. Subcultures are really miniature societies themselves. Some have a whole set of cultural indices which differ from those of the dominant culture, and some share certain indices with the dominant culture but differ in others. Some of them constitute constructive adjuncts to the dominant culture, like the many occupational groups; and some are entirely parasitic, like the many criminal societies. Considerable linguistic differentiation exists in all subcultures, and in some, "standard" English is virtually a foreign tongue. In fact, some evidence suggests that subcultures can be language generated, as in the case of the citizens' band radio aficionados.

Regardless of the realities of the situation, deviations from the mythical norm of the dominant culture tend in turn to produce a reaction, and often an overaction, on the part of certain interests in the mass culture. Already a noticeable trend encourages—sometimes even coerces—everyone to talk alike, dress alike, and think alike, leading often to a form of socialization verging on regimentation. Seemingly forgotten is our historical past in which our diversity, not our social, linguistic, and political uniformity, enabled America to progress so rapidly in various fields.

Therefore, it might be advantageous to go below the surface and study the multifarious subcultures comprising the dominant culture. These, together with their indigenous dialects and languages, have characterized American society from early frontier days to the present. Today, many kinds of subcultures remain clustered within and about the dominant culture. Every organized occupation or profession constitutes, to some extent, a subculture, with the more technical and well-developed ones comprising tight in-groups. Railroading is a good example of one with a voluminous special language and a tight organization which makes entrance from the outside difficult, but not nearly so difficult as entrance to, say, the printers' trade, where apprentices are admitted with something of the same complicated ritual attending the registering of a foal for the Kentucky Derby. All sports form subcultures of sorts, in which members share most of the indices of the dominant culture, except those directly connected with the sport. Horse racing, for instance, cuts across a wide swath of subcultures, each with its appropriate differences, but all overlapping along the way. Racing starts with the breeders, who have an astonishing expertise in connection with horses, and ends with the gamblers, who know nothing about horses but the price on the formsheet. Supporting this sport are millions of racing fans, most of whom know some of that social dialect. By way of contrast, in a sport like cockfighting, still surprisingly widespread though illegal, the specialized language is known only to a limited number of participants. It is secret, ancient, and seems to have escaped study by scholars. There are also religious subcultures like the Trappist monks, the

Amish, and the Mennonites, the Trappists having rejected the dominant culture almost entirely, along with the spoken language, though their sign language shows many features characteristic of the special languages of other subcultures. Many religious, or Utopian, subcultures in the United States have disintegrated because they could not inspire in the younger generations enough hostility to maintain the dichotomy with the dominant culture — so the youngsters joined it; or, like the cult at Jonestown, self-destructed.

Other subcultures are found in the entertainment world past and present (where was there ever a tighter bond than that among old-time circus people?), among the military, among the dozens of subcultures of professional criminals sometimes referred to as the underworld, in public institutions and especially prisons (none of which has ever been thoroughly studied), among sexual deviants, among government bureaucrats, and among law-enforcement officers, to name only a few. The police — once a loose occupational subculture — are now turning into something that may be more sinister; under increasing pressures from both the dominant culture and the criminal element, many large police departments seem, in self-defense, to be tightening their subculture into a force that might some day give us the police state. Some further evidence of this dichotomy is the rather disturbing tendency in many big-city police departments for the police, driven by frustrations with citizens' groups, economic factors, political organizations, the courts, etc., to reinforce their own occupational subculture and strengthen their control over the dominant culture. This is indeed alarming, but symptoms of this malaise surface from time to time in various American cities.

Regional interests can also reinforce and even dominate the social divisions that constitute subcultures. For reasons of convenience, we often assume that social dialects occur in vertical stratification, while regional dialects appear in horizontal distribution. However, the two sometimes combine to create powerful economic and social pressures. Thus, the proliferation of railroads in the nineteenth century made the waterways somewhat obsolescent and influenced the shape of our culture in powerful ways, for large labor pools consisting mainly of immigrants became suddenly mobile and could be shifted rapidly from locale to locale; once the railroads were established, they opened the territory to hordes of other immigrants who developed agriculture, commerce, and industry, all of which introduced nonindigenous personnel. The relative instability of this heterogeneous society has been furthered by several other phenomena that are primarily regional in nature.[1] First, there is the mass migration to the cities leaving only some 15 percent of our population engaged in agriculture or related occupations. Second, there is a mass movement both by individuals and industries, to the so-called sunbelt; this is intensified by other developments in the national economy, especially

1. This tendency has been noted recently by Timothy C. Frazer in "The Speech Island of the American Bottoms: A Problem in Social History," *American Speech* 54, 3 (Fall 1979):175-84.

energy shortages. Third, there is a growing tendency on the part of the federal government to break down national problems according to rather arbitrarily applied (regional) classifications. These geographic considerations cut across many of the social and ethnic subcultures in varying degrees; twenty years ago it would have been difficult to believe that in 1979 three ethnic minorities — blacks, Jews, and Mexican-Americans — would have suddenly had a profound effect on the foreign policy of the United States in two very important spheres: the Middle East and Latin America. A coalition of many subcultures therefore determined the power structure in various communities.

Thus, one thing is certain: subcultures tighten their internal structure and accelerate their differentiation in response to pressure applied either by the dominant culture or by a competing subculture. In fact, without pressures most subcultures would not develop beyond the rudimentary or abortive stage; this is particularly true of criminal subcultures. There must be a threat or implied threat, which intensifies the internal forces already at work. As a specialized language develops there, emphasizing the values, attitudes, and techniques of the subculture (while concurrently downgrading or disparaging those of the dominant culture), it reflects this hostility.[2]

Among criminal groups, for instance, improved technology may excite acute linguistic activity, often with an emphasis on secrecy. The gap between society and the subculture widens. As a subculture becomes more aware of its functional identity, a self-image is generated which must be bolstered by word and deed.[3] Consequently, among criminals the argot becomes a prime factor in triggering criminal behavior. This glorified image may be confused with reality, while the proliferating argot serves to enhance prestige and gratify ego-expansion. Some gangsters appear to build themselves up, partly through verbalization of the invincible self-image, to a state of megalomania suggesting paranoia, while whole criminal subcultures, so deluded, can become formidable threats to any force that the dominant culture can throw against them. We see some of this machinery currently at work in the formation of certain ethnic groups competing for power. We see the finished product in the Mafia. Recently, terrorist groups are establishing this pattern on an international basis.

These principles appear to apply to all subcultures and vary only in degree according to the intensity of conflict between dominant culture and subculture. Subcultures reduplicate, to some extent, the processes already very old by which the dominant culture has learned to symbolize behavior through

2. I have treated the phenomenon of linguistic hostility, still largely unexplored, in greater detail in "Linguistic Hostility as a Factor in Intra-Cultural Conflict," *Actes du Xe Congrès International des Linguistes*, Editions de L'Académie de la République Socialiste de Roumanie (Bucharest, 1969).

3. Illustrations of the connection between the criminal's self-image and the technology of his subculture are listed in *The American Confidence Man* (Springfield, Ill.: Charles C Thomas, 1974), pp. 264–65. Also included in this volume.

language. In the nonlearned and nontechnical subcultures, the tendency is to draw words and phrases from the established language and give them new meanings, which we might call neosemanticisms; in the learned, occupational, or professional subcultures, the tendency is to create neologisms, thus fostering group solidarity, mutual recognition, prestige, and a sense of exclusiveness. The continuity of any subculture is dependent on keeping its language exclusive, since a subculture tends to lose its identity once its language becomes widely known and used by outsiders. When large numbers of words escape from the subculture, this may be an indication of subcultural diffusion and suggest that assimilation is under way with a consequent deterioration of the microsystem. We have good examples of this in the subcultures of the jazz musician and that of the criminal narcotic addict. Words from both these subcultures are now the basis of the slang vocabulary of millions of young people, and neither subculture is nearly so exclusive as it was some forty years ago.

Moreover, there is an increasing tendency for young people from the dominant culture to identify psychologically — and often actually — with criminal and semicriminal subcultures which they romanticize and admire. This psychological identification may be part of what lies behind the upsurge in juvenile delinquency, which is ever on the increase. It is acquired largely through the mass media, which of course depend heavily on language for the transmission of attitudes, techniques, and mores from the subculture to the dominant culture. As an example, I might note that I have in my files a typescript volume of over 300 pages, recording then-obscure argot terms collected nearly forty years ago from denizens of the Harlem brothels, tea-pads, and black-and-tan joints; today this subculture has diffused so that most of these terms are understandable to any teenager who is a fan of certain kinds of music, and many of these words (whose obscure connotations are lost on fond parents and occasionally on the managers of radio stations) are now common currency in the dominant culture. Along with this terminology have come certain attitudes, recreational preoccupations, dress and hair styles, etc., which any urban police force has learned to recognize as stereotypes of the juvenile delinquent. Beyond this we have seen within the last two decades the mass invasion of a definitely criminal subculture by teenagers (and sometimes preteens) from the dominant culture — an invasion that has played havoc with the criminal's cultural pattern as well as his argot. This has taken place in the subculture of the underworld narcotic addict. The diffusion of this subculture is in fact one of the major social problems of our times. Within the range of my observation, it is without precedent.[4]

Argot, therefore, may influence the quality of the language of the dominant culture. Its influence, however, is not always so negative as that de-

4. David W. Maurer, *Whiz Mob: A Correlation of the Technical Argot of Pickpockets with Their Behavior Pattern* (New Haven, Conn.: College and University Press, 1964), p. 5.

scribed above. It provides another valuable source of refreshment and renewal, as with words from other types of social dialects — occupational, ethnic, religious, sports, and so on. This freshening should not be stamped out or discouraged by conformity as our English textbooks would have it; rather, it should be cultivated for the constructive elements it adds to the culture. For example, words that formerly were taboo for women to speak have now reached a station in our language where they are permissible, with few exceptions, for all people to utter without fear of disapproval. Likewise, the roles women can and do play, along with their skills, ideas, productivity, etc., have contributed significantly to our quality of life.[5]

Unfortunately, these somewhat unconventional aspects of the American language have been largely ignored. Slang and colloquial speech, which often enjoy more currency than "standard" English, remained virtually untouched by scholars until Mencken treated slang extensively in *The American Language*, followed by Stuart Flexner's *Dictionary of American Slang*, which appeared in 1960. Flexner's original corpus, by the way, was based largely on criminal and semicriminal lexical items collected in the field. (The study of regional dialects in America started at about the same time as the study of social dialects, with Mencken, Louise Pound, and others establishing the field in the late 1920s. Today, this work is in safe hands under the skilled direction of such dialect geographers as Raven McDavid and Frederic Cassidy.)

Slang, which emanates from conflicts in values among divergent cultural groups, sometimes introduces new concepts and expressions to the cultural mainstream. It represents one of the four optional destinies of argot, the others being that argot becomes standard English (fence, quota), that it remains argot (ding, peeter, fork), or that it is lost (Ken millers, priggers, kates).[6] Often, however, argot shelters refugee words from the subculture which disintegrate, diffuse, etc., until they reappear years later. For example, *pig* for "policeman" is usually thought to be a coinage of the sixties youth culture in America, but was actually listed in the 1811 edition of Francis Grose's *Classical Dictionary of the Vulgar Tongue* (originally published 1785), and was amplified as "China Street pig" which was a Bow Street officer.

Lexicographers are finding argot materials increasingly useful since they frequently explain the etymology of words — slang and otherwise — which have come into the language through underworld subcultures. The lively and often ribald nature of slang frequently derives from the conflict of values existing between the subculture and the dominant culture.[7] Dictionary makers need to know a great deal more than they do about the language before it enters

5. I have dealt with the changing patterns of women's speech in part in "Language and the Sexual Revolution: Part 1," *American Speech* 51 (1976):5-24. Part 2, in preparation.

6. David W. Maurer, "New Words — Where Do They Come From and Where Do They Go: An Experiment in Cavalier Lexicography" with the assistance of Ellesa Clay High, *American Speech* 55, 3 (Fall 1980): 184-94.

7. David W. Maurer, "Slang," *Encyclopedia Britannica,* 1974 ed.

print, since most "new words" have had a long and lively life before appearing in print.[8] New slang words, however, often defy sound etymological work. But if the language of the subculture from which a word springs has been recorded effectively in advance, the history of the term can become universally clear.

So far, however, most social dialects have been explored only on a rather gross level, with criminal argots experiencing conspicuous short shrift. But there are several reasons for this, including the following: there are few trained fieldworkers available; argots are not always easily accessible; and there is not yet enough cross-field work involving linguistics and other disciplines such as psychiatry, criminology, social anthropology, sociology, semantics, law, psychology, and lexicography. Part of the lack of attention may also be due to the feeling among certain academicians that research in this field is not entirely in keeping with the genteel tradition.

The concern over argots, however, transcends the purely academic. They are spoken by groups that have attained an importance out of all relation to their size and are very expensive for the dominant culture to maintain, for professional crime has become one of our major industries. It occupies the headlines in our news media, it gives us a bad reputation abroad, it dominates our magazine fiction, our movies, our television, and — what is worse — these mass media convey a romanticized picture of crime which is far from the truth, largely because most of our writers choose to reflect a popular concept of crime which has little connection with reality. A few happy exceptions, however, such as Nelson Algren, Damon Runyon, and Mario Puzo, indicate a trend in the right direction.[9]

Part of our failure to deal with professional crime is a failure to understand its nature. The study of argots used by criminals gives us not only a tool for penetrating these groups but also some key to their organization, some insight into the nature of their subcultures and their thought processes. Collecting and recording the argots makes available to sociologists, psychiatrists, criminologists, police scientists, etc., a large body of material which could be incorporated into studies within these various fields.

Finally, then, what is really known of the behavior patterns and specialized language features (and they should be studied simultaneously) of this multiplicity of subcultures? Not very much, I can assure you. In fact, we have available more data on some obscure cultures from the South Seas to the Cape

8. David W. Maurer, "Culture, Sub-Culture, and Lexicography," *Annals of the New York Academy of Sciences* 211 (June 8, 1973):184–85.

9. Nelson Algren's *The Man with the Golden Arm* depicts, with great fidelity, both the language and behavior of specific criminal groups. Runyon, with a fluent command of some criminal argots, deals predominantly with stereotypes, slightly caricatured, but drawn with a sure hand. See Jean Wagner, *Runyonese: The Mind and Craft of Damon Runyon* (New York: Stechert-Hafner, 1965). Mario Puzo's novel *The Godfather* reads like an intimate documentary recorded in one of the nerve centers of syndicated crime.

of Good Hope than we have on our own social microsystems. Since all linguists, and especially those who have worked in dialectology, have the needed technology, they constitute one of the logical disciplines to become actively involved. It has become obvious that the life and language patterns of our own subcultures call for systematic study in depth.

Those of us who use language as writers or study it as linguists have a certain responsibility since we are, to some extent, the custodians of one of our most valuable national assets: the English language in America. Since it is language that serves as the catalyst by which groups and individuals interact and transmit many of their culturally important ideas, attitudes, thoughts, beliefs, etc., a constant evaluating and reevaluating of the ubiquitous human exercise of speech can help mitigate the effects of cultural fragmentation. Though no cure-all, the study and creative use of social dialects lead to the discovery of certain commonly held cultural identities which are found within subcultures but are not readily discernible from a singular analysis of the entire American cultural matrix. Clarification of cultural and linguistic matrices composing the dominant culture is facilitated by probing the microsocieties that comprise this complex macrosociety, a knowledge of the languages and dialects of its many divergent groups serving as a precondition for understanding any aspect of it.

DAVID. W. MAURER

GENERAL INDEX

KEY WORD INDEX